The Restoration of
Gregorian Chant

Dom Pierre Combe, O.S.B.
MONK OF SOLESMES

The Restoration of
𝔊regorian 𝔔hant

Solesmes and the Vatican Edition

Translated by †Theodore N. Marier
and William Skinner

The Catholic University of America Press
Washington, D.C.

Originally published under the title *Histoire de la restauration du chant
grégorien d'après des documents inédites: Solesmes et l'Edition Vatican,*
© 1969 by the Abbaye Saint-Pierre de Solesmes.

Library of Congress Cataloging-in-Publication Data
Combe, Pierre.
    [Histoire de la restauration du chant grégorien d'après des documents
inédites. English]
    The restoration of Gregorian chant : Solesmes and the Vatican edition /
Dom Pierre Combe, O.S.B., monk of Solesmes ; translated by Theodore N.
Marier and William Skinner.
       cm.
    Translation of : Histoire de la restauration du chant grégorien d'après des
documents inédites.
    Includes bibliographical references (p.) and index.
    ISBN 0-8132-1348-7 (cloth : alk. paper)
    1. Gregorian chants—History and criticism.   I. Title.
    ML3082 .C5913 2003
    782.32'22'009034—dc21
                         2002153985

CONTENTS

INTRODUCTION

Rev. Robert A. Skeris

The carefully documented narrative of Fr. Pierre Combe's "History of the Restoration of Gregorian Chant," presented to the English-speaking public for the first time in the pages which follow, concludes with the year 1912 when the *Antiphonale Romanum* was published. The chant books printed under the auspices of the Vatican Commission headed by Dom Pothier thus comprised the *Kyriale* (1905), *Cantus Missae* (1907), *Graduale Romanum* (1907), *Officium Defunctorum* (1909), the *Cantorinus* (1911), and the *Antiphonale Romanum*.

The books of Gregorian chant published since 1913 have been edited by the monks of Solesmes, a tradition which continues to the present day. The official chant books prepared at Solesmes during the past century are briefly listed: *Cantus Passionis* (1916), *Officium Hebdomadae Sanctae* (1922), *Officium Nativitatis D.N.J.C.* (1926), *Antiphonarium Monasticum* (1934), as well as the monastic offices of Christmas (1936), *Agendis Mortuorum* (1949), and for feast days (1957). After the Second Vatican Council, the series continued with the *Graduale Simplex* (1967, 2d ed. 1975), the *Ordo Cantus Missae* (1972), and the private edition of the *Graduale Romanum* (1974), *Jubilate Deo* (1974, 2d ed. 1986), the *Liber Cantualis* (1978), the *Psalterium Monasticum* (1981), and the *Liber Hymnarius = Antiphonale Romanum II* (1983), the *Missel Gregorien* (1985) = *Gregorian Missal* (1990), and the second edition of the *Ordo Missae in Cantu* (1995), as well as several reprints of earlier editions.

Such intense publishing activity testifies to the relevance of Gregorian chant for Catholic worship in the new millennium. Many of these new chant books reflect the results of recent researches, which have accordingly influenced the actual chanting of Gregorian melodies today.

The *Liber Hymnarius* and its Preface is a case in point. The RHYTHM of Gregorian chant is once more at the center of attention.

I

When a young cellist by the name of Mocquereau entered the Benedictine monastery at Solesmes in 1875, he found a style of singing which was already "traditional" there, a style which can be traced back to the founder himself, Dom Guéranger. This style was based upon the objective datum then at the disposal of the small choir of this small house: upon the words and phrases of the text. Instead of continuing to hammer out each individual syllable, Abbot Guéranger asked his monks to use their intelligence and good sense: to sing the words, and with those words to form phrases. For Guéranger, the queen of all rules was that, except in cases of pure melody, chant is an intelligent *reading*, well accented, well scanned, well phrased (Gontier 1859).

In 1880, Dom Pothier wrote, "It must be said: in our era, especially since the sixteenth century, the liturgical melodies are no longer what they used to be. They are neither understood nor enjoyed in the way our forefathers understood and enjoyed them, nor are they interpreted in practice as our forefathers interpreted them. We have arrived at a heavy and monotonous style of performance, one that deprives the chant of all rhythm and color, that destroys the charm—how shall I say it?—the very essence of the melody. For sounds that follow one another uniformly, like the syllables of a child spelling his lesson, are no more a chant than the child's syllables are a reading" (*Les Mélodies Grégoriennes* [Tournai 1880] 8).

For Pothier, then, the ancient notes were the *vox* of the chant, its breath, so he advocated a "phonetic" approach to chant in order to "fix" the "broken melodies" which lay fractured in the mouths of modern singers. Later, Dom Mocquereau wished to enumerate the contents of this restored performance: "Before appreciating a text, it is necessary to know how to spell it" ("Notation oratoire ou chironomique": *Paléographie Musicale* 1 [Tournai 1889] 110).

"There is in the Catholic liturgy of the Church (wrote Dom Pothier) a music that . . . is at once a word and a song (*une parole et un chant*), a rich and powerful music that is also simple and natural, a music that does not seek to be music, does not listen to itself, but is released as the spontaneous cry of religious thought and feeling" (*Les Mélodies Grégoriennes* 12). In its most elementary form, this unique fusion of thought and feeling was for Pothier nothing more than what the ancients called an "accent," a term designating the natural rising and falling of the voice. "An art like Gregorian chant borrows its best effects from the science of language . . . and nothing is as delicate as the phenomenon of speech" (ibid.).

And so Gregorian chant was not merely an adornment, a musical layer added to the words of the liturgy, but rather a sound which issued naturally from those sacred words. In the last analysis it was simply—highly expressive speaking, elocution raised to a higher level, capturing in its syllables a music that is the accent of religious devotion. For Dom Pothier, then, rhythm always flowed from the accent of speech as from its primary and natural source. The accented syllable was always "strong without elongation," the unaccented "long, but weak" (*Les Mélodies Grégoriennes* 163). The accent so concentrated the energy of the word that it acted (according to Pothier) as an *élément condensateur*, a "condenser element" forcing the tone of the strong syllable upward without increasing its time value. When that tension was released, the relaxation of both pitch and rhythm produced in the unaccented syllable a slight elongation. In other words, the same speech accent that caused a natural rise and fall in the voice created an equally natural push and pull of rhythm.

With the passage of time (1891, 1895/1900) Pothier developed this insight into a full-fledged notion of rhythmic tension and release expressed by the Greek terms *arsis* and *thesis*. Here, Dom Mocquereau found a starting point for his own reflections on Gregorian musical rhythm.

In the course of time, in other places different interpretations of Gregorian rhythm arose. Some thought the notes reflected long and short quantities arranged according to different schemes in a sort of measured rhythm, while others maintained that one should sing the words with notes as one would speak them without notes. After years of study and reflection upon this problem, Dom André Mocquereau presented a monumental study of Gregorian musical rhythm in two volumes entitled *Le Nombre Musical Grégorien* (1908/1927). Here, beginning with Plato's conception of rhythm as ordered movement, he analyzed the arts of repose and of movement, the movement of sound, the form and matter of rhythm, the rhythmic pulse, and applied these concepts to the free musical rhythm of Gregorian chant. This is the free rhythm proper to and characteristic of the Vatican Edition, in which the basic notes are not distinguished in terms of length as breves, semibreves, long, double longs, etc., but are all theoretically equal to one basic indivisible pulse, save for the case of the *mora vocis* (Dom Ferretti).

Because Mocquereau's approach was consistent and easily understood, it could be explained clearly to others and thus it aided a great many Catholics in their efforts to realize the ideal put forward by the Church: Gregorian chant and active participation of the faithful in song at worship. Indeed, if one marked on a map "the countries which have adopted editions with Dom Mocquereau's rhythmic principles, one would have marked at the same time the countries which best preserved the practice of Gregorian chant" (J. Claire 1955).

In recent years, however, the conclusions which Mocquereau's analysis had reached are regarded by some as superseded. Appeals are made to "the most recent studies of the earliest musical notation" whose rhythmic signs are to be interpreted in singing. The "now outmoded rhythmic markings of Dom Mocquereau" and his "now largely discredited rhythmic theories" are passed over in favor of "the more recent rhythmic theories of Dom Eugène Cardine" and a "subtle reinterpretation" of the traditional Gregorian chant style cultivated in the early years of the twentieth century. The basis of this new approach, much favored by the partisans of "early music" and its "authentic" performance practices, is what is known as Gregorian "semiology" (Dom Sixdenier). Its pioneer was Dom Eugène Cardine (1905–1988).

Like Dom Mocquereau, Cardine was haunted by what he felt was the need for authenticity, to "rediscover" and "respect" the intentions of the Gregorian composers by going back to the sources, the manuscripts. In 1972 Cardine wrote, "We have no other task than to read what the first copyists wished to express in writing. Hence it is needful that we rediscover their state of mind, their habitual practices, the conventions they received from their cultural milieu." And one could accomplish this only by having recourse to the most ancient manuscripts (tenth and eleventh centuries), those closest to the sources since in reality people had "corrected" (!) the Gregorian chant in the name of erroneous principles during the centuries which followed. The *Editio Vati-*

cana, at the beginning of the labors of restoration carried out at Solesmes, began to remedy a declining situation which had lasted for centuries and which was exemplified in the famous Medicean edition of 1614. However, Cardine specifies, any current notation is imperfect from both the melodic and the rhythmical points of view. Thus it is absolutely necessary to pore over the neumes with the most unremitting attention to the most ancient systems of notation used to transfer the Gregorian music into the visual domain. It is only scientifically conducted research which will allow the establishment of an objective execution of this chant. Otherwise, the interpretation will be the performance of a "romanticism" which will inevitably be guided by a rhythm and by nuances borrowed from modern music. . . .

Leaving to others the questions of Gregorian origins, paleography properly so called, melodic restoration, and Gregorian aesthetics, Cardine concentrated his attention upon that extreme diversity of signs found in the most ancient manuscripts. He gradually became convinced that this diversity is intended to express the particularities and the delicate nuances of expression within the interplay of durations and intensities. He will speak of "enthusiastic detection" when confronted with the "inexhaustible richness" of the nuances which the Gregorian composers had desired to convey: "If they used only a small number of basic signs, they labored mightily to combine them in such a multiplicity of ways that this very variety was long considered the result of either disorder or fantasy. But the more one studies these ancient scripts with the same patience and love which their inventors lavished upon them, the more one is astonished at the number and the importance of the discoveries which one can make in them." Their hands followed their voices, and in virtue of this "cheironomic notation" (as Dom Mocquereau called it), Fr. Cardine acknowledged them as theorists "in the best sense of the word," contrasting them with the medieval theorists who held systematic views but only "a purely bookish knowledge" of the music of Antiquity. It is by a path different from that of history that he renews relations with the unknown composers of the Gregorian melodies: through their neumatic writing.

Cardine understood that the neume is a "written gesture," or as we would say, a "written recording" which is presented to us to read, since one cannot hear it again. Paying close attention to these discoveries, the late Dom Hourlier—a colleague of Cardine's and historian of liturgical

MSS at Solesmes—said to their author in 1950 that an "intermediate science" was about to spring up, situated between paleography and aesthetics, a science that needed a precise name. For several years Dom Cardine spoke in terms of "Gregorian diplomatics," but the expression did not seem very felicitous. One of the cantors at San Girolamo in Rome, Dom Sixdenier, suggested substituting the name "Gregorian semiology," and the name was eventually approved and accepted. At that time, the term "semiology" (from the Greek *semeion*, sign) was used chiefly in the medical field.

This new semiology, by which one investigated the meaning of neumatic scripts, is based upon two criteria. The first belongs to the material or graphic order, and considers the design or configuration of the signs. The second belongs to the aesthetic order, and considers the musical context in which each sign is used. It is a matter of investigating the convergence of these two criteria, and of comparing the instances identified in each of the different notations.

Cardine insisted upon two points above all. The first was his discovery of what he called the neumatic break, namely the process of Gregorian writing most widely used in the Middle Ages to emphasize the important note, by an interruption of the normally continued line of the notation. He presented this discovery in 1957 to the III International Church Music Congress at Paris. Afterwards, in a long article in *Études Grégoriennes* (1961) embellished with detailed charts, he produced the paleographic proofs of this constant element of "breaks" among the neumes. Following his path, he was led to what he felt was an even more important discovery, which he set forth at the meeting of the Association for Gregorian Chant Studies in Venice in 1972: the notion of *value*, uniting duration and intensity, the foundation of Gregorian rhythm. He showed that the rhythmic value of the notes is linked to that of the syllables, and that this basic syllabic value (which in general remains obviously the same from one syllable to the next, and hence from one note to the next) can be modified by the Gregorian composer. These are the variations in value which he sought to discern in the neumatic notation and to reproduce in the chant in order to recover the primitive rhythmic inspiration by delighting in its savor and thus making prayer more animated. Having arrived at these foundations of semiology, at the very heart of Gregorian rhythm, he allowed to choirmasters ample space for interpretation while respecting the indications proceeding from the manuscripts.

Semiology, Cardine said repeatedly, has nothing to do with a system, and is not a method but a means, "the" means of making genuine contact with the authentic music. The indications which he furnishes are "elastic" (a term which he returned to frequently); the proportionate "dosage" of the note values in terms of more or less, cannot be determined precisely. As the years passed, Cardine stressed more and more that the achievements of semiology "do not lead ipso facto to a good performance: they must be given life by the interpretation, a very delicate problem which it is proper and expedient to resolve if one desires to avoid a cold performance." In reality, the problem was such that no interpretation of chant recorded up to the time of his death in 1988 received the full and complete approval of Dom Cardine! At any rate, he recognized the merits of some of them, in first place the singing of his own monastery of Solesmes: "The great distinction of Solesmes' chanting" (he said before his death) "is that the text is understood and prayed."

In his musicological "testament" presented during the third international Gregorian chant congress held at Luxemburg in 1984, Cardine beseeched the Gregorianists to whom he had always preached "respect for the sign," to "go beyond" (*surpasser*) or to "exceed" or "be greater than" the sign (*dépasser le signe*). "The danger which awaits us (he explained) is all too familiar: it is to lose oneself among all the details identified . . . and to forget the general effect of the whole. . . . By dint of urging analysis, do we miss the synthesis?" Good judgment and common sense must guide the singer, sustaining him "at an equal distance from inaccessible perfection and from a routine which all too easily contents itself with anything . . . whatever." "Gregorian chant is not simple," he says. "Everyone wants a very easy and simple process. But it is necessary to show that it is the hard work which allows us to approach beauty." He emphasizes without respite, not only that one cannot have any opposition between science and art—in other words, that one cannot set up semiology against interpretation—but also that artistic sense must have a scientific basis. Like the ancient composers whose strength and vigor he left no stone unturned to recover, the semiologist Cardine was profoundly conscious within himself of that Gregorian rhythm which he refused to imprison within formulae: "I believe that one should not lay down rules which do not agree with the genius of the composers. . . . Equal notes? But cannot Gregorian chant give something more? An *élan* or energy which carries higher and farther: the sublimity of the sacred texts and the joy which overflows from them."

In his indefatigable pursuit of Gregorian beauty, Cardine the monk was convinced that such beauty was but the reflection of another Beauty, toward which all praise ascends. One thinks of the words he spoke at Subiaco in 1981: "More than simply *vocal music*, Gregorian chant is a *sung word*, a sacred word which comes to us from God in Holy Writ and which returns to God in praise."

II

On this basic point, there is widespread unanimity within the praying Church today. But there seems to be less agreement on the priorities to be set when it comes to fulfilling the wishes of the Church regarding its practical application to song at Mass. It has been evident for a long time that archaeological researches are one thing, and quite another are the decisions of the Church in matters pertaining to actual practice of liturgical usage.

Some would advance "philological" reasons for rejecting Mocquereau's theory of free musical rhythm as being "mechanical and in part arbitrary." They would favor "free rhythm" understood as non-measurable note values and flexible proportionality in mutual rhythmic relationships of the notes, varying according to the demands of the melodic and linguistic context. In order to realize, in the actual singing of Gregorian chant at daily or weekly liturgies, such results of detailed semiological research, there is required a very high degree of musical literacy. And of course, considerable philological-semiological knowledge would also be needed—requirements whose fulfillment may justly be doubted in most cases. The belief that only in such chanting does "the true beauty of Gregorian chant find expression," seems to imply two presuppositions which ethnomusicological research (among other things) induces us to regard critically:

1. that there exists a notation which is able to record the actual sonic event of monodic art song with all its nuances and details, so that a complete reconstruction would be possible on the basis of the written sketch; and

2. that the aesthetic sonic ideal from which arose the delicate details and nuances now discovered thanks to semiological research, would sufficiently correspond to the musical perception ("beauty") of contemporary Western musical culture.

Admiring knowledge of the richness of an ancient monodic art song is rather limited in its ability to promote the re-animation of lost singing traditions, for otherwise the worship offered by men living at a given time—which is the goal of the efforts at restoration—will be exchanged for a different goal: a likewise quite justifiable but largely historical museum-type research. Such a goal seems less suited to realize the grand musical and pastoral-liturgical ideal of St. Pius X: *actuosa participatio populi* in the liturgical singing of Gregorian chant.

The success of the Gregorian singing style made famous by Dom Mocquereau and Dom Gajard plainly corresponds to the practical needs of daily liturgical life as well as the contemporary musical perceptions and sensitivities of great numbers of people. These two qualities remain of primary importance for any living practice of Gregorian chant according to the mind of the popes of the twentieth century and of the last Vatican Council, and for that reason they rank higher, in case of doubt, than the demand for historical authenticity.

A great modern Gregorian pedagogue put it this way: ". . . the pedagogical experience of my whole life, and that of many others, leads me to believe that as much for teaching children as for unity in people's chants and as for the artists themselves, it is necessary to have marks, reference marks,—in this case, ictus and rhythmic signs—which affirm rhythms, locate the phrases and bring indispensable assistance in realizing rhythmic unity and correct interpretation. In an analogous domain, that of modern music, have editors and musicians ever regretted the time bars (provided they are given an exact meaning) which facilitate performance of the great polyphonic and orchestral works?"

III: Appendix

Fr. André Mocquereau of Solesmes was not only an outstanding musicologist but also a remarkable musician who devoted his life to showing the singers of our own time how to breathe musical life into the dead letters and signs of the ancient manuscripts. Unlike many musicologists who remain locked into a study of the written forms exclusively, Dom Mocquereau studied the signs and then proceeded to transform their meaning into living audible sounds—real music of prayer which can be sung, heard, and appreciated.

Rhythm is the pulse of life, in Gregorian chant as everywhere else, and Dom Mocquereau made clear to us the reality of rhythm, providing us with terms and signs with which we can identify its elements and its reality, and communicate these in workable paedagogy to others. All who are called to labor at this noble task should ponder carefully the implications of an important text like the Preface to the Vatican Gradual (1907), which follows.

An Explanation of the Vatican Edition of the Roman Chant

Holy Mother Church has received from God the task of building up the souls of the faithful in all holiness, and for this noble purpose she has always and most profitably used the sacred Liturgy. To avoid divisive differences, and to foster instead the unbroken unity which is a source of both strength and beauty for the Mystical Body of Christ, the Church tries very carefully to preserve the traditions of the ancients. If in the course of time these traditions have been forgotten, she continually attempts to rediscover them zealously and restore them effectively.

Among all the things which are closely connected with the Church's worship, and which penetrate it in such a way as to add splendor and efficacy, the sacred chant takes the first place. Common experience has shown that it not only adds a certain grandeur to divine worship, but also attracts souls heavenwards in a most wonderful way. Hence the Church, in every age, has recommended the use of this chant, and has taken the greatest pains to see that it lose none of its age-old dignity.

To achieve its purpose, the chant to be used in worship must possess qualities which make it uniquely sacred and beneficial to souls. First and most important, it must possess a religious seriousness. Second, it must be able to draw the understanding of the Christian soul gently toward the truth. Third, it must be universal, in the sense that it fulfills the needs of every race, every country, and every age. Last, it must combine simplicity with the perfection of art.

These qualities are nowhere better exemplified than in the Gregorian chant, "the proper chant of the Roman church, the only chant which she has inherited from the ancient Fathers, which she has jealously kept for so many centuries in her liturgical books, which she offers to the faithful as her own music, and which she insists on being used exclusively in some parts of her liturgy" (*Motu Proprio*, November 22, 1903, no. 3).

In the course of time the purity of Gregorian chant, as a matter of fact, did suffer great harm. This happened principally because the correct rules of chant, received from the tradition of the ancients, were either carelessly overlooked or completely forgotten. Accordingly, we have lost sight of what we call the "liturgical spirit," or the "spirit of prayer," and the style and spirit of sacred music, if not completely extinct, is nearly so.

The Holy Father, Pope Pius X, imitating the efforts of his predecessors in this matter, took measures, by laws and decrees, to prevent further damage to the chant. Any reform must needs begin with principles, and the principles upon which the song of the Church is based, and by which it is governed, were clearly and concisely indicated by the Holy Father in his *Motu Proprio* of November 22, 1903. He also collected the Church's chief decrees against the various abuses which through the years had made inroads upon the chant. There followed on January 8, 1904, a decree of the Sacred Congregation of Rites which urged, even more clearly, the restoration of Gregorian chant.

The Roman church and the others which follow her rite had to prepare books containing the authentic melodies of Gregorian chant. Pope Pius X very clearly foresaw this need, for in his *Motu Proprio* of April 25, 1903 he declared: "The Gregorian melodies are to be restored in their completeness and true nature, according to the testimony of the more ancient manuscripts, taking into consideration not only the legitimate tradition of intervening centuries, but also the common practices of present-day liturgy."

Observing these rules and laws, the men who undertook the work of the restoration at the Pope's bidding began their paleographic research with a diligent and careful examination of the ancient manuscripts. This was a very wise choice, for these documents are valuable not only because of their age (which approaches that of the very beginnings of Gregorian chant), but especially because they were written during the years when chant itself was most vigorously flourishing. Although an earlier date and widespread use among the ancients might make a particular melody worthy of inclusion in a new edition, the factor which actually determines such inclusion must be the accuracy with which it expresses religious art and the strength of liturgical prayer.

Therefore when dealing with the manuscripts one must always remember this: the fact that a manuscript might be older does not mean it must be accepted by reason of its age alone. The restoration of the Church's song must not be based on paleography alone, but also must take into account history, the art of music (and especially chant), and experience in the laws of the sacred liturgy. Otherwise, even though it might be archaeologically correct, it might lack consistency, or offend against Catholic tradition by preventing certain periods from contributing to the heritage of the Church that which is good or even excellent. No one can possibly limit what we call the Gregorian tradition to a fixed period of time, for it includes all the ages which have cultivated Gregorian chant with more or less zeal and success. As the Holy Father says in the above-mentioned *Motu Proprio,* "the Church has always recognized and encouraged all progress in the arts, and has always admitted to the service of her functions whatever is good and beautiful in their development during different centuries, as long as they do not offend against the laws of the liturgy."

In conformity with these wise counsels of the Holy Father the present work of editing has been completed.

However, the Church leaves qualified men at liberty to determine the age and type of any particular Gregorian melody, and to judge its workmanship. One right she reserves to herself, namely, to give and prescribe to bishops and faithful alike the text of the sacred chant, which, carefully restored according to the manuscript tradition, brings a fitting splendor to divine worship and edification to souls.

[Dom Eugène Cardine gave the following musicological testament at the third international conference of the Associazione Internazionale Studi di Canto Gregoriano, which took place in Luxembourg in June, 1984. It is printed here with permission of Solesmes abbey and *Gregoriana,* where it appeared in the issue of July 1988 (No.11). The translation from the French by Virginia A. Schubert originally appeared in *Sacred Music* 115/4 (Winter 1988) 22/7.]

The Limits of Semiology in Gregorian Chant

This is my last will and testament.

If we consider as the subject of semiology all research which, beginning with the oldest and most differentiated neumatic signs, allows us to discover the truth about Gregorian chant, it is necessary to recognize as authentic semiologists certain Gregorian scholars who worked courageously along these lines for more than a century.

In an interesting article, Professor Hans Lonnendonker had the happy idea of stressing the links between several German specialists, as a result of the work of Michael Hermesdorff, organist at the Cathedral of Trier.

In Italy the outstanding personality was without a doubt the canon of Lucca, Raffaello Baralli. More or less quickly, everyone made contact with the monks of Solesmes, who began their research under the energetic leadership of the founder of the abbey, Dom Prosper Guéranger.

Along with the two successive heads of the paleographic workshop of Solesmes, let us name those whose work is of special interest to us here: working with Dom Joseph Pothier was Dom Raphael Andoyer, and with Dom André Mocquereau, two monks whom I was fortunate enough to know at the end of their long careers: Dom Gabriel Bessac and Dom Armand Ménager. Our gratitude and faithful prayers go to these pioneers in the restoration of Gregorian chant and to all the others who preceded us and whose names I would not be able to mention.

Their work constitutes the point of departure for research which was greatly developed later. In 1950, my associate Dom Jacques Hourlier recognized the "intermediary science" which was introduced little by little between Gregorian paleography, a discipline where he himself excelled, and aesthetics, where Dom Gajard preferred being placed. In 1954, Dom Guy Sixdenier proposed to call this new science semiology, a name that was immediately accepted.

Even before being called to Rome in January 1952, and to a much greater extent in the years that followed, by profession and by vocation, I dedicated myself to the study of neumes, by following the path laid out by Dom Mocquereau, a path which always left me in awe. I believed in it from my first reading of his work, and I still believe in it today!

In the scholarly introduction to his *Paléographie musicale* (p. 13), Dom Mocquereau presented the first manuscripts with notation in Gregorian chant in this way: "They are not the ancient masters whose teachings we would like to hear, but the translation into writing of what those masters taught and executed; and from there, for those who know how to read and understand this writing, there is a most perfect expression of 'liturgical cantilena.' Let us emphasize here the phrase "for those who know how to read and understand this writing." This is exactly what semiology consists of: to learn to read in order to understand what Gregorian chant is.

Happily, I was joined in this search by Dom Luigi Agustoni who edit-

ed and published the results of the first research. A little later a courageous cohort of students presented themselves. They agreed to work
on subjects that were sometimes very dry, but their efforts usually resulted in significant research papers and doctoral dissertations. That
precious collaboration enlarged the field of knowledge and assured its
solidity.

At the same time and in a parallel fashion, a collection of outlines
and notes was prepared for the classes at the Pontificio Istituto di Musica Sacra. Along with answers to questions and critiques of readings,
these were carefully assembled in great detail by Dom Godehard Joppich and Dom Rupert Fischer into an organized course. This work was
called *Semiologia gregoriana*, and was soon translated into French, Japan-
ese, English, Spanish and German.

This was the second layer of semiological progress. It presented in
many languages the ensemble of work accomplished over some twenty
years. The written symbols of various schools of notation still gravitat-
ed to signs associated with St. Gall, but they were at the point of detaching themselves and reclaiming their independence. This does not
mean that comparative semiology, which studies the differences and
similarities of various schools, will not always be of the greatest interest
and will not be able to develop indefinitely. To all of those who helped
me in this second period, I send my warmest and most cordial gratitude.

Even before the end of this second period, when it still bore the
promise of rich fruits, a third period had already begun. We had hardly
explained the meaning of each of the neumes in a quick fashion, when
a new group of questions was already raised by the scholars: for what
use were "particular" signs designated? I mean here signs whose design
reveals a choice made among forms which were more or less the same.
Thus one moved from the meaning of the sign to its conscious use.
Here is the progress made: a step was taken toward aesthetics and interpretation. In the *Festschrift* previously referred to (pp. 443–457), Dom
Godehard Joppich gave good examples of the bivirga placed at the end
of a word. Similarly, Professor Heinrich Rumphorst (*Études Grégoriennes*
XIX, pp. 27–88) gave examples of two forms of the pes subbipuncti. Instead of being exhausted, the world of research extended farther and
farther.

Moreover, everything seems to favor this growth. The Associazione

Internationale Studi di Canto Gregoriano, in its tenth year, has more than justified the happy initiative of its two founders; and the third conference currently taking place gives evidence of the zeal and competence of its members. Our secretary, so well assisted by Signora Albarosa, works generously in various scientific and practical areas, especially in the publication of the *Bollettino* and the organization of the courses in Cremona. In addition, the entrance into official teaching and the imminent growth in this area gives us hope of equal progress in depth. Such a balance sheet leads one to profound gratitude to those who are working so devotedly on preparing the future. I sincerely rejoice that there are people to carry on the work; those who are growing up today and those whose presence we can only guess at who will carry on tomorrow.

Thus Gregorian semiology is alive and well. It finds its roots in the "foundation which is the least lacking," that of the first musical notations, and it develops its branches in the most promising milieu. The knowledge which results must bear fruit. Music is only learned in order to be performed and heard, to become pleasure and praise.

Interpretation is necessary in this last stage of bringing the chant to life, just as semiology is necessary to furnish the raw materials. The two must be in harmony or they will fail to reach their goal. If semiology is not respected, the work is treated without dignity and it is deformed. It can even be betrayed. If interpretation is lacking, interest in it will be lacking also. Success rests in the union of these two necessities.

I have affirmed several times that semiology alone is not enough to determine a performance of Gregorian chant. It seems to me correct to say that semiology "is not a method" in the common use of the term, but at the same time the use of this expression is sometimes interpreted too strictly. Some have used it with pleasure as if through it they were freed from a bothersome burden. "It is not a method? Then it has no practical use; let us leave to others this scientific pastime!"

It is impossible to be more seriously mistaken! With Dom Mocquereau we have already seen that the study of the original neumes is the only way to know Gregorian chant, and elsewhere we have proved that this study is indeed worthy of the name of semiology. The conclusion is evident!

Indeed, what do most of our critics want? They pretend that they are faithful to an ideal which they have judged to be perfect once and for all without ever having made the effort to question its value. Since for them the musical world is a question of taste, they are fully satisfied with the comfortable habits they have acquired and enriched with so many memories of people, circumstances and places that they love. Or on the other hand, they believe that if Gregorian chant is music, it has to be this way or that. Thus they think they are dispensed from all research into what sort of music it is. It is too easy! Therefore they cultivate, to their own liking, oppositions in tempo between phrases or clauses in the same piece, using crescendos, accelerandos or their opposites, instead of respecting the variety of syllables and the diverse values of the notes, allowing the Gregorian chant to express its own true character.

All the proposed rhythmic systems which are more or less measured, falter when compared with the first notations, whose obvious differences cannot be made to agree. The very notion of the neume is inconsistent if it is not attached to the syllables of the literary text, for the graphic signs were not conceived of as rhythmic entities. And what is there to be said about the *coupures* (breaks in the neumes), which are evident everywhere in the manuscripts? Only that they are interpreted either more rigidly or with more elasticity, depending on the various schools of notation.

All of these, along with the additions and styles of notation which vary depending on the region, constitute the "semiological givens" that can neither be denied or objected to. These are the beacons of which I have so often spoken!

If we are asked how these well documented "givens" should be applied, it is necessary to answer: "With subtlety!" And once again it is semiology which teaches us. Here is an easy way to prove it. It comes from a research paper presented in 1977 to the Pontificio Istituto di Musica Sacra (No. 33, Sr. Maria Luigina Pelizzoni, *Festschrift*, p. 494). Codex 381 from St. Gall contains a *versicularium* (a book of verses for the introit and the communion), written around the year 1000, which is entirely in *campo aperto* notation. In it there are only eight examples of the virga with an episema ⅄: four times on the word *rex* and four times on *cor*. It is very obvious that the intention was to emphasize these two monosyllables which have a particularly lyric meaning. This is all the more evident because these eight examples always take place in unisonic recitation. However, these two monosyllables, which are sung recto tono, also are notated elsewhere with a simple virga /: three times on *rex* and five times on *cor*. All in all there are the following occurrences: virga with episema, 4 + 4, virga without episema 3 + 5

There is therefore a numerical equality. But since the use of the episema on the isolated virga is very rare in this document, it indicates the will of the author. This is in contrast with those cases when the absence of the episema can, without fearing an error, be attributed to a lack of attention. In general, the scribe preferred the virga with episema "when he thought about it!" Given these conditions, would it be indicated to sing in a heavy fashion the words that were given the episema and to allow those same words to pass unnoticed among the neighboring syllables when their notation is the simple virga? It would be rigorously exact and would conform to the notation, but would it conform to an intelligent understanding of semiology?

It is possible to continue and elaborate on the conclusion. The possibility that we have to analyze this rich collection of psalm verses allows us to note specifically in simple examples what we remark so often in ornate compositions of the Gregorian repertoire. There are examples to be found in the first pages of the recently issued volume (No. XX) of *Études grégoriennes* in the article *"Les formules centons des Alléluias anciens."* In studying these superimposed notations, one sees here and there, next to very rare variants which are clearly opposed to one another, a certain number of imprecisions which cause us to question the attention of the copyists. The ensemble is quite different from a modern work, which is printed and checked several times to eliminate the smallest differences. In this case however, things that are considered as small defects give a certain kind of interest rather than being a detraction. It is like a play of light and shadow which brings out the proportions of the object admired.

Nevertheless, comparisons of this type are extremely profitable. They help us become more intimately connected with those who wrote the notation. If the Gregorian scholar is able to establish a serious contact with similar presentations, he will abandon little by little those aspects of his way of thinking that are too modern and will be able to acquire a sensitivity and a judgment which is more adapted to the music he wishes to bring to life again.

But then an important question is raised. Of what use are the charts of the "values of neumatic signs" that we are daring enough to publish?

Let us recognize first that after having created them patiently, we sometimes hesitate to use them. We do not always know where to place a certain sign even though the value that was assigned to it originally in its context seems evident in most cases. It is the time to repeat once again that neumes are not created to be put in a chart. If in spite of all this we do so, it is to facilitate explanations which are requested of us. A well-organized understanding of the most ordinary cases provides a frame which can be helpful, but we must be careful not to be caught in our own traps. Comparisons can be dangerous. The syllabic value placed between the "diminished" and "augmented" is obvious. But one must not add the two "values" on the left to make the equivalent of the "value" on the right or any other similar calculation. That would certainly be false!

The hesitations I make reference to are an obvious proof of our most perfect submission to the manuscript tradition. Indeed it would be very simple to classify automatically in all the examples in our chart all the signs that we run across, but we do not want to give in to such facility. That is why in more than one case, after having considered the relationship of values on the positive side and on the negative side, we do not want to decide one way or the other. I remember having advised a student to write her examples of a stropha with episema 2 across the vertical line separating the syllabic value and the augmented value, because I could not decide, nor could she, in favor of one attribution or the other.

All this is to say clearly that we are here treating the limits of semiology with regard to the precise determination of values. Let us understand fully the meaning of this affirmation which does not negate the basic progress in this area made in the last few years, but which forbids all automatic classification of the signs, especially of those which are rare. Progress will no doubt be made in the future, but the very nature of a rhythm which is as free as that of Gregorian chant is associated with an elasticity and a suppleness which is opposed to rigorous precisions.

That is why we cannot accept the new Lagal edition which was invented recently to help chanters, but which, I am convinced, offers more difficulties than advantages, in the theoretical as well as the practical areas. It solidifies values in a deadly way and it is especially unable to translate their variety, because their relationship one to the other is relative.

Indeed, thanks to our knowledge of the neumes, when it is understood that a certain note is more important than neighboring notes, or vice versa, it is easy to understand a certain difference, which it will be prudent to reduce rather than augment, unless there are perfectly clear indications. But how to find a precise dimension for that note, such as would be found in clockmaking, but not at all in Gregorian chant? A greater problem still is how to find a printed form of the sign which can be easily measured by the eye of the chanter? It is bringing minutiae to impractical and inexact levels. I never thought of such a thing during my half-century with neumes! The most explicit transcription of neumes is not in any way rigid; it remains supple and human. In general, if the knowledge of plus or minus in the values of notes constitutes the essential part of semiology, the dose is determined by interpretation. On the other hand, instead of paying such scrupulous attention to the signs of the manuscripts, some Gregorian scholars take too great a liberty with the neumes. They clearly separate the syllabic from the melismatic value, affirming that it is impossible to do otherwise. They say that long series of notes cannot be sung syllable by syllable. These series must be clearly heard to be understood.

Let us recognize that examples performed by a virtuoso soloist may be captivating because of the differences established between the slowing down and the hurrying of the sounds. But the beauty of a voice is not enough to be convincing, nor are certain similarities with Eastern music. One cannot manage to bend the notes to these fantasies! The most important thing is to accept this challenge: "If you think that the value of the syllable and the value of the neume can be made equal to each other, prove it!" I willingly return the package to the sender! If a proof must be given, it is through those who attribute different values to the same signs. When we consider a punctum equal to a punctum, and an uncinus equal to a uncinus, proof seems unnecessary. Here we still remain faithful to our total submission to the signs of the first manuscripts! Moreover, if there really was such opposition in the middle ages, would it not be normal to find some trace of that opposition? We are waiting for some evidence that would make us change our mind.

In these conditions, what advice should be given to the Gregorianist who knows semiology at least in its broad outlines and who truly wants to sing and have others sing? How can he make the best use of his knowledge without running the risk of running into the reefs that we just mentioned?

Since semiology is the entrance necessary for all knowledge of Gregorian chant, semiology should be allowed to function freely without encumbrances under the pretext that it could stifle or hinder interpretation! Indeed, if from the beginning, before even having studied the original neumes, one pronounces exclusions against a melodic reconstitution, a vocal technique, or any other musical phenomenon which would be declared contrary to good taste, to accepted practices, to ease of execution or even to the dignity of the liturgy or of prayer, by that very fact, one places an obstacle to the proper functioning of the semiological science and one establishes oneself as a pretentious judge of an art which is much beyond us. It is the duty of the person interpreting to accept all the conclusions of semiology (that is certainly obvious), even those which are surprising or seem abnormal. However, he will try to harmonize them with his own artistic imagination, for it is impossible to imagine a performance which would be judged by the person doing it as a contradiction or an obvious example of ugliness. It will always be possible to present objections which are historical, liturgical, or physiological, or still others which will allow for fruitful debate. The important thing is to arrive at a fundamental understanding which will permit one to apply to concrete cases principles verified in the rest of the repertoire. That is a true semiological type of reasoning which normally ought to be developed and enriched, in relationship to conscientious work, revised constantly and without end. This is a program which is too beautiful for a single researcher, but one that an association like ours can establish and carry out.

If we have referred here exclusively to the values of notes in Gregorian chant, it is not to reduce the area of semiology to that rhythmical given. It is because the variety of values constitutes a very thorny question, in which ignorance greatly harms our performances. It goes without saying that nothing will be neglected with regard to the different schools of notation. Everything must be taken into consideration as historical witnesses; we would be guilty if we allowed them to be lost.

It is at this point that the interpreter comes in. He uses various semiological givens in order to establish a living and harmonious whole. He organizes and places in hierarchical order the various parts of the composition and in each one organizes the subdivisions and principal points, going from one to the other down to the smallest details. In this work he will especially have to take note of breaks in the neumes (graphic separations), recognizing those which are cesuras and those which, quite to the contrary, represent accents. The difference is one of size because for the most part, the accents join the preceding to the following notes, while the cesuras establish one kind of break or the other, from the tiniest hesitation to a real pause (which nevertheless will not be complete because the breaks are found within the neume and thus one must not destroy its unity). This opposition in the meaning of the breaks indicates rather well the necessity for a true interpretation. This is all the more so because between the two extremes, there are many other breaks which are less clear and which should be treated as articulations of the melody which are more or less important. The role of the interpreter is to make a choice between the various possibilities and how much they can be harmonized. In the last analysis it is his work to judge and decide. Without a doubt he will be able to draw much information from the study of contexts and from the signs used for the neumes, but he will also and of necessity need to have taste which is formed by his experience with Gregorian chant.

These varying talents will need to be used when it comes to the immediate preparation of chanters and even more so the actual singing. This will be the time to apply what we have analyzed previously, and even to go beyond it, as must be the case, to create a new living synthesis. If all music begins "beyond the sign," this is even more true of Gregorian chant. Its notation is as supple as its rhythm is free. After having pleaded for respect for the sign, we must beg Gregorianists to surpass it!

The danger that is lying in wait for us is too well known: it is to lose oneself in the details which are identified and learned with difficulty and to forget the whole. In particular, the notes that we pay special attention to become too long. They muddy the movement and make it heavy. Excessive attention paid to a thousand details stifles what is spontaneous and natural. One can hear a voice which is constrained by fear and thus does not produce a good sound. In paying attention to the analysis, will we miss the synthesis? To prevent this, we must so greatly assimilate the result of our work that we end up by forgetting technique so that the listener does not hear it either. This ideal will not be achieved from one day to the next and perhaps never completely, but we will have to try for it as much as possible. May good sense guide us and keep us halfway between inaccessible perfection and a routine which is too easily satisfied with anything at all!

Let us accept this obligation willingly because it will reward greatly both those who look to Gregorian chant for pleasure for themselves, their students or their listeners, and those who consider the sung liturgy as praise of God and a source of spiritual life. For all of you, I wish the abundant fruits whose taste I know, and I hope to meet you in a harmonious progression on the path to Paradise. This is my last will and testament.

Dom Eugene Cardine
SOLESMES, APRIL 11, 1984

TRANSLATORS' NOTE

The layout of this translation of Father Combe's book differs from that of the original French edition in several respects. Quotations of more than two or three lines from letters, documents, and chronicle reports are set as block quotations. Quotations from all foreign-language documents are given in an English translation in the body of the text, with the original language cited by Father Combe presented in the footnotes. Finally, an extensive Index of names and places is provided at the back of the volume.

Father Combe welcomed the preparation of this English translation, and took advantage of the opportunity to make a few substantive changes in the original text. These changes incorporate information that was unavailable when the French edition went to press in 1969.

This translation is intended for readers without knowledge of any of the languages used in the original book. Those who may wish to read the quoted correspondence in the original are urged to consult the French original, available from L'Abbaye de Solesmes, 72300 Sablé-sur-Sarthe, France. For ease of reference, the numbering of footnotes used in the original French edition has been retained in the translation.

Where possible, the English translations of letters and documents are as published in *Papal Legislation on Sacred Music* by Robert F. Hayburn, Liturgical Press, 1979, Collegeville, MN.

We thank the Dom Mocquereau Fund and The Catholic University of America Press for their generous support for the publication of this book.

The Restoration of
Gregorian Chant

FOREWORD

This book is a compilation of numerous articles on the restoration of Gregorian chant that appeared in the *Études Grégoriennes* (Solesmes) from 1963 to 1968. The matter contained in them has been divided into two distinct parts:

Part I. The Gregorian Reform at Solesmes

The Reform of Gregorian Chant and the Chant Books at the Abbey of Solesmes, 1833–1883, Dom Guéranger, Dom Jausions and Dom Pothier (original version in: *Études Grégoriennes* VI, 1963, pp. 185–234).

Part II. The Vatican Edition

The Beginnings of the Gregorian Reform of St. Pius X:
I. Dom André Mocquereau.
II. Father de Santi and Msgr. Carlo Respighi (original version in: *Études Grégoriennes* VII, 1967, pp. 63–145);

The Gregorian Chant Restoration:
III. The Work of St. Pius X (original version in: *Études Grégoriennes* VIII, 1967, pp. 137–198), and

The Gregorian Chant Restoration (continuation): The Work of St. Pius X (original version in *Études Grégoriennes* IX, 1968, pp. 47–100).

These articles are reprinted here essentially as they appeared in *Études Grégoriennes*, resulting in some repetitions for which the author apologizes. However, some improvements have been made and additions have been inserted into the original version; in particular, certain significant documents have been quoted in their entirety. The division of the work into two parts has been retained, although these parts are obviously unequal in length. Chapters, paragraphs, and notes are sequentially numbered in each part. Part II begins again at No. 1. Unless otherwise indicated, the paragraph number or footnote to which the reader is occasionally referred is located in the part where the reader happens to be at the moment.

Three other articles, also published by the author in the *Études Grégoriennes,* are quoted on various pages throughout the book:

Bibliography of Dom André Mocquereau (original version in *Études Grégoriennes* II, 1957, pp. 188–203);

The Initial Publication of the "Revue Grégorienne" (original version in *Études Grégoriennes* V, 1962, pp. 99–108);

The Motu Proprio of November 22, 1903 of St. Pius X, Historical Studies (original version in *Études Grégoriennes* V, 1962, pp. 133–137);

The Vatican Edition, Historical Studies (original version in *Études Grégoriennes* VIII, 1967, pp. 203–221).[1]

It is not our intention here to offer an exhaustive study. In this work, the restoration of Gregorian chant has been viewed solely from a historical perspective. The few paragraphs that have been added at the end on the question of "rhythm" are not irrelevant—quite the contrary. The facts they relate were critical to the final demise of the Vatican Commission.

The sources used in this report are principally to be found in the Archives of the Abbey of Solesmes, especially rich in *unpublished* documents of primary importance that permit light to be shed on many hitherto obscure or misunderstood matters. Very Reverend Father Dom Ignace Dalle, Abbot of Saint-Wandrille, graciously placed the archives of his monastery at our disposal, and we express our thanks to him for this. Unfortunately, this permission was given to us as this book was going to press, so we were unable to take advantage of his gracious offer as much as we would have liked. Whenever there is a question of facts that are well known, we refer to studies that have already been made about them, being content to mention briefly the testimony of the Solesmes Archives.

To allow the reader to view the historical setting of the times clearly, we must (and here we anticipate a bit) give a concise list of the various liturgical chant books that were in use during the nineteenth century.

---

1. Several recent studies have also mentioned the Gregorian restoration; see Appendix V.

When Dom Guéranger restored Solesmes in 1833, only inadequate editions of liturgical chant were in use throughout Europe.

In France, the most widely used editions were derived from that of Nivers. In his *Graduale Romano-Monasticum*, published in Paris in 1658, Nivers, organist at Saint Sulpice, had treated the Gregorian melodies with freedom and, more specifically, had abridged them considerably. The Nivers *Gradual* was intended for monasteries. Many dioceses used this book as a basis for preparing and publishing their own chant books. Among these diocesan editions, those of Digne and Rennes were the best known. At the outset of the restoration of monastic life at Solesmes, Dom Guéranger adopted the then-current edition from Dijon (derived from the "Nivers" book, corrected by Valfré), which, in his view, seemed the least offensive at the time. Dom Guéranger knew that returning directly to the manuscript sources was the essential foundation for a good edition, and he entrusted the task to Dom Jausions and, most especially, to Dom Pothier.

Concurrently with the research undertaken at Solesmes, there appeared various attempts at a Gregorian restoration in editions also based on the ancient manuscripts, but their versions were arbitrarily "corrected": one from the Dioceses of Rheims and Cambrai of 1851 (a *Gradual* and an *Antiphonal*) which, though not perfect, marked an appreciable advance; one by Lambillotte of 1858 (a *Gradual* and an *Antiphonal*), which was wildly inaccurate; and finally, one by Hermesdorff (Trier, 1863–1864) which, while indicating the ancient neumes above the staffs, did not use the traditional notation.

After 1871, the "Medicean" edition, with origins dating back to the seventeenth century, played an especially important role. In 1577, Gregory XIII asked Palestrina and Annibale Zoilo to prepare an edition of chant, but the project was halted due to the justified complaint of a Spanish musician, Fernando de Las Infantas, who warned Philip II about the situation. Fernando rightly asserted that Palestrina and Annibale Zoilo had corrected the ancient melodies according to completely false principles (Palestrina had been involved only with the *Gradual*, and even there, only with the Temporal cycle).

In 1594, Raimondi of the Medicean Press in Rome undertook the project once again, but the Holy See rejected it. In 1614, however, Raimondi achieved his goal and printed the famous Medicean *Gradual* (*Graduale . . . cum Cantu Pauli V, Pont. Max., jussu reformato*). Nevertheless, it has never been demonstrated that Raimondi used Palestrina's work for this purpose.

The Medicean edition of 1614 served as the basis for the Mechlin edition of 1848 (Medicean *Gradual* and *Antiphonal*, after Venice, 1580), with a few attempts at correction. It was this same edition of the *Gradual* that Msgr. Haberl and the publisher Pustet of Ratisbon issued in 1871, claiming it to be the work of Palestrina, a claim that made it an initial success. Also for the *Antiphonal*, they based their work on the Venetian edition of 1580. They obtained a thirty-year privilege for the double publication of the *Gradual* and the *Antiphonal*, as well as a virtual monopoly, given the various commendations of the work emanating from the Holy See.

After the first decree of approbation, dated January 20, 1871, the neo-Medicean edition was in effect presented as containing the *genuinum cantum gregorianum*. As time went on, other documents issued by the Holy See proclaimed the edition *authentic*, and recommended it to the bishops.

The Ratisbon edition was attacked on both musical and historical grounds for the reasons noted above, and even on the grounds of justice, since the value of certain Roman decrees in its favor was hotly debated. The edition became an obstacle to the Gregorian reform that Solesmes was striving to extend to the universal Church, and the monopoly of the Ratisbon edition seemed excessive.[2] Still, it was natural for Pustet to be tenacious in defending its position: its edition had required substantial investment and financial interests of considerable proportions were at stake. Lastly, the issue of nationalism played a significant role in the quarrel. When the Ratisbon edition appeared in 1871, the French had just suffered a crushing defeat at the hands of Germany; hence the French government was also to become involved in the opposition to the Pustet monopoly, which tended to favor German industry.

In 1901, the Ratisbon privilege expired. It was not renewed. That same year, the project of a Vatican Commission was formulated. At first, the project failed to materialize, but it was taken up once again by

---

2. Concerning these facts, see Dom Rafael Molitor, *Die Nach-Tridentinische Choral-Reform zu Rom*, Leipzig 1, 1901, and 2, 1902. Various documents from the Holy See regarding the Medicean edition are found in Franz X. Haberl, *G. P. da Palestrina e il Graduale Romanum Officiale dell'editio medicaea, 1614*, Ratisbon, 1894.—Amédée Gastoué, *Le Graduel et l'Antiphonaire Romains*, Lyon, January 1913.

Pius X in 1904. However, the members of the Vatican Commission, which was chaired by Dom Pothier—with Dom Mocquereau and the monks of Solesmes in charge of editorial work—failed to reach an agreement. After interminable discussions, the edition of liturgical chant officially imposed on the entire Roman Catholic Church as the "Vatican Edition" was the result of a compromise.

The events about to be narrated here are extremely complicated, and the reader will not be surprised if it is sometimes difficult to follow the thread of our exposition.

We would like to express our deepest thanks to Mrs. J. B. Ward and the Dom Mocquereau Foundation, who made publication of this book possible.

LIST OF PLATES

ONE

The Gregorian Reform at Solesmes

I ▪ DOM GUÉRANGER'S RATIONALE

1. New Documents

More than a hundred years have passed since a young monk methodically began studying the elements of Gregorian chant and copying old manuscripts, by order of Dom Guéranger. In his book entitled *L'École Grégorienne de Solesmes*,[1] Msgr. Rousseau established 1856 as the year when the very first work on Gregorian chant research was undertaken at the Abbey. This is indeed the date confirmed by the few, but valuable, authoritative testimonies that have hitherto been assembled. It will be instructive to focus on these early stages of the Gregorian restoration at Solesmes in order to ascertain the main stages of its development and to establish a few dates with certainty. The discovery of very important letters from Father Gontier, of Le Mans,[1bis] Dom Guéranger's friend, and other letters from Dom Jausions and Dom Pothier,[2] allow us to add some detailed information about this subject, and place the role of Dom Guéranger, Abbot of Solesmes, in a clearer light.[3]

---

1. Desclée, 1910, p. 51

1bis. Rev. Augustin-Mathurin Gontier (1802–1881), Dean of Changé-lès-Le Mans, later canon of the Cathedral.

2. All these letters are addressed to the same person, Rev. L. Baptiste, Choirmaster of the Minor Seminary of Saint Gaultier, Diocese of Bourges.

3. On this subject, see also: Dom P. Cagin, *L'œuvre de Solesmes dans la restauration du chant grégorien,* in *Rassegna Gregoriana* 1904, col. 205–206; Dom L. David, *Dom Joseph Pothier, abbé de Saint-Wandrille et la restauration grégorienne,* Saint-Wandrille 1943; M. Blanc, *L'enseignement musical de Solesmes et la prière chrétienne,* Procure générale de Musique, Paris 1952; E. Moneta-Caglio, *Dom André Mocquereau e la restaurazione del Canto gregoriano,* in *Musica Sacra* (Milan), 1960, no. 1ff. This study gives a good overview of the whole Gregorian restoration movement in the nineteenth century.

2. Dom Guéranger's Principles

Comparing the manuscripts

It has become common practice to credit Dom Guéranger[3bis] with the Gregorian restoration, and nothing could be more appropriate, as we shall see. Did not, in fact, the restoration of the liturgy presume a parallel restoration of liturgical chant? In the first volume of his *Institutions Liturgiques,* Guéranger defined the liturgy as the "full array of symbols, of *chants,* and of actions through which the Church expresses her faith in God." He considered that nothing would have been accomplished toward the restoration of the liturgy until the chant was "restored to its ancient traditions."[4] In this first volume, i.e. as early as 1840, as a first step, he posed the principle of a genuine return to the purity of the Gregorian melodies. He wrote: "Clearly we can be quite sure sometimes that—in a particular composition—we have discovered the pure Gregorian phrase *when manuscripts from several remotely separated Churches agree on the same reading.*" In this regard, he also noted that the Fathers of Cîteaux, by their own admission, "had reconstructed the *Antiphonal* of Metz more according to theoretical assumptions than through an examination of manuscripts from various churches" (p. 306). Apologies would be due for quoting Dom Guéranger's oft-cited remark were it not so significant.[5] Besides, insufficient attention has been given to that fact that Dom Guéranger wrote at a time when the study of Gregorian chant was still in its early stages. Until then, only Fétis, a well-known musicologist, had called attention to the notation *in campo aperto,* or staffless neumes, in various articles published after 1808, but he did not offer any explanation of their meaning, nor did he see any evidence of a tradition in them. Moreover, this passage from Dom Guéranger has been the basis for all the research on Gregorian chant done at Solesmes for a hundred years.

3bis. Dom Prosper Guéranger, born April 4, 1805, ordained October 7, 1827, restored Solesmes in 1833, made Abbot of Solesmes on November 1, 1837, and died January 30, 1875.

4. Edition of 1840, p. 1.—Vol. 2, 1841, p. 695.—The present author is responsible for the italics in this quotation from Dom Guéranger and in those that follow.

5. Lambillotte was the first to cite this in his work, as early as 1851, *Clef des Mélodies Grégoriennes,* p. 10.

The testimony of the staffless neume manuscripts

Soon thereafter, Dom Guéranger returned to the question, with regard to Cistercian chant, in an article in *L'Univers* dated November 23, 1843. His comments clarify his thinking on the need for a true restoration of the Gregorian melody. In it we read:

. . . Among the various editions of notated books designated for Roman usage, from the twelfth-century manuscripts to those printed in the nineteenth century, which most clearly reflects the original reading of St. Gregory? This is one of the most important questions in liturgical archaeology, and to answer it satisfactorily, something more is needed than the discovery of the *Gradual* and the *Antiphonal* of Clairvaux in a sacristy at Bar-sur-Aube. This is true first because our encounter with these books is just a discovery—no more, no less. The chant readings at the Abbey of Clairvaux were no different from those at Cîteaux. Indeed many more books from Cîteaux, both manuscripts and published texts, are still extant. Secondly, these books themselves represent the phrasing of Gregorian chant only from the twelfth century on, *thus shedding no light on the true content of Gregorian chant as we can study it in manuscripts using notation that predates the method of Guido d'Arezzo, a notation that has not yet been deciphered.* I am well aware of what can be said in favor of the reading of Cîteaux. Yet therein lies a wealth of unresolved questions, not one of which is even dreamt of by the Gregorian chant *dilettanti* who clutter the public press with panegyrics for a chant of which they may not have heard even a single phrase.[6]

These few sentences are obviously quite significant. Dom Guéranger was well aware from the start of the problems raised by the Gregorian restoration. Above all, he advocated a return to the earliest manuscripts, which were no longer readable and which some long continued to view as useless.[7] Following Fétis, scholars such as Danjou, Lambillotte, Nisard, and Coussemaker[8] tried their hand at deciphering these ancient

6. (Letter) To the editor of *L'Univers* (quoted by M. Blanc, p. 131).

7. See, for example, T. Nisard, *L'archéologie et le vrai chant grégorien*, Lethielleux 1890, p. 40.

8. The main stages of this work were as follows: in Montpellier in 1847, Danjou discovered an *Antiphonal* noted in neumes and in letters, and it was believed to be the type of *Antiphonal* sent by St. Gregory from Rome to the school at Metz. In his journal, Danjou himself gave an inaccurate description of the neumes, which he does not distinguish correctly. In 1849, there followed the studies by Nisard on ancient musical notation in Europe, which shed no new light on neumes. That same year, Father Lambillotte believed that in Codex 359 of St. Gall he had found a manuscript hand-written by St. Gregory and sent to Charlemagne by Pope Adrian I. Lambillotte copied the manuscript and published it in facsimile in 1851. At the same time, he provided a fairly accurate description of the neumes, but his interpretation of the additional signs was poor. He

manuscripts, with greater or lesser degrees of success, but their secrets were ultimately to be uncovered by two of Dom Guéranger's students.

About 1846, it occurred to Fétis to bring out a chant edition based only on a single manuscript.[9] When consulted about this project, the Abbot of Solesmes reaffirmed the principle of the necessity of comparing the manuscripts of various churches in order to rediscover the earliest reading. Moreover, Dom Guéranger's response is interesting in other respects as well, and we will quote from it at some length. The Abbot of Solesmes shows that he was an informed critic and a good judge of the value of the editions then available. He is harsh especially on the Roman editions, but it is well known that they warranted that kind of criticism.

Dom Guéranger wrote:

I regard the publication of Mr. Fétis' Roman books as both an advantage and a disadvantage.

They are a disadvantage, first, because this edition will do nothing to supersede the other divergent editions, and secondly because Mr. Fétis' readings are always necessarily subjective and lack absolute authenticity, since his reading represents only one of the readings that he found in the manuscripts, which are not always in agreement with each other.

His books are an advantage, because Mr. Fétis has studied Gregorian chant sources more than anyone else in the world and because his work, whatever it may be, necessarily carries great authority. He works in the manner of an editor of classical texts, as one who chooses a reading from among *variants*. The more texts he has seen, provided that he is a man of discernment, the more weight can be given to his edition, yet the final reading fails to be completely reassuring.

Basically, I prefer his edition a thousand times over those of the Roman books. I did not mention this unfortunate situation in the *Institutions,* because at the time, I did not have the sources. At the end of the sixteenth century, the

---

was mistaken about the plainchant rhythm he was looking for, and transformed the Gregorian melodies into a measured and heavily accented chant. In 1852, Coussemaker, followed by Dom Schubiger, found the true origin of the neumes, which he derived from grammatical accents. But, like Raillard, who provided another explanation of neumes in 1859, Coussemaker erred with regard to the rhythmic value of the neumes, basing them on measure, and seeking variations in the duration of the notes in the neumes (see Boyer d'Agen, *Introduction aux Mélodies Grégoriennes,* 1894, pp. 92ff.

9. Fétis had thus opened the way for a "return to the sources"; after him, Danjou and Lambillotte unfortunately went off on the wrong track, looking for a hypothetical *Antiphonal* of St. Gregory.

Gregorian chants were corrupted at Rome in the process of shortening them. Strangely enough, the Roman chant books used here in France, despite their many alterations and faults, reflect a thousand times better the readings of the ancient manuscripts than do the books used in Rome, in Italy, and throughout practically the whole world. These unreliable Roman editions of the sixteenth century are found everywhere except in France.[10]

There is no need for additional quotations. These suffice to show Dom Guéranger's rationale, from the very first years of his liturgical work. In fact, each time the occasion warranted, the Abbot of Solesmes touched upon the Gregorian question. Not only did he underscore the contemplative and artistic value of the chant in a romantic way, in keeping with the style of his era, but he also traced its development and transformation down through the centuries. Here, for example, is how he assailed the melodies that were associated with the new liturgies of the seventeenth century:

New texts called for a new chant. . . . That task was addressed and a host of compositions was born, masterpieces of boredom, incompetence, and bad taste. . . . Father Lebœuf, a learned compiler, was asked to notate the Paris *Antiphonal* and *Gradual*. After spending ten years placing notes on lines and lines beneath the notes, he presented to the clergy of Paris a compositional monstrosity, almost all of whose compositions are as tiring to perform as they are to hear. God wanted to make it understood in this way that there are some things that simply should not be imitated, because they should never be changed.[11]

Dom Guéranger reforms the chant at Solesmes.

Everyone knows that the poor editions were deplorable, as was the widespread custom of beating time in order to give the chant some sort of measure that would make it seem more like "music". The Abbot of Solesmes did not hesitate to see "the work of the devil" in this heavily accented, measured chant, which deprived liturgical prayer of all religious character.[12] He judged the return to the authentic interpretation of the Gregorian melodies as important as the return to the original melody. He even said, and rightly so, that it will serve nothing to have good editions of the chant if this bad habit is not corrected, and that he

---

10. Dom Guéranger to Mr. Guignard, August 27, 1846.
11. *Mélanges de liturgie, d'histoire et de théologie* I, p. 37.
12. Gontier to Cloët, June 16, 1859.

would rather make use of a faulty edition, but interpreted according to the traditional rules.[13] From the outset, moreover, in his monastery where poor editions were nonetheless used, Dom Guéranger *managed to give the Gregorian melodies an accent, a rhythm of which the great majority seemed ignorant.*[14] He thus transformed every aspect of the liturgical chant thanks to a relaxed and natural pace, which restored its artistic beauty and value as prayer. This style of chant, basically the free rhythm of prose speech, elated Gontier. It was, in fact, a real revolution, for the true rhythm of the liturgical chant was universally misunderstood at the time, and seemed irrevocably lost. Another witness said, "Dom Guéranger brought to the liturgical functions a warmth and enthusiasm that radiated forth in his sung prayer, with perfect diction and a very supple voice."[15] It is well known that he saw to it that his sons brought the greatest care to the preparation of the chant for the Divine Offices.

From the outset, Dom Guéranger's intent was to restore Gregorian chant so that it might become once again the sung prayer of the Church, and in order to do this, to return to the sources, the most ancient chant manuscripts, and by comparing them, to rediscover the authentic melodies, and to rediscover likewise their traditional interpretation. Although this intent was not set forth in the works dealing with Gregorian chant *ex professo,* it was nonetheless succinctly and accurately expressed, and showed the way for all future work. In addition, this intent was already being tested in the chant sung at the Abbey headed by Dom Guéranger, who was to set in motion the movement to restore the Gregorian melodies. In fact, the daily use of liturgical chant enabled Dom Guéranger to perceive its beauty, to understand its true interpretation and its authentic content.

With such clear concepts as a basis for the true restoration of Gregorian chant, why did Dom Guéranger not apply himself to the task of reforming the chant books? Doubtless, he was waiting to have available to him men who were musically and scientifically competent, since it was a matter of undertaking a work that required both talent and a wide range of knowledge. Dom Fonteinne, Dom Guéranger's precentor, showed considerable musical talent, for he left some beautiful Gregori-

13. Dom Guéranger, *Approbation* of Gontier's *Méthode raisonnée de plain-chant,* Le Mans 1859, p. IX.

14. Dom J. Pothier, *Les Mélodies Grégoriennes d'après la tradition,* Desclée 1880, p. 4.

15. Dom David, *Dom Joseph Pothier,* p. 9.

an compositions that continue to be sung. These have been included in the monastic *Antiphonal* and even in the Vatican *Gradual,* such as his *Stabat mater.* However, doubtless his material concerns—he was cellarer (i.e. steward) of the monastery—did not permit him to apply himself to a task that required a great deal of time. Possibly, too, he was not attracted to this type of study.[15bis]

3. The Chant Books of the Old Solesmes

It is quite relevant to ask what chant books were in use at Solesmes at that time. Dom David pointed out that in the beginning there were no common books, and that various editions were used.[16] They had to get along the best they could with what was available. But this situation lasted only a short while, because a note from Dom Guéranger indicates clearly that, as early as 1833, he bargained for the purchase of choir books (four Graduals, four Antiphonals, eight Processionals) recently published in Dijon and modeled after the Roman edition of Valfré.[17] These books, published in 1827 and 1828, were far from presenting the liturgical chant in all its purity, but Dom Guéranger regarded them, in good conscience it seemed to him, as the "least offensive."[18] Because Solesmes followed the Roman rite at that time, these books could

15bis. Reference has just been made to the chant of Dom Fonteinne. Here is what Dom Savaton said of it *(L'Église de Solesmes,* unpublished notes, p. 53): "What ascended beneath our vaults at that time, directed by Dom Fonteinne, who was quite proud of his voice, his office, and his baton, wielded with gloved hand, went at times all too well, according to Dom Gardereau's testimony in 1837. This same person—then still a novice—wanted his Prior to bring back some good chant books from Rome, of the pure Roman style such as he had heard at Vitré, where the chant, especially for the hymns, was not disfigured by measures and cadences that made three-fourths of the melodies heavy and dull. 'I am taking an increasing dislike to the system of notation used in our *Antiphonal*—as well as in our Passions and Jeremiads *"correctae et concinnatae"* by Nivers in Paris. You may say that my reasoning in this matter is like that of a blind man concerning colors; be that as it may, I am nonetheless certain that there is a truth that corresponds to what I feel in my inmost soul. . . .' (March 22). In Rome, Dom Guéranger responded, 'Gregorian chant is forgotten, mutilated, changed, altered, with no regard for taste and the religion of antiquity; no one is protesting, all are asleep'" (May 24).

16. *Comment les mélodies grégoriennes ont été retrouvées,* in *Rassegna Gregoriana* 1904, col. 226–227.

17. "In 1833, Dom Guéranger purchased 'choir books' from Berlin-Mandar: four *Graduals* (recent Dijon edition after the Roman edition by Valfré), four Antiphonaries as loose sheets bound together, eight Processionals, a bound Missal, all for 225 f" (Dom Savaton, *L'Église de Solesmes,* p. 12).

18. Dom Guéranger's letter to Mr. Guignard, August 26, 1846.

suffice, very likely with some manuscript supplements for the responsorial and for feasts of the Order which were celebrated according to the
monastic rite starting in 1840.[19]

In 1846, however, the problem of books became critical at Solesmes,
where at last the complete monastic rite could be adopted. "The scarci-
ty of old breviaries," writes Dom Delatte, "had prevented the adoption
of the full monastic rite." Since the Benedictine nuns at the Calvaire in
Angers had collected a sufficient number of copies for the Abbey of
Solesmes, it was on the feast of Christmas 1846 that the psalter and
office, which Paul V had established in 1612 for the religious of St. Benedict, were used once again.[20] Nevertheless, the Dijon books were still
kept, doubtless for financial reasons, but also because good editions of
monastic chant did not exist, and it seems that Dom Guéranger was already dreaming of making his own edition. This explains why he did
not adopt the 1851 *Gradual* of Rheims and Cambrai. Though this publication marked notable progress over previous editions, it did not entirely satisfy him. Corrected on the basis of a priori and false principles, this
edition did not present the traditional grouping of the notes. Instead, it
perpetuated the arrangement of the notes as an irregular succession of
longs and shorts, all of which rendered the edition even more deficient,
from the rhythmic point of view.[21]

Since the Benedictine order followed the Roman missal for the Mass,
this *Gradual* did not pose any great practical problem. It was quite another matter with the *Antiphonal*, because the structure of the monastic
Office differs from that of the Roman Office; the distribution of the
Psalter is yet another matter. Nevertheless, the monks were content to
correct the Roman *Antiphonal* of Dijon, and to supplement it with manuscript inserts, as can be seen from the copies in the Abbey's library.

Starting in 1846, the year in which the monastic rite was adopted,
Dom Guéranger set to work preparing the Proper for his monastery.
Dom Delatte wrote: "On March 23, 1852, he addressed a request to Pope
Pius IX to obtain his approval. This was granted in 1856, on the occasion
of a voyage to Rome."[22] The Proper cycle, the chant for which was

19. Dom Savaton, *L'Église de Solesmes*, p. 20.

20. *Dom Guéranger Abbé de Solesmes*, Paris, Plon 1909, vol. I, p. 409. Our first edition of the Bre-
viary was printed by Château-Gontier in 1860.

21. Gontier also judged it harshly (letters of February 23, 1862, and October 22, 1864). Cf. A.
Duclos, *Sa Sainteté Pie X et la musique religieuse*, Desclée 1905, p. 32.

22. Dom Delatte, *Dom Guéranger. . . .* , vol. 2, pp. 121–125.

composed by Dom Fonteinne, a few ancient and very beautiful compositions excepted, was first sung on June 2, 1856, the feast of St. Pothin.[23]

Even for this Proper, the monks felt that they had to be satisfied with improvised solutions. At first, manuscript booklets were used. Later, duplicated notebooks were used in which all the supplements needed for chanting the monastic Office were included: Invitatories, Hymns, Responses, Graduals, and Processional Antiphons. It may be said that this *Supplementum ad Graduale et Antiphonarium* was Solesmes' first publication. The musical text was written in large whole notes (the manuscript notebooks still used diamond-shaped notes) and included some beautiful compositions by Dom Fonteinne.[24]

It should be noted that in 1856, Solesmes published a monastic *Ceremonial*.[25] This publication contained very few chants, and almost all of the *Mandatum* antiphons from the Dijon *Gradual*. From the point of view of melody, the only changes to be noted concerned the musical notation, consisting particularly in the elimination of the bar lines. The effect of this was to render the chant more alive and better phrased. One can also point to a greater number of stemmed *virgas*, together with some diamond-shaped notes. But there is no way of knowing how these details were then interpreted, since chant at the Abbey already had its own special style, as mentioned above.

4. Dom Guéranger's Hesitations

Given the paucity of choir books in use at Solesmes after 1846, it might be supposed that Dom Guéranger was already seriously planning an edition of these books, one that would conform to the traditional principles he had posited.

However, before making contact with the original framers of the Gregorian restoration at Solesmes, it is necessary to go back in time and to mention a circumstance which, in 1853, was not unrelated to the resolution which the Abbot of Solesmes was about to make. Turning back will also allow us to follow the progression of his intent more clearly.

23. *Chronicle* of Dom Bérengier, June 2, 1856.

24. Dom Gajard, *L'Art Grégorien*, in *Maria* (du Manoir), vol. 2.

25. *Cérémonial pour la vêture et la profession des Bénédictins de la Congrégation de France,* Rennes, Vatar, 1856.

The need for books was not felt at the Abbey alone. The dioceses needed them as well. As noted above, the Dioceses of Dijon, Rheims, and Cambrai had published new editions. A few other dioceses did the same.[26] The Diocese of Le Mans also had its own Commission editing its own liturgical chant books, and Dom Guéranger was involved in it. His advice, moreover, was considered crucial.

On August 12, 1853, the Abbot of Solesmes noted for the first time in his *Journal* that he was going to Le Mans "at the invitation of the bishop to take part in the Commission established to prepare the return to Gregorian chant."[27] The minutes of the Commission[28] mention Dom Guéranger twice. It was on Dom Guéranger's advice, according to the minutes, that the Commission rejected all the editions that reproduced the reformed chant of Nivers:

All the true friends of religious chant, in particular Reverend Father Dom Guéranger, Abbot of Solesmes, have risen against this pretended restoration, which is nothing more than a total destruction of this beautiful chant so long honored in the Church.

Dom Guéranger's well-justified severity toward the new liturgical chant compositions is well known, and comes as no surprise. Somewhat more surprising is the advice he gave to the Commission (advice he would repeat in his approval of Gontier's *Method*), to curtail certain repetitions of an identical phrase in the chant. To be sure, the context indicates that there is no question that this meant suppressing what was essential to the melodic line, for, as has been noted, Dom Guéranger was strongly opposed to such alterations. He referred, rather, to what he felt were repetitions added after the Golden Age of Gregorian chant.[29] Even in this form, however, this was a regrettable concession to the fixed practice of the time, and one that the additions of the thirteenth century did not merit.

It is not irrelevant to point out again, in this regard, that at about this

26. The numerous chant methods that saw the light of day at this time gave witness to the growing interest in liturgical chant.

27. He went there again for the same reason, twice in 1854, twice in 1855, and one last time in 1857.

28. T. Nisard, *De la réforme du chant grégorien dans le diocèse du Mans,* Rennes 1853, p. 7. Cf. M. Blanc, *L'enseignement musical de Solesmes,* p. 143.

29. Letter to Mr. Guignard, quoted above, dated August 27, 1846.—*Programme de la commission . . . du Mans,* see M. Blanc, *L'enseignement musical de Solesmes,* p. 144.

time, Dom Guéranger also felt obliged to follow the available editions, notably those of Rheims and Cambrai, with regard to another matter. A note written by Dom Guéranger in about 1855 (so dated because it mentions a book published that year) provided the following information about Dom Guéranger's intent at that time:

A comparison of all the manuscripts of the Middle Ages with the Gothic editions of plainchant leads us to the conclusion that in earlier times there was no concern at all for short syllables in ecclesiastical chant, and that there was no problem whatsoever about elaborating them with several notes, often a great number. A fortunate change, which has the force of law today, has modified this usage of the weak penultimates, and it would be a barbarous archaism to adopt this ancient custom in our time. However, when it is a question of short syllables that are not penultimate, there should be no difficulty in treating them in the same way as the syllables that are not short. We set great store here by Father Petit's book.[30] What he says with regard to the ancients is based on facts, and it follows that there is a reform to be made if we are to enter into the Gregorian tradition. The only possible concession to modern ears is that of the penultimate, in the sense that I expressed at the beginning, and this concession is not contrary to the practice of true antiquity.

With regard to these two comments on Dom Guéranger's intent, let us say right away that we must not be too surprised that the Abbot of Solesmes did not immediately understand all that had to be done to achieve the full restoration of the Gregorian melodies, and that these hesitations quickly disappeared when, at his instruction, the ancient chant manuscripts were studied directly at his monastery. In the end, the clear and sure principles that he himself put forward were to prevail over this trial and error method. Soon, having studied and understood the Gregorian chants better, he offered this excuse for once having thought of shortening them: "I was unaware of all the musical riches contained in our liturgy."[31] As we will see later, Dom Guéranger abandoned his views regarding weak penultimate syllables just as readily.[32]

---

30. *Dissertation sur la Psalmodie et les autres parties du chant dans leurs rapports avec l'accentuation latine*, Paris 1855.

31. Letter from Gontier to Cloët, October 13, 1864.

32. Letter from Gontier dated October 30, 1862, Cf. *infra*, No. 13.

5. Dom Guéranger's Authority

It remains to be noted here that matters pertaining to Gregorian chant were beginning to be directed toward the Abbot of Solesmes. In 1846, as we saw above, Dom Guéranger was consulted on the matter of the issuance of the chant books of Fétis. In 1847, Tesson had also sought his advice regarding the publication of the *Vesperal* (letter of Tesson, August 26). He consulted Dom Guéranger once more, in view of the Commission of which he was a member, and which was to publish the Rheims/Cambrai edition. That same year, Nisard came to consult with Dom Guéranger, whose concern, he said, gave him courage. A while later, Nisard sent Dom Guéranger an article on ancient notations, and asked him to support a request with Mr. de Falloux for a grant for a scientific mission to Montpellier and St. Gall, in view of the publication of the manuscript discovered by Danjou in 1847. Dom Guéranger's response leads us to believe that Danjou had also been in touch with him. In 1853, as we have seen, Dom Guéranger was invited to take part in the Commission of Le Mans. In 1854, Lambillotte came to inform him of the Roman *Antiphonal* and *Gradual* project. Finally, in Rome in 1856, Dom Alfieri spoke to him, too, regarding his Gregorian chant publishing project.[33]

As we have seen, the most eminent names in religious music of that era were among those who consulted with the Abbot of Solesmes. Undoubtedly, this was so because of his authority in matters of liturgy. We can also state that this was because of the renewal he had given to Gregorian chant in his own monastery, and because of the principles he had already articulated in his publications.

---

33. Everyone knew that Dom Guéranger criticized Lambillotte's chant for being "heavily accented and measured." He was no less critical of the Mechlin edition (cf. No. 7), which Dom Alfieri wanted to reproduce, because it was merely a copy of the Medicean edition. Cf. E. Moneta-Caglio, *Dom André Mocquereau, 1960*, p. 8.

II ■ PERIOD OF PREPARATION

6. Dom Paul Jausions

We have arrived at the year 1859, and find a young monk studying Gregorian chant under Dom Guéranger's direction at Solesmes. He was a young cleric from the Diocese of Rennes named Paul Jausions,[33bis] who had requested permission to enter the novitiate on October 21, 1854. The Abbot of Solesmes observed the young monk's love of the liturgy and his great capacity for work. Some family correspondence of the young novice reveals that even before his entrance into the novitiate, he had been deeply interested in liturgical chant. He had a position in his parish choir, and had made an in-depth study of the elements of plainchant. He had also written a brief method to improve its performance.[34]

It is no wonder that Dom Guéranger, far from opposing the favorable disposition of his novice, set about to cultivate it from the outset. Herein lies the first sign, faint though it may be, but significant nonetheless, dating back to 1856. From Rome, where he was attending Holy Week ceremonies, Dom Guéranger shared his impressions of the chant with Frère Jausions, and seemed to allude to the research that they had done together.

33bis. Dom Paul Jausions, born November 15, 1834, professed September 29, 1856, died in Vincennes (USA), September 9, 1870.

34. Here is what someone in his family wrote to him: ". . . I think of all the good advice you gave me . . . Parenthetically, I shall tell you that you will be missed this morning at the poor lectern of St. Jacut" (August 5, 1855).—"As to plainchant, the religious nuns at Miséricorde are making a special study of it, so your little method will be very useful to me" (November 20, 1855).

I thought of you often these days, during the singing of the chant here in the papal chapel. They give the chant "affelonement" (an expression in the region around Le Mans, meaning "to do something with real enthusiasm"), let me tell you. . . . There is nothing else like it in the world, except perhaps . . . at St. Pierre de Solesmes, which filled my thoughts at all times throughout all this pomp and ceremony. Oh, when shall we resume our research in the old books?

It is not until early 1859 that we find more specific evidence of Dom Jausions' activity in Gregorian chant (he was professed on September 29, 1856, and was ordained a priest on December 18, 1858). That evidence is provided in a letter from Gontier to Dom Guéranger, dated March 19, 1859, in which Gontier asked the advice of the Abbot of Solesmes on various chapters of a chant Method that he was preparing. He wrote, "I give you leave, as a master, to trim and to cut as you wish, and it is for this reason that I have sent you these chapters before going to press." Dom Guéranger had already brought the matter to the attention of Dom Jausions, who had prepared his comments. This leads us to believe that Dom Guéranger had given him an obedience in this matter, and that Dom Jausions was already at work on it. Gontier replied, "You thought that I would not reply to Father Jausions, yet I am very grateful for his comments, and shall take note of them." Then, after briefly recalling his basic position regarding the performance of plainchant, he added,

If I were to adopt Father Jausions' ideas on the fixed and proportional value of the notes, my booklet would have no reason for being. I have only one purpose, to combat the musical notation and the scandalous edition of Lambillotte. I shall always maintain that there is no middle ground between prose and poetry, between meter and recitation, between fixed and proportional values and the elastic character of the reciting note.

Surely, the process of trial and error adopted by Dom Jausions is not surprising. In expressing his thought, he did not initially manage to avoid using the prevailing terminology, although in the performance of chant, he was in perfect accord with Gontier, as we shall see.

7. The Labors of Dom Jausions—The Wilton Processional

It is likely that Dom Jausions began by studying the ancient writers, as the nature of his work practically demanded. Moreover, Dom Mocquereau noted that Dom Jausions made constant reference to these ancient writers,[35] and Dom Guépin, one of the older monks at Solesmes, substantiated Dom Mocquereau's position in an article on Dom Jausions published just after his death: "Dom Jausions devoted himself with rare perseverance to the study of the problems raised by the history and performance of Gregorian chant."[36] Dom Jausions certainly studied the ancient authors along with Gontier, who often quotes them in his *Method* and who worked with the Abbey's copies.[37]

It was at this time, as well, that Dom Jausions began to copy the old manuscripts, at the request of Dom Guéranger, and thus founded the Gregorian scriptorium at Solesmes, which Dom Mocquereau was later to expand considerably. We have several of Dom Jausions' copies in our archives. The very first, in fact, seems to date from 1860, if not earlier. It is a copy of the English processional of St. Edith of Wilton, 13th–14th century, which, in the early days of Solesmes, was called the *Rollington Processional*. From Dom Guéranger's letters to Dom Jausions sometime later,[38] we have proof that this was the first manuscript to be copied at Solesmes.

We know of another phase of Dom Jausions' involvement in Gregorian matters. As it happens, an old chronicle of Solesmes tells us, quite fortuitously, that in 1859, Dom Jausions gave ideas to a monk from Belmont that were "very precise on chant and psalmody," and that another monk from Belmont, known in the Gregorian chant circles of the era, a certain J. Lambert, also responsible for the chant at Belmont,[39] met with

35. *Paléographie Musicale*, v. XI, p. 18.

36. Obituary notice published in the *Semaine religieuse du diocèse de Rennes*, no. 46, September 16, 1871, pp. 725ff.

37. In fact, Gontier borrowed the Abbey's copies of Gerbert's *Scriptores* (cf. the letter of August 11, 1859, for example). These books were entered into the records of the Solesmes library in 1844, although they may well have arrived long before that.

38. This letter, dated April 6, 1862, is addressed from Solesmes to Dom Jausions, then in Angers, where he was beginning to copy a missal in pure neumes, manuscript 91 (83), on location at the city library, as we shall see later. Dom Guéranger wrote, "I admire how you copy all of this. The Processional has shaped your writing hand." It can be supposed that the Processional, if it came from England, was brought to Solesmes by Father Shepherd, monk of Belmont, a regular guest of the monastery, or two others from England who came to Solesmes during the summer of 1859, and who shall be discussed later. It is unlikely that the book was brought from England by Dom Guéranger himself at the time of a trip he made there in 1860, although he had seen there several manuscripts in the possession of J. Lambert, one of the two English visitors mentioned above.

39. Dom B. Whelan, *The History of Belmont Abbey*, Bloomsbury 1959, pp. 127–128.

Dom Guéranger and Dom Jausions. Nor did Dom Jausions' lessons fail to yield some good. Dom Guéranger made good use of the experience the following year from where he happened to be, i.e. at Belmont Abbey. Here is what he wrote to Dom Jausions from across the English Channel, where he had gone in 1860:

Mr. Lambert remembers you with affection, as does Father Sweney who always thinks of himself as one of your disciples. I can tell you that he benefited greatly and that he is master of the place. The chant is well sung at Belmont, but they use that worthless Mechlin edition, against which I have often spoken and which I hope to have changed. (September 8, 1860)

Another testimony comes to us from Dom Givelet, one of the singers in the Abbey schola, who expressed himself as follows about Dom Jausions in a letter to Dom Guéranger during the latter's stay in England:

I continue to see Dom Jausions about the chant; from him I am also learning theory, which has always been a weakness of mine and has often been a source of embarrassment to me in actual performance. (September 14, 1860)

These two accounts agree perfectly with that of another contemporary who affirmed that "Dom Jausions' value to Solesmes was in reforming the liturgical readings by the strict application of the tonic accent."[40] Thus from 1859 on, Dom Jausions was giving lectures on chant to his brother monks at Solesmes and to guests at the monastery, especially on the nature of the tonic accent and its role in the singing of Gregorian chant. And, thanks to Dom Guéranger's note quoted above, he was aided in this, prior to the appearance of Gontier's *Méthode*, by Father Petit's *Dissertation sur la psalmodie*, published in 1855, which was based on Latin accentuation. A copy of this work, annotated by Dom Jausions, is found in the library of the Abbey.

8. Gontier's *Méthode Raisonnée* (1859)

That very same year, 1859, Gontier published his *Méthode Raisonnée*,[41] which gave the same basic axioms as those of Solesmes. Gontier had a

40. Dom R. Biron, *Bibliographie des Bénédictins de la Congrégation de France, par les Pères de la même Congrégation*, Paris, Champion, 1906, p. 78.

41. *Méthode raisonnée de plain-chant. Le plain-chant dans son rythme, sa tonalité et ses modes*, Paris, Palme, 1859, 144 p.

close bond of friendship with Dom Guéranger for a long time, and often came to the Abbey of Solesmes; he was, then, among the first to hear the initial Gregorian efforts of the monks. Struck by the ease, the innately religious character of the melody as he heard it at the monastery, as we have already mentioned (No. 2), he was then and there convinced that this method was good, and that the truth was here and not elsewhere. Dom Guéranger, moreover, encouraged him to persevere on this path, while he himself set about to comprehend the secret of the Chant, and to deduce the principles from this performance style which delighted him and which imbued the liturgical chant with its inherent beauty, in spite of the melodic disfigurations to which it had been subjected over a long period of time.

Gontier defined the rhythm of plainchant as being essentially free. In syllabic chant—and this assertion often emerges in his writing—the rhythm of the chant resides entirely in the text, and it ought to be carried over into the melody of syllabic chant. The rhythm is then obtained by observing the accent of the text and the accented note of the melody (November 30, 1861 to L. Baptiste). All these expressions, borrowed from Gontier himself, are drawn from his correspondence. Finally, his personal accomplishment, as he said of himself later, was "to have stated accurately the nature of plainchant and to have given a philosophical reason for the inequality of the notes" (February 7, 1861, to Baptiste). Gontier wrote to Dom Guéranger: "The naturalness, the recitative, the diatonic style, assure the plainchant immutability, perpetuity; this is where its musical system lies, this is what makes it rise above fashions and revolutions" (July 14, 1859). And again:

If we succeed in making plainchant well understood, it will be seen as the religious musical idiom of the people, a music that is not only natural and pious, but I would even say inspired. Its beauty is in its naturalness, a simplicity that excludes any art *(here meaning: any artifice);* it is prayer, fittingly uttered. (August 2, 1859)

So he considered his method, which derives from the most varied and simple ideas, *the* method, the only reasonable one, the only one that preserves the prayerful character of the chant (February 23, 1869, to Baptiste). He justifiably passed on all credit for this resurrection of plainchant's traditional rhythm to Dom Guéranger, who knew that the very essence of plainchant was in its return to its twofold natural source, the word and the liturgy (July 8, 1859).

There can be no doubt that Gontier's method was the Solesmes method. In fact, Gontier could not have been more emphatic on this point. From August 1858, his editing work being well advanced, he expressed the wish to confer with Dom Guéranger, "to discuss the theory and the application of the method . . . I shall only be content when you have approved (it) because no one is more competent than you are" (August 22, 1858). He pleaded with him again to give him "several hours . . . to look over my work on the chant which is coming to its conclusion . . . and makes application of a method which, moreover, is yours and that of Solesmes" (September 11, 1858). It was stated above that he sent his book to Dom Guéranger before it was printed so that the Abbot might read it and correct it, and it was with special insistence that Gontier solicited from him a letter of approbation which he truly wished to have:

One must be able to perform the chant in order to understand all of this, and it is as one who performs, that you appreciate what I have done; the more you think about it, the more convinced you will be that all I did was to analyze your style at the same time I analyzed my own. (July 7, 1859, cf. July 27)

At that same time, Gontier appealed to Dom Guéranger again in order to have his work examined and approved. Therefore, on September 13, 1859, he sent him "a rough sketch that needs your scissors and file"; and on the twenty-first of the same month, a short article, doubtless the same, "on the true notation of chant," all the while telling him that his was to be "the final judgment."

In place of these articles, which cannot be identified, it will suffice to point out only to give an idea of the ancient notation, that in his *Méthode Raisonnée*, Gontier presented a few chant compositions copied from a fifteenth-century manuscript and transcribed into modern notation, then reproduced in photographic facsimiles, affirming that the ancient notation clearly "surpasses the notation of our day in accuracy and expression."[42] "Here are the compositions on trial before the court," he wrote to Dom Guéranger (August 22, 1858).

It is not surprising from this that Dom Guéranger gave his unreserved approval of Gontier's work. On August 1, 1859, he wrote the Preface so often requested and fervently awaited:

42. *Méthode*, p. 118.

I hasten to send you my congratulations for the service you render to our churches by bringing to light the only true theory for the performance of Gregorian chant . . . The publication of your very insightful memorandum is a veritable boon.[43]

Gontier was very pleased because for approbation he knew no one "more competent and more powerful in this matter" (August 11, 1859).

As for d'Ortigue, he was not sparing in his praises of the *Méthode Raisonnée*, which then appeared under the double patronage of Solesmes and that of the famous musician.[44]

All that has been said up to now portraying Dom Guéranger as an innovator ought not diminish Gontier's contribution. His book is, in fact, not lacking in originality, indeed far from it, for the conviction and the confidence that are found in it are surely his. He said one day to d'Ortigue: "I would gladly dedicate my life for the restoration of the true Gregorian plainchant."[45] Gontier was a herald, and it was he who "gave to research the precise direction toward the horizons and principles which, in the future, were to be those of Solesmes" (Rousseau, p. 43).

Nonetheless, it remains true that it was at Solesmes, near his illustrious friend and in listening to the chanting of the monks, that he had the intuition of what was the true traditional Gregorian chant. That he considered himself utterly dependent on Dom Guéranger in this matter cannot be overly emphasized. Here, for example, are the conditions on which he submitted to him an article having to do with the true notation of plainchant mentioned above:

Have you weighed it in the balance and found it wanting? Do you propose to make it the basis of your own article? That will surely be the best thing to do; this was, I believe, your original intention. That is all I ask for. You know that I approve of all that you do, all that you decide. Please, then, take a stand and if you have not done it, accept the challenge of promulgating in France and everywhere the true notation of plainchant, which you understand so well. (September 21, 1859)

And again, with regard to another article, to be mentioned later:

---

43. *Ibid.,* p. VIII.

44. Chapter I and the Preface of the *Méthode raisonnée* appeared in d'Ortigue's review, *La Maîtrise, Journal de Musique religieuse,* July 1859 (Ch. I, July 15, 1859, Preface, August 15), that is to say, before the publication of the book.

45. *La Maîtrise,* July 14, 1859, p. 41.

I have written a paper for the Paris Congress that is to take place next November . . . It is you who should be the final judge of it . . . I shall make a trip to Solesmes to have the pleasure of seeing you and of receiving from you in person counsels that will be of great value . . . My thesis is partly philosophical and partly practical and, from this double point of view, no one is more competent than you are to judge it. (August 5, 1860)

In his letter of approval of Gontier's book, Dom Guéranger estimated that it was of the greatest importance to have found the authentic interpretation of Gregorian chant; he even conjectured that it would be preferable to possess only the faulty editions but to sing according to the traditional principles, than to use St. Gregory's own *Antiphonal* and then ignore the principles of the ancient chant.[46] However, he also hoped for "an edition where first of all the Gregorian melody could be found which might have been altered but which was never lost." Then Gontier replied:

I implore you to make yourself responsible for a new edition. There is no one but you in France capable of causing a revolution and attracting the attention of the hierarchy. (July 24, 1859)

I am not letting you off easily, dear Father, the materials for a new edition must be prepared now. It is only at Solesmes that such a work can be accomplished. (August 11, 1859)

9. The Paris Congress (1860)

From the following year, 1860, onwards, there was considerable discussion about the *Méthode Raisonnée* at the Paris Congress for the restoration of plainchant. Gontier presented a paper on *Le plain chant, son exécution*[47] and proposed his own ideas about the nature of Gregorian chant, which is first of all a prayer, and about its rhythm. He was listened to with interest and favor. In a letter defending plainchant, the Abbot of Solesmes, moreover, recommended the *Méthode* to the Chairman, d'Ortigue, who had the letter inserted into the Acts of the Congress, and had it published in *L'Univers, Le Monde* and *La Maîtrise*. In his letter, Dom Guéranger underscored the "supreme importance" of

---

46. *Méthode raisonnée,* approbation, p. IX.
47. Le Mans, Monnoyer, 1860, 48 pp.

Gontier's theories and asserted that "the truth is here and not else-where." The Bishop of Le Mans likewise praised Gontier's work unre-servedly in strong terms, pointing out that the *Méthode* was adopted at the Cathedral and at the Major Seminary of Le Mans with completely satisfying results.[48] Nevertheless, in spite of d'Ortigue's warm recom-mendation and the favorable reception given to Gontier's theories by the majority of the delegates, Gontier's name was lost in the discussion for various reasons.[49] There was a reluctance to include in the published Proceedings of the Congress some propositions (drafted with Gontier's collaboration, in fact) which rejected any method based upon perform-ing equal notes or proportional note values. This was essential and Gontier declared himself satisfied with it (August 19, 1869 to Baptiste). In spite of everything, Gontier stated his position precisely in a letter to Dom Guéranger dated December 3, 1860: "During the entire Congress, the dominant theme remained that there was only one method, the method of Father Gontier."

10. The First *Directorium Chori*

In 1860 we find two unexpected pieces of evidence: Dom Jausions' Gregorian activity, and the nature of the tasks undertaken at Solesmes under Dom Guéranger's direction. These came to light in a written record of events (Dom Bérengier) dated April 22, 1860, and in Dom Jau-sions' letter from Rennes to his Abbot, dated April 28, 1860. The chroni-cle mentioned earlier informs us that Dom Jausions arrived at Rennes for the printing of the *Directorium chori* because he was the one in charge of "the first printing of our monastic chant." Dom Jausions clearly states this in his letter:

I brought our illustrious manuscript to Mr. Vatar, and the first proof of the Preface would be ready now if he had not been forced to request from Paris

48. *Congrès pour la restauration du plain-chant et de la musique d'église, tenu à Paris les 27, 28, 29, 30 novembre et 1er décembre 1860. Procès-verbaux, documents, mémoires*, Paris, de Mourgues, 1862, 126 pp., see pp. 23–24 (cf. M. Blanc, *L'enseignement musical de Solesmes*, p. 145).

49. See *op. cit.*, p. 31, for what M. Blanc said of this. Much later in 1880, Gontier was to write: "At the Congress, in spite of the approval of Dom Guéranger and Msgr. Nanquette, in spite of the applause and the support of the Congress committee, I can say that I was scarcely under-stood, but the question was posed," to Dom Pothier, February 26, 1880, in a letter published in the *Revue du Chant grégorien*, 1911, p. 186.

certain type-fonts that he did not have. On my return to Solesmes I shall bring it with me.

So from April 1860, Dom Jausions could dream of having his Preface printed along with the *Toni Communes* of the Mass and Office (such, in effect, was the content of the *Directorium chori*). This account presupposes several years of research and study, which takes us back to about 1856, indicated by Msgr. Rousseau as the beginning of the Gregorian restoration at Solesmes and which is the date of Dom Jausions' profession.

As it happened, though the printing of the *Directorium chori* was nearly finished, only a few years later was work on it to be resumed. Dom Guéranger had wished that the rules of accentuation and performance of the chant should precede this book. But we have seen that at that time there were certain differences between Gontier and Dom Jausions, differences, it must be repeated, that seemed certainly to have been expressed verbally and which an open discussion sufficed to eliminate completely, as we shall see.

But if, as we believe, the first proofs of the initial version of the *Règles pour la prononciation correcte de la langue latine* (the Preface mentioned in Dom Jausions' letter), as well as those of the *Directorium chori,* have come down to us, they indicate that Dom Jausions still insisted on the musical notation of the Rheims-Cambrai editions, with the proportional notation and without the traditional grouping of the notes, the only notation known in the editions then in use.

What Gontier thought of Dom Jausions' first efforts comes to mind here, and as was pointed out, he himself made use of photographic plates, since typefaces were lacking, to reproduce the traditional notation in his *Méthode*. In spite of this, he wrote to Dom Guéranger on July 14, 1859:

If we wish to notate syllabic chant with the dactylic brève, how does that concern me, provided that you grant me that the values, the accents, the breaks, in a word that the rhythm is in the text? Whether the modern square, stemmed, or diamond-shaped notes are used doesn't concern me; as for condensing the long vocalises, doing this would threaten the very life of Gregorian chant.[50]

---

50. Eleven years later, the *Méthode* by L. Baptiste, which we shall discuss later, and which was to be patronized by Dom Pothier, still used this defective musical script.

In practice, Dom Jausions expressed certain reservations that showed his embarrassment and allowed him to take quite a few liberties. It is reasonable to surmise that Jausions already suspected that Gontier's principles contained certain inaccuracies.[51]

A meeting between Dom Jausions and Gontier became necessary. Thus the chronicle mentioned above informs us that Dom Guéranger sent Dom Jausions to Le Mans the first time on September 23, 1860, after he returned from Rennes, and a second time, from October 10 to November 5, in order to have "Canon Gontier explain his method of plainchant and his treatise on accentuation to Dom Jausions." But it is certain that the difference of ideas was only superficial and that there was no need to insist on it excessively even if Gontier did advise Dom Jausions, as he told him twenty years later, to burn his manuscript.[52] So, after the first meeting, on September 29, 1860, Gontier wrote to Dom Guéranger:

Dom Jausions must have told you that we cleaned house and that we are in perfect agreement. Here is what we accomplished: we are completely in accord as to theory and practice, and on the nature of the rhythm, and that about sums up the question.

Furthermore, there is no reference to a substantial disagreement in a letter of December 3, 1860, nor in letters over the ensuing years. On the contrary, there was the most perfect understanding between them, especially in the matter of performance practice.

In Le Mans, Dom Jausions consulted ancient manuscripts that were unavailable at Solesmes. He also took steps to bring "one of those important chant manuscripts" to the Abbey, and this was not easy: the Bishop was away, and the librarian of the bishopric "created problems in the name of the chapter." Finally, the bishop allowed him to take the desired manuscript; however, added Dom Jausions, "we shall have it for six months on the condition of giving them a receipt, which was requested, for fear that we might keep it."[53] The manuscript—a Roman

51. We have spoken above about the monastic Ceremonial printed in 1856. It does not seem that we can attribute the musical composition to Dom Jausions, who, at that point, would have been preparing it during his novitiate. The fact that his family, very generous to the Solesmes monastery, paid for the printing of the Ceremonial at the time of Dom Jausions' profession, does not prove that he, somehow, was involved in editing this publication.

52. Gontier's letter to Dom Pothier, February 26, 1880, published in *Revue du Chant grégorien*, 1911, p. 186.

53. Dom Jausions' letter to Dom Guéranger, dated November 3, 1860.

Gradual from Maine—explained Dom Guéranger (May 2, 1861 to the Bishop), was duly returned and, at the same time, the Abbot of Solesmes requested the loan of another manuscript under the same conditions.[54]

11. Dom Jausions and Dom Joseph Pothier— The Reform of the Chant Books Decided at Solesmes

In order to help Dom Jausions in his work,[55] Dom Guéranger, in 1860, assigned to him an assistant, a young priest from the Diocese of Saint-Dié, who, like Dom Jausions himself, had been ordained to the priesthood on December 18, 1858, and had donned the habit of St. Benedict on February 1, 1859, at Solesmes. This was Brother Joseph Pothier, who was to bring to fruition the task undertaken by the Abbot of Solesmes and was to prove himself the restorer of the Gregorian melodies.[55bis]

Dom Joseph Pothier came to Solesmes with a good grounding in Gregorian chant. He learned to love the chant at the parish school of the small village of Bouzemont, in the Lorraine region, a school run by his father, who was also head cantor of the parish. Dom Pothier's biographer wrote: "At the school, the study and practice of the sacred chant was considered to be on the same level—at least—as arithmetic and spelling."[56] Every morning, the children sang a Mass in Gregorian chant. Later, at the major seminary, a musician named Father Hingre encouraged Dom Pothier's special interest in Gregorian chant.

Thus it was not long before Dom Guéranger discerned the talent of his young novice. One day, Dom Guéranger came upon Brother Pothier in the library, deeply engrossed in a recent new book by Father Jules Bonhomme, and

congratulated him on being so "affelonné" (a favorite colloquial expression of his, meaning 'enthusiastic') for sacred chant, a subject of such importance, and encouraged him to study well.[57]

---

54. Chronicle, October 16, 1860, and November 6, 1861.

55. Dom Pothier's letter of September 25, 1897, cited by A. Dabin, *Le chant bénédictin*, p. 15, note 1.

55bis. Dom Joseph Pothier, born December 7, 1835, professed at Solesmes November 1, 1860, Prior of Ligugé, April 9, 1893, Abbot of St. Wandrille, July 24, 1898, died December 8, 1923.

56. Dom David, *Dom Joseph Pothier*, p. 10.

57. Dom David, p. 12.

As a matter of fact, whilst still a novice Brother Pothier taught chant to the novices,[58] and possibly even to the community. Indeed, the novitiate chronicle reports that on July 15, 1860, Brother Pothier gave a lecture to the entire community on chant according to Gontier's method. The details remain unclear, but it seems in any case that from 1860 onward, Brother Pothier gave practical courses in chant at the Abbey itself, and not only in the novitiate. It is also known that around this time, in reply to a question, he made a comment about the first version of the *Directorium chori:* To Dom Jausions, who raised objections to Gontier, he replied without hesitation, "But it is Gontier who is right."[59]

Be that as it may, if it is quite certain, on the testimony of both Dom Jausions[60] and Dom Pothier himself, that it was in 1860 that he became assistant to his senior in Gregorian chant research, it is likely that it was only at the time of his monastic profession, November 1, 1860, that he received this obedience.

At the end of 1860, it will be recalled, Dom Jausions was in full accord with Gontier with regard to the chant. Nevertheless, he was again at home in Le Mans during February and March 1861[61] and Dom Guéranger himself took part in the conversations the exact nature of which is unknown. In August, Dom Jausions was in Brittany, and the letters that Dom Guéranger wrote him at that time provide information on the subject that is of interest to us. Thus, Dom Guéranger points out that "Dom Pothier explained the *podatus* successfully" (August 16). And another time, he mentioned that the printing of a chant book, doubtless the *Directorium chori*, was eagerly awaited, and that its delay annoyed Dom Guéranger. He wrote:

I am sending you a letter from Mr. Vatar with a sample chant, which unfortunately I let grow old on my desk; luckily, you are at the source; could you, on your return, press forward with this important matter, which has been dragging on for six months? Dom Pothier is still very "affelonné," and Father Gontier is giving him an earful. (September 19, 1861)

On September 22, 1861, Dom Jausions was again in Rennes where he mentioned having many things to do at the Vatar printing plant, espe-

---

58. Dom Guéranger named him Zealot of the novices on November 25, 1860. The "Zealot" is assistant to the Master of Novices.

59. Dom David, *Comment les mélodies grégoriennes ont été retrouvées*, col. 229.

60. Dom Jausions' letter of October 26, 1868. Cf. *infra*, No. 30.

61. Dom Guéranger's *Journal* and Dom Bérengier's *Chronicle*, February 19 and March 14.

cially in view of printing the *Directorium chori* according to the new findings. It cannot be doubted but that the manuscript of this book had already been sent to the printer. Quite simply, it was recognizable by its return to the traditional notation, especially in the matter of the grouping and shape of the notes. This book, then, marked a new stage of development, a true resurrection. It was the first book of the Gregorian restoration at Solesmes, and even, it can be said, of the Gregorian restoration anywhere. We shall see further on the reasons for the delay that surrounded its printing and publication.

During the summer, Father Baptiste[62] came to Solesmes. He evinced a keen interest in the Gregorian chant. In a letter addressed to Dom Guéranger, he thanked him for the two half-hours accorded him to speak of chant and the liturgy, and he was happy about the news that Gontier sent him, to know that "you are determined, Reverend Father, to have printed for your monastery the chant from manuscripts of the fifteenth century, with their notation" (October 4, 1861). Moreover, there are two letters from Gontier to Father Baptiste, which will give us more precise details.

The first, on October 7, 1861, lacking more complete data, pointed out the tasks undertaken at Solesmes over a period of years.

Let us speak of Solesmes, since you believe to see in it, if not a solution to all the problems, at least much progress in that direction. I think, as you do, that the name of Dom Guéranger carries great weight, that the adoption of a version and a notation is an event of immense significance; but, between us, my friend, Dom Guéranger is not the most learned person in the community on this matter, but rather Dom Jausions and Dom Pothier. I tell you for sure that the reform of the chant is well along, and that it will be completed as soon as the books are printed. As you know, this reform consists of: (1) not giving a time-value to the notation; and (2) marking the grammatical and melodic accents. I add that, in spite of the natural span of time for any change to take place, there is no one at Solesmes who regrets the change or who holds to the old system.

Gontier's second letter, of November 30, reveals the initial difficulties caused within the Abbey itself by the new way of chanting. Though Gontier considered Dom Jausions and Dom Pothier scholars of this science, a few of the other religious were less skilled. Furthermore, what

---

62. Cf. above, No. 1 and note 2.

the letter says of Dom Guéranger is rather surprising, and these last affirmations by Gontier are to be added to others already mentioned, in which the Canon made Dom Guéranger's competence absolutely clear, and all that he, Gontier, owed him. He wrote to Baptiste:

You know Solesmes, you know what is lacking, rather what is lacking in a good performance of the chant, you know the disputes, the confrontations with some religious. Here are the facts of the matter. I have learned everything from these gentlemen, and you know it is not ignorance or deference on the part of the good Fathers. Father Abbot, who has a deep feeling for the chant, who understands well the text and melodic accentuation, told me that up to now he had not understood the chant, that thanks to me he does understand it today, that he used to be unaware of the musical riches locked up in our liturgy, that he wanted to preserve these riches in all their purity and integrity.

As a result, he is determined to reproduce the fifteenth-century version of the chants with the notation of the beautiful manuscripts that you have seen here in my home. There is a priest at Solesmes, whom perhaps you have seen, Dom Pothier, fully knowledgeable, intelligent, humble, who understands the chant admirably. He is the one whom the Abbot has placed at the head of the chant class and the old teachers are placed under his direction. You would not recognize the chant at Solesmes. What is his style? He has his students sing the chant following the old notation; sometimes he makes copies, according to the old notation, of pieces which should be chanted by a soloist, and I know the pleasure that this chant has given to religious and outsiders. That is not all: in spite of these bad times which place them under the threat of dissolution, since they must absolutely have choir books, Father Abbot is determined to have the books printed. He is adopting all the formulae of the old plainchant.

Thus Dom Pothier gave chant courses to the Solesmes community from the first year of his profession and perhaps even earlier, if we read the quote from Gontier above in this way. In this situation must be seen a special sign indicating the high level of appreciation which Dom Guéranger had for Dom Pothier's musical talents, and that fact is the more unusual in that the Abbot of Solesmes was obliged to tread cautiously in this matter because of some "old timers" with whom he had to deal. Moreover, Dom Pothier made them sing according to the old manuscripts. Neither Dom Guéranger nor Dom Jausions had dared to do this, and thus Dom Pothier was experimenting with this new technique from the very start. But must we link with this resolve of Dom Pothier the determination taken by Dom Guéranger, in view of the *Directorium chori*, to adopt the traditional version of the plainchant in its purity and integrity for the books that he intended to have printed for use in his monastery?[63]

We must concur, if we accept what Dom Pothier wrote later, in 1897:

In the beginning, we thought seriously of joining up with Rheims, but by no means of recasting the chant and reproducing the manuscripts. It was only when, with another priest who died shortly thereafter while on a journey to America (a reference to Dom Jausions), I began working and taking stock of the situation that we realized that we had to return to the sources.[64]

Still, Dom Jausions seems to have set the date for this decision prior to his collaboration with Dom Pothier when he wrote, in his turn, in 1868: "Very little study was made of ecclesiastical chant in those days . . . I was forced to have recourse to the manuscripts."

Only later did he add:

In 1860, one of my confreres, Reverend Father Dom Pothier, joined me, and although from that moment I had been given charge of practically all the research and transcriptions made in the libraries *(Dom Jausions is referring here only to the very first efforts)*, Dom Pothier devoted himself in a manner more exclusively than I was able to do, to the studies we had so long pursued together.[65]

In fact, it was from October 1860 onwards, after Dom Jausions had meetings with Gontier, that the revision of the *Directorium chori* according to the ancient notation was decided on. It is known that Dom Pothier expressed his thought exactly on that occasion, and it is doubtless to this that he was referring in the letter cited above.

12. The First Transcripts of Manuscripts in Staffless Neumes

In any case, it was in 1862 that Dom Jausions and Dom Pothier began the study of the manuscripts notated in staffless neumes, thus going back to the most ancient examples known of Gregorian chants. In fact, at that time, Dom Jausions began to copy a *Gradual*, the manuscript 91

---

63. For that was still all that was at issue at the time, as the Abbot of Solesmes explained to L. Baptiste, who wanted to have the books adopted for use in the Diocese of Bourges: "We are preparing, in fact, an edition of Gregorian chant at Solesmes, but only for our own use" (December 16, 1861).

64. A. Dabin, *Le chant bénédictin*, p. 15, no. 1 (Letter of September 25, 1897).

65. Dom Jausions' letter to Abbot Perriot, October 26, 1868. Cited *infra*, No. 30.

(83) of Angers, in the city library, a task he would pursue until 1867, as circumstances permitted, with the copy of two other *Graduals* on staff lines, as we shall see in due course. In the year 1862, he made three visits to Angers, April 4–12, June 27–July 9, and October 13–31.[66]

The library at Angers still has the descriptions and the notes (recognizable from the beautiful script) that Dom Jausions made, contributing to the liturgical sources in that significant collection.[67]

Dom Jausions had a very skilled hand, and his transcriptions are masterpieces of neatness and precision.

Dom Pothier, for his part, was even more successful; he undertook to transcribe to staff-lines the St. Gall Codex 359, published by Lambillotte in 1851[68] and notated in staffless neumes. A happy circumstance brought to light this transcription, in which the Graduals and Tracts (the only pieces with the Alleluias given in their entirety in the Cantatorium) are grouped according to modes. The first six pages give the neumatic notation above the staff (but the romanian letters and signs were not transcribed by Dom Pothier) and the square notation follows faithfully, indicating even the nuances of the *oriscus*, the *liquescent*, the neumatic divisions—the importance of which he did not fully perceive—and the *quilisma* with two or three elements. The incomplete notebook does not include the Alleluias, and is dated 1862 on the front page, in Dom Pothier's own hand.[69] Even though he was helped in this task by good manuscripts on staff-lines that Dom Jausions sent him from Le Mans, and those that he was able to find there himself, it can be said, nevertheless, that Dom Pothier gave proof from the very beginning of extraordinary accuracy in transcribing the old manuscripts, which for years many had considered untranscribable and, as a result, of no use whatever.

66. Dom Guéranger wrote to him on April 6, 1862: "What a precious thing is this Missal with neumes. Can you not fetch it here? Father Zealot (*Dom Pothier had been Zealot of the novices since November 25, 1860*) will write to you about it. I admire how you copy this. The Processional has shaped your script" (*the Wilton Processional of St. Edith, already mentioned*).

67. Rousseau, *L'École Grégorienne de Solesmes*, p. 17.

68. *Antiphonaire de Saint-Grégoire, fac-simile du manuscrit de Saint-Gall,* authentic copy of the autograph written around the year 790, Brussels, 1851.

69. The notebook of the analytical table of the St. Gall manuscript that he did first bears the date November 3, 1861 (4 nonas novembris) at the top. Originally it read 1861, but the 1 was changed to a 2 by Dom Pothier himself, no doubt when the table was finished. However, in support of the precedence of this analytical table, it must be noted that this table was necessary prior to undertaking the copying of the various pieces in the manuscript by types and modes.

13. Problems in Restoring the Melodies (1862)

At the end of 1862, a serious problem arose in the Gregorian restoration at Solesmes having to do with the treatment of the penultimate syllables. We have already seen what Dom Guéranger thought about this: he was of the opinion that several notes ought not be given to these weak syllables and in this matter the manuscript tradition ought not to be followed. On the occasion of a trip to Le Mans, Dom Jausions mentioned the problem to Gontier and confided to him the Abbot's hesitation, hesitations that he and Gontier wanted to eradicate. Gontier considered the matter important and even wrote a long letter to the Abbot on this matter on October 30. The letter reads as follows:

I received a visit from Dom Jausions and, as you might well imagine, our long conversation had to do with matters of mutual concern. I realized with pleasure that we are in complete accord as to basics and details. He spoke to me of a problem that I consider very serious, namely that neumatic groups must be used on penultimate syllables.

I have thought about this for a long time; now I can say that my opinion is fixed. Surely, there are many who are opposed to this restoration; the changes introduced in recent centuries seem to respect the prosody and the correct pronunciation of Latin. It is said that what exists must be respected, that our ears are not accustomed to these glaring errors, and without doubt the composers wrote at a time when the rules of prosody had been forgotten. I think, dear Reverend Father, that these reasons will not impress you very much; you know enough about St. Ambrose, St. Gregory, Hucbald, Guido, St. Odo, etc. etc. . . . to affirm that these were not ignoramuses, that they knew more than we about quantity and accentuation.

My opinion is one having little weight; but such as it is, I give it to you as well as that of several competent people with whom I have discussed the matter. At Solesmes it is a matter of archaeological restoration: this must be thorough. It cannot be a half-restoration, a provisional effort. It must not be said that it could have been done better. For me, corrections and mutilations are corruption.

We must have plainchant just as it was when plainchant was understood. What can be said in opposition if all you are doing is reproducing antiquity, that is, the work of those who surely knew more about it than all of our contemporary plainchantists?

I consider plainchant to be a liturgical fact that cannot be tampered with lightly. But in the reading of liturgical Latin, must not the values of the syllables be respected in order to render them intelligible? When the chant is syllabic, the text is king, *la letra est la reyna*, there is the value of the strong syllable, weak, final; but as soon as the neumatic phrase begins, there is no longer a strong syllable, nor a weak syllable, there is a melodic motet: *littera est ibi loco subjecti, et cantui servit.* . . .

Do not be afraid of making a mistake, since you are reproducing a text that is not yours, one that belongs to history and liturgy. Father Lambillotte had neither predecessors nor tradition; he could indulge in fantasy. You have on your side all the Benedictines of all ages, back to the seventeenth century.

There is no doubt but that this authoritative letter from Gontier captured the attention of Dom Guéranger, because after this there was no longer a problem. It is supposed that the way was clear: in fact it is known that from this time on, Dom Guéranger was resolutely committed to the path toward a complete return to the manuscript tradition. Thus it was that he had already denounced any kind of reductions of certain long melismas. A note from Dom Pothier dated from this period gives us formal assurance of this. As we have seen, there was a question of certain repetitions that Dom Guéranger believed to be posterior to the golden age of Gregorian chant (No. 4). Regarding this, Dom Pothier wrote that "Reverend Father's current opinion is in opposition to any kind of melodic reduction."[70] Against this, Gontier, in order that the reduction of certain long melismas not be excessively shocking,[71] later changed his position on the issue of weak penultimates, a rather surprising assertion testified to in a letter written some years later:

There is one thing that bothers me with regard to the projected editions, that it is the intention of the Father to leave the long succession of notes on the short penultimates. I can see how this will prevent dioceses from adopting their books and I would like the Solesmes editions to be widely known. (Letter to L. Baptiste, June 2, 1865)

14. Rhythmic Problems (1863)

In June and July of 1863, Dom Jausions was in Rennes supervising the printing of the *Directorium chori*, which was progressing slowly. The

---

70. *Observations sur la Méthode raisonnée de plain-chant publiée par Mr. A. Gontier,* cf. *infra,* No. 15.
71. See his comments on this matter in No. 10.

choice of the traditional notation signs, designed at Solesmes itself,[72] was a settled issue, but the difficulty they were having in casting the new signs explains, though only in part, the slowdown of the printing. In fact, there were other much more serious difficulties causing this delay, as will be seen later.

Nevertheless, by September the printing of the *Directorium chori*, though not completed, was at least well advanced. It appears from a letter of Dom Guéranger that at that time Vatar was also printing for the Solesmes account a small pocket booklet, *Benedictiones mensae* (Letter of September 20th).

Moreover, two letters from Gontier to Baptiste clearly indicate to us where work stood at Solesmes. We do not hesitate to quote them very extensively, in spite of their length, because they are most interesting. In them Gontier comments on the various theoretical and practical aspects of the Gregorian question: the principles, research, the chant itself, everything is examined in them, and there can be no question but that the author of these lines was well informed.

The first of these letters is dated September 26, 1863. Gontier wrote:

At the moment, I am finishing a short treatise on accentuation including rules for reading Latin. I intend to send it to you. . . . This little treatise will be useful certainly for plainchant; because the value of the note in syllabic chant is in the syllable, it is of utmost importance to know the value of the prose syllables. As I have already written to you, Solesmes is going in the right direction, the chant there is generally good. Traces of the old style persist, but there is improvement day by day. The teachers understand and teach the most basic principles, but the guidelines will not be promulgated until the new books are actually in use. At present, these books have not been printed. The *Directorium chori* is in print, as are the invitatories, but the *Gradual* is not yet begun, the reason being that they would like the rules of accentuation to take precedence, which I have here in a manuscript prepared by one of the monks, and about which, at least about some of them, there are misgivings. These rules of Solesmes are the very same as those which I included in my short treatise, with the difference

---

72. De Coussemaker obtained permission to use them in his book *Scriptorium de Musica Medii Aevi* . . . Paris, 1864 (cf. p. XXIII), translated into French under the title *Traités inédits sur la musique du Moyen Age,* 1864. On page 22 of the French edition, the author wrote: "Before closing, we wish to mention that the musical notation typeface used for the printing of our book was graciously placed at our disposal by the Very Reverend Benedictines of Solesmes, who designed it and had it engraved for a new edition of Roman chant, which was printed by Mr. Vatar of Rennes . . ." (cf. Dom Jausions' letter of June 9th).

that my short treatise is appropriate for educational institutions, that of Solesmes for the sung pronunciation of liturgical Latin. Do not expect the Solesmes edition soon, but be assured that it will be a good one. The manuscripts of the tenth and eleventh centuries are being copied, and the melodies of the fourteenth and fifteenth centuries will be used.

The information given in this letter certainly elicited the vital interest of Gontier's correspondent (Father Baptiste), for a second letter followed, containing more detail than the first:

Now let us turn to other matters. I am not surprised that Father Abbot should have been so cautious about his publication. I am going to ask you, with good reason, to remain silent about the confidential details which I know very well, and which I am going to pass on to you.

The *Directorium chori* has been printed, but this is not known in the community, or at least is only surmised. This *Directorium* includes the manner of chanting the various parts of the office, prayers, chapters, epistles, Gospels, short responsories, psalms, etc., and it includes the invitatories for the eight modes, the *Te Deum*, etc. All the remainder is ready for the printer. Then why is it not being printed? The reason is this. There has been some disagreement among the project leaders over some minor details relating to the method.

Father Abbot awaited my work on the accent, in order to compare it with an identical treatise prepared at the community. Now that this is done, there is no opposition.

The working agenda is as follows. After the *Directorium chori*, the rules for the accent will likely be printed, their application to syllabic chant and finally, the rules for melodic chant. These will be promulgated at Solesmes, then the *Gradual* will be printed. Hymnody will not be issued until later. Father Abbot told me that in this matter there are great problems; I told him that to me it did not seem so, that it would suffice to divide the hymns into measured and non-measured, to apply the rules of poetic rhythm and of prose rhythm. Father Abbot also wanted me to have a long discussion with Dom Pothier in order to consider the question of method in depth. Our meeting lasted an hour and a half. I will give you a few comments about this that will not be without interest for you: meanwhile, I will tell you that I have given a written account of this to Father Abbot.

I must first tell you that as for performance, Dom Jausions, Dom Pothier, and I are in complete agreement. Here is the crux of the matter. As for the rules of the accent, these gentlemen have read my treatise, no opposition. As to the syllabic chant, it should be printed in square notes, all the rhythm; the full value of the notes is in the text: all in complete agreement. As to melodic chant, the ancient notation with *virga, podatus, clivis,* etc., should be used, agreed.

The neumatic phrase ought to be divided into musical syllables, which form suspensions, apparent pauses, the *mora ultimae vocis;* here too we are all in agreement.

In melodic chant, the text must never be lost sight of; by voice inflections, the meaning of the text must be understood, linking together the syllables of a word, the words to a phrase; I strongly approve this idea so that in another sense, it can be said that *littera cantui servit.* In pure melody, in the neumatic phrase, there are stronger notes *in quasdam voces majori impulsu efferimus,* what I call melodic accent. We are in complete agreement. No accent, no rhythm: in the text there is grammatical accent, in the neumes, melodic accent. There now, you will say: you agree on every point, the matter is settled, all has been said. Well yes, but not quite: it is here where our discussion begins, as you will see. If there are stressed notes in the melody, should this be reflected in the writing of the notes? If the accent, the stressed beat, is essential, should this be acknowledged in notation? I say Yes, Dom Pothier says No. Dom Pothier says: this stressed beat, this accent, comes about naturally, the voice gives an impulse sometimes on one note, sometimes on another; but not archeologically, nor theoretically, nor practically is this stressed beat given to the *virga,* or the *clivis,* no more than it is given to the *podatus.* To this, I say that the *virga: /.* is an acute accent followed by grave accents and that, if later, when a fixed value was given to notes, it was said that *productio innuitur per caudas,* it was because the accented sign was readily accepted as a long note. As for the *clivis,* it is not unreasonable that it is called "circumflex" because it is made up of a higher note and a lower note; when it is said that the *clivis componitur ex nota et seminota,* it is when the first note has a fullness of sound which the second does not have. On the same page, the same author says: the last note of the *clivis* has a faint sound; however, it enjoys the honor of being a perfect note. If the last has a faint sound, the first then is more prominent. Is this prominence nothing more than an accent? I add that, if the accent were written over the *virga* and over the first note of the *clivis,* nothing points to its being indicated for the first note of the *podatus.* We are agreed that the last note of the *podatus* dissolves ("fondante") when it is not at the end. Then I say that the *torculus* is a *podatus flexus* deprived of an accent, while the inverted *torculus* is a *clivis resupinus* with an accent on the first note. Father Abbot seems to agree with me; in any case, I think that the matter will be settled soon and the promulgation of the new Method will take place before Lent. For the rest, do not count on having the *Directorium chori.* I do not think it will be sold before the edition is finished. Father Cloët has asked for it: he has had no response. My part in the discussion interested Father Abbot very much and he seemed to share my opinion completely.

Another letter of January 4, 1864, must be added, which follows on the heel of the others:

Father Abbot of Solesmes did not understand that the last syllable of accented words is never short; he did not want to accept this principle from Dom Jausions, which he rightly held, but which Father Abbot rejected. I believe I made him understand this and he included it in the Solesmes Method. I am certain that the meeting that I had with Dom Pothier should interest you, even though taken out of context and reduced to a skeleton. You have the essentials, even though abridged. This report should have no interest for the seculars, for those who are not as initiated as you are into the principles and expressions of the matter at hand. We were at the heart of the question, and though in agreement as to the performance, it was necessary to be exact, for it occupies a central place in the method. Suppressing the accent sign in the neume style is, in my opinion, the same as suppressing the accent itself, that is, the rhythm. This would ultimately lead to a return to the equality of the notes, or to a haphazard rhythm, as in the Rheims method, or in Father Lambillotte's. . . .

15. State of the Work in 1864

A few details of these letters of Gontier ought to be reviewed here. Two points must first be examined:

1. The printing of the *Directorium chori* must not have been completed until 1864, because the book carries this date, and not that of 1863;

2. What Gontier was alluding to cannot be understood clearly when he says "all the remainder is ready for the printer," because the preliminary work of copying the manuscripts for the Gradual was certainly not very advanced at this time. Only two copies of ancient manuscripts of staffless neumes were begun: manuscript 91 from Angers by Dom Jausions, and the St. Gall 359, which Dom Pothier was not only copying but reconstructing with the help of good staff manuscripts provided from Le Mans.

But the importance of this letter, despite a few inaccuracies and contradictions, is that it reveals to us the procedure adopted by Dom Guéranger for the restoration of the chant books. Although the purest principles were taught and observed by Solesmes, the Method would be promulgated only when the new books were being used. As for the *Directorium chori* which was being printed, it would not be distributed to the community until after the issuance of the "rules of accent, application to the syllables of chant, and rules for melodic chant."

The *Petit traité de la bonne prononciation de la langue latine*,[73] which Gontier published at this time and which contained the rules for reading Latin, was in his mind a "true method of plainchant."[74] The author stated that he was in total agreement with an identical work prepared by the Abbey. This work done at Solesmes, it seems, is surely the work of Dom Jausions. In a letter written not long after this period, Dom Jausions mentioned, in fact, "the rules of accentuation, nearly all of which were written out by me" (April 25, 1866), and, at the same time, Gontier, alluding for his part to a work of broader dimensions, speaks of "a few pages from a manuscript Method" or "a substantive written work" from the pen of Dom Jausions (to Baptiste, April 13, 1866 and April 1866). Moreover, Dom Jausions was credited with having reformed the liturgical readings and psalmody at Solesmes, through the rigorous application of the tonic accent (No. 7).

As for the disagreement that existed between Gontier and Dom Pothier with regard to the method, it all comes down to this: although Gontier, Dom Pothier, and Dom Jausions all agreed on matters of performance, based on

—the traditional script to be adopted for the published books,
—the rhythm of the syllabic chant in which "all the note values are in the text,"
—the rhythm of the melodic chant, the neume phrase being divided into musical syllables, into incises and phrases and guided only by the text itself,
—the presence of the tonic accent without which there can be no rhythm,

there was nonetheless a difference of opinion when it came to a question of knowing whether this melodic accent, indispensable to the rhythm, is recognizable when written.

While Dom Pothier voted no, Gontier, whom Dom Guéranger seems to follow, gives the note the value of intensity, and voted yes. On July 22, 1859 Gontier wrote to Dom Guéranger: "The difference between the notes comes from the accent (♩), which is performed by having the voice press on the note without prolonging it." This, he insisted, differs essentially from its being a note of length.

---

73. Paris, Palmé 1864, 36 pp.
74. Letter to L. Baptiste dated March 12, 1866.

The important role played by Dom Pothier in this discussion has been mentioned. He was the one assigned by Dom Guéranger to treat the question of method in depth with Gontier. This should not come as a surprise, for Dom Pothier had already given evidence of having a profound knowledge of matters pertaining to Gregorian chant. It is also doubtless necessary to date at this period his *Observations sur la méthode raisonnée de plain-chant de M. Gontier*, which requires a comment here.

This work consists of just four small pages on which Dom Pothier, after reading Gontier's book, wrote a few remarks. In spite of their brevity, these remarks give evidence of a knowledge of the manuscripts that Dom Pothier could have acquired only in recent years, by being in contact with the same Gregorian chant sources. They also reveal the firm position that Dom Pothier had already taken, bearing on the question of Gregorian rhythm and the point of view which was his. Although he was firm in pointing out the weak points of Gontier's book (he disagreed that rhythm is "constituted" by the alternation between accented and non-accented syllables; likewise, he disagreed with the attribution of accents of intensity to the stemmed notes), he fully approved the principles set forth in it. Yet he stated that,

although the chief reason for oratorical rhythm does not reside in the accent, which is not even the principal means, [he is] not disposed to recognize for the formulas an absolute value independent of the position which they occupy on the syllables of the text or in the musical phrase.

Abstracting from this position, he saw "formulae only as notes united in performance as in the written word." At the same time, he showed that he was obstinately opposed to overemphasizing the development of rhythm. He wrote: "Groupings and counting in plainchant only exist in the natural instinct of the ear; there are scarcely any rules to establish the laws of rhythm." But for him, "indeterminate" is not the same as arbitrary: "The notation of plainchant, although *undetermined* is, nevertheless, not *uncertain*."

For Gontier, not specifying the rhythm is the same as leaving it to be determined arbitrarily. This position was later to form the basis of Dom Mocquereau's research, with this essential difference: while Gontier assimilated the rhythmic ictus with the strong beat, Dom Mocquereau developed Dom Pothier's intuition mentioned above, proclaiming it independent of intensity.

Whatever differences there may have been, Gontier remained optimistic and predicted unhesitatingly that the matter would be settled soon, and that the Method would see the light of day in the months ahead.

16. *Benedictiones Mensae* and *Directorium Chori*

On March 1, 1864, copies of the *Benedictiones mensae* were distributed to the members of the community. Thus this little booklet would then be the first book of chant restored by Solesmes, if we did not already know that the printing of the *Directorium chori* was finished, or almost so. On October 13, Gontier wrote that (the Fathers of Solesmes) "have printed the refectory prayers which are only a simple recitation, so only the square note is used; no stemmed or diamond-shaped notes; accent is indicated in the text" (October 13). In other words, all the rhythm is in the text and the proportional written forms were abandoned. Thus in and of itself, this booklet, which offered only syllabic chant, marked a forward step at the time.[75]

As for the *Directorium chori*, Gontier had this to say in the same letter, when the printing of the book was at last finished:

> Their *Directorium chori* is printed, and I have seen it; but the whole run is still at the printer's. . . . I shall have a copy of it as soon as it is distributed to the religious. All the principles that I mentioned to you were followed in the printing. Every isolated note is a square one; signs for the *podatus* have been made, the two notes of the inverted *torculus (porrectus)* are written with one stroke. A very moderate use of bars was made, but there is more of this than I care for. Not a single note is marked strong, not a diamond note for the *torculus*. To give you an idea of the characters, I shall tell you that Mr. de Coussemaker had a few ancient pieces printed, which you may have seen with the Solesmes characters.

Unfortunately, Dom Guéranger delayed in distributing the *Directorium chori*, and the entire edition, except for a few rare copies (only four), was destroyed in a fire at the Vatar Printing Company around 1866.[76] This was really too bad, for it would be necessary to await the *Liber Gradualis*

---

75. For this booklet, a musical design different from that of the *Directorium chori* was used, one better adapted to a manual edition.

76. Dom Biron, *Bibliographie*, p. 139.—The author attributed the composition of the *Directorium chori* to "Dom Jausions, with the collaboration of Dom Pothier" (pages 79 and 139).—Dom Guéranger's hesitations explain this phrase of Dom Pothier, written in 1865, which could have

of 1883 to find an important publication giving the traditional notation.[76bis] (See Plate 5, a page from the *Directorium chori*.)

17. The "Corrected *Gradual*"

Evidently research was on going. In Angers, arriving there on June 3,
1864, Dom Jausions continued copying the neumed *Gradual* at the library. From there, his travels took him to Paris, where he was known to
be on July 3rd, and from where he did not return until the 20th, "so that
he could continue work, for which there was no lack of material," even
though he had already "studied some very curious manuscripts."

On July 3rd, he wrote:

I have been very well received here at the Imperial Library, the only one I have
gone to so far, and at the Ministry of Public Instruction where I went to find a
curious work by Mr. Nisard, which is supposed to be kept there. This manuscript has not been found yet, which, according to its title, ought to be a collection of variants from a large number of manuscripts, a collection that is all
done, it seems, and done doubtless with all the care that Nisard brought to
works of this kind (at the Imperial Library, I saw from a distance a magnificent
copy of the Montpellier *Antiphonal*, as good as the original). They are still looking for this manuscript for me. In the meanwhile, they have given me two
printed works on chant matters, which is nothing to be sneezed at. I shall try to
make my trip as profitable as possible . . . and to stop at Le Mans to see Gontier
in passing, and to speak with him a little about whatever I find here.

As we see, Gontier continued to have an active interest in this research, but work was not progressing fast enough to suit him, and he

only a dilatory meaning: "You ask me about the *Directorium;* it is a matter which, for the moment, is completely dead" (March 17, 1865, to Dom Bastide).

76 bis. Dom Guéranger participated in the making of the *Directorium chori*. Here are some of
the minute details we have as evidence: Dom Cabrol affirms that Dom Guéranger took our chant
for the *Pater* in the Office from an *Antiphonal* of St. Maur (*Antiphonale diurnum . . . monasticum,*
Paris 1699, LXIV—Solesmes WL-25), and from a monastic Psalter, both of 1699. See the *Revue
Grégorienne*, XVI, 1931, p. 18. In fact, it is this chant that appears in the *Directorium chori* of 1864. As
for the litany of the *Kyrie* that precedes the *Pater*, it was first taken from the above-mentioned *Antiphonal*. But in 1856, Dom Guéranger substituted another melody, the one that still appears in the
monastic *Antiphonal* of 1934. Here is its history. The chronicles states on August 14, 1856, that
Dom Guéranger brought from Monte Cassino (he was in Rome that spring) a new chant for the
Pater litany and he thinks that this melody was taken from Greek monks, because he heard it
sung a hundred times at St. Athanasius. It was used for the first time at Solesmes on the feast of
the Assumption in 1856, and the one from the St. Maur *Antiphonal* was reserved for Benediction.

complained about this to his erstwhile correspondent, Baptiste: "I am despairing because of Father Abbot's delay in printing his *Gradual*. I never see him without discussing it with him" (August 30, 1864).

These words of Gontier could only translate his impatience to see this traditional publication in print, which he dreamed about; in another letter, he wrote:

. . . as for the *Gradual,* the copy is partly prepared; but Father Abbot, through whose hands all matters must pass, has not yet given the go-ahead to print, whether he did not have time to think about it, or whether it was because of some minor difference in the wording of the Method. On a recent trip I took to Solesmes, I made some effort to investigate the matter; I do not know when work will be done on it. (October 13, 1864)

But, as noted above, the work was not yet sufficiently advanced at Solesmes for them to dream of printing yet: the copying work being done by Dom Jausions and by Dom Pothier was far from finished. Moreover, it was not just the corrected *Gradual* that was involved. A German monk, Dom Benedict Sauter, who had just finished his novitiate at Solesmes from 1862 to 1863, at the time of the beginning of the Beuron foundations, mentions that *Gradual* and avers categorically:

A secret: we have in our possession a corrected *Gradual* based on the most reliable manuscripts. Without wishing to assert that this version is authentic in every detail, it is at least certain that this book alone allows for a performance of plainchant in a way that is reasonable, sensitive, and harmonious. We owe this treasure to a member of our Order, who, not being able to publish yet the new edition of the *Gradual* which he is preparing in collaboration with several other competent persons, wanted very much, anticipating the results of his research, to supply a new foundation of the Order with the principles of a good performance of liturgical chant.[77]

Dom Mocquereau, to note in passing, asserts that this draft of the corrected *Gradual* imported to Beuron by Dom Sauter was the work of Dom Jausions. But it was still only a correction of an edition then available, most likely that of Rheims-Cambrai, for the purpose of facilitating the performance of the chant. Dom Pothier was to prepare a very similar work for Baptiste.[77bis]

77. *Le plain-chant et la Liturgie,* 1867 (Paris), p. 69.

77bis. Gontier presents Dom Sauter to his correspondent in an earlier letter in the following terms: "I believe you have already mentioned a budding community of Benedictines in Prussia,

18. Agreements and Disagreements

It must be noted that the minor differences mentioned above persisted, and that Dom Guéranger did not always resolve them. Gontier wrote to Baptiste again, and gave more detail: "The *Directorium chori* is printed, but the whole run is still at the bookseller's. The *Psalter* is ready to be printed, as is a section of the *Gradual*. But Father Abbot wishes the Method to be started, and you are well aware of the minor disagreements over the strong note of the melody" (October 22, 1864). So, as we see, Gontier had not managed to convince Dom Pothier, who persisted in his refusal to grant any determined value to the *virga* and, in general, any precision to Gregorian rhythm. As for the Psalter of which Gontier speaks, it has not been possible to identify it.[78]

However matters may have stood with regard to these differences, Gontier continued to admire the chanting of the monks. He wrote to Cloët, an ardent Gregorianist (October 13, 1864), "I do not believe plainchant is better interpreted anywhere." Evidently he spoke about it to Baptiste and lured him to Solesmes a second time in 1865. On May 26, 1865, Baptiste wrote to Dom Guéranger:

Father Gontier of Le Mans has written to say that the singing at Solesmes was even better than when I was there. I cherish the gentle hope of once again hearing the Gregorian melodies perfectly sung, and of studying your method more thoroughly; it is unquestionably the best, because it is the traditional method.

Duchy of Baden. It was at Solesmes that they first acquired their taste for, and then the principles of, the plainchant. For the past six months, they have started to use those principles, and people come from everywhere to hear them. Dom Sauter, a young religious of great piety and rare intelligence, an excellent musician, wrote to me (I quote from his text) that the Reverend Father Prior, his superior, believes that the time has come to begin the struggle in Germany, and to publish my little work *Le plain-chant: son exécution* as a program for what ought to be done, and what ought to be repealed. He adds that this little work, translated, will enter the scientific world and to this first work, he would add my brochure entitled *Méthode raisonnée,* the translation of which is well advanced, and that the religious and novices study it in their lectures" (to L. Baptiste, January 4, 1864).

In 1865, Dom Sauter published, in the form of a memorandum to the German hierarchy, a book entitled *Choral und Liturgie . . .* (Schaffhausen), which was translated into French in 1867 (*Le plain-chant et la Liturgie,* Paris).

78. Without doubt, this was the *Tons des Psaumes,* which was to appear later, in 1873, in the form of lithographed pages for the exclusive use of the monastery (Dom Biron, *Bibliographie,* p. 139).

Thus the interpretation of the chant, as adopted at Solesmes, continued to give satisfaction to Gontier. It is clear that the Solesmes style was well established, and this, it must be added, in spite of certain theoretical differences.

A letter from Gontier in June 1865 informs us of other causes for the delay that he regretted so much, in addition to differences regarding the method and some difficulties encountered in the very heart of the community. The Abbot of Solesmes's health left much to be desired. Thus Dom Guéranger could not give as much time as was necessary to the chant questions so dear to him, and which he followed to the last detail. In fact, on June 2, Gontier wrote:

> The Abbot of Solesmes has been very ill, even gravely so. Today he is better, but requires intensive care. This indisposition has slowed down the preparation of the edition. I suspect that this is not the only reason for the delay. Father Abbot knows that the work does not please several members of the community, and he is hesitant to alienate them. They are already applying the method more or less well, but they shy away from what they do not understand. . . . Father Abbot reserves to himself the control of all the details of the printing, as well as of the method.

> When I am with Father Abbot, he agrees with me, but on some small details that are important in themselves, there are some nuances that separate me from Father Jausions and Dom Pothier, particularly from Dom Pothier. . . . I could tell you what the small differences that separate me from the Fathers regarding the presentation of the method are; I would hasten to say that there are no differences in our manner of performing. I saw Father Abbot two weeks ago; he promised he would resume his discussions with Fathers Jausions and Pothier. (June 2, 1865)

19. Researching the Manuscripts (1865)

Over the course of 1865, Dom Jausions made several trips to Angers, on March 6, June 30, and October 27. It is entirely possible that he continued to be involved in the chant there. That year, however, Dom Jausions was occupied with the publication of a book on the Little Office of the Blessed Virgin.[79] His letters mention it continually. The printing

---

79. *Le petit Office de la B. V. Marie pour les différents temps de l'année, avec une traduction nouvelle et un commentaire en forme de méditations*, XII-314 pp., Angers, Barassé, 1865.

at Angers was completed in late July. The visits Dom Jausions made to Angers after that were certainly related to the chant, because until 1867, he was occupied at the city library with copying in their entirety not only manuscript 91, but also—as we have already mentioned—two other Gregorian manuscripts. It must also be remembered that Dom Jausions' literary activity (he published a historical work every year from 1863 to 1868)[80] could leave him only limited time for the Gregorian cause.

On July 26, Dom Pothier went to Alsace for health reasons, "then to St. Gall to consult Gregorian chant manuscripts" (Dom Guéranger's *Journal*). It seems that on the way, he paid a visit to the Imperial Library. He surely visited Laon, with its rich holdings in manuscripts. He wrote from Soultzmatt on August 6 or 7, 1865:

What I found most interesting on my trip, without exception, was the city of Laon, its cathedral and library. It contains a great number of manuscripts (about 500) including practically all of Prémontré. The *Antiphonal* I wished to see is from the eleventh century, judging from the neumes that resemble those of the Albi and Arles Antiphonaries in the Imperial Library. It is a different system of notation from that of St. Gall. In spite of that, in the Laon manuscripts are found the romanian letters explained by Notker. These letters at Laon, even more so than at St. Gall, confirm, as I have assured myself, Guido d'Arezzo's theory about the long final of the musical symbols, *mora ultima vocis*. I shall go to Colmar on Monday to obtain, if I can, those of Murbach.

Indeed, after a stop at the library in Épinal in July, Dom Pothier arrived at Colmar. The librarian there promised to send him some Murbach manuscripts at Soultzmatt right away (three manuscripts specifically indicated in a note from his brother, Dom Alphonse Pothier). It is also from this last locality that a letter informs us of this visit (August 8). Dom Pothier found there the "manuscripts of the Abbey that the Mayor of Colmar, with extreme kindness, allowed him to take along." And Dom Paquelin added a postscript that the Mayor of Colmar would gladly have given Dom Pothier the entire library had he wanted it. As Dom David has pointed out, from these manuscripts, Dom Pothier "copied the neumes with great animation, on twenty large pages in folio."[81]

---

80. Biron, *Bibliographie*, p. 78.
81. Dom David, *Dom Joseph Pothier*, p. 17; Dom Guéranger's *Journal*, October 11.

From Soultzmatt, Dom Pothier went to Beuron, where he arrived on August 21 or 22, to give chant classes. He stayed there almost a month, then proceeded to St. Gall, where he rejoined Dom Paquelin who was occupied with collating the old manuscripts of St. Gertrude and St. Mechtilde with a view to publishing their works. Dom Pothier helped him—and did so again later[82]—in this work of collating. But at the same time, Dom Pothier was also involved in making a partial copy of the *Antiphonal* of Blessed Hartker. Completed on September 26, this copy comprised no fewer than 171 pages. Moreover, here is what Dom Pothier himself said about his trip to St. Gall:

I could spend only ten days here, during which I profited as much as I could; I saw all the chant manuscripts, and they are numerous. I copied one of them, the one that seemed to me to be the most useful for our projects. These projects are progressing slowly—too slowly. Let us hope, however, that we shall arrive at something worthwhile one day (letter to Dom Bastide, dated January 12, 1866).[83]

20. The "Manuscript" of Dom Jausions (1866)

We have already noted that Dom Jausions was occupied with the printing of a book on the Little Office of the Blessed Virgin. In 1866, it was the publication of a life of Father Carron[84] that interested him. The book had two editions, the first in one volume, the other in two volumes, published in Paris by Dauriol. However, this did not keep Dom Jausions from continuing his work on copying the Graduals in Angers, where he stayed from March 8 to 25.

During this time Gontier, as always, appeared impatient. On March 12, he wrote: I am unaware of where the work stands at Solesmes. They are dependent on Father Abbot's approbation, and that approbation depends on his health. I still do not have a copy of the *Directorium chori* that he promised to send me as soon as it was promulgated.

---

82. Cf. Dom David, *Dom Joseph Pothier*, p. 17.

83. There is one detail worth mentioning here. Dom Guéranger's *Journal* informs us that in July 1865, the Abbot of Solesmes decided that the novices, before profession, should be given a test of their talent for intoning (*Journal*, July 17 and August 18). In the event of a failure, he would let Father Prior be responsible for the reception of their vows. This measure seems at first very severe, but it underscores Dom Guéranger's great concern for the dignity of the Divine Office and the esteem for the official prayer of the Church which he desired to find in his sons.

84. With the collaboration of Dom Bouleau, XI-632 pp.; LXVI pages, Paris, 1866.

A few extracts of a Method that was being studied were, however, being circulated. Gontier, in fact, informed his correspondent that "Dom Jausions has left quite a substantial memorandum at Angers and at Séez which you could ask him for and which he will send you." Gontier became more specific: "He told me what I already knew, that what he had left at Angers, at Séez, and at other places were some pages of a Method in manuscript" (April 13, 1866).

As for Dom Jausions, he speaks of a "chart" or "a page of instructions for the performance of the chant" (April 18, 1866). We shall see later, in an important letter by Dom Jausions dated April 25, 1866, that the few pages mentioned by Gontier are the "rules of accentuation" composed by Dom Jausions, and that the "chart," also composed by Dom Jausions, restated the principal rules for performing plainchant, and was only a summary of a much more extended Method. Moreover, the part played by Dom Jausions in the method that was being worked out was greater still. In fact, in the letter dated April 18 mentioned above, with regard to his page of instructions Dom Jausions says that he was in need of them at the moment to "complete the publication of our Method," and, in the letter dated April 25, he mentions "several trials" on rhythm which he had made in collaboration with Dom Pothier.

21. Dom Pothier's "Memorandum" (1866)

Nevertheless, in his letter of April 13, Gontier informed Baptiste that he had news from Solesmes. Dom Jausions came to Le Mans and Gontier learned from him that Dom Guéranger, wishing to finish it, had taken the chant problem in hand, and charged Dom Pothier with composing an essay intended to appear as a preface to the *Directorium chori*. Gontier wrote:

I had Dom Jausions with me for breakfast at home this morning, and he told me that Father Abbot, feeling better, had taken up again the plainchant question. He gave Dom Pothier orders to prepare a preliminary piece to be printed as a preface to the *Directorium chori*, which would appear as soon as Dom Pothier's work was finished. This preface is a kind of philosophical essay that will be scarcely understood, but will have value among competent persons. (April 13, 1866)

It must be admitted that these lines gave rise to certain difficulties. In fact, the reference is to a text that was to serve as an introduction to the *Directorium chori* and was to be inserted at the front of the book (this is certainly the meaning of Gontier's expression "as a preface to the *Directorium chori*"), even though the *Directorium* was already printed. Moreover, this conforms to the original plan set up by Dom Guéranger, which we already know about (No. 14). But this essay was something other than the Method, because Dom Jausions was soon to say, on April 18, that he was finishing up with writing it. Moreover, the task entrusted to Dom Pothier was to be an essay, not a statement of performance practice as such. The memorandum spoken of by Dom David in his memoirs of Dom Pothier comes readily to mind: "About twenty large pages in which the principles of returning to the manuscripts for the melodic line, the notation, as well as a useful statement about performance are set forth." What strongly supports this hypothesis is that such a memorandum would be appropriate as a preface to the *Directorium chori*, as it was the first book dedicated to the return to traditional notation. Thus it comes as no surprise that Dom Guéranger requested this assignment from Dom Pothier, given the part that he had played up to that point in the orientation of the project.

In any case, this memorandum cannot possibly have been intended, as it might appear at first glance, for the sole use of the Abbot of Solesmes, for the purpose of clarifying the point of discussion that remained between Gontier and Dom Pothier with regard to the "strong note of the melody,"[85] for the essay, Gontier clearly affirms, was intended for publication. But why did Dom Guéranger request the memorandum when the publication of the method was already well advanced? It is difficult to conjecture. Thus, faced with this lack of complete certainty, it is better not to suggest anything.

---

85. Gontier always insisted on this point, maintaining "that the stemmed-note at the top of an ascent produces a melodic accent" (October 13, 1864). "The culminating stemmed-note is a strong beat" (August 30, 1867), cf. *infra*, No. 25. The paper given by Dom Pothier at Arezzo in 1882 is an echo of the discussion that took place during this period on "the *virga* in the neumes" (cf. No. 38).

22. The Work Drafted by Dom Pothier (1866)

Meanwhile, Baptiste asked Dom Jausions to send him his notes on the performance of the chant. Dom Jausions thus had to acknowledge that the Method on which he was working was well along and ready to appear.

On April 18, 1866, Dom Jausions wrote:

First, the page of instructions for the performance of the chant that I have already sent to various places, notably to Séez and Angers, has not been printed yet. Although it has been copied at various establishments, I have in my possession only the one copy that I made for my own use. Nevertheless, I shall gladly send it to you, but I need it right now to finish editing our basic Method that Reverend Father Abbot speaks of publishing three or four months from now. Doubtless you would prefer to wait for the publication, anyway, so as to have something more complete?

Finally, on April 25, another letter from Dom Jausions takes us, one might say, to Solesmes in the midst of the work itself. Dom Jausions sent off his "page on the chant" so eagerly requested by his correspondent and, happily for us, he added to it lengthy explanations on the nature and plan of the method that was talked about for so many years.

Although not everything was yet settled, the plan had been agreed upon, at least in its overall design. There is a valuable letter explaining where matters stood in late April 1866:

I enclose my manuscript chart of instructions for the chant, which obliges me to send you everything as *official documents*. On this point, to respond to what you told me at the beginning of your letter, I can assure you, dear Father, that I have no difficulty whatever about communicating it to you. It is only that, since it is not yet finished in every detail (as you will see by a paragraph which I have marked in parentheses, and which I have annotated), I would wish in no way to contradict the very much more extended Method we are preparing at this time, and which Reverend Father Abbot continually talks of approving.

I hope the Method we are preparing will merit your attention, and I thank you for the early indication of your interest in your request for a number of copies. Nevertheless, perhaps this will require further attention on your part. This method will be basic, and then again not so basic. It will be basic in that we will never produce anything quite so succinct again. It will not be as utterly basic, however, because it will have to run at least some hundred pages to include very important and minute details, and because it will not include everything usually expected in a basic method, namely the theory of the scale, of intervals, and of modes. Rather, assuming that those matters are familiar, it will present only the rules for accentuation, good reading, and good rendition of the chant *from the point of view of rhythm*. I have drawn up almost complete rules for accentuation, and I present them as self-evident. After our several previous trials, Dom Pothier is now writing up the results of our research on the rhythm of the chant. It is a continuation of the ideas contained in the chart I sent you, which I drew up in Angers for the seminarians. He has already written altogether about seventy-five pages, and has not yet finished. Although we have worked on it every day together, I do not have an available copy of this work in progress. I fear that it might be rather advanced for children. On the other hand, things must be clear.

So you will see, dear Father, that we have a decision to make, for, on the one hand, if it is to be printed soon, I can scarcely see how I can send it to you before printing; on the other hand, if you wish a considerable number of copies of it, we would have take this request into account when we go to press as, aside from your order, we were planning on printing a rather small number of copies. In fact, this *method* we are discussing is *merely a practical introduction to get our new books into usage among our religious.* We are in no way seeking to publicize it, as we may later for an extended *Treatise on Plainchant*, on the scale of the works by Dom Jumilhac and others.

What emerges from this long letter of Dom Jausions? First, the work at issue was not a Method as we understand the term today, but rather something like a treatise on *rhythm* (emphasis by Dom Jausions), that was to run "at least some hundred pages to include very important and minute details."

Dom Jausions says that he himself wrote the rules for accentuation, at least to a very large extent, rules that were to include the rules for the accentuation of the syllabic chant and the melodic chant, as we have seen above (No. 14). But it was Dom Pothier who worked on the main part, the section on rhythm. Yet Dom Jausions did point out that this work on rhythm was merely a continuation of the ideas contained in his own "page of instructions for performing the chant." He also noted that he had already done several trials on this subject with Dom Pothier, and that they continued to work on it every day. But we must point out again that it was Dom Pothier who was doing the writing: he had already written seventy-five pages and was not yet finished. Although this was still just a *practical introduction*, it does seem that the introduction was quite lengthy. So this is something quite different from the twenty pages mentioned by Dom David, who wished to see in them the whole of the early Method.[86]

This letter may also hint at the material in Dom Pothier's book entitled *Les Mélodies Grégoriennes*, published in 1880. Doubtless the most important part of that book, the section on rhythm that occupies several chapters (chapters VIII to XVI) and runs some 173 pages, was drafted in 1866. Otherwise, any trace of Dom Pothier's major work under discussion here would have disappeared thereafter. Since Dom Guéranger approved the *Mélodies Grégoriennes* in 1869, long before he died and while Dom Jausions was still living, as we will see below, we have no record of any other work on rhythm by Dom Pothier that would have paved the way for his book.

As for Dom Jausions' collaboration (the Solesmes tradition has always been consistent on this point), there is no doubt about it, at least with regard to writing the chapters on rhythm, if the letter presented here is read objectively. Although Dom Jausions' very first efforts had involved neither a restitution of the ancient melodies nor a return to the traditional notation, it turned out that early on he had come around easily to the way of thinking of Dom Guéranger, Gontier, and Dom Pothier, and that he was then working in full agreement with Dom Pothier.

In a letter dated July 1866, Dom Pothier was not yet envisioning an immediate printing of the Method. (Although he speaks of a *Preface*, it clearly has to do with the method, as proven by the timetable, which corresponds to the dates mentioned by Dom Jausions.) As for the *Directorium chori*, also mentioned in this letter, it had been printed, as we know. What is said of it in the letter can only refer to its promulgation, which was in fact to be done at the same time as the promulgation of the Method.

In July 1866, Dom Pothier wrote to Dom Bastide:

The famous Preface is progressing, but slowly. I thought that surely by bringing it back up and reworking it last Lent, it would be finished by August, but we

---

86. *Un document intéressant,* in *Revue du chant grégorien,* July–August 1911, p. 185.—There may be a reference to these "trials" mentioned by Dom Pothier in a letter he wrote to Dom Bastide on March 17, 1865. After discussing the *Directorium chori* (cf. Note 76), Dom Pothier added, "As for the Preface, I am waiting." This sentence can be understood in various ways, including: "I am waiting to get to work on it." In any event, this cannot possibly be a reference to the essay requested by Dom Guéranger in 1866 (No. 21).

shall have neither it nor the *Directorium* until next Advent at the earliest. Father Gontier calls it a work of science and of patience: this last expression, it must be allowed, is apt. If the delay were to result in a more accurate and practical science, nothing will have been lost by waiting a bit. What seems more urgent to me are the chant books; not a note of either the *Antiphonal* or the *Gradual* has been printed yet. A work of patience! (To Dom Bastide, July 1866)

23. Gregorian Travels (1866)

Baptiste had spoken of possibly going to Solesmes during the summer of 1866. Dom Jausions informed Baptiste that he was planning to visit the Petit Séminaire de Saint-Gaultier on his visit to the monastery of Ligugé "to put a little order in the chant of that abbey" (letter of April 18, 1866), since he could foresee that he would be away from Solesmes for the summer. Dom Pothier, "the only other person besides me who is abreast of the chant question," would also be away. In announcing his trip to Ligugé, Dom Jausions stated clearly that the journey would be brief, and the reason he gives for this is that the Method was not finished:

I am going to Ligugé because it was a trip scheduled for other reasons; but the brief time I must spend there gives you all the more indication that nothing is finished with regard to our Method. Nonetheless, we could discuss many things, and the immediacy of our meeting permits me to set aside at this time many things which can be discussed in person more easily than in writing.

Dom Jausions left Solesmes in late June for the "lengthy musical peregrinations" from which he was to return "full of neumes," as reported in the chronicle. On July 4, he was at Ligugé, where he discussed the *Directorium chori*, according to Gontier.

We next find him in Paris, working hard in libraries—too hard in Dom Guéranger's view, fearing for his young disciple's health. A long letter from Dom Jausions tells us that he had "perused a number of manuscripts intently" at the Imperial Library, noting with deep interest a host of things for his own information, and that he had received word of three Antiphonaries he wanted to copy (two at the Imperial Library and one at Sainte-Geneviève). However, it all involved a great deal of trouble, and he triumphed only after countless efforts, "letters to the ministry, visits to offices, visits to all the librarians, the pleasant and the impossible alike." Finally, he added, "I hope that this trip to Paris has perhaps given me an opening with people who might be useful to us when needed for our projects." (July 27 and September 2, 1866)

These last observations show, if it were necessary, that although Dom Jausions was a "good copyist," he also knew how to take advantage of his contacts with the manuscripts, in order to instruct himself on the many problems raised by the Gregorian question.

In acknowledging receipt of the manuscripts from Paris, Dom Guéranger informs us that Dom Pothier, for his part, was resting at Soultzmatt. He was there from August 16 to September 16, and his biographer assures us that he had resumed work "on the Colmar manuscripts." In fact, at Soultzmatt Dom Pothier was copying a Murbach missal from the Colmar library. He finished work on the copy on September 9. He also went to Laon, Muenster, Basel, and finally Troyes.[87] In these various cities, he doubtless researched new manuscripts, as he did at Basel, from which he later obtained manuscripts by correspondence. At Laon, most especially, the old *Antiphonal* of the Mass,[88] which he had already studied on his previous trip, seemed to draw his attention, and perhaps it was at this time that he took steps for it to be lent to him so that he could copy it, which he deemed indispensable for his work. We will return to this matter later.

24. Various Difficulties (1866)

During these days, the novices at Solesmes, or at least their Father Master, Dom Couturier, who would one day succeed Dom Guéranger, were inclining toward Dom Pothier's restorations. This new chant, with its pure lines, was a foretaste of the *Gradual* being prepared, and aroused their wish to have it emerge from its swaddling clothes:

When will your *Gradual* ever see the light of day? Meanwhile, I want to tell you, as my teacher, and to console you for all the attention you have given me, that during your absence I took on the task of solfeging all the copies of the Graduals your brother *(Dom Alphonse Pothier)* gave me. (Dom David, p. 17)

87. Dom David, *Dom Joseph Pothier*, p. 17. Cf. Also a note from Dom Alphonse Pothier.
88. This was Codex 239 (9th–10th century) at the Library of Laon, which Dom Mocquereau was later to publish in the *Paléographie Musicale*, vol. X (1909).

Nevertheless, Gontier's letter from Cloët, dated August 11, 1866, makes mention again of Dom Guéranger's hesitations; Dom Guéranger did not dare face the opposition raised by some of the religious on this matter:

I believe I told you that nothing has yet been made public; for several years now the *Directorium chori* has been printed; but it has not yet been distributed to the community; and I do not know whether it ever will be. Father Abbot, not at all well, has become timid, not wanting to cope with the deaf ear of an opposition that is fearful of change. Two religious have prepared the *Gradual* and the *Antiphonal;* and if Father Abbot wished, everything could be printed in less than two years.

Whatever were the problems faced by Dom Guéranger in his own monastery regarding the publication of the Method, the persistence of a considerable variance of opinion between Dom Pothier and Gontier on the nature of the stemmed *virga* can be considered one of the principal reasons for his hesitations. Well, this dispute, as we shall soon learn, obstinately remained utterly unresolved.

Another reason for the slowdown of the work was the fact that Dom Jausions and Dom Pothier were still absorbed in other projects. This was noticeable especially in Dom Pothier's case, because he was the one whom Dom Guéranger could count on particularly to bring the restoration of our chant books to a satisfactory conclusion. Then Dom Pothier was placed in charge of the theology course, which evidently occupied most of his attention. So Dom Guéranger decided to relieve him in November 1866, so that Pothier might devote himself entirely to the work of the Gregorian restoration, which had already dragged on for several years. At least for a time, Dom Jausions was going to have to discontinue his historical and liturgical studies; and we have already seen him completely occupied in preparing, with Dom Pothier, the preliminary Method requested by Dom Guéranger.

25. The First Version of the *Mélodies Grégoriennes* (1867)

In spite of Dom Guéranger's decisions, especially that to relieve Dom Pothier, matters continued to drag on. The Abbot of Solesmes became ill in early 1867 and was absorbed with various concerns that prevented him from devoting himself to the examination of the Method, whose composition he followed closely. Dom Jausions and Dom Pothier advised Baptiste of this in a joint letter dated January 15, 1867.

Yet Dom Pothier hoped just the same that "the practical rules of Gregorian chant" could soon be sent to the printer (January 15, 1867). And happily, on April 8, he noted:

You will wait a good while for the Method, on which I am not the only one working. I hope, however, we can send it to the printer very soon after Easter. . . . Independently of the Method, we shall finally start printing the Gradual and Antiphonal, and I hope that once matters are underway, they will move along quite smoothly.

One can thus conclude that the editing of the Method was completed in 1867. Proof of this will be found further on, besides. In the summer of 1868, Baptiste could consult a "manuscript" by Dom Pothier, in view of the editing of a practical Method that he alone was working on. Although the term used seems unclear, it is evident that it could only refer to the Method developed at Solesmes, which alone, in view of his work, could be useful to Baptiste. But let us return to 1867. Cloët, having come to Solesmes in the summer[89] when Dom Jausions was away, had long conversations with Dom Pothier over a period of eight days, but as Gontier said, he (Dom Pothier), "showed him neither the *Directorium chori* nor the Preface of the Solesmes edition" (August 30, 1867). The word Preface could refer simply to the Method—and we have seen that Dom Pothier referred to it thus—or to the essay requested by Dom Guéranger in April 1866, or perhaps to both at once. The task being finished in the summer of 1867, the matter worked itself out, so that Dom Jausions and Dom Pothier were less preoccupied and had more free time. At the end of July, Dom Jausions, this time at his leisure, could give a series of Chant courses at Ligugé, Fontgombault, and Saint-Gaultier, where he "allowed Father Baptiste's students to sing as much as they wished" (August 2, 1867; cf. Dom Jausions to Baptiste, letter of

---

89. Dom Jausions went to see Cloët at his home in February, very likely at the time of a trip to northern France.—In 1863, Cloët published at Lecoffre a *Recueil de Mélodies Liturgiques,* preceded by a method. From the point of view of notation, there is nothing new in this book. A believer in speech rhythm, the author nevertheless gave in to the prejudice of the *long accent,* and his discussions with Gontier on this point and a few other points, as well, had not shaken his convictions (Rousseau, p. 47). According to Gontier, Dom Pothier fared better, in that summer of 1867, and Cloët admitted that "there is no one in France who is stronger in the chant than Dom Pothier" (August 30, 1867).

July 3). Dom Pothier had time to annotate and correct a *Gradual* from Rheims, also at Baptiste's request.

Thus it seems that the two writings of Dom Pothier which plainly constitute the basis for the *Mélodies Grégoriennes* published in 1880, were ready. The first of these was Dom Pothier's essay, still quite short (here one naturally thinks of Chapter I of the *Mélodies Grégoriennes,* which from the historical point of view clearly settles well the problem of returning to tradition). The second writing was the *Méthode* in a much more developed form (already amounting, in 1866, to more than a hundred pages). This text, written by Dom Pothier in close collaboration with Dom Jausions—in this instance, Dom Pothier himself confirms his authorship of the Method, in the letter of April 8 cited above—was still quite general in character, in the form of a treatise on rhythm, as Dom Jausions explained in detail (cf. above, No. 22). Thus it is this second document that seems to correspond best, through its content and scope, to what was to become the *Mélodies Grégoriennes*, a treatise on the rhythm of liturgical chant, of which the *Méthode* would be the first version. It is important to note that without this, all trace of this work would have disappeared, and it is difficult to imagine what other writing of Dom Pothier could be viewed as a preparation for the *Mélodies Grégoriennes* approved by Dom Guéranger in 1869.

But if this was the case, why was the *Méthode* not sent to the printer at the time? The reason is that the differences between Gontier and Dom Pothier, mentioned at the outset, continued to exist even as, otherwise, they were in complete agreement regarding performance practice. A letter from Gontier proves well, in fact, that he held fast to his position:

. . . the more a subject is probed, the more differences become known. I am in full agreement with Dom Jausions and Dom Pothier as to performance; and we sang in unison for a whole day; but I am with Dom Jausions and somewhat against Dom Pothier in saying that customarily, the stemmed note at the top of a melodic rise is an accented note. I say customarily, for I do not think that in the oldest editions, like the beautiful manuscripts that I have here with me, a strong accent should always be made on the first note of the *clivis*, etc. (August 30, 1867)

26. Dom Pothier's Style

Dom Pothier, too, was consistent with his own style, which was based on taking great liberties, the enemy of excessive attention to detail. To Father Baptiste, who asked him to write a method applicable specifically to the Rheims-Cambrai edition, he replied:

What you request can readily be done, but only when the one in preparation is finished. I understand your impatience over this problem, and we would like to be able to comply immediately with your request: meanwhile, continue to work at it, you have the general idea, and for the most part the special technique, and many things you think you cannot resolve will fall into place by themselves; the problems of minute details should not cause you to stop; basically, what is important is to know how to give the chant a movement of natural recitation; this is for the division of the tonal groups or of the syllables necessary to sung language, a language simply accented; to choose, among the various ways of establishing groups, what makes the text more intelligible and, at the same time, makes the melody more agreeable. Doubtless, tradition must be respected as well as the manuscripts, but when the double purpose has really been achieved, which is apparent in the singing, almost always the tradition and the manuscripts are found to be in accord (April 8, 1867).

In replying to a specific question, he added:

One cannot and one should not seek complete and perfect uniformity in terms of supervenient phenomena; in this sense, any absolute system in this regard can only be false, at the very least in the sense that exceptions are always necessary; in the final analysis, it is indeed the ear that can sometimes be the judge and even sometimes the only judge in the matter of chant, as the eye when it judges painting (April 8, 1867).

To this text, we are adding three more, written later, in 1869, but which are relevant here:

As far as syllables, neumes, and distinctions are concerned, I should tell you, if I am not mistaken, that it is very important to teach the singers to follow the sense of the phrase, that is, first of all, to take note of the words, possible even when a knowledge of Latin is lacking; as for the special case where such a division involves a neume and another a simple musical syllable, it is just about impossible. If you try to systematize and analyze the elements of discourse, you will not succeed; the pauses offer too many nuances for you to classify them methodically. One must not try to impose a precise solution on what is, by its nature, imprecise.

However, for the division of the neume, the solution is often clear: it is when the melody ends in an incomplete pause, but one that is still sufficient to provide a satisfactory melodic sense. How can this be expressed? Sing, and you will see that some pauses are impossible to suppress, while others you could skip over quite handily. The first mark the end of the neume, the second, those of simple syllables. (March 21, 1869)

. . . I am far from being settled as to the formation of the principles: I do not find any that are sufficiently broad; the more I proceed, the more I see the need to be freed from any system. I do not say this to discourage you; on the contrary, I only want to say that the simplest things closest to what nature teaches are often the most difficult to explain; however, try we must. (April 25, 1869)

For me, the subdivisions into binary groups within ascending as well as descending phrases—it is all the same. If you wish, speak only of the rising groups, well and good; but it must be clearly understood that these subdivisions in no way lengthen the musical syllables; these subdivisions are intended only to avoid detaching the notes. . . . But there is no longer any need to speak of these subdivisions; this is useful only in the longer series. (August 31, 1869)[90]

27. Preparation of the *Antiphonal*

The task of transcribing the manuscripts progressed slowly. The work required patience, but the "copyists" appreciated the fruits of their labors: a more perfect knowledge of the manuscripts, which their attentive reading of the neumes and their faithful transcription revealed to them. On March 28, 1867, Dom Jausions wrote from Angers, where he was working in the library:

As for our work's progress, it clearly will not be rapid, because of the many impediments that slow us down. I shall mention only one. Our task, being the

90. Several Gregorianists already felt the need for more precise instruction. One of L. Baptiste's correspondents noted (regarding unexpected issues): "Dom Pothier says that it is necessary to follow nature: this leaves the field wide open for capriciousness, and nobody wants that" (Abbé Léonard, January 19, 18. .). Another, Planque, gave an account to Cloët of a letter of Dom Pothier, also asking for greater precision on the very matter of the rhythmic subdivisions and this for the purpose of unifying the chant: "There is a place here to adopt supplementary signs to indicate better the principal incises and the melodic phrase; for the written word we have the period, the colon, the semi-colon, and the comma; in the chant, we have only two kinds of bars, few indeed. For some singers, it is never going too far to dot the i's for them, as they saying goes; moreover, in a large choir, a good system of punctuation can only improve the unity of the ensemble's performance (February 18, 1868).

restoration of the text according to the manuscripts, would be considerable enough if we had at our disposal the manuscripts we need in our cells at Solesmes. Do not forget that, far from having these indispensable documents right at hand, we are obliged to procure them first by the interminable route of a complete transcription. Thus because of this, we shall have lost years; I am wrong to say lost, since these transcriptions are for us a study to familiarize us with the chant that we intend to restore; but quite lost, nonetheless, from the point of view of the advancement of the work.

Hence I am here at the public library, copying two *Graduals*, one from the tenth century, the other from the twelfth. In both of them I am at the Sundays after Pentecost (including the sanctoral cycle, which, in these manuscripts, is intercalated within the Proper of the Time). Now I am approaching the end, and by giant steps, but in order to reach this point, I had to make many trips, spending only a few days each time.—So also, and after much trouble, last year in Paris I obtained three texts of the *Antiphonal*. They have been sent to us for the year; but since we can have them only for that period, we are hurrying to transcribe them; so this year, spent still trying to obtain documents in this way, will yield scanty results, at least directly, in terms of our ultimate work. When we do have all our materials, these three or four *Graduals*, and as many *Antiphonaries*, our work will move along notably faster. But in all, time and patience are needed, and especially in this endeavor. You know, too, that Dom Pothier and I have several other assignments and obstacles. In the midst of all this, we shall do our best; but we cannot do the impossible.

It was in July 1867, before the trip to Ligugé, Fontgombault, and Saint-Gaultier mentioned above, that Dom Jausions completed the transcription of manuscript 91 at the library in Angers. He presented a handsomely bound copy of it to Dom Guéranger on the Feast of the Assumption. At the same time, still in Angers, he copied combined manuscripts 96–97, twelfth-century *Graduals* of which we also have a copy (the verses of the Offertory, at the end of the transcription, are in Dom Pothier's hand). At Solesmes, he also collated the three Antiphonals that he had brought from Paris the year before. He returned them in September, only to obtain a new loan of the Sainte-Geneviève manuscript.

The collation of the *Antiphonal* filled up about thirty notebooks. The three versions are laid out there one beneath the other (we have identified those of the Compiègne *Antiphonal*: B. N. 17.296, and the Beauvais *Antiphonal*: Sainte-Geneviève), but the melodic variants alone are indicated on lines, which are often almost entirely blank. To these copies by

Dom Jausions, we must add various partial copies done at Angers, always in view of the *Antiphonal.*

28. The First Version of the *Liber Gradualis* (1868)

It seems clear to us that the Method prepared at Solesmes was completed in 1867. In 1868, the *Gradual* was also finished. We can follow the final stages of the work in Dom Pothier's correspondence. On April 14, for example, he wrote:

We could print the Introits, the Graduals, and the Tracts right away. All of this has been concluded. But we shall begin to print only when the book of Mass chants is ready; the *Antiphonal* will follow.

And on October 16:

This summer, thanks to the active steps taken by Dom Jausions, we were able to consult and transcribe new documents, which will be valuable to us. Our work for the rest, it seems, has gone well; the Introits, Graduals, Tracts and Alleluias could be printed at once; the Offertories are coming along, the Communions will then follow. All of this requires care and time; be patient.

For his part, Dom Jausions stated specifically that it was Dom Pothier's responsibility to establish the definitive reading. In a letter dated December 22, 1868, he wrote: "... he is the one who is preparing the text that we felt should be adopted." To do this, Dom Pothier laid out the various pieces of the Gradual by types and mode (an arrangement he had used previously in transcribing Codex 359 of St. Gall), without first making use of comparative tables as Dom Jausions had done for the *Antiphonal* (see above), somewhat in the manner generally used by Dom Mocquereau later.

One can therefore conclude that by the end of 1868 practically everything was finished. Professor Amédée Gastoué confirmed as much: "Toward 1868, preparation for this work (the *Gradual*) had been completed, and I can say, since I held it in my hands, dated and signed, that it differs very little from the final edition."[91] Incidentally, the words which Dom Pothier uttered later shew clearly that it was in fact a definitive edition.

91. *Dom Joseph Pothier,* in *Questions liturgiques et paroissiales,* 1924, p. 35.—Cf., by the same author: *L'Édition vaticane,* in *Société Internationale de Musique,* 1909, p. 1025; *Dom Joseph Pothier,* in *Dictionnaire de Connaissances Religieuses.* Cf. Dom David, *Dom Joseph Pothier,* p. 18.

It was for this reason that during the summer of 1868, Dom Jausions had continued his research. At the end of July, he was back in Paris, whence he returned "with various chant manuscripts," as noted in the chronicle. More exactly, these manuscripts, unless still other manuscripts were at issue, were sent to him the following month. On August 28, Dom Jausions wrote: "The manuscripts that I asked for in Paris have arrived. . . . I wrote to speed up the delivery of three others, which I had likewise requested." Unfortunately, it is impossible to determine what were the manuscripts to which Dom Jausions was referring. Perhaps they were Antiphonaries as well, for under the title *Mélanges Dom Jausions* we happen to have several copies of antiphons of the Psalter taken from various Paris and Angers manuscripts. (Seven are from Paris.)

In any event, it does seem that the bilingual Montpellier manuscript[92] was sent to Solesmes at this time or soon after, because the *Liber Gradualis* is in large measure indebted to it and owes it all of its merit. In his letter dated January 15, 1867, Dom Pothier had already mentioned this manuscript in passing, but perhaps it still had to do with Nisard's traced copy, housed in the Imperial Library, and which Dom Jausions knew about from 1864 (letter dated July 3). In any case, mention must be made of the copy of the Missal of Saint-Martial of Limoges (B.N. lat. 1132) made by Dom Pothier in 1868.

At any rate, when Cloët and Planque came to Solesmes in September 1868, they were able to see where things stood, and they had long conversations with Dom Jausions and Dom Pothier. Cloët had brought along an edition about which the Solesmes master entertained serious reservations. On October 9, 1868, Gontier wrote:

These gentlemen stayed from Monday to Saturday, the work of Abbé Cloët was examined in detail. . . . As to the outcome, I think either that Abbé Cloët decided not to go to press, or that Abbé Planque decided not to support the edition.

Thus Cloët was particularly interested in the Solesmes edition, and after his stay at the Abbey, he left an account of his conversations with Dom Jausions and Dom Pothier among his papers, which may be summarized as follows: the Solesmes edition project used the traditional Gregorian script (neumatic grouping of the notes, indication of certain spe-

92. This refers to the eleventh-century *Antiphonale tonale Missarum*, Codex H. 159 of the Bibliothèque de Médecine de Montpellier, which Dom Mocquereau published later in the *Paléographie Musicale*, vol. VII and VIII (1901–1905).

cial neumes, such as the *oriscus* and the *strophicus*) and, from the perspective of rhythm, they indicate the punctuation of the melodic phrase to the extent possible at the time. These were the very areas for which the Rheims-Cambrai edition had been criticized.

29. Baptiste's *Méthode*

In the fall of 1868, Baptiste was preparing his own *Méthode*. This *Méthode* was the subject of an exchange of letters between Baptiste and Gontier, on the one hand, and between Baptiste and Dom Pothier, on the other. We have already made several references to Dom Pothier's characteristic manner of treating questions of detail as revealed in this correspondence. During one of his trips to Solesmes, Baptiste, as we have already seen, was allowed to examine the *Méthode* that Dom Pothier had put together with help from Dom Jausions. He was also allowed to take notes, and he asked permission to use these notes later. To this request, Dom Jausions replied in Dom Pothier's name:

As to the main issue, namely using the notes that you took from Dom Pothier's manuscript, here is what he himself said to me: these notes may be inserted into a *Méthode* to be published, provided that the proofs be sent to us and we have control over what has been borrowed.[93]

Certainly, Baptiste was influenced by Dom Pothier's manuscript in the chapter where he speaks of rhythmic subdivisions. Nevertheless, in any case, whatever use he made of it, Baptiste sent his manuscript to Dom Pothier for review and corrections.

In acknowledging receipt of the package, Dom Pothier replied on October 16:

I shall read your manuscript carefully and also with pleasure. Send it along as agreed. I shall try not to make you wait too long for the comments you want to receive, which I shall make freely and in confidence, if there is a need for this.

Then, after stating where Solesmes stood at that moment in the work of preparing the *Gradual* (this is where the passage cited above, No. 28, fits), he added, without transition, "All this requires care and time. Please then be patient. In its time, your work will be useful to us. But it

---

93. Letter of August 15, 1868.

is too soon for us to be concerned with methodology for the moment."

This last, rather puzzling sentence could be simply a polite way of deferring a decision. Or, it could mean "Since we, too, at Solesmes are thinking about *printing* a Method, your work will be useful when it is time for us to be concerned about this printing," or yet again "Some differences of principle continue to exist *(and we are thinking of those still unresolved between Gontier and Dom Pothier),* so let us wait awhile before becoming involved with printing a Method; besides, your work will doubtless shed light on the subject." Now, if Dom Pothier's reluctance to form precise rules on rhythm are taken into account, this would explain why this long-awaited publication was delayed.

Yet the delay that Dom Pothier predicted was not to be too long. On January 11, 1869, Dom Pothier returned the manuscript to Baptiste, having freely used the permission given him: "I finished the revision of your *Méthode* today, and I am returning it to you more heavily annotated than when it arrived. At my leisure, I allowed myself the freedom to shape and cut it, doubtless a bit too much."

Finally, at the last minute, Dom Pothier was again requested to pass by Saint-Gaultier on returning from a trip to Germany in the summer of 1869, a trip we shall examine later. Baptiste's intention in composing an elementary method was thus to translate into practical terms the principles learned at Solesmes. Dom Pothier, far from disowning this *Méthode,* said once that it was as much "ours" as Baptiste's (letter to Dom Guéranger, August 23, 1869). In 1870, Baptiste's work was to appear under the title *Méthode élémentaire et classique de Plain-chant Romain,* prepared especially for the Rheims-Cambrai edition.[94] For this reason, it retained the notation systems employed in that edition; at the same time it attempted to regulate rhythmic subdivisions, in order to correct the principal fault found in the Rheims edition.

30. A Letter from Dom Jausions

Lastly, let us point out a request for advice that Dom Jausions received in October 1868. Dom Jausions responded at great length,[95] a

---

94. Lecoffre, 58 pp.

95. Letter of October 26, 1868, graciously provided to Solesmes by the Abbey of St. Wandrille.

stroke of good fortune for us, as this is the only document we have that expresses his thinking on Gregorian matters after the experimental efforts early in his musical career. Here are some salient points.

Dom Jausions explains, first of all, how it came to pass that Solesmes undertook an edition of chant conforming to the true Gregorian tradition. This passage has already been quoted, at least in part (No. 11), but must be situated here in its full context. Obviously, Dom Jausions alludes to his frequent trips to libraries, but without intention to diminish at all the equally important role of Dom Pothier in transcribing the manuscripts. He also mentions the decision made by Dom Guéranger in 1866 to allow Dom Pothier to devote all of his time to Gregorian studies. As for himself, he was no longer involved with the transcriptions, at least for a period of time (in 1866 and 1867, once again he worked together with Dom Pothier in editing the *Méthode*), leaving Dom Pothier to pursue his research and to prepare the text of the *Gradual*. The literary activity of Dom Jausions has already been pointed out. Without dissociating himself from Gregorian questions, as this letters shows, his orientation was more and more toward historical research, toward which he felt himself more inclined.

When the house of Solesmes was re-established in 1833, there were but few dioceses where the Roman Liturgy was in use. Ecclesiastical chant was rarely studied at the time. The "Dijon" edition was the best known among our Fathers. They used it, and for the time being we still have it. As for replacing it, we believe, in spite of the remarkable efforts made since then, that not one of the new editions is suitable. It is this that has prompted us to push our research further and to go back to the sources. Because of this, I was obliged to return to the manuscripts. In 1860, one of our brethren, the Reverend Father Dom Pothier, asked me to join him; and though since that moment I have been put in charge of almost all research and transcription done in the libraries, Dom Pothier has devoted himself in a more exclusive manner than I could have done to the studies that we had pursued for a long time together and, right now, it is he who is preparing the text that we think is likely to be adopted.

After explaining how monastic chant is not different from Roman chant, Dom Jausions continues:

It follows that we do not copy this or that manuscript for exclusive use in our Order at a given time; even less do we copy those editions, often very beautiful in terms of typography, but deplorable from the point of view of the chanting traditions to which the Benedictines of Saint-Maur have devoted themselves over the last two centuries; but we study and compare the most ancient Gregorian manuscripts that have been the focus of the learned scholars of our day; lastly, to interpret them, we follow the chain of tradition back to the time when knowledge of plainchant began to show signs of change.

It happens, he continues, that the traditional neumatic script was preserved rather late and it translates the authentic rhythmic design of the Gregorian melody:

It can be said, then, that from the seventh century to the Council of Trent, or thereabouts, the musical work of St. Gregory continued to be reproduced with the signs that he himself used in writing; the notation, from the time of Guido, was not a translation of the ancient neumes, but merely a graphic improvement by means of which the former sign, now made clearer without becoming unrecognizable, could be transferred to a staff with a clef. In this way, the location of the pitch on the tonal scale could be defined.

This notation, you may say, imposes very precise indications on the rhythm of the plainchant. In our opinion, this notation also so well expresses even the most delicate contours of the Gregorian melody that it is nearly impossible, unless one is extraordinarily well-versed in Gregorian formulae, to perform the chant well without having this notation before you as a guide, and that no other notation can replace it. From this, it follows that to attempt a translation of it is an illusion that gave rise to the miscalculations of previous editors.

Dom Jausions went on to state specifically that, although the graphic symbols of the fifteenth and sixteenth centuries duplicate exactly the most ancient neumatic signs, a serious restoration requires comparison of these fifteenth-century manuscripts with the most ancient manuscripts, for there could have been—and often there have been—changes in the original melody over the course of the ages.

The only way to prepare an edition that is at once authentic and suitable for everyday use is to collate the greatest possible number of these manuscripts, from the St. Gall manuscript and ones of similar date, to render them into the script of the fifteenth or sixteenth centuries. This is not at all a translation, but a simple rearrangement of some neumes on a staff which in earlier times were *in campo aperto.*

Interpretation and especially rhythm, he continues, are quite another matter:

Indeed, although the graphic symbols of plainchant have been preserved, as I said before, as recognizable since the time of St. Gregory to the sixteenth century, the interpretation of these symbols has not remained at all consistent. Indeed, far from it. Gerbert's collections contain the theories of several centuries on this subject. One has only to read the writings of the authors included, one after another, to realize that the later ones are a completely different mind-set from those of an earlier period. Similarly, the scholarly research of de Coussemaker bears witness to the birth of modern music. For, just as the new art progressively changed the tonality of plainchant, so too, little by little, did it also change its rhythm.

Dom Jausions developed his thought by showing how the authors cited by Gerbert or Coussemaker defined everything, not from the perspective of plainchant, but from the perspective of measured music:

Even when their quotations are not taken from notes, but from the Gregorian repertory; even when their citations use the names and traditional figures of the ancient formulae *podatus, clivis,* and others, nevertheless they remain in the field of figured music, they attribute conventional values to these ancient signs, different, first of all, from those invented by the ones who, a bit earlier, preceded them in this way of conventional use and arbitrariness, different above all from the ancient and original interpretation of the Gregorian neumes.

So Dom Jausions concludes by condemning the proportional notation still used in the Rheims-Cambrai edition—the same Dom Jausions who at the outset had said of this mistaken view:

We would be at fault if we believed ourselves authorized by the theories of certain authors in the Gerbert and Coussemaker collections to preserve their procedures of notation and performance. Because certain authors in these collections distort Gregorian formulae by isolating notes whose value they determine by a system of mathematical proportionality, they are in the domain of mensuralist music, and no longer give the true notion of plainchant rhythm.

31. The Years 1869–1870

The year 1869 was notable because of Dom Pothier's trip to Germany and the departure of Dom Jausions for America (May 6), where he died the following year.

Dom Jausions, who was very partial to historical studies, went to study on the spot the origins of the church of Vincennes (Indiana), founded by one of his uncles, and the establishment of the faith in the New World. For a second time, Dom Pothier accompanied Dom

Paquelin with a view to publishing the works of St. Gertrude and St. Mechtilde. It is clear from the letters we have relating to this trip that this was its sole purpose. It was only secondarily and occasionally that Dom Pothier became involved with the chant. He himself attested to this: "I have had little spare time to copy the chant, but I was able to study a great number of manuscripts" (Beuron, July 22, 1869).[96]

This is the time to call attention to a copy of manuscript 239 of the Laon Library (Dom Pothier dates his *explicit* March 12, the Feast of St. Gregory the Great). In Volume X of the *Paléographie Musicale*, which reproduces this manuscript in phototype, Dom Mocquereau wrote:

Since 1869, there has existed a nearly complete copy of this manuscript, done by Dom Pothier. It is preceded by a short Latin preface. The copy is excellent, in spite of some inaccuracies. . . . It is in one volume, 222 pages, to which an index of some thirty pages has been added recently.[97]

The manuscript may have been loaned to Dom Pothier when he visited Laon in 1866, although no mention of this is made in the Solesmes correspondence. This is all the more likely a scenario as the almost complete transcription of the manuscript must have taken a great deal of time, and seemingly could not have been done on site at Laon.

32. The *Mélodies Grégoriennes* and the *Liber Gradualis* in 1870

The care with which Dom Pothier corrected Baptiste's work in 1868, and the two prolonged absences of Dom Jausions and Dom Pothier in 1869, are grounds enough for us to believe that the planned publications by Solesmes were already well advanced.

96. Dom David spoke of this trip, without otherwise giving exact details as to what was its real purpose, in the following terms: "On May 27, 1869, he (Dom Pothier) left for a long, two-and-a-half month trip to Germany. What a Gregorian harvest! In his correspondence with Dom Alphonse [Pothier], what delightful personal notes! But I must be brief and content myself with a mere listing of the stops along the way: first Rouen, then Cologne, Wolfenbüttel (where he met Dom Paquelin, still rapt in conversation with his dear St. Gertrude and St. Mechtilde), Magdeburg, Leipzig, Halle, Eisleben, Fulda, Gotha, and Mainz. From Mainz he went on to Beuron, Constance, and St. Gall where, he said, 'I work at the library from seven o'clock to noon and from noon to seven o'clock without stopping.' Finally, he reached Einsiedeln, where there are so many beautiful manuscripts" (*Dom Joseph Pothier*, p. 18).

97. It was from this copy that the *Caecilia* of Trier reproduced a few pieces in its lithographed Supplements for the *Mitglieder des Choralvereins,* 1873, pp. 38–41.

But Dom Pothier informs us that before Dom Jausions left for America, Dom Guéranger had had time to approve his work. Here is Dom Pothier's important text, placed at the beginning of his *Mélodies Grégoriennes:*

A memorandum had been drafted along these lines *(of an authentic traditional restoration of Gregorian chant)* and presented by the humble sons of Dom Guéranger to their revered father and master *(earlier, Dom Pothier had said that Dom Guéranger had assigned to* "two of his religious, long ago, the responsibility of undertaking the necessary research"), which he completely approved of, as well as the noted result of the research conducted under his supervision and direction. . . . . The pages that follow, and which we offer in all simplicity and confidence to the friends of the holy liturgy and sacred chant, reproduce the memorandum approved by Dom Guéranger with the corrections and additions that he himself had in large measure indicated. (Preface to the *Mélodies Grégoriennes,* p. 6)

What emerges from this text is that the book published in 1880 reproduced the memorandum presented to Dom Guéranger, well before his death and while Dom Jausions was still alive, which brings us to 1869, the year of Dom Jausions' departure for America. Moreover, Dom Guéranger approved the memorandum, as mentioned, after having carefully reviewed and corrected it.

This text also tells us that from that point on, in a single work the memorandum provided both the essay that Dom Guéranger requested of Dom Pothier, to be used as a Preface to the chant books for practical use, and a general method, in the form of a treatise on rhythm. Dom Pothier had thus managed to combine these two works in the preceding months, and had expanded the Preface, fleshing it out with all the basics on notation (an expansion of the table that he was to put at the beginning of the *Liber Gradualis*), specifically chapters III and VIII of the *Mélodies Grégoriennes.*

As mentioned above, Dom Pothier paid tribute to Dom Jausions' collaboration, to which he had already alluded, as you will recall, in a letter cited above (No. 25). There is no doubt that its author was Dom Pothier, and his influence was decisive from every point of view. Yet it is clear from any objective reading of the texts that concern this matter that Dom Jausions was not a mere copyist. Rather, he assisted Dom Pothier with his reflection and insight, working in true collaboration.[98]

98. See Note on page 77.

Yet at the time of Dom Jausions' death in America on October 3, 1870, while he was preparing to return to France, there had been no talk of any sort of publication for the previous two years. Nor was there to be any such talk in the years that followed, to the point that a correspondent of Baptiste once complained: "Dom Pothier tells me nothing more, neither of their books, nor of the work related to them" (Abbé Léonard, February 2, 1873). It took the intervention in 1875 of Cardinal Pitra, professed at Solesmes, to convince Dom Pothier to publish something on the chant.

After Dom Jausions' death, Dom Pothier continued his research. Whatever significance may otherwise be attached to the book approved by Dom Guéranger in 1869, it did constitute the charter for the restoration of the liturgical chant and, when it was published in 1880 under the title *Les Mélodies Grégoriennes*, its 260 pages did not add anything essential to that charter.

The *Gradual* seems to have been presented to Dom Guéranger at the same time as the memorandum mentioned by Dom Pothier, the one included in the *Mélodies Grégoriennes*. (Dom Pothier had spoken of the "noted result" approved by Dom Guéranger.) Clearly other ancient manuscripts could have been consulted for more extensive documentation. Moreover, the book benefited from ten years of choral experience together with a much better understanding of Gregorian composition and traditional rhythm. Gastoué asserts that the first version of the *Gradual* "differs only slightly from the final edition" (quoted above). It must be recognized that the years preceding its publication were devoted more to the performance of the chant than to the search for manuscripts.

Thus, at the time of Dom Guéranger's death, the Gregorian restoration already had its charter, whose basic principles had been laid down by the Abbot of Solesmes himself, both from the perspective of performance practice and from that of the restoration of the melodies. The first practical chant books, especially the *Gradual,* were in preparation. The printing of the *Gradual* was already within sight.

Note:—The Solesmes tradition has always been in favor of the collaboration of Dom Jausions with respect to Dom Pothier's book on the *Mélodies Grégoriennes*. Among our "elders," we cite:

Dom Paul Cagin, *L'œuvre de Solesmes dans la Restauration du chant grégorien* (*Rassegna Gregoriana,* 1904, col. 210);

Dom B. Heurtebise, *Solesmes et le chant grégorien* (Le Mans, 1904, p. 3);

Dom Auguste Gatard, *La Musique Grégorienne* (Paris, Laurens, 1913, p.
108); and

Dom André Mocquereau, *Le Révérendissime Dom Joseph Pothier* (*Revue
Grégorienne,* 1924, p. 36).

Furthermore, all saw fit to quote the above passage by Dom Pothier,
taken from the Preface of his book, almost without commentary. That
is to say that, although our "elders" at Solesmes knew of Dom Jausions'
collaboration, they were unaware of the details of how it functioned. In
addition, they were unaware of the recently discovered documents used
in the writing of this book.

Abbé Rousseau's book is also quite restrained, as is that of Abbé
Blanc, who used the letter of April 23, 1866, which was discovered at the
time that book was published.

Based on the letter quoted by Abbé Blanc, Moneta-Caglio (*Dom André Mocquereau e la restaurazione del Canto Gregoriano,* in *Musica Sacra,* Milan, March-April 1960, p. 37) attempts to assign authorship of the various chapters of the *Mélodies Grégoriennes* to Dom Guéranger, Dom
Pothier, and Dom Jausions. Regardless of any value this endeavor may
possess, the fact remains that this book, at least in its final form, was
written in its entirety by Dom Pothier.

As for the dispute that arose on this topic, it is worth mentioning that
it took shape in the troubled atmosphere of the beginnings of the Vatican Edition, at a time when certain laymen were denying to Dom Mocquereau the initiation of the *Paléographie Musicale,* for which he had
fought so hard (an initial whiff of this is found in an article distributed at
the Roman Congress of 1904, *Une réforme de Pie X,* under the pseudonym A. Louis in *Le Gaulois,* March 8, 1904). Moreover, one article published in these circumstances seemed to some to have spoken too
briefly of Dom Jausions (*Rassegna Gregoriana,* 1904, col. 225).

The facts given in these pages provide corrections that need to be
made on both sides (once again, cf. *Revue du Chant Grégorien,* 1911, p. 184,
and 1931, p. 87).

III ∎ THE FIRST PUBLICATIONS

33. Gregorian Chant and the Council (1870)

The sequence of events pertaining to the Gregorian restoration at Solesmes is better known, at least after 1880. It is customary to follow the development of these events to their successful conclusion, even though this may mean summarizing briefly those events that have already been reviewed.

It should be noted, for example, that in 1870, Dom Guéranger was requested on at least two occasions to intervene at the Council with a view to involving Rome itself in the movement of the Gregorian restoration. The time was not ripe, and Dom Guéranger knew it. In fact, there is no proof at all that he followed up on these requests, although he did appear uneasy because of the intrigues being woven in this regard (August 19, 1869 to Baptiste). But is it not significant that a certain Mr. Tesson, of the Rheims-Cambrai Commission should have had recourse to the Abbot of Solesmes to plead with him to intervene in favor of the Gregorian cause, whereas he might have considered himself qualified to do this on his own, pleading with insistence that Dom Guéranger "render this new and important service to the Church"?

For his part, Msgr. Lootens, Bishop of Castaballa, wrote to Dom Guéranger on June 15, 1870:

I find it extraordinary that among the reform projects whose plans we have received, there is no mention at all of the reform of religious chant. I have spoken of this to several Bishops. Many are of the same opinion. But I fear that, with some of them wanting to go too far, we shall obtain little or nothing. I believe it would be sufficient to restate emphatically the existing laws.

Msgr. Lootens then discussed various details because, as he put it, "I wish to plead with you for the love of the sacred liturgy to make use of

your pen one more time, to help in bringing about the necessary reform."

34. The Lithographed *Processional* (1873)

On the first Sunday of Advent, 1873, the monastic processional, composed by Dom Pothier and lithographed by his brother, Dom Alphonse
Pothier, was inaugurated at Solesmes. This first edition of the Processional still contained only 130 pages in traditional notation. Moreover, it
relied on the copy made by Dom Jausions of the English processional of
Wilton and Dom Pothier's copy of the manuscript of Compiègne. Dom
Guépin wrote:

The *maestro* did everything himself, and made up for the imperfection of the
tools available with his patience and ingenious methods of his own devising.
He even acted as a draftsman, and decorated his work with illustrations, histo-
riated letters, tail-pieces, and even full-page drawings representing the mysteries of the Annunciation and Christmas. All of this was taken from the *Heures* of
Simon Vostre and other printers of the earliest period. How delighted we were
when these modest notebooks were given out to us. Little did we imagine that
one day the melodies we were singing, with such great difficulty in the beginning, little by little would make their way throughout all Christianity.[99]

Two years later, on January 30, 1875, the restorer of the Abbey and
the first pioneer of the liturgical reform movement rendered his soul to
God, before witnessing the full flowering in the domain of music of the
liturgical work he had done. On July 22, 1875, the young Dom Mocquereau entered the Solesmes novitiate; he was to become Dom Pothier's collaborator, and was to pursue his work in the Gregorian restoration. Cardinal Pitra was at the Abbey[100] at that time, once again among
his professed brothers. He was deeply interested in the efforts being
made relative to Gregorian chant, and in a letter urgently requested
Dom Couturier, successor to Dom Guéranger, to require Dom Pothier
to publish something on this subject.

---

99. Dom David, *Dom Joseph Pothier,* p. 14.
100. A. Battandier, *Le cardinal Jean-Baptiste Pitra,* Paris, Sauvaitre, 1893, p. 590.

35. The Gregorian Apostolate

It was only two years later, in 1872, that Dom Pothier went to Belgium to negotiate the printing of his book, entitled *Mélodies Grégoriennes*. But as early as February 1876, he announced to one of his colleagues that Desclée of Tournai, the founder of Maredsous, was building a printing establishment "to help the Benedictines in their work of restoring the liturgy, including music." He concluded, "And so we shall set to work, and we shall provide the purest St. Gregory possible."[101]

Of Dom Pothier's trip to Germany in October–November 1878, the only thing of interest to us mentioned by his biographer is

a stay in Wiesbaden where, at the request of his fellow Benedictines, Cardinal Pitra, and for his own personal satisfaction, he collated the manuscripts of St. Gertrude, the great 12th-century visionary, poet, and missionary. He copied all of her musical works, which are very interesting with regard to music and text alike, composed in a flamboyant and highly expressive style (p. 18).[102]

In early 1879, Dom Pothier's first Gregorian publication appeared, revealing his knowledge of the manuscripts and the neumes. In an article entitled *Quelques mots sur la notation du chant grégorien,*[103] Dom Pothier was replying to a study on a missal of Saint-Vougay published in the *Revue de l'Art Chrétien,*[104] and which reproduced an antiphon of manuscript 83 of Angers, copied by Dom Jausions. He explained on this occasion the two systems of Gregorian notation, that of accents and that of dots, and showed how semiology could serve to interpret the delicate nuances of the sacred chant.

In 1879, Dom Alphonse Pothier noted down his brother's travels to

---

101. Dom David, *Dom Joseph Pothier,* p. 19. From Brussels and Tourcoing, Dom Pothier went on to Ghent, Trier, and Termonde in April and May (according to a note by Dom Alphonse Pothier).

102. In 1878, Dom Pothier printed a brief 18-page work on the lithographic presses of the Abbey (doubtless for the sole use of the monastery), entitled *Des signes de la notation neumatique,* which we no longer have, but the title of which is sufficiently evocative. It was surely a short course in paleography, which corresponded to what was to become chapter IV in the *Mélodies Grégoriennes,* and which was republished in 1879 under the title *Des signes neumatiques* (also lithographed).

103. First published in the *Revue de l'Art Chrétien,* vol. 24, 1877, p. 211 and reprinted in *Musica Sacra,* Toulouse, February 1879, pp. 15–19.

104. Article by Dom Plaine, vol. 23, 1877, p. 257.

Paris, Chartres, Autun, Dijon, Mechlin, Brussels, and Bruges. The undated quotation by Dom David (p. 17) seems to be from this time (for Dom Pothier's biographer recounts at this point, pp. 17–22, Gregorian chant-related activities stretching over several years):

> I am here at the rue d'Ulm, at the home of the Réparatrices. After my Mass, I give a chant class to the community . . . Then I go off to the libraries, from which I do not budge from 10 o'clock in the morning until 4 o'clock in the afternoon. I started at Sainte-Geneviève, then the Mazarine; in the third place I went back to the Bibliothèque Nationale to which I shall return tomorrow and thereafter . . . I am planning to go by the Arsenal on Wednesday and to return to Solesmes on Thursday, bearing my harvest. (P. 19)

In any event, these were not just study tours, but a Gregorian apostolate, as well.

36. The First Gregorian Congress of Aiguebelle (1879)

Therefore, at year's end, from November 27 to December 1, Dom Pothier was at the Abbey of Aiguebelle, where the first Gregorian chant Congress was held. The Trappists were the first to join the movement for Gregorian reform, and they did so wholeheartedly. So there were several Cistercian Abbots there, along with their cantors, as well as musical personalities from Lyons, Marseilles, Grenoble, Langres, and Saint-Claude. Dom Pothier, the guiding spirit of the Congress, was also there, accompanied by Dom Bourigaud from the Abbey of Marseilles. Dom Bourigaud had already been to Aiguebelle from May 21–31, and had given ". . . lectures on Gregorian chant according to Dom Pothier's method, in the presence of the Right Rev. Dom Marie-Gabriel, the Abbots and cantors of Bellefontaine and of Notre-Dame du Désert, and the Prior of Igny" (Dom Bérengier's *Chronicle*).[105]

It was at the Trappist monastery in Bellefontaine that Dom Pothier gave a series of lectures, sharing the benefit of his knowledge and experience with the sons of St. Bernard.

---

105. *Musica Sacra*, Toulouse, December 1879, p. 127: *La Trappe d'Aiguebelle et le chant grégorien:* Dom David, p. 22. Cf. T. Nisard, *Que faut-il penser des Nouveaux livres de chant liturgique de Ratisbonne*, Rennes 1880, p. 65, Epilogue.

There were two lectures each day. The morning lecture was for the religious only, and focused on the particular needs of their choirs. The Reverend Father Abbot of Melleray, himself well versed in the techniques of ecclesiastical chant, the Reverend Father Abbot of Notre-Dame-de-Grâce (Diocese of Coutance) and professed cantors of several monasteries were present for this first meeting. In the evening, the lecture was held in the large hall of the Guest House. The religious, who did not want to miss any of the *master's* teaching, were mixed in among numerous ecclesiastics, happy to be able to respond to the invitation that the Reverend Father had extended them. A few lay people also came and participated.[106]

37. The *Mélodies Grégoriennes* (1880)

The *Mélodies Grégoriennes d'après la tradition*, by the Reverend Dom Joseph Pothier, had first appeared in early 1880. The book was sent to the printer by order of Dom Couturier, as Dom Pothier continued to manifest reluctance to face criticism.[107] It contained the confirmation of the principles set forth twenty years earlier by Gontier, but fleshed out and more solidly stated. The book gave the key to the neumes, which the author described and explained clearly and accurately. (In fact, once the book was published, Dom Pothier earned the nickname "the Champollion of neumes," after the decipherer of the hieroglyphics on the Rosetta Stone.) The rules of oratorical rhythm were better defined in it, and the nature and role played by the Latin accent were highlighted in particular. In addition, Dom Pothier drew as much as possible on the treatises of medieval authors and gave various practical and judicious suggestions, the results of his own experience.

Abbé Blanc wrote:

The *Mélodies Grégoriennes* contains the summation of the principles that will govern the reconstruction of the Gregorian phrase and the re-establishment of its rhythm. The norms for deciphering the manuscripts in neumatic notation are presented here as an introduction to the practical principles of performance and to the aesthetic rules of interpretation (*op. cit.*, p. 35).

For his part, Dom Mocquereau wrote:

---

106. *Musica Sacra,* Toulouse, April 1881, p. 42: *Le chant grégorien à la Trappe de Bellefontaine.*

107. Dom Cagin, *L'Œuvre de Solesmes,* col. 211. There is no need to review the origins of this book, which were discussed in detail above (Chapter II).

Two facts result from this study: (1) the traditional melodies of the Roman Church were preserved in the manuscripts, and can be read; (2) the practical rules governing their performance have been rediscovered.

Dom Mocquereau continues: "The book met with absolutely unexpected success. It was translated into German and Italian *(by Dom Serafini)* and caused a veritable revolution in the performance of plainchant."[108]

The Trappists continued to demonstrate their complete dedication to the Gregorian cause. A second Congress was held at Aiguebelle on August 19–20, 1881. In attendance was Dom Pothier's close friend, Father Velluz, whom he had known in the Solesmes novitiate. Author of a brochure entitled *Étude bibliographique sur les Mélodies Grégoriennes de Dom Pothier,*[109] Father Velluz was a self-appointed promoter of Dom Pothier's book, whose teachings he presented in his lectures (cf. Dom Bérengier's *Chronicle,* August 21, 1881). After the Aiguebelle Congress, he also published a short *Introduction aux Mélodies Grégoriennes.*[110]

The same year, Dom Pothier issued a short 12-page study published in the *Revue de l'Art chrétien,* a Gregorian piece taken from the Lyons *Gradual* of 1738 and a fragment notated in staffless neumes.[111] This was to show that an integrated and authentic restoration of Gregorian chant (melody and rhythm) was possible and relatively easy to realize, and also to show that the traditional chant is found as late as the first printed volumes, and at times even much later than that, as the Lyons books show. With mastery, Dom Pothier pursued his demonstration through a detailed study of each neume of the piece he used as an example and reproduced in an exact copy. Once again, he demonstrated his talent as a paleographer and his profound knowledge of Gregorian chant.

This is likewise the moment to mention the establishment of the St.-Pierre de Solesmes Press, which in the future would play a significant role in spreading the Benedictine chant editions. The first trials date from 1879, but it was during the exile of the monks from their monastery that the Abbey's Press became organized and began to flourish.[112]

---

108. *La pensée pontificale et la restauration grégorienne* in *Revue Grégorienne* 1920, p. 18.

109. Grenoble, 80 p.

110. *Souvenir du Congrès d'Aiguebelle,* 19 et 20 août 1881, Grenoble, 20 p., ten of which are chant.

111. *Le chant de l'Église de Lyon, du VIIIe au XVIIIe siècle,* in the *Revue de l'Art Chrétien,* July–September 1881.—As an off-print, Imprimerie de la Société du Pas-de-Calais, Arras 1881, 12 p.

112. Dom L. Guilloreau, *La stamperia di S. Pietro a Solesmes,* in *Rassegna Gregoriana* 1906, c. 115ff.

38. The Arezzo Congress (1882)—
The Papal Brief of April 26, 1883

The European Congress of Arezzo for the study and improvement of liturgical chant took place in 1882. It will suffice[113] to recall the circumstances in which this congress took place. The Medicean Edition had been recommended repeatedly in decrees from the Holy See and, without being imposed, it had become the official edition. Thus, the delegates to the Arezzo Congress, where the Steering Committee had already been forced to impose limits on the agenda, had the feeling that they were heading for a battle. They came from just about everywhere. Solesmes was represented by Dom Pothier and Dom Antonin Schmitt, as well as Dom Étienne Bourigaud, a monk of the French Congregation.

Dom Pothier presented three reports to the Congress printed by the Abbey Press:

Concerning the Virga in the Neumes (48 pp.);
A Small Question of Grammar with regard to Plainchant (24 pp.); and
Tradition in the Notation of Plainchant (32 pp.)

which, on the one hand, justified the nature of Gregorian rhythm and, on the other, the melodic restorations of Solesmes. Dom Schmitt, undoubtedly one of those who helped Dom Pothier in preparing the printing of the *Gradual,* for his part presented a brochure in which the basic propositions of the Gregorian restoration were formulated with precision: *Proposals on Gregorian Chant in accordance with Findings Universally Accepted by Archaeologists* (30 pp.). These four brochures established the state of the question that was at once firm, lucid, and direct, and neatly positioned the School of Solesmes for the Gregorianists present at Arezzo.

Given the importance of Dom Schmitt's brochure, we shall give its basic propositions, in the author's own terms:

113. Regarding the Arezzo Congress, it will be helpful to consult: Dom Cagin: *Le chant grégorien au Congrès d'Arezzo,* Oudin 1883, 44 p.—M. Blanc, *L'enseignement musical de Solesmes,* p. 40ff.—E. Moneta-Caglio, *Dom André Mocquereau e la restaurazione del canto gregoriano,* in *Musica Sacra,* Milan, March–April 1960, p. 39ff.

I. We possess the true version of Gregorian chant in the manuscripts; the few slight and inevitable variants found in them cannot lead us into error regarding the true meaning of the early version.

II. The manuscripts give us the relative pitches of the notes.

III. By giving us the tones fixed according to their relative pitches, the manuscripts also show them united or separate by groupings.

IV. The form of the neumes does not indicate the proportional value of duration or of intensity.

V. The rhythm of chant is the rhythm of prose speech.

Before the Congress, Dom Pothier and his assistant were able to make contact with various people prominent in musical circles, especially Dom Amelli, the organizer of the Congress, who still harbored some reservations.

En route to Arezzo, Dom Schmitt wrote on September 8, 1882:

> The outstanding event of our stay in Milan is the complete conversion of Dom Amelli, who appeared totally devoted to Dom Pothier whom he understands better all the time.
>
> He had to abandon part of his program when Dom Pothier explained to him how the truth simplifies everything. Dom Amelli publicly and on several occasions expressed his personal conviction that Dom Pothier's excellent and all-embracing synthesis was the means by which all was explained and logical. He has been personally and without a doubt won over to our side.

Dom Pothier was the hero of the day. His doctrine was applauded and acclaimed, and a sung Mass with the advance proofs of the *Liber Gradualis* enthused those in attendance "like an echo of ages past". In addition, the resolution "that choir books henceforth should have the closest conformity to the ancient tradition" was passed almost unanimously (cf. *Appendix I*). It was a triumph for Dom Pothier in the two domains of scientific restoration and of the principles of performance practice. As early as this point, there was even some discussion of translating the *Mélodies Grégoriennes* into Italian.

Looking back on the Congress, Leo XIII could not have been more gracious toward the delegates.[114] The Pope expressed concern over the situation of Father Abbot and his monks, who had been driven from their monastery.

Dom Pothier wrote to his Abbot:

---

114. Cf. Dom Marsille's Chronicle, p. 133.

As for the chant itself, there was nothing notable, some general encourage-ment; but we did expect, and should continue to expect, some reaction against the Congress, where the general atmosphere and resolutions did not please everyone; to which I say: Let them react.

However, during the audience, the Pope had said: "Oh, the chant, that is your own business, you Benedictines." Dom Pothier continued:

The name of Solesmes cropped up again in connection with Father Ory, Vicar of Chateauneuf. "Are you choirmaster?" asked the Holy Father. "I am Vicar, and I am very much concerned with the singing of my parish, and I am also near Solesmes," he replied. "Oh then," said the Pope, "that is good, I under-stand."

In conclusion, Dom Pothier wrote to Dom Couturier (September 17, 1882): "In summary, the audience was good, and will continue to give the Congress, which will surely be attacked, more force and authority."

The adversaries had taken refuge in the argument of authority. For his part, Dom Schmitt wrote: "The Pustet delegation arrived with over 70 kilograms of books to distribute to the Congress."

In the end, Rome condemned the Arezzo resolutions. The issuance of the decree *Romanorum Pontificum sollicitudo* on April 26, 1883, uphold-ing the privileges of the Medicean Edition, was a stunning blow causing dismay among the friends of Solesmes, because Solesmes was obvious-ly the target. To all appearances, this meant the collapse of all hope. The time was not yet ripe for the necessary reforms. However, full free-dom was granted to researchers of pure scholarship. This was an open-ing that the Abbot of Solesmes would use to full advantage.

39. The *Liber Gradualis* (1883)— Papal Briefs to Dom Pothier (1884)

It was under these circumstances that the Solesmes *Liber Gradualis* came to be published. We have seen that from 1877 on, Dom Pothier had been negotiating with Desclée in this matter. Thus it was doubtless at this time, perhaps even a little earlier, that Dom Couturier assisted him, though we cannot name names with certainty:

In order to support and comfort Dom Pothier in a practical way, Dom Couturi-er provided him with two or three monks zealous for the work of restoration, but as yet they were inadequately qualified to work competently in this effort.[115]

Problems were resolved with the arrival of the proofs, because practical instruction could not have been given beforehand. In addition, Dom Pothier was annoyed by the greater authority enjoyed by the Ratisbon Edition. These things resulted in undeniable weaknesses, but such failings did not amount to much in comparison with the progress achieved. Nevertheless, if we look at the first transcription onto staff lines of St. Gall Codex 359, accomplished by Dom Pothier in 1862, it is clear that he would have done excellent work right away, had he been free to act as he saw fit.

Had the book perhaps already been printed before the Arezzo Congress but they were not yet available for sale? A statement by Dom Schmitt, in the letter cited above, seems to substantiate this view. In fact, he regrets ". . . that Dom Pothier had insisted on sending half of the *Graduals* to Solesmes, because they would have served his cause well at Arezzo." However, the printing was certainly not completed at that time, as is attested by a letter that will be discussed below. Besides, the *Liber Gradualis* carries a publication date of 1883. What Dom Schmitt mentions must have been advance proofs that would have been quite useful at the Congress. So it was from proof pages that the chants were sung at Arezzo on September 15th, at the Mass of Our Lady of the Seven Sorrows, directed by Dom Pothier. It was also from proof pages, by order of his Abbot, that Dom Mocquereau introduced the new chant on October 5, 1882, for the feast of the Novitiate: "an experiment that succeeded beyond all expectations," noted Dom Delatte (*Vie de Madame C. Bruyère*, chapter IV *in fine*). Finally, a Solesmes chronicle (by Dom Marsille) attests that the printed books from Desclée were received on July 11, 1883, the Feast of St. Benedict and the fiftieth anniversary of the re-establishment of Benedictine life at Solesmes[116] (see Plate 6, a page from the *Liber Gradualis* of Dom Pothier: the Gradual *Universi*).

---

115. Dom Cagin, *L'œuvre de Solesmes*, col. 212.—In a letter of 1886, Dom Schmitt, Dom Andoyer and Dom Cagin were named along with Dom Pothier (Dom Babin, September 7, 1886); we know, moreover, that Dom Mocquereau was appointed to this work as early as 1880.

116. The *Liber Gradualis* was inaugurated at Sainte-Cécile, the monastery of nuns where the Pontifical Office was sung during the exile of the monks in the village. On other days, the Office was sung in the parish church, and the first Masses sung from the new *Gradual*, to the extent that

The *Gradual*, bearing the imprimatur of the Bishop of Tournai (May 23, 1883), was entitled:

The *Liber Gradualis* originally compiled by St. Gregory the Great, subsequently revised and greatly expanded by authority of the Supreme Pontiffs—restored and provided with musical notation in the manner of our forefathers in a manner faithful to the manuscripts, published for the use of the Benedictine Congregation of France by order of its Presiding Abbot[116bis]

Dom Mocquereau called attention to the discretion of this title, and also to the courage of the Abbot of Solesmes who, under the circumstances, could appear to some to be like a revolutionary:

Each word of this title is significant: It is *honest*, for it does not hide the fact that the new *Liber Gradualis* contains the melodies of St. Gregory the Great, restored from the manuscripts; it is *bold*, because these things are said one month after the decree that disapproved these melodies; it is *discreet*, because the *Liber Gradualis* makes no pretense of intending to be imposed upon the Universal Church; it was published by order of the Abbot of Solesmes, *for the exclusive use of his congregation.*[117]

In fact, Dom Couturier did not lose heart. On June 22, 1883, a few days after the decree was published, he wrote to Dom Mocquereau:

This is all quite distressing, but I hope it will not stop you. We are not beaten, not even targeted, with regard to the performance of the traditional chant in our Benedictine churches. Let us therefore move forward. I am happy to learn that your schola continues to set about its work with such great enthusiasm.

This last sentence perhaps refers to the decision, taken earlier by Dom Couturier, to create a schola distinct from the monastic choir, and to entrust its direction to Dom Mocquereau.

Following up on this, Dom Mocquereau wrote:

---

they could be rehearsed, were the Masses of St. Anne, St. Peter in Chains, the Transfiguration, and St. Lawrence. It was at this moment that the Abbot decided to form a schola, distinct from the choir, under the direction of Dom Mocquereau. (Dom Marsille, *Chronicle*, p. 180.—Dom Pothier to L. Baptiste, October 30, 1883.—Dom Couturier to Dom Mocquereau, June 22, 1883.—Dom Cagin, *L'œuvre de Solesmes*, col. 216).

116bis. *Liber Gradualis a S. Gregorio Magno olim ordinatus postea Summorum Pontificum auctoritate recognitus ac plurimum auctus—cum notis musicis ad majorum tramites et codicum fidem figuratis ac restitutis—ad usum Congregationis Benedictinae Galliarum praesidis ejusdem jussu editus.*

117. *La pensée pontificale,* in *Revue Grégorienne,* 1920, p. 188.

What would have happened if the Abbot of Solesmes, intimidated, paralyzed by defeat and abandoned by his friends, had halted the publication of the *Liber Gradualis?* I do not know. The Lord has a thousand ways to achieve his ends. However, by this courageous act of faith in the final triumph of truth in the very bosom of the Church of Rome, our Abbot strode into the future and assured the restoration of the liturgical melodies.

However, in Cardinal Pitra's mind the book arrived too late. Dom Mocquereau wrote to his Abbot about this when the Abbot was away from the monastery, and reported the thinking of the Cardinal verbatim:

I admit I do not understand either Dom Pothier or Desclée. Your book was finished in November and you did not publish it. What ever were you waiting for? If you had taken your position before the Brief, you would have earned the right to be heard. (Dom Mocquereau to Dom Couturier, June 17, 1883)

Cardinal Pitra himself presented the new *Gradual* to the Pope and obtained from Leo XIII a very flattering Brief in honor of Solesmes and of Dom Pothier (March 3, 1884, cf. Appendix II). This Brief praised the zeal and intelligence of the author

to interpret and explain the ancient manuscripts of sacred music in the exact and original form . . . for the Church of Rome has always held this kind of sacred music which bears the name of St. Gregory the Great in high esteem.

Unfortunately, some people claimed victory too soon, and compromised the situation by imprudent and excessive commentaries. Thus, a second Brief addressed to Dom Pothier on May 3, 1884, while confirming the praise contained in the previous one, emphatically stated that

in order to avoid false interpretations to be given to this letter . . . it was not our intention to ignore the content of the public decree *Romanorum Pontificum sollicitudo* and to approve the use of the Solesmes *Gradual* in the Sacred Liturgy. *(The texts of these two Briefs are given in Appendix II.)*

However, the way was open to study. The conflict moved from the domain of authority to that of learning, and success was assured.

40. Various Publications

From Milan, Dom Schmitt closed his letter to Dom Couturier with these words: "There is the matter of translating Dom Pothier's *Méthode* into Italian, so happily announced by Dom Cagin, and of translating the *Mélodies*, as well." Now this seems to reopen the question of the identity of the *Méthode* that was in preparation in 1866, and of the *Mélodies Grégoriennes*. Nevertheless, in our view there is nothing to this. The book that Dom Pothier was preparing, aided by Dom Jausions, could only have been the *Mélodies Grégoriennes*, which Dom Guéranger corrected and approved long before he died. Moreover, Dom Jausions himself said that it was not a matter of a method in the strict and common meaning of the word, and he hesitated to put it in the hands of Baptiste's students (No. 22). When Dom Schmitt spoke of a "method" in 1882, and perhaps when Dom Pothier did so as far back as 1868, as we saw above, it could only have referred to one project, namely to an abridged version of the *Mélodies Grégoriennes* which would reword the instruction in the *Mélodies Grégoriennes* for teaching purposes.[118] In the end, it was Dom Schmitt himself who did the project. His book, *Méthode pratique de chant grégorien, leçons données aux Bénédictines du Temple, rue Monsieur,*[119] totaling 180 small lithographed pages, came out in 1885, and remained at Solesmes for a long time and, in friendly houses, this practical work gave the essential principles of Solesmes concerning Gregorian chant. *Le Monde* printed a review of it on December 31, 1885, under the name Lenoir, but it was really written by Dom Andoyer. As for Dom Pothier's *Méthode*, announced in October 1883 in the catalogue of the St. Pierre de Solesmes Press, there was no mention of it in the 1884 catalogue.

To conclude, let us call attention once more to the first Gregorian transcriptions—in traditional notation, of course—from the Abbey Press: the four pamphlets presented at the Arezzo Congress by Dom Pothier and Dom Schmitt came from the St. Pierre de Solesmes Press (August 1882). These were followed by other chant pamphlets:

—the *Cérémonial de la Vêture et de la Profession* (1883), which, it is true, included only a few scattered chant antiphons;

—a Table of neumes with a few noted examples, 8 pp., 1 table (April 1883);

—the *Cantus in honorem Smi Sacramenti* (August 1883), 16 pp.;

—the *Antiennes pour les Mystères du Rosaire* (October 1883), 8 pp.;

118. The fact is certain, and it is well known that Dom Cagin had wanted to "convince" Dom Pothier to write this practical method.
119. Published by Chauvin, Paris, 1885.

—the *Antiphonae et Responsoria in Vestitione Monalium et Consecratione Virginum* (January 1884);

—the *Toni Communes Officii et Missae ad usum Congregationis Gallicae O.S.B.* (1884), 68 pp.

When the *Hymni de Tempore et Sanctis in textu antiquo et novo cum tonis usitatis*, 244 pp., came out in 1885,[120] the Gregorian chant publications from the Solesmes presses had achieved, by this very fact, great prestige among the public that was interested in liturgical chant.[121]

Conclusion

The purpose of these pages has been to establish the date of the earliest signs of the Gregorian restoration at Solesmes and to indicate the principal stages of its development. From all that has been said, it is clear that the movement of restoration had certainly begun at Solesmes in 1860, and that the printing of the *Directorium chori,* planned before that, leads us to consider an even earlier date. When all is said and done, we can go back no further than 1856, as previously indicated by Msgr. Rousseau from the testimonies of the very early members of the Abbey. But the basic principles for an authentic Gregorian restoration, proposed and formulated by Dom Guéranger and consisting essentially in the return to the free rhythm of discourse for the performance of the chant, and in a comparison of the manuscripts for the restitution of the melodies, entered a new phase in 1860 when Dom Jausions and certainly Dom Pothier began to copy the ancient neumed manuscripts.

The *Directorium chori,* revised according to a new orientation, was printed in 1864; moreover, the editing of a Method had already begun

120. In collaboration with Dom Andoyer. Cf. Biron, *Bibliographie,* p. 141.

121. The first trial printings, the Offertory *Stetit Angelus,* are from 1881 (cf. the catalogue of the Press). Previously there had been various chant leaflets for particular occasions printed on the lithographic presses of the Abbey (Dom Biron, *Bibliographie,* p. 139ff.). Dom Biron mentions, in 1881, an "Office of Saint Anne for the diocese of Vannes," not printed at Solesmes, the chant for which was composed by Dom Pothier. Others, such as Dom Fonteinne, had tried their hand at this exercise before him, and with some measure of success; still others were to do so later.

(discussions relating to that project are recorded starting in 1863), and the work preparatory to the reform of the practical books was back in full swing once the remaining uncertainties regarding the integrity of the restoration were cleared up.

Work had begun in 1862 on revising the *Gradual*, and in 1866 on revising the *Antiphonal*. The year 1866 was decisive for the editing of the Method, completed in 1867. This Method, written by Dom Pothier in cooperation with Dom Jausions, seems to have been the first version of the *Mélodies Grégoriennes*. The work was less a Method *per se* than a treatise on rhythm. The essay that Dom Guéranger had requested from Dom Pothier for use as a Preface to the chant books being prepared was later expanded by Dom Pothier himself, and was incorporated into this Method. All this was approved by Dom Guéranger while Dom Jausions was still living, i.e. in 1869. An edited version of the *Gradual* was also approved by Dom Guéranger in 1869, a Processional was published in 1873, and the preliminary work on the *Antiphonal* was also well advanced at the time the Abbot of Solesmes died.

As to the role played by each, the preceding pages have defined it adequately. Dom Guéranger was the one who inspired and breathed life into the effort. Gontier was the first to formulate the basic rules of the Solesmes method, and his very solid counsel was never found to be faulty. Dom Jausions and Dom Pothier translated the theory into practice, especially Dom Pothier, who, gifted with a remarkable feeling for Gregorian chant, assured the triumph of the liturgical chant restoration. After receiving approval of his efforts from his Abbot, Dom Pothier continued his research. His book on the *Mélodies Grégoriennes,* published in 1880, together with the *Liber Gradualis*, earned him the title of the "restorer of Gregorian chant."

The *Mélodies Grégoriennes* enjoyed enormous success at the Arezzo congress. The same could be said for the *Liber Gradualis*. But these two books were also the targets of many controversies, and it is not our aim to discuss these here. One need only look through the periodical literature of the time to get a sense of the matter.

While awaiting the day when the good cause would finally triumph, Dom Pothier encountered many set-backs. But we have already identified the one who was to help Dom Pothier in his struggle for the Gregorian cause: Dom André Mocquereau, the future founder of the atelier of paleography at Solesmes, and of the *Paléographie Musicale*, the war machine that was destined to deliver the death blow to faulty editions by revealing the sources of the authentic Gregorian chant and revealing the errors in the editions then in use. In the end, the crowning achievement of all this Gregorian activity would be the Vatican Edition, published in 1904 by order of Pius X, after sometimes bitter disputes.

TWO

The Vatican Edition

A ▪ PRELIMINARIES OF THE GREGORIAN REFORM UNDER LEO XIII

I ▪ DOM ANDRÉ MOCQUEREAU AND

THE *PALÉOGRAPHIE MUSICALE*

The second part of the Gregorian restoration concerns the efforts and struggles it took to gain acceptance of the restoration, particularly in Rome. We will focus on this aspect, drawing mainly on the correspondence of Dom Mocquereau, Msgr. Carlo Respighi, consultor of the Congregation of Sacred Rites and pontifical master of ceremonies, and Father Angelo de Santi, editor of *Civiltà Cattolica*, who was to be the mainspring of the Gregorian reform. Dom Mocquereau's great achievement, the *Paléographie Musicale,* was crucial for Father de Santi in this regard, because it showed that Dom Pothier's work was in complete conformity with the manuscript tradition. Even so, once that had been demonstrated, Father de Santi and Msgr. Carlo Respighi had to exert all their influence to have the Gregorian restoration accepted by the Holy See itself, and to have it enter universal practice.

The broad outline of the facts is already known[1] and the following pages are intended merely to provide new testimony and some new information gleaned from many unpublished documents, particularly concerning the role played by Dom Mocquereau and his friends in Rome.

We have presented the facts chronologically, which we feel promotes both the truth and the liveliness of the story.

---

1. These pages are based in part on an article by Dom Mocquereau that appeared in the *Revue Grégorienne* of 1920–1921, *La Pensée pontificale et la restauration grégorienne,* a lecture given in New York at the International Conference on Gregorian chant (June 1–3, 1920). The article has been expanded considerably, and the documents on which it is based have been quoted.

1. Dom Mocquereau at Solesmes (1875)

First, let us consider some essential dates. Dom André Mocquereau was born on June 6, 1849, at La Tessouale (Maine-et-Loire), but his family originally was from Sablé. Almost all of his education was with the Brothers of Saint-Gabriel. Early on, he showed a remarkable aptitude for music, which explains his artistic education. At Cholet, where his family was living, he used to play the cello in an amateur orchestra directed by the violinist Charles Dancla, a professor at the Conservatoire. Dancla thought so highly of his young student's talent that he tried to bring him to the Conservatoire in Paris, convinced that the young Mocquereau had a brilliant career before him.

However, André Mocquereau was already thinking about the religious life. As soon as he was free from certain family responsibilities, he came knocking at the door of the Abbey of Saint-Pierre de Solesmes. He knew the place very well, since one of his sisters had been a cloistered nun since 1873 at the Abbey of Sainte-Cécile, where she was the organist. Thus he had frequent contact with Dom Guéranger, who recognized the seriousness of his monastic vocation and consented in principle to his admission to the novitiate, as soon as that became possible.

When Mocquereau entered the novitiate on July 22, 1875, Dom Guéranger was no longer there, as he had died the previous January 30. However, an illustrious professed monk of Solesmes was staying at the monastery at the time, Cardinal Jean-Baptiste Pitra, Librarian of the Holy Roman Church. Cardinal Pitra was later to encourage the restoration work begun at Solesmes many years before (Part 1, Nos. 35 and 39), particularly that of Dom Mocquereau. André Mocquereau was professed on April 9, 1877, and was ordained a priest on December 28, 1879, by Bishop Mermillod of Geneva.

The year 1880, when Dom Pothier's *Mélodies Grégoriennes* was published, was marked by the forced physical expulsion of the monks from their Abbey, on November 8. This expulsion was to last fifteen years, with the exception of a few months when the monks believed that they could return to their home. They were evicted once again in March 1882, and could not return this time until 1895.

At first, the expelled monks were divided into various groups, forming a number of small monasteries in Solesmes and vicinity. Dom Mocquereau was among those who took refuge in Chesnaies, in the

Mayenne region. There, they lived at the home of the Duc de Chaulnes, where the students were gathered (although a priest, Dom Mocquereau had not completed his theology studies in keeping with the usual course followed in the Congregation). The Abbey's presses had been brought to Chesnaies, whence the Imprimerie Saint-Pierre (the monastery press), which was to render such great service in spreading traditional Gregorian chant, would soon be transferred to Solesmes itself.

In June 1881, the students returned to Solesmes. They resided at "La Rose," the monastery's hostelry, since only the conventual buildings, strictly speaking, were off limits to their rightful owners. Little by little, nearly the entire community had gathered in Solesmes, albeit scattered in various houses in the village. The entire community congregated in various places at various times: all the monks gathered at the parish church or at Sainte-Cécile for the Offices, for meals at the common refectory (although not right away) in an outbuilding of the monastery, and for Chapter in the attic of the Presbytery.[2]

These sad events, which affected the usual development of monastic life at Solesmes, must be mentioned because to a certain extent they also hindered the restoration movement begun at the Abbey. Yet it was at this very time, in the midst of these various events, that Dom Mocquereau had the idea of publishing the sources of Gregorian chant, and brought his project to fruition.

2. Initial Work

It appears that Dom Mocquereau, just after his priestly ordination or perhaps even earlier, was assigned to assist Dom Pothier. In 1880, he was studying the Latin accent. This was an in-depth study indeed, to judge from the sort of books he had on hand (for example, the works of L. Benloew and H. Weil). His correspondence also reveals the orientation of his work. He was also responsible for rehearsing the novices in Gregorian chant. In that role, using galley proofs, he inaugurated the *Liber Gradualis* in 1882, on the feast of St. Placide, patron of the novitiate. It was on that occasion that the Abbot, Dom Couturier, determined to form a schola that would be separate from the choir. Dom Mocquereau was made director of the schola.

2. Cf. Dom A. Savaton, *Dom Paul Delatte, Abbé de Solesmes* (Plon 1954), pp. 71ff.

On this matter concerning the performance of Gregorian chant, there were some differences of opinion between Dom Pothier and Dom Mocquereau. For Dom Pothier,

perfection in Gregorian chant can only be the privilege of an individual, of a small number, but essentially, Gregorian chant does not require perfection. When sung simply and naturally, it is always pleasing. (Notes by Dom Mocquereau)[3]

To this Dom Mocquereau replied that there is some truth in what Dom Pothier says, but does that mean that here at Solesmes we should not try to attain at least a relative degree of perfection? No. For his part, in keeping with Dom Guéranger, Dom Mocquereau believed that careless chanting with little regard to rhythm and expression was part of the reason for the decline of Gregorian chant. Moreover, his Abbot did not contradict him. Even then, the Abbot wanted Solesmes to become a school of chant, "regretting that Dom Pothier did not establish such a school" (letter of F. Velluz, June 9, 1883). In Dom Mocquereau's correspondence, one finds echoes of these differences of opinion between Dom Pothier and him concerning the performance of the chant. The attitude of Dom Couturier himself explains very well why Dom Mocquereau was made conductor of the Schola in 1882, and then general director of the Abbey choir in 1889. There is also an explanation why Dom Mocquereau immediately oriented his research toward greater precision in Gregorian rhythm. Here, too, his correspondents urged him on, particularly Father A. Lhoumeau and Father F. Velluz, a fervent Gregorianist and former novitiate companion of Dom Mocquereau. In fact, we will see that this preoccupation at least partly determined the selection of the manuscripts that Dom Mocquereau would publish in the *Paléographie Musicale*.

The Solesmes *Liber Gradualis* was published in 1883. Before that, however, a decree of the Congregation of Sacred Rites, the decree *Romanorum Pontificum sollicitudo* of April 26, 1883,[4] had disavowed, in practice, the resolutions of the Arezzo Conference, by maintaining the privileges of the Pustet edition (Part 1, No. 38). Dom Mocquereau had written to his Abbot immediately, asking whether it might not be wise to notify Rome before launching the *Gradual*. He said, "It seems almost

---

3. On "Dom Pothier's Manner," cf. Part 1, No. 26.
4. Text and French translation in *Musica Sacra* of Ghent, June 1883, p. 87, cf. Part 1, No. 38.

impossible to me for us to release the *Gradual* without notifying Rome, because (people) would certainly not fail to point Solesmes out to the entire Catholic world as a pack of rebels" (June 17, 1885).

Some specifics must be mentioned regarding the relationship between Dom Pothier and Dom Mocquereau. Dom Mocquereau's esteem for the restorer of the Gregorian melodies never wavered. Let us consider just one example. In 1885, Dom Antonin Schmitt had lithographed the lessons in plainchant that he had given to the Bénédictines du Temple at the Rue Monsieur in Paris. This was a 180-page book entitled *Méthode pratique de Chant Grégorien* (Paris, Chauvin, 1885). It was published at the request of Dom Couturier, who deplored Dom Pothier's slowness in providing a practical method. This displeased Dom Pothier. Thus Dom Mocquereau pleaded his master's cause, writing to his Abbot in his own words; like Dom Pothier, he was unaware of the Abbot's order to Dom Schmitt.

In this whole matter, it seems to me that we are forgetting what Dom Pothier did and suffered for the sacred cause of Gregorian chant, that at a particular point he carried on Dom Guéranger's restoration work, and that he is one of the glories of Solesmes. Let us add that this is even more the result of God's grace than of the intrinsic merit, however great it may be, of the *Mélodies Grégoriennes*. God chose Dom Pothier for this great work of restoration, and without doubt He made Dom Pothier well suited for the goal he was to attain. No man is perfect, and like any individual, Dom Joseph Pothier was to have his failings . . . but, when all things are weighed out in the sight of God, I first recognized that we must give thanks and praise for the goodness, wisdom and intelligence of this man. (April 9, 1885)

Dom Pothier learned of this intervention and, from the monastery in Silos, Spain, where he was accompanying his Abbot, he thanked Dom Mocquereau most warmly.[5]

Twice before (in 1880 and in 1881), Dom Mocquereau had to go to Cauterets to care for his throat, which had caused him a great deal of pain. When passing through Paris in 1883, he visited Don Bosco to seek healing from him.[6] He returned to Cauterets in November 1884. Howev-

---

5. On April 15, Dom Couturier replied to Dom Mocquereau, from the Abbey of Silos, that he had acted as he did for the good of the Gregorian cause. On May 3, the Abbot wrote to Pothier himself: "Rev. Schmitt generously did what I had asked him to do." Dom Andoyer wrote a summary of Dom Schmitt's book in *Le Monde,* under the pen name Lenoir.

6. "You will never have much of a voice," the saint and miracle healer said to him, "but you will have enough for the work that Providence expects of you" (*Bulletin Salésien,* March 1930, p.

er, as early as July of that same year, he spent some time in Paris for the same reason. It was on that occasion that Dom Mocquereau had direct contact with the manuscripts in the Bibliothèque Nationale. He wrote to his Abbot:

Amid all these old liturgical books, I find that I am happy and at ease; I feel at home. They all remind me of the good old monks who wrote them for the Divine Office; and the whole monastic past of the Holy Church reawakens. I am happy and respectful in leafing through them, and cannot refrain from groaning at seeing all these books, Bibles, Missals, Graduals, etc., all holy books of our Religion, in the hands of the secular State. (July 20, 1884)

3. Catalogue of Manuscripts—*Scriptores*

In the last letter, Dom Mocquereau mentioned a "catalogue of noted manuscripts" already begun at Solesmes, and which he hoped to complete. Once again, we find indications of his methodical mind. Before starting in on anything, he began by drawing up as complete a list as possible of the main chant manuscripts, and of the treatises by ancient and medieval authors. We still have these venerable notebooks in our possession. Far from being a dry enumeration, they contain various interesting pieces of information about the manuscripts listed, in the order in which they were registered.

It has already been mentioned that the question of Gregorian rhythm preoccupied Dom Mocquereau. Thus, he thought first of doing a revised and completed edition of the *Scriptores* by Gerbert and Coussemaker, which had been studied at length by Gontier, Dom Jausions, and Dom Pothier. At one point, regarding this project, he wrote: "At Solesmes, there is a sort of dictionary, still in manuscript form, in which extracts from the major authors, musicians, and grammarians of the Middle Ages are collected and arranged by subject matter" (*Paléographie Musicale*, XI, pp. 16–18), and the first copies date from 1884. What Dom Mocquereau does not say is that largely, this dictionary was his own work, and that the project was started at his instigation. The detailed catalogue of the various editions of the *Scriptores* is written entirely in

---

76). Let us also note in passing that it was Dom Mocquereau who composed the Gregorian melodies of the Mass of St. John Bosco. Made of formulas, these melodies are well balanced and tuneful.

his handwriting. We even have a complete copy done by Dom Mocquereau of a treatise that took on special value since the manuscript was lost in the fire at the Library at Chartres in 1944. This was manuscript 130 of that library: *Musica Enchiriadis.*

However, Dom Mocquereau did not take long to realize that to achieve any complete archeological restoration of Gregorian chant, it was the manuscripts that had to be studied in detail.[7]

4. Establishment of the *Paléographie Musicale*

In addition, events themselves brought Dom Mocquereau to change the orientation of his work. As soon as it came out, the *Liber Gradualis* was the object of dispute. On the one hand, there were the partisans of the return to traditional Gregorian chant. On the other hand, there were those who upheld the official Ratisbon edition. The two camps collided. One need only read the musical periodicals of the day to become aware of what was going on. (See Plates 4 and 6, the Gradual *Universi* according to the Ratisbon edition and according to the Solesmes edition. A comparison of the two versions of the music reveals that they reflect two completely different orientations).

Once again, the practical and far-sighted mind of Dom Mocquereau knew immediately what had to be done to prepare the way for and hasten success, without wasting his time in trotting out the same arguments over and over again. In the *Revue Grégorienne* 1921, p. 9, he wrote:

After all, canonical discussions of papal briefs, decrees, and personal interpretations were secondary. The main question lay in the intrinsic value of the two competing editions, the *Neo-Medicean* and the *Benedictine.* If we could manage to prove beyond a doubt that the melodies of the Medicean edition were merely a miserable caricature of the early cantilenas, the battle would be won. All the decrees would fall by the wayside automatically, because once Rome was in possession of all the elements of the matter, it would never allow chants unworthy of divine praise to be used in Catholic churches, as events were to prove. As master and guardian of the arts, the Church possesses these sacred melodies as a treasure. The Church would put them back in a place of honor once their ancient beauty was restored, once their *historic* authenticity had been

---

7. He explains his view in the *Introduction Générale* to the *Paléographie Musicale,* vol. 1. See the passage quoted below, No. 13.

established rather than their *canonical* authenticity. So it was on this purely scientific terrain that the fight was to be waged; there, we were sure of victory. What is more, the modern Mediceans were so unwise as to draw us onto that terrain. After their favorite argument of *authority*, to which we did not want to respond out of respect, their favorite lines of reasoning were (a) that the Solesmes edition could not contain the chant of Saint Gregory, because that chant had been lost; and (b) that even if it were found, it was impossible to decipher the manuscripts that contain it.

A response had to be made to these gratuitous affirmations, but that response had to be unassailable. Should this response be made by means of newspaper articles or articles in periodicals? People were tired of those. That type of light weaponry would no longer do. The fight had been going on for fifteen years (1868–1884), and it had to be brought to an end. In another fifteen years, the famous thirty-year privilege was set to expire. At that point, it was essential for light to have dawned in Rome, a light so bright that the truth would emerge as a triumphant master.

But what war machine could overturn all obstacles and hasten victory? What had to be found was a kind of scientific tank—powerful, invulnerable, and capable of crushing all the enemy's reasoning.

The new war machine that Dom Mocquereau was thinking about was the publication, by phototype, of the main manuscripts of Gregorian chant, with essential commentaries. In his opinion, and future events were to prove him right, this was the best possible response to offer to his opponents, whoever they may be. It would justify the recent publication of the *Liber Gradualis* by Dom Pothier, showing that it was based on indisputable documents, the many chant manuscripts preserved in the libraries, the oldest of which went back to the 9th and 10th centuries. In commenting on a letter of Father Lhoumeau, who was worried that people thought everything had been placed back in doubt, Dom Mocquereau wrote: "It is firmly established that the main goal in publishing the manuscripts is to prove to everyone the truth of Dom Pothier's doctrine and the version of the chant given in his *Gradual, by using the very sources themselves*" (August 3, 1887). Moreover, publication of the manuscripts would also make a more in-depth study of the various problems related to Gregorian chant possible, particularly the question of rhythm. It was Dom Guéranger himself, the founder of the Gregorian restoration movement at Solesmes, who set down the general principle, which applied to this domain as well: "The original documents contain the basic facts of the various sciences, unalloyed and without a system of organization, but doubtless with all their original energy" (*Paléographie Musicale* VI, p. 17).

It must be admitted that although the idea of publishing the sources of Gregorian chant was not absolutely new (Father Lambillotte had published a copy of a Cantatorium from St. Gall, Manuscript 359), it was bold. Dom Pothier's young disciple, who was then thinking of starting a *monumental* collection of that type, was not lacking in courage. He was going to need it. Even at the Abbey itself, he encountered significant resistance, and even opposition. Nevertheless, Dom Mocquereau immediately received his Abbot's approval; once again, the Abbot supported Mocquereau's youthful ardor. There is no need to underscore the fact that the project was significant, and that starting up such a collection posed many problems. First, they needed assurance that an adequate number of subscribers could be guaranteed, all the more so as the temporary scattering of the monks of Saint-Pierre in the various houses in the village imposed a certain burden on the Abbey's finances. The monastery's Cellarer was going to be asked to make great sacrifices.

5. The Project (1887)

The first references to Dom Mocquereau's project date from 1887. In early August, Father Lhoumeau sent his encouragement to Dom Mocquereau. Dom Delpech was already at work recruiting subscribers (August 8), Dom Cabrol was sending Dom Mocquereau information obtained in his name and for this purpose from Léon Gautier (August 18), Dom Andoyer was assisting Dom Mocquereau in his research at the Bibliothèque Nationale with regard to the planned publication (three letters in September), and finally, in December, Dom Mégret offered Dom Mocquereau his assistance.

In rendering an account to Dom Mocquereau of his visit to Léon Gautier, Dom Cabrol mentioned exactly what was at issue: the conditions for the loan of manuscripts, the support that could be expected from musical periodicals, the Prospectus for launching the periodical, and the booksellers. Léon Gautier was charming, noted Dom Cabrol, and said that he was "drawn immediately to the significance and usefulness of the publication," and agreed to assume the responsibility for

PLATE I. Dom André Mocquereau

securing the loans of manuscripts needed from St. Gall, and promising a subscription to the new periodical from the École des Chartes.

As for Father Lhoumeau, he gave his wholehearted support to Dom Mocquereau's idea, and in particular, he pressed Dom Mocquereau to clarify the question of Gregorian rhythm. At the same time, however, he asked that a practical periodical be published as well, since "providing specifics on rhythm is essential so that the rhythm is not lost. With a method or a musical translation, the rhythm will be fixed and stereotyped; interpretation will always have its place, as in music, but there will be built-in protective limitation (August 3).

In October 1887, Dom Mocquereau himself went to Paris to work at the Bibliothèque Nationale with Dom Andoyer. On October 7, Dom Mocquereau noted, "Dom Andoyer has done good work . . . and he is doing me a great service. Tomorrow we will select the manuscript page that will serve as a model" (a reference to the phototype reproduction to appear with the Prospectus). However, Dom Mocquereau was already thinking about publishing his collection of the *Justus ut palma* Graduals, proving that this Gregorian melody had been preserved down through the centuries in various countries. This is evidenced by the fact that Dom Andoyer was researching those pieces for Dom Mocquereau at the Bibliothèque Nationale. In Paris, Dom Mocquereau visited Arthur Loth and told him of his project.

6. Journey for Subscriptions (1888)

The following year, in May 1888, accompanied by Dom Cabrol, Dom Mocquereau made a journey to Paris and the surrounding area to find potential subscribers. They visited Chartres and Versailles, then Ville-d'Avray, Auteuil, and Orléans. In all, they obtained 70 subscriptions, including those of Msgr. Freppel, the École des Chartes, and the Library of Sainte-Geneviève (the Curator offered to write personally to his friends in Germany and at the Conservatory of Music). In Paris, Dom Mocquereau again studied the various practical questions that arose, regarding the loan of manuscripts and matters involving booksellers.[8]

Dom Cabrol had returned to the Abbey slightly earlier than Dom

8. Dom M. Havard, *Révérendissime Dom Fernand Cabrol*, in *Revue Grégorienne*, 1937, p. 203, describes the welcome Msgr. d'Hulst, rector of the Institut Catholique in Paris, gave Dom Mocquereau, based on the correspondence of Dom Cabrol.

Mocquereau, following the death of the Reverend Father Prior of Solesmes. Dom Mocquereau was quite upset by Dom Cabrol's return, because Dom Cabrol was most useful to him on their visitations. Their most recent success had been receiving the subscription of the École des Chartes. However, from Solesmes Dom Mocquereau received the following encouraging news from Dom Cabrol himself. On May 21, 1888, he wrote:

> I can tell you that the Abbot is very pleased with your success, and that he is allowing you to continue your work in Paris, in order to obtain as many subscriptions as possible. I have also seen a certain number of the Fathers, and I am pleased to see that the interest in your work increases the better it is understood. . . . The printers are also very happy, and are taking heart. So, take heart. You will need constancy and energy to bring this business to a happy end, but you have an abundance of both.

7. Opposition—The Vow to Our Lady of Chartres (1888)

We must mention, however briefly, the various objections made to Dom Mocquereau with regard to his publication project.[9]

We know of Dom Pothier's objection, because Dom Mocquereau himself spoke of it, and replied to it.[10] Dom Pothier was somewhat

---

9. With regard to the establishment of the *Paléographie Musicale*, we should point out that new documents have come to our attention since these pages were written, notably letters from Solesmes (Dom Mocquereau and Dom Babin, director of the Imprimerie Saint-Pierre) to Dom Cabrol, which would confirm, if there were still such a need, that the initiative for establishing and producing the periodical came from Dom Mocquereau and from him alone. It has been claimed that it was not Dom Mocquereau who established the *Paléographie Musicale*, but rather Pothier, who was always opposed to the project. Nor have we overlooked what Dom Joseph Gajard wrote about this matter (cf. *La "Paléographie Musicale" et Dom André Mocquereau*, Foreword to Volume XIV of the *Paléographie Musicale*, pp. 9–59). We do not wish to enter into these polemics, which were quite legitimate at the time. The new documents that we have published in the course of this study are sufficient proof that the entire initiative for establishing the *Paléographie Musicale* came from Dom Mocquereau.

10. *Examen des critiques dirigées par dom Jeannin contre l'École de Solesmes* (Desclée 1926, pp. 105–106). "Dom Pothier was opposed to this publication. He had many arguments to oppose it, one of which he repeated in thousands of ways: "Yes," he said, "at first sight this project seems very seductive and full of promise. However, the closer you look at it, the sorrier the results will be. It could ruin the Gregorian restoration that we are attempting at Solesmes . . . we will see a harvest of the most extravagant theories on its origin, on the reading of neumes, on rhythm and the modes of the Gregorian melodies, etc.; in short, there will be fights, controversies, and battles that will certainly delay the restoration for many years, if not ruin it outright."

afraid, which is quite understandable, that the new collection constituted a revision of his *Gradual*. But the most tangible result, and this was certainly the goal sought by Dom Mocquereau, on the contrary, was to show that the *Liber Gradualis* was in conformity with the manuscript tradition. Above all, Dom Pothier was afraid that the manuscripts would be misread and misinterpreted when placed in the hands of the general public. Father Lhoumeau shared this fear. After having encouraged Dom Mocquereau to pursue his project, Lhoumeau requested, as we have seen, that the scientific periodical be accompanied by a practical periodical, "since to offer the manuscripts up for study without guiding instruction is to expose people to the risk of not drawing all the desired benefit from them and to expose the manuscripts to erroneous interpretation" (August 3). That was true, and so Dom Mocquereau proposed that the publication of the manuscripts be accompanied by the various studies needed to interpret them.

There was also the fear of turning Rome itself against Solesmes, at the time when Msgr. Franz Haberl, the defender of the Ratisbon edition, was in great favor.[11] However, Cardinal Pitra applauded the project enthusiastically, and his support was to carry great weight, without doubt, in the decision of the Abbot of Solesmes to support Dom Mocquereau (*Revue Grégorienne* 1921, p. 9).

Finally, there was also opposition from the printers, the monks charged with operating the Abbey's printing works. They were beginning to take heart, thanks to the arguments of Dom Cabrol (cf. No. 6). However, the director of the printing works, Dom Babin, remained to be convinced. On May 23, Dom Cabrol, who had returned to Solesmes before Dom Mocquereau, explained to Dom Mocquereau how he had broached the issue with Dom Babin:

I met with Dom Babin for nearly two hours. . . . I outlined the situation for him clearly, without bringing you into it at all and speaking only in my own name, i.e. as a humble assistant who has no commission whatsoever to make deals or to make commitments on your behalf. At first, he seemed to me rather hostile to the whole undertaking, fearing the risks involved, etc. I showed him, or at least tried to show him, that those risks could be reduced to next to nothing provided that we managed to get the desired number of subscribers together.

---

11. On July 20, 1887, Msgr. Haberl was appointed to the Commission for the Reprinting of the Authentic Books of the Chant (Moneta-Caglio, *Musica Sacra,* 1960, 4, p. 100).

Secondly, I pointed out to him that we were turning to him out of a sense of brotherly commitment, to give him the right of first refusal in an advantageous and honorable undertaking, because from many perspectives it was far better for a work of this nature, which was conceived at Solesmes, to be carried out at Solesmes. . . . Then I described the steps we had taken, the success that we had had, and the favorable opinion of so many specialists with regard to scholarship, the chant, paleography, bookstores, etc. In the end, he was convinced.

However, for a time it looked like the whole business might never see the light of day because of these various sources of opposition, particularly that of Dom Pothier. As soon as he returned to Solesmes—and this information comes from Msgr. Rousseau, who received it directly from Dom Mocquereau—he was called in to see Couturier, who told him, "not without hesitation and sadness, that, because of urgent and powerful approaches to him, the planned publication would have to be abandoned. . . . All he could do was agree."

It was at this point that, to rescue the work then in jeopardy, Dom Mocquereau made his well-known vow to Our Lady of Chartres, on May 26.

It so happened that it was his turn to perform the functions of hebdomadary, that Trinity Sunday, and during Benediction as he knelt before the Blessed Sacrament, Dom Mocquereau was moved to place this laborious undertaking under the protection of the Virgin Mary, promising that, if it were successful, he would offer the first volume to Our Lady of Chartres, which had given the first subscribers. The Right Rev. Dom Couturier, then Abbot of Solesmes, whose position alone it was to ratify this vow, gladly consented to it. From that day on, the obstacles disappeared one after the other.[12]

First of all, the decision of the Abbot was promptly revoked, thanks to the intervention of completely devoted brother monks, Dom Cabrol, and Dom Cagin.

Nevertheless, some time later Dom Cabrol wrote once again to Dom Mocquereau, who was on his way to Switzerland:

I see nothing new to tell you as far as the printers go. They seem generally well disposed (July 11, 1888). . . .

Generally, the disposition (of the printers) is the same as when you saw

---

12. The two texts just quoted, that of Msgr. Rousseau and the second, by Dom de Sainte-Beuve, are found in the *Paléographie Musicale*, vol. XIV, p. 14. In an article in the *Revue Grégorienne*, 1930, p. 42, Dom de Sainte-Beuve says that it was in fact from Chartres that the very first subscriptions came.

them upon your departure, on all three sides. From the first, keen sympathy, but hardly any influence to exert; from the second, confidence, somewhat cool firmness, and an absolute determination to carry on; and from the third, indecision and disbelief which will not disappear, like that of St. Thomas, until he sees the facts, if it would disappear even then (July 22, 1888).[13]

8. Dom Couturier and the Gregorian Movement

In discussing the establishment of the *Paléographie Musicale*, it is fitting to mention the role of Dom Couturier, Abbot of Solesmes. As was proper, the final decision was up to Dom Couturier. We must be grateful to him for supporting Dom Mocquereau and for having approved of his work. Without Dom Couturier, nothing would have been possible. He had already given evidence of decisiveness and courage with Dom Pothier. In fact, it was Dom Couturier's actions that brought Dom Pothier to decide to publish the *Mélodies Grégoriennes*, and then the *Liber Gradualis*. It was said in his day that this act of faith in the ultimate triumph of the truth ensured the restoration of the liturgical melodies. In 1885, distressed at Dom Pothier's slowness in providing a practical Method for the chant, Dom Couturier asked Dom Schmitt to publish the lessons he had given to the Benedictine nuns at the Rue Monsieur in Paris. We also owe to Dom Couturier the establishment of the Imprimerie Saint-Pierre, which was to publish many works starting in 1882, spreading traditional Gregorian chant. Dom Couturier would have liked Dom Pothier to establish "a school of Gregorian chant" (F. Velluz, letter of June 9, 1883). Finally, as we shall see later on, Dom Couturier did not hesitate to appoint Dom Mocquereau choirmaster, in order to ensure the unity of the chant at the Abbey itself, on the one hand, and more widespread development of the work of the Gregorian restoration, on the other hand.[14]

13. Dom Mocquereau, commenting on the letter of Dom Cabrol, noted in the margins: Dom Vannier, most favorable, Dom Lenoble and Dom Babin. Among those who supported Dom Mocquereau, there was also Dom A. Schmitt, author of the memorandum *Les propositions sur le chant grégorien d'après les faits universellement admis par les archéologues, présentés au Congrès d'Arezzo* (Part 1, No. 38).

14. Part 1, No. 39, in particular.

9. The Prospectus

Once the printers were convinced that Dom Mocquereau's project was viable, they set to work on the typographical composition of the Prospectus, written by Dom Mocquereau himself. (We have in our possession the proofs of the two prospectuses in French, corrected by Dom Mocquereau, as well as the rough drafts of the cover letters). Right away, they requested a second, much shorter prospectus intended for the general public. In the absence of Dom Mocquereau, they addressed their request to Dom Cabrol. "The printers have asked me to shorten the Prospectus, so that they can send out a single octavo page," Dom Cabrol wrote to Dom Mocquereau in early July 1888. "They told me that this had been arranged with you. I made up the Prospectus, drawing my inspiration from your version."

Dom Mocquereau's Prospectus comprised eight large quarto pages, with a plate, which, according to Monsignor Battandier, Cardinal Pitra's secretary, "rivaled the best that Dujardin has to offer" (letter to Dom Pothier). The date of the first printing was June 30, 1888. The Prospectus was entitled: *Paléographie Musicale. Les Mélodies Liturgiques ou recueil de Fac-similés phototypiques des principaux manuscrits de chant grégorien, ambrosien, gallican, mozarabe, avec préface explicative publiée par les Révérends Pères Bénédictins de l'Abbaye de Solesmes* (Solesmes, Imprimerie Saint-Pierre, 1888). *Les Mélodies Liturgiques*, then, was the main title used for the new collection. They may have been anticipating later confusion with the title of Dom Pothier's book, *Les Mélodies Grégoriennes*. The Prospectus set forth the goal, scope, and plan of the new collection. The text was a foretaste of the masterful Preface that Dom Mocquereau was preparing for the opening of the periodical.

A second French edition was soon to be issued by the Abbey press, followed by several translations into foreign languages:[15] one edition in Latin and French (printing date: August 29, 1888, 840 copies), one in English (November 26, 1888, 700 copies), and one in German (December 19, 1888, 1,100 copies).[16] These foreign-language editions of the Prospectus refer to the collection as the *Paléographie Musicale*. (There was a third

15. Cf. Dom P. Combe, *Bibliographie de dom André Mocquereau*, in *Études Grégoriennes*, II, 1957, p. 196.

16. We are speaking here only of the quarto editions of the Prospectus, not of the shorter versions.

edition in French, published on November 28, 1889, which obviously bore the same title.) The director of the monastery press sent the announcement of the first fascicle to the subscribers himself (on Sept. 15, Oct. 7, and Oct. 19, 1888).

10. A Trip to Switzerland (1888)

What manuscript was Dom Mocquereau going to use to head his collection? There was no doubt and no hesitation whatsoever on his part: he would use a manuscript from the school of St. Gall.[17] He was seeking to justify the *Liber Gradualis* and to advance studies on Gregorian rhythm, which he felt were essential for the success of the restoration. The St. Gall manuscripts were rich in information that would shed light on this problem.

However, he had to go choose the desired manuscript on site. Dom Pothier, who was already familiar with St. Gall, and who wanted to look at some more manuscripts there, went with Dom Mocquereau, which must have been a great pleasure for Mocquereau. In fact, Dom Mocquereau was afraid that his request for the loan of a manuscript would be denied, particularly for the phototype reproduction of the manuscript, and he was counting on Dom Pothier's presence to obtain such permission. This is also why Dom Mocquereau had Cardinal Pitra get involved. Dom Pothier, who had known Cardinal Pitra at Solesmes, was assigned to ask the Cardinal to plead the cause of his brothers at Solesmes with the Dean of the Chapter at St. Gall. The Cardinal graciously agreed to do so, glad once again to support the work undertaken by Dom Guéranger toward the restoration of Gregorian chant.

For Dom Mocquereau, the trip to St. Gall was an opportunity to go around to the major libraries in Switzerland, the first of a series of visits abroad that he took himself, or that others did on his behalf. Dom Mocquereau much preferred the silent work of the monastic cell. This varied research was to enable him to form the paleographical workshop at Solesmes that is one of the monastery's treasures.

---

17. Pothier could only encourage Dom Mocquereau along these lines, because Pothier also attributed great significance to the manuscripts from the school of St. Gall: "The school of St. Gall," he wrote on September 18, 1863, "seems to be the school where the chant was cultivated with the greatest care and preserved with greater purity."

For the moment, let us follow him on his trip to St. Gall. This will be easy, since, as was his custom, Dom Mocquereau left a detailed account of his travels for his sister, the Benedictine nun. After stopping at Delle, Dom Pothier and Dom Mocquereau went on to Basel, Constance, and Rheinau, visiting libraries (Dom Mocquereau, as usual, has left various paleographical notes taken during this trip). Once at St. Gall, the two travelers got down to work. Dom Mocquereau noted that he worked "from 8:00 AM to noon, and from 2:00 PM to 7:00 PM."

On July 12 he wrote to his Abbot:

> At the library, Mr. Idtenson was very nice. He made available to us eleven old manuscripts that contain the *Liber Gradualis*. We made our choice as early as yesterday, and we were quite clear in expressing our objectives to the librarian. With almost no difficulty at all, he promised to do what he could to provide us with the manuscript we selected. He is taking care of that. Although we do not have a final answer, we are sure of getting our manuscript. So, God be praised.
>
> It is a 10th-century manuscript, its notation is very clear, it has the romanian letters and signs, it includes the Offertory verses, and finally, and most importantly, we know the name of its author, a monk of St. Gall. This, in and of itself, "dates" the manuscript.
>
> The Cardinal's letter carried great weight for our success, and Dom Pothier intends to thank him for it.
>
> As soon as the final answer concerning the manuscript is given, I will send Dom Babin the few lines to be added to the Prospectus.[17bis]

The trip continued with a visit to Chur, stopping very briefly at Wartegg castle, the residence of Her Royal Highness the Duchess of Parma, whose mother was a cloistered nun at St. Cecilia at Solesmes,[18] where three of her own daughters were to enter. At Chur, Dom Mocquereau immediately set out to look for manuscripts, but this time without success. From there, with Dom Pothier he went on to Einsiedeln, then to Zurich, where Dom Pothier left his companion to return to France.

On July 22, Dom Mocquereau wrote:

17bis. For his part, Dom Pothier was copying prose texts and sequences, doubtless with an eye toward his *Variae Preces* that he was preparing at the time. ("Our territories are quite distinct," Dom Mocquereau noted pleasantly.)

18. The Reverend Mother Adelaide de Braganza, widow of Don Miguel, King of Portugal, entered St. Cecilia in 1886. Two princesses of her family had entered St. Cecilia before her.

I was sorry that Dom Pothier did not want to stay in Zurich, because after taking him to the station, I went to the Cantonal library, where I found a veritable nest of manuscripts of liturgical chant, Graduals, Antiphonaries, Hymnaries, etc., all from the Abbey of Rheinau. With these documents, it would be easy to write the history of the music and liturgical notation, and the story of their decline, at that Abbey. (Letter to Dom Couturier)

From Zurich, Dom Mocquereau went on to Beuron, where he received a fraternal welcome. Dom Kienle had also thought of publishing a manuscript, the one from Montpellier discovered by Danjou in 1847, but in light of Dom Mocquereau's grand project, Dom Kienle permanently renounced going ahead with his own project. From Beuron, Dom Mocquereau returned to St. Gall, and to Zurich, to continue working there.

11. The Manuscript Chosen for Publication

We noted that the manuscript Dom Mocquereau chose to publish was a St. Gall manuscript from the tenth century, noted *in campo aperto* and decorated with Romanian letters and signs. Some were astonished at the choice, believing as they did that it would have been better to use the bilingual manuscript from Montpellier first, one that was noted in neumes and in letters (Ms. H. 159). However, Dom Mocquereau did not want to open his collection with a manuscript that strictly speaking was not a liturgical book, but rather a school book. The manuscript from Montpellier presented the chant pieces in groups by type and by tone. In any event, he did plan to publish it eventually (in volumes VII and VIII of the *Paléographie Musicale*). Moreover, as he explained in a note on this subject, it was only appropriate to proceed chronologically. Manuscripts *in campo aperto* are the oldest, and, according to Dom Pothier, the Montpellier manuscript is not always in conformity with the pure Gregorian tradition.

Furthermore, even as he wanted to justify the reading of the *Liber Gradualis*, Dom Mocquereau wanted to shed light as quickly as possible on the question of Gregorian rhythm. He explained this desire in the following terms to a correspondent:

The main question at issue now among musical scholars is not that of the translation of the neume; everyone now acknowledges the possibility of this transposition by means of comparisons with the Guidonian and alphabetic manuscripts. What is more, this transposition is done in several periodicals and particularly in the *Liber Gradualis*. The problem occupying minds today is rhythm. . . . The oldest manuscripts, i.e. the manuscripts *in campo aperto*, retain the grouping of the notes more faithfully than do the more modern manuscripts. The St. Gall manuscripts, moreover, have the romanian letters and signs to which we attach very great importance in determining the rhythm and the nuances of expression. . . . We have subjected Manuscripts 359 (Lambillotte) and 339 from St. Gall to detailed analysis once again, which has resulted in quite important and absolutely certain discoveries regarding the use of these signs. These discoveries will be presented in a booklet which will be published in the first few months of 1889, and will, we hope, provide the fullest possible justification for the selection we are making among the St. Gall-Romanus manuscripts. (To Father Morelot, September 1888)

The selected manuscript, St. Gall 339, did not reach Solesmes until Sunday, September 9, the feast of the Holy Name of Mary, as Dom Mocquereau noted with satisfaction at the bottom of the cover letter. The delay resulted from the fact that permission had first to be obtained from the Library Committee. At that time, Dom Mocquereau had just issued the second Prospectus (the printing date is September 3). It met with the expected success, partly due to the devotion of faithful friends who placed themselves at Dom Mocquereau's disposal. Subscriptions were coming in, and some of them were particularly welcome, such as those of Alexandre Guilmant and of his Society, as well as that of the Société Française d'Archéologie.

12. Episcopal Approvals

Among the episcopal approvals, particular note must be made of that from Cardinal Langénieux, Archbishop of Rheims, because its wording differed from the regular formulas:

Your studies of the plainchant are all the more useful in that, since they have an edition that has won the praise of your own Fathers,[19] you make the interpretation of the ancient phrases and melodies easier for us, retained as they were with all due care by the Rheims-Cambrai Commission.

Since we take advantage of every possible opportunity to encourage proper

19. A reference to the Rheims-Cambrai edition of 1851.

performance in our diocese of the chant placed into use by Cardinal Gousset, friend of the learned and pious abbot Dom Guéranger, we look upon everything that you are doing to help our priests and the faithful to achieve this goal as a service for which we are most grateful. (November 12, 1888)

Above all, one approval was particularly well received at Solesmes. This was a "practically apostolic" word, a letter from Cardinal Parocchi, Vicar of His Holiness, which read: "As for the *Mélodies Liturgiques*, I welcome them as a nearly prophetic sign of the complete restoration of sacred music in the churches" (October 15, 1888). The correspondent who passed this word along to Dom Mocquereau concluded,

The letter in which His Eminence, Cardinal Parocchi, makes quite a consoling prediction, in a few lines that you will certainly appreciate, . . . such approval, coming from so high up, is well worth a subscription. (Dom Bourigaud, October 21, 1888)[20]

This last approval was soon to be followed by another even more appreciable one, since it was made in the name of the Pope himself, approval from Cardinal Rampolla, Secretary of State, which was to appear at the head of the first volume of the *Paléographie Musicale*.

13. Volume I (1889)

Volume I of the *Paléographie Musicale* was first published in January 1889, the date that the first fascicles were delivered. In fact, even though the publication was a collection of volumes, and not a periodical, the notebooks were sent to subscribers as they were printed, in the form of fascicles similar to the issues of a periodical.

The letter dated April 23, 1889, from Cardinal Rampolla, Secretary of State, appeared at the top of the volume. This letter conveyed the congratulations, encouragement, and blessing of the Sovereign Pontiff. There followed an impressive list of subscribers: the name of the Minister of Public Education and of the Fine Arts, who had subscribed for 50 copies, was followed by the names of eight cardinals, the Apostolic Nuncio to Paris, nineteen bishops, three Princes or Princesses, eighteen State Academies or Libraries, and twenty-four other libraries, and final-

---

20. See E. Moneta-Caglio, in *Musica Sacra*, 1960, 4, p. 110, on Cardinal Lucido Maria Parocchi (1833–1903).

ly, many other subscribers. Then there was a dedication to Leo XIII. Finally came the masterful Preface or General Introduction by Dom Mocquereau, dated November 22, 1888, on the feast of St. Cecilia. The subheadings of the Preface were as follows:

I. Influence of new reproduction techniques on the progress of archeological studies.

II. The use of facsimiles in musical archaeology from the seventeenth century to our day (with a copious bibliography).

III. Musical treatises and noted manuscripts: their respective significance from the perspective of the archaeological restoration of the chant.

IV. The current state of mind with regard to questions concerning Gregorian music.

V. Musical philology.

VI. Musical paleography.

VII. Plan and implementation.

Here we will reproduce just a few passages of special interest from the Introduction because, beyond the immediate goal sought by Dom Mocquereau, as previously mentioned, these passages also show the more remote and broader purpose that he sought, and the hopes that he placed in this new collection.

In acknowledging his teacher Dom Pothier, who had already shed some light upon the texts of the ancient medieval authors of the Middle Ages in *Les Mélodies Grégoriennes*, precisely by using the monuments that transmit to us the chants themselves in traditional musical notation, Dom Mocquereau wrote:

For archaeologists, these monuments have the distinct advantage over musical treatises that they are the raw material of their research. In and of themselves, they contain everything we want to know about the version, modality, rhythm, and notation of the ecclesiastical melodies. They are not exposés on the principles of chant; rather, they contain substantially both the theory and the practice. They are not the ancient masters whose readings we would like to hear, but they are the written translation of what those masters taught and did, and thus, for those who know how to read and understand this writing, they are the most perfect expression of the liturgical songs. That is why they are important, and why they are ranked above the authors. (p. 23)

He makes a similar statement a little further on:

The musical texts form the most solid basis for our studies; let us add that a deeper understanding of these very same documents would remedy the incessant divisions that continue to occur among archaeologists who work on the sacred chant. (P. 27)

These are just glimpses, and we still have not mentioned the Mozarabic and Gallican psalmodies; yet one can already sense all the riches of this mine that science must exploit, and the usefulness of a collection of the kind we are undertaking. Once armed with the texts, scholars will be able to analyze at their leisure each musical work, each phrase, each neume, and will be able to trace its history. For each dialect, they will be able to classify the various intonations and successions of intervals that constitute the modes, study the combinations that the rhythm may assume, the cadences that are like the declensions and inflexions of the musical language. The prejudices, confusion, and doubts that still prevail against our liturgical chants will gradually fall by the wayside, in light of the facts and of history when these are better known and better appreciated. (P. 44)

The presentation of the manuscript itself included:

A few words on Manuscript 339 of St. Gall and on its notation (pp. 51–54, by Dom Mocquereau).

Codex 339 from the Library of St. Gall:

I. *The Library and the monastery of St. Gall* (pp. 57–70, by Dom Cabrol);
II. *Description of the Codex* . . . (pp. 71–95, by Dom Cagin and Dom Mocquereau);
III. *Origin and classification of the various neume scripts* (pp. 96–160, by Dom Mocquereau).

These were followed by the plates of the manuscript.

That the printing and presentation of the volume were extremely painstaking was to contribute enormously to the reputation of the Imprimerie Saint-Pierre. Dom Mocquereau wrote: "Comparison between this manuscript and our *Liber Gradualis* proves that we reprinted, nearly note-for-note, group-for-group, the true melodies of the Roman Church" (*Revue Grégorienne,* 1921, p. 10). This comment reveals the immediate goal that Dom Mocquereau was pursuing in response to those opposed to tradition. In fact, we will see that this goal was attained—though some were not convinced, or pretended not to be—because it was easy to make the comparison that Dom Mocquereau suggested; the neume script of St. Gall, all things considered, was the easiest to decipher, and the manuscript was in a perfect state of conservation.

14. Publications by Dom Pothier

For his part, in 1888 Dom Pothier published the *Variae Preces ad Bene-dictionem SS. Sacramenti praesertim cantandae* (152 pp.; there was a second edition in 1889), and particularly the *Processionale Monasticum* (382 pp., in cooperation with Dom Andoyer), a new edition of which came out in 1893). These books from the Imprimerie Saint-Pierre were welcomed enthusiastically not only in monasteries, but all over. They provided a repertory of varied and select chants, which brought many Gregorian pieces back to life from the oblivion into which they had fallen, particularly the beautiful Responsories of the Divine Office which were no longer sung, many other pieces taken from old antiphonaries, and exquisite sequences.

The Processional had been preceded by an *Officium ultimi Tridui Majoris Hebdomadae* (1886), an *Officium pro Defunctis* (1887), an *Officium et Missa in Festis praecipuis* (1888) and some extracts from the *Liber Gradualis*. Other choral books were underway, particularly the monastic *Antiphonal* and *Responsorial*. Dom Pothier was also composing various propers for dioceses or religious congregations.

In addition, he was continuing his Gregorian apostolate, which began around 1879. The bishops themselves were issuing urgent appeals for him to come teach the clergy, seminarians, and the faithful. In 1885, he went with his Abbot to Spain where a daughter house of Solesmes, the Abbey of Silos, had already been established. His biographer wrote,

Among other documents, the Abbey had the precious noted *Liber Ordinum* dating from the eleventh century. The text was to be published by Father Férotin, and Dom Pothier made a complete copy of it for us on one hundred fifty-two large pages. I cannot leaf through with you the daily account of this *iter hispanicum* that Dom Pothier's correspondence provides, at all times a vibrant and picturesque account with rapid descriptions: stays in Toledo, a circuit through Burgos, Valladolid, Salamanca, Seville, and Segovia where the two travelers [Dom Pothier and Dom Férotin] discovered two chests of documents from Silos; another trip through Seville, Grenada, Cordoba, Tortosa, Barcelona and finally Montserrat.[21]

---

21. Dom David, *Dom Joseph Pothier, Abbé de Saint-Wandrille et la restauration grégorienne,* St. Wandrille 1943, p. 28.

It also happened that Dom Mocquereau had occasion to sow the seeds of good Gregorian doctrine. For example, in Paris the Benedictine nuns of St.-Louis-du-Temple requested lessons from him whenever the opportunity arose. At Solesmes itself, in fact, Dom Mocquereau was called upon to accept the position of precentor, and thus of choirmaster, in 1889. The first fascicle of the *Paléographie Musicale* came out in January 1889 (the volume was to end with 1890). However, Dom Mocquereau did not go out much, and did so only with evident reluctance. Yet there was research that had to be done, if only to secure the loan of manuscripts, or to obtain photographs of them.

This was, in fact, the beginning of the paleography studio[22] that was brought about through his efforts, though at that time it contained only a few dozen copies of manuscripts made by Dom Jausions and Dom Pothier. In his library research, Dom Mocquereau was assisted by Dom Cabrol and Dom Cagin. In 1889, Dom Cagin made a trip through the north of France in May and June, while Dom Cabrol headed to the east in November. Dom Cagin was also assisting Dom Mocquereau at the monastery itself, as was another young monk. But outside Solesmes Dom Mocquereau had volunteer assistants, collaborators as far away as Spain, who required much personal attention from him since it was not always a matter of simple inquiries, as Dom Mocquereau's correspondence testifies. For example, in Paris the cloistered nuns were making magnificent copies for him (among others, we have a splendid copy of the *Antiphonal* of Hartker, which is a true and perfect copy, as well as a copy of an *Antiphonal* from Saint-Maur-des-Fossés (B. N. 12044), also extremely well reproduced, with text and dropped capitals). Dom Mégret and Dom Delpech also made several copies of manuscripts.

15. Dom Mocquereau in Rome (1890)

The publication of volume I of the *Paléographie Musicale* had demonstrated that the Solesmes *Liber Gradualis* gave the authentic chant of the Church of Rome. Nevertheless, this proof did not convince the adversaries. To answer the objection that a single manuscript

22. Dom Pierre Combe, *Bibliographie de dom André Mocquereau*, in *Études Grégoriennes*, II, pp. 189ff.

proved nothing, Dom Mocquereau had the wonderful idea of publishing a single piece of music (the Gradual *Justus ut palma*, the formula of which appears several times in the Gregorian repertory), according to a very large number of manuscripts (volumes two and three of the *Paléographie Musicale* reproduced this piece according to 219 Graduals of various origins, from the ninth to seventeenth centuries). In fact, Dom Mocquereau had already foreseen this objection, and as early as 1887 he was already looking for the piece he had selected to illustrate his proof. In September 1887, Dom Andoyer was looking for it for him at the Bibliothèque Nationale, at the same time that he was also on the lookout for treatises by medieval scholars of music. Others in addition to Dom Andoyer had been called upon for contribution, as Dom Mocquereau's correspondence for 1888 shows. However, such an undertaking required a vast canvassing of libraries. That is why the first stage in this process required that Dom Mocquereau travel to Italy in 1890, where he stayed with Dom Cabrol from January 18 until May 24. Moreover, Dom Mocquereau wanted to reassure himself that Solesmes could print a *Liber Vesperalis*, to follow up on the *Liber Gradualis*, without risk.

It was quite understandable that the first stop was Turin (January 18), where Dom Mocquereau stayed with the Salesian Fathers. The tomb of Don Bosco, whom Dom Mocquereau had met in Paris in 1883 during his triumphant tour of France, drew Dom Mocquereau to Turin. But he also knew that at the Salesian Seminary in Turin, they sang the chant according to the Solesmes *Gradual*. Don Bosco had hoped that the Gregorian reform would spread throughout Italy from Turin, so the study of plainchant was emphasized there, and was included amongst the examination subjects.

On January 24, accompanied by Don Musso, a Salesian kindly placed at his disposition, Dom Mocquereau left Turin after visiting the City Library, the archives of the Cathedral of Ivrea and the archives at the Cathedral of Aosta,[23] where he was received especially warmly by the bishop. Photographs were taken of the *Justus ut palma*, but Dom Mocquereau also took advantage of the occasion to continue work on the catalogue of Gregorian chant manuscripts begun in 1884. He noted that

---

23. Cf. Dom J. Marsille, *La restauration du chant grégorien*, in *Échos de Santa-Chiara*, Nov.–Dec. 1904, p. 113.

the Ivrea archives bore witness to the history of the notation in that diocese, and the Turin archives did the same for the Bobbio notation. At the same time, he took the opportunity to point out the beautiful organization of the traditional chant, the regularity of its formulas and the recitative nature of its style. One detail should be underscored: before leaving Turin, a Salesian gave Dom Mocquereau the address of Father Angelo de Santi, whom Dom Mocquereau wanted to meet.

Dom Mocquereau then went on to Rome directly, after a brief stopover in Genoa. He met up with Dom Cabrol once again in Rome. The two of them were to remain there for several months (until late April), spending their time visiting libraries. It must be noted right away, to avoid the need to address this point later on, that after his stay in Rome, Dom Mocquereau's research brought him and Dom Cabrol to Naples, La Cava, Salerno, Assisi, Capua, Loretto, Perugia, Florence, Cortona, Arezzo, Fiesole, Lucca, Pistoia, Bologna, Modena, Nonantola, Venice, Padua, Verona, Monza, and Milan. With his companion, Dom Mocquereau visited Monte Cassino and Subiaco during their stay in Rome. Finally, both returned through Switzerland, which Dom Mocquereau had visited previously in 1888, to take some more photographs of the *Justus ut palma*.

16. Dom Mocquereau and Father de Santi

The very day after he arrived (January 26), Dom Mocquereau went to visit Father de Santi.[24] Immediately he understood the significance of this meeting, knowing that this Jesuit priest from *Civiltà Cattolica* was in the thick of things. Moreover, Dom Mocquereau was intent on discussing Father de Santi's articles with him, in which Father de Santi always spoke of Solesmes with considerable deference. In a brief report, for example, Father de Santi praised Dom Ambrose Kienle for having attempted to apply Dom Pothier's method "to the only authentic and official books of the Church of Rome," i.e. the Ratisbon edition (*Civiltà Cattolica*, May 1888). Most importantly, at the Soave Congress (September 14, 1889), Father de Santi had very recently spoken in favor of the re-

---

24. Born in Trieste on July 12, 1847; professor of music at the Seminary in Zara in 1880. Brilliantly successful at the *Schola Puerorum* in Padua, musical contributor to the Trent *La Voce Cattolica* (E. Moneta-Caglio, *Musica Sacra*, 1960, 4. p. 103).

form movement that was slowly taking shape, after having restated his submission to the Roman decrees as far as practical application was concerned, of course, in terms of the choice of edition. The consequences of this Congress will be seen below.

In his first conversation with Father de Santi, Dom Mocquereau got right down to the heart of the matter immediately, namely the adoption of the ancient traditional melodies. Father de Santi explained to Dom Mocquereau how he had been called to Rome by Leo XIII in 1887 to discuss religious music in *Civiltà Cattolica*. The Pope, it seems, was well aware of the musical movement in France and Germany, and did not want Italy to fall behind. He even followed what was being said very attentively, as he had just reviewed an article by Father de Santi prior to its being printed. Father de Santi admitted that he had never been concerned with such questions before receiving this particular commission, and now it was his duty to defend the official edition. Needless to say, this state of affairs was to put Father de Santi in an awkward position on occasion, but he had managed to reach the following solution, which left his conscience quite clear: Pustet was for practical use; Dom Pothier was archeology. Father de Santi willingly acknowledged that, although it was everyone's duty to submit to the decrees of the Holy See in terms of practice, Solesmes had every right to pursue its research and to publish the results of that research in all freedom.

The discussion was closely conducted. Dom Mocquereau managed to get Father de Santi to admit that Rome could review the Gregorian issue from the historical perspective, that originally the Holy See did not want an abridged edition, but a *"genuinus cantus gregorianus"* (decree of January 20, 1871), for it was only later that Roman chant was mentioned, when they realized that the Ratisbon edition did not contain the traditional chant. Once Father de Santi relaxed, he began to speak in confidence, and said that the members of the Commission responsible for preparing the edition did not know anything about the issue, and that the decree to which Dom Mocquereau had just alluded had in fact simply been suppressed in the Bullarium, and that he himself acknowledged the contradictions in the Pustet edition (he gave some examples, and also admitted that he had had to give up on having one particular piece sung), and that at Rome, the official edition was hardly ever used any more, but was accepted musically. Then he took the offensive himself, and complained of certain articles that had appeared in France recently, merely poisoning the issue and assuring the success of the Ratisbon edition. It was easy for Dom Mocquereau to prove that Solesmes was uninvolved in any such polemic.

Finally, they took leave of each other, promising to meet again. In summing up this initial meeting, Dom Mocquereau wrote in his Notes:

From our long conversation, it was clear to us [Dom Cabrol and himself] that we were not dealing with an impassioned individual, an implacable opponent; he was searching for the truth. He acknowledged the order that he had received from Leo XIII, and wanted to obey it; all the while recognizing, in his straightforwardness, the superior value of our "method." He did not yet fully appreciate the superiority of the Solesmes edition. For the moment, he wanted to study, in order better to serve the cause of art and the Church.—In sum, he was the Holy Father's man; through him, we might possibly reach His Holiness and, in the long run, shed light on the real status of things for him. (*Revue Grégorienne*, 1921, p. 12)

Dom Mocquereau saw Father de Santi again on February 3, but the only subject they discussed was the Congress that was to be held at Rome for the thirteenth centennial of the Exaltation of St. Gregory the Great. They arranged to meet the following morning, when, in the absence of indiscreet witnesses, the two religious could continue their free conversation, which had started a few days earlier. That same evening, Dom Mocquereau, who was accompanied by Dom Cabrol, wrote to Dom Pothier about the encounter:

This evening I saw Father de Santi, and we understand each other very well. . . . If I were to publish the interview that Dom Cabrol and I had with him, he would be *sunk* in Rome.

When we arrived, he went to fetch Father Grisar, and it was only then that the conversation began. I kept strictly to the line of reasoning you laid out for me in your letter. He, Pustet in hand, and I, with my Pothier edition, sang one after the other an Introit, a Gradual, and an Alleluia; and I did not fail to point out on every line the outrageous rhythmic and melodic blunders in his Pustet.

He admitted everything with remarkable candor; in the end, he was so well educated that he himself was finding the errors. He had no idea about our manner of performance, and believed, in keeping with a ridiculous reputation that people ascribe to us, that our chant was *vivace*, one endless *allegro*.—Moreover, he had no idea about Gregorian rhythm, the construction of a Gregorian phrase, nor any concept of the beauty of this chant.

Then we spoke of neumes. . . . How can we read this illegible scrawl? I took the *Paléographie* and sang a piece for him, and he asked, "How can you read a third, a fourth?" "Read the answer yourself," I said, "it's on page so-and-so in the *Paléographie*." The comparison with the word "timbre" shed light on the subject for him, and even more so for Father Grisar, who was delighted.

At another point, I had the opportunity to see how much prejudice there was against us. I showed him a photograph of the *Justus XII* or *XIV* on lines. . . . He looked at it carefully, then started singing the *Justus*, and said, "But then Dom Pothier didn't just make up his own notation, as they say he did, because here it is, in a 13th-century manuscript. . . ." So that's where he is for the time being, but this won't last long because he is a hard worker. He is frank, loyal, and wants to discover the truth; but what a tight spot he finds himself in when he finds it! Yet he is a good Jesuit, and he will certainly find a way to defend authority without praising the authentic edition, because he recognizes its errors. He may even find a way to praise our own edition. He is counting on his cleverness to avoid all the difficulties surrounding him, in order to obey the Holy Father to the letter, yet without harming the truth.

However, here is another thing, which you may already know from the papers, concerning the centennial of St. Gregory: they want to hold a Roman Congress of liturgical arts and sciences. I am sending you the general program drawn up by Father de Santi. There will be a section on music, and it is he, Father de Santi, who will chair it. The general chairmanship of the Congress is reserved for Cardinal Parocchi. The dates have not yet been settled. Father de Santi is preparing an issue on the program for the *Musica Sacra* of Milan [March 1890], which will focus solely on St. Gregory. . . .

We are making the rounds of all the libraries, one after the other, starting with the smallest ones. We have not yet been to the Vatican; that will be the crowning moment. The *Angelica* and the *Vallicelliana* are still occupying our time. There is a lot in this depository. . . . (February 4, 1890)

A few days later, Dom Mocquereau met Father de Santi again at Holy Apostles, on the occasion of the funeral services for Cardinal Pecci. Dom Mocquereau noted:

The Sistine Chapel choir sang; Father de Santi sat next to me, as did the son of General Kanzler, a plainchant enthusiast. . . . The voices are magnificent and the music is performed with great perfection, but the plainchant is hammered out, with a heavy beat, and shouted; one would not believe that these are the same artists. . . . At the end of the ceremony, Father de Santi said to me: "See of what stuff the unity of the chant is made; in my hands, I have the Pustet edition, from which the Sistine Chapel choir did not sing, and I am quite sure that they didn't sing from your edition either."

Dom Mocquereau noted these avowals, and saw with pleasure the evolution that was soon to become so pronounced in Father de Santi.

17. At the French Seminary

An event that was small enough in and of itself soon occurred, but under circumstances that were to prove decisive. The evening of February 11, at the invitation of the superior of the French Seminary, Dom Mocquereau gave a lecture on Gregorian chant to all the students at Santa Chiara. In his journal, he wrote: "I tried to prove to them that Gregorian chant is a recitative. I had a reading, some psalmody, and an ornate chant performed." The superior did not stop at that, however. A few days later, on February 23, he asked Dom Mocquereau if he would kindly have the Mass of the Second Sunday of Lent sung at the Seminary. In truth, it was the two students responsible for chant at the Seminary who, by their insistence, made up the Superior's mind to take this step, a step that he did not take without a certain amount of hesitation, fearing that he might upset the bishops of France in so doing.

Dom Mocquereau accepted the invitation, but, since he wanted the Gregorian cause to benefit from the experience, he wanted everything to turn out for the best, and he made his acceptance subject to certain conditions: (1) There would be a schola of only 12 to 15 students to sing; (2) they would sing from the Solesmes *Gradual;* (3) finally, there would be a one-half hour lesson every day. Dom Mocquereau wrote: "I have one week in which to work. I do not know if I will succeed, because they have serious errors to overcome and must learn a rhythm with which they are unfamiliar." Without regard to his own discomfort and this excess of work, Dom Mocquereau got right down to work, encouraged by the good will of the seminarians.

On March 2, the second Sunday of Lent, the small schola of Santa Chiara acquitted itself quite honorably. The choir sang its responses to the schola according to the Rheims-Cambrai edition. "The length, the confusion and the disjunction of the voices in the choir showed off the disciplined performance of the schola to its advantage. . . . In all, our fifteen students sang well, and it was a success for our cause."

Clearly, the matter could not be left as it stood, and Dom Mocquereau was invited to rehearse the Mass of the following Sunday, Laetare Sunday. On March 10, he noted, "The lessons begin tonight, and if the students sing well, we will invite Father de Santi, etc. In God's hands!"

Father de Santi had been shaken by his conversations with Dom

Mocquereau, and now was asking him "how to speak of the *Paléographie* in the *Civiltà*, he, the official representative of the Pustet edition." It was on this occasion that Dom Mocquereau invited him to come to Santa Chiara on Laetare Sunday. He also invited the choirmaster of the Collegio Germanico, who was becoming interested in what was going on at the French Seminary. For their part, the seminarians had turned into apostles.

They invited their confreres, and on Laetare Sunday, students from the various Colleges of Rome were all gathered at the chapel of the French Seminary. There were students there of every stripe, some even wearing red habits, the *Germanics* with their choir director, sworn supporters of the neo-Medicean edition.[25]

Father de Santi was there, along with priests invited by the students at Santa Chiara as well. Dom Mocquereau noted: "I was a bit frightened by this assembly; I was calling upon St. Gregory and St. Cecilia most vigorously." With the exception of the *Kyriale*, everything was sung correctly, without accompaniment. After the Mass, Father de Santi went to Dom Mocquereau's room, accompanied by Baron Kanzler. Father de Santi said: "It is clear that this chant will be the chant of the Roman Church some day."

Baron Kanzler subscribed to the *Paléographie Musicale* on the spot, and the superior of Santa Chiara decided to keep the schola on an ongoing basis.

From then on, every Sunday brought new listeners to Santa Chiara; everyone was struck, delighted with the beauty of the Gregorian melodies.—Soon, the French schola became well known at Rome. It was often invited to sing at ceremonies. It also soon had imitators and rivals. (*Revue Grégorienne* 1921, p. 12)

The Gregorian chant restoration movement out of France found a natural home at the French Seminary. Yet it was above all the ultimate conversion to traditional Gregorian chant of Father de Santi that marked Laetare Sunday, 1890.

---

25. Dom Mocquereau wrote: "I knew that the Belgian seminarians were quite pleased; as for the *Germanics*, they found this chant so beautiful that they could not believe that it is the chant of St. Gregory. They no longer recognize it. Naively, they had brought along their Pustet editions to follow along (to Madame Bruyère, May 17, 1890).

18. Pustet's Visit

Clearly, Dom Mocquereau's success at the French Seminary could not go unnoticed. Pustet himself was, no doubt, the first to be disturbed by it. He requested an interview with Dom Mocquereau, through the good offices of Father de Santi. No sooner was the visit over than Dom Mocquereau sent an account of it to his Abbot.

Of course the conversation focused not on the performance at Santa Chiara, but rather on the respective rights of the two competing editions. Pustet did acknowledge rather easily that his edition was merely the approved and privileged one, but it did not exclude other editions that maintained their place. He agreed, as well, that his edition was not perfect, and that he would like to have revised it, but that such as it was, he said, it was capable of being well sung (that, one will recall, was Father de Santi's position, as well), a point that Dom Mocquereau disputed. As for the attacks in the French press, it was easy for Dom Mocquereau to separate the cause of Solesmes from that of the individuals given to excess (according to a letter from Dom Cabrol to Dom Couturier dated April 20).

The position taken by the main proponent of the Pustet edition in Rome itself was becoming quite interesting. Nevertheless, one might wonder under what conditions the Congress in honor of St. Gregory, planned for 1891, would take place. Plenty of talk was going around on this subject, as reflected in Dom Mocquereau's notes. At a recent meeting with him, on March 28, Father de Santi had told him that no one wanted to hear talk of a Congress as such in Rome itself, but rather at Monte Cassino, for example, because they were afraid of a repeat of the Arezzo Congress, which had dared to pass resolutions in support of a return to traditional Gregorian chant. Now, Father de Santi was informing Dom Mocquereau that a Congress in Rome would be accepted, provided that music was not discussed at it. Dom Mocquereau himself deemed it useless to raise such a problem, while minds were as yet unready to accept the changes that were necessary. It would appear that Father de Santi was of like mind.

19. Discovery of the "Old Roman" Chant

The purpose of Dom Mocquereau's trip to Italy was to visit libraries, where he spent most of his working time, obtaining as much information as possible, assisted by Dom Cabrol, while still finding time to satisfy his pious inclination in the venerable churches of the Rome, and to write a travel journal, from which we have drawn in this book.

We must point out the discovery of Graduals containing the special chant, since then called "old Roman", that Dom Mocquereau made in the Archives of St. Peter's. As soon as he made this unusual discovery, Dom Mocquereau wrote a letter about it to his Abbot:

I must tell you of a discovery we made at the Vatican, and that continues to astonish us. Perhaps Dom Pothier will be able to explain what I am going to say? It is a 12th-century *Gradual,* certainly of the Roman liturgy, with the exception of some slight peculiarities, but in which *the chant is not the one used in all manuscripts in all countries.* This is a singular exception that intrigues me. For a time, I had thought that the *Ambrosian* chant had replaced the *Gregorian* chant; but this is not the case, because in this new chant the universal Gregorian chant is easy to recognize, but with constant variations that give it a very special character. This is surely an Italian manuscript, as proven by the notation. One note that I found, I no longer know where, advances the unsubstantiated notion that it belonged to St. John Lateran. We have yet to see the Archives at that Basilica; are surprises of this kind awaiting us there, perhaps? I have no idea. But I would be most interested to know what the Reverend Father Dom Joseph Pothier[26] thinks about all this. I have not yet studied this curious manuscript in detail, because I had hoped to manage to get it to Solesmes."

On the 19th, Dom Mocquereau wrote in his journal:

How astonished I am to come upon a second *Gradual* with the Roman liturgical text and a different version of the Gregorian chant, and this at St. Peter's itself, in Rome! One of these manuscripts absolutely must be copied so that we can study this chant at our leisure at Solesmes . . . These two manuscripts are from the same school, have the same writing and the same Roman liturgy with a few variations, the same chant. . . . We do not have an Ambrosian *Gradual* at

26. On April 8, Pothier answered: ". . . bring us as many details as possible. What do the variations in the chant or the text consist of? . . . we must have a good analysis of it; it is on that analysis that we will base the research needed to understand the nature of the variations, their origins and their cause . . . the more numerous and the more accurate the details, the narrower the scope of guesswork will be. . . . Traditions thrived in prior times; at St. Peter's they still use not only ancient hymns, but even a special Psalter that dates from far back."

hand; in Milan, we will be able to compare the relationships between these two chants easily.

Dom Mocquereau published the results of his study of the special chant in the *Graduals* of the Vatican (Manuscript 5319) and of the Archives at St. Peter's (Manuscript F. 22 and B. 79), in volume II of the *Paléographie Musicale*, p. 4, note 1:

Most of the chants used in these codices are not related to tradition either by the economy of the distribution of their neumes, or by the series of musical intervals. These are no longer variations or alterations being offered to us: this is truly a distinct chant, as far removed from Ambrosian as from Gregorian. Yet the melodic basis is generally borrowed from Gregorian song: one recognizes the original design behind the flourishes, embroidery or, as they also say, the embellishments that disfigure it. These melodies seem to date from a relatively recent period, when the rules of Gregorian composition were beginning to fall into disuse. That is what the often incorrect or awkward manner in which the words are applied to the music reveals, not to mention the other indications that would take too long to discuss here.

The reader can decide how prudent was Dom Mocquereau's judgment. This simple note sufficed, moreover, to explain the reason why he viewed the melodies found in those Roman manuscripts as outside the general stream of melodies studied earlier. That was also his view of the Ambrosian melodies.

20. Travel within Italy

Dom Mocquereau left Rome in late April, to continue his travels toward Loretto, Perugia, and so forth, accompanied all the while by Dom Cabrol. His return brought a note of triumph. Of course, he was feted at the French Seminary upon his departure, and saw that the students at the Collegio Germanico themselves were beginning to be swayed. He was pleased to announce: "Next Sunday, the students at the Germanicum are going to sing the two Alleluias of St. Joseph in our *Gradual*. It is scarcely to be believed."

At Lucca, after his visit to the Chapter Library with its rich holdings in liturgical antiquities, the academy of music, to honor the Benedictines, assembled not only the seminarians, but the canons of the Cathedral and some notable personalities from the town. In Bologna, the monks from Solesmes received an enthusiastic welcome from Don Gamberini, author of a chant method in the manner of Dom Pothier. In Venice, things were even better. Father Tebaldini, a professor at the Schola Cantorum founded by Cardinal Agostini, invited Dom Mocquereau to hear his Schola. "The Cardinal came and presided at the gathering. Speech by the Cardinal on sacred music. Tebaldini introduces the Benedictines and their scholarly work in the *Paléographie*."

In Milan, after the visit to the libraries, it was Father Magistretti who brought together

the chief cantor of the Cathedral, a few canons and several students from the Seminary at the Archbishop's residence. From 8:00 to 10:00 we sang Gregorian chant and Ambrosian Chant, and I think that here, too, we have sown good seed.

All, or nearly all, the names listed above are quite familiar in the Gregorian chant world, and the welcome extended to Dom Mocquereau bears witness to the interest expressed even that early on in the restoration of Gregorian chant then underway. In fact, several of these Gregorian chant scholars from Italy stayed in contact with Solesmes.

His return from Italy brought him to Switzerland: Einsiedeln, Zurich and St. Gall, where Dom Mocquereau had some photographs yet to take in the libraries (by mail, he asked for his Notes taken in 1888). Dom Mocquereau and Dom Cabrol returned to Solesmes about May 24. Dom Mocquereau was anxiously awaited. On April 8, Couturier wrote to him: "We stand in great need of the return of our choir director, so that he can take over the chant lessons. Whether they like it or not, Solesmes must remain the center of the movement." Dom Mocquereau returned with a good harvest of notes and photographs, not just of the *Justus ut palma*, but also of anything that might be of interest for his Gregorian chant research and study, particularly concerning notation.

21. The Influence of the French Seminary

The trip to Italy had other fortunate results, as well. The work done at the French Seminary was considerable. From Milan, on his return trip, Dom Mocquereau had received encouraging news. On May 17, he sent the following report to his Abbot:

The news from Rome is quite interesting, as I learned in a letter from M. Ginisty. The French Seminary is being called upon to do good things for our cause.
I received proof of this most recently at Verona. A canon from there, Father
Bonuzzi, had occasion to go to Rome for a few days. Father de Santi sent him
to the French Seminary, where he heard the Mass of St. Monica. This good
canon told us that he thought he was in heaven, when he heard the plainchant,
the Gregorian chant, performed by these young French seminarians. He could-
n't stop talking about it. He said, "I have finally found what I have been looking
for for forty years." He also told us, "What amazed me even more was to hear
Father de Santi, our leader, praising and advocating Dom Joseph Pothier's *Gradual* and his method of performance. It is a complete turnaround in our favor,
and for you, the Benedictines, this conquest is of capital importance." I was
glad to hear Father Bonuzzi thus confirm everything that Father de Santi had
told us, i.e. Dom Cabrol and me. If we had stayed longer in Milan, it would
have been easy to bring about a similar revolution. We saw everyone at the *Musica Sacra*.

Once back at Solesmes, Dom Mocquereau stayed in close contact
with Father Ginisty. Every Sunday brought more and more visitors to
Santa Chiara. Father Ginisty told Dom Mocquereau of his successes,
and also of his difficulties and fears. On May 8, he wrote:

The seminarians at the Germanicum performed true plainchant from our
Gradual on two occasions. Among them, some, particularly the musicians,
were filled with wonder; the others accused this style of chant of excessive sen-
timentalism. The authorities (of the College) became involved, and forbade
chanting from Dom Pothier's *Gradual* from then on.

The opposition was to take advantage of such slight incidents to forbid
everywhere the use of the *Liber Gradualis*.

22. The Gregorian Conversion of Father de Santi

Above all, Father de Santi's complete conversion to traditional Gregorian chant was a great satisfaction for Dom Mocquereau. As early as
August 15, in one of the first letters in a long correspondence between
Rome and Solesmes, Father de Santi congratulated Dom Mocquereau
on the *Paléographie Musicale*,[27] persuaded as he was that it was thanks to

27. "My heartfelt congratulations on the extraordinary and fascinating work which is the
Paléographie. I am convinced that all doubts will be cleared up, and that whatever becomes of the

it that doubts concerning the adoption of the traditional melodies would be dispelled. What he feared was the intemperate language used in certain periodicals. One newspaper, *Le Matin*, had recently antagonized the Holy Father by claiming that, in this whole question of the chant, the Holy See had allowed itself to be taken in by speculators. On August 21, Father de Santi pointed out to Dom Pothier that he understood the attitude of the Holy See in this regard. The Holy See could do nothing other than stay with the neo-Medicean edition when a new edition of liturgical books had to be made, specifically because of the lack of clarity on the questions raised at that time on the legitimate form of the traditional melodies. Now, however, he added that many questions had been resolved,

particularly since 1883 *(Liber Gradualis)* and following the publication of the *Paléographie Musicale*, to the point that one can see that the Benedictine edition truly corresponds to the demands of the art and that it reproduces faithfully the original and legitimate form of the Gregorian chant. Consequently, this edition could be considered as liturgical, and can be recommended.[28]

However, Father de Santi insisted on silence regarding such confidential statements, because his duty was to support the official editions. Yet he said that he knew that the Pope's private thinking on this matter was "less strict than the wording of the decrees." On August 18, 1890, Father de Santi went to His Holiness to present the acts of the Soave Congress (1889), and the action plan of the Standing Committee on Sacred Music, of which he was president.

---

question of practice (for now), attacks on the principles themselves will cease henceforth." ("Mi congratulo ex toto corde dello stupendo e sempre più interessante lavoro che è la *Paléographie*. Sono persuaso che i dubii si dissiperanno, e che *quidquid sit* della questione practica (per ora), si lascerà oramai d'attaccare i principii") (August 15, 1890).—This is one of many expressions of esteem that greeted the appearance of the *Paléographie Musicale*.

28. Although he complained about certain advertisers, Father de Santi did not question the Benedictines of Solesmes in any way. In an article published on August 21 in the *Osservatore Romano*, which was a response to the newspaper mentioned above, he clearly stated: "In France, there are many distinguished men who love their traditional chant, or who are involved in archaeological studies on the original form of the Gregorian melodies. The first take advantage of the freedom granted to them by the Holy See, the others are encouraged in their studies by the words of the Holy Father himself [Brief of March 3, 1884], which blesses and sustains everything that is true art and true science. We are convinced that neither the first group nor the second is involved in the bad intentions, the impertinence and the sectarian spirit of *Le Matin* and its correspondents" (August 21, 1890). The Brief of March 3, 1884 was addressed to Pothier after the publication of the *Liber Gradualis* (see Appendix II).

The address of the Soave Congress, signed by Father de Santi, on behalf of the Managing Committee of that Congress, and by Mr. Gallignani, on behalf of the Committee on Sacred Music in Italy, protested the submission of those attending the Congress to the decrees of the Congregation [of Sacred Rites], and thanked the Holy Father for the encouragement he had given to the movement to reform Church music, which is building steam slowly, but with a certain degree of success, in Italy.

The Pope demonstrated that he was very much up to speed on everything, and had said, particularly: "You are aware that you are defending the truth, and fighting for what is right and just. Carry on ardently: truth always finds a way, and eventually, it triumphs."[29]

At the end of the year, Father de Santi himself told Dom Cabrol, who was then in Rome, what he knew personally of the private thinking of the Holy Father: yes, the Pope wanted freedom for all the editions. He was still advancing his favorable consideration by supporting his actions in *Civiltà Cattolica*, actions already attacked by the adversaries of the traditional chant, who were quite well aware of his change of view in this field (Dom Cabrol to Dom Mocquereau).

Once this is clear, one understands why Father de Santi, knowing the Pope's thought, did not hesitate to promote the Benedictine editions, at least indirectly. We have already seen that he sent Verona's Father Bonuzzi to the French Seminary. Here is further testimony, provided by Father Ginisty:

Father de Santi gave the young Apollinarists "a good lesson" in the parlor; he gave them the principles for proper performance, and encouraged them to go to the French Seminary as often as possible to hear and to understand the rhythm of our melodies, so that they could incorporate it into their singing from the Pustet edition. He reminded them of the example of the choirmaster from the Germanicum, who compares his text to Dom Pothier's text each time, re-inserts some *pressus* here, some *strophicus* there, which he has his singers perform as best they can. But that is the work of a Roman. One day, not all that far off, tired of this partially futile labor, they will abandon their Pustet editions and will adopt your edition plain and simple: it will be easier for them that way. The other day, Father de Santi told me, "When will I see this edition at the Apollinare? When will we hear these melodies at this Roman Seminary? That hour has not yet come." (To Dom Mocquereau, December 9, 1890)

---

29. Msgr. de T'Serclaes: *Le Pape Léon XIII, sa vie, son action religieuse, politique et sociale*, vol. 3,

23. Volume II—Trip to Belgium and Holland (1891)

The first shipment of Volume II of the *Paléographie Musicale* appeared in January 1891.[30] Along with the presentation of the first plates of the *Justus ut palma*, this volume was to include a long study by Dom Mocquereau on the accent-neumes. But a second volume of plates (volume III) was needed to show even more fully that Dom Pothier's *Liber Gradualis* was identical to the manuscript tradition. Thus Dom Mocquereau went off once again, on the hunt for manuscripts. This time, he and Dom Cagin traveled to Belgium and Holland, from March 7 to the end of April. Their itinerary took them to Namur, Maredsous, Liège, Maastricht, Averbode, Tongerloo, Brussels, Louvain, Mechlin, Ghent, Bruges, and Ypres. At that point, Dom Mocquereau returned to France, having been called back by Dom Delatte, successor to Dom Couturier as Abbot of Solesmes, who sent Dom Mocquereau to Rome with Dom Pothier, for the Congress on the Centennial of the Exaltation of St. Gregory the Great. Father Abbot had been invited by Cardinal Parocchi (on February 10), who requested that he come in person, or that he send personal delegates to these Gregorian celebrations. Clearly Father de Santi had a hand in these invitations (see the letter from Father de Santi on February 18, 1891).

Dom Cagin visited the libraries in Holland by himself, in The Hague, Leiden, Katwijk, Warmond, Haarlem, Amsterdam, Utrecht, Groningen, Dordrecht, and Delft.

From the very beginning, Dom Cagin kept the travel journal; Dom Mocquereau took up his pen only once, from Brussels (on March 16), to tell his Abbot some important news:

I was delighted to handle all these manuscripts, and I have been able to see all the types of notation used in Belgium and Luxembourg. One of the goals of this trip has been achieved. The study of complete manuscripts has confirmed my theory.

---

p. 446, Desclée 1906.—Father de Santi's address to the Holy Father is printed in the Ghent *Musica Sacra*, September 25, 1890, pp. 13ff., and in the Toulouse *Musica Sacra*, October 1890, p. 19.

    30. Volume II contained: *Le Répons-Graduel "Justus ut palma" reproduit en fac-similé d'après plus de deux cents antiphonaires manuscrits d'origines diverses, du IXe au XVIIe siècle. Préface*, pp. 1–26 (Dom Mocquereau), *Étude sur les neumes-accents* (ordinary neumes, liquescent or semi-vocal accent-neumes), pp. 27–88 (Dom Mocquereau), and the first 107 plates of the *Justus ut palma*.

It is possible that Dom Mocquereau was alluding to his rhythmic system, but he could equally have been alluding to the results he had achieved regarding the rules of composition of Gregorian melodies, which he was going to publish in Volume III of the *Paléographie Musicale*, then in preparation.

They brought back quite a few photographs of the *Justus ut palma* from Belgium and Holland, and even a good selection of manuscript fragments graciously made available to them by generous librarians.

24. Congress of St. Gregory the Great (1891)

Before following Dom Pothier and Dom Mocquereau to Rome, we must review how this Congress in honor of St. Gregory the Great came about. Dom Mocquereau writes:

On January 29 (1891), at the inaugural meeting[31] at the French Seminary, in the presence of the Prefect of the Congregation of Sacred Rites and Cardinal Parocchi, Vicar of the Pope, Reverend Father Grisar, from the *Civiltà*:

a. openly praised the book of *Mélodies Grégoriennes* by Dom Joseph Pothier;

b. made solemn mention of the archaeological and musical studies by the Benedictines at Solesmes, and of their *Paléographie Musicale*, and

c. finally, was not afraid to congratulate the young students at the Seminary. He said: "In Rome, everyone knows the artistic perfection and deep piety with which they perform the ancient Gregorian melodies at their church of Santa Chiara."

Such a beginning for the celebration was a good indication that it would be truly worthy of our great St. Gregory.

In fact, on the following March 5, there was another meeting. This time, it

---

31. *Revue Grégorienne* 1921, p. 13.—On the inauguration day, Father Ginisty gave Dom Mocquereau a detailed account of this session: "(Father Grisar) mentioned the work of the Benedictines at Solesmes, with effusive praise, particularly the *Paléographie Musicale,* which is the most striking archaeological *confirmatur* of Pothier's *Mélodies Grégoriennes.*" "What is this Gregorian chant? Where is it heard? You don't have to leave Rome, or even the French Seminary. . . . All Rome knows *(e noto a Roma)* the perfection and piety with which the students at this Seminary perform the ancient melodies every "Sunday" in their church."—"This compliment, which is quite flattering to us, but also quite useful for the cause of St. Gregory, caused a *silence* and a thrill that nearly triggered a burst of applause . . . as well as a few comments made between the two cardinals" (Cardinal Parocchi, and the Cardinal Prefect of Sacred Rites who were presiding). Letter of January 29 to Dom Mocquereau.—As for the speech by Father de Santi, dated March 5, the text is printed in the Ghent *Musica Sacra*, March 25, 1891, pp. 57ff.

was the students at the Vatican Seminary who offered the Sovereign Pontiff a *test of sacred music,* under the direction of the Reverend Father de Santi.—The first part of the program was devoted to Gregorian chant. Father de Santi outlined its history in broad strokes, and drew parallels that were striking in their truth between St. Gregory the Great and Leo XIII, the first having presided over the *organization* of the melodies, the second over their *renaissance.* Essentially, he said that *revertimini ad fontes S. Gregorii* is the watchword given by the Pontiff. Under his reign, archaeologists have sifted through antiquity, and uncovered and deciphered the manuscripts. Even better, they have restored life to and rediscovered the rhythm of the ancient melodies. In his enthusiasm, Father de Santi said: "The Gregorian notes are like the fields of sparse and dried bones that Ezekiel saw . . . *Fili hominis, putasne vivent ossa ista?* And a new Ezekiel appeared, and answered: *Ecce ego intromittam in vos spiritum et vivetis . . .* This new Ezekiel is Dom Joseph Pothier, of the Abbey of Solesmes." Father de Santi elaborated his theme with captivating eloquence. . . .

Then Father de Santi had his schola, now an emulator of the one at the French Seminary, perform two Gregorian melodies the texts of which were contained in the archives of St. Peter's, entirely in conformity with the Solesmes *Gradual.* Other similar performances followed in Rome during the month of March. Cardinal Parocchi, hearing only what confirmed the judgment of his piety, officially invited the French Seminary to crown these celebrations of the centennial of St. Gregory with their chants at the Coelius on April 11 and 12.

The steps taken the previous year, forbidding all discussion of sacred music during this Congress, had thus been revoked. Father de Santi wrote to Dom Mocquereau on February 18 about this whole business, but without mentioning that it was he, Father de Santi, who had intervened with the Pope the previous August 18. Shortly thereafter, the Cardinal Vicar had set up a Commission, on which Father de Santi was called to sit. At one of its meetings, the question of the chant was discussed, as was the possibility of intervening on behalf of the Benedictines at Solesmes (Father de Santi, February 18, 1891).

At an audience granted to him, the Pope congratulated Father de Santi on his speech, delivered on March 5, a speech that was circumspect with regard to the attitude of the Holy See as far as Gregorian chant was concerned. In a March 17 letter to Dom Mocquereau telling of his audience, Father de Santi summed up his position as follows:

In my speech, which had to be read at such a solemn session and presented to the Holy Father, I strove to raise the question in such a way that the truth was safeguarded, yet without divulging the entire truth, in keeping with St. Paul's advice: *Omnia mihi licent, sed non omnia expediunt.* Dom Amelli would prefer the *est est, non non,* which comes from the same mouth that told us *Estote prudentes,* etc., and that inspired St. Paul. No, neither the Holy Father nor the Congregation of Sacred Rites will ever accept any demonstration whose purpose is to make them say *Ergo erravimus.* We would just be greeted with yet more decrees. But if we say (1) that the Authorities have done well to limit themselves to the archaeologists during this period of debate, and (2) that the discovery of Dom Pothier, although dating from before 1880, has not been supported by proof until our own time in the *Paléographie,* and that consequently the Congregation was justified in not addressing the issue until now, then the door is open for us to take the steps that we can, to bring about a satisfactory solution. We will need time to do it, but we will get there. Dom Amelli, I hope, will be wise enough not to compromise a cause that has been so dear to him. . . . I went to the Holy Father to offer the speech to him. I know that he has read and praised it. That in itself is something.[32]

25. Dom Pothier and Dom Mocquereau in Rome (1891)

After an enthusiastic welcome by the Salesians in Turin, the two monks from Solesmes arrived in Rome on April 4 (in fact, Dom Pothier did not arrive until April 5, since he was obliged to give a lesson in chant to the Salesian seminarians). When they reached Rome, they learned that at an important meeting, the Pope had said how happy he was to know that the traditional Gregorian chant would be sung at St. Gregory at the Coelius under the direction of Dom Pothier. In addition, as Dom Mocquereau recorded in his journal, Father de Santi assured them that "everyone was well disposed in our favor, and that the Holy Father was entirely on our side."

In another visit with Father de Santi, Dom Mocquereau, who was still following up on his idea, showed Father de Santi the charts of the modes that had been prepared for Volume III of the *Paléographie Musicale,* as well as other similar work.[33] It was a true success, the very suc-

---

32. In a letter written in French, Father de Santi spoke once again of the possibility of applying the Solesmes rhythmic system to the Pustet editions; he saw this as a means for gradually achieving the adoption of traditional chant.

33. It was these same comparative charts of the various versions of melodies that Dom Mocquereau had prepared that made such a strong impression on Father de Santi in 1904.

cess that Dom Mocquereau was looking for. They sang together, as well.

The feast of St. Gregory at the Coelius was celebrated with Cardinal Parocchi presiding, on April 11 and 12. Dom Pothier and Dom Mocquereau had prepared the schola of the French Seminary, but it was Dom Mocquereau who directed the Gregorian chants during the Mass and at Vespers, the eve and on the day of the feast.[34] The effect of the Mass was decisive. Said *Civiltà Cattolica:*

The students of the French Seminary, directed by Dom Mocquereau (Dom Pothier had yielded the honor of directing to his eminent colleague), admirably performed their program, enabling all to taste the beauty of the Gregorian melodies in their true rhythm, which appeared to a great many of the listeners as a musical novelty, or, to put it better, a return to antiquity, worthy of the highest praise. We can attest to this not only in our own name, but also in the name of many highly competent music directors, excellent judges, with whom we discussed this performance.[35]

On April 13, there was a literary meeting. Dom Pothier spoke after Dom Amelli from Monte Cassino, and at the invitation of Cardinal Parocchi. Dom Mocquereau wrote: "Before he had said a single word, Dom Pothier was greeted by one of those endless waves of applause that attest to the sympathy and enthusiasm of the assembly. It was a real triumph for him and for our cause." Dom Pothier outlined the distinct character of the Gregorian and Ambrosian chants, and their relationship to each other.

The next day, Tuesday, April 14, Dom Pothier spoke once again, summarizing several chapters of his *Mélodies Grégoriennes* in a most interesting and delightful talk. He highlighted the nature, origins, and incomparable beauty of the musical works of St. Gregory. At the same time, he explained the scrupulous fidelity through which these works were handed down over the centuries, and how the countless copies that he had found and consulted in the libraries of Europe were in accord with each other and, with few exceptions, present the same single traditional melodic text.[35bis]

---

34. "Great was the astonishment of the Romans, accustomed to hearing offices that take up a quarter of the day, with psalms the shortest of which were well over half an hour in length; in under three quarters of an hour, everything was finished at the Coelius, and more than a few of those in attendance heard, for the first time in their lives, possibly, the entire office of Vespers, in a church in Rome, on a major feast day" (Abbé Ginisty, *Échos grégoriens des deux Centenaires,* p. 51, Paris).

35. Ch. Ginisty, *op. cit.,* p. 53.   35bis. Ch. Ginisty, *op cit.,* p. 55.

Significantly, Dom Mocquereau noted that:

There was no direct or indirect reference to Pustet. . . . We know that they are quite pleased at the Congregation of Sacred Rites, and one might even say that this marked the beginning of a solution to the difficult situation in which they found themselves, because now it is no longer possible to say (so they affirm) that we are not allowing the greatest possible degree of freedom in the matter of Gregorian chant to the French as well.

That evening, Dom Pothier and Dom Mocquereau gave a course in Gregorian chant at the Vatican Seminary itself, where Father de Santi had brought them, and where he had gathered the leading choir masters, Gallignani and Magistretti from Milan, Bonuzzi from Verona, several prelates and a few monks from St. Anselm. The meeting lasted three hours, and Dom Pothier and Dom Mocquereau took turns directing the chants.

26. Results

The April 12 Gregorian chant demonstration had not been to everyone's liking. Dom Mocquereau points out irate articles published against the chant and the French. But that was of little significance in comparison to the Pope's benevolence. In fact, the Pope received those attending the Congress in a private audience on April 19. Cardinal Parocchi introduced them to Leo XIII who, in a prepared speech,

highly praised the organizers of the centennial, and was pleased to take note of its success. As for sacred music, the Sistine Chapel was the object of well-deserved compliments. Then Leo XIII clearly showed his contentment with the fact that, during these Gregorian feasts, at the Coelius the French Seminary had sung the chant of St. Gregory, returned to its ancient purity, *richiamato alla sua antica purezza.* (*Revue Grégorienne*, 1921, p. 14)

The Pope spoke a word to Dom Pothier, then Dom Mocquereau was introduced by Father de Santi as the founder of the *Paléographie Musicale* and the one who had conducted the chants at the Coelius: "Oh, that's good, that's good," said Leo XIII.

Dom Mocquereau concluded:

In the end, despite the little inconveniences of the trip, I am happy, the results will be significant, quite significant, I believe. This performance at St. Gregory produced an extraordinary effect in Rome: the ant hill has been kicked over. The fight is going to begin now, at the very time it is ending in France. Father de Santi was not frightened, because he has the truth and the Pope on his side, along with a good number of partisans. Father de Santi is an upright, daring man who is not afraid of struggle or contradiction. What's good is that he is feared quite a bit, because of his pen and his personal value. It is to him that the Vatican sends bishops so that they will have precise information on matters of the chant. Yesterday, the Archbishop of Dublin went to see him and told him, "I no longer understand what's going on in Rome. How is it that a few years ago you were inviting us *vehementer* to use the Medicean edition, and now the preference is all in favor of Solesmes; yesterday, the Cardinal Vicar himself was telling me that the Pustet edition, the edition of Rome, was the worst of them all." And the poor archbishop went on and on with his groaning. Upon which Father de Santi told him the whole truth. . . .[36] The archbishop went off regretting that he had adopted the Pustet edition in his diocese. (*Journal* of Dom Mocquereau)

Father de Santi would soon bear public witness to his feelings with regard to Solesmes. Shortly after his return from Rome, Dom Mocquereau was pleased to read, from the pen of Father de Santi himself, in the *Musica Sacra* of Milan, a piece praising the Gregorian chant work done by Solesmes. In a review of a posthumous book by Nisard, *L'Archéologie musicale et le vrai chant grégorien*, in which the author concluded that "Here scholars are faced with an insoluble problem," Father de Santi had written:

Those whose minds are not prejudiced by passion and who have followed the course of Gregorian studies and the marvelous results achieved by the Benedictines at Solesmes must conclude, without any fear of error, first that the period for discussions of the Gregorian problem is now past, once and for all; secondly, that the period for solutions is beginning under favorable auspices, especially since the start-up of publication of the *Paléographie Musicale* on January 1, 1889; and thirdly, that in the archaeological and historical field, everything is pointing toward a stunning victory, such that the Benedictines of Solesmes could write this beautiful sentence on their books: Here scholars find themselves in the presence of a problem solved.[37]

---

36. Father de Santi had asked Dom Mocquereau for a report on the history of the Pustet matter.

37. *Musica Sacra* 1891, p. 29. Translation in *Musica Sacra* of Ghent, February 1891.—On this same subject, see also the *Lettre du Père de Santi à M. A. Kunc*, in *Musica Sacra*, of Toulouse, August 1891, and *Musica Sacra*, of Ghent, September 1891.—An impartial testimonial written by the

Once again, on a card sent from Rome as he was leaving, Dom Mocquereau had written: "The fight goes on, and this is good, but the Italians will have to work hard to fight against the current and achieve an understanding of the pious and pacific music of St. Gregory." Later on, he was to write:

Finally, we, the Benedictines and our friends, were no longer *revolutionaries, Jansenists,* and *heretics*—for all of that had been said. Much to the contrary, we were on the right path—we had heard that from the mouth of the Holy Father himself—on the path traced out by the successor of St. Gregory. We were merely profiting from the *freedom* that he had asserted so many times and that assured us, with the help of God, full victory in a relatively near future.

It is true that we had to quit Rome; but we left there a group of true friends, devoted to the Gregorian cause. And at their head was the Reverend Father de Santi. We knew that he had the Holy Father's confidence. . . .

Word of the celebration in honor of St. Gregory quickly spread throughout the entire world. The *Revertimini ad fontes sancti Gregorii,* the *Richiamato alla sua antica purezza* were repeated in newspapers, magazines, and in speeches, and hope was on the rise everywhere. Increasingly our friends took heart. In the years that followed—I can merely summarize—the congresses and performances of Gregorian chant increased in number. Admirers of the restored melodies became countless in number. (*Revue Grégorienne* 1921, p. 14)[38]

27. Dom Mocquereau's Assistants

On the return from Rome, Dom Mocquereau stopped once again at various libraries in Florence, Vercelli, and Montpellier, where he wanted to get some idea of the possibility of reproducing in phototype the famous manuscript discovered by Danjou (the bilingual manuscript H. 159 of the School of Medicine). Dom Mocquereau also stopped at Aix and Apt. Dom Pothier, for his part, took another route back.

Since the opportunity presents itself here, we must note the assis-

---

Rev. Eugène Chaminade, a zealous partisan of the Ratisbon edition, on the perfection of the chant of Solesmes directed by Dom Mocquereau is available in the *Semaine Religieuse du Diocèse de Périgueux et Sarlat* (November 14, 1891).

38. In November 1891, there was a Congress of Religious Music at Milan: "Father Angelo de Santi (was) prevented for reasons pertaining to his Order from taking part in the work that his zeal had prepared in such an intelligent way" (*Musica Sacra* of Ghent, April 25, 1892, p. 92). One can see in this the beginning of the difficulties that the music director of *Civiltà Cattolica* was to encounter.

tants to Dom Mocquereau in this work of finding manuscripts. We have already mentioned Dom Cabrol, wandering through the East of France (1889) and Dom Cagin in the North (1889 and 1891), but we must also mention Dom Delpech in the South (1890, 1891 and 1893),[39] Dom Roullin from the Abbey of Silos, who visited libraries in Madrid and Toledo (in 1891). There were many other people of good will—as attested by Dom Mocquereau's correspondence—who helped him, if only in sending him photographs of a manuscript that he had pointed out to them. The harvest grew to a total of 1,145 photographs, a collection of specimens of manuscripts that was quite valuable for studying various Gregorian notations. This was the beginning of the great collection that Dom Mocquereau was soon to undertake and that was to contain hundreds of manuscripts photographed in their entirety.[40]

28. Journey to Chartres (1891)

On July 10, 1891, at the first Vespers of the Translation of St. Benedict, the Monastic *Antiphonal* restored by Dom Pothier was inaugurated at Solesmes. This book, which also included an edition for the Roman Office, thus completed the restoration of the Gregorian melodies begun in 1883 with the *Liber Gradualis*. Shortly thereafter, as soon as he could, the Abbot, Dom Delatte, went to Chartres to fulfill the vow of Dom Mocquereau at the founding of the *Paléographie Musicale* and ratified by his predecessor, Dom Couturier. Thus on August 7, 1891, the Abbot of Solesmes, accompanied by Dom Mocquereau, placed the first volume of the collection, decorated with a splendid binding, at the feet of the Virgin. The other volumes were to be added to it gradually, although the vow specified only that the first volume would be offered. But Dom Mocquereau, whose Marian devotion is well known—many references to it are found in his correspondence and in his travel notes—insisted on extending this sign of the consecration of the work to the Virgin of Chartres.

39. Dom Mocquereau himself was there in 1892.

40. Other paleographical journeys were to take place in 1904 (August–December, to Italy), in 1905 (July–December, to Germany and Belgium), and in 1914 (April–August, to Austria). England was visited during the monks' exile on the Isle of Wight, beginning in 1901, and Spain was visited in 1905 (April 1905–January 1906) (see below).

II ◼ FATHER DE SANTI AND

MONSIGNOR CARLO RESPIGHI

29. New Orientation

Once he returned to Solesmes, Dom Mocquereau soon had good news from Rome. On October 19, 1891, Father de Santi told him, in fact, that the Pope had ordered the Congregation of Sacred Rites to review the Regulation of September 14, 1884, which had followed the decree of April 26, 1883, published after the Arezzo Congress to maintain the privilege of the Ratisbon edition,[41] and to publish another, the interpretation of which would leave no room for hesitation concerning the Gregorian question, and which could serve as the rule for all Churches. Father de Santi also knew, through Cardinal Rampolla, that the leading musicians in Italy and abroad would be consulted. Yet, he added, it does not seem that the question of the editions was to be addressed. But still, "the Holy Father seriously desires musical reform, and I believe that stricter rules of order than before will come out of this" (October 19, 1891).

Unfortunately, there were behind-the-scenes maneuvers that ran the risk of compromising everything. For example, the Chambre Syndicale des Imprimeurs Français [Employers' Federation of French Printers], through the French Embassy, was trying to obtain a clearer statement of freedom from the Holy See with respect to the editions, but using means that could only result in displeasure (Father de Santi, November 27, 1891).

Nevertheless, Father de Santi wrote reassuringly:

41. The decree *Romanorum Pontificum sollicitudo* of April 26, 1883, cf. *supra,* Part I, Nos. 38 and 39. These documents are published in the *Musica Sacra* of Ghent, June 1883, pp. 87–92 (decree) and November 1884, pp. 23–27 (regulation).

I was able to discuss at length with Monsignor Nussi (Secretary of the Congregation of Sacred Rites) everything that concerns our cause. From it all, one can conclude that our studies have been taken into consideration, and that they are no longer thinking of issuing a reconfirmation of past decrees. (December 9, 1891)

Father de Santi invited Dom Mocquereau to prepare a comparison of the Medicean edition with the manuscripts (which was to be the object of a study published in volumes III and IV of the *Paléographie Musicale*). Regarding Msgr. Haberl himself, Father de Santi added this curious detail: "Haberl left last night. He went to Santa Chiara and told me that he came away quite satisfied." Yet Father de Santi had pointed out a few days earlier (November 27) that any discussion was difficult with him. Msgr. Haberl appealed to authority, Father de Santi to tradition and art (December 9, 1891).

30. The Report by Father de Santi (1892)

Father de Santi alluded not only to the studies published in the *Paléographie Musicale*, but also to his own work. The reference was certainly to his own articles in *Civiltà Cattolica*, but to other studies as well, particularly a work on the editions of the chant for which he had requested assistance from Solesmes. He sought that assistance from Dom Pothier (August 26, 1890, cf. February 5, 1892) and from Dom Mocquereau (February 18, 1891, cf. December 9, 1891).

Encouraged by the steps taken by the Pope regarding the revision of the Regulation of 1884, Father de Santi was thus able to present an historical report to the Congregation of Sacred Rites in 1892, on the errors and contradictions of the decrees concerning the Medicean edition. On May 5, 1892, he wrote to Dom Mocquereau:

In part with the notes sent by Dom J. Pothier or by Your Reverence, and in part with the fruit of my own studies, I have written a report containing twenty major observations on the decree *Romanorum Pontificum* (of April 26, 1883). Father Chatillon has summarized it and presented it to the meeting of the consultors for the revision of the decrees of the Congregation of Sacred Rites. All the consultors, in a unanimous vote, decided to forego the decreeing of the new authentic collection that is in preparation. This resolution of the consultors will be submitted in September to the cardinals at the regular Congregation. If the suppression of the decree runs into any trouble, the consultors will protest, and will defer to the Holy Father in the matter. So we can consider it a certainty even now that the decree will be, as it were, tacitly suppressed. The seriousness of the matter consists only in the fact that Gardellini had already published it at the same time as the others. Therefore, its suppression is quite significant in the present circumstances.

Nevertheless, this is merely a first step. It seems that the consultors are of the opinion that the Congregation must no longer propose any official edition, but merely recommend the true Gregorian chant. For my part, I believe that the truth and the beauty of the Gregorian melodies will make their way all by themselves, without the outside support of a privilege, a recommendation, or imposition.

In a recent book, Monsignor Romita has pointed out that this historical report was accompanied by a draft Regulation intended to replace that of 1884. Prepared as early as 1891, these two documents were submitted to the Congregation of Sacred Rites in January 1892 *(La preformazione del motu proprio di S. Pio X sulla musica sacra, con documenti inediti*, Rome, Desclée, 1961, p. 20). We will return to these two documents later on.

31. Miscellaneous Efforts

In an earlier letter, Father de Santi had asked Dom Mocquereau for a study comparing the Pustet edition with the manuscripts (December 9, 1891), a study that Dom Mocquereau had discussed with him in Rome itself in 1890, showing him the charts prepared for that purpose on psalmody. To assuage his impatience, Dom Mocquereau had already sent him two tableaux on psalmody in mode 1. On February 5, 1892, Father de Santi answered him: "In truth, they are crushing and serve to demonstrate the truth, even to those who understand nothing about notes and melody."[42] Later on, Father de Santi received other "tavole parlanti e eloquenti," which he promised to show to the Secretary of the Congregation of Sacred Rites, Monsignor Nussi (April 25, 1892).

Finally, in June 1892, Dom Mocquereau sent a work that Father de Santi wanted to have printed for the use of the consultors of the Con-

---

42. "Davvero sono schiaccianti e servono a mostrare l'evidenza della verità anche a chi non capisce nulla di note e di melodia" (February 5, 1892).

gregation of Sacred Rites. Doubtless this was a memorandum on the errors in the Pustet edition, in which case this document would be a summary that we possess of the study that was to appear shortly in volume III of the *Paléographie Musicale* (comparison between Pustet and Solesmes concerning the three psalmodic styles: simple, ornate, and neumed). After a few observations, Father de Santi concluded: "The demonstration, in and of itself, is so strong and eloquent that it stands in no need of commentary" (June 15, 1892).[43]

On September 28, once again Father de Santi acknowledged receipt of a *stupendo* extract from the *Paléographie Musicale*, most likely an offprint of the Preface on the Response *Justus ut palma*, or of the study on the neume-accents, which he quickly distributed to the consultors.[44] Father de Santi added that the consultors already had in their possession a report on the decree of 1883, that is, his own report mentioned above. In this regard, he noted that the Congregation of Cardinals would not be examining the matter in September, as originally planned, but in November. Yet everything looked quite promising, because Father de Santi wrote shortly thereafter (October 7, 1892) that the consultors were still in favor of suppressing the decree of 1883 in the new edition of the Bullarium.

32. The Gregorian Apostolate of Father de Santi—Volume III (1892)

While waiting, Father de Santi continued his work of introducing the traditional Gregorian chant into the Roman milieu. In May 1892, on the occasion of the inauguration of the organ at its church, the Vatican Seminary had held a meeting at which Father de Santi had given those in attendance a taste of the gentle character of the Gregorian melody,

43. "Nel resto la dimostrazione è per se stessa tanto forte ed eloquente che non ha bisogno di commenti" (June 15, 1892).

44. "I received the wonderful excerpt from the *Paléographie*. I distributed four copies of it to the consultors of the Congregation. They have already cast their votes against decree 83 so that Gardellini will withdraw it. But the Congregation of Cardinals will not take up the matter until November." ("Ho ricevuto lo stupendo estratto della *Paléographie*. Ho distribuito 4 copie ai consultori della Congr. Essi hanno già dato il loro voto contro il Decreto 83 perchè sia espunto del Gardellini. Ma la Congreg. dei Cardinali non esaminera la cosa che in novembre") (September 28, 1892).

an experience that was, for many, "something new and a true revelation." The *Musica Sacra* of Ghent noted, in this regard, that a real revolution had taken place in Rome in this area, and that several institutes, specifically the Vatican Seminary and the Capranica College, had adopted the Benedictine editions, which the authorities viewed with pleasure. Likewise, on June 8, 1892, the Vatican Seminary once again, still under the direction of Father de Santi, sang two melodies taken from Dom Pothier's *Liber Gradualis* for the Pope at a concert (the Introit *Dispersit* and the Alleluia *Loquebantur*). "Father de Santi's harmonious and perfect interpretation" was singled out (*Musica Sacra*, Ghent, 1892, p. 103).

The first copies of volume III of the *Paléographie Musicale (Justus ut palma II)* were delivered to subscribers beginning in July 1892.[45] The volume was to open with a study by Dom Mocquereau, entitled *L'influence de l'accent tonique latin et du cursus sur la structure mélodique et rythmique de la phrase grégorienne* (I. *L'accent tonique et la psalmodie*), pp. 1–77. The continuation of the plates of the *Justus ut palma* (Plates 108–211) followed, along with a *Précis d'histoire de la notation neumatique d'après les fac-similés publiés dans la Paléographie Musicale*, also by Dom Mocquereau (pp. 79–82), and various tables.

The study of the neume-accents, begun in volume II, was therefore interrupted, and the chapter on *The Apostropha and its derivatives* (the *strophicus*, the *pressus* and the *oriscus*) in the delivery of April 1892 was not followed up. Why this change in plans? Dom Mocquereau explained it this way to one of his correspondents, in November 1892:

I had to yield to unforeseen circumstances, and to pressing demands that required the immediate publication of the study in progress. Although it entails a certain amount of inconvenience, this change does have its advantages . . . it allows us to demonstrate earlier, through intrinsic proof, the truth of our teaching with respect to the recitative rhythm of Gregorian chant, and at the same time to answer the unfair criticisms leveled so often at the ancient chant of the Roman Church. The practical and artistic value of the Ratisbon writing is revealed in the process. At the very least, you will allow that we are proceeding with the help of scientific and pacific discussions. Facts, nothing but facts, not a word of criticism." (To Father Chaminade, November 1892, from a rough draft by Dom Mocquereau)

---

45. Volume II (*Justus ut palma*) had begun with the deliveries of January 1891 and concluded with the delivery of April 1892.

We have seen Father de Santi's great interest in this study by Dom Mocquereau on psalmody, and the tables that accompanied it. As soon as he was able, he distributed extracts of it to the Cardinals and consultors interested in the Gregorian question (April 1, 1893). For his part, Dom Mocquereau saw to it that the study, which he viewed as very important, was translated into German for the Ratisbon supporters.[46]

The goal that Dom Mocquereau intended to achieve by publishing the Gradual responsory *Justus ut palma* has already been indicated above: to show that the manuscripts spread out across all of Europe were in agreement with each other, and that the restitution of the true Gregorian chant was possible. Dom Mocquereau wrote:

A piece of music was selected and reproduced from two hundred nineteen antiphonaries of various origins, dating from the ninth to seventeenth centuries. All the Churches, those of Italy, Switzerland, France, Belgium, England and Spain, were called upon to bear witness to this quest, and all testified in favor of the Gregorian musical tradition of the Roman Church, by contributing to our collection the same melody in all cases, that of the Solesmes *Liber Gradualis*, with the exception of some insignificant variations in detail. The proof was there for those with honest minds. (*Revue Grégorienne* 1921, p. 10)

Dom Mocquereau continued, pointing out the conclusions of his study on the Latin tonic accent and its relationship with Gregorian melody, or better yet on the rules of composition for Gregorian chant, which was, at the same time, a timely condemnation of the Ratisbon edition:

After having determined the external shape of the melody and its historic authenticity, the Benedictines pushed ahead. Through precise analysis, and entering into the most minute detail, they rediscovered the laws of composition of this ancient musical language:

rules for applying words to the melody,
rules for tonic accentuation,
rules concerning weak penultimate syllables,
rules for the melodic "cursus" copied from the "cursus" of the text,
rules for musical rhyme, etc.

In the organization of the melodies, they noticed a whole series of ingenious and artistic procedures transferred from everyday language to the musical art;

---

46. *Der Einfluss des Tonischen Accents auf die Melodische und Rhythmische Struktur der Gregorianischen Psalmodie* (Herder 1894).

for example, in a given melodic formula, the *suppression* or *addition* of notes, required by the modification of texts; or yet again *contractions, divisions,* or even
permutations of notes or groups, all used by the composers according to well
and duly verified rules, based on countless examples taken from the oldest Gregorian pieces. These unexpected discoveries came to light in due course, and
gave the defenders of Gregorian art the happy opportunity of having at their
disposition an entire arsenal of proof, new, irrefutable proof of the soundest
sort, which would bear witness against the neo-Medicean edition and save this
art, this inestimable treasure of the Church, from becoming shipwrecked. Until
then, the *Paléographie Musicale* had been engaged solely in defense and reconstruction. From that point on, it was in a position to go on a strong offensive,
and to transform itself into the war machine I mentioned before, intended to
wipe out the chants that claim to be Gregorian in the Ratisbon edition.

To achieve this goal, all that needed to be done was to draw up tables comparing the two editions. On one side, the ancient version with a short summary
of its laws of composition. On the other, the neo-Medicean version, with its
mutilations and its total ignorance of the rules. There was no need for any
commentary; the mere sight of these tables was convincing. (*Revue Grégorienne,*
1921)

33. Father de Santi's *Method*

Dom Mocquereau, as you will recall, had met several choirmasters
in Italy, all of whom were won over to the Gregorian reform. Three of
them came to Solesmes as early as the summer of 1892. In August, Don
Bonuzzi came from Verona, along with Don Minetti from Genoa.
Then, somewhat later, Don Tebaldini came from Venice.

Father de Santi envied them. Thus the idea of coming to the Abbey
himself occurred to him, apparently for the first time. Nevertheless, he
did not think that he could undertake such a trip for the time being,
even though he wanted to have his Rules *(Guida)* for the performance
of Gregorian chant printed at Solesmes, for the use of the Vatican Seminary. This book, he added, would not be redundant with regard to the
Method that Bonuzzi was also going to have printed at Solesmes.[47]
There was no reason for concern about obtaining the requisite approval. The approval of the Master of the Sacred Palace and that of the
Vicar General of St. Peter, Ordinary of the Vatican Seminary, were cer-

---

47. *Metodo teorico-pratico de Canto gregoriano* (Solesmes, 1894, 361 p.).

tain (August 3, 1892). Even better, a few weeks later he told Dom Mocquereau that the Pope approved of his plan, and was sending him with
his blessing (September 28, 1892).

Dom Pothier and Dom Cabrol, the latter being at Rome at that
point, pressed Father de Santi to come to Solesmes. Dom Mocquereau
did the same, because Father de Santi had sent him his manuscript, and
there were several matters to clear up before the printing.[48]

The trip was on the verge of taking place, in October 1892. The Very
Reverend Father General of the Jesuits had granted his permission, but
he did ask Father de Santi to put off publication of his book. Given the
circumstances, the General wanted explicit permission from the Pope
(October 17), and Father de Santi's Rector had already asked him not to
continue his articles in *Civiltà Cattolica* on the Church's tradition regarding religious music (October 7, 1892). Finally, the plan for a visit to
Solesmes was dropped, and Father de Santi was all the more upset by
this fact because he was truly moved by Dom Mocquereau's criticisms
of his book, and even more so concerning the performance of the Gregorian melodies.

In this regard, Father de Santi spoke for the first time of the maneuvers of his adversaries to drive him out of Rome, where his influence
really was too strong for their liking. The Cardinal Vicar, at the urging
of Father de Santi, of course, had just imposed the study of the
Solesmes *Liber Gradualis* on the Roman Seminary (October 7, 1892), after all. Yet Father de Santi remained calm throughout all this, because

48. On October 4, 1892, Dom Mocquereau wrote, "It is because we sense the significance of
your work, all the responsibility that you are going to assume, that Pothier and I have not hesitated to critique your initial work on certain points, and to indicate *in grosso* several corrections
to be made, some slight, others more serious. As for the *substance,* it can and it must remain. For
my part, provided that certain modifications are made in these matters and in the terms used, I
accept the theory of rhythmic feet, and the analogy that exists between the rhythm of the words
and that of the neumes, on condition that you reduce this latter theory to a simple school system intended to help students better understand the rhythm of the neumatic periods. What I
mean is that your Guide is *correctable.* This is easy enough to say, but it does require prior agreement for reworking the second part of your work."

". . . And then again, just imagine how fruitful it will be for you to *hear* the Gregorian
melodies at Solesmes, particularly at Sainte Cécile with our Benedictine sisters. In your Guide,
there are certain instructions (on the *expression* to be given to the Gregorian melodies, for example) the exaggeration of which you will not understand fully except through savoring and hearing these sweet and pious songs over and over, an act of listening which cannot be replaced by
books or even discussion. Fortunately, Rev. Bonuzzi has experienced what I am telling you"
(Dom Mocquereau's copy).

he still hoped in the uprightness of the Holy Father (December 18, 1892).

In addition, Father de Santi did not neglect the practical aspects. We have seen his influence in Rome, particularly at the Vatican Seminary, but his actions extended beyond there, to Fiesole and to Reggio, of which he spoke enthusiastically in a letter dated January 6, 1893. Under his influence, others were working in the same direction and, for the first time, Father de Santi mentioned Perosi and the success that he had had at Vigevano (Piedmont). All of this, particularly the benevolence of Leo XIII ("The Holy Father is fully disposed in favor of the right cause"), was a consolation, even though the newspapers announced that the document expected from the Congregation of Sacred Rites, supporting freedom, had been put off (January 6, 1893). And so Father de Santi bravely continued his efforts to support the traditional chant, and announced a study in which he wanted to compare the Pustet edition with that of Solesmes, and another in which he wanted to show that the Council of Trent had never passed any resolution in favor of abbreviating the Gregorian melodies, and that Pius IV had never set up a commission for that purpose (February 25, 1893).

The matter of a visit to Solesmes by Father de Santi came up once more at Easter, 1893.[49] But in the end, he gave up on that plan of his own accord, since he could not have his *Method* printed (May 1, 1893). The moment was not well chosen, in fact, and soon he would be forbidden to write about Gregorian chant, not only in *Civiltà Cattolica*, but even in the *Musica Sacra* of Milan or in any other publication (July 7, 1893).[50]

34. The Work of Dom Pothier

In April 1893, Dom Pothier left Solesmes for the Abbey of Liguégé, where he received the title of Monastic Prior. Dom David wrote: "The

49. De Santi, October 23, 1892. According to a letter from Dom Cabrol, then passing through Rome, Father de Santi was once again thinking of coming to Solesmes in June (April 1893).

50. Having gotten word via Tebaldini that Dom Mocquereau was thinking of coming to the Congress held at Thiene, Father de Santi advised him not to draw attention to his presence there, and to go there "as if by chance" (July 7, 1893).—In an article in *Civiltà Cattolica*, the Reverend Father Bauducco spoke of Cardinal Aloysi Masella's violent opposition to Father de Santi (who often discussed the matter in his letters to Dom Mocquereau) (*Il p. Angelo de Santi S.J. e l'edizione vaticana dei libri gregoriani dal 1904 al 1912*, p. 246).

Abbot and the entire Community of that monastery pressed Dom De-latte at Solesmes, begging him to send Dom Pothier to them; Dom Pothier could hardly refuse, despite his deep attachment to Solesmes.[51]

In 1891 Dom Pothier had published the *Liber Antiphonarius* at the Solesmes press. Apparently the book was received with the greatest joy, and all the more so as there was one edition for the Order of St. Bene-dict, one for the Benedictine Congregation of Solesmes, and one for the Roman Church (in two volumes: Lauds and the Minor Hours, Vespers and Compline). In 1891 as well, Dom Pothier published his *Principes pour la bonne exécution du chant grégorien* (Solesmes, 16 pp.), which was distrib-uted very widely. In 1892, he came out with a new edition of the *Variae Preces,* and in 1893, one of the Monastic Processional, not to mention other excerpts from books published before then. We must also point out several Diocesan Propers and Propers for Religious Congregations that he composed. Finally, beginning in 1892, Dom Pothier had started a long collaboration with the *Revue du Chant Grégorien* founded at Greno-ble by Father Vincent-Martin (the first issue came out on August 15, 1892). As if there were any need to say so, Dom Pothier's commentaries were to contribute substantially in helping others savor and appreciate the ancient Gregorian melodies. Dom Pothier was also to exercise this apostolate through his practical conferences, which he gave in many places.

In this context, let us also point out two trips that Dom Mocquereau made to the Abbey of En-Calcat in February and August 1892. The first trip was primarily to go to Lourdes. The new Office of the Apparitions of Our Lady, composed by Dom Pothier, was sung there for the first time on February 11, and it was Dom Mocquereau who rehearsed and directed the performance.

35. The *Votum* of Cardinal Sarto (1893)

Following various tactless steps taken by French typographers, which the press (*Le Matin, Le Génie* and *L'Éclair,* for example) orchestrat-ed and to which we have previously referred,[52] the situation had deterio-rated for the supporters of the old traditional chant. Thus the most con-

---

51. *Dom Joseph Pothier,* p. 32.
52. For example, see the commentary by the *Courrier de Saint-Grégoire* (Liège), 1893, pp. 78–81.

tradictory news was circulating, and especially the announcement of a new decree in favor of Pustet (July 7, 1893), or even of a decree that would impose the Ratisbon edition excepting France alone (November 23). "This exception will be a consolation for the French," Father de Santi wrote, "but what about for us?"[53] In any event, a note in the *Osservatore Romano* (August 2, 1893) confirmed that "the Holy See never intended to impose on the bishops the obligation to introduce the chant books published by Pustet in their dioceses." Thus, concluded Father de Santi, "these tactless steps taken by the French typographers ended up producing a positive result, which is that no one will dare do anything further in support of the Ratisbon edition."

Father de Santi was correct in saying that Leo XIII was well disposed in favor of the reform of sacred music, and particularly of Gregorian chant. We have seen that he had decided to revise the Regulation of 1884 and to consult the most famous church musicians, as well as the Chairmen of the Episcopal Conferences in Italy. A commission had then been charged with collecting the wishes of the musicians and to draw conclusions from them, then to draw up a schedule of modifications to be made to the Regulation of 1884, a schedule that was sent to the Chairmen of the Episcopal Conferences on June 13, 1893.[54]

According to Father de Santi (July 16, 1893), Leo XIII was not very pleased *(non fosse troppo contento)* with the wishes of the musicians, and furthermore, he wished to settle the matter of the books of liturgical chant. To do that, Father de Santi was relying heavily on the influence of Monsignor Sarto, recently made a cardinal on May 31, 1893, and Patriarch of Venice on June 11. He was among the first of the prelates to be consulted. Thus Father de Santi thought that the document desired for so long would soon be in hand—as early as November, he hoped. Twice before, he had told Dom Mocquereau the opinion of the consultors of the Commission, in favor of a revision of the decrees. They were unanimously in favor of suppressing the decree of April 26, 1883 (May 5 and October 7, 1892), the one that had preceded the Regulation of 1884. So there were grounds for having confidence despite the tenacious opposition and tactless maneuvers of some.

53. "L'eccezione per la Francia, consolera i Francesi. Ma noi?"

54. We have drawn this detail, and those that follow, from the book by Monsignor Romita, *La preformazione del motu proprio di S. Pio X sulla musica sacra (con documenti inediti)*. Desclée, Rome, pp. 14ff.

Furthermore, Father de Santi was still continuing to study the historical aspect of the problem in greater depth: on the one hand, the decrees themselves (August 14, 1893),[55] and on the other hand, the work attributed to Palestrina, which posed a number of problems in its own right. How had Palestrina been able to create so unmusical a work? (December 2, 1893).

In July 1893, Cardinal Sarto, consulted on the Regulation of 1884, turned to Father de Santi to prepare the response that he was to provide. On July 9, the Cardinal, who was still in Mantua and who was preparing to take possession of the Patriarchal See of Venice, essentially asked Father de Santi to prepare a report for him, which he said he wanted to present to the Congregation of Sacred Rites. The Cardinal was incapable of dealing with this matter at the time he was being transferred to the See of Venice and, moreover, he protested that he was completely in agreement with the ideas of the music director of *Civiltà Cattolica* in matters of religious music. Father de Santi certainly rejoiced in this unhoped-for opportunity to have a Cardinal present documents that he had written in 1891, a report on the reform of sacred music and a draft of a new Regulation, which was discussed above. Thanks to the benevolence of the Secretary of the Congregation of Sacred Rites, he was able to retrieve the documents that he had submitted to him in January 1892, and send them to Cardinal Sarto, who thanked him most deeply for them as early as July 30, 1893.

It was already known that the *motu proprio* of November 22, 1903 reproduced a *votum* submitted by Cardinal Sarto to the Congregation of Sacred Rites in 1893, and a recent study has shown that the *motu proprio* of Pius X relied upon the writings of Father de Santi.[56] Now we know the precise origin of the pontifical document. The *votum* of 1893 comprised the report on the reform of sacred music and the draft of a new Regulation on sacred music prepared by Father de Santi, in part with the help of his friends from Solesmes. All this was collected into a single document:

The report:

---

55. Letter of August 6, 1893. Father de Santi had sent some documentation on this topic to the *Courrier de Bruxelles*.

56. *Dom André Mocquereau e la restaurazione del Canto gregoriano*, in *Musica Sacra*, 1961, nos. 1, 2, and 3.

1. General considerations (on the role of the Church in matters of religious music), seven printed pages;

2. Special observations (on desirable reforms), four pages; and

The Regulation:

3. Instruction on sacred music, fifteen pages with indications of the sources used.

Father de Santi reworked this document before sending it to Cardinal Sarto in July 1893. The Regulation or Instruction on sacred music became the *motu proprio* of November 1903, or more precisely the Instruction that followed it and that he promulgated, with the same titles, the same sub-titles, and nearly the same text.[57] We will specify below the changes that were made.

Father de Santi had merely told Dom Mocquereau that he was counting on the influence of Cardinal Sarto (July 16, 1893), but he did not seem to doubt that some persons were dead set against him. At the end of the year, he spoke of having a *Liber Tonarius (Toni Communes)* printed at Solesmes, a project for which he had his Rector's consent (November 18, 1893).

36. The Exiling of Father de Santi (1894)

In January 1894, the news that Father de Santi had been exiled and was required to leave Rome hit Solesmes like a thunderbolt. Dom Mocquereau wrote to him immediately, and Father de Santi's reply was dated from Modena on February 16, stating that he had, in fact, left Rome on January 20. This response was, nevertheless, full of hope. Father de Santi had left bearing the Pope's blessing. Thus he was confident in the triumph of truth and justice. On March 22, writing from Piacenza, Father de Santi reminded Dom Mocquereau that the Palm Sunday *Hosanna* was followed by the *Crucifige* of the Passion, but also by the *Alleluia* of the Resurrection.

The reasons for this persecutory measure are easy enough to discern. Father de Santi had taken a position practically against the official edition, and was using all his influence to see to it that the traditional

57. F. Romita, *op. cit.,* p. 22, note; text of the *votum,* pp. 70–95.—Cf. Appendix III.

chant was adopted. He was already being criticized for the fact that he had revived the Cecilian movement in Italy.[58] Ultimately, it was not difficult for the Congregation of Sacred Rites to pick up the scent of Father de Santi's style in the *votum* of Cardinal Sarto, just as it had perceived his style in the program at the Soave Congress.

A Roman correspondent of Dom Mocquereau, however, provides an even more specific cause for this exile:

The opinion of the most highly regarded choirmasters had been sought (on the Regulation of 1884). Several did not answer at all, and the others had submitted their *parere;* the responses were bound together in a volume, and that volume had been placed in the archives with a prohibition against communicating its contents to certain individuals whose extremely competent adversarial position was feared. What happened? Someone, clearly a traitor, immediately offered the first fruits of the collection to the very people from whom it was to be kept. . . . The most obvious outcome of all this was that Father de Santi was sent away from Rome. (Reverend Father Vincent Laporte, O.P., March 23, 1894)

For its part, the *Musica Sacra* of Ghent[59] provided an even more discreet explanation, and Father de Santi complained bitterly to Dom Mocquereau about the indiscretions that placed some of his brothers in religion in question, accused of having compromised with his adversaries (Piacenza, April 15; Padua, August 2, 1894), indiscretions that could do nothing but harm to him. In fact, it seems that they contributed to prolonging his exile.

In truth, the friends of Father de Santi committed certain errors of their own which did him disservice. For example, one of them took advantage of his exile to have his *Method* printed in Italian and French. Father de Santi had to take decisive action to see that this plan was halted, first with Dom Mocquereau, who had already received a copy of the manuscript (Padua, August 2; Piacenza, August 15, 1894).

Despite all this, Father de Santi did not lose interest in musical matters. He spoke of Monsignor Nussi, who remained supportive of the cause and, as necessary, sometimes had spirited debates with the Cardinal-Prefect of Sacred Rites (Padua, June 17, 1894).[60] He said that the

---

58. Moneta-Caglio, in *Musica Sacra,* 1960, 4, p. 113.

59. *Lettre de Rome* in *Musica Sacra,* Ghent, February 1894, pp. 52–54.

60. Cf. Moneta-Caglio, *L'attività musicale di S. Pio X,* in *Bollettino Ceciliano,* November 1964, p. 248. Cf. De Santi, June 17, 1894, announcing the resignation of Msgr. Nussi, who was replaced by Msgr. Tripepi, "mi ottimo amico."

Pope did not want to renew the Pustet privilege, but rather that he wanted to leave all completely free, under the supervision of the bishops (June 17). On another occasion, he expressed the wish to see a calmly presented report on the imprecision of the 1883 decree (Piacenza, August 15, 1894).

37. Perosi at Solesmes (1894)

It was at this same time that Father de Santi was occupied with a trip to Solesmes by Perosi, who had expressed a desire to come to the Abbey (Padua, May 26, 1894).[61] In a previous letter, he had already introduced the famous conductor to Dom Mocquereau (January 6, 1893). More recently still, he told Dom Mocquereau of Perosi's appointment as choirmaster at the Basilica of St. Mark in Venice. "He is an ardent friend of Solesmes," he added, "and during the upcoming vacation he hopes to go there. How glad I would be to accompany him!" (Padua, May 26, 1894). Father de Santi, too, hoped that Perosi would be his strong ally on behalf of the cause he was defending (Padua, August 2, 1894). On June 17, from Padua, Father de Santi specified that Perosi desired to come to Solesmes in July, and that through de Santi's mediation he requested hospitality "in that same monastery." Perosi, added de Santi, had already studied Gregorian chant at Monte Cassino as well as with de San-

61. On Perosi's trip to Solesmes, cf. the *Musica Sacra* of Milan, 1894, p. 96; *Rassegna Gregoriana*, 1906, col. 560–561: *Un aneddoto.*—On the first page of his *Gradual,* Perosi was accustomed to note down significant dates. There are thirteen of them, the seventh of them being: "Solesmes, July 1894" (Capra Catalogue, p. 8).—Contrary to what has been said on this topic, Perosi was not sent to Solesmes by Cardinal Sarto; he went there of his own accord, and his trip was prepared by Father de Santi, as appears from two excerpts, presented here, from Father de Santi to Dom Mocquereau: "May 26, 1894, Padua. The young Perosi, who has taken the ecclesiastical habit at Imola, has been appointed to St. Mark's Basilica in Venice. He is an ardent friend of Solesmes and, during the upcoming holidays, he plans to visit there. How I would love to accompany him." "June 17, 1894, Padua. You are well aware that Perosi, now Father Perosi, has been appointed choirmaster at St. Mark's Basilica in Venice.... Now Perosi intends to make the pilgrimage to Solesmes this coming July, when he is free, and he has asked me to request your generous hospitality at the monastery. I am certain that Father Abbot and you will welcome him, knowing that, in doing so, you are doing a great good. He is now entirely on the side of Solesmes. As for the manner of performing the melodies, he had learned very little at Monte Cassino, then he studied under me for a few days two years ago. He will perfect his understanding by listening to the monks of Solesmes. Would that I, too, could accompany him! But I am do not despair; it is unclear whether I will be able to come now. But who knows, perhaps things will work out later."

ti himself, but perfect understanding would come to him at Solesmes. For himself, de Santi had not abandoned hope of coming to the Abbey in his turn, but somewhat later (Padua, June 17, 1894).

Perosi did come to Solesmes in July 1894. He found only Dom Mocquereau there, as Dom Pothier had already left the monastery where he was professed for the Abbey of Ligugé. It was at Solesmes that Perosi received a famous letter from Cardinal Sarto, which is well worth reproducing here. The letter is dated July 11 at Mantua. The Cardinal wrote:

> I am most grateful for your greetings, and I am profoundly happy that you have arrived safe and sound at the first stop on your tour. The mere mention of the Vespers that you heard sung by the venerable monks has stirred in me the desire to hear the Lord praised in a similar fashion in Italy, as well. The wait will be long, but I hope that I shall not die before tasting of its fruits. According to a notice that I read in the newspapers, it would seem that the Holy Father has already submitted the new Regulation for music to the Cardinal Prefect of the Congregation of Sacred Rites, which will be printed before long. Let us hope that everything will be in keeping with our wishes. Try to relax a bit. Please pay my respects by kissing the hand of Reverend Father Abbot on my behalf. I wish you a very joyful and happy continuation of your travels. Most affectionately yours in Jesus Christ.[62]

In his letter, Cardinal Sarto was referring to the impending and long-awaited publication of the document on sacred music (signed on the same day that Perosi arrived at Solesmes, July 7, 1894). Alluding to the *votum* that he had sent to the Congregation of Sacred Rites in 1892, he hoped that the document would be in keeping with his wishes. We will see that he would not have much cause for rejoicing.

38. The Decree of July 1894

The decree on sacred music *Quod Sanctus Augustinus* was published in Rome on July 7, 1894. It was in response to the consultation of the Bishops of Italy with musicians, as discussed above. The decree published a new Regulation that recommended Gregorian chant "as it is found in the books approved by the Holy See" and Palestrinian music. The new decree upheld former decisions in the matter of plainchant and once

---

62. *Études Grégoriennes* V, 1962, p. 137.

again exhorted bishops to adopt the official Ratisbon edition "in order to achieve uniformity, yet without imposing it on each Church, according to the very wise conduct of the Holy See." A Letter from the Congregation of Sacred Rites to the Bishops of Italy, dated July 21, 1894, drew the following conclusions about the Gregorian question:

As the old debate about plainchant has been revived in recent years, despite the many statements of the Holy See on this matter, His Holiness wished that this subject be reconsidered, and that the questions raised be examined and resolved by the Congregation of Sacred Rites. That Congregation, having taken into consideration all that was suitably proposed in this regard, determined that there was no cause to revise any of the previous orders.[62bis]

Although the decree of April 26, 1883, had not been suppressed, as had been hoped, at least the new document said that the bishops were left free to choose from among the editions of plainchant, and this freedom indicated progress on the road to reform and to the return to the ancient Gregorian melodies.

Yet this was a disappointment for the supporters of traditional chant. This turn of events was to be expected, however. It was still too early to speak of reform, because minds were not yet sufficiently prepared for that. It must also be acknowledged that the press campaign waged in France had contributed substantially to hardening the situation. In addition, at that same time the supporters of the Ratisbon edition were little inclined to capitulate, since Msgr. Haberl had discovered a document establishing that the Medicean edition was indeed the work of Palestrina (a thesis that opponents were soon to demolish).

Msgr. Moneta-Caglio notes that the new Regulation disorganized the restoration movement in Italy, by suppressing any reform effort at the national level, limiting initiatives to the diocesan level at a time when the sympathies of Italian scholars were being won over to the traditional chant. The National Congress of Sacred Music held at Parma in November 1894 was authorized reluctantly. The Standing Committee on Sacred Music in Italy had to resign. Yet the decisions in Rome galvanized the Italian bishops, who strove to outdo each other in commenting on the new Regulation.[63]

62bis. These documents are found in the *Musica Sacra* of Ghent 1894, pp. 102–108, and in F. Romita, *Jus Musicae Liturgicae,* Rome 1947, p. 277 and p. 287.

63. Moneta-Caglio, in *Musica Sacra* 1960, 5, pp. 132–133.—Cf., by the same author, *L'attività*

Father de Santi's return to Rome was greeted as a sign of détente. On November 1, 1894, Father de Santi notified Dom Mocquereau of his return, saying that he would even get into the business of his *Method*, which some had wanted to print without his knowledge, as early as September. Yet although he returned to the Eternal City, it was through the desire of the Cardinal Prefect of the Congregation of Sacred Rites, on condition that he not become involved in either religious music or Gregorian chant. He was "to play dead," as Father de Santi put it, and he bemoaned the fact that the defense of the Gregorian cause had caused him so many problems and so much humiliation (November 1). *Raucae factae sunt fauces meae.—In salicibus suspendimus organa nostra.—Perdidi promptae modulas loquelæ*—all these laments appear in his letters to Dom Mocquereau (April 13–August 27, 1895).

Reduced to silence, Father de Santi still followed the Gregorian movement very closely. Every piece of good news caused him to rejoice greatly, such as the *Pastoral Letter* on sacred music, written by Cardinal Sarto and published in Venice on May 1, 1895. This letter presented Gregorian chant and the classical polyphony of Palestrina as models of religious music *(Tribune de Saint-Gervais*, July 1895, pp. 5ff.). Father de Santi wrote enthusiastically about it to Dom Mocquereau, yet without noting that the letter was based on the ideas in the *votum* that he himself had prepared in 1893, although the form of the Letter was the personal work of the Patriarch of Venice. Father de Santi added that the Cardinal had adopted the melodies of the *Liber Gradualis*, and he mentioned once again the good that was on the horizon in this regard in Reggio Emilia, Piacenza and Modena (April 13, 1895).—In this regard, it must be noted that as early as 1894, Charles Bordes had founded the *Schola Cantorum* in Paris, to "encourage the performance of plainchant according to the Gregorian tradition," and to restore the music of Palestrina to its place of honor. The *Tribune de Saint-Gervais,* founded in January 1895, was the monthly bulletin of the *Schola Cantorum*.[63bis]

In July 1895, a Diocesan Congress on religious music and plainchant was held at Rodez, a congress that drew its main inspiration from the Abbé Ginisty, a former student of Dom Mocquereau at the French Sem-

---

musicale di S. Pio X, p. 251, in *Bollettino Ceciliano,* November 1964.—See also the commentaries by the Italian episcopate in the *Musica Sacra* of Milan.

63bis. On the *Pastoral Letter* of Cardinal Sarto, see Moneta-Caglio, *Musica Sacra* (Milan) 1961, nos. 1, 2, and 3.

inary. The work of Dom Pothier was praised and acclaimed. For his part, Dom Mocquereau, who was taking part in the Congress, met with great success. The directing of the chant had been entrusted to him, and to Dom Delpech, and Dom Mocquereau gave a well received conference on *Roman Psalmody and the Latin Tonic Accent* (Rodez 1895, 42 pp.). The topic was familiar to readers of the *Paléographie Musicale*, but the conference was accompanied by musical examples sung by the schola that Dom Mocquereau had trained. Concisely but firmly, Dom Mocquereau himself stated the conclusion:

The tonic accent and the cursus are the elements that generate the liturgical melody. In other words: the tonic accent and the cursus have exercised a considerable influence on the melodic and rhythmic formation of the chants.

At the conclusion of the Congress, Cardinal Bourret, Bishop of Rodez, recommended the Solesmes chant method, even as he temporarily retained the edition of Digne (*Tribune de Saint-Gervais*, November 1895, p. 4). Although the Benedictine school had not been present long before the Congress of Religious Music at Bordeaux, "its spirit was present and led the Cenacle" (*Tribune de Saint-Gervais*, June 1895). The next year, the Congress of Rheims, where Dom Andoyer praised the work of the *Paléographie Musicale*, was to adopt the same approach (*Tribune de Saint-Gervais*, September 1896, p. 136, note 1).[64]

Father de Santi congratulated Dom Mocquereau on all of this. But what made him most happy was the success of the *Paléographie Musicale* and the fascicles that Father de Santi asked to be sent to him in Rome (he had been unable to receive them during his exile) (April 13–August 27, 1895).

39. Volume IV (1893–1894)

Volume IV of the *Paléographie Musicale* began to appear in October 1893. It reproduced an *Antiphonal* of the Mass from the tenth or eleventh centuries, from the monastery at Einsiedeln (Codex 121) and the School of St. Gall. This manuscript, which is particularly rich in Romanian let-

---

64. On this Congress, see also the *Revue du Chant Grégorien* 1895–1896. Dom Mocquereau's conference at Rodez is found in it on p. 20. On p. 27: Dom Mocquereau conducts the chants at Aniane on the occasion of the millennium of St. Benedict of Aniane, February 1895.

ters and signs that complete and perfect the neumatic accents, proved that not only had the traditional melody and rhythm of the Gregorian melodies been preserved, but the expressive nuances as well. After a twenty-four page Preface on those signs, Dom Mocquereau continued his study of *The Influence of the Latin Tonic Accent and the Cursus on the Melodic and Rhythmic Structure of the Gregorian Phrase. (II. The Cursus and Psalmody*, pp. 25–204), in which he outlined the laws of composition of the ancient liturgical chants. Dom Mocquereau demonstrated by this very fact the errors in the Ratisbon edition, thanks to comparative tables of the melodies. Certain conclusions from this study may be disputed (such as the date of composition of the Gregorian melodies), but that does not diminish in any way the objective value of the detailed demonstration.[65]

40. The *Gradual* of 1895

On August 25, 1895, the monks of Solesmes, exiled in the town of Solesmes since 1880, returned to their monastery. Their exile at the very doors of the Abbey had not slowed the growth of the Abbey Press (Imprimerie Saint-Pierre de Solesmes). Much to the contrary, the Press had gone on perfecting its techniques and increasing in size. Thus when the 1883 edition of the *Gradual,* printed by Desclée, had sold out, the Abbey requested a new edition from Dom Pothier, an edition that the Imprimerie Saint-Pierre de Solesmes published in 1895. The Preface noted some improvements (increases or decreases in the spacing between neumes, for example); other improvements did not amount to much (a few *b naturals* added, liquescents eliminated). There were also many additions (new Masses).[66]

Likewise, in 1895 the monks of Solesmes published the *Liber Responsorialis* for the Night Office, with an extract for the Roman Office, *Cantus officii nocturni de Communi Sanctorum ad normam Breviarii romani* (102 pp.). These two books were mainly the work of Dom Pothier, who also continued with his effective Gregorian apostolate, through his articles

---

65. In must be noted that on p. 9 Dom Mocquereau announced his treatise on rhythm that was already in preparation.

66. *Revue du Chant Grégorien*, 1895–1896, p. 127 and pp. 165ff.

and practical conferences.[67] Similarly, his recent elevation to Prior of Saint-Wandrille (December 25, 1894) did not dry up his genius as a composer. He composed melodies for many Masses and offices.[68]

41. New Hopes (1896–1898)

Upon his return from exile, Father de Santi had been reduced to silence. By February 1896, he was showing signs of melancholy at no longer being able to speak out on an issue that was of the greatest interest to him and for which he had already suffered so much, and of his interest in everything that was said or done in this area.

In February 1896, he told Dom Mocquereau that the French Embassy was once again involved (as in 1891) with presenting memoranda to the Vatican denouncing Pustet's *de facto* monopoly. Father de Santi did not believe that much could be achieved through such pressure tactics. Nevertheless, the situation did seem to be evolving slowly. In the same letter, for example, he noted something that was said by the Cardinal Prefect of the Congregation of Sacred Rites, Pustet's protector and defender, which indicated a reversal on the Cardinal's part. Recently, on the issue of the editions of Gregorian chant, he had said to the Abbot Primate of the Benedictine Order: "Let the Benedictines do whatever they think is right, according to their own traditions" (February 26, 1896).

Father de Santi also noted the modest advances made by Gregorian chant in Rome itself. On October 29, 1896, he said that at the marriage of the prince heir to the throne of Italy, at Santa Maria degli Angeli, the Introit *Deus Israel* had been sung according to the Benedictine edition, and *con tutte le regole di Solesmes*, which had made an excellent impression on all the musicians in attendance.

But, while congratulating Dom Mocquereau on the *Paléographie Musicale* (the latest fascicles of Volume IV), he complained that for his part, he could not say anything regarding music (February 28, 1896). He went so far as to say that he could not even accept the responsibility for tak-

---

67. Dom Delpech also went on a tour giving conferences and practical courses in the south of France in April 1895.

68. A list of Pothier's articles and Gregorian compositions (Masses and offices) is given in Biron, *Bibliographie des Bénédictins de la Congrégation de France* (1906), p. 138.

ing photographs of manuscripts for Dom Mocquereau, and left that up to Baron Kanzler because, as he said, "For me, that would be major excommunication *latae sententiae ipso facto incurrenda*" (June 20, 1896). It was all too true that he had to remain on his guard. For example, he reported, the *Voce della Verità* had recently spoken of him in complimentary terms; the Cardinal Prefect of the Congregation of Sacred Rites, who was quite displeased, had brought the matter up with the Very Reverend Father General of the Jesuits (July 10, 1896).

Nevertheless, they could not prevent Father de Santi from working and from pursuing his historical research on the decrees that supported Pustet. Here is a translation of a letter he sent to Dom Mocquereau on November 29, 1896. After congratulating his correspondent on the *Paroissien Romain* or *Liber Usualis* (its first edition), which included the chants of the *Gradual* and the *Antiphonal* for Sundays and the major feasts of the year in a single volume, he told him of the discovery he had just made in the Vatican Library:

On the occasion of your feast, I would like to give you some news that will make you happy. In a manuscript at the Vatican Library, I found a previously unknown letter from Fernando de Las Infantas (cf. Fétis) to Gregory XIII against the corrections of the Gregorian chant. He says that the errors that some well-intentioned eminent musicians *(virtuosi)* were pointing out in that chant were not errors at all, but rather an admirable artifice of music. He added that it is not right to do such harm to him *(to St. Gregory the Great)*, and that in his own homeland and under the reign of another Gregory. He concluded that: "it is up to the Pope *(tocca al Papa)* once again to prohibit any similar attempts at correction, by ordering that the manuscripts that had been prepared for printing should be burned." What is more, this letter opens up a new horizon:

1. Las Infantas mentions a long report that he had written on this issue the year before.

2. He asserts that Palestrina acknowledged the accuracy of his observations, and was quite astonished by them *(fu tutto sospeso)*,

3. He says that some musicians were continuing their efforts in view of the printing, that Philip II had written in his own hand to the Sovereign Pontiff, and that he was still protesting through his Ambassador,

4. Gregory XIII gave the formal order to suspend all corrections,

5. Despite this, the musicians *in their own interest* were plotting to succeed in the end, and that perhaps all the errors in Gregorian chant derived from that, and

6. This is why Las Infantas was protesting once again.

As Your Reverence can see, here we have a whole series of steps taken under Gregory XIII against these corrections; that is why Palestrina did nothing, and it was not until Paul V that the musicians brought to light what they did.

Now we must go on the hunt for the other documents related to this issue, even though this is already sufficient to shed new light on the matter. I am telling you of all this as a token of friendship, because I reserve the right to publish this document myself as soon as I am freed, in some way or other, from ex-communication. [This weighed heavily on him; see above].

We point out this discovery by Father de Santi because it was not he who published the documents by Las Infantas. He sent them to Dom Janssens for publication in a German periodical; Dom Janssens in turn sent them on to Dom Molitor of Beuron (Father de Santi, August 27, 1898). In the end, it was Msgr. Carlo Respighi who published them first, as we shall see.[68bis]

The last fascicles of Volume IV of the *Paléographie Musicale* edited by Dom Mocquereau appeared in April 1896.[69] The next volume, on an *Ambrosian Antiphonal* (Additional Codex 34 209 of the British Museum) was entirely the work of Dom Cagin.[70] The reason was that Dom Mocquereau was, by that time, nearly fully occupied with the study of Gregorian rhythm, in preparation for writing a theoretical and practical method, the main thrust of which he had already worked out.

In February 1897, he sent Father de Santi a little work that was presented as an extract from that method in preparation, namely a *Petit traité de la Psalmodie*, which was extremely well received because of its clarity and precision. In fact, that little book went through several French-language editions, as well as four editions in foreign languages. Father de Santi was among the first to congratulate Dom Mocquereau. Here is what he wrote to Dom Mocquereau on February 18, 1897:

Thank you for your latest letter, and the very handsome little book on Psalmody. This is the first time that this matter is seen so clearly. . . . So I am looking forward to the full method, which will be what we can and should expect of Solesmes. I certainly hope that my situation has changed by the time

68bis. Msgr. Carlo Respighi, born in Bologna in 1873, nephew of Cardinal Vicar Pietro Respighi. He was the director of the *Rassegna Gregoriana* (1902–1914), member of the Congregation of Sacred Rites, Prefect of Pontifical Ceremonies, and Secretary of the Pontifical Commission of Sacred Archaeology. He died in 1947.

69. This volume was discussed previously in this book; see above.

70. In 1897, Dom Mocquereau published *Notes sur l'influence de l'accent et du cursus toniques latins dans le chant ambrosien*, Milan, Cagliati, 1897, 59 p.

your method finally is published, so that I can translate it into Italian immediately, thereby making up for *ignorantias juventutis meae*, when, in all good faith, I set about translating the *Magister Choralis.*"

Father de Santi then gave various items of news that augured well:

Here a glimmer of light is starting to be seen. In Rome itself, there is a movement in favor of sacred music that, if well directed, may yield excellent results. In the meantime, the adversaries are changing their minds a little, and hardly a day goes by, it seems, that I don't hear an *ergo erravimus* from one of them. A Society of St. Gregory is being formed, whose members will be choir directors and church singers. It is Msgr. Gessi, a longtime close friend of mine, who is the driving force behind it all. I do not know the particulars of their statutes, but I am sure that they are acceptable, at the very least. They are doing everything they can to get me involved in it somehow, but I am remaining quite cool, as is my duty.

In the meantime, in addition to the news I have already given you concerning the performance of Gregorian melodies at the marriage of the Princes, I must tell you the news about the Offertory at the anniversary Mass of Victor-Emmanuel at the Pantheon. It was also taken from the *Liber Gradualis*, and performed in keeping with your method. A chair of Gregorian chant has been established at the Royal School of Saint Cecilia, a chair held by Professor Mattoni. The exercise book is the *Compendium* from Solesmes, and they sing in accordance with the teaching and principles of our schola. That at least is something.[71]

The Society of St. Gregory, which dealt with sacred music, founded in Rome in March 1897,[72] was in a position to provide significant support for the return to traditional Gregorian chant. Father de Santi as well was following its development with great interest and often spoke of it in his correspondence. The presiding board of the Society consisted of musicians, all of whom were friends of Father de Santi (July 9, 1897). At one point, everyone believed that all was going forward for the best. On January 16, 1898, Father de Santi announced that the Society was sailing on the high seas, and that the Pope wanted to make it a pon-

71. A little later, on July 13, 1897, he wrote to a French correspondent: "By contrast, in Rome you will find not only a place uneducated on this issue, but even rebellious, in some respects. There are precious few even interested in it. But Rome is the seat of truth, and sooner or later the truth will make its own way, and, I hope, it will manage to break through in the very near future" (to the Abbé H. Villetard).

72. This society was founded on March 15, 1897, thanks to the good offices of Msgr. Angelo Gessi (*Civiltà Cattolica*, April 1897), cf. *Musica Sacra* of Toulouse, June 1897, p. 82.

tifical academy. Unfortunately, there was opposition and even some cardinals opposed the Society (January 16, 1898). Thus the high hopes of the early days were short-lived. "The Society is enduring the brunt of the storm," Father de Santi wrote on April 30, 1898. Then, the following June 15, he announced that the Society was utterly moribund.

The reasons for this failure were twofold, as Father de Santi saw it. Although the Society represented the right principles, it was wrong not to come out frankly in favor of the Benedictine editions (January 16, 1898). Yet the failure was also due to the fact that, because it had not wanted to compromise itself with Pustet, the Society had drawn the wrath of those who supported the Ratisbon edition (August 27, 1898). Pustet had already suffered one defeat with the Society. Pustet had sent its books to the Society—at the request of the Congregation of Sacred Rites. Instead of the public letter he expected, the only thanks he received was a private letter that contained nothing that could be interpreted as any sort of support for the Ratisbon cause (July 9, 1897). Still more recently, the vice-president had refused to serve on the Commission *peritissimorum virorum* for the Pustet publishing company (August 27, 1898).

Despite all this, Father de Santi said, there was still room to hope that no further action would be taken against the traditional chant. In fact, several months previously a new Prefect of Sacred Rites, Cardinal Camille Mazzella, had replaced Cardinal Aloysi Masella. Masella had protected the Society of St. Gregory, and in the end had shown less aversion than in the past toward Father de Santi (July 9, 1897). Cardinal Mazzella was more reasonable and more prudent than his predecessor. Father de Santi had even gone so far as to hope for a response from the Congregation of Sacred Rites affirming that the Gregorian melodies from the Solesmes edition were not contrary to the spirit of that Congregation. But the cardinal was reticent and, as a Jesuit, did not want to show excessive favor to someone of his own order (July 9, 1897).

Thus vigilance remained the watchword. The Pope had requested that a *motu proprio* be prepared to support the Society of St. Gregory, and a text was drawn up that actually imposed the Ratisbon chant and repeated all the errors of the decrees, particularly those that concerned the role played by Palestrina. Happily, the President of the Society managed to enlighten the Holy Father, who suspended publication of the document (August 27, 1898).

For several months, Msgr. Antonio Rella, a student of Father de San-ti, had been teaching Gregorian chant at the Vatican Seminary, thus following there the lead of his teacher (January 16, 1898). Msgr. Rella was also handling the chant at the monastery of St. Benedict-de-Urbe, with the English Benedictine nuns (April 30, 1898), who were providing an example of a complete Gregorian practice (June 16, 1898). Many came from all over Rome to hear it.[73] Cardinal Parocchi encouraged them fully in this direction (June 15, 1898), praising their performance "of the very gentle melodies of the legitimate chant according to tradition" (November 20, 1898), just as he had exhorted the Salesians to follow the Solesmes method which, he said, would inevitably be approved at some time or another (card from Don Grosso, no date). Likewise, at the French Seminary, the Cardinal had said:

This chant is a sermon full of life and eloquence, because the religion, the Church that was capable of inspiring such a chant, could be none other than divine. Love Gregorian chant always. Once, Rome gave it to France through St. Gregory; today, we have lost it, and now it is France that will return it to us. (*Revue du Chant Grégorien* 1898, p. 156)

42. The Gregorian Apostolate of Dom Mocquereau

Although Dom Mocquereau was completely wrapped up in studying rhythm and preparing his method, on rare occasions he did give lectures. On March 14, 1896, he gave an address at the Institut Catholique in Paris, before a large and select audience, on *The Gregorian Art, Its Purpose, Its Procedures, and Its Characters.*[74] Alternating with portions of his address, the schola directed by Dom Delpech performed chants that demonstrated the application of the principles developed by the speaker (*Revue du Chant Grégorien* 1896, p. 128).—Dom Mocquereau gave the same speech, also accompanied by chants under the direction of Dom

---

73. "Yesterday I, too, went there for the feast of St. Scholastica. There were several students from the Germanicum there, with the *Liber Gradualis,* two foreign German priests, several from the French College of Santa Chiara and from the Ecclesiastical Academy. There were a few Frati dressed all in white, some bearded missionaries, an archbishop, several ladies and gentlemen, etc." (Father de Santi to Dom Mocquereau, February 11, 1898).

74. The text was published in several magazines, particularly in the *Revue du Chant Grégorien* 1896–1897.—Cf. *Audition de chants ambrosiens et grégoriens,* Solesmes, March 14, 1896, 11 p.

Delpech, at the Cercle Catholique of Besançon on May 18, 1896. This conference had been preceded by chant lessons at the Major Seminary and at the Choir School of the Cathedral, in preparation for the feast of the Ascension (*Revue du Chant Grégorien*, 1896).

On April 1, 1897, Dom Mocquereau gave a lecture at Poitiers, with slides, on the Gregorian timbres and on the errors contained in the modern editions, a lecture that he gave at St. Jean de Luz, as well, in August 1897 (*Revue du Chant Grégorien* 1897, p. 147).[75]

There was no dearth of visitors at Solesmes, either. Since 1889, as you will recall, Dom Mocquereau had been directing the chant, which he had managed to bring to a high degree of refinement. The *Schola Cantorum*, founded by Charles Bordes, came to Solesmes in July 1897, and for a full week studied with Dom Mocquereau and Dom Delpech. Dom Mocquereau introduced them to the secrets of paleography, while Delpech gave practical courses in the chant. At the same time, the members of the *Schola Cantorum* listened to the chanting of the monks of St. Pierre, and to that of the nuns at St. Cécile. Charles Bordes even convinced the Abbot to allow Dom Mocquereau to come to Paris to repeat the lessons he had given at the Abbey before a larger audience. As early as December 1897, therefore, Dom Mocquereau went to Paris, and gave eight lectures on paleography at the *Schola Cantorum*, in the presence of many artists and musicologists.[76] He covered the origin and evolution of the neumes, and Gregorian rhythm. Dom Delpech accompanied him once again, to direct the chants (*Revue du Chant Grégorien*, 1897–1898).[77]

Charles Bordes was to return to Solesmes with his singers in June 1899. For several days, the children even joined the monks in the psalmody, and sang the brief Response at Vespers by themselves. On June 24, on the feast of St. John the Baptist, the full *Schola* sang with the monks, the children in red cassocks standing in the choir, the older singers in the first row of the nave with the choir of the Lay Brothers. On that day, the congregation included Camille Bellaigue, music critic for the *Revue des Deux Mondes* (Chronicle of Solesmes).

Let us go back a bit. A group of some twenty Englishmen belonging

---

75. Dom Mocquereau had gone to the south of France from September 15 to October 4, 1896.

76. Those in attendance included C. Bellaigue, A. Hallays, M. Brenet, J. Tiersot, J. Combarieu, P. Aubry, A. Coquard, and A. Marty.

77. *Timbres Grégoriens transcrits en notation moderne,* December 10, 1897, Schola Publications.

to the Anglican Church closest to Catholicism, came to the Abbey in August 1897, to study Gregorian chant (*Revue du Chant Grégorien*, 1897–1898). Another well-known visitor, J. K. Huysmans, often came to Solesmes and admired the chant of the nuns at St. Cécile, in particular.[78] All agreed that Dom Mocquereau had been able to give the chant great firmness and precision, while also imbuing it with vigor and enthusiasm.

Let us also note in passing one fact that is of interest, in one way or another, to the entire Gregorian world. In July 1898, Dom Pothier, who had been prior at Saint Wandrille since 1894, was elevated to the rank of Abbot. The installation ceremony was presided over by the Abbot of Solesmes, whom Dom Mocquereau accompanied. The Abbatial Blessing took place the following September 29. The "restorer of the Gregorian melodies," as busy as he was with restoring the monastic life at Saint Wandrille, did not lose sight of the Gregorian movement, as witnessed by his assiduous work on the *Revue du Chant Grégorien*.[79]

43. Suppression of the Decree of April 26, 1883 (1899)

In 1899, the ancient Gregorian chant had made its way everywhere, even to Bavaria, just steps from the citadel of Ratisbon. Father de Santi then returned to a project that he had had to abandon in 1891. As you will recall, at that point he had wanted to have the decree of April 26, 1882, *Romanorum Pontificum sollicitudo*, suppressed. A memorandum to that effect had been well received by the competent Commission of the Congregation of Sacred Rites, and they had agreed to suppress the decree. But, after the incidents that occurred in 1894 (the exile of Father de Santi), everything had been questioned once again. Father de Santi met with greater success in 1899, thanks to the effective assistance of Msgr. Carlo Respighi. While Respighi was seeing to it that a report reached Cardinal Mazzella, Prefect of the Congregation of Sacred Rites, and the competent Commission, Father de Santi had Cardinal Richard, the

---

78. Ch. H. Villetard, *J. K. Huysmans, Souvenirs et quelques lettres*, in *Le Lutrin* (Geneva), 1949, p. 75.

79. In 1898, Dom Mocquereau made a Gregorian tour of the south of France (Bayonne, Dax) in January–February, then went to Montpellier in December. He went to the north (Minor Seminary at Arras, and the Abbey of Wisques) in November 1899.

Archbishop of Paris who was in Rome at that time,[80] speak with the Prefect of the Congregation of Sacred Rites, as well, and with the Pope himself. All these moves were well received, and, in fact, in March 1899, the pages of the new edition of the *Decreta authentica S. R. C.* no longer list the decree of April 26, 1883 (Father de Santi, March 1, 1899).

The time seemed to be at hand for rendering obsolete the other decrees that had been handed down in support of the Ratisbon edition, by taking the opportunity of the imminent end of the privilege granted to that edition. Father de Santi and Msgr. Respighi specifically wanted to have the decree of 1894, *Quod Sanctus Augustinus* (cf. *supra*, No. 38), suppressed. But that was impossible, out of respect for the Cardinal who had signed that decree, who was still living.[81] Thus, even though he was still threatened by another period of exile, Father de Santi did not lose confidence: "a change in circumstances could grant us victory from one moment to the next," he said to Dom Mocquereau at the time (March 1, 1899).

Father de Santi even hoped to obtain a favorable response regarding the chant of the manuscripts (cf. March 28, 1899), not a direct approval of the work of Solesmes, but a response that would be an indirect approval of its editions. He said: "Our idea is to recommend printing of the melodies at the Vatican Press after a comparison *specie tenus et honoris causa* of the text of Solesmes with the manuscripts of Rome." Nevertheless, he noted sadly that not all people were moved by the beauty of the ancient melodies. He said that it was essential to point out quite clearly the errors in the decree of 1894 (Father de Santi, March 1, 1899, cf. March 29, 1899).

44. Perosi's Actions (1899–1900)

On May 28, 1899, however, a piece of news reached Solesmes that was bound to bring joy and exultation. A telegram signed Baron Kanzler read: "Alleluia. This morning, opening of the American Council

80. It was Dom Janssens who spoke to Cardinal Richard about the matter, at Father de Santi's request.

81. For his part Dom Janssens wanted to have the decree of 1894 suppressed. He only managed to have it modified, through the suppression of anything that derived from the decree of 1883 (letter of March 28, 1899).

(this was a council of American bishops). Sistine Choir under the direction of Perosi inaugurates Gregorian melodies."

Two letters from Father de Santi followed, back to back, speaking of his consolation and satisfaction, after so much suffering on his part for the success of the Gregorian cause. This consolation was felt all the more deeply because at the same time, the representative of Pustet was mopping up after a stunning reversal of fortune in Rome itself. Having gone there to give a series of conferences on Ratisbon chant to the American bishops, he drew twelve out of forty of them on the first day, only two on the second day, and that was all. . . . He had suffered a previous setback in March. The Society of St. Gregory, which had been forbidden to sing the Gregorian melodies in 1896, had invited the French Seminary that year, which sang the Mass in pure Gregorian chant on the occasion of their patronal feast day, March 12 (May 28 and May 30, 1899).[82]

On December 14, 1898, Father de Santi had informed Dom Mocquereau of the appointment of Perosi to the Sistine position, following the huge success of his oratorio on the Resurrection of Christ, and from that early date, Father de Santi told him that Perosi had shown "the firm desire to work with all his strength toward the complete and imminent triumph of Solesmes," a claim to which the maestro had taken care to append his own signature (*Revue du Chant Grégorien* 1921, p. 18). Father de Santi then added, however, that he had not believed that it would be possible to introduce the Gregorian melodies at the Sistine Chapel from the very first day that Perosi became its director. Someone other than Perosi would have introduced the reform gradually, but he, with his sovereign independence, wanted to strike a great blow right away, declaring that he would rather resign if he could not have his way. There was great resistance among the singers, who immediately complained, "But here, this is Father de Santi's chant!" They did not know that the two Gregorian pieces sung on the feast of the Holy Trinity, the Introit and the Alleluia, had been transcribed into modern notation by

---

82. The *Musica Sacra* of Ghent (*Le Plain-chant grégorien à Rome*, June–July 1899, p. 96) mentions another ceremony at which the French Seminary drew attention for its perfect performance of the Gregorian melodies, on Sunday, May 14, when the Society of Sacred Archaeology celebrated the twenty-fifth anniversary of the discovery of the Basilica of St. Petronilla. They sang the *Rosa vernans*, taken from a 12th-century manuscript, which had been recently published by Dom Mocquereau.

Father de Santi himself, from the Vatican manuscripts, so that the name of Solesmes was not even mentioned (Father de Santi, May 28 and May 30, 1899).

Protests reached even the Pope's ears, accusing Perosi of having unapproved chant performed, thereby setting a bad example. Documents in hand, it was easy to show that the two Gregorian pieces that had been sung were found in the manuscripts of the Vatican and the Sistine. The Pope's majordomo, upon whom he had called, concluded that in any case, the Sistine Chapel should not take direction from anyone, but rather on the contrary, it should establish officially what should be considered authentic sacred music (Father de Santi, May 31, 1899).

Father de Santi's idea was that the Gregorian melodies had already been approved for centuries and needed no further approbation, merely a statement asserting that they were the legitimate chant of the Church (and moreover, there was no possibility of obtaining anything more, as long as the Pustet privilege stood). Father de Santi had even drawn up a *Dubium*[83] that could be submitted to the Congregation of Sacred Rites for purposes of obtaining an authentic statement along these lines. Perosi was working along the same lines. Even though he had already obtained assurances from the Congregation of Sacred Rites that the Pustet privilege would not be renewed, he did not feel reassured, and wanted to obtain the answer desired by all the friends of Gregorian chant from the Pope himself (May 31 and June 18, 1899). Moreover, since the representative of Pustet saw his position threatened, he himself was suggesting that their edition be corrected. The Holy Father would have agreed to that, but only on condition that the new edition be submitted once more for approval by the Congregation of Sacred Rites.

Therefore, Father de Santi concluded, "these are serious times, and a momentous explosion may occur at any time." Thus, with his friends Msgr. Carlo Respighi, the Baron Kanzler, and Perosi, he was on constant alert (Father de Santi, May 31, and June 18, 1899).

83. On July 12, Father de Santi wrote to Dom Mocquereau: "As for the request, rest assured that it will not be presented until we know for sure that the response will be what we want. So far, nothing has been done and it is better to wait for more favorable circumstances." Here is the wording of the *Dubium: Quæritur an probandus sit venerabilis cantus gregorianus quem ex veteris Ecclesiæ universæ codicibus Schola Solesmensis diligenter transcripsit additis ex earundem melodiarum more novis officiis? Resp.: Talem venerabilem cantum ab Ecclesia jamdiu receptum atque Romanis Pontificibus summis laudibus exornatum legitimum semper fuisse et nunc esse, ideoque nulla nova approbatione indigere* (De Santi, June 18, 1899).

Perosi still had a battle on his hands with the singers at the Sistine Chapel (on June 30 he had them perform a few more pieces of Gregorian chant), despite the fact that he was supported by the Pope himself, who was threatening to disband the recalcitrant Pontifical Choir. Father de Santi was still exposed to the adverse mentality of his opponents.

They have a grudge against me, and Father General has told me that, once again, I have been accused before the Pope as the author of the suppression of the decree of 1883, but that the matter could not be proven. (July 12, 1899, cf. June 16, 1900)[84]

Despite all this, the ancient Gregorian melodies were continuing to forge a path, slowly, into the very heart of the city of Rome. After the Vatican Seminary, the Salesians and the English Benedictine nuns, the Réparatrices and the Dames du Sacré-Coeur also began to study Gregorian chant. They were followed by the Collegio Pio Latino-Americano, whose Rector had taken the advice of Father de Santi after the conferences by the Pustet representative, which displeased everyone.[85] On January 21, 1900, Father de Santi wrote:

This morning, the young men of the South American College inaugurated the Gregorian melodies. They sang very well for this, their first time, but everything will go even better from now on, because they have a strong will and great enthusiasm for our chant. (Cf. June 16 and Christmas, 1900)

The Germanicum also wanted "to be done with Pustet" (Father de Santi, May 30 and November 19, 1899; August 5, 1900).[86]

It was to meet the needs of the schools, colleges and boarding schools that Father de Santi had the idea of printing a Gregorian *Vade mecum* in modern notation,[87] which would include an extract from the

84. "During this time at Rome, serious opposition began against Perosi. There was a lot of talk about the Gregorian melodies performed at the Sistine Chapel, and they were trying to pin it on me. Reverend Father General warned me that my enemies were spying on me constantly, trying to catch me in some wrongdoing" (de Santi, August 1, 1899).

85. Returning to this episode, on February 21, 1900 Father de Santi wrote: "The students were so dissatisfied with the Haberl readings that they opted for Solesmes. Now, they sing their Gregorian chant Mass every Sunday, and I am pleased with their performance. You are well aware that at this school, we have the elite clergy of Latin America. So it is a great victory for Solesmes to have won over these good students" (to the Abbé H. Villetard).

86. In another place, Father de Santi said that the "Ladies of the Roman patrician class wanted to establish a Gregorian schola so that they themselves could sing on the feasts of their Catholic association" (May 30, 1899).

87. Father de Santi had to argue against Pothier about the benefit of these transcriptions of

Kyriale and other melodies that can be used most often. He entrusted publication of the book to Solesmes (Father de Santi, June 18, 1899).

45. The *Paléographie Musicale* in 1900

Still, the *Paléographie Musicale* continued its scientific research, comparing the intrinsic value of the two competing editions, the neo-Medicean and the Benedictine. That was the purpose for which it had been founded.

Volume VI (1900–1901) presented a transcription onto lines of the Ambrosian *Antiphonal* (British Museum, cod. addit. 34 209), published in phototype in Volume V. This was, you will recall, the oldest known manuscript in which the tradition of the Milanese chant was preserved. Yet at the same time, Dom Mocquereau began a new "monumental" series of the *Paléographie Musicale* (Series II), the volumes of which would not come out in fascicles, but all at once. The first volume in that series was a tenth-century *Antiphonale Officii monastici*, written by the Blessed Hartker, monk of St. Gall (nos. 390–391 of the Library of St. Gall). It came out in 1900, preceded by a brief Preface by Dom Mocquereau, and a notice on the *Antiphonal* (pp. 9–15), and on the *Tonale* restored to its original order (pp. 16–22). The manuscript itself ran to 458 pages. You will also recall that Dom Mocquereau had made an extremely faithful copy of this manuscript, to which he attributed great significance because of its wealth of rhythmic indications and expressive nuances. Msgr. Rousseau wrote:[88]

The *Paléographie Musicale* had taken on such significance among the scientific works of that time that at the Second Congress of Christian Archaeology, held in April 1900 at Rome, the illustrious historian Rev. Father Grisar deemed it a duty of justice to intervene in order to acknowledge the success of the paleographers at Solesmes, and to bring them to the attention of modern scholars.

Gregorian chant into modern notation. The square notation, which there was no discussion of eliminating, was, in fact, a stumbling block to the spread of the traditional melodies, and Father de Santi stressed the significance of the successes already achieved thanks to these transcriptions (de Santi, January 14, 1900).

88. *L'École Grégorienne de Solesmes*, Desclée 1910, pp. 27–29. Cited in *Atti del II Congresso internazionale di Archeologia cristiana tenuto in Roma nell'aprile 1900. Dissertazioni lette o presentate e resoconto di tutte le sedute*. Rome, Spithöver 1902, pp. 408–409 and 415–416. Cf. *Musica Sacra* (Toulouse), December 1900, p. 140.

Since he himself was unable to attend the meeting, he asked the secretary to submit the following resolution for the approval of the 4th Session: "Considering the special significance of the archaeological study of *Gregorian chant* in understanding the influence of ancient Latin and Greek music on the music of the *Middle Ages*, the Congress highly recommends studies such as those of the Benedictines of Solesmes, in their very valuable *Paléographie Musicale*, and further recommends the practical study of Gregorian chant."

It seems that such a proposal, written up in such laudatory terms for scholars whose work was beyond question, should have been accepted unanimously with gratitude, particularly by the members of the Benedictine family. It was, in effect, the placement of the *Paléographie Musicale* on the agenda. "Reverend Father Janssens thinks that the resolution must be worded in a more general manner, without placing so much emphasis on the *Paléographie Musicale*, since everyone knows that this work is the most remarkable and interesting on the subject, and the best known by those devoted to musical researches."

"Father Amelli, the chairman, agreed with Dom Janssens, noting in turn how widely known was the work of Solesmes. By contrast, others felt that Father Grisar's resolution had to be accepted in its entirety. Father Morin, Mr. Blumenstihl and others wanted mention to be made of the very significant work of the Solesmes *Paléographie*. Baron Kanzler showed that this would be the most suitable solution, and suggested merely that some expressions be modified. Others expressed the wish that mention be made of the studies on the ancient music of the Hebrews.

"The Chairman recommended that the resolutions be studied by a committee, to include Dom Janssens and Baron Kanzler. At the following day's meeting, the corrections and modifications that may seem suitable would be suggested and debated. . . ."

"At the opening of the meeting the next day, April 20, 1900, Chairman Dom Ambrogio Amelli recalled the debate of the previous day regarding the resolutions proposed by Father Grisar, and submitted a new wording written by the Committee and fully accepted by Father Grisar himself, and by the General Chairmanship of the Congress: '*On the study of the relationship between ancient music and the liturgy of the Middle Ages.* The Second Congress of Christian Archaeology, in light of the singular significance of the archaeological study of Gregorian chant in order to understand the influence of ancient Hebraic, Greek and Roman music on the music of the Middle Ages, highly recommends these studies.'"

"Baron Kanzler commented briefly on the very great importance of the publication of the *Paléographie Musicale* of Solesmes, as an aid for the science of the archaeology of music, and provided numerous testimonies."

It has been necessary to quote *in extenso* both the resolution proposed by Father Grisar and the debate that it engendered, in order to indicate the considerable position assumed very early on by the *Paléographie Musicale* in scientific work, and also to note the high regard in which it was held by the best critics in contemporary science.[89]

In October 1900, Dom Mocquereau went to England. He gave courses in chant at the monastery of Farnborough and at the seminary nearby. Dom Cabrol, former Prior of Solesmes, was governing the monastery founded and entrusted to Solesmes in 1896 by the Empress Eugénie. It housed the tomb of Napoleon III. For Dom Mocquereau, this was an opportunity to visit the British Museum, with its vast collection of manuscripts. Other circumstances that could not be foreseen at the time were to bring Dom Mocquereau and his brethren at Solesmes to England—for a twenty-year stay.

46. Msgr. Respighi vs. Msgr. Haberl (1899–1900)

While Dom Mocquereau was preparing for the future by publishing the authentic sources of Gregorian chant, Msgr. Respighi was attacking the poor Medicean edition on historical grounds, using documents discovered by Father de Santi in 1896 (cf. Father de Santi, November 29, 1896; cf. No. 41), and was overturning the theory that Palestrina was the author of the Medicean edition. On November 19, 1899, Father de Santi informed Dom Mocquereau that Respighi had published the documents of Fernando de Las Infantas in the *Ciudad de Dios*,[90] in Madrid (October 1899), and that the article was also going to be published in Rome.[91]

Msgr. Respighi argued against Msgr. Haberl, a defender of Palestrina's authorship,[92] first that, although Palestrina had received a commission from the Pope to revise the *Gradual*, the renowned musician, as a

89. According to a letter from Father de Santi to Dom Mocquereau dated April 28, 1900, it was Cardinal Parocchi who caused praise for the *Paléographie Musicale* to be suppressed, at the request of Cardinal Aloysi Masella. Masella also maintained that the decree *Quod Sanctus Augustinus* contained errors, and that it had been snatched away from him.

90. This article was published without the knowledge of Father de Santi.—Cf. November 15, 1899: "Msgr. Respighi has published the documents of Fernando de Las Infantas in the *Ciudad de Dios*. I knew absolutely nothing about this, and I was more than a bit surprised when I saw the publication of that wonderful article."

91. *Giovanni Pier Luigi da Palestrina e l'emendazione del Gradual Romano,* Rome, Desclée, n. d.

92. In his brochure entitled *Jean Pierluigi Palestrina et le Graduel romain officiel de l'édition médicéenne* (French translation in 1894), he affirmed that Palestrina was the author of the

result of the pressing claims of Don Fernando de Las Infantas to Gregory XIII, stopped his work of correction around 1580; secondly, that it
was impossible to prove historically that the Palestrina manuscript was
the same thing as the Medicean edition, and therefore that it was unfair
to use the name Palestrina in defense of that type of plainchant.[93]

As has been said before, following the discovery of the letter from
Don Fernando de Las Infantas, Father de Santi turned to Dom Janssens
since he could not publish it himself. Dom Janssens, in turn, approached Dom Molitor from the Benedictine Abbey of Beuron. Msgr.
Respighi had used the letter in his memorandum on suppressing the decree of April 26, 1883. The reason that Msgr. Respighi managed to publish the letter first, without Father de Santi's knowledge,[94] was that time
was of the essence. As Respighi saw it, the time was right for revealing
the truth about the origins of the Medicean edition. Yet because Dom
Molitor added new elements to the debate, things that he had found on
his own since Dom Janssens told him of Father de Santi's discovery (Father de Santi, August 27, 1898), Father de Santi told Dom Mocquereau,
and Msgr. Respighi published a new article on January 14, 1900:

[Msgr. Respighi's] pamphlet has caused quite a stir here, and Haberl's authority
has been sharply attacked. Now, the *Roemische Quartalschrift* (Dom Molitor's article) is publishing documents not found by Msgr. Respighi, i.e. the letter from
Don Fernando to the king, the king's response to Don Fernando, the letter
from the king to the ambassador and to the Pope. The issue is quite clear.
Msgr. Respighi will respond to Msgr. Haberl, and his new pamphlet will be
published.[95]

Msgr. Respighi's pamphlet was published, a new study on this most
interesting topic.[96] According to a contemporary report, the author in-
tensified his arguments:

Medicean edition, an edition of plainchant done in 1614 by order of Paul V, and reproduced by
the Pustet publishers of Ratisbon.

93. A. Martin, *Palestrina et l'édition médicéenne,* in the *Revue du Chant Grégorien,* March 1900,
pp. 127–131; April 1900, pp. 142–149.

94. Cf. Note 90, and Venice 1901, n.d. (Letter from Father de Santi).

95. Cf. *Revue du Chant Grégorien* 1900, p. 145, note 1. On August 5, 1900, Father de Santi wrote,
"Msgr. Respighi has finished his work, and in a few days it will be put before the public. He has
sent me a few printed sheets, and it seems to me that his demonstration is obvious, and that
Haberl has definitively been beaten." Msgr. Respighi, for his part, kept Dom Mocquereau abreast
of his work.

96. *Nuovo studio su Giovanni Pier Luigi da Palestrina e l'emendazione del Graduale Romano* (Rome,

Msgr. Respighi has valiantly and happily declared himself an opponent of the German doctor. Since he discovered valuable documents in the Vatican Library, he felt that it was his duty to clarify matters concerning the origins of the *editio medicea* attributed to Palestrina by Haberl. He has proven that: (1) the correction of the Roman *Gradual* that Palestrina began under Gregory XIII was abandoned by order of that Pope, as Palestrina himself said; (2) there is absolutely no proof that the master's manuscript, in this interrupted state of affairs, was ever brought to the Medici printing house; (3) even if it were proven that the Medici printing house did receive the manuscript, it must nonetheless be agreed that Palestrina had nothing to do with getting it there.[97]

The Ratisbon *Musica Sacra* denounced the source of the threat against the official edition:

The stronghold of these adversaries of the choral books of Rome is called Solesmes, as opposed to Ratisbon. From Solesmes, a new branch of the Benedictine Order is acting through the spoken and written word on behalf of the "pure traditional chant of St. Gregory, without alteration. . .". The attacks have begun, and we take up the fight under the protection of authority, in the interests of sacred art and with the weapons of science, while not turning a blind eye to the work done toward reviving and fostering Church music in Germany.[98]

Dom Molitor collected all the documents related to this issue in a two-volume work published in 1901 and 1902 (*Die nachtridentinische Choralreform*, Leipzig).

47. Liberating Words (1901)

All this work was even more opportune, in that there was still talk of renewing the privilege of the Ratisbon edition (June 15 and August 5, 1900). At Christmas, Father de Santi went so far as to say that there had been talk of imposing the neo-Medicean edition on the Diocese of Rome, and of having it acknowledged as containing the authentic chant of the Church.

Desclée 1900, 140 pp.). Cf. "Palestrina et l'édition médicéenne," *Revue du Chant Grégorien*, August 1900, pp. 20–22.

97. Henri de Surrel, "La question du chant grégorien et la S. Congrégation des Rites," *Revue du Chant Grégorien*, December 1900, p. 91.

98. Signed by Msgr. Haberl, a member of the Pontifical Commission for *the* revision of choir books.

Happily on January 12, 1901 (and Father de Santi notified Dom Mocquereau of this at once), the Pope had spoken some liberating words at
the request of the Cardinal Vicar, saying:

Tell the Rectors of the Colleges and all those who are involved that they should
set their minds at rest, and that they should sing and cause to be sung what they
feel is best and most suitable. There will be no new decrees. We must take another path than the one we have followed so far, and We Ourselves shall think
in these terms.

Our Roman friends had gone all out to obtain this response, or at
least to pave the way for it. On December 22, 1900, Father de Santi had
sent a memorandum to Cardinal Ferratta, now Prefect of the Congregation of Sacred Rites,[99] in which the errors into which that Congregation had been led were exposed. This arrival of the memorandum
was timely, because the decision to impose the Ratisbon edition on the
Diocese of Rome had already been made, although it had not yet been
implemented. Dom Janssens wrote to the Cardinal on December 30. Finally, Msgr. Carlo Respighi was working, as well, keeping Cardinal
Oreglia and Cardinal Rampolla well informed. Cardinal Rampolla approached Cardinal Ferratta and the Cardinal Vicar personally, asking
him "to favor freedom in all things, and not to make any decision in this
area."

In various settings, other cardinals showed their support for the
effort to return to tradition, especially following publication of an article that Father de Santi was wrongly suspected of writing, or at least of
inspiring.[100] Cardinal Vivès, for example, protector of the Latin-Ameri-
can College, supported the actions of the Rector of that College, who
was accused of not following the decrees in force and of setting a bad
example. The same thing had been done with regard to the Superior of
the French Seminary.

It was following these actions that the Cardinal Vicar felt that it was
his duty to mention them to the Pope, and that he obtained the liberating words mentioned above. At the time, Father de Santi wrote: "It is incredible how much effort Msgr. Carlo Respighi has devoted to these
matters. Solesmes and the Gregorian cause must be forever grateful to
him. We must also admire Providence, which stirs men to action as

99. Father de Santi had announced his appointment on October 24, 1900.
100. *Osservatore Cattolico*, December 27–28.

needs arise."[101] Father de Santi did not speak of himself, but his correspondence attests to the role that he, too, played in the fight for the ancient melodies of St. Gregory (January 12, 1901).

48. The Memorandum Requested of Solesmes (1901)

Msgr. Respighi had another project in mind at that point, one that he shared with Dom Mocquereau on January 17, 1901. In his opinion, a new age was beginning, the dawn of the triumph of the Gregorian cause was breaking thanks to the devoted efforts of the intrepid defenders of the ancient Gregorian melodies. He wrote: "In all your prayers, as a debt of gratitude, recommend to the Lord the three great Cardinals Oreglia, Rampolla, and the Cardinal Vicar, and don't forget Perosi, Kanzler, Father de Santi, etc."

The favorable intentions of the Pope were now widely known, and the horizon, which appeared so dark and stormy at Christmas, suddenly cleared. The Pope wanted to resolve the Gregorian question in keeping with the constant tradition of the Roman Church and with the demands of art and science. Msgr. Respighi pointed out one further reason for having confidence:

The Cardinal Vicar has just appointed a Commission on Sacred Music in Rome, with the approval of the Holy Father. The Commission will include Capocci, Parisotti, Kanzler, Mattoni, and Mancini. This will be very useful, indirectly, for Gregorian chant: they are all in favor of Solesmes.[102]

Consequently Msgr. Respighi asked that a short but complete memorandum be prepared at Solesmes as soon as possible "because we must strike while the iron is hot." The memorandum was to include all the theoretical and practical studies published in support of the Gregorian restoration. He also requested a catalogue of all of Solesmes' publications on this issue, thus placing "at the service of the Holy Father and of the Holy See the results of lengthy studies done to discover the true *cantus Ecclesiae Romanae.*"

101. On August 1, 1899, Father de Santi had written, "He is our faithful friend, the one who led the fight for abolition of the decree of 1883."

102. "Musique et plain-chant à Rome," *Revue du Chant Grégorien,* February 1901, pp. 110–112.—Father de Santi told Dom Mocquereau the news on February 20, 1901.—The Cardinal-Vicar mentioned here is Cardinal Pietro Respighi, uncle of Msgr. Carlo Respighi.

Msgr. Respighi wanted major emphasis to be placed "on the truth of the Roman tradition," on the *Cantus Ecclesiae Romanae*. He also wanted the melodies of the *Pontificale Romanum* prepared at Solesmes to be mentioned.

It was at Msgr. Respighi's instigation[103] that Father de Santi had asked Solesmes, on July 12, 1899, to have the melodies of the *Pontificale Romanum*, which was about to be reprinted, in readiness. This was the former Roman edition, a copy of which the Pope was in the habit of giving to new bishops.[104] Obviously, there was fear that advantage might be taken of the reprinting of this old edition in order to insert the chants from the German edition. Dom Mocquereau was quick to assent to this proposal, and on August 1, 1899, he assured Father de Santi that everything would be ready.

In Msgr. Respighi's opinion, Leo XIII, being the protector of the arts and sciences, would necessarily appreciate the honor of this work by the sons of St. Benedict, and the action planned could be vital in advancing and resolving the Gregorian question. In his view, Cardinal Rampolla was the perfect intermediary to present the memorandum to the Holy Father.[105]

The work was done quickly at Solesmes because as early as February 5, 1901, Msgr. Respighi had read and annotated it. Besides, the Memorandum corresponded perfectly to the desire of both Msgr. Respighi and Father de Santi, who were predicting a positive outcome of the effort. Msgr. Respighi hoped only that the decree of 1883 would not be discussed too explicitly, recalling that there was a time when the traditional melodies were prohibited. He then recommended to Dom Mocquereau that he approach Cardinal Satolli, the Prefect of Studies, who was very supportive of the cause, in order to have the Memorandum reach the Pope, or at least to request his support in his role as Prefect of

---

103. "Msgr. Respighi (and this must remain a secret between us) is responsible for correcting some rubrics in the *Pontificale Romanum*. He is deliberately slowing the work down to stall for time, hoping for some change that might help us out" (de Santi, January 14, 1900).

104. The Roman edition of the *Pontificale* (called the *camerale* edition) used melodies different from those in the Ratisbon edition, melodies that continued the ancient tradition fairly well. It was important to keep the edition that was in preparation from following the lead of the German edition in this regard. We know that some of these melodies in the Roman edition come from the repertory known as "Old Roman." Dom Gatard went to the British Museum in 1901 at the behest of Dom Mocquereau, to study this aspect of the editions of the *Pontificale* there.

105. At the same time, Msgr. Respighi advised the monks at Beuron to write to the Pope and to Cardinal Rampolla.

Studies. Finally, Msgr. Respighi closed with a long and detailed list of the churches, colleges, and institutes in Rome where the Benedictine editions were used as the basis for the chant.

Cardinal Satolli agreed to present the Memorandum, and greetings from Solesmes, to the Pope. The Cardinal readily acknowledged that the Congregation of Sacred Studies could intervene *toto jure* in a matter involving scientific studies and reports. In reporting this news to Solesmes, Msgr. Respighi said once more that the fight was not over, and that their adversaries were still strong, but that they should take confidence from the Pope's firm and resolute statements to the Cardinal Vicar on January 12, 1901, statements that had just been repeated to Cardinal Svampa, the Archbishop of Bologna. The day after the feast of St. Gregory, the Pope had told Cardinal Svampa (who had broached the issue of Gregorian chant with the Pope at the request of Msgr. Respighi) that he wished "to resolve the matter worthily, taking into account the studies that have been done, and appoint a commission of true specialists for this purpose." The Pope thus confirmed what he had said to the Cardinal Vicar two months earlier.

It was Msgr. Respighi who gave copies of the Memorandum printed at Solesmes and intended for distribution, as well as the volumes of the *Paléographie Musicale*, to Cardinal Satolli, who was "well disposed to do all that was within his power in support of the holy cause." He had lovingly prepared the tributes intended for the Pope:

I have taken the liberty of having a white box made for the Memorandum intended for His Holiness, a strong black box for the Hartker volume, and three cases done in black cloth to put all the other books together into three sets, in other words: (1) The books of the Roman Rite, (2) The books of the Monastic Rite, and (3) Extracts, the *Liber Usualis*, etc. I had the soft-cover books bound in black cloth. They will be ready tomorrow evening, and I will bring them to His Eminence, who will attend the Holy Father's audience Saturday morning at 10:00. Let us hope that His Holiness will receive the offering favorably, and that he will say a word in favor of the Gregorian work done by the Benedictines. May Your Reverence pray for this lofty goal, and ask for prayers for this intention. (Respighi, Vigil of the Feast of St. Benedict, 1901)[105bis]

The Memorandum was one of the last works published by the Imprimerie Saint-Pierre de Solesmes before the exodus of the monks.

105bis. Our friends Dom Janssens and Dom Perosi applauded Msgr. Respighi's project wholeheartedly (Respighi, Vigil of the Feast of St. Benedict, 1901).

Signed by the Abbot of Solesmes, but actually written by Dom Moc-quereau, it was entitled: *To His Holiness Leo XIII. A Memorandum on the Studies by the Benedictines of Solesmes on the Restoration of the Liturgical Melodies of the Roman Church.*—Imprimerie St.-Pierre de Solesmes, n.d., 20 pages. It was divided as follows: Initial Work, Initial Publications (Dom Pothier):

A. Scientific Section: The *Paléographie Musicale*
    1. The photocopied manuscripts (the seven volumes that have appeared to date).
    2. The explanatory text in the *Paléographie Musicale:*
        1. Reading and deciphering the neumatic notations;
        2. Classifying the neumatic notations of Europe. Certain foundations are laid for the science of the *Paléographie Musicale.*
        3. Refutation of an objection drawn from the variety of neumatic scripts versus the agreement among the manuscripts.
        4. Study of the melody itself, its laws, its speech rhythm, its procedures, its beauty.
        5. Comparison of this beautiful Roman melody with the Medicean Ratisbon edition.
        6. The Ambrosian liturgy.

B. Practical Section (a total of 19 first editions).
    Books for the practice of teaching.
    Worldwide movement in favor of the Roman tradition.
    Appendix (other publications: Propers of dioceses, etc., 62 in all).

Cardinal Satolli gave the Memorandum and the Solesmes works on the chant to Leo XIII on March 23. Msgr. Respighi wrote to Dom Moc-quereau about it immediately:

This morning, His Eminence Cardinal Satolli gave the Memorandum and the books to the Holy Father. I do not yet know the details of their meeting. I saw His Eminence, who was returning from the meeting by car. His Eminence had the car brought to a stop, and he told me that the Holy Father welcomed the offering and the Memorandum with "great goodness and benevolence." He appeared to be quite pleased, and he inquired specifically about the project of the *Pontificale,* approving it in substance. For my part, I know nothing more, but it seems to me that it was an immense success.

On March 25, Msgr. Respighi wrote once again providing further details:

I visited Cardinal Satolli once again. He gave me a few more details about his meeting the day before yesterday. The Holy Father is well disposed in support of our cause. He accepted the Memorandum with pleasure, and approved of the idea of printing the *Pontificale* with the restored melodies. On this matter, however, His Holiness reserved the right to speak with the Cardinal Vicar to make use of the *Roman Commission*, exactly as we had foreseen.[106]

At that point, Msgr. Respighi recommended sending the Memorandum to Cardinal Rampolla, who was "very knowledgeable in archaeology and history," and to Cardinals Oreglia and Respighi. Msgr. Respighi said that this would guarantee the protection and assistance of four cardinals. Nevertheless, he cautioned that the strictest possible silence be maintained to avoid compromising everything.

The Memorandum was sent to other prelates, too, as confirmed by Father de Santi:

In Rome, only Cardinal Oreglia, the Cardinal Vicar, Cardinal Rampolla, and a few prelates who are interested in us received the Memorandum, which was entrusted to their discretion. In a few days, I will easily arrange to have a copy reach Cardinal Parocchi, Cardinal Gotti, Cardinal Vivès, and a few other cardinals. In this way, no noise will be made, and we will not have sounded the alarm in the enemy camp. This gives us greater hopes for a happy outcome. Any action or word whatsoever from the Holy Father, *at this moment*, would be extremely valuable,—a *simple* word of praise in favor of Solesmes, *at this moment*, would carry great weight. (Father de Santi, April 20, 1901)

49. The Plan for an International Commission (1901)

We have already noted that the Cardinal Vicar had appointed a Roman Commission on sacred music for the Diocese of Rome, the establishment of which was a terrible blow for the adversaries of traditional chant. Msgr. Respighi was nursing another project along at the moment, that of an international commission. He had already asked Dom Mocquereau for a list of musicians from all countries who, in his judg-

---

106. On April 19, Father de Santi wrote, once more, "The Holy Father's outlook remains unchanged, and today I learned from a highly-placed source how pleased he was to receive the books and the Memorandum."

ment, would be capable of taking part in this Commission (Respighi, February 18, 1901). Now the prelate's hopes were taking shape. He was hoping, in fact, that the Pope, who was interested in the project, would charge the Roman Commission with presenting names for the International Commission. In any event, any matter related to Gregorian chant would be submitted to the Roman Commission, at least in its capacity as an advisory body (Respighi, March 23, 1901).

Yet Father de Santi was even more explicit in a letter dated March 26, 1901. Regarding the Gregorian question, "the Pope wishes to make use of the Roman Commission established by the Cardinal Vicar." In this way, they could hope to see the melodies of the *Pontificale Romanum*[107] approved. Nevertheless, he added, the Commission is not competent:

They must be artists, and the purpose of the Roman Commission should be to appoint these men, to examine their work and the evidence that they provide in order to be approved. I believe that the monks of Solesmes are these artists par excellence, and that it will be necessary for Your Reverence to come to Rome for a while, in order to collate the manuscripts once again.

Writing on March 26, 1901, Father de Santi continued in the same vein:

When he came to Rome a few days ago, Cardinal Svampa thanked the Holy Father for his statements on the Gregorian question. Once again, the Holy Father confirmed everything. When the Cardinal added that it would be appropriate for me to write on this subject in order to educate the public about the terms of the matter, the Holy Father said that this was his desire, as well, and that he had spoken of the matter with the Superiors of *Civiltà Cattolica*. I have no illusions about this; to the contrary, I think that absolutely nothing will come of it. Nevertheless, I must remain ready.

It is clear that despite the happiness that recent successes had brought him ("I share *ex toto corde* in your domestic joy, which is also a joy shared by all your friends"), Father de Santi felt that he had to be prudent. He was not counting much on being freed from the threats that weighed against him.[108]

---

107. On April 19, Father de Santi wrote as follows on this matter: "Let us hope that the new *Pontificale* will become a reality. . . . It seems to me that the printing of a *Pontificale* at the Vatican, with the Solesmes melodies, is a matter of such importance that it is well worth a trip to Rome by Your Reverence."

108. One cardinal (Cardinal Ferratta) who had previously favored the Ratisbon edition was now thinking along the same lines as the Pope, and was speaking of full "freedom" for all, while continuing to proclaim the inalienable rights of Pustet (de Santi, April 19, 1901).

Furthermore, the traditional melodies continued to take root pretty much all over, and even in Rome itself:

The day before yesterday, I went again to hear the Schola at the South American College. I was quite pleased: now everyone has been won over, and the students are spreading the word in America by sending copies of the *Liber Usualis* as presents to their friends. That is why they are asking for so many. The curious thing is that through a contract that they have with Pustet, they send their books to Pustet to be bound; consequently, the Solesmes books go there, and return very well bound, indeed. Another piece of news: in the upcoming Holy Week triduum, the Basilica of St. Peter has entrusted the Gregorian chant to the Vatican Seminarians,[109] who, of course, will sing using the Solesmes books. Furthermore, after Easter, a Schola of 30 children or youths will be founded at the Basilica of St. Peter, under the direction of our professor Msgr. Antonio Rella. In this way, our chant will certainly make its way into St. Peter's. A similar Schola is being founded at St. John Lateran, and as we know, Capocci, the director, is on our side.

50. The Brief *Nos Quidem* to the Abbot of Solesmes (1901)

As we have already seen, Father de Santi said that "any action or word whatsoever from the Holy Father, at this moment, would be extremely valuable,—a simple word of praise in favor of Solesmes, at this moment, would carry great weight" April 20, 1901). In fact, both Father de Santi and Msgr. Respighi had an ardent desire for a document favoring the Gregorian cause, in response to the Memorandum and the tributes from Solesmes. After all, that was the goal they had pursued in suggesting this approach to Dom Mocquereau.

The Pope demonstrated his satisfaction right away. Thus the idea of a Brief addressed to the Abbot of Solesmes occurred to him. Msgr. Volpini was assigned to write the Brief, but in order to do so, he turned to Msgr. Respighi who, of course, consulted Father de Santi. On April 27, 1901, Father de Santi sent Dom Mocquereau a draft of the document that he was planning: "I am including here a draft of the Pontifical Brief that I have composed with great love, in keeping with the feelings expressed by the Holy Father to Msgr. Volpini."

---

109. De Santi, March 26, 1901; cf. March 31.

Leo XIII willed that the praises to be bestowed upon the labors of Solesmes would not, on the one hand, constitute a direct and formal approval, and on the other hand would not directly disparage the work of the Congregation of Sacred Rites. Yet Father de Santi had managed to insert enough praise into the text to give the document the importance that he expected it to have. He dwelt on the *Roman* origin of the traditional melodies, on the conservation of those melodies in the manuscripts, on the encouragement already given by the Pope to the work of Dom Pothier[110] (mentioning, too, that Dom Guéranger had been his inspiration), and on the practical nature, not merely the scientific nature, of the Benedictine editions which had revived traditional performance and were spreading everywhere, including in the Eternal City and at the Vatican Seminary.

Msgr. Respighi transformed Father de Santi's text before sending it to Msgr. Volpini. Father de Santi had certain regrets about the changes, since he had written the document with the greatest possible care, making certain not to compromise the authority of the Pope in any way.[111] Nevertheless, Msgr. Respighi's intention was not to diminish the importance of the document, because he said that the text he had sent, after touching it up, to Msgr. Volpini was "very flattering to Solesmes."[112] Might he have judged Father de Santi's text insufficiently prudent?

Nonetheless, on May 10 Msgr. Respighi wrote: "Everything nearly went up in smoke last week. There was an intervention that was hostile to us." Perhaps the Nuncio to Paris, Msgr. Lorenzelli who was then in Rome, had heatedly defended Pustet's cause. Yet Msgr. Respighi concluded:

The Holy Father, and this comes as a consolation, did not change how he feels about Solesmes, it's just that he feared Cardinal Aloysi [Masella] and the other adversaries. Yet these days the horizon is clearing once again, and the Holy Father has *once again* returned to his initial idea. So he will draw up a Brief, but perhaps a *very vague* one, though still useful.

110. This refers to the Brief of March 3, 1884, addressed to Dom Pothier when the *Liber Gradualis* was published.

111. For this reason Father de Santi complained of being left out, to a certain extent (cf. April 27, 1901), but there were fears of compromising everything by placing him too much in evidence.

112. Moneta-Caglio notes that the Pope had to overcome Msgr. Volpini's fears (*Musica Sacra*, 1960, p. 162).

In closing, Msgr. Respighi urged Dom Mocquereau to be patient: "Everything moves very slowly here in Rome." He said that this slowness should be expected in this case, in particular, given the importance of the document they were hoping for (May 10, 1901).

The Brief was submitted for the Pope's signature on May 18, a Saturday, noted Dom Mocquereau. Msgr. Respighi said, "No one told me of any reservations whatsoever made by His Holiness." He added that it had been impossible to make mention of Dom Pothier, solely because of the demands of the Curia. He said that the Brief was critically important despite its vague nature, because it praised the practice of the Benedictine editions (which eliminated the weight of the Counter-Brief of May 2, 1884, addressed to Dom Pothier),[113] and constituted indirect approbation regarding the use of these editions in the liturgy. He noted that under the present circumstances, one could not have hoped for anything more.[114] Finally, Msgr. Respighi concluded, even though its form is vague, the Brief would be exceptionally important, taken together with the *"importance of the timing* of its publication, since no sooner has the Pustet privilege expired than the Pope, saying nothing in support of Ratisbon, is turning rather toward Solesmes, with words of praise" (Respighi, May 19, 1901).

Father de Santi, for his part, expressed his satisfaction with the "new ideas and statements, which are most timely and effective," that were included in the Brief, although he continued to regret that his own, more explicit draft was not used. In *Civiltà Cattolica*, he wrote enthusiastic commentary on the pontifical document, which solved an apparently inextricable and thorny problem. It praised not only the purely scientific and theoretical work in support of the restoration of the traditional melodies preserved in the manuscripts, but also the use of the melodies at long last restored in the liturgy, and even the benefits of the method of performance that cast into sharp relief the beauty and loveliness of these original melodies, as well as their value as prayer. Above all, it placed emphasis on the encouragement and freedom proclaimed in support of similar work *(sollerter et libere)*. All in all, the document showed the way to be followed in the future in this area: the way of sci-

---

113. This counter-brief had restricted the practical implications of an earlier brief addressed to Dom Pothier on March 3, 1884, following the publication of the *Liber Gradualis* (Part 1, No. 39).

114. "We could have wished for more, but in Rome, everyone is accustomed to proceeding *piano*" (Respighi, May 19, 1901).

ence and art, of history and tradition.[115] In his letter, Father de Santi also added that Msgr. Respighi had heard from a reliable source that "His Holiness was speaking with evident satisfaction about the Brief that had been issued and that, as a result, our adversaries can no longer make their hostile insinuations" (Father de Santi, May 30, 1901).

Nevertheless, Father de Santi was still hesitant to have his name mentioned, despite the *sollerter et libere*, and it was through the good offices of Dom Janssens (Msgr. Respighi had taken the appropriate steps in this regard since he knew he would be away from Rome) that the Brief was communicated to the press, as soon as Solesmes had acknowledged receiving the document sent to it. The Brief was sent to *Germania* in Berlin, and to the *Voce della Verità*, which published it on Wednesday, May 29, while several copies had been sent to Berlin, Salzburg, Beuron, and to close friends on the evening of the 28th.

Msgr. Respighi expressed his satisfaction with even greater enthusiasm on June 2, from Monte Cassino, where he was staying:

Deo gratias! The Brief reached me at Benevento, where I had gone to visit some friends, who are themselves Gregorian enthusiasts. They were most pleased with it. I examined the Brief very attentively. I find it significant and excellent. The first reasons of exceptional importance come from the importance of the historical moment and the resolute manner in which the Holy Father desired that the Brief be issued, without worrying about the past, or any recriminations from Cardinal Aloysi [Masella], from the S.C.R., etc. We must also recall that five months ago, there was talk of imposing the Medicean edition in Rome. Let us also recall the large number of cardinals who exerted their influence in this happy outcome (of the matter): Oreglia, Rampolla, Satolli, the Cardinal Vicar, Svampa, Sarto, Parocchi, and so many others who did not, as these cardinals did, take direct action, but were with them in the communion of ideas. I will not list all the illustrious individuals, musicians, Italian and foreign artists, Catholic and non-Catholics, etc. The Brief was favored with a quasi-official promulgation in Friday's *Osservatore Romano*, copies of which will be sent to Your Reverence.

"The Brief is perfect," continued Msgr. Respighi, who produced a detailed analysis of it. Let us consider his comments on the word *constan-*

115. *Civiltà Cattolica*, 1901, vol. 2, pp. 726–727 (cf. *Revue du Chant Grégorien*, 1901, p. 31). The article is unsigned, as usual. Note, however, that although Father de Santi was unable to write about the sacred chant, "nonetheless," he himself said, "a few brief bibliographies are tolerated, and I take advantage of that to spread the word as best I can in support of our chant" (to Abbé H. Villetard, February 21, 1900).

ter, praise for perseverance in work despite contradictions and consequences: "so we were not rebels;"—approval of the use of the Benedictine editions, which the Counter-Brief of 1884 suppressed.

Here is the text of this document, which should be considered to
have been the *charter of the Gregorian restoration* until Saint Pius X.[116] At
Solesmes, the Brief was read in Chapter, and at the French Seminary, in
the refectory. Perosi was there, and witnessed the applause that greeted
the reading (Chronicle).

To Our dear Son, Dom Paul Delatte, of the Order of St. Benedict, Abbey of
Solesmes, Leo XIII, Pope

Dear Son, greetings and Apostolic Benediction.

We know indeed, and We have praised elsewhere the enlightened efforts
you have devoted to the science of those sacred chants whose origin is attributed by tradition to St. Gregory the Great.

In like manner We cannot fail to express approbation of the unremitting toil
which you have so painstakingly and unceasingly dedicated to research and to
publication of ancient monuments in this field. We have before us the various
fruits of your labors in the many volumes which you have graciously presented
to Us on different occasions and which, as We have learned, have already received widespread notice and which are even, in some places, in daily use.
Every undertaking which aims toward explaining and propagating the science
of plainchant, which is the ever-faithful subsidiary of the sacred rites, is worthy
of high praise not only for the spirit and the energy expended, but for the benefit which necessarily results for divine worship. For it was to make clear the
meaning of the words in the first place, that the Gregorian melodies were composed with perfect skill and taste. Provided only that they are sung artfully,
there is in those melodies a great power, at once gentle and solemn, to enter
easily into the hearts of the hearers and to arouse in them the movements of
prayer and of salutary thoughts. Hence it is fitting that all, in both the secular
clergy and the religious, who feel disposed toward the science or the art of ecclesiastical chant, apply themselves to it skillfully and freely *(sollerter et libere)*,
each according to his own ability. Their labors, as well as your own up to the
present, can exercise a beneficial influence on the issue, always presuming, of
course, that the precept of fraternal charity be observed, along with that of respectful obedience to Holy Church.

As a pledge of divine graces and in testimony of Our benevolence, We willingly grant to you and to your brethren the Apostolic Benediction.

---

116. Msgr. Moneta-Caglio points out the various comments made in the press on the Brief

Given at Rome, from St. Peter's, May 17, 1901, in the twenty-fourth year of Our Pontificate.

Leo XIII, Pope.

51. First Draft of the Vatican Edition (1901)

The supportive attitude of Leo XIII concerning traditional Gregorian chant and the possible despoilment of the property of religious congregations in France had already caught the attention of one publisher in Paris, whose representative was in Rome when the Brief to the Abbot of Solesmes appeared. Here is what Father de Santi wrote about it to Dom Mocquereau on May 30, 1901:

Another piece of news: for about a month now, a certain Mr. Etienne Védie has been here in Rome; he is handling a major edition of Gregorian books that the Poussielgue publishing company is planning to bring out. At first, he had some very unusual ideas; he was thinking of having all the principal manuscripts photographed, and of beginning the whole effort all over again, as though nothing had been done so far. Quickly he adopted a far wiser attitude, acknowledging that it would be absurd to proceed without Solesmes as the basis. Yet he added that there is some antagonism between Dom Pothier and Solesmes, and that he would side with Dom Pothier rather than with Solesmes. Finally, he recognized that although there may be divergent opinions, they cannot be very substantial, and he said that Poussielgue would reach an agreement with Solesmes for the new Paris edition. He says that he has the support of sixteen dioceses already, and that he expects sixty to support him in all.

If the Holy See is thinking of publishing an edition at the Vatican Press, he is offering to cover all costs, not in exchange for a monopoly or privilege, but to be the first to republish the Vatican Edition, the bulk of which would be done in Paris and, for the sake of appearances only, would be published with the Vatican frontispiece. Our triumvirs[117] and I have used our influence with this man—who seems to be a loyal individual, besides—to get him to agree not to do anything without Solesmes. It will then be up to Solesmes to deal with Poussielgue. I thought it a good idea to bring all this to your attention, although I would ask Your Reverence, naturally, to be discreet as to the source of this information.

Nos quidem, Musica Sacra 1960, p. 162.—The original text appears in Romita, *Jus Musicæ Liturgicæ,* 1947, p. 281.

117. Msgr. Respighi, Kanzler, and Perosi.

Védie submitted his request to Cardinal Rampolla, who spoke of it with the Pope. The Pope welcomed the idea, and forwarded the request to Cardinal Ferratta, Prefect of the Congregation of Sacred Rites (Father de Santi, June 14), where a thousand objections were raised. The traditional chant is hard to perform because it is very long; besides, the Gregorianists are far from reaching any mutual agreement, and the Ratisbon edition can be corrected; finally, authority wishes to remain free to publish an official edition whenever it might deem appropriate (Father de Santi, June 14).

On June 14, Father de Santi wrote:

Everyone is still convinced that the Prefect of Sacred Rites is powerless to object, given the Brief *Nos quidem* [the opening words of the Brief to the Abbot of Solesmes] and the firm desire of the Holy Father to follow the course He has set. So Mr. Védie enjoys great protection, and it does seem that he will manage to secure an even more explicit statement of freedom. Mainly, he is insisting that the Holy See have the Vatican Press begin an edition of liturgical books, seeking (as I wrote to you) to obtain preference for publishing ordinary editions, especially if the Holy See accepts the proposal of the Poussielgue publishing company, which is prepared to pay for the Roman edition. Mr. Védie has also said, in explicit terms in his Memorandum, that he wishes to proceed in joint agreement with the Benedictines of Solesmes. It would not have been possible to prevent Mr. Védie from acting here, and he is happy that he did not work independent of our influence.

In an audience with the Pope, Poussielgue's agent explained his project directly, and insisted that the freedom conceded to Solesmes be granted to everyone. The Pope responded (1) that for the time being, he had no plans to begin an edition of the chant, (2) that he had already presented his position on Gregorian chant in the Brief addressed to Solesmes, and (3) that the freedom in question applied to all, but that, for certain reasons, he did not deem it necessary to come out with a new statement (Father de Santi, June 23, 1901).—Védie was not very satisfied, and said so out loud; for a moment, Father de Santi feared that the situation may have been worsened. But now he was assured that Védie would reach an agreement with Solesmes. "Poussielgue stated emphatically that a new edition would be done under the direction of Dom Pothier and the Benedictines of Solesmes. And he wants me to be on the Steering Committee" (Father de Santi, July 12, 1901).

After two months of insistence and proposals, Védie did manage to obtain something, in the form of a rescript that established (1) the suppression of the Pustet privilege, and (2) the recognition of the editions legitimately in use. Here is a translation of the rescript: [118]

July 10, 1901
To Mr. Charles Poussielgue, Paris.

In response to the request that you presented through Mr. Étienne Védie regarding a new edition of Gregorian chant, the Congregation of Sacred Rites has declared that since the privilege granted to Herr Pustet of Ratisbon regarding the Medicean edition has expired, there is no objection on the part of the Congregation to printers, provided that they observe the customary rules, issuing new editions of the Medicean or of other editions legitimately in use in accordance with the declarations issued on this subject by the Holy See.

This is the response that the Congregation of Sacred Rites can make at this time to your request, as it would to any similar request presented to it either by the printers of the Congregation of Sacred Rites, or by others.

With sentiments of highest esteem, I profess myself to be your devoted servant,

†D. Panici, Archbishop of Laodicea
Secretary of the Congregation of Sacred Rites

At the last minute, Védie had obtained a slight change in favor of the Benedictine editions. The first version of the rescript allowed publishers to publish new editions of the Medicean or other notations in use according to the previous statements of the Holy See, phrasing that referred to the Brief sent to Dom Delatte. The final version was more explicit, and spoke of other notations that were *legitimately* in use according to statements issued on this matter by the Holy See, i.e. only the notations of Solesmes, so far.

On July 17, 1901, Father de Santi wrote:

The definitive text, therefore is as follows: *or of other editions legitimately in use in accordance with the declarations issued on this subject by the Holy See.* He (Védie) was unable to obtain anything more, but Cardinal Ferratta visited the ambassador, assuring him that these words implied the legitimacy of the Solesmes editions, and the power to print them; and finally, that reasons relating only to the Curia had prevented mentioning the Brief expressly in the document. They

<hr/>

118. *Tribune S. Gervais,* Sept.–Oct. 1901, p. 288.—*Revue du Chant Grégorien,* August 1901, p. 15.— See the Italian in F. Romita, *Jus Musicæ Liturgicæ,* 1947, p. 132.

only wanted to take a first step by removing the privilege of the Ratisbon books, placing them henceforth at the same level as the others. Later, open and explicit approval can be granted to the traditional chant.

On the same day (Respighi, July 17, 1901), Msgr. Respighi concluded:

This, then, is a reversal of everything that has been done so laboriously in 32 years. . . . Thanks to his activities, Mr. Védie has certainly achieved good results. He will go to Solesmes! In fact, he will have to act in perfect accord with the Benedictines. Oh, if only all publishers could come to such an understanding with Solesmes! The matter would then be resolved.

Father de Santi was hoping that Poussielgue would reach an agreement promptly with Solesmes, because he saw in such a move the unhoped-for means, immediately following the liberating Brief from Leo XIII, to expand yet further the traditional melodies printed in the Benedictine editions. On July 17, 1901, he wrote:

In his memoranda submitted to the Vatican and to the Congregation, he (Védie) always spoke of Solesmes with high esteem, telling everyone that the edition that Poussielgue wants to publish will be the Solesmes edition with any corrections or changes that might be made by mutual agreement by Dom Pothier and Solesmes. It was in this manner, and also on this condition, that we came to his assistance, and promised to do so in the future. So please keep me informed of everything, while keeping everything that I have told you on this matter to yourself.

Mr. Védie went to Solesmes in August 1901. He proposed that the Abbey take Poussielgue as its publisher, and work out an arrangement with him regarding a complete edition of all the books of plainchant. The idea was received even more favorably because the Imprimerie Saint-Pierre had never been an adequate instrument of propaganda, and besides, the departure of the Benedictines had already been decided upon, pursuant to the laws on Associations.

The Poussielgue project was immediately disclosed by the press as follows:

Relying on the freedom already officially indicated by pontifical acts and now reconfirmed, as of today Mr. C. Poussielgue is undertaking the publication of a major collection of Church chants in the Gregorian tradition, in concert with the Benedictines. In order to push the scientific and artistic perfection of these books as far as possible, while retaining their essentially practical nature, he has just founded an international commission of competent scholars and artists under the chairmanship of Dom Pothier, Abbot of Saint-Wandrille, the restorer of the Gregorian melodies, and of Dom Mocquereau, the Benedictine scholar at Solesmes, director of the *Paléographie Musicale*. (Tribune de S. Gervais, VII, p. 288)

Cooperation with Solesmes was, therefore, presented in this notice as something already achieved. This hasty statement was to harm the negotiations to a certain extent. The idea for the international commission certainly came from Father de Santi, and especially from Msgr. Respighi, who had already planned for one shortly after the Roman Commission on Sacred Music was established (see No. 49). In fact, there can be little doubt that they were the ones who got Poussielgue to accept the idea, along with the notion of working with Solesmes. The following letter may provide additional proof of this, as well.

Father de Santi was listening closely. On August 26, he wrote to Dom Mocquereau:

I would like to believe that any problems related to the Poussielgue matter have been smoothed out to your mutual satisfaction by now. The letter of invitation sent to the members of the Commission seems very well done, to me, and under the direction of Your Reverence and of Dom Pothier, everything will go smoothly. The international commission could appear necessary if the plan to produce a Vatican edition had been carried out, for the honor of the Holy See. But even in that case, the Commission would have had to decide whether to use the Solesmes edition as the basis for the Vatican Edition. No doubt, the answer would have been entirely favorable and the changes or corrections to be made would have been quite secondary, the very same ones that the Benedictines themselves would make in their reprints. This has always been my way of thinking, and so it was that I presented these ideas to Mr. Védie. Since the Holy See has not agreed to produce the edition, there remained this idea of a commission, but now its task is easier. Nevertheless, let the first questions that will be posed to the members of the Commission be asked. It is appropriate to obtain full approval from the Commission on behalf of the Benedictine edition, as it stands, and then to proceed promptly with a reprinting, making only those corrections deemed necessary for further improvement of the [musical] instruction. With regard to the idea of shortening the verses of the Graduals, and Alleluias, it seems that Mr. Védie did not express himself well, or that he was misunderstood. He wrote to me that he had simply wanted to say what I myself had said; but I never spoke of abbreviating anything, but I did say that the melodies must remain as they are and that singers who do not know them or cannot sing them could omit them, replacing them with the organ, or performing the psalms in another manner. We hope that everything will proceed with complete understanding on both sides and to the full satisfaction of the Benedictines at Solesmes.

The laws on Associations passed by the French legislature on July 1, 1901, imperiled the freedom and very existence of religious congregations. In an unsigned article, *L'examen de conscience d'un religieux*, an article of great dignity and nobility, the Abbot of Solesmes, Dom Delatte, expressed his point of view in the face of the persecutory laws, and chose exile for himself and his monks. The initial departures for the estate at Appuldurcombe,[119] on the Isle of Wight (England) took place in August, and the Divine Office was last celebrated at the abbey church of Solesmes on September 20, 1901. Dom Mocquereau left Solesmes on August 21. A few days earlier, on August 17, Dom Pothier had come to discuss Poussielgue's plans with Dom Delatte (Chronicles).

For Father de Santi, the fate of Solesmes was of critical interest in resolving the Gregorian question. Therefore, he and Msgr. Respighi wished to be "reassured on the new position" resulting from the departure of the monks and their exile in England. On October 25, 1901, Msgr. Respighi wrote: "Poussielgue has invited me, and a few others, to join the Commission for the new edition. But Perosi, Kanzler, and I have not yet responded. We are awaiting your instructions."

A month later, on November 20, 1901, Msgr. Respighi shared some of his fears with Dom Mocquereau:

I believe it useful to bring the following point to your attention. I know that Védie and Poussielgue are putting forward the name and the authority of Dom Pothier. I wrote to Dom Pothier about this, and, in a very interesting letter, he replied, word for word, that he conditionally approves the decision of Solesmes. I believe it necessary to send you Dom Pothier's letter, requesting that you return it to me as soon as possible. It seems to me that Pécoul is fanning the flames.

Finally, in the same letter, Msgr. Respighi spoke once more of the Pontifical, and asked whether someone from Solesmes might come to Rome to review the melodies.

This letter of Dom Pothier (to Msgr. Respighi, October 27, 1901) read as follows:

---

119. In 1908, the monks took up residence at Quarr Abbey, which they restored, also on the Isle of Wight. Dom Paul Bellot had built a monastery and a magnificent church there.

With regard to the matter initiated by Mr. Védie in the name of Mr. Poussielgue, I must say that I was informed rather late. It was after his long sojourn at Rome, and a visit to Solesmes, that Mr. Védie came to St. Wandrille to bring me up to date on the negotiations at Rome and Solesmes, and to ask for my cooperation. I promised him my support conditionally, i.e. after he had made firm arrangements with Solesmes and signed a formal agreement. So far everything has been verbal. But at this juncture, Solesmes is transferring its Imprimerie Saint-Pierre to Desclée. What will be the consequences of this sudden transfer, done hastily before the dispersal of the community? I have no idea. All I know is that there are discussions now underway between Solesmes and the Poussielgue publishing house, which plans to pursue the work, as announced with the approval of Solesmes and a real, if unsigned, understanding.[119bis]

Dom Pothier's letter alludes to the sale (although the matter was still at the negotiation stage) of the Abbey's press to the Desclée company in Tournai. Some explanation is needed to understand this move by Solesmes. The fact of transferring the press to a foreign publishing company that had already published the *Mélodies Grégoriennes* and the *Liber Gradualis* explains the choice. Perhaps they were hoping to escape more easily from the rapacious grasp of the liquidator of the religious congregations. But there was something else. In August 1901, at the same time the Poussielgue project was disclosed in the press, a brochure was published with the title *Le Chant Grégorien*, signed with the pseudonym *a Gallo-Roman*. The brochure was, in fact, the work of A. Pécoul, a former postulant at Solesmes who had become its furious adversary. Father de Santi had already pointed out that Pécoul was in Rome, where he was scheming.[120] Msgr. Respighi referred to him in the previous passage. In this brochure, which was published by Poussielgue, the name of Solesmes was never mentioned, not even in regard to the Brief of Leo XIII. The alert had been sounded at the Abbey, and there is no doubt that the involvement of the author of the brochure in the affairs of Poussielgue changed the course of events.

Furthermore, Solesmes considered itself the sole proprietor of the chant editions, on various grounds.[121] The initiative had come from Dom Guéranger; his successor had pursued the work tenaciously: the

---

119bis. Pothier's first reaction was more animated (Moneta-Caglio, *Musica Sacra* 1962, p. 72).

120. De Santi, June 23 and July 21, 1901.

121. This information, and the information that follows, is taken from a memorandum by Dom Noetinger, the Abbey Cellerar.

cost of the work had been paid by the Abbey and by it alone. The work was the fruit of the collaboration of several monks. Finally, monastic law recognized that the profits for the monks' work belong to the monastery and not to the monks themselves. But Poussielgue, advised by Pécoul, was opposing, in practice, the interests of Solesmes and those of Dom Pothier, who claimed to have acquired the copyright to the Solesmes chant editions. In this way, the Paris-based publisher could claim to have acquired ownership of the Benedictine editions, the monks of Solesmes and Dom Pothier being reduced to the role of merely cooperating in the work. Indeed, Dom Pothier wasted no time in signing a secret agreement with Poussielgue, on November 20, 1901.

In a letter dated February 11, 1902, sent to the Abbot of Solesmes, Dom Pothier explained his intentions by saying that he believed he was authorized to sign the agreement because, in the eyes of the law, he thought he was the lawful owner. He added:

This made it seem to me that not only was I allowed, but I was truly obligated to accept the arrangement being offered by the publisher, while observing, of course, the reservations imposed by canon law and the rules of religious congregations, limitations that were drawn up in writing and deposited separately. These are the current circumstances, which enable me to save all or part of the inventory of the Imprimerie Saint-Pierre, which imposes on me the duty to find the means to do so. I have been assured that these means are the arrangement I mentioned above. The grounds have been tested, they assure me, and claims based upon them will be accepted.[122]

Since the Imprimerie Saint-Pierre had been closed, on the other hand, and it was no longer possible to prevent the publications from appearing, the Abbot of Solesmes contacted M. Desclée, who had already published Dom Pothier's *Les Mélodies Grégoriennes* in 1880 and the *Liber Gradualis* in 1883, ultimately signing an agreement with him (in April 1902).[123] But it was agreed with Mr. Desclée that if Mr. Poussielgue were to prove more understanding, he would be given preference. Mr. Desclée immediately entered into discussions with him. As a result, on November 25, 1901, Dom Mocquereau replied to Msgr. Respighi that al-

---

122. Cf. Moneta-Caglio, Musica Sacra, p. 73, note 264. Letter in the same vein from Dom Pothier to Msgr. Respighi, December 27, 1901.

123. First to continue publication of the *Paléographie Musicale,* and then, somewhat later, to publish the chant books of Solesmes.

though the sale of the Press certainly changed the question, Solesmes was not refusing to deal with Mr. Poussielgue:

It is clear that the transfer of our press to Mr. Desclée has changed our relationship with the Poussielgue company completely. The agreement made with Mr. Desclée no longer allows us to make any deals with Mr. Poussielgue without the involvement of Mr. Desclée. We have been aware of the details of this agreement at Appuldurcombe for a few days now. Therefore, if Mr. Poussielgue intends to implement his plans, he must come to an agreement not only with us, but with Mr. Desclée, as well. This is the general tenor of what we will write to Mr. Poussielgue. If the two companies manage to reach an understanding, then fine; we will not stand in the way of that. But no matter what, it must remain clearly understood that under no circumstances may the agreement mention a third party as co-proprietor of the publications. The Abbot of Solesmes, like his predecessors, intends to remain the sole proprietor of the liturgical publications already produced, and of those yet to come. He reserves the right to assign the work as he sees fit. It is easy to appreciate the fairness and wisdom of this decision: it avoids the countless problems that would arise among monasteries were it not followed. We find it utterly repugnant to deal with Poussielgue for the simple reason that Pécoul . . . is involved in this matter.

The negotiations between Solesmes-Desclée and Poussielgue dragged on until late in 1902, without resolution. Poussielgue, a Paris-based publisher, maintained a relationship with Pécoul, who was in contact with Ménage, the liquidator of the religious congregations. It is curious to note that the conclusions reached by the liquidator concerning the Benedictines' literary proprietorship coincided precisely with the termination of negotiations between Poussielgue and Desclée. The liquidator filed suit against Desclée, whose claims regarding the monastery Press—which was included in the liquidation—were rejected.[124]

There is no reason to dwell further on this affair. Our purpose was simply to point out the reasons for the failure of negotiations with Solesmes. Yet it is also important to retain this idea of an international commission presided over by Dom Pothier, because it is an idea that was to resurface in 1904 with the Vatican Commission.

Our Roman friends were deeply saddened by the failure of the discussions between Solesmes and Poussielgue, for they had been hoping for a quick solution of the matter of the chant books, immediately fol-

---

124. The sale of the press to Mr. Desclée was dated September 8 and 10, 1901. The sale was recorded at Sablé on October 2, cf. Dom L. Guilloreau, *La Stamperia di S. Pietro a Solesmes*, in *Rassegna Gregoriana*, 1906, col. 115–126.

lowing the Brief to the Abbot of Solesmes and the failure to renew the Pustet privilege. They had no reason to believe that such an occasion would come their way again any time soon.

In addition, in a draft letter to Dom Mocquereau that is undated, was never sent, and certainly dates from before the letter of November 20, 1901 cited above, Msgr. Respighi wrote:

I have been assured, and I can assure Your Reverence, *in modo riservato*, that the Poussielgue affair has recently been emphasized at the Congregation of Sacred Rites, in order to prevent the Pope from speaking more clearly in support of Solesmes.

In fact, there had been a great deal of talk about the project, and there was even talk of a truce between Ratisbon and Solesmes (Msgr. Moneta-Caglio, *Musica Sacra*, 1962, pp. 75, 98, and 112).

The Brief to Dom Delatte had other immediate and effective results. At Fribourg, Dr. Peter Wagner immediately conceived the idea of establishing a Gregorian Academy, for which he sought and received the Apostolic Blessing, through the good offices of Cardinal Satolli, Prefect of the Congregation of Studies. In the letter that Cardinal Satolli sent to Wagner on June 18, 1901, there is explicit mention of the Brief *Nos quidem* (to Dom Delatte), as a succinct indication of the Pope's thinking with regard to this matter. The Academy of Fribourg opened in November 1901, and at the same time, in Rome, Father Hartmann of the Friars Minor was launching a School of Sacred Music, under the patronage of Cardinal Vicar Pietro Respighi. Msgr. Carlo Respighi and Father de Santi were counting heavily on this school, but unfortunately, it did not survive for long.[125]

52. The Rhythmic Synthesis of Dom Mocquereau— Volume VII (1901)

Since October 1900, the fascicles of Volume VII of the *Paléographie Musicale* had been publishing the eleventh-century *Antiphonale Tonale Missarum*, Codex H. 159 from the library of the École de Médecine in Montpellier. The volume began with a brief Notice (pp. 9–18) on this

125. *Civiltà Cattolica,* 1901, vol. 3, pp. 222–223: *Scuola Romana di Musica Sacra;—Musica Sacra,* Toulouse, October 1901, pp. 116, 121;—*Revue du Chant Grégorien,* 1901, pp. 10–11.

bilingual manuscript, in which the sung pieces are grouped by mode and are notated in neumes accompanied by alphabetic notation of the pitches. From the time the series began to appear, Dom Mocquereau had been asked to publish this manuscript, but he had wanted to place greater emphasis on manuscripts for liturgical use, rather than a "school" manuscript.

The manuscript was accompanied by a long treatise entitled *Du rôle et de la place de l'accent tonique latin dans le rythme grégorien*. This essay was the fruit of many years of effort. Dom Mocquereau may well have had the intuition for his rhythmic synthesis as early on as 1891 (cf. No. 23). In any event, his studies of the Latin tonic accent and the *cursus* published in the *Paléographie Musicale* revealed to him the secrets of the structure of the Gregorian melodies, the spiritual nature of the Latin accent, and the preeminence of musical rhythm over the rhythm of the words.[126]

In 1897, at the beginning of his *Petit Traité de Psalmodie*, Dom Mocquereau had announced the publication of a practical method of Gregorian chant. But this practical method was to be preceded by a treatise that would be a broad inquiry and a great synthesis of Gregorian rhythm. This was the subject of Volume VII, the study accompanying the phototype publication of the Montpellier manuscript. That study was divided into the following sections:

L'accent tonique et les compositeurs de musique religieuse (pp. 25–127).

L'accent tonique latin dans l'enseignement de l'École de Solesmes (pp. 128–165).

Le rythme et le mot latin (pp. 166–242).

Le membre de phrase et le mot latin (pp. 243–257).

La période (pp. 258–296).

Chironomie du mouvement rythmique (pp. 297–308).

Le rythme et l'harmonie (pp. 309–341).

Vue d'ensemble sur le plan de ce volume (pp. 342–344).

Appendices (pp. 345–368).

Tables.

---

126. For his discussion of this issue, see *La Psalmodie romaine et l'accent tonique latin* (Rodez, 1895) and in *L'Art grégorien, son but, ses procédés, ses caractères* (1896).

The rhythmic synthesis of Dom Mocquereau is well known. Indeed, to discuss it here would be to stray from our subject. Let us merely note that for Dom Mocquereau, Gregorian rhythm is no longer the rhythm of speech, but musical rhythm, depending more on the melody than on the text. In this sense, he was fully aware that he was in line with his predecessors, whose teachings he was merely perfecting. For him, rhythm was still free, not subject to measures, combining at will binary and ternary elements; yet the rhythm is also precise, because it is made up of precise values, as are the elementary rhythms and compound rhythms. Rhythm, according to Dom Mocquereau, is also emancipated from intensity, and rhythmic footfalls often come to rest on the soft final syllables of words with the light and lively Latin tonic accent.[127]

In practical terms, the first rhythmic indications appeared in 1897, in a small volume published by Dom Mocquereau with the Schola Cantorum press. It contained a selection of Gregorian chants and medieval music taken from the books of Dom Pothier and transcribed into modern notation by Dom Mocquereau. The rhythm was transcribed in this work by means of a complicated system of points placed above the melodies. Later, Dom Mocquereau published various books of Gregorian chant in modern notation, and he simplified his system of rhythmic notation: only the ictus were marked, by a point placed above the musical staff, a form of writing that he also used for modern notation until the appearance of the Vatican Edition.

The notation using points within the musical staff in square notation appeared in 1899,[128] with the *Missae Propriae Ordinis Minorum Sancti Francisci Cappuc.* (Solesmes), where we also find the *oriscus* and the quarter bar. Vertical episemas attached to the notes[129] and horizontal episemas appear in 1900 in various publications from the monastery Press or from the Biton Press.[130] In 1901, we find, for the first time, a Preface addressing the binary and ternary groups and subgroups, as an introduction to a *Kyriale* (Solesmes, 1901). In addition, at the front of the

127. Dom Mocquereau expanded on his teachings in a more didactic format in the *Nombre Musical Grégorien* (I, 1908 and II, 1927). But the first chapters were published as early as 1906 in *Church Music* (Philadelphia) under the title *Gregorian Rhythm. A Theoretical and Practical Course* (1906–1909) (cf. *infra*, No. 86 and note 245bis).

128. As well as in 1897, in a Sequence from an Office of St. Hilary of Poitiers.

129. It was later, following the decree of February 14, 1906, that Dom Mocquereau detached the ictus from the note.

130. *Chants des Offices extraits du Paroissien noté de Solesmes et des Variae Preces* . . . (Ordinary of the Mass, hymns, etc.). Biton, 1900.

Manuel de la Messe et des Offices extrait du Paroissien Romain et des Variæ Preces de Solesmes, published by Desclée in 1902, a foreword explained the reason for this change of publisher, the exile of the monks in England, and the sale of the monastery Press to Mr. Desclée.

The most significant of these books was the *Paroissien Romain* published by Desclée in late 1903. This was a new edition of the *Paroissien* and of the *Liber Usualis* of 1896, with the same format (in-12) and the same layout (texts and chants of the Mass and the Office for all Sundays and double feasts). The book bore the Imprimatur of the Master of the Sacred Palace, dated October 9, 1903 (and soon it was also to bear the Imprimatur of the Congregation of Sacred Rites, dated February 24, 1904). The rhythmic indications and the expressive signs taken from the St. Gall manuscripts were used much more extensively in these publications than in previous works, since the rhythm was marked throughout these books according to the principles advanced by Dom Mocquereau. The musical writing was perfected: the neumes were transcribed with greater accuracy, and they contained new neumes, as well (the *oriscus* and the *salicus*), the bars of the notation were distributed more wisely, and the quarter bar replaced the half bar at the incises. In addition, the melodies themselves had been revised and corrected in part. We say "in part" because the comparative tables that Dom Mocquereau had drawn up for this purpose were generally limited to the study of formulas: more than a hundred, however, were revised in accordance with some twenty manuscripts, which made it possible to provide various improvements in the details of melodies restored by Dom Pothier in the *Liber Gradualis* and the *Antiphonal*.[131] There had been a precedent for this revision of the melodies in the *Officium et Missae Nativitatis D.N.J.C. juxta Missale et Breviarium Romanum* (Desclée, 1902, No. 571, 47 pp.). It is easy to discern the reason: the government of the French Republic had taken possession of the Solesmes press, and of the entire stockpile of books legitimately sold to Messrs. Desclée. The old Benedictine editions would have to be cleared of added marks if they wanted to begin publishing them again.[131bis] The *Paroissien Romain* was a great success,

131. Cf. C. Gaborit, *Le Nouveau Manuel grégorien*, in *Tribune de S. Gervais* 1903, p. 12.

131bis. Here is how Dom Mocquereau explained this matter to Msgr. Respighi on April 28, 1903: "The legal proceedings between Ménage and the Desclée firm will begin soon. To save the chant of Solesmes, it has become necessary to provide a demonstration, even a public demonstration, by which I mean in the newspapers, of the new works, and of the new research done on the manuscripts in order to perfect our old editions, and thereby, to make it possible for us to

and went through five editions in 1903 and 1904. The Latin-language editions of the work, published under the title *Liber Usualis*, were the most widely distributed of them all.

Once the *Manuel de la Messe et des Offices* was approved, Father de Santi and Msgr. Respighi told Dom Mocquereau of their surprise at these changes. According to them, the introduction of rhythmic indications into the Solesmes books could only result in difficulties for the hoped-for approval by the Congregation of Sacred Rites. In fact, there was no such difficulty, as the editions of Solesmes were approved by that Congregation on February 24, 1904.

However, Dom Mocquereau received a veritable indictment from Father de Santi in late November 1902, to which he responded point by point on November 27. The lack of books, he wrote, cannot be attributed to Solesmes, which was required to go into exile and was deprived of its press. The signs for rhythmic punctuation indisputably make the performance of the chant easier and, in general, they have been well received. Besides, the episemas do not deform the Gregorian writing, but, on the contrary, they perfect it

in the manner of the points, dashes, boldface dashes, and countless romanian letters in the oldest manuscripts. Thus, far from leading us astray from the ancient tradition, we are taking steps that draw us ever closer to it. . . . Nothing is easier to prove than the fact that the *main reason* for the decadence and ruin of the chant of Holy Mother Church was the inadequacy of ecclesiastical notation to express rhythm. It was inadequate from the *tonal* perspective, as well . . . So I believe, Father, that in order to prevent decline and to assure unity, it is necessary to establish now a rhythmic tradition that is as close as possible to that of the ancient masterpieces.

Dom Mocquereau concluded by announcing the revision of the musical notation of the preceding Solesmes editions, which was to be yet another source of discontent among our friends in Rome.

In passing, Dom Mocquereau had also criticized the accompaniments of Giulio Bas, advocated by Father de Santi.

The accent that is always struck, the accent that always coincides with the chord on the down pulse of the rhythm, in a word the "metric principle" with all its attendant harshness, there is the great error of the moderns when it

escape the greed of that sad person and of those who are pushing him from behind the scenes" (Moneta-Caglio, *Musica Sacra,* 1962, p. 78).

comes to the rhythm. Dom Pothier pointed that out a long time ago. Read carefully his article on the *Ave maris stella (Revue du Chant Grégorien*, January 15, 1895, p. 84); the matter cannot be stated better or more accurately. I adopt this theory in its entirety, and I taught it already in 1896, in my lecture on *L'Art Grégorien*. Daily practice confirms us in these principles. Dom Gatard teaches exactly the same thing at Westminster Cathedral.

This is of enormous importance in coming to understand all the beauty, all the suppleness, I would say the *spirituality* of the Gregorian rhythm. Many musicians, I know, do not even have the slightest inkling about the theory of the freedom of the accent, the theory of pure rhythm; they find that scandalous, but a great many others, broader-minded, more welcoming, accept it fully. One of them—and I could list many others as well—M. Laloy, editor-in-chief of the *Revue d'Histoire et de Critique Musicale* in Paris, whom I saw at Solesmes and to whom I explained our entire theory of rhythm, wrote to me not long ago: "Your study [on accent and rhythm] seems quite incontrovertible. . . . I would be happy to make whatever modest contribution I could to this work where science and musical feeling will find equal consideration, and *from which art will emerge freer and more alive.*"

In a memorandum sent to Bas on January 19, 1903, Dom Mocquereau wrote, with regard to the accompaniment of Gregorian chant:

The role of the accompaniment, relative to the rhythm, is to follow the rhythm of the Gregorian melody. The accompaniment must proceed *at the same pace* as the melody, rest where the melody itself pauses. The ordinary place of the chords, therefore, is entirely indicated in the rhythmic alighting places. But given the infinite suppleness, the movement, the soaring flight, the spirituality of the Gregorian rhythm, accompaniment is always a threat to it; it is akin to clothing the melody in heavy armor. The lighter, the more subtle it is, the better. No accompaniment would be best of all. In all our major renditions, we have always eliminated accompaniment.

53. The *Rassegna Gregoriana* (1901–1902)

As early as 1895, there had been talk of establishing a journal of Gregorian chant for Italy. The original idea for this journal seems to have come from Father de Santi, the first to conceive of the project. On June 4, 1895, he told Dom Mocquereau that he wanted the Italian Benedictines to publish a review along the lines of the Grenoble-based *Revue du Chant Grégorien,* founded in 1892 by Father Vincent-Martin.[132] But on November 3, 1900, it was Msgr. Respighi who stated that he, as well as Perosi, had decided to publish a Gregorian journal, and he had asked Dom Mocquereau to agree to work on it. On February 20, 1901, it was once again Father de Santi who stated that he had always wanted a Gregorian journal to be published in Italy, but, he added, who should be entrusted with publishing it, since he himself was still condemned to silence? A letter from Msgr. Respighi dated May 19, 1901, sheds little light on this matter. In that letter, he asked for cooperation from Solesmes, and spoke of the project they had going with Father de Santi and himself:

We are in the process of putting together a *Rivista Romana di Canto gregoriano,* but the journal needs the cooperation of Solesmes. Therefore, please let me know if it would be possible for Solesmes to make a contribution to the journal, through an agreement of some kind, and a few articles . . . at least *six* per year. The *Revue Romaine* would be the coup de grâce *(ictus gratiae)* for Ratisbon.

Similarly, a letter from Father de Santi dated May 30 adds little in the way of clarification. In the letter, he states that, an understanding with Desclée having been reached, the journal would be published starting July 1, 1901, and he added, "We are counting heavily on support from Solesmes"—the "we" referring to Msgr. Respighi and himself. This request for cooperation was repeated more urgently on June 14, 1901:

Desclée has already started the new publication of the *Rassegna Gregoriana,* a journal that I have always wanted so very much. Here we are in mid June, and almost no one is doing anything . . . It seems to me that such a journal in Rome can be of extraordinary helpfulness to the Gregorian cause, and that everyone must work hard to support this publication and to maintain its scientific character, without neglecting practice, as well.

The good Jesuit, always so prudent, continued: "Remember that I cannot do any writing. I can provide them some assistance in an indirect way. . . . It is critical for Solesmes to help us . . ." (June 14, 1901). In this letter, and in another dated June 23, 1901, we find evidence that the initiative for the proposal for a journal comes from Father de Santi, who had always been so desirous of it, and who finally found someone who could take over management of the journal in his place. On June

132. In December 1892, he had already written to Dom Mocquereau about this journal: "Give me some information, if you can, about the Gregorian journal" (December 18, 1892).

23, 1902, he wrote: "Msgr. Respighi is taking charge of the *Rassegna*, and he tells me that he would be delighted to accept your work on the Psalmody of the Mass and the Responses."[132bis] On July 12, 1901, Father de Santi spoke of "Msgr. Respighi's *Rassegna*, which cannot be published yet because the Right Rev. Dom Pothier has not sent the articles he promised, and because of other problems as well. . . . The journal will be called *Gregorius*. . . ." In November and December 1901,[133] it was Msgr. Respighi who finally announced the imminent publication of the *Rassegna Gregoriana* (the title they kept), the first issue of which dates from January 1902. Father de Santi remained quite interested in the project. On March 21, 1902, he complained that the *Rassegna* had few subscribers, and he was still asking for Solesmes' cooperation for articles on the liturgy.

In fact, Solesmes contributed significantly to the editing of the journal. Not only did Dom Mocquereau (starting in 1904) write some ten articles on Gregorian paleography, along with Dom G. Beyssac, but Dom Cagin and Dom Pierre de Puniet made other contributions, as well, on liturgical matters. Soon, in 1910, Solesmes became involved in editing the bibliography.

The first issue of the *Rassegna* appeared in January 1902. The first article was the 1901 Brief from Leo XIII to Dom Delatte, the "Charter of the Gregorian Restoration" as our Roman friends called it. On March 12, the feast of St. Gregory the Great, the first three issues were presented to the Pope, with a letter signed by the main contributors in Rome. But none of the articles on chant were signed by Father de Santi, even though he wrote to Dom Mocquereau, on July 26, that the full burden of producing the journal fell to him: corrections, translations, and articles that Msgr. Respighi signed. "Since I am not yet free," he wrote, "I must do my work as though in hiding. . .". The issue was that his Superior General did not want him to be involved in chant matters (a point about which Father de Santi often complained to Dom Mocquereau),[134]

132bis. Nonetheless, on July 25, 1901 Father de Santi was still thinking of Father Hartmann for the position of Director of the Journal—which would have been the publication of his School of Sacred Music in Rome (Moneta-Caglio, *Musica Sacra* 1962, p. 74, no. 266, from a letter of De Santi to Casimiri).—On the cooperation of Dom Mocquereau in the *Rassegna*, cf. *Études Grégoriennes* II, 1957, pp. 188–203.

133. November 20 and December 12.

134. Cf. June 23, 1901, and August 26, 1901.—On June 10, 1902, he said to Father Villetard: "The soul of the new journal is Msgr. Respighi. I fan the flames from behind; that must suffice for now."

which made the Pope's good disposition where he was concerned rather pointless (cf. November 20 and December 12, 1901).

54. A Time for Waiting—Congress of Bruges (1902)

One year after the memorable date when Leo XIII had opened a new path for traditional Gregorian chant by pronouncing the liberating words that had been so long awaited, Msgr. Respighi told Dom Mocquereau that the Pope had decided to have the in-folio edition of the *Pontificale Romanum* printed at the Vatican Press. Msgr. Respighi added,

As for the chant section, the Holy Father has entrusted that to the Benedictine priests. I am to notify you of this in the name of the Cardinal Vicar. I would ask you to pass word of this along to Reverend Father Abbot, confidentially.

After giving various details, Msgr. Respighi concluded by saying that the issue was of great importance, for this might well prove to be a precedent that could be invoked in support of other editions (January 12, 1902). He also passed along the request, through Father de Santi, that the chants proper to the Consecration of Churches be prepared first of all.[135] The Abbot hastily agreed to the cooperation requested of Solesmes, with regard to liturgy and music alike, for both of these elements had been foreseen by Msgr. Respighi, while pointing out that preparation of the chants had been entrusted by him to Dom Pothier in July 1901 (Dom Mocquereau, January 18, 1902).

Another anniversary came around in May 1902, that of the Brief to Dom Delatte. Our friends in Rome, who were always prepared to seize any occasion that came along to clarify and shore up the situation regarding the Gregorian cause, made this date into an occasion. Indeed, Msgr. Respighi took it upon himself to send a letter of thanks to the Pope, as did Dr. Wagner and Dom Horn on behalf of the *Rassegna*, the Académie Grégorienne in Fribourg, and the *Rundschau* founded in 1902. So he asked the Abbot of Solesmes to write to the Holy Father, as well (Respighi, May 10, 1902).

The time for action seemed all the more propitious to him as the struggle continued and the *sollerter et libere* of Leo XIII still remained a

---

135. The volume appeared in 1904, under the title *Ritus consecrationis Ecclesiae juxta Pontificale Romanum* (Desclée 1904). Dom Delatte entrusted the work of preparing this edition to Dom Pothier, whom he also had prepare the Monastic *Responsory* (Dom Mocquereau, January 18, 1902).

dead letter, and he recommended that Cardinal Rampolla be brought in to intervene in that regard (May 10, 1902).

On August 6, 1902, he notified Dom Mocquereau that the Congregation of Sacred Rites seemed to wish to readdress the Gregorian question, and that there were grounds to fear that all might be lost. Then he asked, once more, to do something to make the situation clearer and more solidly established:

All I could send to the Pope was a brief memorandum that was well received. I wrote a strongly worded letter to the Cardinal Secretary of State, but I can do a little more. It has been suggested to me in high places, as well, that I ask our friends to act. I begin by asking you to explain to Father Abbot the difficulty of the moment, and the need for us to get moving, as well. I believe that Reverend Father Abbot could write to Cardinal Rampolla and to His Eminence Satolli, and to the Pope himself, in whatever terms he thinks most fitting.

At the same time, Msgr. Respighi was writing to Dom Pothier. Then, on August 7, he sent the following note to Dom Mocquereau:

As a follow-up to today's letter, let me add that I know that the Congregation of Sacred Rites will take up this matter in an extraordinary session, sometime shortly after the 15th, without questioning any of us. I give you this news in the strictest confidence, so that you may alert Father Abbot.

At that time, from August 7–10, 1902, the Musical Workshop of the Schola Cantorum of Charles Bordes was being held at Bruges. The occasion was a great success for the cause of traditional Gregorian chant and for sacred music worthy of the name. There were four hundred delegates from eight countries in attendance.

Father H. Villetard represented the *Rassegna Gregoriana* at the meeting, and Dom Gatard went on behalf of Solesmes. Father Villetard made a presentation about the new Italian journal, and summarized the situation in support of traditional Gregorian chant in Italy, particularly in Rome. Msgr. Respighi had warned him of the intentions of the Congregation of Sacred Rites in favor of Pustet and, while counseling him to adopt a prudent stance, suggested that the Congress pass a tribute to Leo XIII in gratitude for "the new path opened by the Brief to the Abbot of Solesmes, in total harmony with science and art." Cardinal Rampolla responded to it with equal prudence. Professor Wagner repeated Msgr. Respighi's request, and on August 7, he wrote to Charles Bordes:

I have just learned that the Ratisbon supporters in Rome are growing active again, and that a new act of the Congregation of Sacred Rites is threatening us. I ask you to send a strongly worded protest to Cardinal Rampolla against any new favor [with regard to] the Ratisbon books, in the name of scholarship and Christian art, signed by the Congress itself, or if that should prove impossible, by you, as Director of the Chanteurs de Saint-Gervais and of the Schola Cantorum; by M. Tinel as Director of the École Belge de Musique Sacrée, and by all our friends. *This matter is most urgent. Videatis, consules!*

During one of the meetings, the following telegram was read aloud. The telegram had been sent from Padua and was signed by several notable Italian figures in music and Gregorian chant, including Father de Santi, Msgr. L. Bottazzo, and Msgr. Casimiri: "We proclaim our support of this music Congress, applauding the triumph of the Gregorian cause."

A few days later, on August 23, 1902, Msgr. Respighi wrote:

The Pope is still immutably attached to the Brief to Solesmes and to the position created through it for the traditional melodies. In this spirit, His Eminence Cardinal Rampolla responded aloud and in writing, and this when the Congregation of Sacred Rites is threatening to adopt a new pro-Ratisbon position. (To Casimiri, quoted by Msgr. Moneta-Caglio, *Musica Sacra*, 1962, p. 75, No. 269.)[136]

Finally, on December 24, Father de Santi sent more reassuring news:

You were aware of the forming of the Liturgical Commission, recently set up by Cardinal Ferratta for the Congregation of Sacred Rites. This is a serious matter, one destined to do great good. They have already met once, and Father Ehrle came away from it very pleased. The Commission is authorized to consult other scholars, according to the needs and special competence of each. They talked about the *Pontifical*, as being the most pressing matter. And so the thinking is that the other liturgical books, as well, will be subjected to a new revision, and that the infamous "typical" editions of Pustet will ultimately fall by the wayside as chant books.

In the midst of these conjectures, Father de Santi continued to regret the fact that no understanding was reached with Poussielgue, all the

---

136. On the Congress of Bruges: H. Villetard, Personal files—*Revue du Chant Grégorien* 1902–1903, pp. 40, 60—(French translation of the *Rassegna Gregoriana*, 1902, col. 155ff).—To gain some idea of the displeasure among the partisans of Ratisbon occasioned by the success of the Congress, see the report of it published in the *Courrier de Saint Grégoire*, of Liège (A. Dirven, *Le Congrès de Bruges*), August 1902, pp. 54–60.

more so in that Cardinal Ferratta had committed himself to a certain extent to approve its editions (Respighi, April 16, 1902).

On April 12, 1902, Dom Mocquereau was chosen by his abbot as claustral prior of Solesmes in exile at Appuldurcombe, a position he retained until June 18, 1908. The following year he had to return to France for health reasons, from early June until mid August. It was at Dax, where he was being treated, that he completed an article written for the *Tribune de Saint-Gervais*.[137] In this long study entitled *À travers les manuscrits, étude sur une cadence des traits du VIIIᵉ mode* (signed at Dax, July 10, 1903), he wished

to give all the friends of Gregorian chant an example of the procedures that we use in correcting our books. These procedures are slow and very laborious, but they lead us to results that are as accurate as they are solid, that are an even greater delight for the artist and the monk desirous of the beauty of the divine office as for the archaeologist and the paleographer.

We include this sentence here, for it truly reveals the profound piety of Dom Mocquereau. In the same journal, Dom Mocquereau published his *Préface du Manuel de la Messe et de l'Office*[138] that was intended for the editions in modern notation; he justified the use of that notation in this preface. In truth, Father de Santi had used it first in his initial Gregorian performances in Rome, in order to facilitate the task of the chanters who had little experience with the square notation.

We must also point out the publication entitled *Officium Majoris Hebdomadae juxta Missale et Breviarium Romanum* (Desclée 1903, No. 578), a revised and corrected edition with rhythmic indications. We have already seen that these changes in the melody and rhythm were not to the liking of our Roman friends. The year 1903 was spent in discussions between Father de Santi and Dom Mocquereau, as witnessed by the correspondence received from Rome. Nonetheless, Father de Santi was quick to recognize the legitimacy of these melodic changes, and the usefulness of these rhythmic indications. On this latter point, Father de Santi wrote in December 1903: "I personally recommend the punctuated Gregorian edition warmly, because I believe that it is very useful for the seminarians" (December 20, 1903).

137. *Tribune de Saint-Gervais* 1903, pp. 202, 275, 327.
138. *Tribune de Saint-Gervais* 1903, p. 420; 1904, p. 35.

B ■ THE WORK OF ST. PIUS X

III ■ THE NEW LEGISLATION OF PIUS X

It was St. Pius X, elected Pope in August 1903, who brought the Gregorian restoration movement to its fulfillment. We will see the assistance provided to Pius X by Father de Santi, with regard to both the wording of the *motu proprio* of November 22, 1903, and that of April 25, 1904, and the establishment of the Vatican Commission responsible for reforming the liturgical books of Gregorian chant. Yet, although the honor for this restoration is justly due to this great Pope, it is equally just to point out those who promoted that movement.[139]

55. The Initial Thought of Pius X

On August 4, 1903, Cardinal Sarto was elected Pope. Msgr. Carlo Respighi and Father de Santi immediately shared their joy and their hopes with Dom Mocquereau.

As early as August 27, Msgr. Respighi obtained a blessing for the *Rassegna Gregoriana* and a word of encouragement in favor of musical reform in general. But in the view of Father de Santi, who was then away from Rome, Msgr. Respighi had lost the opportunity to obtain an immediate public declaration in favor of traditional Gregorian chant (Father de Santi, September 16, 1903).

It was on September 18, during an audience, that Msgr. Respighi sought a blessing for those who were involved in the cause of Gregorian chant and spoke to the Pope of his friends from Solesmes and of Dom Pothier. In addition to the text of the Brief *Nos quidem* of Leo XIII to

---

139. The letters of Msgr. Respighi and Father de Santi are addressed to Dom Mocquereau unless otherwise indicated.

Dom Delatte, he gave the Pope the Memorandum of the Abbot of Solesmes to Leo XIII on the work of the *Paléographie Musicale*, a memorandum with which Pius X was unfamiliar. In this regard, the Pope expressed his desire to see published the chant manuscripts of the churches of Italy.

On September 18, 1903, immediately after this audience, Msgr. Respighi wrote to Dom Mocquereau:

> I have just this moment returned from the audience that His Holiness Pius IX [*sic*] consented to grant to me. I have not written to you earlier about our new Pope, nor about the matter of the manuscripts sent to the *Rassegna*, because nothing truly significant is contained in them about Gregorian chant. Given the situation in Rome, it was timely to obtain immediately a word from His Holiness on the subject of musical reform; I was waiting for the right moment to speak with His Holiness in person about Gregorian chant, and the audience this evening focused on this topic alone.
>
> His Holiness was very agreeable and we spoke of this important subject for about a half an hour. Before all else, I asked for a blessing on those who are interested in Gregorian chant, and I added, by name, for the monks of Solesmes, for the Very Reverend Abbot Delatte, the Very Reverend Abbot Dom Pothier, *Dom Mocquereau*, Dom Cabrol, Dom Cagin, Leclerc, etc. His Holiness, with a great deal of consideration, told me to pass along [this blessing] to their Reverences.
>
> Still speaking of Gregorian chant and the work at Solesmes, His Holiness talked about conservation of the manuscripts in the churches of Italy, of the usefulness of publishing them, etc. I took the liberty of offering His Holiness a copy, which had been given to me, of the Memorandum presented by the Very Reverend Father Abbot to Leo XIII, a memorandum with which His Holiness was unfamiliar, and which he accepted with great interest. Then we spoke of the Brief *Nos quidem*, a copy of which I also left with him, although His Holiness was already thoroughly familiar with it.
>
> It was especially pleasant for me, on the first occasion I had to speak quietly with His Holiness, to remind him of the monks of Solesmes and to make myself, as it were, the interpreter of their feelings with respect to His Holiness. He is certainly a good friend of our cause. Long live Pius X.

The Pope was even more explicit with Father de Santi in his audience on September 23: Pius X did not want there to be any monopoly on the part of any publisher, which would mean a return to the same difficulties as in the past. He did want the major Churches that had preserved their manuscripts to restore their ancient melodies. Although those melodies, said the Pope, may differ a little from each other from church to church, they still present the traditional chant substantially the same everywhere (Father de Santi, October 22).

Pius X repeated these very clear statements to the publisher Pustet of Ratisbon on October 18. Once again, the Pope said that he did not want to favor any one publisher over another, and he invited Pustet to publish the melodies drawn from the German manuscripts. Later he advisedly added that Leo XIII had opened a new path in this area, in his Brief *Nos quidem* to the Abbot of Solesmes, a point that he repeated once again in December to Cardinal Fischer, for the benefit of the *Cäcilien-Verein* association, and to Msgr. Lans, president of the Dutch Society of St. Gregory the Great.[140] Traditional Gregorian chant, in fact, possesses truth and art, two qualities that are indispensable for sacred chant: therefore, it is this chant that must be restored. Thus, on that same day, October 18, the Pope congratulated Count Lefebvre, an associate of the publisher Desclée, on his cooperation with Solesmes. Here is a translation of the letter from Father de Santi to Dom Mocquereau on October 22, 1903, which relates these facts [the full text appears in Appendix IV].

We have also been told that the publication of the *Liber Usualis* has now been completed. God be praised that, finally, we have been able to overcome the difficulties regarding the books, and that we will be able to satisfy so many friends who are asking for them. We also hope that Desclée will deliver them long before Christmas . . .

The way things stand, and thus the future, are now clear. Since the Pope knows this issue and judges it for himself, he will reveal his thinking himself, without having others suggesting it to him. At the audience I had with him on September 23, the Holy Father told Msgr. Respighi and me that he does not want a monopoly on liturgical books to pass to another. It was his opinion that the principal Churches, which have good manuscripts, should publish them in manual editions, thereby reviving the ancient melodies everywhere. He said

---

140. Cf. F. Romita, *Jus Musicae Liturgicae*, pp. 132 and 282;—cf. *Rassegna Gregoriana*, col. 16 and 130.—The Pope expressed his desire that the *Cäcilien-Verein* association submit joyfully to the instructions that the Holy See was about to give with regard to religious music. The same exhortation was made to J. A. Lans, president of the Cecilian Association of Holland. That association did not make public the letter that the Pope sent to it until several months after it was sent. Msgr. Haberl published the letter sent to Cardinal Fischer, Archbishop of Cologne, immediately, but without any commentary. Rather, in a circular letter, Haberl decried the banning of the Medicean edition. Finally, he edified everyone through his obedience to the instructions of the Holy See (E. Moneta-Caglio, *Musica Sacra* 1961, p. 157).

222 THE WORK OF ST. PIUS X

that they would differ slightly from each other in some small parts of the melody, but after all, we would then have the traditional chant in each country.

Last Sunday, the Holy Father received Count Lefebvre and congratulated him; he is pleased with the chant editions that he prepared with the assistance of Your Reverence and the Benedictine Fathers. He added that it would be a good idea to publish the choir books in folio editions, as well, because, he said, these folio books are used in many cathedral or collegial churches, and because the canons would be grudging in their adjustment to the manual editions.

The same day the Holy Father also received Mr. Pustet of Ratisbon. The statement of His Holiness was very clear. He declared that he had no preferences for anyone, and any publisher would be equally favored by him. But he added: "In the Gregorian chant the Holy Father Pope Leo XIII has opened a new horizon, has traced a new path, and this is the road that should be maintained. In the chant of the Church, we must search out truth and art. These two qualities are found only in the ancient traditional chant, and this chant must now be restored. Then he urged Pustet to publish books of traditional chant himself, taking the melodies, if he so pleased, from the manuscripts of Churches of Germany.

I heard these things that very evening from Msgr. Bressan, and they were in keeping with the information we had received about that audience from others. If the Pope's advice is followed, competition among publishers will not be far behind. . . .

Shortly after the audience granted to Father de Santi, the Pope even told the Archbishop of Westminster that he wished to see the Benedictine editions adopted everywhere. The archbishop told the Rector of the Seminary of Wonersh:

I have seen the Holy Father on the subject of the Cathedral of Westminster, and he said to me that he was happy to know that the chant of Solesmes had been adopted there, and that he wished to see it adopted universally, and that it will no longer be necessary to hold to the Ratisbon edition. I believe that you would do well yourselves to prepare to change to the books of Solesmes. It is clearly the desire of the Holy Father that all do it. (From the copy of Dom Gatard, November 13, 1903)[141]

Father de Santi's statement in the *Rassegna Gregoriana*, therefore, seems a bit exaggerated:

---

141. The Wonersh Seminary adopted the Solesmes books at Christmas, 1903 (*Revue du Chant Grégorien* 1904, p. 187).

(Haberl) has informed us that the Holy Father invited Mr. Pustet, the pontifical typographer, to prepare an edition of the Gregorian chant himself in conformity with the manuscripts, and he has told us that he is persuaded that the Holy Father now personally prefers the Solesmes edition. We believe that we can state with great reassurance that *this second piece of information is not quite accurate.* The Holy Father is above any question of publishers or editions. He wishes, and we can now say this openly, he desires the traditional chant of the Church to be restored, independently of any particular edition.[142]

56. Preparation of the *Motu Proprio* of November 22, 1903

In November 1903, Father de Santi was deeply involved in preparation of the pontifical document that was to set the reform of sacred music in motion. After having received various individuals interested in musical reform in audiences, specifically Father de Santi and Msgr. Carlo Respighi,[143] the Pope had given the order, on October 18, the same day on which he received Pustet and Count Lefebvre, to prepare the necessary studies that would serve as the basis for a document on the subject for the Diocese of Rome:

The order was given to the Cardinal Vicar, Msgr. Pietro Respighi, who left the matter up to his nephew, Msgr. Carlo Respighi. It was at that point that Father de Santi entered the picture, suggesting that the instruction on sacred music contained in the *votum* of 1893 be used for this purpose, and that it should be turned into a pontifical document affecting the Church as a whole.[144]

Here is Father de Santi's account of how it all happened:

In early November, the Cardinal Vicar wanted to publish a circular letter on sacred music, to advocate the observance of the ecclesiastical directives that were already known. When Msgr. Respighi showed me the galley proofs, it was my opinion that something more could be done. I knew of the existence of, and was quite familiar with, the *votum* that Cardinal Sarto had sent to the Congregation of Sacred Rites in 1893. The *Pastoral Letter* of 1895 had already come

142. *Rassegna Gregoriana,* December 1903, col. 553. Emphasis added. See also Father de Santi's letter of January 1904, cf. *infra.*

143. And others, such as Camille Bellaigue, who recounts the audience granted to him by Pius X upon his elevation to the Sovereign Pontificate (*Pie X et Rome,* Librairie Nationale 1916, p. 13).

144. Romita, *La preformazione del "motu proprio" di S. Pio X sulla musica sacra (con documenti inediti),* Rome 1961, p. 101.

PLATE 2. Saint Pius X

from that *votum*. Why not base a pontifical *motu proprio* on it, as well? I made the suggestion to the Holy Father immediately, and he deigned to approve it, and charged me with putting the document together. There was no need to go search out the *votum;* I had a copy of it in my papers. The work was quickly done: all I needed to do was add the directives concerning Gregorian chant. (Father de Santi to Dom Mocquereau, January 4, 1904; full text in Appendix IV.)

In fact, Father de Santi was extremely familiar with the *votum* submitted by Cardinal Sarto to the Congregation of Sacred Rites in 1893, and which had already inspired the *Pastoral Letter* on sacred music from the patriarch of Venice in 1895. Father de Santi was the one who drafted it, in circumstances we have already discussed, partly with the help of his friends from Solesmes.[145] Nonetheless, the *motu proprio* uses only one part of the *votum* of 1893: 3. *Instruction on sacred music*, fifteen pages, with an indication of the sources used. It is this last part only that was integrated into the *motu proprio* as the Instruction that it promulgates for the entire Latin Church. Both documents use the same main headings, subheadings, and text.[146] Father de Santi had to update the pontifical document to reflect the intentions that Pius X had just manifested with regard to Gregorian chant. That is why the *motu proprio* states: the Gregorian chant that the Church "has jealously preserved for many centuries in its liturgical manuscripts" and that "recent work has so happily restored in its integrity and purity" (i.e. the work by Dom Pothier and Dom Mocquereau) has always been considered "as the most perfect model of sacred music"; therefore, it is necessary "that it be restored widely in the offices of worship." Nonetheless, the *motu proprio* does show evidence of the approval of Pius X, and there are corrections made in his hand.[147]

Father de Santi also prepared the letter sent by the Pope to the Cardinal Vicar of Rome, the letter that Pius X had initially intended, dated December 8, 1903. This letter demanded that the traditional Gregorian chant be reestablished and studied in Rome itself, from where it would spread throughout Christianity. This letter again praised "Gregorian chant restored in such a satisfactory way to its early purity, as it was handed down by the Fathers and is found in the codices of the various churches." In his letter of January 4, 1904, Father de Santi states:

145. Cf. Nos. 30 and 35, and Appendix III.
146. Romita, *La preformazione*, pp. 70–95 gives the text of the *votum*.
147. Romita, p. 22, note.

The Letter to the Cardinal Vicar was also drawn up according to ideas suggested by the Pope, and everything was then ready by early December. Publication was delayed because of the Christmas holidays so that the poor choirmasters would not be caught unawares. They could not possibly have responded in such a short time. I also prepared the draft of the Sacred Rites decree . . . and now the Holy Father has it, and I hope that there will not be any impediment to publishing it. (Full text in Appendix IV.)

The decree that Father de Santi mentions was published on January 9, 1904, promulgating the *motu proprio* for the entire Latin Church, and marking the end of the incorrect, altered, or truncated editions.

57. The New Solesmes Edition—A Request of Father de Santi

In Rome, the issue of practical chant books was posed immediately. This was inevitable. That is why Father de Santi had written to Dom Mocquereau on November 28 to complain about delays in publishing the new *Liber Usualis* that was then being prepared.[148]

But there were good reasons to explain, and even justify, the slowness of the work. On December 2, Dom Mocquereau wrote:

The *Liber Usualis* has been finished for a long time now. I would like you to let it be known in your circles, and *even publicly*, that in such a serious undertaking, it is our duty to advance with sure footing. The greater the confidence the Holy Father places in us, the more we must respond by doubling our efforts and our attentiveness in our research. . . . I assure you that we are not wasting a single minute. There are at least twelve of us monks assigned to this work. Transcriptions, photographs, comparative tables, correcting proofs, rubrics, Propers. etc. Everything is moving ahead at the same time. Father Germain Morin, who visited our work area and saw our organization and method, in order to write an article, did not hide his astonishment and his admiration. But all this takes time, and your good friendship must help us to win over those who are impatient. (See Plate 10: by way of example, an extract from the comparative tables prepared at Solesmes.)

At the same time, moreover, the Cellarer of Solesmes wrote a letter to Desclée that gives an excellent picture of how the work was considered with such detachment:

148. Desclée had just published the *Paroissien Romain,* but Father de Santi was awaiting the Latin edition impatiently. Cf. No. 52.

... It is sufficient for the Holy Father to express his desire to adopt our chant generally for us to modify the old editions completely, and for us to lay out an entirely new program and work load. First, this is not the chant of Solesmes, but Gregorian chant, restored, it is true, by the School of Solesmes, but it is still the chant of the Church, and not our own. It is not a question of monopolizing it, but of spreading it around. It would be shameful to make money with the approval of the Sovereign Pontiff, and to use it to create a commercial monopoly. . . ."

But on December 20, 1903, on the eve of the publication of the liberating *motu proprio*, signed on November 22 and then delayed, as we saw above, to spare choirmasters great confusion at Christmas, Father de Santi decided to write to the Abbot of Solesmes himself. After announcing, in confidence, the impending publication of the pontifical document, which would form a Code of sacred music and would be a very serious document in support of the return to tradition,[149] and also after mentioning the letter to the Cardinal Vicar and the decrees imposing the reform, he came to the issue of practical books. Where, in fact, can the books we need be found, books that everyone would soon be demanding to replace the editions that would be condemned from then on? Moreover, the Pope found that the editions of the *Liber Usualis* from Solesmes were too small. Father de Santi begged Dom Delatte *(supplichiamo vivamente)* to enjoin Dom Mocquereau to produce books in a larger format, like the format of the *Liber Gradualis* of 1883, and without rhythmic markings, which were invaluable for performance but still too controversial.

Finally, Father de Santi insisted that Dom Mocquereau must accept these conditions, otherwise those who did not want to adopt the traditional Gregorian chant and did not want to change their habits would be given a reason for obtaining their books in another manner. It was necessary, he continued, for Solesmes to engage itself on this point, so that he himself could give the Pope the assurance that the various demands could be met, demands that were sure to come for books of the sort that the Pope desired.

149. Dom Mocquereau had already been alerted by Bas, who wrote to him on November 25: "We are on the verge of receiving a new document from the Pope regarding liturgical chant, and our cause in particular. I have been assured that this will be a definitive statement" (letter written in French). But it does not seem that Dom Mocquereau paid much attention to it; his focus was entirely on the printing of the new editions at that point.

In a letter addressed to Dom Mocquereau himself, a few days later on December 31, Father de Santi repeated his pressing demand concerning the typical editions, and this at a time when the pontifical document had been published:

The Holy Father complained to Haberl that the current Solesmes editions are too small in terms of the notes and the text. We implore the Fathers of Solesmes, and I have already written about this matter to the Abbot, to get to work immediately on typical editions of Gregorian chant, in the manner of the *Liber Gradualis*, without dots and without rhythmic indications.

Here is a translation of the letter from Father de Santi to Dom Delatte, dated December 20, 1903 (full text in Appendix IV):

Most Reverend Father,

Please accept my wishes for the approaching Christmas feast. I write to bring you some news which doubtless will be most consoling to yourself and all your monks. Truth to tell, this news is *not* yet to be made public, but I trust myself to *your* discretion, since public documents will not confirm it.

During the Christmas holidays, the Holy Father will publish a solemn *motu proprio* on the restoration of sacred music. In it is taken, at last, the final step in favor of Gregorian chant according to the manuscripts, which is expressed each time the chant is mentioned. This *motu proprio* is given the force of law, *as to a juridical code of sacred music,* which is why the affirmations made regarding Gregorian chant take on an extraordinary significance.

The Holy Father communicates the new document with a very beautiful letter to the Cardinal Vicar of Rome in which he enjoins in paternal yet strong terms the observance of his regulations in all the churches and basilicas of Rome. The conclusion is directed to the colleges and seminaries of Rome, and praises Gregorian chant splendidly, recalling its happy restoration through the labors of illustrious personages who have served the cause of sacred art long and well. At the end, he imposes upon all the institutions at Rome the study of traditional Gregorian chant, expressing a desire that just as in the past this chant had been spread from Rome throughout the Church, so too the young students educated in the seminaries and colleges of Rome might in their turn go back from Rome to their dioceses. As you see, Father Abbot, the change is total and profound, the return to tradition solemnly affirmed by the Supreme Pontiff in a most weighty document. The formal revocation of the decrees of the Congregation of Rites is a self-evident conclusion and we have requested the Holy Father to add such a declaration to the documents; all the more because in order to avoid an avalanche of requests to the Sacred Congregation it seems necessary to state that the Ratisbon editions can be maintained, in those places where they are being used *donec quam primum fieri poterit*—until the earliest possible moment that the traditional chant replaces them.

However, I cannot deny to you that the question of the books is exceedingly important. If a cathedral or collegiate church wishes to introduce the traditional chant, where does one find the texts? The small books we have at present are completely unsatisfactory for great churches, although most useful for seminaries and colleges. In addition the Holy Father complained to Dr. Haberl that these books are rather poorly printed in type which is too small, and he advised Herr Pustet to print the chant in larger type. We earnestly beg you, Father Abbot, to restrain the efforts of the excellent Dom Mocquereau and to order that work be started at once on larger books with larger type, as the *Liber Gradualis* was originally. The rhythmic signs are certainly excellent for instructional purposes, but since they also present at the very least an *occasion for doubt*, we earnestly entreat you and beg that for now, in the typical edition of the chant books, such signs be omitted. Otherwise you will never obtain ecclesiastical approval and indeed will furnish a reason for taking other measures if the monks of Solesmes do not agree. It is absolutely necessary that we receive this promise from Solesmes in order thus to assure the Holy Father that we shall have as soon as possible the typical edition of the chant books as he desires them, and in order to reply to the requests which the various dioceses might make as to which books they should buy. I entreat you with the greatest insistence that in the decisions which are taken regarding the chant, you hear also the view of Rome and not leave us in the lurch, ignorant of your undertakings. You will pardon the liberty we are taking, but believe that nothing else motivates us except the desire to see the triumph of a cause for which so much has been endured.

Unfortunately, we do not have a verbatim copy of the response sent by Dom Delatte, but the contents of his response can be established on the basis of other letters from Solesmes.

On the one hand, Dom Noetinger, Cellarer of Solesmes, confirms that Dom Delatte responded in the sense indicated by Father de Santi: a medium-size format for the edition, as the Pope desired, and an edition without the rhythmic indications, in conformity with the wishes of Father de Santi (letter of December 23, 1903 to Mr. Desclée); at the same time, Dom Noetinger announces that the *Antiphonal* was far along, and that most of the work on the *Gradual* had already been completed, editions that included all the chants of the Office and of the Mass (not just those of Sundays and feasts):

We are preparing large-format editions as the Holy Father wishes, and editions without the rhythmic indications, to please Father de Santi. Work will have to be organized at Tournai to ensure that the *Antiphonal* and the *Gradual* do not languish. Here, work on the first of them is far along, and work on the second will not be long. . . . The Abbot responded to Father de Santi in the terms indicated above. . . .

On the other hand, Dom Delatte himself, following Dom Mocquereau, pointed out that the preparation of this edition would take effort and time. In late December, he wrote:

The movement is so sudden that the definitive editions will not be able to be completed at once. From a private undertaking, our work has become a work of the Church. And, while we pursue our work with a critical eye and maturity, we are being hounded and pressed. . . . I just wrote two letters to two great pontiffs of the Centenary [no doubt Msgr. Carlo Respighi and Father de Santi] urging them to be patient, pointing out to them how unwise it would be to provide the universal Church with an ill-conceived work under the title *traditional chant*, a work whose inconsistency with the manuscripts would easily be discerned by the critics.[150]

As soon as he heard Dom Delatte's response, Father de Santi informed the Pope immediately, and just as promptly, he expressed his joy and confidence to Dom Mocquereau:

The one thing that worried all of us was the matter of the books. It is undeniable that books with dots alone are not enough, and at a time of such radical change it seemed absolutely necessary to avoid any discussion of uncertain or doubtful points. But we trust the monks of Solesmes and we have given assurance of it to the Holy Father as well, and for now we are satisfied with the statements of Father Abbot. And so the twelve monks working on the books should set to work and give us as quickly as possible the books of medium size, without rhythmic signs. For my part, I recommend as strongly as possible the Gregorian edition with dots, because I believe it most useful in seminaries etc. I only have a few reservations about certain subdivisions which in my view could also be indicated in some other fashion, except of course where it is clear that the manuscripts have it that way, or that mutual comparison of the different melodies requires it. (Father de Santi, January 4, 1904. Full text in Appendix IV.)

It is clear from the facts we have just presented that Father de Santi was counting on Solesmes to realize in practice the reform that the

---

150. Letter quoted by Dom A. Savaton, *Dom Paul Delatte, Abbé de Solesmes*, Plon 1954, p. 229.

motu proprio, which had not yet been published, would promulgate. His urgency in turning to Solesmes, and directly to Dom Delatte,—and his insistence that the books should appear as Pius X, and he himself, wanted them—and his promptness in keeping the Pope up to date on the steps he was taking are adequate proof of this.

Moreover, a few days later he made the following statement in *Civiltà Cattolica:*

The Holy Father did not designate any particular edition of traditional Gregorian chant, and some have deduced from this that before the traditional chant is introduced, we must wait for a new, official edition to be approved by the supreme authority; we believe that we can state that such an edition is out of the question, at least for now, and that it is probable that no such edition will ever appear. In the meanwhile, we have the Benedictine edition, already praised and approved by Leo XIII in the Brief *Nos quidem*, and which fulfills the intentions of the *motu proprio* rather well. If, subsequently, others should be able to provide editions of equal or greater value, those editions will be most welcome.[151]

Nevertheless, although the Pope was kept up to date on Father de Santi's exchanges of letters with Solesmes, this was not an official, or even unofficial, measure,[152] but rather a completely personal approach by Father de Santi to Dom Delatte. Moreover, we must conclude that by *typical edition*, Father de Santi understood not an official edition, but one that would give the last word from Solesmes regarding the restoration of the melodies, and that would prevail over the other editions, given its scientific value and its adoption in Rome itself. Msgr. Moneta-Caglio thus writes quite correctly:

Father de Santi did not understand this as an official edition, but he wanted a work that would be the definitive word of Solesmes regarding the Gregorian reconstruction, and which could be taken as the most authorized expression of that School. According to his predictions, this edition should ultimately have prevailed over all the other editions solely on account of its internal virtues and of the fact that it would be adopted in Rome as a sort of *textus receptus.* . . .—

---

151. *I nuovi documenti pontifici sulla restaurazione della musica sacra,* in *Civiltà Cattolica* 1904, January, vol. 1, pp. 257–276, note on page 2 (unsigned article).

152. Moneta-Caglio, *Musica Sacra,* 1962, pp. 81–83. The author arrives at this conclusion on the basis of other texts by Father de Santi which appeared in the *Rassegna Gregoriana,* December 1903, col. 553 (quoted above); February 1904, col. 89; March 1904, col. 189, and May–June 1904, col. 273.—In an article in the *Revue Grégorienne* (1954, p. 118), we spoke of an *unofficial* measure, for the reasons outlined above, but we concur with the view of Msgr. Moneta-Caglio.

The tactic adopted was, therefore, to put off the notion of a Vatican edition and to let things evolve on their own, favoring in the meantime the Benedictine edition, which was the one that enjoyed the right of priority—*melior est conditio possidentis*—and that belonged canonically to the monastery of Solesmes. If it was the true traditional chant that people wanted, they would necessarily have to end up there.[153]

We have already seen that Father de Santi did not accept the rhythmic theory of Dom Mocquereau. And that is why he was asking Solesmes to prepare editions without the rhythmic indications, which he could offer to the various churches that would ask for it in order to implement the *motu proprio*. Nonetheless, as we have also seen, he thought that these rhythmic indications were quite useful in practice. Thus he wanted the chant fascicle that was planned for the celebrations of the Centenary of the death of St. Gregory the Great to appear in a double edition: one without rhythmic indications, and another one with the rhythmic indications for use by the singers (Father de Santi, December 31, 1903). As for the melodic improvements that Dom Mocquereau was introducing in the *Liber Usualis*, and which were not to Father de Santi's liking initially, because, in his view, they could do harm to the unity of the chant at a moment that was particularly critical, they no longer drew any objection, and in fact, the fascicle for the feasts of St. Gregory the Great (Office and Mass) drew all its melodies from the new *Liber Usualis*.[154]

58. Publication of the *Motu Proprio*

The *motu proprio* on sacred music appeared in the closing days of December 1903, for the reasons already outlined above. A *Circular Letter* from the Cardinal Vicar, dated December 29, announced the pontifical documents to the various interested parties in the Diocese of Rome. At the same time, it announced that the Roman Commission on Sacred Music, established in 1901, was charged with overseeing the implementation of the new discipline. There followed the names of the members of the Commission: Perosi, Capocci, Mancini, Kanzler, Parisotti, Rella,

---

153. Moneta-Caglio, *Musica Sacra*, 1962, pp. 81 and 83.
154. Cf. No. 52.

and Mattoni. Finally, it was noted that Perosi and Rella were specifically responsible for Gregorian chant in the seminaries, colleges, and ecclesiastical institutes of Rome.[155]

Father de Santi, who had just told the Abbot of Solesmes about the pontifical document in confidence, immediately wrote to Dom Mocquereau. At the same time, he told Dom Mocquereau of his attempt to introduce the name of Solesmes into the pontifical document:

> At present the pontifical documents will bring some joy to the bitter exile of the good Fathers of Solesmes. Worthily and much sooner than one could have reasonably expected, the Lord has crowned your learned labors. And all of us congratulate you from the very depths of our heart. An explicit mention of Solesmes or at least of the Benedictine order may perhaps have been desirable. We had made that request to the Holy Father, since he had deigned to entrust the revision of the document to a few of us who therefore met together with Father Janssens on the Aventine. But His Holiness replied that it was not needful, that there would be no dearth of opportunity for him to show his pleasure at the work of the Benedictines, but that in documents of this type it was necessary to avoid any personal reference, also in order that there would not be the slightest chance of claiming that the Pope showed any preference for particular publishers. Perhaps it will be good to have Rev. Father Abbot write a letter of thanks to the Holy Father in his name and on behalf of the monks. (Letter of December 31, 1903 to Dom Mocquereau. Full text in Appendix IV.)

Father de Santi presented the *motu proprio* in *Civiltà Cattolica* in January 1904.[156] He dwelt on a few points in particular: the earlier Venice Letter of Cardinal Sarto (1895);—the importance of the pontifical document that was without precedent, and was presented as a *Legal code of sacred music*, an initial application of Pius X's program *instaurare omnia in Christo;*—the part relating to Gregorian chant defined as the chant proper to the Roman Church, possessing to the highest degree the qualities of sacred music, of which it is considered the perfect model, and which must serve as a rule for judging other compositions permitted in divine worship. This chant, Father de Santi continued, has just been restored to the state in which it is found in the manuscripts, thanks to the work of Dom Pothier and Dom Mocquereau in the *Paléographie Musicale*. Father de Santi then quickly retraced the history of the Medicean

---

155. Cf. *Rassegna Gregoriana* 1904, col. 444–445.

156. (De Santi), *I nuovi documenti,* pp. 257–276 (unsigned). Text of the *Motu Proprio* in Romita, pp. 290ff.

edition, whose enormities and errors had been indicated through the recent work of Solesmes.

Finally, we must point out that the decree of January 8, 1904, prepared by Father de Santi and Msgr. Carlo Respighi[157] to promulgate the *motu proprio* throughout the Latin Church and to condemn the use of incorrect editions, caused some commotion in the Ratisbon camp and, of course, in Germany particularly. The prospect of the eventual adoption of an edition printed in France or in Belgium roused their fears, and Msgr. Haberl immediately began to campaign in favor of a new official edition. As early as January 20, 1904, he wrote, in fact, a Circular to all the presidents of the diocesan Caecilian Societies, "asking that it be considered opportune to take steps in Rome in favor of soliciting an official edition."[158]

59. Dom Pothier's Project

The situation changed when Dom Pothier intervened, and we must note immediately that Dom Pothier was quite unaware of the steps that Father de Santi was taking with Solesmes.

Dom Lucien David, a monk of Saint-Wandrille who was then a student at St. Anselm, the Benedictine college in Rome, wrote to Father de Santi in early January 1904, asking him for an interview, unbeknownst to the Abbot-Primate and the Rector of St. Anselm—who, as we will soon see, had their own plans for a Gregorian edition (*Journal* of Dom Noetinger, Cellarer of Solesmes, December 4, 1905).[159] At that first meeting, which took place on January 13, Dom David merely sounded out the terrain with regard to the possibility of making a Gregorian edition in Rome, and Father de Santi shared with him his objections concerning the last edition of Solesmes, the *Liber Usualis* with the rhythmic indications (*Journal* of Father de Santi, published in Appendix IV, January 13, 1904).

A few days later, on January 28, Pécoul, the adversary of Solesmes whom we already encountered in 1901 during the first project of Poussielgue (see *supra*, No. 51), wrote to Father de Santi suggesting that

---

157. Cf. Moneta-Caglio, *Musica Sacra* 1961, p. 151, note 217.

158. Moneta-Caglio, *Musica Sacra* 1962, p. 83.

159. This is a note made following a conversation with Father de Santi in December 1905.

he should prepare a typical edition, printed at the Vatican Polyglot Press, which publishers would have to reproduce. Then he suggested that Solesmes not be informed, and announced the arrival in Rome of Dom Pothier (Pécoul, January 28, 1904).

Dom Pothier first sent a letter to the Pope. Seizing the occasion of his gift to the Pope of his *Cantus Mariales,*[160] Dom Pothier placed himself at the Pope's disposal for any purpose the Pope should see fit. That much is clear from the response of Pius X, in the form of a Brief[161] dated February 14, 1904, a response which contains, in fact, nothing but a general acceptance of Dom Pothier's offer of service. Father de Santi was informed of Dom Pothier's letter by the Pope himself, at his audience of January 31, during which the matter of Dom Delatte's letter of December 1903 and of musical reform was raised once again. In his *Journal* on January 31, Father de Santi refers, in fact, either to the response of Dom Delatte to his letter of December 20 or to the letter that he had asked Dom Delatte to send to the Pope, following the publication of the *motu proprio* of November 22.

Instructed by the events of 1901, Father de Santi understood immediately what was going to happen. He wrote the following note on February 5: "Dom Pothier will come to Rome to create an edition opposed to the Solesmes edition." The next day, on February 6, Dom David confirmed to Father de Santi that Dom Pothier would soon arrive in Rome, and told him of Dom Pothier's plan to create the edition himself (Father de Santi *Journal*, February 6).

Why this opposition from Dom Pothier? We have seen that he was opposed to establishing the *Paléographie Musicale*, and the reasons for his stance (cf. No. 7, above). In 1901, several years after his departure from Solesmes for Ligugé and Saint-Wandrille, he had reached an agreement with Poussielgue, during the first project for a Vatican edition, and had pressed claims to his alleged rights to the Solesmes chant editions (cf. No. 51, above). Suffice to it say, once again, that according to monastic

160. Offices of the *Revue du Chant Grégorien*, Grenoble.

161. The Brief is found in *Revue du Chant Grégorien* 1904, p. 129, and in *Rassegna Gregoriana* 1904, col. 133.—The passage to which we allude here is as follows: "As for the assurance that you give us that you will always provide, in support of this cause, the assistance of your activities, we accept this good disposition with paternal eagerness . . ." The author of the commentary in the *Revue du Chant Grégorien* (Professor Amédée Gastoué) is wrong, therefore, in saying that Dom Pothier was *called* to Rome in February 1904.

legislation, and as long as Dom Pothier was at Solesmes, the fruits of his work belonged rightly to his monastery of profession, which, moreover, had taken the initiative in the Gregorian restoration, and was paying all the expenses for it. In these circumstances, Dom Pothier seems indeed to have been advised by Pécoul, who was no friend of Solesmes, and it was because of Pécoul that the 1901 project failed. Dom Pothier, still being advised by Pécoul (see the letter in note 168), continued to have the same attitude with respect to Solesmes in spring 1904, as we shall see. But it does not seem possible that Dom Mocquereau's theory of rhythm could, by itself, explain this attitude on the part of the Abbot of Saint-Wandrille, as has too often been asserted. Besides, as we shall see, Dom Mocquereau never dreamed of imposing his rhythmic indications on the Vatican Edition: the discussions and differences of opinion within the Vatican Commission related only to the *melodic* restitution of Gregorian chant. In any event, it was long before the publication of volume VII of the *Paléographie Musicale* (1901), in which Dom Mocquereau first presented his rhythmic principles, and the publication of the *Liber Usualis* (1903), that Dom Pothier had become detached from his monastery of profession. His opposition does seem to stem from a number of concerns that have nothing to do with music, but are strictly monastic in nature (cf. Dom A. Savaton, *Dom Paul Delatte*, Plon 1954, pp. 163–167).

The day after his arrival in Rome, Dom Pothier went to visit Father de Santi, on February 13, and in fact suggested preparing a Vatican edition under his own direction (de Santi *Journal*, February 13). Dom Pothier was accompanied by a representative of Poussielgue, and there was a discussion of Poussielgue's project that had failed in 1901, but which could be revived with the assistance of the Vatican press, with the Poussielgue company "having either to take on responsibility for everything, or provide photographs for the Vatican press" (*Journal* of Dom Noetinger, December 4, 1905). Father de Santi imposed one condition: Nothing could be done without Solesmes, and the Abbey's copyright would be respected.

A report by Father de Santi in 1908 at the request of Dom Mocquereau confirms this information, and provides other interesting information, as well.

The letter, dated November 28, 1908, presents the situation as it stood in February 1904 (we provide the reference to the *Journal* of Father de Santi along with the letter, the full text of which appears in Appendix IV):

. . . Regarding the events of 1904 there is not much to say beyond that which I have already indicated. Dom Pothier came to Rome without being invited by anyone, but on his own initiative with the intention of proposing to the Holy See an edition under the auspices of the Pope, to appear, if desired, at the expense of the Poussielgue firm at Rome or at Paris, as desired, with the understanding that Poussielgue would publish the edition first, and later other publishers would be permitted to reproduce it. Therefore he came accompanied by an agent of that company. Basically, they wanted to repeat the proposals already made by Védie in 1901. I laid down the explicit condition that the Benedictines of Solesmes would have to take part in the editorial work, and Dom Pothier agreed. Furthermore, I discouraged presentation of the proposal to the Holy Father before knowing Signor Scotti's opinion on it. It seemed to me that by eliminating the difficulties which could have arisen on the part of subordinates, one might more certainly achieve one's purpose. And so I spoke with Signor Scotti and he excluded most definitely any interference of Poussielgue, saying that he was ready to publish the edition himself and proposing his plan to separate the publishers from the question of expenses in the manner as it had been done before. (The agent of Poussielgue departed Rome as soon as he learned of Scotti's decision.) However, he did raise two questions: ownership of the notation and copyright of the melodies [cf. de Santi *Journal*, February 15]. Dom Pothier said it was unnecessary to worry about the first point; as to the second he declared his readiness to turn over to the Holy See all the rights which he might have had to his labors, adding that certain difficulties might perhaps arise with the French Government, which at that time had confiscated the Solesmes editions. He also added that in order to move ahead without hindrance it would be good to have a statement of renunciation from Solesmes as well for that which was their contribution. At that time I wrote to Pécoul to ask the terms in which the property matters stood at Paris. I had had no connection with Pécoul at all, but after the publication of the *Motu proprio* on sacred music he had written me a letter of congratulation, and Dom Pothier told me that he was able to do a great deal to prevent government interference with an edition which one might wish to publish at Rome. I pointed out that Dom Pothier, although he had advised also contacting Solesmes for the transfer of their property rights, he did not however put the matter as absolutely necessary, at least for the greater part of the work already done. Matters having been settled thus, on the evening of Monday, February 22, I reported on all of this to the Holy Father, formally proposing the preparation of a Vatican edition with the cooperation of Dom Pothier and the Benedictines of Solesmes. The Holy Father welcomed the proposal with great pleasure and lavishly praised the plan of Scotti regarding expenses [cf. de Santi *Journal*, February 22 and 25, and April 27]. In the meantime Pécoul began to bombard me with letters, which remained unanswered. Dom Pothier presented a written declaration transferring to the Holy See all his literary rights and on the evening of March 9, Scotti came to me to say that the Holy Father had ordered that a letter be written to the Benedictines of Solesmes inviting them also to transfer their portion of the copyrights, and to collaborate in the edition [cf. de Santi *Journal*, March 9, 10, and 11]. Dom Pothier came to Rome with another monk of his abbey whose name I do not recall. I do remember that he and Dom David spoke to me continually of honoraria which one would have to pay, and of percentages on the edition, be they in compensation for Dom Pothier's work, or to assist the catastrophic financial state of the abbey. Scotti's proposal to publish the edition in a way that would not cost the Holy See a penny was not at all to their liking. I spoke of this with the Holy Father, and the Holy Father told me that he could not pay anything, but if it were necessary, that he would gladly meet the expenses which Dom Pothier had to incur because of his stay at Rome. I think that the original idea of Dom Pothier was to strike a bargain with Poussielgue, putting the Holy See in the middle in order to avoid upsetting Solesmes. But the scheme failed in part.[161bis] As far as the guidelines for producing the edition were concerned, it was originally proposed to make a good edition based on the earlier one. But when the monks of Solesmes demonstrated that the copyright was theirs and the Holy Father recognized the need to give them some compensation of honor in return for the transfer of rights by officially declaring them editors of the Vatican Edition, we thought in terms of a criterion more strictly scientific, such as had been proposed in the *Motu proprio*. [We will return to this last sentence later.]

60. Initial Decisions

On February 22, Father de Santi submitted the proposal for a Vatican edition to the Pope, to be done with the cooperation of Dom Pothier and the Benedictines of Solesmes. No mention was made of forming a special commission responsible for revising the musical text. However, on March 2, the Pope confirmed the authority of the Commission for the revision of the chant books of the Congregation of Sacred Rites, by naming new members, specifically Dom Pothier, Dom Janssens, Father de Santi, Msgr. Carlo Respighi, and Baron Kanzler. This was the Liturgi-

161bis. Cf. the letter from Pécoul cited in note 168.

cal Commission established in 1901 by Cardinal Ferratta (cf. *supra*, No. 54), which was different from the Roman Commission for Sacred Music, which was diocesan and not attached to the Congregation of Sacred Rites.[162] At the time, Father de Santi adds, the only intent was to "produce a good edition based on the earlier ones."

The Pope was very pleased with the proposal submitted to him by Father de Santi (de Santi *Journal*, February 25). So was Father de Santi, certainly, for both he and Msgr. Respighi had abandoned the 1901 project with great regret. In November 1903, once again Mr. Desclée sent word of this to Dom Mocquereau. He wrote,

In Rome, Father de Santi does not appear to have completely abandoned Poussielgue's initial idea, i.e. to have the new editions prepared in Rome itself, by a committee working on the information from Solesmes. (November 13, 1903)[163]

Msgr. Moneta-Caglio has published a reflection by Father de Santi that leaves absolutely no doubt on this point. In fact, Father de Santi wrote to Msgr. Respighi on August 30, 1903, immediately after the arrival of Pius X, an arrival that wakened his hopes: "Then, when all of us will be in Rome, we must attempt to abolish the decrees and, if possible, to print the melodies at the Vatican." The intervention of Dom Pothier, therefore, provided an opportunity for Father de Santi to return to this plan.

61. An Invitation for Solesmes

Father de Santi wrote to Dom Mocquereau on February 28. Without mentioning Dom Pothier, Poussielgue, or the audience of February 22, he merely implied that the Holy See was preparing to reach a decision about the Gregorian editions. The Pope had given the order to inform

162. Moneta-Caglio, *Musica Sacra*, 1962, p. 112, cites the Journal of Father de Santi: "March 2. I received the decree appointing me to the Commission for the revision of the Gregorian books. From the phrasing they use and from the notice in the *Osservatore Romano*, it does not seem that the old Commission has been suppressed."—Here is the note from the *Osservatore Romano*, on March 3: "The Holy Father has graciously deigned to order, by letter of the Secretary of State, that the following persons shall also be members of the Commission for the revision of the books of choral chant, which is assigned to the Congregation of Sacred Rites: Dom Joseph Pothier, O.S.B., Abbot, Dom Laurent Janssens O.S.B., Rector of St. Anselm's College, Father Angelo de Santi, S.J., Msgr. Carlo Respighi, Choirmaster Father Lorenzo Perosi, and Baron Rudolf Kanzler." Cf. No. 54, and *Tribune de Saint-Gervais*, 1904, pp. 50–51.

163. Moneta-Caglio, *Musica Sacra*, 1962, p. 79.

the representatives of Pustet and of Desclée "not to make any decisions about future editions of the traditional chant, and to await word from the Pope." For the moment, and especially in writing, Father de Santi did not want to say any more, but in closing his letter, he did hint more clearly that something was in the works, and he insisted that Dom Mocquereau should come to Rome. He wrote:

Several matters of the greatest importance are slowly developing to maturity, and as soon as I am able to say something, I shall not neglect to inform you at once. For the moment my lips are sealed. But everything comes down from higher up and all will surely turn out satisfactorily. I ask you to keep this information to yourself, even if it be so sibylline. Come to Rome quickly. Maestro Perosi had even given me the news that you had already arived; I called San Anselmo at once and was disappointed. (Full text in Appendix IV)

Dom Mocquereau did not pay much attention to Father de Santi's sibylline words, for he did not reply until March 4, to say that he was hoping the Abbot would not allow him to attend the Congress in honor of the Thirteenth Centenary of the death of St. Gregory the Great. Coming immediately after the *motu proprio* of the previous November 22, this Congress was of singular importance, and it was to be expected that the issue of Gregorian chant and sacred music would be addressed there. But, as we now know, it was for an entirely different reason that Father de Santi was so ardent in his desire for Dom Mocquereau to come to Rome. Thus, on March 7, he renewed his invitation. For his part, Bas was forceful in his insistence that Dom Mocquereau should come to Rome where, he said, the situation was grave and the presence of Solesmes necessary.[164]

At Appuldurcombe, the first refuge of Solesmes in England, Dom Delatte immediately understood that it was in the best interest of the Abbey to be in attendance at the Congress and not to be absent if there was a question of preparing an edition in Rome itself. Thus he decided to send Dom Mocquereau and Dom Cagin, the Abbey's knowledgeable liturgist, and for practical reasons Dom Noetinger, the Cellarer, whose presence was rendered all the more essential in that Pustet had just done some typographic test runs of the Solesmes *Liber Gradualis* (de Santi, February 28).

164. Letter of March 8, 1904; Father Holly wrote along the same lines on February 12 and as early as January 23.

62. Letter from Msgr. Bressan to Dom Delatte

In inviting Dom Mocquereau to Rome, Father de Santi was thus pursuing the project of a Gregorian edition. In fact, if this project were really to come to fruition, using the Benedictine editions, one preliminary question had to be settled, namely the copyright held by the Abbey of Solesmes. This issue had been a stumbling block in 1901, and the matter was made all the more delicate now since the property of the Abbey had been confiscated after the departure of the religious into exile. Before all else, therefore, there had to be contact with Solesmes. This was an issue that Scotti, the pontifical publisher, understood immediately even as he rejected any possible collaboration with Poussielgue (de Santi *Journal*, February 15, and letter of November 18, 1908).

Scotti spoke of the matter directly with the Pope on March 9, and it was through Scotti that the Pope charged Father de Santi with preparing the letter sent to the Abbot of Solesmes. By the next day, March 10, the letter was ready and Father de Santi submitted it to the Pope. It was sent immediately with the signature of Msgr. Bressan, private secretary of Pius X (de Santi *Journal*, March 9, 10, and 11). The letter arrived at Appuldurcombe after the three monks of Solesmes had already left for Rome.

Here is a translation of the letter (the full text appears in Appendix IV):

Right Rev. Father!

His Holiness has arrived at the decision to publish at the Vatican Press the edition of liturgical books containing the chant of the Roman Church. This edition, produced under the auspices of the Holy See, will not have restricted copyright but any publisher will be permitted to reprint it as may please him best. The edition will be limited to the typical books alone, such as the *Liber Gradualis*, the *Liber Antiphonarius*, the *Pontificale*, the *Ritual*, etc.

At the same time His Holiness has deigned to entrust to the Rt. Rev. Father Joseph Pothier O.S.B. of the Solesmes congregation, presently Abbot of Saint-Wandrille, the honorable task of furnishing the text of the Gregorian melodies and of directing the editorial labors which, prior to being approved by His Holiness, will be diligently examined by persons regarded as more competent in this material, with final revision by the Liturgical Commission for the publication of Gregorian chant books recently established by the same Holy Father.

Rev. Father Pothier, grateful for the honor conferred upon him, has renounced in favor of the Holy See, by a formal declaration and for the sole purpose of the aforementioned edition, all rights and every copyright which he might have in the melodies copied by him from the ancient manuscripts, or adapted, or newly composed, such as have already been published in the Solesmes edition.

But the Holy Father in his very special predilection for the illustrious order of St. Benedict, recognizing with deep satisfaction the indefatigable labors performed by Benedictine monks in the restoration of the genuine Gregorian melodies, in particular by the religious of the above-mentioned abbey of Solesmes, has deigned to order that also in future the editing of the Gregorian liturgical books as well as the composition of any new melodies which may occur in eventual new offices, be always reserved to the Benedictine order and in particular to the monks of Solesmes.

His Holiness does not doubt in the least that you and the monks of your monastery will only receive with gratitude this act of sovereign benevolence, remembering well how Your Reverence, writing in 1901 to his predecessor Pope Leo XIII of holy memory, placed at the disposition of the Holy See all of your efforts so that they might serve in their way for the greater glory of God and for the good of the Church.

In communicating to Your Reverence these sovereign resolutions, I have the high honor by the express wish of His Holiness, to invite Your Reverence and the monks subject to you to collaborate diligently and skillfully in the work desired, under the guidance and direction of the Rt. Rev. Abbot of Saint-Wandrille and in accord with the norms indicated above, which will in due time be made public by means of a special pontifical act.

I take this occasion to present to you, Father Abbot, my sentiments of most profound esteem and I sign myself as the most humble servant of Your Reverence

Giovanni Bressan
Private Chamberlain to His Holiness

Thus the Pope was asking the monks of Solesmes to work with Dom Pothier on editing the planned edition, and was inviting them to transfer the Abbey's copyright on the chant books used as the basis of the Vatican Edition to the Holy See. The letter from Msgr. Bressan noted the gesture of Dom Pothier, who had transferred in writing, on March 8, the rights he wrongly believed he held for the Solesmes editions to the Holy See. Along the same lines, the letter recalled that in 1901, in the memorandum requested by Father de Santi and submitted to Leo XIII, the Abbot of Solesmes had already placed at the feet of the Sovereign Pontiff all the previous work of the Abbey in this area. The wording, you will recall, was suggested by Msgr. Respighi,[165] but as Dom Noetinger writes, "the offer was never accepted and made final" (cf. de Santi letter of November 28, 1908, *supra*, and the Memorandum of Dom Noetinger).

Thus in mid March, although no firm decision had yet been made—as we shall soon see—the project was nonetheless taking shape with increasing clarity. It is clear from the letter of Msgr. Bressan that the edition would be subject not only to the Liturgical Commission of the Congregation of Sacred Rites, but also to examination of competent individuals.

63. The Project of the Abbot-Primate

Neither the letter of Father de Santi quoted above nor the letter of Msgr. Bressan make reference to a proposal of the Right Rev. Father Abbot-Primate of the Benedictine Order.[166] Father de Santi was informed of this proposal by Dom Pothier on his second visit, on February 14:

Dom Pothier is back. He says that the Abbot-Primate wishes to take the matter of the chant in hand himself, in order to ensure its future ties to the Benedictine Order. With that, Dom Pothier remains bound and the situation changes. The proposal must be made to the Pope in another manner. (*Journal*, February 14, in the Appendix)

Dom Hildebrand de Hemptinne did want to handle the planned edition, as soon as Dom Pothier spoke of it to him (for it seems that his only knowledge of the project came from Dom Pothier). He believed that through the mediation of the Benedictine Order, traditional Gregorian chant would spread more easily throughout the entire Church. Although this plan was quickly dropped, it is nonetheless true that Father de Santi first had to take the project into account and speak to the Pope about it. Moreover, as we shall see, the Abbot-Primate was none too keen on dropping his project.

165. Cf. above, No. 48. Here is the wording: In closing, Holy Father, the sons of Dom Guéranger place at your feet all the scientific and practical work that they have undertaken for the restoration of the liturgical melodies of the Roman Church, the object of their love and veneration, praying Your Holiness to dispose of it as Your Holiness sees fit for the greater glory of God.

166. The Abbot-Primate at the time was Dom Hildebrand de Hemptinne, in residence at St. Anselm College. At his side was Dom Janssens, rector of St. Anselm and a fervent Gregorianist.

As soon as he learned that Dom Mocquereau had left for Rome, on March 12, Dom de Hemptinne wrote to the Abbot of Solesmes from Maredsous, where he was staying at the time, to inform him of his project. Taking advantage of the difference that existed between Dom Pothier and Dom Mocquereau, he wrote:

Very Reverend Father Abbot,

The reform of the liturgical chant undertaken with such ardent zeal by the Sovereign Pontiff now places extraordinary importance on the work in this area begun and brought to a satisfactory conclusion by the Congregation of France.

One might even be tempted to believe, at certain moments, that the rapidity of the change that has been accomplished not only offers all the advantages of a great victory, but also involves all the inconveniences of a conquest that remains to be organized.

Living in Rome, at the very heart of this evolution, I am well aware of the advantages obtained and the dangers to be avoided, and that is why I am writing to Your Reverence, in order to bring you further up to date than you already are on this situation.

Traditional chant has triumphed, and it is beyond dispute that your editions are the ones most in agreement with tradition. That is generally accepted.

The twofold question now posed, quite understandably, is whether the editions are in absolutely perfect agreement with tradition, and whether they will be accepted as official editions.

The Holy Father is, I believe, very devoted to your work, and I have reason to believe that He is taking into consideration the material advantages to which you are entitled on account of this work.

I personally feel great satisfaction, need I say, in seeing that our holy Order is being of use to the Holy Church, and I defend the glory of this work and the material rights won for your Congregation as part of our heritage. In order to succeed in safeguarding these advantages, it seems to me of great importance that the Congregation of France remain united, and that it remain closely united with all the rest of the Order.

The little controversies between Dom Pothier and Solesmes, unfortunately, have leaked out a bit, and they are greatly to be regretted, as I see it. Mr. Poussielgue has already attempted to turn them to his own advantage, and I would not be the least bit surprised if certain individuals in Rome were viewing them as a means for turning the course of Solesmes into a different direction.

I will not enter into great detail, because the facts that I might present have already been explained to a great or lesser extent, but nevertheless, I believe that there is a general tendency toward diminishing the importance of Solesmes in the movement of the future. I believe that it is necessary and fair for me to oppose this trend insofar as I am able.

I took energetic steps before my departure, and Dom Pothier has sent me a letter in which he promises not to transfer to anyone any copyright he may hold for the chant books without prior authorization from his Superiors. I have learned that Dom Mocquereau and another of your monks have left for Rome. I will see them there at Easter. But until then, they should do whatever is possible to reach an understanding with Dom Pothier.

It seems to me that all Benedictines should come to an understanding about the path to be taken, so that the same editions are introduced in the majority of our monasteries. The Right Rev. Dom Pothier, your monks, Dom Laurent Janssens, and Dom Hugues Gaisser could form the initial core of a Monastic Commission to which other members could be admitted, such as the Right Reverend Procurator General of England, Dom Amelli, a representative of the Congregation of Subiaco, etc. Once all were agreed, this Commission would wield considerable influence on the course of things, all the more so in that, being an international body, it would not be exposed to objections from the various nationalities.

Please let me know, Reverend Father, if this project seems good to you. If necessary, you could mention it to your sons in Rome, but I believe that it would be better not to do anything in that regard until my return. The essential thing for now is to do everything possible to ensure a perfect harmony of viewpoints and actions between your representatives and Dom Pothier.

Moreover, I know that those in high places are well aware of the differences of opinion, and that the decision has been made to put an end to those differences. How much more preferable it would be, then, for us to put an end to them ourselves.[166bis]

Very truly yours, etc.

> . . . Hildebrand, *Abbot-Primate O.S.B.*
> Abbey of Maredsous, March 12, Feast of St. Gregory the Great, 1904.

The composition of the Commission envisaged by the Abbot-Primate would not allay suspicions. The issue clearly was to prepare an edition intended for the entire Church of the Roman rite, as were the Solesmes editions (obviously the Benedictine Order uses the Roman *Gradual,* and the other books of the monastic Divine Office contain all the chant pieces of the Roman Office, which is shorter).

The Abbot-Primate did not return to Rome until April 8. The next day he scheduled a meeting with the envoys of Solesmes for April 10,

---

166bis. In this letter, the Abbot-Primate mentions Dom Pothier's alleged copyright to the Solesmes editions of the chant, and other differences of opinion of a musical or monastic nature. See the discussion of this point in Nos. 51 and 59.

when he spoke with them at length about his project. On April 11, he went to pay an extended personal visit to them himself. Soon word came of the project that he was presenting to the Pope and to the Cardinal Secretary of State:

(1) The editing of the Vatican Edition should be done at St. Anselm, for which purpose the Primate would bring together individuals from the various Benedictine Congregations as he saw fit; (2) The publishers who wanted to reproduce this edition would have to seek permission to do so from the Abbot-Primate; (3) In exchange for that permission, the publishers would pay a fee to the Abbot-Primate. The monks of Solesmes would be compensated from these fees. [Note from Rome.]

Dom de Hemptinne had won over Mr. Desclée of Tournai and his compatriots to his project. They subsequently advised the monks of Solesmes to reach an agreement with him. Nonetheless, the project was most certainly rejected immediately by the Pope, as early as the audience of February 22, since we find no trace of it in the letter from Msgr. Bressan to the Abbot of Solesmes. If the Abbot-Primate did not lose hope of seeing his point of view triumph, this was no doubt because he was not kept informed of the negotiations.

64. Initial Difficulties

A word must also be said about an exchange of letters that was at the origin of certain misunderstandings. Solesmes' agreement to cooperate unleashed the ill humor of Pécoul,[167] whom Father de Santi had consulted on the matter of the copyright of the Solesmes editions. Over the course of March and April, he wrote at least a dozen letters to Father de Santi, impassioned letters to which Father de Santi alluded above, and which he gave to Dom Mocquereau in December 1905.

In his letters to Father de Santi, Pécoul revealed a large-scale plan worked out the previous January: to give the Poussielgue publishing company exclusive rights for the Vatican typical edition for France (March 9); to create a Commission of competent and universally recognized individuals charged with granting or refusing authorization to reproduce the typical edition (March 12); to place this Commission under

167. Cf. No. 51.

the control of the Secretary of State, and not of the Congregation of Sacred Rites (March 12). Since the Solesmes editions had to be used as the basis for the planned edition, Pécoul, given his relationship with the Minister of Cults and the Liquidator of the Religious Congregations, would take responsibility for smoothing over the difficulties that might arise owing to the confiscation of the property of Solesmes [a significant letter from Pécoul[168]], particularly the Imprimerie Saint-Pierre (March 9–10, and March 21).

In Pécoul's plans, some ulterior motives concerning Solesmes are quite obvious: exclusive rights for France, thereby excluding Solesmes as a publisher; a Commission of competent and universally recognized individuals . . . In addition, Pécoul specified that the Vatican Edition should be reproduced only *exclusis aliis* [to the exclusion of other editions] (March 9), *ne varietur* [without any variation] (March 19). He even threatened to stir up trouble if the editions of Desclée were to be declared *typical*. In other words, he was recommending that the work of the Abbey of Solesmes be used, while keeping the Abbey on the sidelines (March 27–29).

But Father de Santi remained firm in his resolve to work with Solesmes, and soon stopped answering such impassioned letters. Finally, as soon as the *motu proprio* of April 25 was published, Pécoul wrote him a note full of scorn, as follows:

How is it that pure gold
Has changed into vile lead? (Racine)
Certified accurate: A. Pécoul.

We will come back to Mr. Pécoul; let us merely say at this point that he was laying the groundwork to welcome Dom Mocquereau to Rome

---

168. He suggested that the Pope separate the works of Dom Pothier from the property of the Congregation of France (March 9): "Without the complications caused by the *mystics* [emphasis added] of Solesmes, everything would be easy: done in due time, the full and complete restitution to Dom Pothier of his copyright with regard to Solesmes, by a direct act of the Pope, would have settled everything. Today, that act would still simplify matters in more than one respect; but there must not be any further delay; the Cardinal Secretary of State would send a letter notifying the Abbot of Solesmes, along with the other decisions of the Holy Father concerning Dom Pothier and Dom Guerrin, his indispensable socius.—On account of all this procrastination, anything that is a *work of Solesmes* has been confiscated by the Government by virtue of the law on the Congregations, liturgical books just like all the others. I have had several meeting on this matter with the Director of Cults, Mr. Dumay, and the liquidator of the property of the Congregations, Mr. Ménage, even with the attorney in charge of inventorying the property. I have not overlooked any-

in his own special way. Pécoul was stirring up opinion against Dom Mocquereau, and even went so far as to advise the Superior of the French Seminary, where Dom Mocquereau had been so warmly welcomed in 1890 and in 1891, not to receive him. This explains why Dom Mocquereau, the choir master of Solesmes, was put off at first when he arrived at the French Seminary (letters from Rome, April 2, and from Father Frey, March 7). So, as in 1901, Pécoul's maneuvering did nothing to simplify matters; to the contrary, they were the source of many misunderstandings (cf. note 174).

65. The Actions of Father de Santi

The monks from Solesmes left a detailed journal of the conversations in which they engaged during their stay in Rome in March and April 1904, in the form of letters written every day by one or the other of them, and even by all three at once, on occasion. The object of these conversations was, on the one hand, to settle with Solesmes alone the matter of the copyright to the Benedictine editions of Gregorian chant, and, on the other hand, to prepare the *motu proprio* of April 25 regarding the Vatican Edition announced by Msgr. Bressan in his letter to the Abbot of Solesmes. The monks from Solesmes also speak, in their journal, of the Congress of the Centenary of the Death of St. Gregory the Great.

They visited Father de Santi on March 13, the day after their arrival in Rome. Father de Santi brought them up to date on everything. Thus, they learned (since they had already left England when the letters from Msgr. Bressan and the Abbot-Primate arrived there) that the Holy See wanted to prepare an edition of Gregorian chant in Rome itself, an edition based on the previous Benedictine editions. Dom Mocquereau then showed Father de Santi, using some comparative tables that he had prepared, in which each melody was represented by some thirty manuscripts whose versions matched neume for neume in vertical columns, that it was necessary to return to the manuscripts if serious work was to

---

thing. I would have been able to come to some arrangement, but I had no authority to strike a deal" [emphasis added]. It is clear from these letters that Father de Santi was still corresponding with Pécoul in early April; on March 29, Pécoul wrote to ask for a draft that he had sent to Father de Santi: "rules of order aiming to prevent any recurrence of the abuses of the monopoly."

be accomplished. Father de Santi noted in his journal that the reasons advanced by Dom Mocquereau impressed him deeply (*Journal*, March 13), and that same evening, he wrote to Msgr. Bressan (Dom Cagin, March 14). On March 15, following another meeting with Dom Mocquereau, Father de Santi informed Dom Pothier, who was visiting him, of the resulting change in the situation (*Journal*, March 15).

What was this change? Without doubt, Dom Mocquereau's tables definitively convinced Father de Santi that there was still room to improve the previous Benedictine editions, particularly the edition of the *Liber Gradualis* done by Dom Pothier in 1883, in terms of melody—for, as we shall see, the issue of rhythm was not open to discussion. As you will recall, Father de Santi had criticized Dom Mocquereau for having introduced melodic variations in the *Liber Usualis* of 1903 (No. 52), then came around to his point of view, but not very enthusiastically (No. 57, above). Dom Mocquereau's tables were equally successful in winning over Don Giovanni Mercati, Perosi, Don Molitor, and especially Wagner (Dom Cagin, March 13, 18, 19 and 30; Dom Noetinger, April 7). Wagner was already vehemently opposed to Dom Mocquereau's system of rhythm. From this fact, we can conclude that there was no question, for Dom Mocquereau, of proving the scientific value of his method for rhythm, but of justifying his melodic restorations.

But there is more. Dom Mocquereau prepared a memorandum for the Pope on this subject. The memorandum was presented to Father de Santi, who revised it (Dom Noetinger, March 15 and 17), and the monks from Solesmes submitted the memorandum to Msgr. Bressan on March 20 (Dom Cagin, March 23, cf. Dom Mocquereau, March 18, memoranda of March 14 and 18). Specifically, this memorandum stated:

> Therefore, in a process that can be accomplished only with the aid of the manuscripts belonging to all the Churches and to all periods, we must extract from all these chants the true text; we must reconstitute the truly traditional reading through delicate and patient comparison. (March 18)

The memorandum added that Solesmes would gladly accept verification of its work by a Commission.

From that point on, Father de Santi was thinking not just of having Dom Mocquereau involved in editing the work, but of having him appointed as the man in charge of the editing process, under the oversight of a Commission. Thus, as of March 18, Dom Mocquereau noted that it was to Solesmes alone that the Pope wished to entrust the task of *edit-*

ing the chant books,—and he added that the Pope did not want to hear anything about the project of the Abbot-Primate (Dom Mocquereau, March 18).

Dom Gajard states that he was told by Dom Mocquereau (*Paléographie Musicale* XIV, p. 16) that Father de Santi first thought of appointing him as chairman of the editing Commission, and that Dom Mocquereau allegedly refused that duty in deference to Dom Pothier. We have not found any trace of this fact in the files available to us, and we think that if Father de Santi did think of placing Dom Mocquereau at the head of the Commission for a time, it could have taken place only at this point in time, namely when he made up his mind to entrust the editing of the Vatican Edition to Dom Mocquereau. But this was merely a wish that was quickly dispelled, and by Dom Mocquereau himself, who immediately realized, as did Father de Santi, that he could not be the judge of his own work, and that Dom Pothier could not be cast aside.[169]

The memorandum prepared with Father de Santi's assistance had also addressed the delicate matter of copyright to the Benedictine editions that were to serve as the basis for the Vatican Edition. The issue was addressed again in a memorandum from Dom Noetinger, submitted to the Cardinal Secretary of State on March 21, in response to the letter of Msgr. Bressan to the Abbot of Solesmes (Dom Noetinger, letter of March 21, cf. Dom Cagin, March 23). For his part, Dom Delatte wrote a letter to the Pope "which filled Us with joy" (Brief to Dom Delatte, May 22, 1904).[170]

On March 21 as well, Father de Santi read to the monks from Solesmes the draft of a pontifical document on the Vatican Edition announced by Msgr. Bressan in his letter to Dom Delatte (Dom Cagin, March 23). This document entrusted editing of the Vatican Edition to the Congregation of France, specifically to the Abbey of Solesmes; it specified that the edition would not be made available in the commercial market, but would simply be reserved for publishers, and that any other edition based on the manuscripts could be approved; finally, the composition of new offices that are not found in the manuscripts would be entrusted to the Abbey of Solesmes (Dom Cagin, March 22 and 23).

The very next day, March 22, Father de Santi submitted the draft to the Pope (Dom Cagin, March 23; Father de Santi *Journal*, March 22) and

169. Cf. Moneta-Caglio, *Musica Sacra,* 1962, p. 115.
170. Cf. No. 69.

told the Solesmes contingent about the audience. Dom Mocquereau suggested that the document should contain an appeal to the Bishops and Chapters who have manuscripts, in order to facilitate access to and reproduction of the manuscripts.

Finally, on March 23, Father de Santi accompanied Dom Mocquereau and his companions to the audience with the Pope (de Santi *Journal*, March 23; Dom Cagin, March 23). The Pope spoke in Latin, revisiting the ideas already advanced by Father de Santi: He did not wish to favor any one publisher;—he wanted Solesmes to be involved in editing the work, as Father de Santi had suggested to him (if necessary, he said, a monk could come to Rome for this purpose, a suggestion discarded by Dom Mocquereau, and by Father de Santi who noted that the task of the monks of Solesmes was to edit the chant books, which could be done only at Solesmes where the requisite documentation was found);—but the Pope still wanted an oversight Commission to be presided over by Dom Pothier, a commission which, he thought, would be strictly *pro forma;*—finally, the Congregation of Sacred Rites would not be involved, given prior experience in this area (March 23), a solution suggested to Father de Santi by Pécoul (March 12).

Dom Noetinger, as Cellarer of the Abbey, asked what exactly the Pope wanted, and acting as the representative of Dom Delatte, Noetinger transferred all necessary rights to the Holy See so that the edition might become a reality[170bis] (Dom Noetinger, March 25).

Nevertheless, the donation of the Abbey of Solesmes could be accomplished only in total agreement with the Desclée publishing company of Tournai, to which the Abbey, by contract, had leased its rights to the chant editions when the Monastery Press was despoiled. Received by the Pope on March 27, Count Lefebvre, an associate of Mr. Desclée,

---

170bis. Here is the precise wording of the deed signed by the three representatives of Solesmes: "Most Holy Father, March 23: The envoys of the Abbot of Solesmes have come to Rome to express to Your Holiness their devotion to the Holy See and to work in its name in carrying out the intentions of Your Holiness with regard to Gregorian chant. Having been informed that a Vatican edition is to be prepared under the auspices of and on order of Your Holiness, they are pleased to place at Your disposal the effort and work of Solesmes in any manner necessary for completion of this project, under the conditions that have been presented to them. They are hopeful that an accord may soon be reached between the Holy See and Messrs. Desclée and Lefebvre rendering this offer final. They place at the feet of Your Holiness this expression of feelings of profound respect and filial veneration, Holy Father, as the very humble and very obedient sons of Your Holiness."

joined in the generous gesture of the Abbot of Solesmes.[171] The very next day, March 28, the Pope revealed his determination to pursue this project of an edition of the books of Gregorian chant, after consultation with the Cardinal Secretary of State. Father de Santi, who was present at the audience, acted as interpreter for Solesmes, and the Pope gave him the file of documents received to date on the matter of the planned edition (Dom Cagin, March 28).

The Chapter of Solesmes ratified the donation of Dom Delatte on April 5[171bis] (Dom Delatte, April 6). But as early as April 2, Msgr. Bressan had written to the Abbot of Solesmes on behalf of the Pope to thank him for his eagerness and generosity.[172] Here is a translation of that letter (full text in Appendix IV):

Right Rev. Father!

His Holiness was profoundly moved by the piety and filial devotion, by the spirit of disinterestedness and no small sacrifice, as well as by the marvelous promptness with which Your Reverence accepted the invitation of His Holiness to collaborate in the preparation of a Vatican Edition containing the melodies of the Church and intended for the free use of all the churches throughout the world. The Holy Father has consequently ordered me to manifest his august pleasure to you, with the expression of his gratitude, whilst he wholeheartedly imparts to Your Reverence, to the monks of your monastery, and to their labors, as also to the entire Congregation of France O.S.B. which Your Reverence so excellently governs, the Apostolic blessing. In fulfilling this pleasing and honorable task, kissing your hand I have the honor to repeat that I am

Your Reverence's most humble servant

Giovanni Bressan
Private Chamberlain to His Holiness

171. When they arrived in Rome, the monks from Solesmes learned that the Pope first wanted to entrust publication of the Vatican edition to Desclée, in order to show consideration for the publisher's interests (Dom Noetinger, March 13).

171bis. Here is the wording of the minutes of the meeting of April 5, 1904: "The Sovereign Pontiff having manifested His intention to have a typical edition made at Rome in conformity with the Gregorian traditions, Reverend Father Abbot has suggested to the Convent that the copyrights of Saint-Pierre de Solesmes for the chant books be released into the hands of His Holiness to the extent that this transfer may serve the designs of the Sovereign Pontiff. The votes being unanimous in the affirmative, the meeting was concluded."

172. Msgr. Bressan was similarly instructed to write to the Messrs. Desclée on April 2. The text of that letter is reprinted in A. Duclos, *Sa Sainteté Pie X et la musique religieuse,* Desclée 1905, p. 37.

The Abbot of Solesmes added even more to his sacrifice—and truly it was a sacrifice, particularly at the time it was made, following closely upon the expulsions and at a time when the community of Solesmes had not yet found a stable place of refuge; the Abbot did not wish to receive any compensation for the involvement asked of Solesmes. On March 28, he congratulated Dom Noetinger on having anticipated his thoughts by refusing any form of financial assistance (Dom Delatte, March 28). Later, in May, Dom Delatte again stated that he wanted to assume all costs associated with research in the principal libraries of Europe, for which he was thanked profusely by Father de Santi (May 28) and the Vatican Commission itself in the name of the Pope (cf. *infra*, No. 70).

It was at the audience of March 23 that Pius X granted Solesmes permission to reproduce the Vatican Edition with the rhythmic indications already used by Dom Mocquereau in the *Liber Usualis* of 1903, which Father de Santi did not want to use as the official edition. This concession was not the subject of a written document, but it was tacitly understood, so to speak, in the document given to the Pope by Dom Noetinger and his companions. In 1911, when attacks against the rhythmic editions became more virulent, Father de Santi, a negotiator present at the audiences of March 23 and March 28, bore witness to what had been agreed upon at that time:

I am prepared to swear on the Holy Gospels that it is true that the Benedictines placed this reservation on their donation; that the Holy Father acknowledged as much on two occasions *(repetutamente)*, and that I was instructed by the Holy Father to give assurances on this matter in his name to the monks of Solesmes.

It is understandable, then, that efforts by the opponents of the rhythmic editions to have those editions forbidden by the Holy See always met with the resistance of Pius X.[173]

173. See the comments of Dom Mocquereau on this matter (*Le décret du 14 février 1906 de la S. Congrégation des Rites et les signes rythmiques des Bénédictins de Solesmes*, Desclée 1906, pp. 8 and 9).—Cf. F. M. Bauducco, *Il Padre Angelo de Santi, s.j., e la questione dei "segni ritmici" dal 1904 al 1912*, in *Bolletino Ceciliano* 1964, pp. 75–92.

Here is the original text by Father de Santi quoted above: "Io sono pronto a giurare sui Santi Vangeli che così è veramente che i Benedettini hanno messo questa riserva alla loro cessione, che il S. Padre l'ha repetutamente riconosciuta ed accettata e che io fui incaricato dal S. Padre di assicurarne in suo nome i monaci di Solesmes" (February 6, 1911).

One often hears that the dissension that arose within the Vatican Commission derived from the rhythmic theory of Dom Mocquereau (for example, the article *Solesmes* in the dictionary *Die Musik in Geschichte und Gegenwart* (Blume); this is not the case for, as we shall see, Dom Moc-

Let us return now to the conclusion of Father de Santi's letter to Dom Mocquereau on November 28, 1908, quoted above (see No. 59). In fact, at that time, Father de Santi did not indicate the initial reason that led him to entrust the editing of the Vatican Edition to Solesmes. In November 1908, he wrote:

As far as the guidelines for producing the edition were concerned, it was originally proposed to make a good edition based on the earlier one. But when the monks of Solesmes demonstrated that the copyright was theirs and the Holy Father recognized the need to give them some compensation of honor in return for the transfer of rights by officially declaring them editors of the Vatican Edition, we thought in terms of a criterion more strictly scientific, such as had been proposed in the *Motu proprio*(of April 25, 1904). (Full text in Appendix IV.)

Yet in Father de Santi's *Journal*, written *at the very time of the events*, and in the correspondence of Solesmes, it is quite clear that it was the scientific evidence brought forth by Dom Mocquereau that convinced Father de Santi to act as he did. On March 13, he wrote:

In the afternoon Dom Mocquereau, Dom Cagin, and Dom Noetinger come. They are aware of some things and I have told them the rest. The reasons they advance in support of their edition are very weighty and I am impressed by them.

And again on March 15:

Dom Mocquereau comes bringing his comparative charts. In the afternoon Dom Pothier comes and I tell him frankly my views on the changed situation. (Appendix IV)

So Dom Mocquereau managed to convince Father de Santi that Dom Pothier's restoration of the melodies was still imperfect, and that it was

---

quereau never intended to impose his rhythmic system on the Vatican Commission, something that he could not aspire to do in any event. In fact, Father de Santi did not want it used in an official edition (cf. *supra*, No. 57). Further confirmation is provided below in No. 70, concerning a memorandum from Father Moissenet against the rhythmic editions of Solesmes, a memorandum that the Commission rejected because it was written at a time when the author could not have known of the intentions of the Holy See in this regard.—Finally, the minutes of the Vatican Commission prove that the debate focused on the melodic restoration itself, not on the question of rhythm (cf. *infra*, No. 70). In his booklet on the *Décret du 14 février 1906*, Dom Mocquereau wrote: "It [the Commission] did not have to debate or decide on the use or rejection for the Vatican edition of the Solesmes rhythmic indications which it could not use" (reference to the authorization allowed to Solesmes to publish rhythmic editions which Father de Santi did not want).

possible to proceed with greater scientific rigor. Consequently, Father de Santi agreed that the editorship of the planned edition should be entrusted to him.

Shortly thereafter, on March 30, Father de Santi sent off the printed draft copy of the *motu proprio* for the Vatican Edition (Dom Cagin, March 30). On March 31, Father de Santi learned from the Pope himself that he had made the decision to produce the edition in Rome (de Santi *Journal*, March 31). The printed draft will be analyzed in comparison with the final wording of the *motu proprio* (see No. 68, below).

66. Final Discussions

At that point, Dom Mocquereau was invited to participate in the preparations for the papal document. Msgr. Moneta-Caglio quoted Father de Santi's journal concerning the meeting of April 4, during which there had been objections in the matter of the role assigned to Solesmes in the draft of the *motu proprio*.

April 4. Meeting of the Roman Commission to discuss the page proofs. We agree on the first three paragraphs. But when we get to the point of the editing by Solesmes we reach a deadlock for one reason or another. The gist of it is that Dom Pothier and Dom Janssens do not wish to be present because they are against Solesmes.

The Solesmes correspondence clearly indicates that the incriminating phrase of the *motu proprio* was what the Pope had wished (Dom Cagin, April 3–4; Dom Noetinger, April 6), and that after the meeting the opponents wrote about it once again to Father de Santi[173bis] (Dom Noetinger, April 6) and Dom Pothier to the Pope himself (Dom Cagin, April 9). As for Father de Santi, after having explained everything personally to the Pope, he sent off a memo (Dom Cagin, April 10; Dom Noetinger, April 14–15), in which he defended his point of view: the editorship to be confided to Solesmes with an oversight committee presided over by Dom Pothier. At the same time, Father de Santi offered a refutation of two other suggestions: Father Ehrle's note, in which the

---

173bis. The privileges accorded to Solesmes deserved to outweigh the protestations (Dom Pothier) and they proposed to have the editing done at Saint Anselm (Dom Janssens, according to a letter from Dom Noetinger dated April 6).

writer proposed that the Commission being organized for the *motu pro-prio* should itself be responsible for editing the publication;—and the proposal by Dom Janssens that the editing should be done at Saint Anselm on the basis of the Benedictine editions under the aegis of Dom Pothier (Noetinger, April 6, 24, 15, and 16) and not that of the Abbot Primate. The Messrs. Desclée, meanwhile, hoped that this last proposal would be found acceptable. On April 8, in fact, they advised Solesmes to align themselves with the Abbot Primate, who shortly thereafter communicated his plan to the Cardinal Secretary of State. On the eve of signing the *motu proprio*, the problem was still unresolved (de Santi *Journal*, April 18, 22, 23; Dom Noetinger, April 19 and 25; Dom Cagin, April 21).

Father de Santi's journal reflects the ill-humor of the pontifical publisher, who wished to bypass the Benedictines. Msgr. Bressan and Scotti himself were, in fact, supportive of Father de Santi on April 18. Hence the Solesmians thought it wise to make a protest to the Pope directly, making it known that they had nothing whatsoever to do with the new projects (Dom Noetinger, April 22). Their request was communicated to Father de Santi by Msgr. Bressan, who provided the necessary clarifications for Father de Santi, who then passed them along to the Pope on April 23. The result confirmed the Pope's resolution, which he indicated to Father de Santi on the same day, April 23 (cf. de Santi *Journal*, April 18, 22, and 23; Dom Cagin, April 23; and Dom Noetinger, April 24). However, on April 24, Baron Kanzler and Msgr. Respighi conferred with Father de Santi and succeeded in letting the Pope know that they wished to see to it that the editing of the Vatican Edition be confided to Solesmes (Dom Noetinger, April 25).

Father de Santi tried very hard to convince the Pope, doubtless still hesitant, to adopt his point of view. He had thought of making a recording of the chant sung by the students of the French Seminary who had been rehearsed by Dom Mocquereau.[174]

In this way the Pope will be informed *de visu* by Father de Santi of the practical functioning, and would thus understand *ex auditu* what Gregorian chant sounds like at Solesmes under the direction of Dom Mocquereau . . . (Dom Cagin, April 23)

---

174. Dom Noetinger's letter of April 3 reads as follows: "Today the Prior (Dom Mocquereau) went to conduct the Mass at the French Seminary. It went well and it so completely convinced

In fact, the Gramophone Company recorded the Centenary of St. Gregory the Great under the direction of Msgr. Rella, Dom Pothier, Dom Janssens, and Dom Mocquereau. This last performance included the Alleluia *Fac nos innocuam*, the Easter Introit, Gradual, and Sequence, plus the Introit *Sacerdotes Dei*.

On April 27, Father de Santi was received in an audience with Pius X and charged with putting the final touches on the pontifical document about the Vatican Edition. That is to say, this document was predated, because it carries the official date of April 25, the Feast of St. Mark, Patron of Venice (de Santi *Journal*, April 27). It was as Father de Santi had wanted, but with the following changes: the editing was no longer entrusted to the Benedictine Order (this was to bypass the proposal of the Abbot Primate), but to the O.S.B. Congregation of France, and to the Solesmes monastery. The phrase concerning the supervision of the edition by the Abbot of Solesmes was suppressed, in order to satisfy the objections that had been made. The Pope deemed it needless to mention this, since everything had to be done in proper hierarchic order within the French Congregation. But he did retain the mention of the Abbey of Solesmes, despite the opposition. On April 27, Dom Noetinger wrote:

Up to the last minute, even yesterday, our adversaries tried to erase the mention of the Solesmes monastery; they did not succeed in this, but they did succeed in suppressing the phrase: under the direction of the Right Reverend . . . etc. The Pope considered the phrase inappropriate because everything must follow the hierarchical order to pass through the Congregation, and moreover, Father de Santi says that the Pope planned to send us a Brief in which whatever is lacking in the *motu proprio* will be completed .(Dom Noetinger, April 17)

The first draft read as follows (emphasis added to indicate the principal changes made in the final text):

In view of our special affection for the celebrated Benedictine Order, thankful with true satisfaction for the untiring efforts given by the Benedictine monks to the restoration of the Church's authentic melodies, We wish that in the future also the editing of those segments of the liturgical books that contain the chant and the composition of new melodies which will be included in the new Offices of the Roman Church, should always be *reserved for the Benedictine Order*

---

the teachers and professors that at the dinner they gave him an ovation, and to give further impulse to the ovation, they confessed that it was because of Pécoul's letters that they had refused to receive him" (Dom Cagin, April 2).

and in particular for the Congregation and to the monastery of Solesmes *under the direction and authority of the Right Reverend Fr. Abbot* "pro tempore" Superior General of the above-mentioned congregation, as has been done in the past with regard to these monks.[174bis]

(The Appendix to the draft read: under the direction of the Right Rev. Abbot of Solesmes, Superior General of that Congregation.) The definitive text reads as follows:

Because of our special predilection for the Order of Saint Benedict, recognizing the work done by the Benedictine monks in the restoration of the genuine melodies of the Roman Church, particularly the work done by the Congregation of France and of the monastery of Solesmes, we wish that for this edition the editing of those parts that contain the chant, and the composition of the new melodies for the new offices of the Roman Church, should at all times be *reserved for the Benedictine Order* and in a special way for the Congregation and monastery of Solesmes.[174ter]

67. The St. Gregory the Great Congress

We must go back in time to say a few words about the celebrations accompanying the Thirteen Centenary of the death of St. Gregory the Great.[175] The celebrations were marked first by a Congress, from April 6–9, which was especially encouraged by the *motu proprio* on sacred music dated November 22, 1903, and which brought together more than 800 participants. From the moment of the opening session on April 7,

---

174bis. Per la specialissima Nostra predilezione verso l'inclito Ordine di S. Benedetto, riconoscendo con vera soddisfazione l'opera indefessa prestata dai monaci benedettini nella restaurazione delle genuine melodie della Chiesa romana, particolarmente poi dai religiosi della Congregazione e del monastero di Solesmes, vogliamo che anche in seguito, la redazione di quelle parti dei libri liturgici, che contengono il canto, e la composizione delle nuove melodie che occorressero per le nuove officiature della Chiesa romana, siano sempre *riservate all'Ordine Benedettino* ed in particolare alla Congregazione ed al monastero di Solesmes, *sotto la guida e la dipendenza del Rev.mo Abbate* Superiore Generale "pro tempore" della detta Congregazione, come presso quei monaci si è sempre in addietro praticato.

174ter. Per la speciale Nostra predilezione verso l'Ordine si S. Benedetto riconoscendo l'opera prestata dai monaci benedettini nella restaurazione delle genuine melodie della Chiesa romana, particolarmente poi da quelli della Congregazione di Francia e del Monastero di Solesmes, vogliamo che per questa edizione, la redazione delle parti che contengono il canto, sia affidata in modo particolare ai monaci della Congregazione di Francia ed al Monastero di Solesmes.

175. *Rassegna Gregoriana* 1904, col. 263ff.—*Revue du Chant Grégorien* 1904, pp. 148–161.

Father de Santi and Dr. Peter Wagner paid tribute to Dom Pothier and Dom Mocquereau (Dom Noetinger, April 7). But even before that, during one of the preparatory meetings on March 30, Dr. Wagner had requested an ovation for Solesmes because of the work done by the Abbey in restoring the traditional Gregorian chant in the domain of practicality as well as in the domain of science (Dom Cagin, March 30).

Dom Pothier and Dom Mocquereau addressed the delegates, Dom Mocquereau on April 7, at the First General Meeting, and Dom Pothier on April 9, at the Third General Meeting. Dom Mocquereau explained the method followed at Solesmes in restoring a melody according to the most rigid rules of paleography. Dom Pothier took for his topic *Le chant grégorien est un art*, emphasizing the artistic side of Gregorian chant.[176] Consciously or not, each side took up differing positions even before the creation of the Pontifical Commission that dealt with publication of the Gregorian chant books. In one segment of his lecture entitled *Evolution in aesthetics and the Gregorian tradition*, Dom Mocquereau replied to a recent article by Dom Pothier on the same subject, in which the author justified beforehand his principle for the restoration of the Gregorian melodies taking into account their development over the centuries down to modern times, i.e. not overlooking changes that occurred in the melodies after the golden age of Gregorian chant. Here is the key passage:

It has always been the way with tradition down through the ages, whether pre-Gregorian or Gregorian, that as a living tradition it is consequently susceptible, as is every form of life, to constant change and development, but always by means of evolution and not revolution.[177]

Dom Pothier had this point of view admitted in the *motu proprio* during the preparatory stage, and it became the basis for disputes relating to the Vatican Edition (Dom Cagin, April 2).

It was during his lecture that Dom Mocquereau estimated that it

---

176. The two lectures are printed in the *Rassegna Gregoriana* of 1904, Dom Pothier's (*Le chant grégorien est un art*) at col. 325–332, and Dom Mocquereau's (*L'École Grégorienne de Solesmes: I. Sa Méthode critique*, col. 233–244; II. *Histoire d'un neume*, col. 311–326; III. *L'évolution dans l'esthétique et la tradition grégorienne*, col. 397–420). Dom Mocquereau's lecture was translated into Italian and Spanish (*Études Grégoriennes* II, 1957, p. 199). Both lectures were recorded by the Gramophone Company.

177. *La question du plain-chant. Une lettre de Dom Pothier,* in *Le XXe Siècle*, Brussels, February 15, 1904.

would take fifty years to prepare a definitive edition: "Even with our charts, some areas of our work remain provisional . . . It would be inadvisable and premature to offer an edition as being definitive. Perhaps in fifty years such an edition may be within the realm of possibility. Not today."[178] This statement was to be used against future publications, and against Dom Mocquereau himself. Msgr. Moneta-Caglio commented in this respect: "But upon sufficient reflection, this is one of the most judicious statements ever made by Dom Mocquereau. It gives a full picture of his conscience as a paleographer."[179]

We must also point out the April 9 lecture given by Dom David, entitled *Comment les mélodies grégoriennes ont été retrouvées*, which dealt rather briefly with the history of the beginnings of the Gregorian restoration at Solesmes.[180] Dom Cagin also responded to this in the *Rassegna Gregoriana* by developing the subject more fully, with the documentation that he had at hand in Rome. That article, entitled *L'oeuvre de Solesmes dans la restauration du chant grégorien* (cf. *Rassegna Gregoriana* 1904, col. 295ff.), in turn elicited reactions which intimated that the proposed publication project would not be accomplished without difficulty.

At the sidelines of the Congress, Pécoul was also distributing an article from *Le Gaulois* that was at least inspired, if not actually written, by him. The article makes Dom Pothier out to be the founder of the *Paléographie Musicale*.[181] Moreover, faced with the success of Dom Mocquereau's "tables," this same person started the rumor that the Solesmes choirmaster followed the manuscripts too closely, and this after having accused him of not giving them sufficient attention.

On April 9, the Vatican Edition was officially announced during the Third General Meeting by Msgr. Foucault, Bishop of Saint Denis, Honorary President of the Gregorian section. The night before, on April 8, at the Second General Meeting, Father de Santi was pleased to say that the Pope did not favor any particular publisher, and that, although for the time being the Solesmes publications were the only ones considered

178. *Rassegna Gregoriana*, col. 243.

179. Moneta-Caglio, *Musica Sacra* 1962, p. 115, notes 308–309.

180. The lecture is published in the *Rassegna Gregoriana*, col. 225. Father de Santi made some changes in the lecture when it went to press (Dom Cagin, April 4, and Dom Noetinger, April 12).

181. A. Louis, *Une réforme de Pie X, La musique sacrée et le chant grégorien*, in *Le Gaulois* of March 8, 1904. This historic error was often repeated in the years that followed. Therefore, from that time on, announcement of the *Paléographie Musicale* included this subtitle: "Under the direction of André Mocquereau, Prior of Solesmes."

as conforming to the *motu proprio* of November 22, 1903, and had come to be approved by the Congregation of Sacred Rites of February 24—on the favorable advice of Perosi[182] and according to a formula designed by the Holy Father himself (Dom Noetinger, March 12, cf. Desclée to Dom Noetinger, February 26, 1904)—this approbation did not provide a privilege in their favor, since it was given to every other publisher who would offer the same guarantee of fidelity to the manuscripts.

These same assurances were given by the Pope himself to Msgr. Foucault, who then communicated them, in turn, to those attending the Congress at the same time that he announced the official Vatican Edition. In fact, the Vatican Edition was announced in the following terms, in wording personally approved by Pius X:

> His Holiness does not wish to establish a privilege of a monopoly for any publisher.
>
> As soon as possible after the Congress, His Holiness will form a Commission to prepare the Typical Edition.
>
> As the pages are issued by the Vatican Press, they will be placed at the disposal of the publishers who will have the right to reproduce them but without change.
>
> Meanwhile, each diocese can continue to utilize its current books without being obliged to adopt others before the publication of the Typical Edition.

Each person interpreted the first part of the statement according to his own mind set. For some, Poussielgue was seen as the publisher, whose hope relative to the publishing project was mentioned above—and this, it seems, is what Father de Santi had in mind;[183] for others, only Desclée, Solesmes's publisher, could be viewed as the publisher (cf. *infra*, No. 71). As for the second part of the declaration, while it announced the formation of a Commission instructed to prepare the Vatican Edition, it did not define its role, and it made no mention of the *editors* for the publication. At this time, in fact, the Pope's determination had not yet taken shape relative to these two bodies. What is more, the correspondence at Solesmes attests to the fact that Pius X was still quite ambivalent as to the matter of the edition itself (letters of April 8, 10, and 11).

On April 11, Pius X celebrated a Papal Mass in the Vatican Basilica.

---

182. Cf. *Sulla restaurazione della Musica Sacra e del Canto gregoriano secondo il motu proprio di S. S. Pio X Papa* (supplement to the *Rassegna Gregoriana* of 1904), pp. 8–9; *Un giudizio del Maestro Perosi sul Canto Gregoriano*.

183. Moneta-Caglio, *Musica Sacra* 1962, p. 116. Cf. *infra* No. 71.

According to his wishes, as previously expressed in his letter of December 8, 1903 to the Cardinal Vicar, the chants were Gregorian. The Proper was sung by a schola of 150 singers from St. Anselm, under the direction of Dom Janssens, and the Ordinary, the Mass of the Angels, was sung by more than 1,000 clerics from 36 different institutes, under the direction of Msgr. Rella. All these chants were taken from the latest Solesmes publication, according to the Pope's wishes, and reproduced in leaflet form without the rhythmic indications for the Prelates and with rhythmic indications for the singers.[184] The *Alma cohors* Sequence had been restored by the Anglican pastor H. M. Bannister, a well-known paleographer.

The Pope followed the Mass from a parchment Missal, transcribed and decorated in the style of the most richly decorated manuscripts by the nuns of Saint Cecilia of Solesmes. At the time, the nuns were refugees at Ryde, Isle of Wight. The volume offered to the Pope by the Solesmians on April 9 (Dom Cagin, April 9) contained the *Ordo Romanus* used for the service, the Office of Tierce, as well as the chants for the Mass of St. Gregory. Camille Bellaigue wrote:

Pius X was finishing singing the Preface. The Cardinal Deacon who was assisting him turned the page of the Sanctus, where the Benedictine nuns had painted a golden lyre with the figure of Christ on the Cross stretched out across it. This symbolic miniature charmed the Pope, we know, and held his attention for a moment. Art and faith combined could not offer a more subtle expression of thanks to the Pontiff whose firm and steady hand had just placed the image of the Crucified Lord back onto the lyre.[185]

Mention has been made of Bannister. He was the one who, at the beginning of the April 11 ceremony, stunned by how little attention was being given to Dom Mocquereau, made him step out of the crowd and take his place in the front row (Dom Cagin, April 12). A witness wrote: "Why have the Benedictines of Solesmes in these solemn feasts taken such a self-effacing role? Or rather, why did they play no role at all? The majority of the Congress attendees were visibly troubled by this."[186]

184. *Officium et Missa Sancti Gregorii Papae et Confessoris et Ecclesiae Doctoris juxta antiquorum codicum fidem restituta*, Desclée 1904, 33 pp.

185. *Pie X et Rome*, Librairie National 1913. Cf. *Rassegna Gregoriana* 1904, col. 391–396, with two photographs of the Missal and a Brief of thanks addressed to the Reverend Abbess of Sainte-Cécile de Solesmes.

186. Reverend H. Villetard, *Les fêtes de la Musique Liturgique et le XIIIᵉ Centenaire de la mort de saint Grégoire le Grand à Rome* (April 6–14, 1904), Paris 1904, p. 14.

On April 13, the Pope received the delegates and exhorted them to imitate the holiness of St. Gregory. Then he gave each a commemorative medal of the Congress (Dom Noetinger, April 14).

68. Publication of the *Motu Proprio* Dated April 25, 1904

As mentioned earlier, the *motu proprio* for the Vatican Edition was signed on April 27—and thus was antedated, since it bears the date of April 25, the Feast of St. Mark. Below is a translation of it, with references to the draft discussed above, which differs from the final text on certain points. The Pope said:

With Our *motu proprio* of November 22, 1903, and with the subsequent decree, published by Our command through the Congregation of Sacred Rites, January 8, 1904, We have restored to the Roman Church Her ancient Gregorian chant, the chant which She inherited from the Fathers and which She has jealously preserved in Her liturgical codices, and which the more recent studies have happily brought back to its primitive purity. [The same terms were used in the *motu proprio* of November 22, 1903.]

In order to accomplish the work begun, as is proper, and to provide Our Roman Church and all Churches of the same Rite with the common text of the liturgical Gregorian melodies, We have decreed the publication of the liturgical books containing the chant of the Holy Roman Church as restored by Us, by Our Vatican Press.

[In a practical Appendix, the draft stated that publication would be limited to typical and essential books only: "Publication will be limited to the typical and essential books only, such as the *Liber Gradualis, Liber Antiphonarius, Rituale Romanum, Pontificale Romanum*, etc. The chant shall be expressed in the appropriate traditional Gregorian notation, without particular rhythmical indications."]

In order that everything may proceed with full comprehension by all those who are or will be called by Us [the draft also added: "or by our Congregation of Sacred Rites," see above] to offer the tribute of their studies to a work of such great importance, and so that the work may proceed with the fitting diligence and alacrity, We have established the following norms:

a. The melodies of the Church, so called Gregorian, will be restored in their integrity and purity in accordance with the true text of the most ancient codices, in such a way, however, that due attention be given to the true tradition contained in the manuscripts throughout the centuries, and to the practical usage of contemporary liturgy. [This last sentence, as we have already pointed out, was suggested by Dom Pothier and was destined to trigger endless debate later on.]

b. Because of Our special predilection for the Order of St. Benedict, recognizing the work done by the Benedictine monks in the restoration of the genuine melodies of the Roman Church, particularly the work done by the Congregation of France, and of the Monastery of Solesmes, We wish that for this edition, the editing of those parts containing the chant be especially entrusted to the monks of the Congregation of France, and to the Monastery of Solesmes. [This text was discussed in No. 66.]

c. The works thus prepared will be submitted for examination and revision to the special Roman Commission recently instituted by Us for this purpose. It has the obligation of sworn secrecy for all that regards the compilation of the texts and the manner of printing.[187] This same obligation must also be extended to all other persons outside the Commission who may be called upon to render their services to this same end. The Commission must proceed in its examination with maximum diligence, permitting nothing to be published for which sufficient and certain proof cannot be given. In case of doubt, the opinion shall be sought of persons who are outside the Commission and the editorial staff who are recognized as competent in this field of study and are capable of rendering an authoritative judgment. During revision of the melodies, if difficulties should arise concerning the liturgical text, the Commission will consult the historical-liturgical Commission previously instituted under the auspices of Our Congregation of Sacred Rites, so that both Commissions proceed concordantly with respect to those portions of the books common to the work of both Commissions. [In case of persistent difficulties, the draft (Appendix) referred the issue back to the supreme authority: "If a mutual understanding cannot be achieved even in this manner, the problem shall be decided by the Supreme Authority."]

d. The approval to be obtained from Us and from Our Congregation of Sacred Rites for the books of chant thus compiled and published will be of such a nature that no one else shall be permitted to approve liturgical books, even in the parts which contain the chant, unless they either altogether conform with the editions published by the Vatican press under Our auspices, or at least in

187. With regard to the secrecy demanded of the members of the Vatican Commission, Father de Santi noted in 1907, in the *Rassegna Gregoriana,* that the "obligation to secrecy had to do only with the compilation of the texts and the printing schedule, as indicated in the *motu proprio,* so that publishers would not issue anything ahead of the Vatican Press" (*Rassegna Gregoriana* 1907, col. 92), cf. Moneta-Caglio, *Musica Sacra* 1962, p. 70 and note 260).—As to the texts relating to the deliberations of the Commission, if they, too, were included in the secrecy, it must be acknowledged that the Commission scarcely felt bound by it; from 1905–1906, the *Revue du Chant Grégorien* published two letters from the Cardinal Secretary of State intended only for the Commission members (*Revue du Chant Grégorien* 1905, p. 145 and 1906, p. 105).

the judgment of the Commission they conform in such a way that the variations introduced prove themselves to come from the authority of other good Gregorian codices. [This last option expressly referred to the Solesmes editions already in use.]

e. The literary copyrights of the Vatican Edition are reserved to the Holy See. The editors and printers of every nation may request from Us permission to print this edition. Those who under certain fixed conditions will give sure guarantees of their capability to accomplish the work satisfactorily will be granted permission to reproduce these freely as they wish, and to make extracts therefrom, and to spread the copies everywhere. [The draft differed on this point, since it stated that the edition did not have copyright status as St. Pius X had at first wished (cf. letter of Msgr. Bressan to Dom Delatte): "The Roman edition will be limited to the typical and essential books only, and will not have copyright status, so that all publishers will be permitted to reproduce it as they see fit, to make excerpts from it, and to distribute copies of it according to their own interests" (cf. No. 65).]

Thus, with the help of God, We hope to be able to restore to the Church the unity of Her traditional chant, in a manner corresponding to the science, the history, the art, and the dignity of liturgical worship, at least insofar as Our present studies permit, and We reserve to Ourselves and to Our successors the right to dispose otherwise.

Given at Rome at St. Peter's on April 25, 1904, on the Feast of St. Mark the Evangelist, in the first year of our Pontificate.

Pius X, Pope.

It is interesting to note two provisions of the draft that were retained in practice, even though they do not appear in the *motu proprio* itself:

a. One concerned the new Offices, which are not in the manuscripts and which had to be composed according to the ancient models: "But the melodies composed for the new Offices, which for this reason are not found in the ancient manuscripts, ought always to correspond exactly to those published by Us; they ought to conform in every respect to those of the Vatican Edition."

b. The other requested that the Commission issue the *Kyriale* first (which was done, as the Vatican Commission had already made this decision during its initial meetings).

The Pontifical Commission for the Vatican Edition of the Gregorian liturgical books instituted by the *motu proprio* included ten members and ten consultors:

Members of the Commission:

Right Rev. Dom Joseph Pothier, O.S.B., Abbot of Saint-Wandrille, *President*

Msgr. Carlo Respighi, Pontifical Master of Ceremonies, of Rome

Msgr. Lorenzo Perosi, Perpetual Director of the Sistine Chapel, of Rome

Msgr. Antonio Rella, of Rome

Rev. Dom André Mocquereau, O.S.B., Prior of Solesmes

Rev. Dom Laurent Janssens, O.S.B., Rector of St. Anselm, of Rome

Rev. Father Angelo de Santi, S.J., of Rome

Professor Baron Rudolf Kanzler, of Rome

Professor Dr. Peter Wagner, of Fribourg, Switzerland

Professor H. G. Worth, of London

Consultors of the Commission:

Rev. Father Raffaello Baralli, of Lucca

Rev. Father François Perriot, of Langres

Rev. Father René Moissenet, of Dijon

Rev. Father Norman Holly, of New York

Rev. Father Ambrogio Amelli, O.S.B., Prior of Monte Cassino

Rev. Father Hugo Gaisser, O.S.B., of the Greek College at Rome

Rev. Father Michael Horn, O.S.B., of the Monastery of Seckau

Rev. Father Raphael Molitor, O.S.B., of the Monastery of Beuron

Professor Amedée Gastoué, of Paris[187bis]

On April 29, the Pope received the members and consultors who were in Rome.

The *Minutes of the Pontifical Commission for the Vatican Edition of Gregorian Liturgical Books* begin as follows:

The Holy Father received the Commission in an audience on April 29, 1904, at 10 o'clock in the hall of the Library. Present were: Right Rev. Dom Pothier, Dom Mocquereau, Dom Janssens, Msgr. Respighi, Msgr. Rella, Father de Santi, and Baron Kanzler.

187bis. The announcement of Dom Mocquereau's appointment is dated April 30, 1904, with the signature of Cardinal L. Tripepi, Pro-Prefect of the Congregation of Sacred Rites.

In very affectionate terms, the Holy Father thanked the Commission "for the kindness shown toward the Holy See and to him personally" by offering its work for the Vatican Edition of the liturgical books. He said, "With Dom Pothier, Dom Mocquereau, and Dom Janssens, we are an *iron barrel* [i.e., *we are sure to succeed*] and we are unafraid of our critics. We shall respond to them; as for those critics who add the prefix *hyper* that is so prevalent these days, we need not be concerned by them." The Pope read the list of consultors, praising the choice of membership. He singled out for special commendation the Director of the Vatican Press, Commander Scotti, and recommended that all should keep him informed of their deliberations and actions. Finally, he gave each one a copy of the text of the *motu proprio* of April 25 and, at the same time, a silver medal enclosed in a small case emblazoned with his coat of arms. After imparting his blessing to each, He ended the audience by thanking them again and encouraging them in the task ahead.

69. Brief of 1904, *Ex Quo Tempore*, to Dom Delatte

On May 22, 1904, the Abbot of Solesmes was honored by a Pontifical Brief. In this document, the Pope not only recalled and praised the work of Solesmes on Gregorian chant and thanked the Abbot for his promised collaboration in favor of the Vatican Edition, and for his generosity, but also praised again the manner in which, up to the present, Solesmes had pursued the work of restoring the Gregorian melodies. We know that this method was to be practically rejected by certain members of the Vatican Commission because it seemed too rigid, not allowing optional choices of melodic variants and for adopting certain changes conforming to modern taste and introduced in the old melodies over the centuries of its history. A word must be said on the origin of this document.

Father de Santi was saddened at witnessing the first lively opposition, and lost no time in conceiving the idea of a Brief to the Abbot of Solesmes to regain the terrain lost during the heated discussion in preparation for the *motu proprio* of April 25. This is what Dom Noetinger wrote on April 27: "Father de Santi says that the Holy Father intends to send us a Brief in which what is lacking in the *motu proprio* will be filled in" (letter quoted above). On the same day, Dom Mocquereau noted: "Father de Santi, seeing how much I regretted the omission of the Abbot of Solesmes *(motu proprio)*, repeated several times that this omission will be rectified very clearly in the Brief that the Holy Father will soon send you."

Father de Santi wanted to have the method employed by Dom Mocquereau approved, a method that he could judge himself thanks to the comparative tables shown him. In 1905, he based his defense of Solesmes' work on this document. The Brief is not a mandate, at least not in the sense indicated by Father de Santi, because Msgr. Bressan had already transmitted the Pope's thanks to the Abbot of Solesmes in a letter dated April 2 (cf. No. 65), and to Dom Mocquereau in a letter of April 7. This second letter announced the shipment of two chalices intended for the monasteries of St. Peter and of St. Cecilia of Solesmes. Msgr. Moneta-Caglio did not call attention to this Brief in his article in the *Musica Sacra* of Milan. This is why we are dwelling on the elements that characterize it, and provide a complete translation of it below, since the Brief outlines the main lines of Solesmes' work in the matter of Gregorian chant. We have underscored the principal passage.[188]

To our dear Son, Paul Delatte, O.S.B., President of the Benedictine Congregation of France, Abbot of Solesmes

Pius X, Pope.

Dear Son, Greeting and Apostolic Benediction.

Ever since Prosper Guéranger of illustrious memory, your first predecessor, by his wholehearted devotion to liturgical science, aroused and inflamed your endeavors by his own, everyone has been acquainted with the renowned name of the monastery of Solesmes, especially through the skillful work of restoration of the ancient teaching of Gregorian melodies. And you, who were pressing forward this both difficult and fruitful undertaking, did not, and indeed could not, lack signs of praise from the Apostolic See.

For Leo XIII of blessed memory more than once testified to this, and particularly in a letter addressed to you by name in May 1901; and, moreover, quite recently in the month of February, the Congregation of Sacred Rites both confirmed and willingly approved the liturgical books of plainchant edited under your care and already widely in use.

188. On May 28, Father de Santi wrote to Dom Mocquereau: "Msgr. Galli said that the Holy Father holds firmly to the details of the Brief, except he crossed out what was said about the equality between the Vatican edition and that of Solesmes."—This Brief is found in the *Rassegna Gregoriana* 1904, col. 387–390. Msgr. Fernessole, *Pie X, essai historique,* vol. 2, p. 118 (Lethielleux 1953) remarked that the tone of the pontifical document "was moreover one of high praise and endearment."

We, however, hold that the time has come for Our office to deal authoritatively with the work of restoring the Gregorian chant according to the old traditional order, and We have shown quite recently that We hold your labors in this area in very high esteem, as We have frequently testified elsewhere. For in the solemn ceremonies which We celebrated at the tomb of Gregory the Great in honor of his centenary anniversary, when We wished, as it were, to consecrate the beginnings of the restoration of the Gregorian chant, We ordered the Solesmes melodies to be used as an example.

Now, moreover, there is a special reason why We should extol, in addition to this great skill of yours, your sentiments of devotion towards the Roman Pontiff. For when We were thinking of deciding on a Vatican Edition of liturgical melodies, which should be adopted everywhere under Our authority, and appealed to your zeal with this object, We received from you, Our beloved son, in the month of March, a most gratifying letter saying that you were not only ready and prepared to help with the desired work, but were willing for that purpose to yield Us even the fruits of your toils which had already been published.

It is then easy to understand how highly We value such a signal indication of your love and regard, as well as the gratification it affords Us. And in order to express the thanks deserved by such an exceptional service, as by Our *motu proprio,* We have charged chosen men to prepare Our said official edition, so at the same time *We wish it to be the work of the congregation of which you are the Superior, and especially the duty of the community of Solesmes, in their own manner and method,* to go through the entire field of ancient records now existing, and when they have thence elaborated and arranged the materials of this edition, to submit them to the examination and approval of those whom We have appointed for that purpose.

And as to this toilsome but most honorable duty, although you had already been informed of it, We gladly appraise you by Our own hand that We have laid it upon you, beloved Son, whose chief care it is to see that your companions carry it out. We know your great love for the Apostolic See and Church, your zeal for the seemliness of divine worship, and your care for the holy rule of the monastic life. The further practice of these virtues will assure you hereafter, as it has done hitherto, a happy issue to your labors; and verily the saying, which Gregory uttered concerning the Father of the Rule, may not unfittingly be applied to you his children: "His teaching could not differ from his life."

But We trust that abundant assistance will be afforded to you in your endeavors to carry through the work committed to your care, and particularly that there will be no hindrance to your investigation of the ancient codices; and We are sure that the principal factor, the divine assistance, which We earnestly implore, will not be wanting. As a presage whereof, and in testimony of Our singular benevolence, We most affectionately grant to you, beloved Son, and to your monks Our Apostolic blessing in the Lord.

Given at Rome at St. Peter's on the Feast of Pentecost, May 22, 1904, in the first year of Our Pontificate.

Pius X, Pope.

We shall not give the original Latin of this document, titled *Ex quo tempore*, which has been frequently reprinted in journals almost as often as the Brief *Nos quidem* of May 17, 1901, addressed to the Abbot of Solesmes by Leo XIII (cf. No. 50).

IV ▪ THE MEETINGS OF THE

COMMISSION HELD IN 1904

70. The Initial Meetings of the Commission

The meetings of the Commission began on the afternoon of April 29. Six meetings were held between April 29 and June 27 at the Circle of St. Peter, at the offices of the Congregation of the Propagation of the Faith, and at St. Anselm, the Benedictine house. The purpose of these meetings was purely practical: to organize the work, and to determine the steps to be taken. In these first six meetings, there were never more than seven members of the Commission present: Dom Pothier, the President, took part in the first meeting only, and Dom Mocquereau participated only in the first three. Dom Janssens came to only four meetings, Gaisser and Kanzler to three. Perosi attended two. Only Respighi, Father de Santi and Msgr. Rella, attended all the meetings.

The major decisions taken, which were sent to the other members and consultors on June 29, were as follows:

1. The Vatican Edition will not feature the rhythmic indications of the latest Benedictine editions, but will limit itself to the method already in use in the initial editions of Dom Pothier, retaining only those signs related to the groupings of notes and of members of phrases.

2. The pages of the *Kyriale* will be printed first, so that publishers can reproduce them immediately as an excerpt.

3. The *Liber Gradualis* and the *Liber Antiphonarius* will be printed simultaneously, to enable publishers to produce the excerpts that are appropriate for them right away.

4. We wish to take advantage of the opportunity at hand to revive some ancient melodies, either within the body of the books or in an Appendix; for ex-

ample, other cadences for the chant of the lessons, and other melodies for the hymns. Please send your suggestions on this point.

5. During printing, we wish to publish the following parts as separate off-prints intended for publishers only: *Officium et Missa Nativitatis, Hebdomada Sancta, Officium et Missa Defunctorum.*

6. The most direct work on the Vatican Edition is reserved for the members of the Commission. Everyone, including the consultors, will be kept up to date on what the Commission is doing and, if they are present in Rome, they shall participate in the ordinary meetings and may exercise their voting rights.

7. The members of the Commission review the printer's proofs. The proofs shall be sent to those consultors who request them. However, everyone has the right to send in comments on any particular reading of the melody, basing those comments on the latest Benedictine editions from Solesmes.

8. In the Vatican Edition, the *morae vocis* shall be indicated by a blank space of equal and unchanging width, and four sorts of bars shall be used: a small bar, a medium bar, a large bar, and a double bar. After the intonations, the double bar shall be omitted, and replaced by a star or asterisk.

9. A copy of the circular (not confidential) sent to the major masters of Gregorian chant shall be sent to all members of the Commission, with the request that they, too, answer the questions posed in the circular.

10. Please send comments on changes to be made in the literary text to the Editorial Board (Reverend Father Dom Mocquereau, Appuldurcombe, Isle of Wight) as soon as possible.

11. We would like to submit a request to the Congregation of Sacred Rites asking it to decree that from now on, no liturgical Office proper to particular dioceses shall be approved unless the corresponding chant is presented at the same time; that chant must be reviewed by the Commission, which shall make its decision in conformity with the Vatican Typical Edition. If the dioceses do not present the chant, the Commission shall be responsible for providing it, at the expense of the dioceses.

12. We would like to hear everyone's opinion about the approval to be granted at a later date to books that, while containing the chant of the Vatican Edition, add other rhythmic indications to it and that present the melodies in modern notation. This issue has been debated at various meetings, and so far, our opinion is that these editions must be approved by the bishops only, not by the Congregation of Sacred Rites.

In effect, the *motu proprio* of April 25, 1904 offers only two formulas for granting approval: absolute conformity with the Vatican Edition, and conformity with certain variants derived from good manuscripts. If we start approving the addition of rhythmic indications and of translations, it will not be possible to limit ourselves to the editions of Solesmes alone. [Excerpt from the minutes.]

We must now return to certain points that require explanation, or that are not included in the Circular of June 29. This information is drawn from the minutes of the Commission and from the correspondence of the monks of Solesmes.

At the first meeting on April 29, after a brief speech by Dom Pothier commenting on the first paragraph of the *motu proprio* of April 25 that established the Vatican Commission, Father de Santi noted that the Commission was *new*, i.e. that it was different from the one to which new members had been appointed by the Congregation of Sacred Rites the previous March 2 (cf. *supra*, No. 60). When he went on to suggest that the opinions of the *consultors* should be sought on certain general matters, Dom Janssens noted that the Commission had nothing to do until the text was submitted to it by Solesmes. Father de Santi responded by saying that Dom Mocquereau was already in a position to indicate the musical text that he would be recommending. In fact, the letters received from Solesmes state that it had been decided that the *current* Solesmes edition—the edition of 1903—would be used as the basis for the Vatican Edition (Dom Noetinger, April 30, 1904).[189] Dom Mocquereau noted, in this regard, that Dom Janssens' ill humor had not abated, and that he was creating "as much of a road block as possible by claiming to want to have every note of the text suggested by Solesmes checked" (Dom Noetinger, April 30, Dom Mocquereau, May 7, cf. *supra*, No. 66). The same remark appears in the correspondence of Father de Santi (to Dom Mocquereau, May 28, and to Dom Delatte, June 18, 1904).

We have already seen that it was decided—at the first meeting—that the Vatican Edition "would not have special rhythmic indications like those in the most recent Solesmes edition" (Minutes). But at the second meeting (May 7), Dom Mocquereau asked that the manner of marking the *morae vocis* be decided; he recommended that they should be

---

189. The correspondence from Solesmes also indicates that, at the second meeting, the point was made once again that the Vatican edition would be *limited* to the essential books only: the *Liber Gradualis,* the *Liber Antiphonarius,* the *Pontificale,* the *Rituale,* etc., as had been specified in the draft of the *motu proprio* (in the Appendix), but not stated explicitly in the final version of the text (cf. *supra*, No. 68—Dom Noetinger, April 30, 1904).

marked with a space of *equal and unchanging* length (which was not the course followed later on), and that the four types of bars used in the Solesmes editions should be adopted. Similarly, he proposed that at the intonation, an asterisk should replace the double bar, which interrupted the melody in an inopportune way. These suggestions were adopted unanimously.

It should be pointed out that the Abbé Moissenet of Dijon, wrongly supposing that the existing Benedictine editions would be printed as is, sent a letter dated April 29 to the Pope, by way of Msgr. Bressan, accompanied by a memorandum in opposition to those editions. But the Commission rejected the memorandum, noting that the letter had been written before the publication of the *motu proprio* of April 25 and that, as a result, the Abbé Moissenet could not have known the intentions of the Holy See at the time (3rd Meeting, May 11). In fact, except for the issue of the rhythmic indications, the most recent Benedictine edition was used as the basis of the Vatican Edition in terms of the *melodic content*, strictly speaking. At the meeting on May 11, Father de Santi had actually asked whether, in the Vatican Edition, it might not be possible to indicate by means of a *tenete* the note that, according to the Romanian signs, should be slightly lengthened. But that idea was rejected out of consideration for Solesmes, which was already using those long marks in its punctuated editions.

At the fourth meeting, on May 27, Father de Santi presented a letter from Dom Mocquereau dated May 23, in which the Abbot of Solesmes waived the subsidies offered by the Pope for the photographing of the manuscripts needed for editing the Vatican Edition. The letter was sent to the Pope, who instructed the Commission to express his thanks to Dom Delatte (5th and 6th Meetings).

At the sixth meeting, on June 27, Father de Santi read two letters from Father Grospellier of Grenoble and from the Abbé Paquet of Annecy, concerning a response from Msgr. Bressan to Msgr. Turinaz, Bishop of Nancy. Bressan's response stated not only that the Benedictine editions would not be the only sources taken into account in editing the Vatican Edition (Msgr. Turinaz feared that they might be creating an edition that would be inaccessible to the Christian people), but also that the Vatican Edition would not be forced on the dioceses that already have a Gregorian tradition of their own. That second phrase, in particular, might "open the door for all the editions in use in the dioceses of

France." So the Commission expressed the desire that from then on, it should be consulted before responses of this kind were issued in the name of the Pope. The Commission also agreed to publish a brief article in the *Rassegna Gregoriana* concerning the letter of Msgr. Bressan to the Bishop of Nancy.[190]

On May 11, the same day as the third meeting, Dom Mocquereau was received by the Pope, as was Dom Cagin (Dom Noetinger had already left to return to England). Pius X had just sent them two very beautiful chalices intended for the Abbeys of Saint-Pierre and of Sainte-Cécile, and at the audience—"a delightful audience," wrote Dom Mocquereau—the Pope expressed to them his great appreciation and affection for Solesmes (Dom Mocquereau, May 11).

On May 12, Father de Santi and Msgr. Rella came to say goodbye to the two monks from Solesmes. "They are going away happy," Father de Santi noted. He also stated his own satisfaction with his last conversation with Dom Mocquereau: "I had a good and useful conversation with Dom Mocquereau, and it is quite obvious how well he knows the manuscripts" (de Santi *Journal*, May 12).[191]

Dom Mocquereau thanked Father de Santi once more for everything he had done on behalf of Solesmes (cf. De Santi *Journal*, May 2), for without him, quite clearly, Solesmes would have been completely ignored.

190. Cf. *Rassegna Gregoriana* 1904, col. 564—*Revue du Chant Grégorien,* September–October 1904, pp. 43–45 (article by A. Grospellier).—Here are some additional issues dealt with by the Commission during its first six meetings:

Appointments: Father de Santi, recording secretary; Msgr. Antonio Rella, treasurer; Giulio Bas, reviser;—expansion of the Commission;—the process for revising the melodies;—printing and final printer's proofs;—consultation with libraries.

Review of works submitted to the Commission: (the following list contains only those that were accepted): letter from A. Dabin and D. Gaisser on the "pausa correpta"; and a paper from Dom Maurice (Solesmes), pointed out by Dom Mocquereau (May 7) on the changes of the literary text brought about as a result of the restoration of the authentic melodies (cf. Dom Maurice, *La revisione del testo liturgico delle parti di canto (Graduale) al XVI e XVII secolo* in *Rassegna Gregoriana* 1905, col. 49–59; col. 107–115).

191. Quoted by Moneta-Caglio, *Musica Sacra* 1962, p. 118.

71. The Publishers' Concerns

We have already addressed the legitimate concerns of the publishers, particularly the concerns of the publishers based in Paris.[192] Thus, on April 13, during the Congress of St. Gregory the Great, Msgr. Foucault, in his capacity as honorary chairman of the Gregorian section, was charged with preparing a statement to calm the publishers with respect to the intentions of the Holy See: "His Holiness does not wish to institute any privilege or monopoly for any publisher." As for the Vatican Edition, the publishers "will have the right to reproduce it, but without any changes." The first part of this statement, as we have said, was interpreted in various ways. Some saw it as a statement aimed at Poussielgue, who had just proposed that he himself create the edition under the auspices of the Holy See, or Desclée, the printers that Solesmes used. On the previous February 24, Desclée's editions had been declared in conformity with the *motu proprio* of November 22, 1903 (cf. Nos. 59 and 67).

But the *motu proprio* of April 25, 1904, on the Vatican Edition was not entirely to the liking of the publishers. In effect, the document stated that "the Holy See would retain the copyright for the edition," whereas it had initially been said that the edition would not be copyrighted. In addition, it had also been mentioned early on that the edition would be limited to the essential books, such as the *Liber Gradualis*, the *Liber Antiphonarius*, the *Pontificale*, the *Rituale*, etc., which the definitive text of the *motu proprio* no longer specified (cf. *supra*, No. 68). Finally, for the publishers, approvals already granted for the Solesmes editions seemed to create a sort of privilege in favor of those editions,[193] all the more so since one paragraph of the *motu proprio* specifically addressed the Solesmes editions already in use (paragraph d).

Thus, on May 13, 1904, the *Fédération des Travailleurs du Livre* sent a

---

192. Cf. Nos. 29 and 35, and especially No. 51;—*supra*, No. 59.

193. Cf. *Revue du Chant Grégorien*, March 1904, p. 132: "The present edition has been found to be in conformity with the typical one in regard to the text. In regard to the chant it is in accordance with the *motu proprio* of His Holiness, Pope Pius X, issued on November 22, 1903, and also with the decree of the Congregation of Sacred Rites given on January 8, 1904. In testimony of the authenticity of this decree, I have been authorized by the Cardinal Prefect of the Congregation of Sacred Rites to make this known. From the Secretariat of the Congregation of Sacred Rites, on the 24th day of February, 1904. D. Panici, Archbishop of Laodicea, Secretary of the Congregation of Sacred Rites."

Note to the Minister of Trade. In it, on the one hand, they stated that the *motu proprio* of April 25 "made it possible to annul anything liberal that the statement issued by the Bishop of Saint-Dié (Msgr. Foucault) had contained," and, on the other hand, that the Desclée company, which had become the owner of the Solesmes Press (Desclée was in negotiations with the Liquidator of the properties of religious congregations) was seeking to obtain a monopoly. As a result, their *Note* requested that the Minister instruct the Ambassador of France to intervene with the Holy See to warn it about the Desclée company and about the Vatican Commission itself, where Desclée had powerful support from Dom Mocquereau and another religious (Father de Santi). Likewise, the *Note* requested that the Minister instruct the President of the Council and Minister of Religion to intervene with the bishops of France, to demand that they not purchase their books of liturgical chant from a foreign supplier (Desclée).

On July 10, Father de Santi informed Dom Mocquereau that the *Note de la Fédération des Travailleurs du Livre* had been sent to the Vatican through the good offices of the Embassy, and in the name of the French Government. Father de Santi pointed out:

It is very well known in the Vatican that this is simply a ploy by Mr. Pécoul, and it was extremely displeasing for its insolent form and for its statement of facts absolutely contrary to truth. I too am involved, though not mentioned by name. An answer has already been given by His Eminence, the Cardinal Secretary of State and it was easy to give it in exhaustive fashion.[194]

Father de Santi was quite correct in identifying the inspiration behind the *Note*, who took his revenge in this way for not having been able to dislodge his support for Solesmes.[195] The evidence comes straight from the pen of Msgr. Foucault, in a letter that he wrote to Pécoul on May 25, 1904:

I had just finished writing a letter when I received the document from the *Fédération du Livre* along with your letter. I will be in Paris tomorrow . . . I am taking the liberty of arranging a meeting with you there at 2:15. If the secretary

---

194. "Si sa benissimo in Vaticano che essa è manipolazione del Sig. Pécoul e dispiacque assai per la sua forma insolente e per l'esposizione dei fatti assolutamente contrarii alla verità. Io pure, sebbene non col mio nome, sono messo in ballo. La risposta è gia stata data dell'Emo Card. Segretario di Stato ed era facile il darla esauriente" (de Santi, July 10, 1904).

195. On A. Pécoul, cf. *supra*, Nos. 64 and 51.

of the Federation is able to join us there, we could exchange our impressions, and decide on a course of action.

Shortly before that, Msgr. Foucault had announced to the Pope "a *memorandum* on Gregorian chant." (The response from the Cardinal Secretary of State to the letter announcing its despatch was published in the *Revue du Chant Grégorien* in May 1904, p. 185, and is dated May 23.) On July 3, Father de Santi told Dom Mocquereau that it had arrived: "Msgr. Foucault's memorandum has arrived at the Vatican, and I have been told that it will be sent along to us." (Nonetheless, there is no trace of it in the minutes of the Vatican Commission.) No doubt, Msgr. Foucault believed that this memorandum obviated the need for him to respond to the questionnaire sent by the Vatican Commission to the leading Church musicians, for the Commission's records for the meeting on September 6, 1904, held at Appuldurcombe—Solesmes in exile—show that Msgr. Foucault refused to respond. All of this, it would seem, clearly indicated a bit of ill will on the part of the individual who had been responsible for announcing the Vatican Edition at the Congress of Rome on April 9.—Let us also point out that Dom Pothier promised, at the same moment, that he would write to the Pope on the matter of the chant (A. Bonnaire to Pécoul, May 30, 1904).[196]

Father de Santi's letter shows that the promised intervention with the Pope happened right away, and that the answer came promptly. On July 4, the Minister of Religion, Émile Combes, sent a *Circular to the Bishops of France*, saying:

I am convinced that, under these conditions [those described above], you will be the first to imagine, Bishop, that since the Holy See is granting full freedom, there is no reason, in this matter, to harm the interests of French industry to the benefit of foreign industries, and particularly that it will be your view, in this regard, to issue the Imprimatur only to French editions made in France, in French workshops, and issuing from publishing houses that truly belong to individuals of French nationality.[197]

In conclusion, let us note that at the Congress of the *Fédération des Travailleurs du Livres* held at Rome shortly thereafter, the printer J. Dumoulin said the following, in an attempt to reassure the Master Printers:

---

196. Cf. *Revue du Chant Grégorien,* November 1904, p. 75 (*La Croix,* December 1, 1904).

197. Circular reproduced in Dom André Mocquereau, *Le Décret du 14 février 1906* . . . , Desclée, 1906, p. 16.—On these matters, cf. Archives of Solesmes.

The Pope does not want to profit from this work by granting to the Holy See the monopoly denied to Mr. Pustet. On the contrary, everyone knows, despite the silence of the *motu proprio* in this regard, that the *Editio Vaticana*, printed in a relatively small number of copies and offered for sale without adding any profit margin, will be made available to the bishops and to interested parties. . . . Besides, we should not believe that the *Editio Vaticana*, entrusted to the disciples of Dom Delatte, will be entirely in conformity with the previous Solesmes editions. The religious are renouncing any copyright on the noted text of their current edition, in favor of the Holy See, and they are going back to work so that the new manual will truly be an *Editio Vaticana*, and not an *Editio Solesmensis*. On this point, fairness requires that we acknowledge that the houses of Desclée in Tournai and Pustet in Ratisbon have joined Solesmes in renouncing their copyrights. So the implementation of the plans of Pius X, like the project itself, provides complete reassurance for French printers.[198]

72. The Congress of Arras—Summer School at Appuldurcombe

From August 3–5, 1904, a Congress of Religious Music was held at Arras. The Congress was the brainchild of the Abbé Delépine, choirmaster of the Cathedral. On June 22, the Abbé Delépine had sent a message to the Pope, requesting the apostolic benediction and specifying the goal he was pursuing:

To work effectively for the reform of sacred music and to study the means for ensuring proper performance of Gregorian chant and classical polyphony . . . and to organize in France a St. Cecilia Society on the model of the one now flourishing in Germany.

Delépine added that a large number of bishops had already sent expressions of support for the Congress. The Sovereign Pontiff, not content merely to grant the blessing that had been requested, wrote in his own hand, at the bottom of the request, that he "earnestly recommended" the Congress. Then he sent his blessing a second time, in response to an address from the participants.

It does not appear that the Congress was as successful as had been

---

198. J. Dumoulin, *Le Chant liturgique. Le Motu Proprio de S. S. Pie X et l'impression des livres liturgiques en France. Rapport lu au Congrès des Maîtres-Imprimeurs*, in *La Fonderie Typographique*, Vol. 6, No. 69, pp. 278–279.

hoped. Only one bishop was present—the Bishop of Arras. Although the spectrum of choirmasters who surrounded the Very Reverend Dom Pothier was quite varied, their numbers remained, nonetheless, rather modest. Despite the desire expressed by the Abbé Delépine, Solesmes was not represented at the Congress. Preparations for the Vatican Edition and for a Gregorian "Summer School" commanded the full attention of Dom Mocquereau and his colleagues.

There were two offices (benedictions), two performances of Gregorian music and of ancient and modern polyphonic music, and four study sessions in keeping with the *motu proprio*. The Congress was clearly a success for Dom Pothier: "Between two sessions, those attending the Congress took up the matter of establishing a general St. Cecilia Society in France. The idea was approved in principle . . .but that was as far as it went."[199]

Dom Mocquereau was both a man of science and a practical person. The momentum he gave the choir at Solesmes, which he directed from 1889 on, is well known. He had always attached great importance to the proper performance of the Gregorian melodies, without which it is impossible to comprehend the full import of the artistic and spiritual riches that the melodies contain. Solesmes was the place to go for a thorough grounding in singing, even more than for initiation into Gregorian paleography. When the monks were expelled from France and arrived in England, at the Appuldurcombe estate where they remained until the restoration of Quarr Abbey in 1908, Catholic and Anglican priests began to attend the monks' Offices. Thirty to forty attended Vespers during the week, with 100 to 150 in attendance on Sundays.

One priest from the chapter of Westminster, the Reverend Moloney, came up with the idea of a "Summer School" or Gregorian Session, during the summer of 1904. The Session took place in the last two weeks of August, from August 18–30, and was attended by forty-five Englishmen or Irishmen (and one American who came at the last minute), twenty-two of whom were priests, with one bishop, Msgr. Donnelly, Auxiliary Bishop of Dublin, who took a very active interest in the conference sessions.

There were two lectures on performance practice every day, after

---

199. Cf. *Revue du Chant Grégorien*, June 1904, p. 204 (program); July 1904, pp. 216–217 (address to the Pope); September–October 1904, pp. 46–47 (report).—Cf. *Tribune de Saint-Gervais* 1904, pp. 281–284.

Mass and after Vespers, which were held in the temporary wooden chapel. At the first lecture, Reverend Moloney underscored the continuity of the Gregorian work of Solesmes, from Dom Guéranger to Dom Mocquereau. Then Dom Mocquereau, Dom Eudine, Dom Sergent, and Dom Mégret began their practical lessons, as one roguish chronicler noted, to "make the ears of the sons of green Erin and blond Albion sensitive to the charms of the Gregorian melodies." On August 23, those attending the Congress went to Cowes, where the religious of Sainte-Cécile de Solesmes had taken refuge. They visited the royal castle of Osbourne on their way there. On August 29, the evening before the closing session, the Schola gave a performance in the Chapter of the most beautiful Gregorian pieces—and that evening, at tea, speeches were given by the Reverend Moloney, by the Reverend Colgan, in Gaelic, and by an Irish organist, on behalf of the laymen present.[200]

During the session, Reverend Moloney sought the blessing of the Pope in these terms:

The 15 priests and 30 laymen meeting at Appuldurcombe in England to be trained in the Gregorian chant by the Monks of Solesmes for two weeks pay tribute to Pius X, worthy successor of St. Gregory, and seek his blessing. Father Moloney, Promotor of the Gregorian Chant Summer School, Appuldurcombe, Wroxall.

He received the following telegram from Cardinal Merry del Val: "To Father Moloney: The Holy Father thanks you and those meeting with you, and extends his most affectionate blessing. Cardinal Merry del Val."[200bis]

The momentum was there, and it did not diminish. In following years, there were similar meetings at Appuldurcombe, the ancestors, so to speak, of our summer Gregorian sessions in France.

---

200. Chronicle of Solesmes—Giulio Bas, *La scuola solesmense di Appuldurcombe e le riunioni della Commissione pontificia per l'Edizione Vaticana delle melodie gregoriane*, in *Rassegna Gregoriana* 1904, col. 485–488 (Bas had been staying at Appuldurcombe at the time, since July).—Cf. *Revue du Chant Grégorien*, 1904, p. 15.

200bis. Sacerdotes et Laici XV et XXX congregati apud Appuldurcombe in Anglia ut, per disciplinas XV dierum, efformentur in cantu gregoriano a Monachis Solesmensibus, Pio X, digno Gregorii successori, obsequium testantur, benedictionem petunt. Moloney sacerdos, Scholae Aestivae Gregorianae promotor, Appuldurcombe, Wroxall.

Moloney sacerdos . . . Tibi, tuisque sociis una tecum congregatis, beatissimus Pater gratias agit et amantissimus benedicit. Cardinalis Merry del Val.

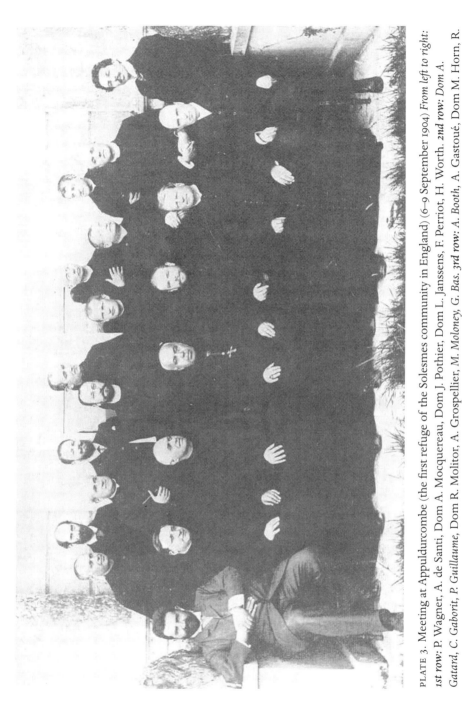

PLATE 3. Meeting at Appuldurcombe (the first refuge of the Solesmes community in England) (6–9 September 1904) *From left to right:* *1st row:* P. Wagner, A. de Santi, Dom A. Mocquereau, Dom J. Pothier, Dom L. Janssens, F. Perriot, H. Worth. *2nd row: Dom A. Gatard, C. Gaborit, P. Guillaume,* Dom R. Molitor, A. Grospellier, *M. Moloney, G. Bas. 3rd row: A. Booth,* A. Gastoué, Dom M. Horn, R. Moissenet, *Dom W. Corney.* The names of the experts, who were not members of the Vatican Commission, are italicized.

73. Meeting of the Vatican Commission at Appuldurcombe

From September 6–9, 1904, the Vatican Commission held several meetings at Appuldurcombe, at the initiative of Dom Mocquereau. He felt that it was essential for the members of the Commission to gain personal knowledge of the Gregorian manuscripts, and to judge the Editorial Board's work on the Vatican Edition for itself. He wrote: "My hope is that they will agree to work with us for a short time on the restoration of a Gregorian phrase, just for the experience of it."[201] His fervent wish was for the members of the Commission to come to Appuldurcombe, either as a group or even one by one, if it proved impossible to schedule a meeting (to Father de Santi, July 27, 1904).

From the private letters that Father de Santi wrote to Dom Mocquereau at the time, it is clear that the Pope was thoroughly aware of the feelings that were being expressed within the Commission, and he hoped that the meeting at Appuldurcombe would produce the union of minds he desired.

To provide support for Dom Mocquereau's request even before it was made, Father de Santi sent the following circular letter, dated August 9, to the members and consultors of the Vatican Commission, and to other well-known Gregorianists, in keeping with the Pope's wishes:

> The Benedictines of Solesmes feel that it is absolutely necessary for all the members of the Commission, to the extent possible, to meet at their residence at Appuldurcombe, on the Isle of Wight in England, to define together the matters that relate to the Vatican Edition, and to examine and to debate the resolutions of the Commission, and the responses from musicians to the circular letter of June 12. The Commission will receive an invitation directly from Dom Mocquereau, and I, too, urgently request that the Commission not fail to attend this important meeting.
>
> In the circumstances in which the Holy See now finds itself, however, it is difficult for us to request the subsidies that would be needed to make such a trip. But the generosity of each person will, no doubt, suggest ways in which this sacrifice can be made, a sacrifice that will be of extraordinary usefulness for all, and will make the difficult task entrusted to us far easier.
>
> The date of the meeting is September 1–8. In my capacity as Recording Secretary of the Commission, I will attend. I am also in a position to add that His

---

201. Quotation from Dom Mocquereau, in *L'Univers: Chronique Grégorienne*, March 20, 1905 (signed J. Dupont, a pseudonym of Étienne Bourigaud).

Holiness was particularly welcoming of the proposal for our meeting with the Editorial Board of the Commission, and grants a special Apostolic Benediction to us and to our work.

On August 12, Dom Mocquereau sent the invitation that Father de Santi had announced:

We have advanced sufficiently in our work editing and correcting the *Kyriale* to be able usefully to present the results of that work to those members of the Commission who would like to see our work and our method in person.

You must already have received a circular letter from Father de Santi, expressing our strong desire to have this meeting. I know that several members or consultors of the Commission are preparing to come, and I now invite you, in the name of the Reverend Father Abbot of Solesmes, to join them. We would be delighted to welcome you.

It would seem best for us all to meet here together. Your visit would thus be even more fruitful.

Unfortunately, the straitened circumstances of our encampment in exile do not permit us to offer lodging for the members of the Commission, but our closeness (12 to 15 minutes) to the town of Wroxall will give you opportunities for a quite suitable place to stay, at very reasonable prices.[201bis]

After various exchanges of letters, the dates for the meeting were set for September 6–9. Only twelve members (six actual members, and six consultors) of the Commission attended the meeting—so, strictly speaking, it was not a plenary session—as well as seven experts from among the Gregorianists who had been invited at the request of the Holy Father, in order to give greater weight to the decisions to be made. The members of the Commission who attended were:

Right Rev. Dom Joseph Pothier, President
Dom André Mocquereau
Dom L. Janssens
Reverend Father A. de Santi
Dr. P. Wagner
Mr. H. Worth
The consultors who attended were:
Rev. Father François Perriot
Father Alexandre Grospellier

201bis. See also a letter from Dom Mocquereau to Father Baralli, quoted by Moneta-Caglio (*Musica Sacra,* 1963, p. 7).

Abbé René Moissenet
Dom Michael Horn
Dom Raphael Molitor
Professor Amédée Gastoué
Among the experts who attended were:
Father C. Gaborit (Poitiers)
Father M. Moloney (Westminster)
Dom A. Gatard (Farnborough)
Dom W. Corney (Downside)
Reverend Father Guillaume (Trappist Monastery of Oka, Canada)[202]
Mr. A. Booth (Liverpool)
Mr. Giulio Bas (Italy)

Eight countries were thus represented at the meeting, and only one Italian, Bas, attended—and he was not a member of the Vatican Commission (Father de Santi was still of Austrian nationality). None of the Germans who were invited as experts responded to this appeal.

There were seven sessions in all: one the first day, two (morning and evening) on the days thereafter. These were the most important ones, not merely because of the number of members of consultors who participated in them, but also because of the positive decisions that were made during them. Bas was appointed secretary, at Dom Pothier's suggestion. His minutes are used as the basis for the account given here.

The first session was held on September 6. Dom Pothier addressed the meeting to pay tribute to Pius X, restorer of the liturgical chant, and read the following telegram, which was dictated by the Pope himself:

Rome, September 4, 1904, 6:25 PM. To: Abbot Pothier, Appuldurcombe, Wroxall. His Holiness, most pleased with the meeting of the illustrious members of the Gregorian Commission being held at the monastery of the worthy monks of Solesmes, extends his fullest apostolic blessing and with the wish for much benefit from the union of minds and efforts. (Signed) Respighi.[202bis]

---

202. The Reverend Father Guillaume from the Abbey of Oka did not arrive until the third session, so his signature does not appear in the missive sent to the Pope (*Rassegna Gregoriana* 1904, col. 487–488); however, he does appear in the photograph published in *Rassegna Gregoriana* 1904, col. 529–530.—Cf. *The Catholic Choirmaster* 1903, no. 1.

202bis. Roma 4 Sett. 1904, ore 6,25 pom.—Abate Pothier, Appuldurcombe, Wroxall. Sua Santità, lietissima della riunione degli illustri membri della Commissione Gregoriana presso gli ammirandi monachi Solesmensi, invia a tutti amplissima apostolica benedizione, augurando dall'unione di animi e studii proficuo risultato. Respighi.

The members of the Commission responded to the Pope in these words:

Most Holy Father. The members of the Pontifical Commission for the Vatican Edition of the chant, and all those who have been invited to take part in their deliberations, meeting together at the residence of the Benedictines of Solesmes at Appuldurcombe, prostrate at the feet of Your Holiness, express their earnest feelings of acknowledgment and filial devotion for the goodness with which Your Holiness has deigned to send them a new Apostolic Blessing, for the most precious encouragement for the work entrusted to them, and which they wish to pursue with zeal for the glory of the Holy Church, and the satisfaction of Your Holiness. [Signatures]

Then Dom Pothier underscored

the responsibilities to the Church, art, and science that were incumbent on all with regard to the research to be done and the decisions to be made. That is why everyone must have the same objective: the interests of art itself, the destiny of which has been, in a way, entrusted to the Commission. Even the inevitable divergence in points of view must work together for the good of the common effort: they must tend to unite, rather than to divide.

Dom Pothier also called to mind paragraph *a* of the *motu proprio* of April 25, in which the task of the Commission is spelled out:

The melodies of the Church, so called Gregorian, will be restored in their integrity and in their purity in accordance with the true text of the most ancient manuscripts, in such a way, however, that due attention be given to the true tradition contained in the codices throughout the centuries, and to the practical usage of contemporary liturgy.

Father de Santi spoke next. "He assured the group that the Holy Father was pleased with these meetings held at Appuldurcombe,"—and he added specifically that it was at "the wishes of the Holy Father" that other Gregorian scholars from outside the Commission had been invited to attend,[203] since the work of restoring the Gregorian melodies benefitted from the scholarly work and the efforts of all. Father de Santi continued, saying, "It is truly unfortunate that many of the Germans invited to these meetings were unable to attend. . . . Their presence would have help mitigate, to some extent, the mistrust that still exists in Germany with regard to our work."

---

203. Dom Mocquereau is thus wrongly accused of having issued these invitations on his own.

Then Dom Mocquereau noted that the *Kyriale* that was planned for publication first is the part of the Gregorian repertory that poses the most problems—it is the least ancient part—and, as a result, he asked for a few months' reprieve, in order to work on determining his definitive version. In this regard, he announced that two monks were traveling at that very moment to photograph the manuscripts, and that they were sending back reproductions every day. By contrast, he noted that the Proper of the *Gradual* was almost finished. At the second session, Dom Mocquereau was in a position to agree to supply the text of the *Kyriale* in January 1905, which was unanimously approved.

During that first session, Father de Santi began providing information about the answers to the questionnaire that had been sent to the members and consultors of the Commission on June 12, and to other musicians and Gregorian scholars.

That circular letter, announced in the decisions of the first sessions held in Rome, asked the opinion of each person on the following points:

1. Do you have any reservations on the last editions by Solesmes, published by Desclée? What changes should be made, beginning with the *Kyriale* and the first part of the *Graduale?*

2. How, in psalmody, might the mediant better be handled when it falls on a monosyllable or on a Hebrew word?

3. What rules should be followed in adapting the text to psalmodic cadences when there are words that have an unaccented penultimate syllable?

Father de Santi informed the meeting of the answers received during the various sessions. These responses were quite brief, except for a few more detailed ones, such as those provided by Dom Pothier, Msgr. Grassi-Landi, canon of St. Peter's in Rome,[204] Father Gaborit, Father Grospellier, Father Perriot, Dom Janssens, Dom Molitor, Reverend Father Dechevrens, Reverend Father Olmeda, Dr. Wagner, and Professor Amédée Gastoué.

The file of responses was then available to anyone. It contained nearly fifty responses (49, to be precise). Curiously, Msgr. Foucault, Bishop

---

204. Canon of St. Peter's in Rome who, according to a confidential remark by Father de Santi, believed that he was quite talented when it came to things Gregorian (*Iter Italicum,* manuscript of Dom Blanchon, pp. 89–91).

of Saint-Dié, and Edgar Tinel, of Mechlin, declined to give their opinions. Bishop Foucault did so because he was unable "to follow the Commission into the territory in which it had moved," and Tinel because he
restricted that honor "to the eminent individuals who have been officially appointed to be part of the Commission at issue, and among whom
clearly I had no right to be counted." There was also a letter in support
of the restoration of the ancient Hymns, signed by a group of seminarians from Saint-Sulpice, some fifty of them, among whom were Abbé
Maurice Feltin (later Archbishop of Paris), and Abbé Yves Delaporte.

At the second session, on September 7, after some responses to the
Commission's questionnaire were read, the following agenda was
adopted for the sessions:

1. Notation of the Vatican Edition, and the relationship of the notation to the rhythm.

2. Approval of the Vatican and other editions or popular transcriptions.

3. Diocesan Propers.

4. Psalmody, interrupted cadences.

5. General lines of the Commission's work.

The discussion on the notation of the Vatican Edition began immediately. "It was decided unanimously that no notation would be accepted
unless the grouping of the notes is in conformity with the traditional
grouping." In the afternoon, the morning's discussion of notation continued, and the Commission decided to allow publishers the freedom to
choose the form of writing that they would adopt (for example, certain
neumes could be written with the two forms, vertical or slanted), and it
rejected a resolution from Dr. Wagner that was worded as follows: "Dr.
Wagner proposes issuing a categorical exclusion of any other notation
(other than that adopted by the Commission), but the proposition was
not accepted." Finally, the Commission did pass a resolution that the
Vatican Edition would be "mandatory for all Churches of the Roman
rite."[204bis]

The question of approving the editions of Gregorian chant was addressed on September 8. Two lines of thought surfaced regarding the

204bis. This decision concerning Gregorian notation would be annulled by the decree of the
Congregation of Sacred Rites of August 11, 1905 (cf. No. 86).

interpretation of the paragraph in the *motu proprio* that dealt with this matter:

> One tends to legitimize the various individual traditions, provided that they are confirmed by good manuscripts; the other, to the contrary, admits that the purpose of the Vatican Edition is specifically to put an end to these various traditions, and that paragraph *d* of the *motu proprio* is intended to protect only those variants of versions that are supported by good manuscripts. Dom Pothier . . . stated that he considers the variants of the versions more dangerous and subject to confusion than the complete diversity of several melodies for the same liturgical text. But Father de Santi, backed by Dom Janssens, noted that the objective of paragraph *d* of the *motu proprio*[205] was quite a worthy one, and that it was very prudent with respect to scientific studies and the work of Gregorian scholars, and therefore it should not be diminished in any way by the decisions of the Commission. It was then agreed to define the subject very precisely.
>
> . . . The Very Reverend President took the occasion to note that the diversity of variants is a rather secondary aspect, in the face of the real and substantial unity of the Gregorian tradition. That unity must not be threatened in any manner. . . .

Those words ended the debate, and at the next session, in the afternoon "Father de Santi's proposal (made at the previous session) regarding the approval of the texts with variants, which will be mentioned in the wording of the approval, was adopted."

In the morning session, the discussion had led Father de Santi to ask Dom Mocquereau for a demonstration, to be done in front of everyone, of the method used in restoring the melodic text. That evening, Dom Mocquereau

> presented the comparative table of the various versions of the manuscripts for the *Kyrie Fons bonitatis*, and he read some explanations which he then expanded upon in additional remarks, and which the members commented upon at length . . . Dr. Wagner then moved for a motion of confidence in favor of the editors and asked the members of the Commission to offer any of their own comments that they felt would be useful on the suggested text. Dom Moc-

---

205. Paragraph *d* of the *motu proprio* of April 25, 1904 was annulled by the decree of the Congregation of Sacred Rites of August 14, 1905 (cf. No. 86). The paragraph addressed the Solesmes editions that had already been approved and declared in conformity with the *motu proprio* of November 22, 1903, on February 24, 1904. It should also be noted the Dom Mocquereau did not seek any support for his editions at the session on September 7.

quereau agreed, but asked that detailed reasons be provided to substantiate the comments.

Dom Janssens noted that the proposed motion would imply that there had been a lack of confidence at times, which was not accurate. To the contrary, the Holy Father had expressed his own confidence with singular solemnity [an allusion to the Brief addressed to Dom Delatte on May 22, 1904] and in Rome the Commission itself had manifested its confidence. For these reasons, he felt that a new motion was unnecessary. It was Father de Santi's opinion that Dr. Wagner's proposal should be considered a confirmation of the resolution taken in Rome, being made more solemn by the number of those in attendance, all the more so since many of the members had not been present in Rome.

The next day, on September 9, Dr. Wagner's motion was recorded with the following addition: Upon reading the minutes of the previous session, Dr. Wagner added to the motion of confidence in support of the monks of Solesmes, which he proposed the day before, another motion worded as follows: The Commission desires that in all cases where the data of the manuscripts is insufficient for a definitive reconstruction, preference shall be given to the versions already used by Gregorian scholars and contained in the books of Solesmes. The Commission approved the resolution. But Dom Janssens proposed a resolution worded as follows: "The Commission expresses its wish that, in cases where paleographical research does not provide a definite solution, esthetic considerations can cause the most beautiful version to prevail, even if an examination of the manuscripts would tend to favor another version." The Commission approved that resolution, as well.

It is regrettable to see Dom Janssens opposing Dom Mocquereau once again, and all the more so since the opposition was a long-standing one. At the Conference of Christian Archaeology held at Rome in April 1900, Dom Janssens had opposed a resolution in favor of the *Paléographie Musicale* (cf. No. 45). We have already examined his subsequent actions in March 1904, during the preparation of the *motu proprio* of April 25 (cf. Nos. 65–66). Again on May 28, Father de Santi had drawn Dom Mocquereau's attention to the fact that if the Commission failed to meet, the reason was Dom Janssens: "Dom Janssens always says that he is ill, and in fact he did not show up yesterday. Might this perhaps be a diplomatic illness?" Finally, on June 18, Father de Santi notes that the Brief that the Pope sent to Dom Delatte had disturbed him:

Reverend Father Janssens now seems to me to be taking the edition very much to heart; but in speaking with me the other day of the latest Brief addressed to you, he told me that it gave the impression that there was a desire to put the

Right Rev. Dom Pothier completely to one side. I do not understand where anyone could derive such an idea. (To Dom Delatte)[206]

Father Grospellier has given the following impartial eyewitness account of the impression left by the visit to the paleography workshop:

Aside from the sessions, the members of the assembly were especially interested in their visit to the paleography workshop, where the work of restoring the Gregorian melodies takes place. At the sight of these manuscripts, which have been gathered from all over, and of the photographs of the manuscripts—thousands of which have already been collected, and the number of which is growing daily in this new style of scriptorium—one had to concede that one could not possibly imagine a richer and more varied collection of materials for preparing the Vatican Edition. It is truly the entire tradition of Gregorian chant that is spread out before your eyes, represented by hordes of witnesses from every century and every country.

Although some entered the scriptorium with some residual caution and defiance, they left with confidence in their souls and with praise on their lips for Dom Mocquereau and his worthy team. All were unanimous in their proclamation that an edition based on such a wealth of materials, such an expert staff, and such refined and conscientious working methods would be worthy of the destiny that the Sovereign Pontiff is preparing for it throughout the entire Church.

The same impression was made even more strongly in a session where Dom Mocquereau presented to the assembly the complete table of a Kyrie, with the whole critical apparatus of the variants from all the manuscripts, and the reasoned and documented justification for each reading adopted for the typical edition. Once again, the conviction unanimously expressed was that it would be impossible to have more abundant information available or to implement a more perfect method of work. (A. Grospellier, "Appuldurcombe et la réunion de la Commission grégorienne," in *Revue du Chant Grégorien*, September–October 1904, pp. 31–32.)

In the March–April 1905 issue of the *Revue du Chant Grégorien*, shortly before the Vatican Commission was dissolved, the following notice appeared: "The editors are using the surest means and the most earnest and conscientious work methods to give the Church as accurate and as perfect an edition as is humanly possible" (*Échos et Mélanges*, unsigned, p. 137).

206. Dom Janssens carefully avoided the two monks responsible for photographing the Gregorian manuscripts, when they passed through St. Anselm's in 1904 (*Iter Italicum*, p. 109).

Let us return to the session of the morning of September 8. Dr. Wagner offered a resolution that, in a certain manner, has just been taken up once again by Vatican Council II. It was worded as follows:

> Dr. Wagner, underscoring the conditions of small Churches in non-Latin countries, where the integral chanting of very ornate melodies is impossible, and the recitation of the texts in place of the chant is no less difficult owing to pronunciation and ignorance of the Latin language, asks whether it would be possible to allow the chants between the Epistle and the Gospel to be omitted. Dom Horn seconded this resolution, at the request of many Germans. Father de Santi recalled that in Rome, at the Gregorian Congress, he had suggested introducing some more or less ornate formulas to which the various texts mentioned by Dr. Wagner could be suitably adapted. Dom Pothier and Dom Mocquereau averred that such formulas could be found in the manuscripts, without any need for composing new ones.
>
> Dom Janssens suggested preparing an abridged edition, made according to all the criteria and means available today, thanks to which a truly artistic result could be achieved. However, the Commission did not share Dom Janssens' opinion. Some commented, as well, that they did not have the authority for such work. To this, Dom Janssens responded that he was only asking that some thought be given to the topic.

With regard to this last suggestion, it must be noted that there could be, in fact, no question of abridging the traditional melodies, thereby falling into the errors of the Medicean edition—nor even of adapting ancient formulas to new texts (and that is doubtless why the 1904 project was abandoned)—but of providing, with the permission of the Holy See, a new repertory of ancient, very short pieces that could be sung in small parish churches, or when it is truly impossible to provide for worthy performance of the traditional Gregorian repertoire.

That afternoon, Dr. Wagner returned to the question:

> With regard to the formulas to be adopted for the simple chanting of the Graduals, Tracts, Alleluia verses, Dr. Wagner proposes that, to this end, reference be made to the formulas of the responsorial psalms that have fallen into disuse. The liturgical nature of these chants would thus be maintained. Dom Mocquereau shares this opinion.
>
> . . . Dr. Wagner, therefore, proposes that the editors of the Vatican Edition be formally charged with selecting simple formulas . . . formulas that should be published at the same time as the rest of the edition, and submitted to the Commissioners as early as possible. Father de Santi also proposes that the

Commission authorize the *Rassegna Gregoriana* to publish them. The Commission approves. The matters relating to the previous session were concluded, and the minutes of that session were approved.

In the afternoon of September 8, a heated debate concerning the "interrupted mediants" took place.

Father de Santi read separately the responses received on this matter, according to the questionnaire that had been sent out. Dom Pothier immediately drew a distinction between the medieval psalm formulae and those more commonly used today. Before comments could be made, he said, it was necessary to know which psalmody was being discussed. In this regard, Dr. Wagner suggested a resolution in favor of returning to the medieval psalm formulae for the psalmody of the Introit and the Communion, which the Commission approved. Then discussion turned to the "interrupted mediants." Father Grospellier read an interesting paper to prove that during the Gregorian era, no special treatment was given in the chant to final monosyllables. At the end of the reading, the Commission was unanimous in its applause.

Dom Pothier admitted that there was no interrupted mediant when the formula is melodic, no matter how little; but that it does exist when the psalmody is merely an accentuation. Professor Gastoué remarked that in many cases, the accented monosyllabic final is illogical and contrary to grammar, and that the truncated final is thus not logical, whereas in the case of oxytonic accentuation, it is legitimate, or at least is not a source of difficulty.

After considerable exchange of ideas on ancient and modern pronunciation of Hebrew words in the liturgical texts, and on the practical opportuneness of maintaining one or another of the forms discussed, Dom Janssens, in agreement with Dr. Wagner, proposed allowing free choice, and the decision was approved to introduce in the Vatican Edition the ordinary formula of the psalmody in any case, placing the interrupted mediant as an alternative at the bottom of the page, for instances in which it might be applicable, for the Lessons, Epistles, and Gospels and in the psalmody of Modes 2, 5, and 8. [Ultimately, it was the contrary that was implemented.]

Finally, there was a debate on psalmody, on September 9, during both sessions:

Father de Santi conveyed various comments and requests sent to the Commission, following which Dom Mocquereau moved that discussion be limited to the psalmody of the Introit. Dom Pothier spoke about the variants that occur on this point, and about their note groupings, and defended his reasoning, in part. Dom Mocquereau and Father Grospellier stated that there was nothing to debate, since the manuscripts are unanimous on the issue. Professor Gastoué responded that certain medieval authors gave norms that were contrary to the manuscripts. That is why both sources must be consulted.

In the afternoon, debate once again focused on this issue:

Dom Pothier spoke at length in favor of the version in which the accent coincides with the neume. Dr. Wagner then asked whether the group wanted to exhaust such a topic on the spot. However, Father Grospellier, in agreement with Dom Mocquereau, answered that the group could and should decide immediately, since the unanimity of the manuscripts left no doubt on what should be done. Therefore, at the specific suggestion of Dr. Wagner, the Commission unanimously decided to follow the uniform tradition of the manuscripts.

In the morning, Father de Santi had made an important suggestion.

He proposed promoting an international Gregorian congress, which would be held at Strasbourg the following year, before the Catholic Congress scheduled to be held there, as well. He suggested making Dr. Wagner responsible for forming an organizing committee, and he proposed that the Pontifical Commission hold a meeting during that Congress. The proposal was approved unanimously.

After the discussion on psalmody discussed above, Father de Santi took the initiative to adjourn the meeting:

The work of the Commission being thus concluded, Father de Santi proposed that special thanks be expressed to the Reverend Father Abbot of Solesmes who had extended such warm hospitality to the Commission, and all applauded loudly. Dr. Wagner said that before the group went its separate ways, it was appropriate to adopt a resolution of thanks to the Reverend President. May God reward fifty years of activity and scholarship devoted to the service of the Church and of art by Dom Pothier! All applauded, and Dom Pothier responded by speaking about the history of the Gregorian restoration accomplished at Solesmes. He thanked those who had helped him, those who had continued and strengthened his work, and those who will continue to work on it. Dom Mocquereau thanked him in the name of all the monks of Solesmes, and after a resolution of thanks to Pius X proposed by Dom Janssens, the final session was adjourned. *Pax in virtute!*

The main decisions of the meeting have been presented above, at times summarizing everything that was said about a particular subject (at the session of the debate and at the following session when the minutes were submitted for approval by all). However, there were other decisions, generally of secondary importance, that have not yet been addressed. As they appear in the official list of decisions made by the Commission at Appuldurcombe, in concluding this section, the full list is presented below, with some additional information provided in parentheses:

1. The Commission meeting at Appuldurcombe confirms the motion of full confidence that it issued at Rome in support of the Benedictine fathers of Solesmes as Editors of the Vatican Edition of Gregorian chant.

2. The Commission expresses its desire that, in all cases where the information of the manuscripts is insufficient to establish a definitive reconstruction of the melodies, preference shall be given to the versions already used by Gregorian scholars and contained in the books of Solesmes.

3. The Commission expresses its desire that, in cases where paleographical research does not provide a definitive solution, esthetic considerations may cause the most beautiful version to prevail, even if the study of the manuscripts may tend to favor another version.

4. In every country, an individual shall be made responsible for gathering correspondence concerning Gregorian chant addressed to the Commission, and to forward such correspondence to Rome.

5. The Commission, limiting itself to the obvious meaning of the *motu proprio*, decides to approve only those editions that contain the melodies of the Vatican Edition. In cases where there may be several variants of versions confirmed by good manuscripts, the wording of the approval shall indicate the legitimate presence of the traditional variants. (This decision was annulled by the decree of the Congregation of Sacred Rites of August 14, 1905.)

6. The Commission expresses its wish that the Vatican Edition be declared mandatory for all Churches of the Roman rite.

7. In the Vatican Edition and in reproductions of it, no notation shall be accepted unless the grouping of the notes is in conformity with the traditional grouping.

8 to 15. [These paragraphs relate to the writing of the neumes, for which a certain degree of freedom was granted to publishers, as mentioned above—vertical or slanted shapes; the liquescent notes and the quilisma are mandatory. A decree of the Congregation of Sacred Rites of August 11, 1905, imposed absolute uniformity in these matters.]

16. The Editorial Board of the Vatican Edition has until January 1905 to produce the melodies of the *Ordinarium Missae* and they undertake to send the recommended musical texts to the Commission from time to time, as they are restored.

17. Other Masses, including a Mass taken from the Ambrosian chants, shall be added to the *Ordinarium Missae* currently in use. [The Editorial Board did, in fact, prepare an Ambrosian Mass, which appears in the initial proofs of the *Kyriale*.]

18. The traditional titles of certain Masses and melodies shall be retained (e.g. *Kyrie Fons bonitatis, Kyrie Deus sempiterne,* etc.), and certain more widely known chants and Masses shall be distributed according to the importance and the class of the (liturgical) functions, leaving all the other chants *ad libitum.*

19. The Royal Mass of Dumont shall not be included in the Vatican Edition, but the *Missa de Angelis* shall be retained.

20. Certain good melodies for the Credo, if any are found, shall be introduced into the *Ordinarium Missae.*

21. In the formulae to be placed at the end of the *Ordinarium* for recitative chants, a return shall be made to the ancient variety and richness, and for the Preface, as well.

22. The Congregation of Sacred Rites shall be requested to return to the medieval text of the Hymns (a) because the text corrected by Urban VIII is ill-suited to the needs of the chant; (b) in consideration of the artistic unity of the whole of the liturgical work; and (c) out of respect for the ancient and holy authors of a great portion of these chants.

23. Authorization to add certain ancient sequences as an Appendix to the Missal shall be sought from the Holy See. [At the suggestion of Father Grospellier.]

24. The Congregation of Sacred Rites shall be petitioned for authorization to sing the Benedictus of the Mass as a single unit with the Sanctus, in conformity with ancient liturgical usage.

25. The medieval psalm formulae shall be used once again for the psalmody of the Introit.

26. With respect to the psalmody of the Introit, the uniform tradition of the manuscripts must be followed.

27. The Editorial Board of the Vatican Edition is charged with selecting more or less ornate recitative formulae that may be introduced as a simple chant for the Graduals, Tracts, and Alleluia verses, and which are

to be published at the same time as the official edition. The Commission invites the Editorial Board to submit these formulae to it as soon as possible. The *Rassegna Gregoriana* of Rome is authorized to publish them as soon as the Commission receives them.

28. For the psalmody, the ordinary formulae shall be introduced in the Vatican Edition in all cases, placing the interrupted mediant at the bottom of the page as an option, when it is applicable. The same shall be done for the formulae of the verses, lessons, Epistles, and Gospels.

29. A complete list of corrections to the liturgical texts to be recommended to the Congregation of Sacred Rites must be drawn up, indicating with a special sign those corrections that relate to the chant; an explanatory note must be provided for all corrections.

30. The Congregation of Sacred Rites shall be asked (a) for approval of the diocesan Propers, not only the texts but their melodies, as well, and to submit them to the Commission; (b) if there are already any existing parts in the Propers, that the melody to be adopted shall be the melody already in use; and (c) that not too many different Masses shall be granted for the same feast.

Father Grospellier noted that the wishes expressed by the Pope in his telegram to the Commission had been fulfilled, and that the meeting had taken place in the harmony "of minds and scholarship." Nearly all the decisions had been made unanimously. That is clearly what the minutes show. Yet if one looks back at the events of March, when the *motu proprio* issued in April was being drafted and the membership of the Vatican Commission was being determined, and if one then examines carefully the minutes of the sessions, it is clear that a certain amount of mistrust was forming with regard to the Editorial Board, and it becomes evident that this unanimity was quite fragile. That everything went so smoothly can be explained by the fact that the hot topics were not tackled, or were mentioned only briefly in passing: the interpretation of paragraph *a* of the *motu proprio* of April 25, 1904 (cf. above). The future was soon to show that this somewhat pessimistic assessment was well founded. When the problem was addressed head-on and openly, the Commission split into two camps, and soon fell to pieces, in fact if not in theory.

Nonetheless, at this meeting in September, there was no dearth of high praise, and very sincere praise, for the work of the scriptorium at Solesmes, and even with regard to the chanting of the monks, which was performed according to rhythmic principles that some of the group had already rejected and which were, at least in part, at the origin of the misunderstanding.

Let us return to the chanting of the monks.

These performances were not merely an artistic delight, but an instructive lesson for all. One did not tire of admiring the perfect ensemble singing of these sixty men's voices, admirably blended into one, nor of the sweetness of the psalmody, of the melodies, in which everything seemed so natural, so devoid of studied effects, as is appropriate for prayer. Thus we were not surprised at the considerable number of Protestants who attended Vespers each evening. (A. Grospellier, *Appuldurcombe*, p. 32)

Msgr. Foucault had declined to respond to the questionnaire sent to him by the Commission. We have also seen that he shared the concerns of the French publishers (cf. No. 71). This did not augur well for the Vatican Edition. However, the edition of Rheims-Cambrai—certainly the best of the French editions published before Dom Pothier's edition—seemed to him to suffice for the French. Thus he was planning on reprinting that edition, to defeat the Vatican Edition in France. An envoy from the Bishop of Saint-Dié, went to Cambrai, as a very well-informed correspondent wrote to Dom Mocquereau,

to ask that the diocese join him in reprinting the Rheims and Cambrai edition. There are four dioceses that have already agreed, and if the number is large enough, one could speedily proceed with the task. Without any doubt, the objective is to obstruct the Vatican Edition. (To Dom Sergent, September 12, 1904)

Nonetheless, despite his differences of opinion with Dom Pothier, Msgr. Foucault found himself with him in Belgium (where Dom Pothier had taken refuge with his community), at Andenne, on September 29. In the company of Dom Pothier, he took part in a large meeting held under the auspices of the Association of St. Gregory, of the Diocese of Namur, chaired by Father Sosson, a musicologist.[207]

207. Cf. *Courrier de Saint-Grégoire* (Liège), October–December 1904, pp. 77–79. On the meeting at Appuldurcombe, cf. *Musica Sacra* (Milan), October 1904, p. 149, an article by Father de Santi: *La Commissione Pontificia per la nuova edizione dei libri di canto gregoriano nell'Isola di Wight* (excerpted from *Civiltà Cattolica* 1904, vol. 4, pp. 142–159).

74. Paleographical Wanderings in England and Italy

Dom Mocquereau had long wanted to create at Solesmes a vast collection of Gregorian chant manuscripts, through photography. However, these manuscripts had to be sought out in the public or capitular libraries, whose conservators were often hardly supportive of, if not outright hostile to, the reproduction of their treasures. Dom Mocquereau was already familiar with the primary collections in France, Switzerland, Italy, Belgium, and the Netherlands, where he had traveled looking for manuscripts, and he was very eager to study the libraries of England, Austro-Hungary, and Spain. The editing of the Vatican Edition, for which he was responsible, was an opportunity for him to fulfill his dream of visiting these countries.

During his stay in Rome, Dom Mocquereau had insisted that he be given every possible assistance in this matter, and he finally obtained a letter from the Cardinal Secretary of State, dated August 8, 1904, to the conservators of the libraries, recommending the delegates of the Abbot of Solesmes who were assigned to photograph the manuscripts.

Armed with the recommendation from Cardinal Merry del Val and, soon, from the Minister of Public Instruction of the Kingdom of Italy, two monks set off on August 17, 1904, and did not return to Appuldurcombe until December 14. They were Dom Paul Blanchon-Lasserve and Dom Amand Ménager, who explored the major libraries of Italy. A new photographic technique (the use of an erecting prism) enabled them to acquire a few hundred definitive proofs in just a few hours. The photographs were taken directly on paper, without the intermediary of a plate or film. Once exposed, the sensitive paper was packaged on site to protect it from light (in the dark room to which Dom Blanchon alludes below), and immediately sent to Appuldurcombe. There, the photographs were simply developed and fixed. At that point, they had a negative reproduction of the manuscripts, which could be used immediately to transcribe the melodies onto the comparative tables.

Let us now quickly join our travelers as they cross the peninsula, taking selections from Dom Blanchon's chronicle, focusing primarily on how warmly they were received everywhere.

The tour through Italy was preceded, in June, by visits to the libraries at Oxford and Worcester, visits that were also made by Dom

Blanchon and Dom Ménager. The librarians were most hospitable, such as the dean (of the Anglican cathedral) of Worcester, who

welcomed us with a warmth that we had hardly hoped for. We worked up in the rafters of the cathedral. The day was far from perfect, but we made do, at the cost of some stiffness that is inevitable when one has to spend a long time in a little nook in the rafters, which I transformed into my darkroom. (June 21)

In early August, the two monks also visited the British Museum, thanks to the recommendation of the Duke of Norfolk and of Msgr. Cahill, Bishop of Portsmouth. Their departure for Italy took place on the 18th. On the 19th, our travelers had reached Milan, and by the twentieth, they were at the Ambrosian Library.

Dr. Ceriani and Professor Ratti [the future Pius XI] were most welcoming, and readily granted us permission to photograph the chant manuscripts that we wanted. We kept up this schedule for eight days at the Ambrosian. Father Garbagnati often came to see us. He is quite friendly, a great admirer of the chant of Solesmes . . . ; he is quite interested in the manuscripts, and makes every effort to help us.

On the 29th, we set up our operation at the Brera, where we were to photograph a manuscript and several fragments. We were very warmly received, and we learned that a telegram had arrived that very morning, urging the Librarian to give us whatever support he could provide for our work. From that point on, we would encounter no more problems . . . The steps taken by Msgr. Bressan resulted in our obtaining a letter from the Director of Public Instruction, and in notice being sent of our arrival to all the Italian libraries.

Archpriest Msgr. Rossi received them equally warmly in Monza on August 30 (they returned to Milan every evening). There were a great number of manuscripts there:

all these manuscripts are marked with the stamp of France's Bibliothèque Nationale, and they are bound in red morocco leather with the insignia of Napoleon. The Emperor had had them all brought to Paris. They were returned to their Church under the Restoration.

They went on from Monza to Vercelli, from September 15–23: "We are able to put in solid days here, from 8:00 AM to 6:00 PM, or even 6:30 PM, the only interruption being for dinner (on the grass in the inner court of the Duomo)." Then they headed to Ivrea, to the library of the Chapter (the two monks lodged at the seminary and went to visit the Salesians). On the 27th, they continued on to Turin, where they stayed with Don

Bosco. "We bring our equipment into the room where they have brought together what remained of the manuscripts, following the fire last January."

On Sunday, October 2, our travelers reached Piacenza; our Msgr. Piacenza,[207bis] a friend of Bannister and Father de Santi, "showed us all its treasures, including a splendid 12th-century *Antiphonal*, a large folio with perfect writing and excellently preserved." On Thursday, October 6, they left Piacenza after being received by the Carmelites for four days "that may well count among the most pleasant of our travels."

After a night on the train, in a car that was completely full and stacked with their awkward baggage, our travelers arrived in Lucca, on Friday, October 7. They were cordially welcomed there by Father Baralli, thanks to whom the canons, ardent supporters of Pustet, agreed to allow their manuscripts to be photographed, although they did request (as was the practice in public libraries) a written promise not to publish the photographs. Gregorian chant enthusiasts met one evening at Father Baralli's residence—an event that was to be repeated elsewhere— and the monks of Solesmes could hardly refuse to provide a few samples of the chant of Solesmes, "even though Baralli, who had never set foot there, sings much better than we do." On Friday, October 14, they reached the Archbishop's offices and the various libraries of Florence. On the 17th, they left for Perugia, where they stayed until the 20th, the date they departed for Rome.

They arrived in Rome on October 21. Their first visit was to Father de Santi. On October 22, they visited Msgr. Bressan, who had received the letter from the Italian government. Then they visited Cardinal Rampolla, the archpriest of St. Peter's. The cardinal "received us right away, and as soon as he learned of the purpose of our visit, he stated that he would cooperate fully with us, and that he would convene the Chapter the next day, Sunday, following the Mass" (with regard to the authorization they had requested). That same day, again with an eye to reproducing manuscripts from public libraries, they had to go to the Ministry of the Interior, where they received a friendly welcome, then to Felici, who was to photograph the manuscripts selected in Rome. Although the archives of St. Peter's were rich particularly in Palestrina's music, the other libraries were more satisfying.

207bis. *Sic:* It so happened that the city and its bishop shared the same name.

On Wednesday, October 26, the Pope granted a 22-minute audience to the monks from Solesmes, and showed them that he was very well informed about everything. He said,

you are having fewer problems than those who were here a few months ago [for the preparation of the motu proprio of April 25]; they worked well, and it was difficult at times, but now everything has calmed down and there is general agreement.

Then the Pope added:

Be patient. We are going to produce a good edition, and the Pope who will come after Us will see to it that everyone accepts it. The work of the Church proceeds slowly. Just consider the Council of Trent: some of its decrees have still not been promulgated, and they would already stand in need of amendment! And those decrees were passed 342, 341 . . . no, 339 years ago!

While performing this little calculation, Pius X smiled and blinked his eyes, and his expression was truly wonderful.

On November 6, the monks from Solesmes saw the Pope once more, but this time in the company of other pilgrims.

On November 7, our travelers left Rome after making a pilgrimage to Subiaco. They learned before leaving that the Marciana library in Venice, which was on the verge of collapsing in ruins, had been closed, and they decided against traveling there. Instead, they headed for Bari by way of Monte Cassino. It was there that they reached "our highest output, managing to produce 600 photographs in seven hours of work" (at which point, they noted, they had used four kilometers worth of paper). On Monday, November 14, they were in Benevento,[208] followed by Loretto on November 20 after an overnight trip, Bologna on the 21st, Modena on the 25th, Nonantola, where the work proceeded very quickly, and Verona on the 29th.[209] In Bologna, Cardinal Svampa welcomed them very cordially, and reminded them that he had been one of the first defenders of the Solesmes chant against Pustet (see above, No. 48). He gave them a letter of recommendation for the Archbishop of Modena and the Cardinal of Verona, who welcomed them with the greatest possible cordiality. On December 4, the travelers were back in Milan

---

208. Father Antonio di Rienzo: *I Benedettini di Solesmes a Benevento*, in *Musica Sacra* (Milan), January 1905, p. 9. Cf. p. 15, *Note Italiane*.

209. *Fiori Solesmiani*, in *Verona Fidele*, December 3, 1904 (chant course at the Seminary).

once again, but this time to rest at the Benedictine house, where they had been so warmly welcomed at the outset.

After being away for four months, the travelers returned to Appuldurcombe on December 9, after a brief stop at Andenne, where there were a few manuscripts to be photographed.[210]

This first journey for the Vatican Edition brought more than 15,000 photographic proofs to Appuldurcombe, and at that point, the workshop had more than 250 complete manuscripts.[211] These photographs were sent to England immediately, after each stage of the journey, which enabled the twelve monks working as copyists to use them right away for the preparation of the *Kyriale*, which had been promised to the Commission for January 1905. Dom Mocquereau was very well aware of the objections that would be raised, and he thus took the wisest course by positioning himself immediately to answer his critics. On this issue, Msgr. Moneta-Caglio wrote:

In this climate of naïve optimism (which arose following the meeting at Appuldurcombe), Dom Mocquereau was the one person who, more than anyone else, kept his head on his shoulders and understood that he was faced with a task that required all his strength. So he got down to work right away, since he wanted the version that he had to submit as editor to be very thoroughly documented. (*Musica Sacra*, 1963, p. 6)

The *Revue du Chant Grégorien* alludes to these objections:

All those who will make the effort to obtain accurate information on the preparation of the chant books will say, along with the Commission, that an edition that has such thorough documentation at its service, such expert scholars, and such refined and conscientious methods, will be suitable for the plans that the Sovereign Pontiff has for it throughout the entire Church.

Another element that supports this affirmation are the Notes on the *Kyrie Fons bonitatis* that Dom Gabriel Beyssac, one of the young editors of the Gregorian school of Solesmes, has just published in the *Rassegna Gregoriana* (November–December 1904, col. 531–544). The 46 neumes of that piece are reviewed

---

210. *Iter Italicum* by Dom Blanchon; cf. *Revue du Chant Grégorien*, 1905, p. 102; *Musica Sacra* (Milan), January 1905, p. 15. Two other paleographical tours took place in 1905, one to Germany, the other to Spain. Finally, another trip took place in 1914 (Germany, Austro-Hungary, and once again in Northern Italy). Cf. *infra*, No. 85.

211. J. Dupont (pseudonym of Dom Étienne Bourigaud) in *L'Univers* of March 20, 1905 (*Chronique Grégorienne*).

one after the other in his article, according to the manuscripts at the paleographical scriptorium. There are 42 manuscripts for this *Kyrie*, grouped into six classes or schools; several date back to the tenth and eleventh centuries. From this exceedingly detailed study, Dom Beyssac has come up with a dozen small corrections, based on the best and most numerous manuscripts. No method could be more scientific, more serious, and more sure of uncovering the authentic teaching. (November–December 1904, p. 75)

The following text appeared in the same publication somewhat later:

This does not keep some detractors, in certain publications dedicated to the chant and to music, from denigrating beforehand the edition now in progress, and abandoning themselves to fanciful tales of doubtful taste on what they call the "Benedictine Commission" selected by the Pope. These impassioned, *a priori* judgments can stem only from ignorance, prejudice, or other even less respectable feelings. (March–April 1905, p. 138)

A confidential remark of Dom Mocquereau, regarding the "fifty years" that a definitive edition would allegedly take to produce, was also used against the upcoming edition. This supposedly confidential remark was in fact something that Dom Mocquereau had said quite publicly, at the lecture he gave in Rome itself during the Congress of St. Gregory the Great, and at the time he was speaking only of "some less ancient pieces and certain irreducible variants" (*Revue du Chant Grégorien*, March–April 1905, p. 138; cf. *supra*, No. 67).

Thus, despite a work that ensured great accuracy, there were doubts and criticisms already being raised concerning the edition that was yet to be created. Msgr. Moneta-Caglio presents these criticisms as follows, justifying Dom Mocquereau's point of view which, ultimately, failed to carry any weight within the Commission:

. . . Outside the Commission, the question of the future edition was being debated among the learned scholars who were raising a number of concerns. G. Houdard, free professor at the Sorbonne and a recognized mensuralist, published articles in reviews and journals with the intention of proving that, as the studies then stood, the *princeps* edition of the Gregorian melodies as envisaged by the Vatican was not yet possible. The work of the renowned Gregorian scholar in Seckau, Dom Célestin Vivell, was somewhat more measured. Written on the model of the Brief *Nos quidem* of Leo XIII, it had obviously been prepared before the publication of the *motu proprio*, and yet it remained a valid piece that should have recommended it to the Commission charged with preparing the new Gregorian teaching. In the summary of this work, H.

Müller, a professor at Paderborn, said, in fact, that "the work of restoring the authentic text is not considered to have been completed with the work of Dom Pothier. . .". In Strasbourg, the periodical *Caecilia* reported that "It is difficult for us to believe that the Vatican Edition is about to be published. Such work cannot just be churned out, for it must have lasting value. As it must be supposed, several years shall pass before we have it in hand." That was to prove a prophetic remark, even though the *Rassegna Gregoriana* responded by saying, "The pontifical *motu proprio* does not demand absolute perfection, which, given the nature of the critical research on the manuscripts, may never be achieved. It is enough for the edition to correspond appropriately to the current state of scholarship." Two years later, the same publication was to deplore the imperfection—both absolute and relative—with which the edition was being managed. In quite the opposite sense, the Bishop of Nancy, Msgr. Charles François Turinaz, was concerned with the fact that the thorough restoration of the melismas, dictated for artistic and not pastoral reasons, would make Gregorian chant inaccessible to the people, and he wrote to the Holy Father requesting that *carte blanche* not be given to the Benedictines alone. In the name of the Pope, Msgr. Bressan responded by assuring him that work done outside the sphere of Solesmes would also be taken into account. (*Musica Sacra*, 1963, pp. 5–6, cf. *supra*, No. 70)

V ▪ THE MEETINGS OF THE

COMMISSION HELD IN 1905

75. Preparation of the *Kyriale*

Dom Pothier returned to Rome at the beginning of February 1905, and was received by the Pope on February 15 (*Revue du Chant Grégorien*, March–April 1905, p. 137). The meetings of the Commission had resumed February 12. In spite of Father de Santi's wishes and those of Dom Mocquereau, the number of consultors remained the same. On November 12, 1904, Father de Santi had nonetheless written to Dom Mocquereau that the Pope agreed that there should be a greater number of consultors so that the preparation of the Vatican Edition might be given the best possible guarantee of success.

At Appuldurcombe (where Solesmes was in exile), the work was intense, and there was no cause for complaints about the slow progress, except from those who had no idea of the method being followed under Dom Mocquereau's direction or of the problems that came to light. Moreover, it had been conceded the preceding September, at the time of the plenary session of the Commission at Appuldurcombe, that the *Kyriale* could not be ready before January 1905. As early as mid November, the beginning of the *Kyriale*—four settings of *Asperges me* and the *Vidi aquam*—had been sent to Dom Pothier. In proposing several melodies for the *Asperges me*, Dom Mocquereau was merely responding to the wishes of the Commission, whose members requested more variety. For all that, Dom Pothier's response on November 22 was a bit discouraging, because he rejected the *Cantus brevior* of the Asperges me as "superfluous," though more ancient, and the Ambrosian *Asperges me* as "useless." Moreover, Dom Pothier affirmed his preference for DO, instead of SI, as the reciting tone of Mode 3 and Mode 8. SI is given in the manuscripts, but Dom Pothier judged it "harsh, difficult, and dull" (now it was not yet a matter of modifying the dominant of the psalms, rather only of establishing SI in the interior of melodic phrases.)[212] It was to Father de Santi that Dom Mocquereau sent his response to Dom Pothier's objections, on December 3.

Finally, on December 30 and on January 2, 1905, the "pieces reviewed from the ancient *Kyriale*" (from the *Liber Gradualis* by Dom Pothier, published at Solesmes in 1895) were sent to Dom Pothier; on January 20, Dom Pothier returned them to Dom Mocquereau, who sent them on in two mailings to Father de Santi, on January 22 and 26. The new pieces which were due to appear in the Appendix were sent at a later date.[213]

Dom Pothier's Memorandum

In returning the text of the *Kyriale*, Dom Pothier included a *brief memorandum*, replying in part to some questions of Dom Mocquereau. In this memorandum, he clearly dismissed two suggestions proposed by Dom Mocquereau. It is well known that in the Middle Ages, there was a custom of writing *Kyrieleison*, as if the two words made only one. Dom Pothier replied that a similar tradition cannot be maintained, and by necessity one should not be "fearful of amputating (the melody) and altering its form, even if fidelity to manuscript notation suffers because of this."—Another common tradition in every *Kyrie* was to make but one syllable of the *lei* in *eleison*, and Dom Pothier insisted that there should not be a diphthong here, but two distinct syllables.—Other detailed remarks on the *Kyriale* followed.

But above all, Dom Pothier took the occasion to present his great principle in a few lines (and credit is due him for having posed at once and openly the problem which had not been frankly exposed at Appuldurcombe in September 1904), namely that of the melodies in the *Kyriale,* "there are some among them which can and even ought to be given important retouching, sometimes to correct them, at other times to im-

212. On the reciting tones of these modes, see Dom J. Gajard, *Les récitations modales des IIIe et IVe modes et les manuscrits bénéventains et aquitains,* in *Études Grégoriennes,* I, pp. 9–45. In the discussions of the Vatican Commission, note that this issue of choosing between SI and DO as the reciting tone applied to Mode 8 (not just to Mode 3). In fact, in some passages in Mode 8, the reciting tone is on SI.

213. With five *Agnus Dei* or *Sanctus* from the ancient *Kyriale,* which are not found in the manuscripts.

prove them by enriching the melody and by giving them developments suggested by circumstances."

Dom Mocquereau's Memorandum

On his own initiative, Dom Mocquereau, with the help of Dom Gabriel Beyssac, prepared a lengthy memorandum in Latin (the *motu proprio* of April 25, 1904, required that nothing be published that could not be justified). In it, he said that the editing of the *Kyriale* had been done according to about 120 manuscripts from the tenth to the seventeenth century; a few of the *Kyries* were studied according to about fifty manuscripts; that "the research procedures and comparison of these numerous early documents had already been set forth in the *Rassegna Gregoriana . . .*"[214] and that "the Editors had but one regret: nine months was insufficient time to complete the most difficult phase of the work . . . that with somewhat more time we might perhaps have been able to do better."

In the memorandum, Dom Mocquereau then restated Dom Pothier's general principle, as mentioned above, because it clearly set forth the explanation of the changes that he required. However, the Editors did not want to reply to Dom Pothier other than to set forth the facts as they became known. Dom Mocquereau, in fact, was naive enough to believe that the evidence of the manuscripts would speak for itself, without need of further explanation.

There followed a detailed analysis of the problems encountered, of Dom Pothier's objections, and the solution for these offered by the Editors. In the event of a disagreement with Dom Pothier, the Editors left it to the Commission to come to a decision.

The Solesmes memorandum was printed in Rome under the title *Animadversiones in Kyriale Pontificiae Commissioni propositum simul cum Responsis ad ea quae Solesmensibus a Rev. D. Pothier obiciebantur.* It contained three parts, the first published on March 17 (pp. 1–23), the second arriving at Appuldurcombe on April 1 (pp. 24–39) with the first proofs of the *Kyriale*, and the third a few days later (pp. 40–50).

The first two parts were prefaced by a brief *Monitum* by Dom Poth-

---

214. Dom G. Beyssac, Notes on the *Kyrie Fons bonitatis, Rassegna Gregoriana* 1904, col. 531–544.—Dom. A. Mocquereau, *L'École grégorienne de Solesmes : I. Sa méthode critique (Rassegna Gregoriana,* col. 233–244); *II. Histoire d'un neume* (col. 311–326); *III. L'évolution dans l'esthétique et la tradition grégoriennes* (col. 397–420).

ier (undated) and, at the end of the text, a few reflections by the chairman to justify his point of view.

Regrettably, the printing of these *Animadversiones in Kyriale*, which arrived well after the resumption of the meetings (February 12) was delayed because Dom Pothier wanted to make some annotations, as noted above, before sending them to the printer. Thus, discussion and
correction of the Solesmes text were begun without waiting for the justification of the text. Therefore, it could be predicted that the positions
so clearly taken by each party would merely become increasingly hard-
ened, and that further discussion would soon become impossible.
When the fascicles of the *Kyriale* edition arrived, it was too late: the position of each player had already become set.

76. Resumption of the Meetings in Rome

The meetings of the Commission in Rome resumed on February 12.
There were fourteen of these meetings, numbers seven through twenty,
before Dom Mocquereau arrived. The meetings took place first at the
Chancery, then, starting with the eighth one, at the Greek College. Father de Santi, recording secretary, was not present for the ninth (March
12), fifteenth (March 26), and nineteenth (April 11) meetings. Therefore,
the minutes of these meetings are very brief. All that is known is that
the examination of the printed proofs continued, and no attention was
paid to who was present at the meeting of March 26 (the fifteenth meeting), except for Dom Amelli, whose name was singled out.

The list presented below details the attendance at these meetings in
1905.

At the outset, it should be noted that the first meeting in 1905 picked
up right where the sixth meeting held in Rome in June 1904 had left off;
so the meetings held at Appuldurcombe in June 1904 had their own
numbering sequence.—We have left the column for the fifteenth meeting (for which there are no minutes), and we have added Father Holly
to that of the twenty-third, since we know from Dom Mocquereau that
he attended that meeting (Dom Mocquereau added his name to his
own copy of the minutes of that meeting).—Finally, although the last
meeting scheduled is the twenty-sixth meeting, on May 7, we know

1905 Meetings

	7	8	9	10	11	12	13	14	15	16	17	18	19	20	21	22	23	24	25	26
Date	2-12	2-19	3-12	3-15	3-17	3-20	3-22	3-24	3-26	4-5	4-7	4-9	4-11	4-16	4-18	4-22	4-28	4-30	5-4	5-7
Members:																				
Dom Pothier	7	8	9	10	11	12	13	14		16	17	18	19	20	21	22	23	24	25	26
Mgr. Respighi	7	8	9	10	11	12	13	14		16		18		20	21	22	23	24	25	26
Nos Perosi	7			10	11	12	13					18								
Don Rella		8	9							16		18			21		23	24	25	26
D. Mocquereau															21	22	23	24	25	26
Dom Janssens	7	8		10	11	12	13	14		16		18	19	20	21	22	23	24	25	26
Père de Santi	7	8		10	11	12	13	14		16	17	18		20	21	22	23	24	25	26
Baron Kanzler	7					12	13					18		20		22				
Dr. Wagner			9	10	11	12	13	14		16	17	18	19	20	21	22				
Absent: H. Worth																				
Consultants:																				
Don Baralli															21	22	23	24	25	
Ch. Moissenet																	23	24	25	
Rev. Holly		8	9	10	11	12	13	14		16	17	18	19				23	24	25	26
Dom Amelli		8							15											
Dom Gaisser	7	8	9	10	11	12	13	14		16	17	18	19	20	21	22	23	24	25	26

Absent: Chan. Perriot, Chan. Grospellier, Dom Horn, Dom Molitor, A. Gastoue

that there was one more meeting on May 11, according to Father de Santi.

Of the twenty commissioners (ten members and ten consultors), fourteen participated in the meetings of 1905, of which nine were members and five consultors. (Don Mercati, appointed on May 6, did not have time to participate.) The line-up of those present is as follows (the names of consultors are in italics):

Dom Pothier	19 meetings attended
Dom Gaisser	19 meetings attended
Msgr. Respighi	17 meetings attended
Father de Santi	17 meetings attended
Dom Janssens	16 meetings attended
Father Holly	15 meetings attended
Dr. Wagner	13 meetings attended
Msgr. Rella	8 meetings attended
M. Perosi	6 meetings attended
Baron Kanzler	6 meetings attended
Dom Mocquereau	6 meetings attended
Rev. Father Baralli	5 meetings attended
Abbé Moissenet	3 meetings attended
Don Amelli	2 meetings attended

Those who never participated in the meetings were H. Worth, *Father Perriot, Father Grospellier, Dom Horn, Dom Molitor,* and *Professor Amédée Gastoué.*

Before Dom Mocquereau's arrival in Rome, those who participated in the meetings as *members* of the Commission were: Dom Pothier, (*President,* at 13 meetings), Msgr. Carlo Respighi (at 11), Father de Santi (at 11), Dr. Wagner (at 11), Dom Janssens (at 10), Perosi (at 6), Baron Kanzler (at 5), Msgr. Rella (at 4);—as *consultors:* Dom Gaisser (at 13), Father Holly (at 11), and Dom Amelli (at 2). So there were eleven commissioners present for these important meetings: eight out of ten members, and three out of ten consultors, particularly Dom Gaisser (13 times present) and Father Holly (11 times present), who were faithful in their attendance, while among the members, Perosi (at 6 meetings), Baron Kanzler (at 5 meetings), and Msgr. Rella (at 4 meetings) participated less frequently, even though they lived in Rome.

Now we arrive at the subjects discussed by the Commission, leaving aside details and practical matters that did not go to the heart of the problem facing the panel. The best approach is to follow in chronological order the Minutes of the meetings, of which we have one faithful copy by Dom Cagin, as well as some added notes, all usually in Italian (we believe that the report is complete up to the end of June 1905).

Meeting No. 7, February 12. Father de Santi asked for a summary of the Appuldurcombe meeting (cf. No. 73). Then it was decided to resolve to keep "everything relating to the compilation of the texts and the process of the printing" in secrecy, and it was decided to maintain the Commission in the *statu quo* by naming no more than a few additional member correspondents and a few honorary members. Then, after presenting the first proofs of the *Kyriale*, it was decided to "reduce the *morae vocis* and to return them to the form already used in the Solesmes *Liber Gradualis*," and the President agreed to assume the task of directing the work. On this matter, Perosi declared that "it is necessary to be faithful to the *motu proprio*. Basically, the Edition is a critical edition; above all, the manuscripts must be followed, unless a solid reason based on good tradition or current performance of the chant suggest a change. There is agreement on this point."

Father de Santi, for his part, proposed that Solesmes be asked to produce a memorandum justifying its text, and announced that he had handed over the entire content of the *Kyriale* to the printing office, and had turned the *Appendix* over to the office of the President for examination.

Meeting No. 8, February 19. It was announced that Solesmes was preparing a research trip to Spain and that, for this purpose, the Cardinal Secretary of State had sent a letter of recommendation. Then the appointment of new consultors was reconsidered, and several names were proposed, but no decision was reached on the matter.

Meeting No. 9, March 12. In the absence of Father de Santi, there was no report of the minutes. The examination of the *Kyriale* proofs was started.

Meeting No. 10, March 15. As to the matter of the proofs and the evaluations of the reviewers already received, the recording secretary notes: "It is not possible to indicate each one of the changes, but probably they will be summarized eventually in a special memorandum."

Meeting No. 11, March 17. The *Animadversiones* (Part 1) of the Editors, preceded by a *monitum* of the President, and the corrected proofs up to the Easter Mass, were sent to the consultors in Rome. On this matter, Father de Santi expressed the wish that the personal communications of the President be made in his name and signed by him.

Then, Msgr. Respighi presented a sort of rules of order for the Commission, based on what is currently in use in other Roman commissions, and which doubtless would be useful in dealing with our business more clearly, more quickly, and with better documentation. The memorandum was read and praised, but no real decision was made on the matter. Father de Santi merely recommended that, for the moment, Father Holly collect the arguments for and against the corrections that have either been recommended or actually made in the proofs examined up to this point. Father Holly graciously agreed to do this.

We must note, in this regard, that Father de Santi appended the following observation to the minutes of the meeting:

In my position as recording secretary, I must note that our Commission lacks a regulating and unifying principle. Time is lost returning to the same questions without any definitive resolution. My advice is that first a memorandum ought to be drawn up which will summarize the opinions reached on the various points discussed; these ought to be studied privately by each member, accepted or rejected, and always for well-founded reasons. Only then should questions be submitted to the Commission, and each one would be better prepared to make his definitive judgment. . . .

Meeting No. 12, March 20. "The need to establish rules of order for the Commission was the primary focus . . . Everyone feels the need for keeping a written record of all matters, especially the reasons for corrections to be made on the melodies proposed by Solesmes." Father de Santi recommended Msgr. Rella for the task, but meanwhile Father Holly offered graciously to step in to cover the need. "The debate on the matter of the SI and the DO came up again; Wagner and Dom Gaisser cite several good reasons for preference to be given to the DO, as will be summarized by Father Holly in particular. (Holly's notes are very brief.)[215]

215. Here is a summary of the debate written by Father Holly, and communicated, no doubt, to the Members of the Commission: "At the sessions of March 12 and 15, 1905, the general matter of the choice to be made between the notes SI and DO as Dominants in Mode 8 and Mode 3 arose.—The Right Reverend President read out the opinions of absent consultors, with the exception of Father Baralli and Baron Kanzler. Most of these gentlemen agreed with the Right

Meeting No. 13, March 22.

The minutes of the meeting were read (from the preceding meeting), and again the need for rules of order was of great concern. . . . In addition, it was proposed that, on the basis of the notebook containing the debates, an official report should be established summarizing the reasons for the corrections introduced in the proofs, and the readings definitely fixed. This report, signed by the President and the Secretary, will remain as an official document of the work of the Commission. All are agreed on this point. [To our knowledge, such a report was not done.]

The entry continues: "Progress is being made scrupulously, and not a single correction is accepted unless it has the support of the manuscripts, even though the general tendency is to consult the tradition [the living tradition] and to exclude forms that are too archaic." (At the preceding meeting, for example, the model of a *Kyrie* proposed by the editors was rejected.)

Meeting No. 14, March 24. Father de Santi reported on the content of a private letter from Dom Mocquereau, who protested certain corrections, in his opinion, as unsustainable. Dom Mocquereau realized that his presence in Rome was necessary but, at the same time, he could not distance himself from the archives collected at Solesmes. However, "he said that if the observations were sent to him successively, he could respond by return mail with a substantiated yes or no." As a result, "the earlier decision to notify the Editors officially of any corrections made, before they are definitively adopted and entered into the printer's proofs, was confirmed." Father de Santi also proposed that an official report on corrections made to the Editors' manuscript should be kept in

Reverend President in preferring the DO.—Dr. Wagner then took the floor, and he pointed out to us that it would be impossible for us to re-establish in its entirety the practice of the eighth and ninth centuries on this matter: (1) because the SI of that day was sharper than ours (i.e. between the SI and the DO of our scale), and (2) in light of the great inconvenience that would arise from establishing a difference between the Dominant of the antiphon and that of the psalm. Besides, he said that we must take legitimate tradition into account that, for reasons relating to the development of Roman chant over the subsequent centuries, had solidly established the Dominants of Modes 3 and 8 on the note DO.—The debate then turned to the phrase *et omnes ad quod* . . . from the *Vidi aquam.*—Father de Santi preferred SI. Dom Gaisser initially wanted SI, but ultimately preferred DO, as more in conformity with a well-founded tradition and, in any event, much easier in practice. Finally, everyone came out in favor of DO (1) in cases where there is a reciting tone in the course of the antiphon, and (2) anywhere that adopting the SI might lend itself to the danger of creating a FA sharp (a danger pointed out for us by Dom Gaisser)."

the attendance register, with a brief indication of the reasons for those changes.

Meeting No. 15, March 26. Since Father de Santi was not in attendance, no minutes were kept for this meeting. We know only that the examination of printed proofs continued.

A note (written later) mentions that the rest of the *Kyriale* proofs were distributed (pp. 25–28), along with the second part of the *Animadversiones* of Solesmes (pp. 23–39), and also that Dom Mocquereau had sent two strongly worded circulars, on March 25 and 28, to defend his work as editor of the Vatican Edition.

77. At the Heart of the Problem

The reason for Dom Mocquereau's two letters, of March 25 and 28, must be clarified. On February 13, Father de Santi had written to him: "All of us on the Commission have agreed to avoid any hurt feelings and to support the Editorial Board in everything that is truly important. . . . However, we all think that it is necessary for Your Reverence to come to Rome." A few days later, on February 19, Father Baralli, who was not in Rome but was evidently kept abreast of all matters by Father de Santi, complained bitterly at the character of the turn of events.[216]

Surely, Dom Mocquereau, who had already received Dom Pothier's memorandum on the matter, a memorandum to which his *Animadversiones in Kyriale* had replied, could have himself formed an idea of the situation from the corrections made to his text, corrections in his view often without justification. Moreover, it could be seen from the foregoing, by following the Minutes of the first meetings of 1905, that the Commission was continuing without a guiding principle and without method, and also, obviously without sufficient basic documentation, which left the door wide open to fantasy and whimsy. The resolutions adopted at Father de Santi's suggestion—(1) to inform the Editors of the corrections made to its text and (2) to draw up a memorandum detailing the modifications adopted, together with the reasons for them—were not yet known at Solesmes. They would remain a dead issue in any event. Thus the need for some rules of order became increasingly

216. Baralli letter of February 19, 1905 (Moneta-Caglio, *Musica Sacra*, 1963, pp. 9–10).

urgent, at least among those who wanted to take the instruction of the Pope seriously and to proceed with the greatest possible scientific rigor.

First Circular from Solesmes

In the first of his circulars, dated March 25 (four large duplicated pages), Dom Mocquereau recounted what the principles of the Editorial Board were: the same as those given in the *motu proprio* of April 25, 1904, in the Brief to the Abbot of Solesmes dated May 22, 1904, and in the decisions reached at Appuldurcombe,—and he said that he was prepared to accept all the proposed changes, "provided that they were well substantiated, based on solid reasons and on specific, designated documents just as we provide substantiation and a foundation for our own texts," something which, for its part, the Commission had not done up until that point.—Dom Mocquereau further stated that the Editors, in many cases, had already considered the legitimate tradition; furthermore, the principle of the legitimate tradition must not be applied willy-nilly, and that the revisionists should give proof of (a) the *legitimacy of the tradition* of their versions, and (b) the *reasons* that made them select a later and altered tradition over the pure and ancient tradition.—He also noted that several modifications introduced by the revisionists departed clearly from the resolutions adopted at Appuldurcombe.—He added once more that he had promised to justify and defend the work of the Commission, that he would then have to take responsibility for all these changes,—and finally, by continuing on the way they were going, they were exposing themselves to producing a "bastard work, indefensible, unworthy of the Commission, of Pius X, and of the Holy Church."

Second Circular from Solesmes

In the second circular, dated March 28 (five large duplicated pages), Dom Mocquereau wished to point out the danger of the criteria followed by the Commission and to outline the responsibility of the Editors, and he gave examples of publications that in the past had withered away after a brief period of success;—he then made clear what he meant by *legitimate* tradition, that "which does not contradict the source from which it comes: tradition called continuity, transmission. However, something that contradicts its sources is undeserving of this venerable name!" (at which point Dom Mocquereau gave the example of the settings of the *Asperges me* proposed by the Commission);—finally, he recalled what the Pope had demanded in the *motu proprio* of April 25, 1904, and in the Brief to the Abbot of Solesmes dated May 22, 1904.

Dom Pothier's Memorandum

This second circular by Dom Mocquereau was in response to a printed memorandum in Latin by Dom Pothier: *Nonnullae Animadversiones ex parte D. Praesidis Commissionis (Some Comments by the President of the Commission)* comprising four large pages (undated, as was customary). In it, Dom Pothier, the President of the Commission, defended his principle of the living tradition and gave as an example the gradual improvement over the centuries *renovata in melius* ("renewed for the better") by the rise of the Dominant to DO in Mode 3 and Mode 8: "However, this was done well, indeed for the purpose of saving the chant from a confusion of tones or modes, or even from losing them entirely." Several remarks followed on the *Kyriale*. Dom Pothier had this to say regarding the *Asperges me* (1st *ad libitum*) of Mode 7: "The shorter melody of the *Asperges me* antiphon must be rejected ultimately, or rather should be deleted. *The reason:* it has fallen into disuse for some time now." Dom Mocquereau wrote in his circular of March 28:

So it is expelled, eliminated, cancelled because it is archaic, because this delicate antiphon had the misfortune in the 13th century of falling into the hands of people of ponderous tastes who weighed it down and ornamented it in their fashion, and so it passed into the modern editions through their hands.[217]

Letters of Father de Santi and Father Holly

While Dom Mocquereau was preparing the long defensive memorandum requested by Father de Santi, a memorandum that he had been thinking about for a long time anyway (at the time, it already ran to some twenty large pages of manuscript, on the first six Masses of the *Kyriale*), suddenly two letters arrived back to back, one from Father de Santi and the other from Father Holly, with a Note from the President of the Commission.

217. Writing to Dom Pothier on March 29, Dom Molitor wrote [in Latin] about this issue (and informed Dom Mocquereau of his letter): "Besides, I greatly fear that, by withdrawing from the authority of the ancient manuscripts, we might not know where to base our understanding of that extremely complex question of the Dominant, SI or DO, in tones VIII and III" (St. Joseph near Billerbeck, March 29, 1905).

Father de Santi's letter was dated March 25, and was written following the fourteenth meeting of the Commission. It arrived after a series of cards and letters that came in rapid succession (dated February 16, 20, 24, 27 and March 3, 8, 13, 14, 18, 20, and 23), and replied to a personal letter of Dom Mocquereau (cf. Meeting 14). Father de Santi spoke with severity about the Commission and the President, but added:

we hope to establish some rules of order, so that matters will proceed with order and speed. Meanwhile, the Commission has decided to ask the Editors please to add any comments on the manuscript that it deems opportune, but never in the form of a polemic that seems unpleasant to everyone. Henceforth, Your Reverence can give as a pretext the general tendency of the Commission, which is to avoid any model that is too archaic and too skeletal, and then it will not be difficult for you to justify by special reasoning the changes from the first edition (of the *Liber Gradualis* of 1883, republished in 1895), that you find the most essential . . .

Father de Santi added, in an allusion to the disorder of the meetings:

If matters continue as they have, I intend no longer to attend the meetings, which have caused me to lose an infinite amount of time. . . . (And moreover) my studies do not give me any special competence to decide in favor of one version rather than another.

Father Holly's letter (written in French) was dated March 20. He insisted strongly that Dom Mocquereau should come to Rome:

. . . Father de Santi does what he can to save a few fragments of the numerous phrases you have challenged. Mr. Wagner, thanks to the authority of the German manuscripts that he quotes at every turn, has been of value to you in a small way. However, in general, I must tell you quite simply that the majority of the voting is in favor of the version of the *Liber Gradualis*, every time that, in the better known chants, that version is contradicted by your instructions. This is ridiculous, because no one of us is qualified to sit in judgment against the work of Solesmes. What reconciles me to this is the perfect confidence that what we do will be submitted to your monks, and that it is you who will always have the last word. It's just that you have to be present *here to protect your rights* . . . As I see it, certain individuals here are convinced that this referral back to you is done only as a courtesy, and that the Commission as it is constituted at the Greek College has the right to treat your text *however it sees fit.* So you can see what we need: not your archaeological weaponry from Solesmes, but some canonical weaponry from Rome. You yourself must wield these weapons. What is needed is a *leader.* For there is no one here strong enough to *wage* a campaign in favor of Solesmes. If you were there, you could easily form and direct a *parliamentary block*, which would give you a majority of votes on all questions under discussion. Father de Santi has tried hard to line us up and lead us in the attack, or rather, to organize the defense. However, lately he is discouraged. . . . Last year, you came (at my urging or on your own initiative, no matter) and you were able to prevail in each of the opposing arguments. Now, if you hold firm in your decision to stay at home, you will certainly lose the fight. You still have time to regain the lost terrain, and to organize the defense of the ground others covet. . . . *P.S.* It seems to me that you would do well to invite Mr. Worth and Father Baralli to come, and also one of your monks who is better able than I to write up the acts and discussions of the Commission. . . . [As we have seen, Father Holly had been assigned the task of preparing certain documentation.]

The President's Memorandum

The Memorandum received from the President that arrived at Appuldurcombe on April 5 was another matter. This Memorandum, dated April 2 (though the postage cancellation date was April 1), addressed to all the members and consultors of the Commission, was printed, and comprised twenty-one lines in all, wherein was explained the procedure followed when examining the texts proposed by the Editors.

It could possibly be useful and certainly acceptable to the members of the Commission who are not in a position to participate in the deliberations to know the procedure that is followed at the meetings when the texts proposed by the Editors are examined.

Each one present has a copy of the proofs to be examined. The President has written on his copy the various proposals from absent members so as to be able to tell how many are favorable or unfavorable to such-and-such a reading. When a passage emerges about which one of the members has a comment to make, or when one of the absent members has written a question or remark, the President stops and the problem is discussed, reading the absent member's own text or observation, if necessary. If the feelings of the gathering are clear, the debate is closed. If no agreement is evident, however, the President asks each member his opinion in turn, and when a majority is reached, a decision is made. One of the members has been assigned to recapitulate in writing the reasons for arriving at a decision. To help him in his task, he gathers the various folders of proofs on which each one has recorded his observations.

Clearly, the method is detailed enough, but orderly and sure.

Rome, April 2, 1905.
Dom Joseph Pothier, President.

This Memorandum was in response to Dom Mocquereau's circulars, at least to the first one, dated March 25. The Memorandum arrived at Appuldurcombe and immediately Dom Mocquereau sent a telegram of protest "at the haphazard method described in the President's Memorandum."

Third Circular from Solesmes

The same day, April 5, Dom Mocquereau sent a third circular to the Commission (comprising five long duplicated pages) in which he showed once again how meaningless the reasons were for opposing the archaeological tradition, noting that "the archaic and the antique are not the same thing," that all art, every expression of beauty, has its hour of maturity, of perfection, and that Gregorian chant, too, had its hour. "It blossomed forth in its absolute beauty, inspired, definitive, after centuries of persecution and following the great centuries of doctrine. Supernatural civilization was at its zenith." After a vibrant page—actually written by Dom Delatte—, Dom Mocquereau recalled that Dom Pothier did not think otherwise. In fact, in 1896 he wrote: "The simpler, more open manner of the early melody is also the softest and most distinctive, a manner that combines the advantage of art and taste with that of antiquity" (*Revue du Chant Grégorien*, December 1896, p. 70). Finally, Dom Mocquereau did not deny that there had been a tradition of development and adoption of new formulae, but "the truth is that the further away one gets from the ages of faith, the more the Gregorian musical art follows the lamentable downturn of a long-term decline."

78. The First Letter from the Cardinal Secretary of State, April 3, 1905

At *Meeting No. 16, held on April 5,*

Dom Pothier informed the Commission of a letter from the Cardinal Secretary of State dated April 3, in which he set forth, with the authority of His Holiness, the interpretation given to the *motu proprio* of April 25, 1904, pertaining to the criterion of tradition in the presence of the most ancient manuscripts. Dom Janssens read the document aloud:

Most Reverend Father:

It has come to the attention of the Holy Father that, among those who are working to prepare the Vatican Edition of the liturgical books, a doubt has arisen as to the best manner of responding to the intentions of His Holiness relative to the restoration of sacred music. The August Pontiff is pleased to state that the differences between one side and the other have arisen out of a desire to respond to his intentions in the best way possible. However, in order to eliminate any occasion and any pretext of doubt and incertitude, His Holiness has instructed me to inform Your Reverence that when He decided on the return to the ancient Gregorian chant, He did not intend to make this work exclusively favorable to the archaeology of the chant, to the point that models of Gregorian melodies that have been received over the course of the centuries cannot be accepted today. In his *motu proprio* of November 22, 1903, the Holy Father recalled very opportunely that "the Church has always recognized and encouraged the advancement of the arts, allowing for use in its worship services anything that artistic genius has found good and beautiful over the course of the centuries, as long as liturgical rules are respected at all times."

In his second *motu proprio* of April 25, 1904, establishing the rules of order with regard to the Vatican Edition of the liturgical books, His Holiness wisely decided that "the integrity and purity of the melodies of the Church, known as Gregorian chant, will be restored according to the most ancient manuscripts, but particularly bearing in mind the legitimate tradition contained in the manuscripts over the course of the centuries, as well as the practical use in current liturgy."

According to these principles, which express the true tradition of the Church, it will not be against the intention of His Holiness that the Pontifical Commission for the Vatican Edition of Gregorian liturgical books should give preference to some less ancient compositions, provided that they have the true character of Gregorian music. In fact, it cannot be demonstrated that the most ancient chant is necessarily and always the best for practical adaptation. Because of certain subsequent developments in the art, the ancient melodies could have evolved logically, or even could have acquired certain embellishments, without causing harm to their original purity.

Please share these authoritative explanations with the Commission over which you preside with such dignity, so that the Commission might take them as a norm and guide in doing its work, and may the Commission continue to prove ever more worthy of the trust that His Holiness has placed in it.

In the meanwhile, I am happy to take this opportunity to express to you my distinguished expressions of esteem, and remain

Yours very affectionately in the Lord,

R. Card. *Merry del Val,*
Rome, April 3, 1905.

Dom Pothier sent this letter on April 5 and, according to Father Holly, it was inspired by Dr. Wagner (Holly, June 27, 1906 to Dom Mocquereau). After it was read aloud by Dom Janssens at the April 5th meeting, there followed "a lively discussion of the document which had just been read, and of other current topics."[218]

Father de Santi said that he accepted this authoritative instruction as was appropriate, but at the same time, he protested against recourse to the Holy See in a case where, in his opinion, the authority of the Commission would have sufficed, especially since the decisions reached at the various regular meetings and at the plenary meeting at Appuldurcombe had already in substance fixed the same principles as contained in the new letter. The Commission could then affirm and impose them once again. He recognized that the Editors were prone to prefer the oldest manuscripts alone, but at the same time he believed that, on the other hand, too much weight was given easily to subsequent tradition. The Cardinal's letter now caused the balance to tip more in favor of subsequent tradition whereas, in his opinion, it would have been preferable to refer to the principles that had already been laid down and, always, to the correct criterion alone.

Dom Gaisser noted that the new document did not impose this tendency, and that it merely affirmed that this was not contrary to the intentions of the Holy Father.

Father de Santi replied that the new document, by not being more precise in explaining the problem, left the question at the same point as before. Finally, he declared that it would have been better not to make this appeal without first seeking the advice of the Commission, and that such remedies, which are always extreme, should rather be reserved for those instances where every other means seems to be exhausted.

Dom Pothier, Dom Janssens, and Dr. Wagner thought the document very opportune, for it was required because of the Solesmes circulars, and it provides a more reliable rule for resolving practical difficulties.

Father de Santi added that the criterion of subsequent tradition could have been invoked when it seemed right to do so, as is the case specifically for the *Kyriale*, or at least for several pieces of the *Kyriale*, and he cited some very clear examples. He maintained that the strictest critical criteria ought always to be affirmed as the sound basis for our work.

---

218. This letter—from the Cardinal Secretary of State on April 3—which had been written for the Commission (and which was thus intended to remain secret) was published first in excerpts by Dr. Wagner in his pamphlet *Über traditionellen Choral,* and then in its entirety by the Strasbourg *Caecilia,* and finally by the *Revue du Chant Grégorien,* January–February 1906, p. 105.

Msgr. Respighi returned to the absolute necessity of establishing rules of order, such as those followed in the Congregations and in the other Commissions in Rome, where difficult and very important matters are settled with reasonable speed and in a prescribed order. He referred to the French Circular [President's Memorandum of April 2], recently circulated by the Very Reverend President, in which certain things that do not seem to correspond to reality are affirmed.

In that regard, Father de Santi read a commentary that arrived today by telegram from Solesmes against the Circular of April 2 from the Very Reverend President, and he declared that regretfully he would have to add his own protestation to it. Specifically, the method followed by the Commission had been discussed and various proposals made to remedy it: it should not have been declared good. Moreover, it would have been good for such communications to have been proposed first in committee. Various comments were made by the Very Reverend President and Dom Janssens to defend the Circular, namely that the method also had its good points and that a detailed account had been kept of the various opinions and points conscientiously discussed, points, moreover, that were not presented as definitive. Father de Santi replied that in Rome, we know that these decisions are not final, but that those away from Rome will readily abide by what the Circular has stated.

Father Holly noted that procedures had been uncertain in the initial meetings, but that he had felt renewed hope when the principle was adopted that solutions would not be definitive, but would first be sent to Solesmes. . . . Msgr. Rella voiced the same opinion.

Everyone agreed that rules of order must be established, and Dom Gaisser proposed that Father de Santi draft these rules, and present them at the next meeting. He accepted, and said that he would focus primarily on the proposals already made by the members at the various meetings. Everyone agreed that without the experience acquired on this issue, it would have been impossible to design rules of order.

In a note, the recording secretary added, certainly at the request of Wagner himself:

Dr. Wagner read a page of an essay that he planned to publish. He said that the Fathers at Solesmes wrote their missive in vinegar rather than ink. He said that they showed neither a knowledge of history nor musical taste, two things absolutely necessary to perform well the task of editing. They merely copy manuscripts. Father de Santi observed that Dr. Wagner's statements against the Editors were too strong.

Father de Santi wrote to Dom Mocquereau on April 6:

I read the hasty telegraph of protest against the Circular in French, and to it I joined my own protest energetically; others joined in with the protests. It all has to do with the internal rules of order, where all matters are controlled. The meeting was very stormy, but we hope that it will bear fruit.

Father de Santi wrote to Dom Mocquereau again on April 7:

At the meeting on the 5th, after the President informed us of the letter [from the Cardinal], I made the following protest: I protest against having recourse to the Holy See without the advice of the Commission in those matters for which the Commission has complete competence, before exhausting every possible avenue requiring this ultimate solution, and especially that this was done by someone who had a particular interest in the matter. I am convinced that the *motu proprio*, just as it has always been interpreted in the obvious sense in the inner workings of the Commission, is adequate for our needs. Thus I am convinced that both sides are going a bit too far, the Editors in giving too much, perhaps exclusive, consideration to the most ancient manuscripts, the President in placing too much reliance, sometimes without convincing reasons, on subsequent tradition.

Then I read your telegram protesting the *Circular of April 2*, and I added my own protest to it, because the Circular had been sent without the consent of the Commission, without considering some of the comments made by the Commission against the regularity [*sic*] of the process, and especially in declaring definitive certain conclusions that, many times, are different from what was agreed in the meetings.

Finally, it was resolutely decided that the Commission's internal rules of order would be developed, spelling out the authority of the President, the standard to be followed for revision (of the proofs), and the procedure that applies to all necessary steps.

I should like to hope that things will improve now, and that we will finally make some headway. I believe that your presence in Rome is now imperative. In any event, for my part, I will always argue that justice must be done for all.

Father de Santi added the following post-script:

The content of the letter (from the Cardinal) leaves me neither hot nor cold. The matter can readily, and even ought to be, interpreted in the sense of the *motu proprio*, as we have always held.

In his protest, which was deposited in the Archives of the Commission and is dated April 5, Father de Santi added not only that the President's Memorandum had been "distributed without the consent of the

Commission," but that it claimed as "perfect and certain" a method that others had criticized in the meetings as "uncertain and disorderly,"[219] and, finally, it had been decided in the meeting to await Solesmes' response to the correctors' revisions and to make an official report of the reviewers' work before "closing the debate."

Before this, in a letter sent to Dom Pothier on April 1 and deposited in the official record, Father de Santi had complained that the Commission was being conducted without a plan—which resulted in a considerable loss of time—and that the decisions to be made to remedy this condition remained without effect.[219bis] As a result, Father de Santi confessed that his assignment as "recording secretary" had been rendered difficult, and that he would be very happy were it to pass into other hands. Dom Pothier replied on April 2, by referring to his Memorandum that was released the same day.

For his part, Dom Janssens wrote to Father de Santi (the statement is in the official record, undated) to protest what he had said in the meeting about the Cardinal's letter and the role of the President, when nothing had been said about the circulars from Appuldurcombe, the tone of which he found offensive. In fact, Father de Santi himself had complained to Dom Mocquereau about the controversial tone of his circulars.

On April 6, Father de Santi replied to Dom Janssens, repeating and clarifying the object of his criticism: not the Cardinal's letter, which he accepted, but the fact that Dom Pothier had had recourse to the Holy See without the advice of the Commission, which was fully authorized to act independently. He agreed that the Editors were overly reliant on the manuscripts, and that Dom Pothier was overly reliant on the subsequent tradition, and without sufficient reason.

---

219. "I am very sorry that I, too, must protest against this note. Above all, because it was distributed without the consent of the Commission on a matter that was not a personal concern of the President, but common to all and concerning the procedure followed by the Commission itself. Secondly, because the comment was made repeatedly in the sessions that things are proceeding in an uncertain and disorderly manner. If there was disagreement on this point, it should have been discussed in the Commission. Now the President, in his note, simply states that the method being used, which has now been placed into doubt, is perfect and certain" (de Santi, April 5, 1905).

219bis. Here is the main passage from Father de Santi's letter to Dom Pothier: "A few decisions were made by the Commission specifically to avoid these obstacles, but I note that that these decisions were not followed in practice" (de Santi, April 1, 1905, to Dom Pothier).

Speaking of an audience with the Pope, Father de Santi added:

At any rate, I only repeated in the Commission the same thing I said the evening before in the presence of the Holy Father, when His Holiness wished to question me on the matter of the letter (of the Cardinal); since I had to tell him that I knew absolutely nothing about it; on the spur of the moment His Holiness deigned to tell me the steps taken to obtain it. If necessary, at the proper time, I shall relate the counsels His Holiness gave me on this subject . . .[220]

Finally Father de Santi declared:

As for the rest, it is very obvious that disorder reigns everywhere. Imploring, insisting in private and in the Commission have always been in vain. A protest was absolutely necessary: it took place and was vigorously debated, and it is the serious state of affairs that provoked it. Given the circumstances, it is our conviction that the Very Reverend President should guarantee the impersonal authority of the Commission in all his resolutions. Otherwise, the idea will germinate that the President does not direct, but that he governs despotically.

In a report to Dom Mocquereau written in 1906, Father Holly noted that it was the reference to rules of order [regolamento, "regulation"] made by Msgr. Respighi (cf. Meeting No. 11) that convinced the President to have recourse to higher authority directly, in order to get out in front of the issue.

In fact, Father Bauducco notes specifically that the letter from the Cardinal was triggered by a memorandum from Dom Pothier dated March 26 (Il P. Angelo de Santi e l'edizione vaticana dei libri gregoriani dal 1904 al 1912, Civiltà Cattolica, 1903, I, pp. 240–253). Msgr. Moneta-Caglio adds that he also had "the memoranda of P. Wagner, A. Gastoué, D. M. Horn, all in support of the living tradition" (Dom André Mocquereau e la restaurazione del canto gregoriano, Musica Sacra, January–February 1963, note 351).

New Memorandum from Dom Pothier

Before proceeding further, a word must be said about a memorandum from Dom Pothier circulated at the same time as the letter of the

220. Ad ogni modo in Commissione non ho fatto altro che ripetere quel medesimo che la sera innanzi al S. Padre, quando Sua Santità volle interrogarmi intorno la lettera e poichè io dovetti dichiarargli che non ne sapevo assolutamenta nullo, si degnà spontaneamente di narrarmi i passi fatti per ottenerla. Se sarò necessario comunicherò a suo tempo gli avvisi dati me in proposito dalla medesima Santità Sua (Father de Santi to Dom Janssens, April 6, 1905).

Cardinal, entitled: "Explanatory Memorandum with regard to the two letters (March 25 and 28) sent by the Reverend Father Dom Mocquereau to the President and several other members of the Pontifical Commission on Gregorian Chant." This memorandum contained six large duplicated pages; it is not dated, as was Dom Pothier's custom, but he said that it accompanied the Cardinal's letter.

The President of the Commission hoped that his memorandum of April 2 "was satisfactory and reassuring"—he stated that the difference between the Commission and the Editors lay less in principles than in the manner of interpretation—in his view, the unforeseen changes in the chant over the centuries:

more than once enriched it. . . . In fact each century is part of this tradition, which is not at all a fixed language, halted in one epoch, but an ancient language, handed down and modified on occasion and perfected by the generations that knew it, understood it, loved it, and practiced it; . . . what was done in the seventeenth and eighteenth centuries is not always to be held in disdain.

Consequently, a later variation should be condemned only "if it clearly proves to be an alteration," and

if the antiquity of a manuscript is to be given prime consideration, relative antiquity is not at all the only criterion . . . and the unexpected changes over the course of the centuries could be accepted as seriously motivated, without the support of more ancient manuscripts which, besides, it is not always our good fortune to possess.

Dom Pothier continues:

Art and performance (in fact) partake of the intimate formation of the chant [and performance always] has wisely modified and in the West gradually refined the scale itself and tonality. Archaeology ought to have the first word, if it will not always be the last. [In the case of a disagreement] performance will have more weight, for Gregorian chant is not a piece of museum furniture.

Finally, Dom Pothier concludes:

The Editors' line of conduct thus becomes more clear. Surely, the ancient manuscripts and even the most ancient among them must be followed, but without placing in them the legitimate tradition as a unique haven of refuge without discovering in them the necessary perfecting of the art, without recognizing constantly improved conditions for performance. At the same time what we call the *living tradition* will be followed.

Pointing out in closing the two Gregorian heresies of our age (very modern infatuation with erudition and ignorance of the manuscripts), the President declared that the providential mission of the Commission is to safeguard against the two extremes and to halt at the truth, *"in medio stat virtus."* There followed the examination of an example chosen by Dom Mocquereau in his second circular, the *Asperges me* of Mode 7.

Reply from Solesmes

Dom Mocquereau assuredly was not contradicting all this, but the question was of a practical nature. In fact, how did the Commission function? The President's memorandum of April 2 had indicated it, and Dom Mocquereau noted in his first circular, dated March 25:

Changes are being proposed to or imposed on us—we do not know which it is—in the following form: This now is what we wish . . . that change is desired . . . This thing does not please us . . . No one can deny that there are convincing enough reasons to preserve the ancient version of the *Kyrie fons bonitatis;* here and there, one reads on the proofs: "the manuscripts say . . .", without further explanation.

Was it not to remedy this state of affairs that Father de Santi called for creating a memorandum in which all the Commission's corrections of the Editors' texts would be justified? Too often, the Commission gave no reasons that were truly justifiable. Furthermore, on certain points, Dom Mocquereau was without doubt ahead of his time. For example, it seems that the world indeed today appreciates the beauty of the recitations on SI, which were rejected by the Commission and adopted by the Monastic *Antiphonal* of 1934.

Dom Mocquereau made lengthy annotations on Dom Pothier's memorandum. He left unfinished a detailed draft of an article which his work did not afford him time to put into final form, but which Dom Cagin redrafted and which appeared under his name in the *Rassegna Gregoriana* of July–August 1905, that is to say, very much too late, and entitled: *Archaïsme et Progrès dans la restauration des mélodies grégoriennes (Origines et Apogée du chant grégorien—Décadence du chant grégorien—La Restauration des mélodies grégoriennes peut-elle trouver dans cette décadence un principe d'esthétique grégorienne?* [Archaism and Progress in the Restoration of the Gregorian Melodies (Origins and Apogee of Gregorian Chant—Decline of Gregorian Chant—Can the Restoration of the Gregorian Melodies Discover a Principle of Gregorian Esthetics in this

Decline?] 19 col.). Moreover, it is doubtful that, even arriving on time, these pages would have modified the situation. Since this article can readily be found, we will merely sketch out its main idea here. After having established the definitions and necessary distinctions, and after having painted a large tableau of the history of the Gregorian cantilena, Dom Cagin concluded that it was erroneous to affirm that

the Gregorian art has continued to progress, to improve up to our own day, when there is, on the contrary, a new musical art, born late, which continued to develop in parallel alongside it from the 10th century onward, having influence on it only to corrupt and disfigure it. (*Rassegna Gregoriana* 1905, col. 314)

With the assistance of Dom Beyssac, Dom Mocquereau prepared a lengthy paper, *Observations sur les corrections proposées*, a paper that was not printed or even duplicated. He justified the text adopted by the Editors, when this was necessary. In addition, Dom Beyssac, declaring that Gastoué's observations had the force of law, added a *Réponse au Résumé des principales observations de M. Gastoué*. All of this still concerned only the first twenty-four pages of proofs of the *Kyriale* (6 Masses) and was the beginning of the memorandum justifying the Vatican Edition that Dom Mocquereau had promised to provide (cf. 1st Circular of March 25th).

At this point, we must call attention to two letters from consultors (to be discussed further on) announcing the shipment of reports to the Commission and declaring adherence to the principles set forth in the Appuldurcombe circulars. The reports had to do with letters from Father Perriot of April 2nd, and another from Father Grospellier of April 27th. Father Perriot wrote:

I have enclosed the reasons [he was returning the Kyriale proofs] why I think that we should not admit later modifications in the well-established earlier versions. It is on this point that I insisted at greater length in my first letter, which I did not send to you.

Father Grospellier noted:

When I returned the first 24 proof pages, I included a very clear refutation of Dom Pothier's principle relating to tradition. It is exactly the same point of view I discovered in your various Circulars . . . I fear that these pages were not even sent around.

And as for Dom Pothier's Memorandum of April 2:

Sending this Memorandum around did serve a purpose. However, although it sheds light on the method employed regarding the proposed variants for the chant, neither the Memorandum nor the *Animadversiones* we have received show that the Commission addressed any of the other specific desiderata or more general comments that members who were not present may have submitted for the entire Commission, but only the variants themselves.

Father Perriot's report was sent to Rome on March 1, and by April 26, it had not been distributed to the Commission. Dom Mocquereau himself noted: "In a conversation I had with Father de Santi at the French seminary on Good Friday (April 21), he told me that Dom Pothier had neither communicated Perriot's letter nor even its content to the Commission." Father Grospellier's report was dated March 26, but it had not been sent around to the Commission by April 25.

Father de Santi acting as moderator—Memorandum addressed to the Pope

At the 17th Meeting of the Commission, April 7, Dr. Wagner read a written statement and requested that it be included in the Acts of the Commission. This statement defended the President and included three points: (1) The President has the right to consult with higher authority without the consent of the members and the counter-signature of the Secretary. (2) He has the right to send notes bearing his signature to members and non-members. (3) The official declarations and treasurer's reports ought to bear the signature of the President and Secretary.

Father de Santi remarked that statements made in the name of the Commission ought to be made by common consent. Then, he protested once again against having recourse to the highest authority, and read the following note sent to the Pope because of "the wish spontaneously expressed by His Holiness to have his [Father de Santi's] opinion":

The *motu proprio* on the Vatican Edition (of April 25, 1904) has been studied, examined, discussed with the greatest weight given to each of its parts, and in particular the paragraph that indicates the principles for the reconstruction of the melodies. This paragraph was considered by all as a model in the critical sense, and one of exquisite tact. This appreciation was given, specifically on the matter of the two currents that have appeared since then: One of extreme rigidity in favor of the teachings of paleography, and one with a tendency to follow subsequent tradition. Thus the Holy See, leaning neither to one side nor to the other, remained completely free of all responsibility for everything that we would accomplish later on. Our task is very difficult, and it will not be possible always to remain exactly in the middle as indicated by the *motu proprio*. But in the case when accusations are made that we are following a path toward one extreme or the other, the supreme authority will, nevertheless, remain unscathed and inviolate, and it is to us that the fault will be directed for not having followed, as we ought, the way which had been so wisely pointed out.

The new document [the Cardinal's letter of April 3] tends to favor the broader course, but after reflecting upon it at length, I see that it does not alter the sense of the *motu proprio;* rather, it explains that sense. The only danger is that it may be abused, but the diligent watchfulness of the Commission will keep an eye on it.

Father de Santi ends by expressing the desire that the responsibility for everything should always be taken *in solidum*. Then, in a spirit of very laudable reconciliation, he proposes that, for the *Kyriale*, which belongs to a relatively late tradition, "our work should be limited to revising the current traditional text, a revision to be made based on observations by the Editors and the revisers." In a report intended for Dom Mocquereau written in 1906 (and mentioned above), Father Holly noted, in fact, that Father de Santi proposed "that the Commission adopt the *Kyriale* of 1895 without further ceremony. This is the only way to save the Commission," Father de Santi thought at the time.

At the 18th Meeting, on April 9, starting with an objection by Dom Mocquereau, Dom Pothier read a motion on the subject of the *Kyriale*. He noted the fact that the *Kyriale* came from an epoch when Gregorian chant was already corrupt, and that it was popular, which is the reason for the variants, that certain (modern) tastes must be taken into account, that Gregorian chant is universal, and that it is improper to restrict its development to one epoch and to one country.

Father de Santi then circulated a letter received from Solesmes, surely for private use, in which Dom Mocquereau rightly "affirms that thirty-four of the pieces in the *Kyriale* are from the 10th century, and twenty-six from the eleventh century, thus from the best Gregorian period." Following this declaration, it was considered inopportune to circulate Dom Pothier's motion to the absentees, but noting that Dom Pothier's motion addressed the *Kyriale* as a whole.

At that point, Dr. Wagner declared that he had lost all confidence in Solesmes. Dom Pothier, while agreeing with Father de Santi on the considerable and valuable work furnished by the Editors, also declared that his confidence in Solesmes had lessened, for he "saw a subjective element in archeology itself." Moreover, he was of the opinion that the Editors ought not criticize the Commission.

Father de Santi and Baron Kanzler expressed disapproval of the tone of Dom Mocquereau's circulars and the immoderate interpretation of the *motu proprio:*

Dom Janssens proposes that a courteous formal letter be sent to Solesmes, in which the bad impression given by the circulars is to be deplored. This letter could be sent along with the *ex officio* shipment of the list of corrections that the Commission intended to make. Moreover, he proposed that two or three members of the Commission be sent to Appuldurcombe, invested with full authority to state precisely the entire text of the *Kyriale.*

Father de Santi, recording secretary for the Commission, not being present at the *19th Meeting on April 11*, the account of the proceedings was taken from Father Holly's notes and includes nothing of importance.

Fourth circular from Solesmes—Dom Pothier's circular

The *20th Meeting on April 16th*, the last that Dom Mocquereau did not attend, was even more lively. Father de Santi had announced the arrival of the Prior of Solesmes to Dom Pothier. Dom Pothier replied—and the letter was entered into the minutes by Father de Santi—that "he hoped that this would mean that an amiable settlement would be reached . . . on the solid terrain of the *motu proprio*, honestly and totally accepted in all and each of its components . . . and clarified in the letter of the Cardinal Secretary of State" (April 13, 1905).

At the start of this twentieth meeting, the President announced that Dom Mocquereau was in Rome, but that the invitation to attend this meeting had probably arrived too late. He took advantage of this absence to communicate a circular from the Editors dated April 10, and another in response to it from the Chairman, dated April 14.

In the circular of April 10, Dom Mocquereau in turn protested—as had Father de Santi—against having recourse to the supreme authority outside the Commission: "Is it not up to the Commission to determine whether to consult the higher authority, if it deems such a move useful or opportune?" Dom Mocquereau added that he feared that this action would merely create a precedent that would be invoked (and this was exactly what was to take place in June) every time there is discontentment with a decision or a general approach.

On April 14, Dom Pothier replied that the Cardinal's letter

was not in any way intended to *supplant* the Commission, but to uphold the principles and conclusions of its work which came under attack from the Editors in its Circulars. By giving its blessing to the Commission's mode of operation, the letter was intended to safeguard its reason for being, because the Editors, through their narrow interpretation of the *motu proprio*, tended to diminish the role of the Commission to nothing more than an illusion.

Dom Pothier continued:

Assuredly, the two sides have always sought to respond in the most perfect way possible to the intentions of the Holy Father. However, since both sides rely on the same texts to support their differing points of view, it may seem necessary to have some kind of clarification. It is not only the President, but several members of the Commission who, on their own initiative, have felt the need to express their worries in this matter, and even their deep concerns.

Nevertheless, the President did not explain why these petitions had not been done with the full agreement and consent of all. There followed a lively discussion. The President agreed that "while it is always necessary to work on the basis of the oldest manuscripts, subsequent tradition and contemporary liturgical usage ought to be considered at all times." Father de Santi, for his part, affirmed that "even if the melodies varies in a thousand ways, to the point that it would be difficult to reconstruct them according to the total tradition, in such cases it is appropriate to focus upon the oldest manuscripts, or to the group of variants deemed best." Dr. Wagner, finally, maintained that "this widespread variation in the earliest melody proves that it was not satisfactory to begin with, and that it would continue to be unsatisfactory today."

The Declaration of April 16

When it came time to decide on the motion, Father de Santi made the observation that it would be better to await the arrival of Dom Mocquereau at the next meeting, but Dr. Wagner carried the day by remarking that this was needless, "since there is already a majority." This effectively closed the door for subsequent, convincing explanations, for it was well known that Dom Mocquereau himself worked on the manuscripts and could demolish superficial arguments. However, to clear his conscience, Father de Santi

insisted that it should be more clearly stated in the motion that work must always begin with the manuscripts and be based on them. A diplomatic edition is not the goal; rather, the aim is to produce a critical edition, come what may. It is only thus that the edition can be defended vigorously. The proposed modifications are recorded, but there is not enough time to examine them properly. The President declared that he would submit the copy to be sent, for the usual signatures.

The copy referred to was the following declaration, which must be cited in full, noting that it was regrettable that Dom Mocquereau, *who was invited only at the last minute*, could not be present at this meeting, which could have been continued the next day since the meeting closed without exhausting the subject. He could have cleared up both the theoretical and practical ambiguities (the very thing that was feared he might do). The practical ambiguities were not resolved, and no mention whatsoever was made in this document as to the Rule of Order that was intended to put the workings of the Commission into good order.

The Commission, meeting in a regular meeting on April 16, 1905, discussed and approved the following resolution or declaration, with the unanimous consent of the members present:

Considering that:

1. At the time when the Commission is preparing to send the first pages of the Vatican Edition to the printer, it is important to settle the difficulties that have arisen, and to anticipate those which may arise and that may harm the gratifying success of its work.

2. As perfect an agreement as possible ought to be established between the Editors, to whom is due the gratitude of all for the attention they have given in carrying out their task, and the Commission, which has been appointed to examine and judge what is submitted for its consideration.

3. The *motu proprio,* carefully explained in the letter of the Cardinal Secretary of State, ought to be the solid and sole basis for operations and decisions for all, as all agree.

4. The criterion for the Gregorian restoration, according to the *motu proprio,* should be based on the following three things: first archeology, then tradition, and then practical and liturgical needs and adaptations of the present day.

5. It is important to explain with the greatest possible clarity the manner in which this criterion is applied.

Declare that:

1. These three critical elements are not subordinated one below the other, in the sense that the second or third are adopted only when the first does not apply.

2. As a result, in considering the oldest manuscripts above all, the subsequent testimony of tradition should never be lost from sight.

3. It is appropriate to take into account the legitimate development and adjustments that art and circumstances may have contributed to these melodies, without changing their character.

4. The work of the Gregorian restoration, although based on the ancient manuscripts, may admit the introduction of justified variations for practical or liturgical reasons.

The Commission further decides that:

The content of this declaration shall be communicated to those Members who are absent from Rome.

> President: Dom Joseph Pothier, Abbot of Saint-Wandrille
> The Secretary: Msgr. Carlo Respighi.

Let us merely cite, and emphasize, the annotations that Dom Mocquereau made on his copy: "Considering . . . 2) . . . and to judge *with knowledge of the reason*—3) sole . . . *there shall be a Regulation*—4) . . . *to accept the legitimate tradition, reject illegitimate traditions.*"

79. Dom Mocquereau in Rome

Before introducing Dom Mocquereau in the meetings, it would seem useful to point out his relationship to the other members of the Commission. The minutes of the preceding meeting provide us a perfect opening to do so, because four letters addressed to Father de Santi are included in the Appendix—letters not yet sent to the members of the Commission. One was from Father Baralli, dated March 24, two from Mr. Worth in early April and on April 15, and one from Dom Molitor on April 14, to which we will return. Before that, however, let us examine the position of other members of the Commission whose testimony is known to us.

Dom Mocquereau's supporters and adversaries

We know where Wagner stood. On March 2, he sent a long memorandum of seven large pages to the Commission, *Observations concerning the first part of the Vatican Edition of the Kyriale.* In it, he first praised the work of the Editors, declaring that his reservations related not to the work itself, but to the principles that guided it: work "of pure archeology, insufficiently suited to performance practice." In his opinion, "All work of this kind can only be a kind of compromise, and the editor must furnish proof that he is the master of the material on which he is working." Moreover, with regard to the modifications that Gregorian chant underwent over the centuries, he stated: "From the Gregorian perspective, all these changes were real improvements, and we must preserve them. We see evidence of them throughout the Middle Ages, and these are truly traditional, not the early form." Finally, after praising the work of the Editors, he concluded that it was not scientific.

Dom Michael Horn, from Seckau, expressed similar thoughts in two letters filed for the record and addressed to Dom Pothier (February 28 and March 5, 1905). "Solesmes' reasoning [with regard to the SI] are not convincing. To accept the SI is to turn back the art of music 1200 years . . . Germany and Austria will reject such melodies with scorn" (March 30, 1905).

The comments of Professor Gastoué *(Résumé des principales observations sur les pages 1 à 24, et 25 à 26)* on the beginning of the *Kyriale* have already been noted. This is not a memorandum. In it, the author does not formulate any guiding principles, but simply indicates the corrections he proposes, on seven long duplicated pages. Dom Beyssac refuted these suggested corrections point by point.

However, other members of the Commission fully agreed with Dom Mocquereau. Father Perriot of Langres wrote as follows on March 1 and April 16 (letters not yet presented at the meetings by April 26; reference was made above to the second of these letters):

> The two other principles, taking into account both a long and legitimate tradition and current liturgical practice, must not weaken the first and key principle (the return to antiquity), nor open the door to the deplorable changes which have, in the long run, corrupted the ecclesiastical chant. . . .
>
> [The first of these principles], the return to antiquity, is very explicit. It is amply motivated by the state of degradation into which plainchant has fallen as a result of these modifications, which have been introduced since the high Gregorian era and all, or almost all, of which are veritable degradations. (March 1)
>
> To return to the earliest origins seems to be the true purpose of the restoration desired by the *motu proprio.* (April 2)

As we noted above, Father Perriot informed Dom Mocquereau that he was going to be sending these letters.

Father Grospellier of Grenoble paid tribute to the work of Solesmes (and his letter had still not been presented to the Commission by April 25). He affirmed that the so-called improvements of Gregorian chant were anything but, because the new theoreticians "were unable to grasp the principles of art and accentuation followed by the early composers, such as have been revealed to us in the studies undertaken by the Benedictines for a quarter of a century." He concluded as follows:

This proves that an existing tradition is not legitimate by the sole fact that it was established for a given number of centuries. Facing a diversity of tradition, the Commission cannot thus be obliged by a general rule always to follow the most recent; the *motu proprio* obliges the Commission to rely, in each case, on what reason, art, and science say is the most legitimate. It seems to me, in fact, that this decision, *a priori* and in the absence of proof to the contrary, necessarily favors the early and authentic reading; this reading will always be the preferred way of proceeding when it has not been shown for sure that another more recent reading is, in fact, more legitimate. It may be that, merely because of our familiarity with a different and more modern form, the restored reading of the most ancient manuscripts at first might seem somewhat shocking. As we well know, however, these first impressions are not long lasting, and gradually are replaced by an entirely different and more independent feeling.

As mentioned above, Grospellier had also informed Dom Mocquereau that he was going to be submitting this letter.

On March 24, Rev. Father Baralli of Lucca gave a passionate presentation objecting to the living tradition and the confusion of the principal directors of the Commission:

I find the following criteria of the Commission—archaeology, esthetic tradition, pitfalls for the singers, rejection of archaism, ease of performance—so confusing that I do not understand any of it. I challenge the stance that it is by these means that we will arrive at the early purity of the sacred chant.

He encouraged the Editors to follow the solid path laid out in the *motu proprio*, and suggested that they publish their edition without further ado, which could be used as a reference point from the scientific perspective.

On April 14, after stating that he found the changes proposed in the name of the Commission to be arbitrary, Dom Raphael Molitor of Beuron concluded:

It is clear that the goal and ultimate outcome proposed in the two *motu proprio* documents is early purity, and our understanding of the ancient Gregorian chant is so widespread today that it does not take much effort to realize that other, different principles have come into play at the Vatican.

Finally, Mr. H. Worth of London, in an initial letter sent in early April, stated that in England, "a mediocre edition that does not conform to the most ancient manuscripts will not be accepted." Then he recalled the resolutions made at Appuldurcombe: "We want only an edition of Gregorian chant that is truly authentic and in conformity with the purest sources, not a work that is certain to come under attack and be demolished."

In a second letter, dated April 15, Worth wrote to say that he joined in the letter of protest sent from Appuldurcombe against the attitude of the President, and that he placed his confidence in the "extremely conscientious work of the Editors."

Others were also favorable to the Editors, as evidenced by the reports of the meeting, and the comments made on the pages of the *Kyriale*. First, of course, there was Father de Santi who, at the time, thought that Dom Mocquereau followed the manuscripts too slavishly. In any case, on April 27, shortly after he arrived in Rome, Dom Mocquereau said:

He [Father de Santi] wanted to count the members who are favorable to our cause, and he also says that we have the majority, 11 to 9. We count Kanzler among those nine. He tells us that he is, in fact, hesitant, but leans more toward our side, as an archaeologist. Baralli, who has recently seen Kanzler, told us the same thing.

In his June 27, 1906 report referred to above, Father Holly said:

Little by little, the Commission is becoming neatly divided into two factions, of which Father de Santi and Dom Janssens set themselves up as leaders; Msgrs. Respighi and Rella, as disciples of Father de Santi, are aligned with him, while Perosi, Kanzler, Wagner and Dom Pothier stand with Dom Janssens. Dom Gaisser always remains independent. As for myself, after I recovered from my initial surprise and disillusionment, I did not hesitate to join Father de Santi. I was named Recording Secretary at the third or fourth meeting.[221]

A note from Dom Cagin likewise divided the members of the Commission, at a later date (in his list, he mentions Don Mercati, who was appointed to the Commission on May 6):

221. Cf. Norman Holly, *The Vatican Edition*, in *Church Music*, Philadelphia, December 1905, pp. 44–48.

- Aside from Dom Mocquereau,
- *In favor of the Editors:* Msgr. Respighi, Father de Santi, Msgr. Rella, Father Baralli, Don Molitor, Father Perriot, Father Grospellier, Father Holly, H. Worth, and Don Mercati.
- *Not in favor of the Editors:* Dom Pothier, Dom Janssens, Dom Horn, Msgr. Perosi, Father Moissenet, Dr. Wagner, Professor A. Gastoué.
- *Hesitating:* Don Amelli, Dom Gaisser, and Baron Kanzler.

Mention must be made here of the paleographic research done in Spain by two monks of En-Calcat, at the request of Solesmes. Because this work was not finished until early 1906, we will discuss it again, along with the research done in Germany by Dom Paul Blanchon and Dom Benoît de Malherbe.

The information that follows has been taken from the official reports of the Commission, and from correspondence that Dom Mocquereau and Dom Cagin sent to Solesmes, as well as correspondence from Father de Santi and Msgr. Respighi to Dom Mocquereau.

Papal Audience

On his arrival in Rome, Dom Mocquereau, accompanied by Dom Cagin, paid a visit to Father de Santi. Father de Santi told him that he had it from the Pope that the Cardinal's letter of April 3 had been wrested from him and that a Regulation was envisioned to return to the criterion given in the *motu proprio.*

The Pope explained [to de Santi] the origin of that letter and how much pressure had been brought to bear, so that, to end the confusion, he had given in . . . The Pope told Father de Santi that if the letter stood in the way or contradicted the *motu proprio*, there were ways to readdress the issue. That was when Father de Santi suggested the ploy of the Regulation regarding procedure and, if necessary, one article of the Regulation could straighten things out . . . (Cagin, April 15; cf. Dom Mocquereau and Cagin, April 22)

At the same time, Father de Santi pleaded the cause of the living tradition because he found the Editors too intransigent. Dom Mocquereau also learned from Father de Santi how the April 16 meeting had proceeded, the meeting that he was unable to attend because he was invited too late. The purpose of that meeting was to provide an *interpretation of the interpretation* of the *motu proprio* already given in the Cardinal's letter!

On April 18, Dom Mocquereau and Cagin were received in an audience with Pius X, who had previously received a letter from Father de Santi. The Pope repeated the complaints expressed by Father de Santi concerning the intransigence of the Editors, but Dom Mocquereau was able to explain his point of view to the Pope so clearly that the Pope enjoined him to speak to the Commission in exactly the same terms. *"State fortiter! Pugnate fortiter!"* (Stand firm! Struggle bravely!) the Pope said several times, striking the table with his fist for emphasis.

Have pity on this poor soul. I am all too familiar with everything that has been written about the Pustet business to start this adventure all over again. I would rather that there be no Vatican Edition at all than an edition in which not everyone has come around to your way of thinking! (Dom Cagin, April 19; cf. April 22)

Dom Mocquereau brought to the Pope's attention the letters mentioned above (from Dom Molitor, Baralli, and Worth), and when the monks from Solesmes were taking their leave, the Pope insisted that they come back to see him again.

Dom Mocquereau at the Commission

The first meeting attended by Dom Mocquereau was *the 21st Meeting, on April 18.* This was also the first meeting attended by Rev. Father Raffaello Baralli, whom Dom Mocquereau (pressed, in part, by Father Holly; cf. *supra*) had urged to come to Rome. After the reading of the minutes of the preceding meeting, Father de Santi stated that

the edition ought to be made according to the most ancient and purest manuscripts. If tradition and practical use in the present-day liturgy call for certain modifications, the reasons for such modifications will always be given. These reasons must always be weighty enough to provide a reasonable counterbalance to the authority of the manuscripts. Dom Mocquereau accepts these declarations, and agrees with the resolution of the Commission.

Father de Santi then read the letters to which we referred above and not yet communicated to the Commission (cf. beginning of No. 79), and alluded to a similar letter received from Father Grospellier. There was indeed some murmuring, but Father de Santi maintained that the Commission ought to have "objective knowledge of what our colleagues are thinking." Then Dom Mocquereau said,

The Editors have always taken into account the legitimate subsequent tradition, and several times already they have established the reading based on such tradition. Taken as a whole, the manuscripts are always the scientific and esthetic basis of the melody. Professor Wagner concedes that the manuscripts are the scientific basis of the melody, but he denies that they are always the esthetic basis. In that regard, he recalls a Papal audience during which (His Holiness) made the following timely comparison, namely that today, the sacred images as they are seen in the catacombs cannot be restored in the churches . . .

Father de Santi then proposed that the Commission begin examining the Rules of Order. It was agreed that this examination should be postponed until the final version was completed and printed. In connection with this exercise, Dom Mocquereau requested

that the course to be followed in revising and correcting the melodies be clearly set forth. The President, Dom Janssens, Father de Santi, Dr. Wagner, and others participated in the discussion. Dom Mocquereau's proposal, approved unanimously, will thus be included in the Regulation. All comments of the examiners will be sent directly to Solesmes, where the final scrutiny will be made. Through lithographed circulars, the reasons that led the Editors not to accept one correction or another will be explained. After this second exchange of ideas, the text will be set definitively, and the file of documents will be sent to Rome for verification and inclusion in the archives of the Commission.

Professor Wagner took the occasion to praise the workshop at Solesmes. He recalled how, on every occasion, the Right Rev. Dom Pothier had spoken with gratitude and with praise for the efforts of the Editors. He said that there was not another scholar in the world who had at his disposal such extensive and complete archives as those at Solesmes, and that, with the aid of these manuscripts, the monks will no doubt be capable of resolving any question easily. He recalled a motion that he had made earlier, and wished to mention it again, namely that if the variations proposed by the examiners are not pleasing, other, better ones might be proposed. Dom Mocquereau stated, and with great pleasure, that this could always be done.

At this point, Dom Janssens proposed that Dom Pothier should come to Appuldurcombe as plenipotentiary of the Commission. Dom Mocquereau immediately accepted, and everyone applauded the proposal. Finally, after Wagner suggest that the flat sign be introduced *ad libitum* on the music staff of the last *Kyrie Rex Genitor*, Father de Santi noted that "the criterion of the *motu proprio* for practical usage in the liturgy ought to dissuade us from introducing variations *ad libitum.*"

In a letter, Dom Mocquereau noted that he had set up a *modus viven-*

342 THE WORK OF ST. PIUS X

di together with Father de Santi, in which the final word goes to those who have the manuscripts at hand. This was accepted as a point that would be included in the Regulation (Dom Mocquereau, April 19).[222]

The 22nd Meeting, on April 22, was very painful. First of all, the President read a memorandum criticizing the letters read at the preceding meeting (the letters from Molitor, Baralli, and Worth; cf. beginning of No. 79). "He mentioned mistakes that are made in them" and produced a letter from Gastoué criticizing not the Commission, but the Editors. There followed another discussion of the meaning to be attributed to legitimate tradition. For Wagner,

a legitimate tradition is one that departs from the most ancient manuscripts. In his opinion, Dom Mocquereau's position that recognizes as a legitimate tradition one that preserves the early melody intact over the centuries, is too narrow. Dom Gaisser also believes that Dom Mocquereau is a bit too strict on this point. He also thinks that, as difficult as it is to define the principle in theory, it is easy to make practical application of it in each case. There followed a new discussion on the criterion of esthetics, on the tradition of the SI or the DO in the *Vidi Aquam.*

Prof. Wagner took his leave, as his departure was imminent. He expressed regret at leaving matters undecided. He recalled the refined taste of the Germans in matters of music, and the severity that they would express in evaluating the Vatican Edition if it were to present the rough edges of a bygone era which can no longer be tolerated today. He predicted a disaster if sufficient attention is not given to this matter.

The meeting ended immediately, and Father de Santi inserted this note in the minutes: "The recording secretary avers that henceforth it is impossible for him to recapitulate the meetings if they take place with such little order, and without a well-defined agenda."

The same day, Dom Cagin informs us, the Pope told Father de Santi

222. Here is the wording of this *modus vivendi:* "1. Our copies are sent to the Vatican Press; 2. The proofs are returned and corrected at Appuldurcombe. Provisional release of final correction proofs; 3. Vatican Press sends these proofs to all members and consultors of the Commission; 4. These proofs are returned to Appuldurcombe with comments, corrections, and suggestions from the members; 5. All these proofs are examined at Appuldurcombe. Accepted or rejected; 6. The work thus amended is sent to the Commission in Rome; 7. The Commission examines the proofs, and does not make any corrections without consulting with the Editorial Board; 8. The Editorial Board releases the final corrected proof. In case of a dispute between the Commission and the Editorial Board, what will be the course of action? I did not want to address this point. But after the meeting, I told Father de Santi that at the next meeting, I would ask that the last word be given to the Editorial Board.

that there would be no Vatican Edition if the Commission failed to reach an agreement with the Editors, and that if necessary, he would annul the Cardinal's letter of April 3 if it were used to oppose the *motu proprio:*

Fortunately, we have the Pope's word: Hold fast! He also said that he would prefer not to have a Vatican edition at all unless everyone agreed with the Editors . . . Dom Janssens responded (at the meeting) that since the letter from the Secretary of State had changed matters in that respect, he was siding with its point of view. Father de Santi, not content merely to deny that the letter from the Cardinal Secretary of State had introduced any change whatsoever, affirmed that he had it from the Pope himself that if there were any effort to interpret the Cardinal's letter in that way, the Pope would rescind the letter. (Dom Cagin, April 22)

Dom Mocquereau added that during this meeting, there had been a heated discussion between Father Baralli and Dom Janssens on the criterion of esthetics, and that they failed to set a date for the next meeting.

On April 24, Dom Cagin reported that Father de Santi wrote to the Pope after the meeting on April 22. His idea was: (1) to entrust the whole business to Solesmes, which would in turn send the work to His Holiness; (2) that a Rule of Order seemed increasingly necessary, but that it ought not be voted upon after deliberation. He even mentioned *drafting a pontifical letter to Dom Pothier*, to notify him that the Pope was taking matters into his own hands. Msgr. Bressan, private secretary to the Holy Father, responded that the Pope did not believe that he could take on this responsibility, and that his wish was to submit the Rule to the Commission. The friends of Father de Santi held a private meeting on this matter on April 25 (Dom Cagin, April 24 and 26).

Audience with the Cardinal Secretary of State

Meanwhile, Dom Mocquereau was received in an audience with the Cardinal Secretary of State on April 25. The welcome he received was less cordial than that extended by the Pope. The Cardinal actually reproached Dom Mocquereau for the protest he had made against his letter, and declared that the Pope wanted a practical edition. Dom Mocquereau replied by making a distinction between the Cardinal's letter and the procedures followed to obtain it (without consulting the Commission). Dom Mocquereau also explained his point of view on the living tradition, which was, in fact, a corruption and a historic error, given the manner in which it was being used. Then Dom Mocquereau explained how the Editors did their work. Then the Cardinal suggested that a cardinal be made President of the Commission, recognizing that Dom Pothier was both judge of and party to the discussion, but also adding that in his view, Father de Santi was too closely aligned with Solesmes. Finally, Dom Mocquereau remarked that it was not the responsibility of the Commission to draft the text, and that the Editors had only one vote to defend their work (Father de Santi's idea was that the Editors should be given three to five votes; Dom Cagin, April 26). He added, in this regard, that the letter supporting the Editors had not been read in the meetings (Dom Mocquereau and Dom Cagin, April 25).

While waiting for the next meeting to be called, the two factions strengthened their positions: while Father de Santi and his friends were preparing the Rule of Order, the others went to the Cardinal, threatening to resign (Dom Cagin, April 25).

However, Dom Mocquereau was not altogether satisfied with the draft of Father de Santi's Rule. Although Father de Santi was of the opinion that the Presidency of the Commission should be entrusted to a cardinal who would impose the Rule, and though he wanted to give five votes to the Editors, he was leaving open a door that they wanted to close, by allowing the Commission to correct the submitted text.

Msgr. Respighi remained optimistic through it all: having seen the Cardinal, he said that there was hope for adopting a good Rule of Order. This Rule, which G. Mercati and Father H. Ehrle (a Jesuit), both working at the Vatican Library and future cardinals, were to examine, would bring everything back to where they had started from: the Editors would be responsible for the version of the melody, while the Commission would handle publication (Dom Cagin, April 26 and 29; Dom Mocquereau, April 27).

The 23rd Meeting was held on April 28, Easter Friday. This time, after the reading of the minutes of the preceding meeting, there was a brief discussion between Dom Mocquereau and Dom Gaisser

on the subject of the exact meaning of the expression *legitimate tradition*. During this exchange of ideas, Dom Gaisser cited the example of the *Kyrie Fons Bonitatis*, and said that, in this case, since the tradition is divided into two currents that are well documented in the manuscripts, he was inclined to favor the version presented by the Editors, because there were proper and sufficient reasons to support that version.

The principle of the *ad libitum* variants was proposed again, and was unanimously rejected. Dom Mocquereau then said that "the Editors would be quite willing to accept full responsibility for the edition," an idea that Father de Santi had already mentioned to the Pope (cf. *supra*). This led to a lively discussion of the matter, and Father de Santi tried to describe the role of the Commission clearly:

It seemed to him that the Commission ought to examine whether the work of the Editors corresponded to the conditions imposed by the *motu proprio;* the Commission could propose corrections which would be accepted by the Editors; finally, the Commission ought to decide if the work was worthy of publication, to honor the Holy See.

There followed a discussion on the order of Masses in the *Kyriale*. It was voted that the Appendix would be eliminated, and that all the pieces would be included in the main section of the *Kyriale*.

The 24th Meeting was held on April 30. After reading the minutes of the preceding meeting, discussion focused mainly on the order of the pieces in the *Kyriale*. The order proposed by the Editors, "although well composed in the copy submitted by Solesmes," was not adopted. Two adaptations made by the President (*Sanctus* and *Agnus de Beata*), even though rejected by the Commission, were kept in, while the *Asperges me* of the Ambrosian Mass, although approved, was not included. Finally, the Appendix to the *Kyriale* was kept as is, even though the decision had been made to incorporate it into the body of the *Kyriale* (cf. *supra*). "Dom Mocquereau requested that he be given a clear account of everything that the Very Reverend President wanted, promising to give it his full attention."

On the matter of this meeting, Dom Cagin adds an interesting detail that he heard from Father de Santi himself:

Did (Dom Mocquereau) speak to you about this afternoon's meeting (Father de Santi told me about it)? Just picture this: the question of the SI, which took up so much time and occasioned so much turmoil, has just been settled in Dom Mocquereau's favor unanimously . . . All voted as one, Dom Pothier along with all the others . . . Father Prior confirmed this to me when I came in. They have completely caved in. Wagner is no longer there. . . . (Dom Cagin, May 1)

80. The "De Santi Regulation"

The Pope's favorable opinion

On May 1, the Regulation (*Regolamento,* "Rules of Order") was forwarded to Msgr. Bressan by Father de Santi, after it was reviewed by Don Mercati and Father Grisar, S.J., of *Civiltà Cattolica.* Dom Cagin wrote:

The Regulation, amended by Father de Santi in keeping with our recommendations, was forwarded to him [no doubt to Father de Santi by Don Mercati and Grisar]) yesterday evening, on Sunday, after the meeting of the Commission. He sent it this morning to Msgr. Bressan, with a letter assuring him that Respighi had seen the Cardinal Secretary of State, and that all the problems have now been explained and all details clarified. Father de Santi spoke to Msgr. Bressan about the Regulation which, he said, had been reviewed and approved by Grisar and Don Mercati, as it would have been without any doubt by Father Ehrle, if he could have reached him. There cannot be a divided opinion, he added, among the experts. He asked him to request that the Holy Father agree to authorize the printing at the Vatican Press as soon as possible. (Dom Cagin, May 1)[223]

The Pope and the Cardinal seemed satisfied with the Regulation, but they did not want to force it on the Commission (Dom Cagin, May 1 and 3), and the Cardinal was to request "written comments from Commission members" (Dom Mocquereau, May 10). In addition, the decision was made that it would be printed up before it was submitted to the Commission for discussion. Dom Mocquereau noted, finally, that he, too, was pleased with the Regulation, since the edition would benefit from it as well, because the Editors would have to be more exacting in their work (Dom Mocquereau, May 5). As for the five votes requested by the Editors, he disagreed with Dom Delatte, who wrote on May 9: "I would prefer that the Editors retain only one vote. Our strength is in our reasoning." Dom Mocquereau expressed his position as follows: "I do not believe that there is any lack of dignity at all in accepting four or five votes for the Editors; since we are occupying the majority position, accept it we must." At the same time, he announced that he had just fin-

223. On May 14, Dom Mocquereau wrote to Father Baralli: "We are awaiting the Regulation. It was submitted for review by Father Grisar, who approves of it entirely, and who suggested a few additions in an even more scientific direction" (quoted by Moneta-Caglio, *Musica Sacra,* 1963, p. 40, note 359).

ished the memorandum on the first twenty-four pages of the *Kyriale* (Dom Mocquereau, May 3).[224]

The following session, *the 25th Meeting, on May 4*, was a stormy one. First of all, the minutes of the preceding meeting were read and Dom Pothier succeeded in having his two adaptations "composed on two ancient and authentic Gregorian melodies" adopted. Then,

the recording secretary announced a memorandum from Father Perriot on the *Credo* proposed for the *Kyriale*, and handed it to the President. Then he rendered an account of the Regulation, which was completed by then. It had been given to Father de Santi at the meeting on April 5 (cf. *supra*, 16th Meeting). Several times, Father de Santi proposed that a discussion be held on the prepared topics. The Commission decided to postpone the examination until after the work on the printer's proofs. The manuscript was sent to Msgr. Bressan, so that he could ask permission of the Holy Father to have it printed at the Press. The Holy Father wanted to read it, and passed it to the Cardinal Secretary of State. His Holiness and the Cardinal stated that they were satisfied, and the manuscript was sent to the Press.

Then Msgr. Respighi disclosed to the Commission a proposal from very high up, upon which the Commission's opinion was being sought. The proposal concerned the protection and the authoritative guidance of a cardinal, specifically of the Cardinal Secretary of State. The proposal was accepted unanimously, but Dom Gaisser expressed his wish that having recourse to His Eminence should be limited to matters of the utmost urgency.

At that point, the President proposed a draft agreement between the Commission and the Editors, on the matter of examining the proofs, but Father de Santi called attention to the need to wait for the Regulation, since it was going to deal with that very issue. Nonetheless, the minutes of the meeting include a note that contains a brief written proposal from Dom Janssens on the same subject.[225]

---

224. Dom Cagin informs us that Father Holly visited the Cardinal Secretary of State and spoke to him about the Commission on May 1 (Dom Cagin, May 1, 1905).

225. Note on the manner of proceeding for revising the proofs. Father Janssens added a proposal, which he later submitted in writing, and which is attached here: "If the Editorial Board agrees to the modifications suggested by the Commission, the approval sanctioned by the President is final.—If the Editorial Board does not accept the modifications with the supporting reasons provided, and at the same time suggests other solutions that the President accepts, in this case the agreement between the Editorial Board and the President must be confirmed by the Commission.—If the Editorial Board and the President disagree, the Commission will adopt the

Likewise, Dom Pothier returned to the matter of the order to be followed in the *Kyriale*, and the remark was made that this question should be considered closed. But the examination of the corrections that were suggested for the Eastertide *Kyrie* and the *Gloria* (the question of SI or DO, again!) elicited a lively discussion, even though

Dom Mocquereau's demonstration seemed overwhelming to most members, and no significant response was directed toward it . . . So Father de Santi proposed that the Editors' text for the Eastertide *Kyrie* and *Gloria* be definitively adopted, as is. With great difficulty and after repeated attempts, he managed to have his motion acknowledged for consideration and brought to a vote.

The same discussion took place with regard to the final *Amen* of the *Gloria*, which had occasioned an objection from Dom Janssens regarding the distribution of the syllables.

The session was much more turbulent than the Minutes would have us believe. In fact, the President wanted to prevent Dom Mocquereau from reading his observations on the *Kyriale*, and was forced to acknowledge that he himself was adopting corrections not based in reality. It was doubtless at that point that Msgr. Respighi handed over to Dom Mocquereau the following written note: "In patientia vestra possidebitis animas vestras" ("In your patience you shall possess your souls") (Dom Cagin, May 5).

On May 6, the Cardinal Secretary of State received Dom Mocquereau once again. "A good audience!" In fact, the Cardinal showed that he fully understood what the Editors wanted, as well as their objections regarding the living tradition as it was too frequently understood (Dom Cagin, May 6).

The next day, at the meeting on May 7 (Meeting 26), the President announced the appointment of Don Mercati as a member of the Commission, and read the Cardinal's letter:

May 6. In order to assure a more perfect uniformity of effort and principles between the historical-liturgical Commission and the Pontifical Commission for the Vatican Edition of the Gregorian liturgical books, His Holiness has wished to direct that the first of these said Commissions be represented in the second by Msgr. Giovanni Mercati, and to that end His Holiness has named him member of the latter Commission, since he is already a member of the first. This is

---

solution deemed preferable by the majority of votes." (This entire note is taken from the minutes of the meeting.)

being sent for information and guidance to the Right Rev. Father Pothier, President of the above-mentioned Commission for the liturgical books containing the Gregorian melodies. R. Cardinal Merry del Val.

Then, after the reading of the Minutes of the preceding meeting, Msgr. Respighi presented the letter that he had sent to His Eminence:

The Commission approved with satisfaction the proposal that the Most Eminent Cardinal Secretary of State, who has the chief supervision of the printing of the edition, will in future, by his high protectorate, greatly facilitate the work of the Commission itself.

The meeting ended with an examination of the proofs of the Eastertide Mass and the *Kyrie Fons bonitatis*.

A brief discussion arose concerning free variants (defended by Dom Janssens), that could legitimately be introduced in view of the letter from the Cardinal Secretary of State. Father de Santi said that this authorization is not found in the *motu proprio*. If one were to open the door to such fantasies, there would be no telling where they would end, and there would be no effective way of preventing them.

To our knowledge, the Minutes of the meetings stop here, and so there were no further meetings of significance. Father de Santi clearly shows a meeting for May 11 as being the last, but it was doubtless not recorded in the Minutes (cf. Moneta-Caglio, *Musica Sacra*, 1963, note 356). Dom Mocquereau's *Journal* (i.e., the letters of Dom Mocquereau and of Dom Cagin) will now be our main source of information, and the Regulation that was being prepared became, from this point on, the sole focus of that correspondence.

The Document

The printed Regulation was sent to Dom Mocquereau on May 7. Dom Cagin wrote (May 7): "I believe that the proofs of the Regulation that Father Prior received are first proofs, and that the members residing in Rome did not receive them. Otherwise, it is quite likely that [the Regulation] will be discussed at the meeting." Father de Santi had sent it to the Cardinal Secretary of State on May 6. In a long cover letter, Father de Santi explained that he had received instruction from the Commission by unanimous vote to prepare this document. Then he gave the reasoning behind it, namely the opposition toward the Editors by the President and the minority, *sostenuto dalla minoranza della Commissione.*

The intent of the document was to indicate exactly the rights and the obligations of the Commission and the Editors, their relationship, and the scientific criteria that ought to govern the restoration of the Gregorian chant, as the Holy Father wanted it.

Father de Santi added that he had shown his draft to competent persons capable of clarifying it, especially to two Benedictines from Solesmes present in Rome, and that they had approved it. He scarcely hoped that the majority of the Commission would also approve it. He was pessimistic about its chances, and did not conceal his discouragement:

I have some very good reasons to fear that if the Regulation is offered for examination during the regular meetings of the Commission, regrettable and absolutely useless discussions will start all over again, once again losing precious time. I am inclined to abandon the work of the Commission and to toss out the hundred or more pages already composed and typeset.

He also requested permission to submit his draft Regulation to an *ad hoc* Commission composed of three well known men of science: Father Ehrle and Don Mercati of the Vatican Library, and Father Grisar of *Civiltà Cattolica*. A few days later, Dom Mocquereau noted:

In reply to Father de Santi's letter, the Cardinal Secretary of State instructed him to shoulder the responsibility himself of having the Regulation examined by the priests he had named. He preferred not to insist on such an examination. The outcome would still be the same. The Cardinal asked for written comments from the members of the Commission, and will make his decision after that. (May 10)

The original text of the Regulation was *in French* (Father de Santi, who spoke and wrote French very well, was assisted by Dom Mocquereau and Dom Cagin). It was fourteen large handwritten pages long. It mentioned the Brief *Ex quo tempore*, addressed to the Abbot of Solesmes on May 22, 1904, which praised the method of work in the scriptorium at Solesmes, as well as the motion of confidence in support of the Benedictines at the plenary session at Appuldurcombe. The *Editorial Board* was composed of a President and four monks of Solesmes chosen by the Father Abbot; it had a consulting and deliberative vote. The draft read in part as follows:

XV. The editing of the manuscript of the Vatican Edition is directly and exclusively consigned by the Holy See to the Benedictines of Solesmes, according to paragraph b) of the *motu proprio* and the Brief *Ex quo tempore* addressed to Dom Delatte. As a result, all the melodies that will be brought together in this edition ought to be presented by the Editorial Board, or at least accepted and approved by it.

Section XXV stipulated that the responsibility for the definitive text devolves upon the Editorial Board, while responsibility for publication rests with the Commission. Section XVIII read as follows: "The corrections proposed by the Commission ought to be submitted to the Editorial Board which shall then make the corrections as requested, or shall explain the reasons that militate in favor of the early reading adopted." Section XXIII states that the comments of the reviewers ought to be based on specific documents, with an indication of their date, value, and origin, and that they should not deviate from legitimate tradition.

The document also stated specifically that during the regular meetings, the President ought to present correspondence concerning the Commission without delay; that he should make no final decisions without first mentioning the proposal during regular meetings, nor without authorization by a general resolution; and that he should not send any official communication regarding the Commission and the work of the Commission that had not previously been discussed, approved by a majority of votes, and marked with the Secretary's countersignature (XI).

The translation *into Italian* added a few corrections to the text, for example: "The melodies ought to be presented by the Editorial Board not as material to be worked on, but as work already carefully prepared and completed, and as a consequence ready for printing" (XV). And especially:

This Regulation nullifies any provisions that run more or less to the contrary that may have been adopted during the meetings of the Commission; it cannot be changed or modified in any part without the authority of the Holy See. (XXX)

Therefore, the text of the Editorial Board was to be presented in a form that was ready for the printer. On May 7, Dom Cagin wrote: "The last paragraph declared null and void anything that had been decided upon at the meetings held so far that runs counter to the provisions of the Regulation" (Dom Cagin, May 7).

The opinion of Don Mercati and of Father Ehrle

So the document was sent to Don Mercati and to Father Ehrle, for a more careful reading for, as you will recall, Don Mercati had already examined it.

Now, Don Mercati found it "too wordy", and in the letter he sent on May 13 to the Cardinal Secretary of State to present his observations, he pointed out its "procedural difficulties, omissions, and contradictions. . . ." Nonetheless, his own comments went on to fill fourteen large handwritten pages, and on May 16, Don Mercati added two more supplementary comments (1 page).

Dom Cagin summed up Don Mercati's position on May 20:

To clear up the inaccuracies that bother Don Mercati on the issue of the members, the consultors, the Commission, the Editorial Board, this is how he views things: There is a Pontifical Commission under the honorary presidency of the Cardinal Secretary of State. The Commission has two Committees: the Editorial Committee, which he calls the Recension Committee, a term commonly used in philology, which is chaired by Dom Mocquereau; and a Review Committee, an exclusively Roman entity. Its sole purpose is to see whether the Recension Committee has completed its work according to the scientific criteria imposed on the various groups, and it does not agree that it can do anything else, i.e. edit on its own account. It receives the organ, and states whether the organ is or is not the organ that was ordered. If that is true, then the Recension Committee would simply submit its recension, without having to vote on what it receives, any more than it does on the organ builder. In its turn, not only does the Review Committee have nothing to do with establishing the text at any point, it is also forbidden to withhold its approval when the work that has been submitted meets the conditions provided for in the criteria. So it is on these criteria that Don Mercati, too, focuses all his attention, but resolutely eliminating all the vague expressions that have previously stirred up so many storms and errors, his spirit freed from having to mince words with regard to the prejudices of the left, and to the Cardinal's letter and to the unsuitable terms of the *motu proprio*.

Don Mercati felt that the Editorial Committee could not be the judge of its own work, but Dom Mocquereau, in a Note (undated), insisted on his right to attend the meetings to defend his work, although he did not take part in the voting. This was to be included in the definitive printed text, and not in the initial proofs (cf. no. 32 of the Regulation).

Father Ehrle's memo was very severe toward the Commission. He did not recommend a definitive Regulation, but one that would be *ad experimentum* for a year to a year and a half. At the end of the copy he made of it on May 20, Dom Mocquereau appended this note, dated May 22, which will give a clear idea of the Regulation:

These comments by Father Ehrle were accompanied by a letter to the Cardinal Secretary of State that was so strongly worded that his Eminence did not want to send it on to Father de Santi. However, he did read it to Msgr. C. Respighi. In it, among other things, Father Ehrle requests that the Commission be overhauled, the first to be ousted being the President, D.J.P., then the useless members; to belong to it, one must be a philologist, an editor, and a paleographer.

It should be pointed out that this letter from Father Ehrle was erroneously attributed to Don Mercati, and it was falsely surmised that Father de Santi and Dom Mocquereau had inspired it. This matter will be addressed in greater detail below.

Father de Santi also prepared a memo that ran to six large handwritten pages, signed May 19, entitled *On the comments of Rev. Ehrle and Don Mercati concerning the proposed Regulation of the Pontifical Commission.* Similarly, Msgr. Respighi wrote a brief note of five small pages to Dom Mocquereau. In it, he said:

As I see it, (a) the Mercati Regulation seems adequate, but the topics we wish to reserve for the general review must be spelled out more clearly. (b) The de Santi Regulation does not displease me either: it gives those living in Rome a freer hand; he gives the vote to Editors, as well, and to the other members, on questions that are not purely editorial matters, and it seems to guarantee standards of procedure, with the request for the written opinion of absent members.

81. The "Mercati Regulation"

Overhauling the document

On May 19, Dom Mocquereau informs us that the Cardinal had submitted the Regulation to Msgr. Respighi, and that Father de Santi had to redo the whole statement, in a sense even more favorable to the Editors:

. . . the Cardinal gave him the Regulation and Don Mercati's comments. He put everything back in Father de Santi's hands, but poor Father de Santi must recast the entire Regulation in a sense that is even more favorable to the Editors. The Cardinal has approved Don Mercati's comments. I believe that Father de Santi is pleased (*sic*) with the suggested improvements. We will find out what they are tonight.

Father de Santi's text was the memo mentioned above, signed May 19, in response to Don Mercati's comments.

There was a meeting on May 21 at Don Mercati's residence.[226] Don Mercati expounded his point of view with the greatest clarity. Dom Cagin writes (May 22):

For him, the Editorial Committee is everything. He wants to put the Editorial Committee and its criteria ahead of everything else. When I spoke to him about the pain he had caused Father de Santi, Dom Cagin wrote: "I grew angry about it," he answered, "because I like Father de Santi very much, but for me, the honor of the Church is more important than anything else. The Holy See must not place itself in a compromising position by taking ambiguous measures. . .". In another passage, he writes, "A legislative text is not a literary exercise. It should contain only what must be said, everything that must be said, and it should do so clearly and without beating around the bush."

On May 23, Dom Mocquereau wrote:

Yesterday evening at 8:00 I went to Father de Santi, who gave me his second version of the Regulation. We went over it yesterday evening and this morning, then we went to bring it to Msgr. Mercati, with my comments. That good man wants to strengthen the Regulation even more in our favor, so as to reduce the revising role of the Commission as much as possible.

On May 26, the *Journal* of Solesmes points out a few more improvements by Don Mercati:

So there had been no provision for timely notice of the meetings, a written agenda, holding the meetings in strict accordance with the written agenda, orderliness in the debate, internal rules of order, any member being able to recall the rules of order, or the order of precedence in the voting. What is more, Don Mercati chairs nearly all the meetings. (Dom Cagin, May 26)

226. Those in attendance were Respighi, Father de Santi, Dom Mocquereau, Dom Cagin, and Don Mercati. The Pope would be displeased, but could the Regulation have been prepared in any other way than by prior agreement among all those who had felt the urgent need for it? (Cf. Bauducco, *Civiltà Cattolica* 1963, 1, 250).

So Don Mercati wanted to make additional changes to the Regulation, even though the cardinal was giving *carte blanche* to Msgr. Respighi to send the document to the printer at the same time, knowing only that it had been entirely redone (Dom Cagin, May 26). Msgr. Respighi was delighted with Don Mercati's new ideas, who made such quick work of the matter that the document was ready for the printer on June 2 (Dom Cagin, June 1 and 3). On June 4, Msgr. Respighi delivered it to Dom Mocquereau: "Msgr. Respighi brought us the *printed* Regulation this morning. He left it with us so that we could make some comments. . . ." (Dom Mocquereau, June 4).

Dom Mocquereau found some of Don Mercati's clauses excessive: one provided internal rules of order applicable to the Editorial Committee; another was relatively secret:

Don Mercati would like the Revision Commission to be bound to secrecy, as well as the entire Editorial Committee, with respect to any discussion of the musical text supplied by the Editorial Committee. We would not even have the right to consult the minutes of meetings where matters of approving or rejecting our text were discussed. (Dom Mocquereau, June 4)

The viewpoint of Don Mercati and Father Ehrle was quite uncompromising. Don Mercati wanted the Editorial Committee "not to be present for the revision work," while Father Ehrle wanted to get rid of all those in opposition (Dom Cagin, June 1, and Dom Mocquereau, June 6):

We have arrived at this very specific point: Don Mercati, in an extremely radical position, does not want the revision board to be involved in the editing, but he also wants the members of the Editorial Committee not to be able to attend the meetings of the Revision Council. We reject that article entirely: we have the right to attend the contentious debates on our musical text, at least as *advocates*. We agree not to vote, but we wish to be present, we want at least to have that right, for it will be quite rare that we will have the opportunity to attend those meetings . . . (Dom Mocquereau, June 6)

On June 8, Dom Mocquereau noted once again: "The fight is still between Don Mercati and Father de Santi as far as the Regulation goes . . . Respighi intervened yesterday evening . . . after a long meeting, he managed to bring the two adversaries closer together." A little further on, he writes:

An article was drafted more or less in the following wording: The Editors shall be able to attend the revision meetings in order to provide the explanations that may be requested of them, but they shall not vote. This evening, Respighi is to see Don Mercati once again, to hammer out with him the text that will be submitted *tomorrow morning* to the Cardinal by Respighi.

On June 10, Dom Mocquereau noted that our friends had not yet come to an agreement, and that the definitive text had not yet been established. In any event, he added: ". . . it is impossible to submit the first draft in any dignified manner to the cardinal, owing to the corrections; it will have to go to the printer again." Finally, on June 12, Msgr. Respighi brought the Regulation to the Vatican Press, and all the corrections were made on the spot. Then he gave Dom Mocquereau the request to Pius X asking for approval of the document, a request he said he would present to the Pope on June 15: "Tomorrow evening, he [Father de Santi] is to see the Holy Father and present the Regulation to him" (Dom Mocquereau, June 13–14).

Finally, on June 16, Dom Mocquereau notes that Msgr. Respighi was able to see the Cardinal and give him the document. Then Msgr. Respighi wrote to the Pope to inform him of the four votes (in addition to the vote of Dom Mocquereau) submitted by the Editorial Committee: Dom Blanchon, Dom Ménager, Dom Maurice, and Dom Beyssac. At the last minute, there was some question of additional changes by Father de Santi, but Msgr. Respighi, in a *"very strong"* letter, managed to convinced him to leave things as they stood (Dom Mocquereau, June 16 and 17).

The next step was to have the Regulation reviewed by the members of the Commission, whose comments were to be made in writing, according to the instructions of the Cardinal Secretary of State (cf. Dom Mocquereau, May 10). Here are the main ideas of the document, which runs to fourteen large printed pages:

The *Internal Regulation of the Pontifical Commission for the Vatican Edition of the Liturgical Books of Gregorian Chant* contains five chapters.

I.—*Concerning the Commission in General.* This chapter mentions the *motu proprio* of April 25, 1904, and the Brief *Ex quo tempore* sent to the Abbot of Solesmes on May 22, 1904.—The Commission comprises an Editorial unit, made up of monks of Solesmes, and a Revision board, under the direction of the Cardinal Secretary of State. The composition and specific activities of each of these units were spelled out in chapters II and III.

With regard to the restoration of the Gregorian melodies, the document states: "They [the melodies] shall all be restored in accordance with the great number of manuscripts, especially the oldest and incorrupt ones, without changing anything, under the pretext of some local variant or a later development, regardless of how beautiful it may be, even less for doubtful reasons of personal taste or similar reasons."

II.—*Concerning the Editorial Committee.* The Editorial Committee comprised four monks of Solesmes appointed by the Abbot of that monastery who were confirmed in their role by the Sovereign Pontiff. The Chairman of the Editorial Committee was also selected from among the monks of Solesmes and appointed by the Sovereign Pontiff at the recommendation of the Abbot of Solesmes.

The task of the Editorial Committee was to edit the musical text, and to that end, to do all the research necessary, to classify and collate the melodies, to write supplementary notes listing variant readings, to prepare the manuscript for publication and an explanatory memorandum, to correct the proofs, to gather the corrections from the revisers, and to accept substantiated improvements, to provide the melodies for the new Offices, and to participate in the work of reviewing the proofs whenever it should prove necessary to consult the manuscripts once again.

III.—*Concerning the Board of Revision.* The Board of Revision comprised a President, a vice-president and a secretary, a recording secretary, a corrector, and experts selected and appointed by the Sovereign Pontiff . . . Its role was to determine, with the greatest possible diligence, whether the musical text from the Editorial Committee corresponded to the standards that had been established, to issue the *nihil obstat*, and to oversee the printing process . . . The steps involved in this work were described in the greatest possible detail.

IV.—*Concerning Meetings.* Note paragraph 32, which was added to the final proofs: "At the private meetings of the Revision Committee, the members of the Editorial Committee may speak in order to explain their reasons more conveniently; but they shall have no right to vote, except for the matters covered under article 15, with regard to which they shall cast their own personal vote."[226bis]

226bis. Here is the original text of the two passages cited: (I) Si ristabiliranno tutte secondo la

V.—*Various Provisions: Confidentiality, Archives.*
VI.—*Status of the Regulation.* The Regulation is mandatory. Compliance with it is overseen by the distinguished presidency of the Commission (the Cardinal Secretary of State) and the presidents of the two committees which comprise it. The Regulation must be considered the legitimate interpretation of the *motu proprio* of April 25, 1904 and of the Brief *Ex quo tempore* to the Abbot of Solesmes dated May 22, 1904: "As to the section in which the principles and institutions contained in the *motu proprio* of April 25, 1904 and in the Brief *Ex quo tempore*, the Regulation must be considered the legitimate interpretation."

The situation grows worse

The efforts made by Father de Santi, Dom Mocquereau, and their friends will come as no great surprise. It was Respighi and Father de Santi who had conceived the idea of a Regulation, and one might say that they and their friends were the only ones with a sincere desire for one. We have seen how essential it was that this Regulation should come about. In 1906, Father Holly wrote a memorandum for Dom Mocquereau (a memorandum discussed several times in this book), which is quite harsh on the Commission. However, our friends had lost a great deal of time in their procrastination, and their opponents managed to use that precious time to mount a defense. One might have guessed as much, seeing musicians who were not members of the Commission arriving in Rome, as well as other individuals who were neither musicians nor members of the Commission. They, too, had audiences with the Pope or the Cardinal Secretary of State. Gastoué, for his part, wrote a harsh letter to the Cardinal (Dom Cagin, June 1 and June 16).

The rumor was circulating that Dom Pothier was thinking of leaving Rome at one point (Dom Mocquereau, May 16 and May 18). This is confirmed in a letter that Dom Pothier wrote on May 7 to the Prior of Saint-Wandrille:

---

grande massa dei manoscritti, specialmente dei più antichi ed integri, senza alterarvi nulla, nè col pretesto di qualche variante locale o d'un posteriore sviluppo, sia pure specioso, nè molto meno per ragioni incerte di gusto individuale e simili.

(IV) Alle adunanze particolari del Consiglio di revisione potranno intervenire anche i membri della Redazione per ispiegare più comodamente le loro ragioni: essi però non avranno diritto alcuno di voto ad eccezione delle faccende accennate nell'art. 15 . . . , nelle quali essi potranno dare il loro voto personale.

Just a little note, but an important one, nonetheless: to let you know that I am packing my bags. Stay calm, I won't be slamming any doors as I leave. I am leaving because I must: my presence in Rome has become useless under the new conditions in which the work of the Commission is proceeding, even though I remain its President. That is all I can tell you . . . (quoted by Dom David; manuscript kept in the Archives of Saint-Wandrille)

Dom David adds (ibid.):

While he was "packing his bags," and when Dom Lucien [Dom David] was with him to help him, suddenly the Right Reverend Father Abbot Primate arrived. He had gotten wind of this business, no doubt through the Rector of the College [Dom Janssens]. Surprise and astonishment: "What? You're packing your suitcases? But you cannot leave like this. It would be a sort of scandal that would have an impact on the entire Benedictine Order. At the very least, the Holy Father must be told about this before you go. . . ."

That same evening, the Right Reverend Abbot Primate went to see the Cardinal Secretary of State, who would speak to Pius X about it, who, in turn, enjoined the Right Rev. Dom Pothier to put off his departure.

Dom Pothier's backers have dwelt at great length on this incident and have accused Dom Mocquereau of having pushed Dom Pothier to such extremes. In any event, if this attempted departure is linked, as is asserted, to a *factum* that allegedly indisposed the Pope, Dom Mocquereau had absolutely nothing to do with it. He was not the author of that *factum*. He never even knew anything about it. Similarly, it is inaccurate to allege that it was at the instigation of Father de Santi and Dom Mocquereau that this *factum* was written (cf. Moneta-Caglio, Musica Sacra, 1963, p. 42, note 363). Thus Father de Santi came to Dom Mocquereau's defense at the Congress of Strasbourg in August 1905 (cf. *infra*). Nor was Don Mercati the author of the *factum*, and Father de Santi, who initially and incorrectly held him responsible for it, later issued a retraction and sent a *Note* to the members of the Commission about this matter on October 15, 1905. Father Bauducco and Msgr. Moneta-Caglio are resolute in their affirmation that it was the letter from Father Ehrle, discussed above in relation to the De Santi Regulation, which was the cause of this reversal (cf. *infra*, Congress of Strasbourg; Father de Santi to Dom Mocquereau, September 6 and 21, and November 30, 1905).

On Wednesday, June 21, after a visit to the Cardinal, Respighi brought the following news, which Dom Mocquereau sent along to

Solesmes: (a) the Regulation that had been prepared was being rejected, and Dom Pothier was charged with preparing another one, which would be imposed:

This time, the matter is something new and serious. Respighi came at half past noon; he saw the Cardinal this morning. The Regulation has been rejected, and D.J.P. is responsible for preparing a third one! The Cardinal accused poor Respighi and all of us of *maneuvering;* he put up a valiant defense, showing and proving that the Cardinal had been kept up to date on everything, day by day . . . (Dom Mocquereau, June 21)

(b) Dom Mocquereau added that Wagner, Dom Horn, Perosi, Gastoué and Dom Janssens had defended the President, orally or in writing. The same day, he wrote to Father Baralli, telling him that Dom Pothier had been charged with preparing a third Regulation.[227]

However, it seems quite clear that it was Camille Bellaigue, in whom Pius X had great confidence, who had the most influence over him as far as music, properly speaking, was concerned, taking the defense of the living tradition (but he was a great friend of Solesmes and of Dom Mocquereau). He had an audience around May 13 (Dom Cagin, May 13), an audience of which he speaks in the letters published after his death (*Revue des Deux Mondes*, July 15, 1935). In considering these letters, Dom David informs us that the Abbot Primate of the Order of St. Benedict also intervened in support of the President of the Commission (*Revue du Chant Grégorien*, 1935, pp. 166–168). He, too, had an audience with the Pope on May 15.

Msgr. Respighi had said "clearly to the Cardinal what the Vatican Edition would be in the hands of the Commission" (Dom Mocquereau, June 21), and Father de Santi attempted—fruitlessly—to obtain an audience with the Pope (Dom Mocquereau, June 22). On June 23, Dom Mocquereau wrote:

Father de Santi is thinking of asking the Holy Father to intervene directly, by means of a Brief to the Commission, in which he would ask that the members make peace, and request that work begin again, affirming that the editorial work was reserved for the Editorial Board alone, and that revision was up to the Commission.

227. "This morning, Msgr. Respighi saw the Cardinal. Mercati's Regulation has been rejected, and Dom Pothier has been invited to prepare a third, simpler one" (Dom Mocquereau, June 21, 1905, quoted by Moneta-Caglio, *Musica Sacra*, 1963, p. 45).

Since he was unable to see the Pope, Father de Santi explained his point of view to Msgr. Bressan by telephone. In response, Bressan assured him that the Pope was still very much disposed in his favor, but that he was tired of the whole business, for which he did not see any solution (Dom Mocquereau, June 23–24).[228]

Thus our friends determined to send a Declaration in support of the Editorial Board to the Holy Father. Msgr. Respighi took charge of obtaining signatures for the declaration. He, too, suggested writing to Msgr. Bressan (Dom Mocquereau, June 23–24). It is sure that Father de Santi, Holly, and Msgr. Rella signed the declaration, but there were others, as well. On June 21, Dom Mocquereau wrote: "We have the majority here in Rome, and even on the Commission as a whole." Among the opponents, some were sincerely sorry at the turn of events, including Perosi, who had a long conversation with Dom Cagin a few days later (Dom Cagin, June 27).

Here is the text of the Declaration submitted to the Pope:

The undersigned members of the Pontifical Commission for the Vatican Edition feel that it is their absolute duty to declare that the monks of Solesmes, charged by the Holy Father with editing the Gregorian melodies that will be used for that edition, merit their full confidence in this work, despite the difficulties raised against them in recent days.

The incomparable scientific means that the monks have at their disposal, the serious and truly critical method that they use, the esthetic sense that they have demonstrated, confirmed by their daily performance of the liturgical offices, the total disinterest that they have shown in all things and in circumstances that are singularly difficult for them, are arguments that cannot be outweighed by anything else in the world.

Since the School of Solesmes, consequently, offers such a set of guarantees and since, to the contrary, the difficulties raised in opposition are without substance, even to the point of lacking any scientific basis, the undersigned members declare that they are ready firmly to uphold the authors of a work undertaken for the honor of the Church, a work that, until now, not only justifies, but surpasses the hopes that the Holy Father has expressed.

228. From Father de Santi's *Journal*, dated June 23: "I telephoned Bressan, wishing to speak to the Holy Father about the matters of the Commission. He told me that it was better to keep a respectful distance, as the Holy Father was unhappy. I remain fearful... The Pope has been told that we wanted to pull one over on Dom Pothier, by drawing up a Regulation without his knowing anything about it. And then, the Holy Father is unhappy at the fact that, after we were all in agreement with Dom Pothier, now we have declared war on him" (quoted by Moneta-Caglio, *Musica Sacra*, 1963, note 364).

It would be most regrettable if the difficulties raised should now stand in opposition to the rapid execution of the work entrusted to us, or, an even more painful consideration, should entirely compromise the work itself of the edition, by violating the honor of the Holy See and dashing the great hopes fostered by the Holy Father.

For all these reasons, the undersigned members humbly present their declaration before the Pontifical throne, in the confidence that it will be welcomed with benevolence and that work will be started up once again without further delay on the unshakable basis of the *motu proprio* of His Holiness and of the Brief *Ex quo tempore*.

For his part, Dom Mocquereau advised the Abbot of Solesmes to write to the Pope (Dom Mocquereau, June 25), but it was too late. On June 26, he telegraphed Appuldurcombe to say that a new document was going to be issued. This document was the letter from the Cardinal Secretary of State dated June 24, 1905, addressed to Dom Pothier. This letter was supposed to remain secret, and the Cardinal refused to allow it to be published in the *Osservatore Romano*, but all the newspapers carried it on June 27. All the copies of the letter emanated from St. Anselm's. Thus Dom David sent a copy to *L'Univers*, with an explanatory note which the newspaper did not include, just as it refused a commentary from Msgr. Battandier (Dom Mocquereau, June 27, Dom Cagin, June 27; cf. Dom Logerot, July 8, sending the letter of Dom David dated June 26 and the commentary of Msgr. Battandier).[229]

82. The Second Letter from the Cardinal Secretary of State, June 24, 1905

The letter from the Cardinal Secretary of State to Dom Pothier, dated June 24, 1905, announced a simplification of the work of the Editorial Board. After expressing praise for the monks of Solesmes, the letter stated, in effect, that the Vatican Edition would be based on the Solesmes edition of 1895, the work of Dom Pothier, yet still taking into account the valuable paleographical studies undertaken at Solesmes. Here is a translation of the letter:

229. It was Dom Logerot who sent Dom David's note to Solesmes, along with the commentary of Msgr. Battandier. He himself had obtained them from the Editors of *L'Univers*.

Very Reverend Father:

The preparatory work of the Pontifical Commission for the Vatican Edition of the Gregorian liturgical books has clarified the many advantages to be gained by simplifying the work of the editors, which will make it possible to gain greater profit from the results achieved so far by those who initiated the Gregorian restoration.

Accordingly, the Holy Father, after having once more paid a due tribute of praise to the Benedictine monks, particularly those of the French Congregation and of the monastery of Solesmes, for their enlightened and fruitful labors toward the reform of the sacred melodies of the Church, has deigned to decide that the forthcoming Vatican Edition should be based on the Benedictine edition published at Solesmes in 1895, thus recognizing the just value of that well-executed reform.

To Your Reverence, then, as President of the Pontifical Commission, the Holy Father entrusts the delicate task of revising and correcting the edition in question. In this work you will ask the assistance of the different members of the Commission, availing yourself, when necessary *(all'uopo)*, of the precious palaeographical studies carried out under the wise direction of the Right Reverend Father Abbot of Solesmes. And in order that this important work may be carried out with greater alacrity and concord, His Holiness proposes to appeal to the various members of the Commission to apply their researches more directly to those liturgical books, the reform of which is as yet not far advanced.

To guarantee the execution of these provisions, the Holy Father has also deigned to make the following decisions, which I make known to you in the name of His Holiness:

1. The Holy See will take under its supreme authority and its high protection the special edition of the liturgical books which it recommends as typical, whilst at the same time leaving free scope for the researches of scholars competent in Gregorian studies.

2. To avoid the possibility of any monopoly, whether of law or of fact, the Vatican typical edition may be freely reproduced by publishers provided they fulfill the conditions set forth in the *motu proprio* of April 25, 1904.

3. The members and consultors of the Commission shall readily lend themselves in aiding the President in his task by their insights and their scientific knowledge. They shall also be at the disposal of the Holy See for other tasks of a similar nature, and to examine the publications submitted to the Congregation of Sacred Rites for approval.

4. In order to safeguard both now and in future the indisputable rights of the Holy See to the plain chant which is an integral part of the patrimony of the Church, general direction of the work involving the composition of the liturgical books and the approval to be granted to the various liturgical publica-

tions, specifically the Propers and the new Offices, is entrusted to His Eminence the Cardinal Prefect of the Congregation of Sacred Rites, who shall take counsel with the President of the Commission regarding the opportune dispositions and measures to be taken. These shall then be put into execution with the consent of the undersigned Cardinal Secretary of State.

5. The copyright of the Holy See, namely, proprietary rights concerning the printing by the Holy See itself and by the publishers whom it has already authorized to reproduce the Vatican Edition, are guaranteed by the nature of the publication, by the special physical characteristics of the Edition itself, and by the formal renunciation so generously made in favor of the Holy See by the Father Abbot of Solesmes and by Your Reverence, of all the previously published results of their and your preceding labors.

6. These provisions, particularly that by which the edition done at Solesmes in 1895 is taken as the basis for the Vatican Edition, will serve to safeguard the letter and the spirit of the previous pontifical documents, including the letter addressed to the Abbot of Solesmes on May 22, 1904, and to bring about the best scientific and practical solution.

In making known to Your Reverence these dispositions of the Holy Father with the perfect assurance that you will, with your wonted zeal, devote your most earnest solicitude to the task of carrying them out, I avail myself of this opportunity to declare myself again, with most sincere sentiments of esteem to Your Right Rev'd Paternity,

Affectionately yours in the Lord,

> R. Card. Merry del Val,
> Rome, June 24, 1905[230]

Clearly this letter was not at all in the spirit of a Regulation, nor did it announce any future rules of order. Msgr. Moneta-Caglio has commented on this situation as follows:

So it was decided to set aside the Mercati Regulation and to draw up another, simpler one, a euphemistic way of saying that they were giving up on having the Commission actually function. The outlines of the document were provided by Dom David. (*Musica Sacra*, 1963, p. 45)

Dom David did supposedly boast that he drew up the Cardinal's letter, but it seems more likely that Dom Janssens wrote it (that is the opinion of Father de Santi, in a letter to Dom Mocquereau dated July 17), ex-

---

230. Translation from: *Tablet* 69 (London, July 8, 1905) p. 51. Here is the original wording of the key passage of this letter: "Alla si fara coadiuvare dai diversi membri della Commissione, valendosi all'uopo dei preziosi studi paleografici eseguiti sotto la sapiente direzione del Rmo Abate di Solesmes."

cept, perhaps, for the introduction and the conclusion, which the Cardinal likely added (Dom Marini to Dom Mocquereau, September 5, 1905).

In September, Father de Santi confided the following information to Dom Mocquereau:

At first, the Holy Father wanted to give up completely on this edition, which was off to such a bad start. His Holiness wanted to get rid of it all: the Commission, the edition, and all the rest. Mr. Scotti saved the edition, by helping him understand that it was impossible to go back on the commitments that had been made. (September 21, 1905)

As for the effect it produced, needless to say that the letter caused quite a sensation in the musical world.

The attitude of Solesmes

On June 25, Dom Pothier sent the Cardinal's letter to Dom Mocquereau, and added that he had been within his rights to propose changes to the 1895 edition, but that he had been too intransigent in doing so, and that in any event, the new document reestablished unity within the Commission.

On June 26, Father de Santi informed Dom Mocquereau of the following lines, which Dom Pothier had written to him on June 24: "I have just received a new document: it is a reaffirmation of the broad understanding to be applied to the *motu proprio*, and I hope, also a means for managing to bring out something more quickly, and well." Father de Santi added:

Let's have a good look at what this is really all about. There is no need to hurry, and in any case, if you do not believe that you can make a decision before consulting with Father Abbot [Dom Mocquereau was planning to leave], you can tell that to the Cardinal and to the Holy Father. At the same time, you will have the means to explain your reasons. I have done everything that was in my power to defend justice and truth. We have failed, it seems, and in any case, the confidence that they had in me is lost, and I can no longer do anything directly.[230bis]

A letter from Dom Mocquereau to Father Baralli explains the reaction at Solesmes in great detail. It is dated July 7 at Appuldurcombe, after the return of the monks of Solesmes (letter published by Msgr. Moneta-Caglio, *Musica Sacra*, 1963, pp. 45–46):

230bis. On the same day, Dom Molitor sent this singularly laconic telegram to Dom Mocquereau: "What more is there to be done?"

Dear Baralli. Your letter of June 27 has reached me here. Here is our story. On the evening of the 25th, I received a letter from Dom Pothier telling me of a document from the Cardinal, a hard letter, at once triumphant and syrupy. On the 26th, foreseeing a great disaster, I went to say Mass at St. Cecilia's. When I came back, at 8:00 AM, I found the document on my table. Respighi arrived at the same time. "A great iniquity," he told me. He is truly sorry. I sent a telegram to the Abbot of Solesmes, telling him of the document, and I gave him our address at Poppio Mertato, St. Valentin, the country residence of the French Seminary. We have been here since Tuesday, the 27th. On the 28th, in the evening, we received a telegram from Father Abbot: "Return immediately." On the 29th, the Feast of St. Peter, after saying our Masses, we left for Florence, Milan, Basel, Paris, etc. On Sunday morning we arrived at the Isle of Wight, at the residence of our sisters of St. Cecilia, where Father Abbot was receiving the profession of a religious sister. Finally, I returned to Appuldurcombe. I need not tell you how stunned we are at this outcome. What will we decide to do? I have no idea. The only thing I can tell you is that our Right Reverend Father Abbot has written to the Holy Father and to the Cardinal. What will come of all this? The Commission will do nothing; they are all dismayed. This morning, I received a letter from Dom Pothier, who invites me to assist him in his task. I shall no longer answer him. He is asking for the proofs of the *Kyriale* and the comments from the members. I left everything with Msgr. Respighi. You can ask him for the proofs and tell him not to give them to Dom Pothier. If you think it worthwhile to write to the Cardinal or even to the Holy Father, through Msgr. Bressan, you can do so right away, telling them what you have seen, of course.

The President of the Commission had obtained authorization to consult the members and consultors in writing, that is, by correspondence (*Monitum* of July 11, 1905). Several would never respond again. This was, in fact, a dislocation of the organization established by Pius X in 1904. However, it must be acknowledged that it was no longer possible to work together seriously after the incidents of the previous few months.

Yet, in the thinking of the Pope and the Cardinal, nothing had changed. Now, it is important to note the resolution adopted by the Abbot of Solesmes, which was never a secret. Dom Delatte believed that he was personally targeted in the opposition raised against his monastery, and he had good reason to think so,[231] especially recalling

231. For the background leading up to this crisis, see Dom A. Savaton, *Dom Paul Delatte,* Plon 1954, pp. 163–167; pp. 230–235 of the first edition.

the heavy sacrifices that he had made in favor of the Holy See in 1904 (No. 65). Following the Letter of June 24, Dom Delatte offered his resignation to Pius X, on June 28. In his letter, he recalled in passing that Solesmes "has worked in accordance with the principles of the *motu proprio* and of the Plenary Assembly of the Vatican Commission at Appuldurcombe." On July 3, the Cardinal responded that nothing had changed, and therefore his resignation was not accepted:

Nothing has changed, therefore, with respect to the previous provisions made by His Holiness for the Typical Edition at issue, and consequently the conclusions that you have drawn from the publication of my Letter, as referenced above, crumble away, as they are utterly unfounded. The Holy Father maintains without change his benevolent regard for the Monastery of Solesmes, and his full confidence in the Abbot of that Monastery.

Nonetheless, on July 6 Dom Delatte repeated his offer of resignation to the Cardinal, and on July 21 to the Holy Father. He was reelected on October 5. We will dwell no further on this delicate subject.[232]

Father de Santi wrote, in the *Rassegna Gregoriana:*

Nonetheless, this singular opinion of Father Janssens [the alleged attack by Solesmes against Dom Pothier] must have served as the pretext for the upheaval that has recently occurred in the Commission, following the Letter of June 24 from His Eminence, the Cardinal Secretary of State. *As a pretext*, we repeat, for, if one wanted to speak the truth, it would seem that other things are at stake here, monastic issues that have nothing to do with the Gregorian edition; a look back at the last five years would show us that this is a disagreement among the Benedictines themselves. (1905, col. 545–546)

On July 3, Dom Pothier wrote to Dom Mocquereau, saying that he had always applauded the research of Solesmes, and again on July 14, saying that he had not wanted to do without our assistance, and he was counting on our useful and valuable cooperation.

The interventions of Father de Santi

Father de Santi was attempting to straighten out the situation. On July 17, from Arezzo, he told Dom Mocquereau that he had sent a memorandum to the Pope on July 7. In it, he dwelt at length

---

232. Cf. Bauducco, *Civiltà Cattolica*, 1963, I, 248.—Moneta-Caglio, *Musica Sacra*, 1963, p. 47.

especially on the monastic question, . . . on the copyright issue (for the chant editions), and on the commitment made by the Holy See to the monks of Solesmes . . . , on the maneuvering, plotting, and calumnies used to present matters in a false light, . . . on the exclusion [from the Commission] of the *motu proprio* and of the Brief (to Dom Delatte). . . . The Holy Father prepared a draft response which Msgr. Bressan copied and sent to me on July 9. [In it, the Pope said] that there was no deceit or maneuvering, [except perhaps on the part of the friends of Father de Santi], that the letter from the Cardinal was limited to prescribing what the Commission [itself] had decided by unanimous resolution [an allusion to the Commission's resolution to use the Solesmes edition as the basis], that absolutely nothing had changed with respect to the *motu proprio* and the Brief *Ex quo tempore,*—and that I should rest easy and continue in my former Gregorian thinking.

Father de Santi added that he had an audience on July 13:

The Holy Father was exceptionally good to me, laughing at my fears. He told me that, after he read my memorandum, he wanted to reread the *motu proprio* and the Brief, and that truly he had found nothing changed. He affirmed with the greatest possible insistence that the Editorial Board of Solesmes remained intact with all its right, as the Commission remained intact with its rights, that Dom Pothier simply was to take the votes into account, make the corrections that were suggested, and reach a decision in case of uncertainty.

Then the Pope spoke of a letter from Don Mercati, which the Pope found too harsh, in his opinion (cf. *infra*, No. 83, Congress of Strasbourg).

Regarding this audience of July 13, Msgr. Moneta-Caglio quotes the *Journal* of Father de Santi: "Audience with the Holy Father. He stated categorically that nothing has changed with the *motu proprio* and the Brief; that he became convinced of this in rereading the documents *à propos* of my memorandum" (*Musica Sacra*, 1963, p. 82, note 416).

In the same letter of July 17, Father de Santi said that he had planned to present the Pope with a Declaration intended for the *Osservatore Romano*

in which he would affirm that nothing had changed with respect to the provisions of the *motu proprio*, etc. However, my audience was interrupted when another person was announced. I left everything in the hands of Msgr. Respighi, and so far I have had no news about what he did or what he was planning to do.

Finally, Father de Santi said—still in the same letter—that

the Holy Father had given the order to abandon the whole business of the edition, but that (Scotti) had raised serious objections about that, with regard to expenses already incurred and commitments made to publishers. So the arrangement that we have come to know was made. Of course, Dom Janssens managed to seize the opportunity to present what he had prepared a long time ago.

In conclusion, Father de Santi wrote: "I remain firm in my intention to abandon the question of the chant for good, so long as one will not reach a suitable agreement."

Finally, on July 24, and again from Arezzo, Father de Santi wrote to Dom Mocquereau once more:

On July 19, I made once last attempt, thinking that I could do so after the statements the Holy Father had made to me at his last audience. So I wrote, referring to the letters arriving from all sides, and the various interpretations that were being given to the Letter of June 24, even in the newspapers. I said that it would be appropriate to make the Holy Father's declaration public, both to calm tempers and to have Dom Pothier understand that, although there is an Editorial Board and there is a Commission, there is also a desire for control of the work of the President, so that matters can function in a regular manner.

The Holy Father had a response sent to me on July 21, in these exact terms: The Holy Father has read your letter, and has asked me to tell you not to be alarmed, not to respond to the letters from partisans or adversaries, to have full confidence in Dom Pothier, who will take into account the vote of the consultors, without sending the sheets for a second and third revision, which would delay the edition until the Last Judgment.

. . . and yet, we could still salvage something, perhaps, if the Holy Father entrusted to Solesmes the formal editing of the *Liber Gradualis*, in just exactly the same way that he did with Dom Pothier for the *Kyriale*, and with the same method indicated by him in his most recent *Monitum*. After all, doesn't the Letter of June 24 say that the Holy Father reserves the right to entrust one part or another of the work to certain members of the Commission?

I have received your letter of the 21st. I understand why you do not believe that you can submit any longer to a Commission such as ours. Given the anti-scientific principles that have been manifested within the Commission, what has happened—dissension—was bound to occur.

Father de Santi concluded the letter by saying: "As far as I'm concerned, all revision work has been completed, and any proofs they send me shall go unanswered." He even wanted to discontinue his work with the *Rassegna Gregoriana*—as did Msgr. Respighi, as well (cf. *infra*, letter of August 6)—and asked Dom Mocquereau for his opinion on the matter. However, if he was to remain with the periodical, he demanded that it publish a critique of the Vatican *Kyriale:* "After all, the Cardinal's letter does leave the door open for better work, and assures the Congregation's approval for other editions."

Finally, his opinion on the edition could be summed up in this sentence, written to Dom Mocquereau on August 6:

No one can keep me from judging the things that have happened in accordance with the knowledge that I have of those events, and according to a forthright conscience; but as to the outcome of these events, I must accept the edition as it is given by authority. So, before the public my attitude must be this alone: that the edition is good, perhaps even relatively the best among the many editions available, but certainly less perfect than was initially supposed. No one can say anything contrary to this reservation.

It is important to note that Father Baralli visited Appuldurcombe from early August until the first days of November 1905. Those were unforgettable days for him. He was able to work with the team in the scriptorium, and the older monks had very warm memories of him. Father Baralli wrote an account of the paleography atelier for the American periodical *Church Music* (*The atelier of Solesmes at Appuldurcombe House*, in *Church Music*, Philadelphia, 1906, pp. 291ff. and pp. 475ff.).

83. The International Gregorian Chant Congress of Strasbourg (1905)

Things had reached a point where it was no longer possible to plan an official meeting of the Vatican Commission at the Congress of Strasbourg, as had been decided initially at Appuldurcombe in September 1904. Dom Pothier sent word to the Commission about this in the following letter, dated at Rome, August 2:

The President of the Commission is honored to inform the Members that, in light of the special difficulties encountered by several members in going to Strasbourg for the period of the Congress, it will not be possible to hold official sessions of the Commission on that occasion, as was discussed at the Appuldurcombe meeting. He hopes, however, that as many Members of the Commission as possible will be able to meet there.

The Congress of Strasbourg, which was conceived, in fact, at Appuldurcombe as a result of the desire to provide better support for the Pope's wishes by advancing the movement of the Gregorian restoration, will give the Members a happy opportunity to contribute to the success of the Gregorian cause, and will enable them to engage in exchanges of views that will greatly benefit the work of the Vatican Edition.

Note: The information contained in this communication may be shared with others, without restriction.

In November 1904, Dom Mocquereau had been invited by Dr. Wagner to take a position on the Preparatory Committee, an offer that Dom Mocquereau accepted (Wagner, November 18, 1904). However, one might rightly assume that he did not take part in the Congress. Our friends, as well, were hesitant to attend. Nonetheless some did, as we shall see.

Father de Santi decided to go, so that his absence would not be interpreted in a negative light. On August 6, he wrote from Arezzo:

The decision is in the hands of Father General, and I have not been told yet what that decision will be. If it is affirmative, I will go, but as a representative of the periodical *(Civiltà Cattolica)*, and I will not participate in the Congress at all. I will observe, I will assess the Congress, I will write a summary, and after all, it will not be a bad thing to have some eyewitness account of what goes on there. However, the local committee, at least in the private letters that have been sent to us, has always been supportive of Solesmes and pained by the change that has taken place . . .

The Congress was held August 16–19. Bas gave a long account of it in the *Rassegna Gregoriana*, the essential points of which are presented here.

The author underscored first the significance of the Congress, which was put under the patronage of Cardinal Fischer, Archbishop of Cologne, and of Cardinal von Skrebensky, Prince-Bishop of Prague, and under the protection of Msgr. Fritzen, Bishop of Strasbourg. He also listed twenty-one bishops, and many others sent representatives. Some 650 people attended the Congress, from all over the world. Dom Pothier was appointed President of the Congress. All the members and consultors of the Vatican Gregorian Commission who were present were named vice-presidents attached to the president, as were Msgr. Franz Haberl, President of the *Cäcilien-Verein*, and the other diocesan presidents who were in attendance. Thus the quality of those attending the Congress contributed to giving the meeting a truly scientific and artistic stamp.

Of course, there were solemn ceremonies, concerts, conferences, and private sessions. There were even some practical exercises that "made clear the relative easiness of traditional Gregorian chant, as well as the excellence and natural quality of our method of performance." The author also noted the addresses by Msgr. Foucault, Bishop of St. Dié, who was known for his mensuralist approach. With regard to the performance of the Abbé Fleury, who had the *Christus factus est* sung according to the method of Father Dechevrens, he noted the silence of the assembly, a mark of its disapproval, whereas the same melody, sung using free rhythm, won the approval of everyone. The performances by the cathedral choir, under the direction of Mr. Victori, provided perfect examples of Gregorian chant sung by an ensemble.

However, there was another side to the Congress, one that was less apparent but no less important. The presence of Msgr. Haberl was a sign of the Germans' loyalty to the Gregorian restoration (recall that none of the Germans invited to Appuldurcombe in September 1904 came, cf. No. 73). Msgr. Haberl had stated that the Congress was premature, since the official Gregorian books were not yet available. Similarly, he had stated that recent events concerning the Vatican Commission were a sign that the Pope had broken with science in this area. Despite all this, at the Congress he said that he was prepared to accept the Vatican Edition because "it came from authority." So in this sense, the Congress was a triumph for the Gregorian cause.

This Congress had been desired by all those who were following the trials and tribulations of the Vatican Commission and wanted some explanation of the most recent positions adopted by the Holy Father. The Pope had clearly demonstrated his desire for the Vatican Edition to be justified in scientific terms, and Solesmes had agreed to provide that justification.

Yet at Strasbourg, not only was the issue not on the agenda, but a speech by Dr. Wagner announced in the agenda of the general session of August 18, under the promising title *Sul Canto tradizionale e l'edizione vaticana*, was cancelled at the last minute, at the urging, word was, of the local Committee.

(That speech was to be a discussion of the ideas that Dr. Wagner had expressed in a pamphlet distributed during the Congress.) The name of

Solesmes, the place where the Gregorian restoration began, was scarcely mentioned. But the role played by Solesmes was mentioned, as Bas
himself relates:

Nonetheless Solesmes was not forgotten. On August 18, in the second public
session, Father Holly, a consultor of the Pontifical Commission, aimed to remedy this painful silence by proposing a resolution of congratulation and tribute
to the Gregorian School of Solesmes. But . . . Dr. Wagner, who was chairing
the sessions, opposed it, saying that the same thing was going to be offered the
following day at the initiative of the President. In the afternoon of that same
day, a meeting was held of the members and consultors of the Pontifical Commission who were in attendance. These were the Right Rev. Dom Joseph Pothier, Dr. Wagner, Dom Michael Horn, Father Moissenet, Professor Gastoué, Father Perriot, Dom Amelli, Father de Santi, Father Grospellier, and Father
Holly—barely half the Commission. The apparent result of the meeting was
the announcement read the next day by Dr. Wagner in the last public session.
Here is a translation of the text: "The Pontifical Commission for the Vatican
Edition of the books of liturgical chant has the honor of bringing to the attention of the Congress that the sheets of the Kyriale of the Vatican Edition have
received the final approval for printing. The Commission can also announce
that this work, while based on the 1895 edition, and in accordance with the dispositions of the Holy See in this regard, represents the fruit of the patient and
enlightened research of the Reverend Fathers of Solesmes."

An examination of the *Kyriale* will show, in due course, just how close to the
truth this announcement is. Whatever the case may be, this announcement
seemed to be a declaration of fidelity to the rules set forth in the pontifical documents, rather than a tribute by the Commission to the Abbey of Solesmes.
That is why Father Holly asked for the floor. At first, Dr. Wagner seemed determined not to recognize him, citing some rule or other. Finally, faced with the
insistence of the assembly in support of Holly, and thinking perhaps that it
would be a serious matter to prevent a vice-president of the Congress from
speaking, Dr. Wagner gave in. Father Holly then offered the resolution of tribute that had been turned down the day before. He was greeted with loud and
sustained applause. No sooner had the applause died down than Dr. Wagner
felt compelled to express regret that such a resolution had been presented by a
member of the Pontifical Commission. We do not know what those who were
hoping to hear a word of guaranty concerning the working methods for the
editing of the new liturgical books were thinking at that point.[233]

233. Giulio Bas, *Il secondo Congresso Internazionale di Canto Gregoriano*, in *Rassegna Gregoriana*
1905, col. 421–430.—On this Congress, see also *Acta Generalis Cantus Gregoriani Studiosorum*

In a letter to Dom Mocquereau written in Venice on September 6, Bas wrote:

As for the sessions of the Commission, I know that Father de Santi set forth the events as they happened, showing how they had been twisted . . . All that was said, I was told, with a singular sense of calm and dignity. Of course, no one responded and, to the contrary, the speech by Wagner on tradition and the Vatican Edition was not given, even though it was announced in the program, printed, and for sale.

In November, he added that Wagner's statement concerning the *Kyriale* was not to Dom Janssens' liking: "Dom Janssens told me that, if he had been present at the Congress, it would not have happened" (this is a reference to Wagner's mention of Solesmes; cf. Bas, November 14, 1905).

The statements by Bas were confirmed or expanded upon for Dom Mocquereau by Father C. Gaborit and Mr. Eloy, Desclée's agent. One particularly important document is a precious letter from Father de Santi, dated September 6. Here is the passage concerning the unofficial meeting of the Commission:

. . . We were invited to a meeting on Friday, August 18, at 3:00 PM. Dom Pothier said that the *Kyriale* was ready and that he had sent the approval for printing from Strasbourg. Then he spoke of the Preface, but without entering into detail. I had not yet received it from Msgr. Respighi, otherwise I would have registered a protest. Wagner suggested that a declaration should be made to the Congress in the name of the Commission that the *Kyriale* was ready, and that it contained the results of the latest work of Solesmes. I commented that I could not judge, in good conscience, whether the latest work of Solesmes had been adopted broadly enough to affirm what Wagner was proposing. But the others approved, and the resolution passed.

Then I asked permission to make a few comments in the presence of the Commission, on a personal matter:

1. I told the story of the Regulation, and I protested vigorously against the lie being spread that we had wished to impose this Regulation without its first being discussed by the Commission, and in such a way that it was pleasing to His Eminence, Cardinal Merry del Val.

Conventus Argentinensis, 16–19 Aug. 1905, Strasbourg, printed by F. X. Le Roux, 1905; H. Villetard and A. Grospellier: *Le Congrès international de chant grégorien de Strasbourg*, in *Revue du Chant Grégorien*, August–October 1905, p. 23. On page 36, we read that the chants "had been carefully printed in a special collection, in accordance with the editions of Solesmes" (*Cantus varii ad usum Conventus cultorum cantus gregoriani collecti*, Argentorati, August 1905, Rome, Desclée, 31 p.). See also in *Revue du Chant Grégorien*, January–February 1905, p. 101, March–April, p. 139, July, p. 187.

2. I said how the Pope had attributed [responsibility for] Msgr. Mercati's *Memorandum* (cf. *infra*) to me, and once again I objected with the greatest firmness to the hateful lie that said that I had suggested this *Memorandum*, even though I had no knowledge of it. I stated that the Commission was my own work, that I had recommended the members and consultors, and that I was incapable of doing anything to destroy the work of my hands by excluding Dom Pothier and other members from the Commission.

3. I stated that, to my knowledge, neither Your Reverence nor Dom Cagin had worked on that *Memorandum*, even though that lie had been believed by the Holy Father.

4. Finally, as a logical deduction from my statements, I said openly that the Holy Father had been deceived in a hateful manner, and that, consequently, all the new arrangements were based on a lie. I added that I was not accusing anyone, because I would not know whom to accuse, but the person who caused this deplorable misunderstanding would answer for it before God and before history. These words made a great impression: everyone declared, Dom Pothier first among them, that they had never thought that I inspired the Mercati *Memorandum!*

Next I spoke of the withdrawal of the monks of Solesmes from the Editorial Board, and of the sad consequences that would result for the Vatican Edition. I then saw that they all regretted this withdrawal. Dom Pothier said that he was prepared to go to Appuldurcombe, to consult with Your Reverence and to consult your archives. Wagner then suggested that, in the name of the Commission, the monks of Solesmes should be asked to continue their cooperation with the Commission. Dom Pothier took responsibility for communicating this resolution, sincerely accepted by everyone, to all appearances. Then the session was adjourned.

At Strasbourg, I was treated with the greatest possible coldness by all of Solesmes' opponents. They even pretended not to know me, I who was once the mainstay of the restoration movement. For the rest, it is of little importance to me. The only thing that bothers me, what truly pains me deeply, is the ruin of the edition that began under such great auspices, with such love and, on your part, such great sacrifice. [The letter is dated September 6, from Terme di Salice.]

Since the Commission had charged Dom Pothier to tell Solesmes that the Commission continued to count on its precious cooperation, Dom Pothier wrote to Dom Mocquereau about this matter on August 26:

I have been charged to inform you that everyone wishes and hopes that you will continue to assist the Vatican Edition with the precious fruits of your collations of manuscripts (there is no longer any question of *editing*), as, indeed, the Holy See supposes and demands in its most recent provisions. These provisions do not do away with any of the organizational machinery previously established, and are intended merely to regulate the operation and the driving force of that machinery.

But the letter of June 24 specifically gave no instruction on the steps to be followed in practice, and it was not the Regulation for which everyone had felt such an urgent need!

Finally, a correction must be given regarding the memorandum then attributed by Father de Santi to Don Mercati (de Santi, September 6). It was the Pope who spoke to Father de Santi about a memorandum of Don Mercati (cf. de Santi, July 17), but he was confusing it with the *Comments* of Father Ehrle, and particularly with the letter that accompanied those comments (cf. De Santi Regulation, *supra*). Father Ehrle was so widely known as the author of that memorandum that Mr. Eloy, Desclée's agent, mentioned it to Dom Mocquereau in his report on the Congress. Being better informed, Father de Santi addressed the following correction to the members of the Commission, dated October 15, and sent to Dom Mocquereau on November 30:

> To the Members and Consultors of the Pontifical Commission of Gregorian chant, assembled in Strasbourg on the occasion of the meeting of the Commission on August 18, 1905.
>
> Msgr. Giovanni Mercati, a member of the Commission, firmly and categorically states that he knows absolutely nothing about, still less is the author of, the memorandum that he is said to have sent to the Holy Father last June, a memorandum that allegedly caused the immediate change that has occurred in the business of the Commission, in consequence of [*in forza*] the Letter of His Eminence the Cardinal Secretary of State dated June 24, 1905.
>
> It was the absolute duty of the undersigned to make this statement, in light of what was reported during the meeting in Strasbourg mentioned above, even though, at that time, he was in possession of information that, in good faith, he believed he had to accept.
>
> Rome, Via Ripetta 246, October 15, 1905, Angelo de Santi, member of the Pontifical Commission.

Don Mercati did draw up a memorandum to present his Regulation to the Pope—as reviewed earlier in this book—and he insisted on showing it to Dom Cabrol, who was passing through Rome on October 21, 1905, but that memorandum did not include anything contained in the accusations (Note from Dom Cabrol).

Father Ehrle was also defended by Father de Santi, who reprinted in the *Rassegna Gregoriana* (1905, col. 362) an article from the *Kölnische Kirchenzeitung* of December 5, 1905, which stated that Father Ehrle's judgment had been given in an entirely private capacity. This is what Father Bauducco expresses so clearly in *Civiltà Cattolica:*

An accusation of high treason was present within the Commission, and Father de Santi was designated as the author, even though it all came down to a private judgment of Father Ehrle [the future cardinal] who, when asked by Cardinal Merry del Val, had said that a Commission appointed for scientific work should be composed of scientists. (*Civiltà Cattolica*, 1963, I, 250—cf. Moneta-Caglio, *Musica Sacra*, 1903, p. 42)

84. The Vatican *Kyriale*

In a letter dated September 6, Father de Santi told Dom Mocquereau that on August 28, he had informed the Pope that the Preface prepared for the *Kyriale* had been rejected by the majority of the Commission, which did not accept the principles expressed in it (those of the living tradition):

I am sending you what Msgr. Respighi wrote to me on August 25 about the Preface. On August 28, I wrote to the Holy Father from Luxembourg, entreating him *in visceribus* not to allow such a serious error. I told him that it was a true and clear insult to the majority of the Commission, which does not accept these principles, some of which are inaccurate, other absolutely false, all the more so in that everything in them is presented in the name of the Commission, even though it had not even been consulted on such a serious matter. I did not receive any response, and I do not expect to receive one. We are utterly powerless.

Then, on September 21, he added the following additional details about the same matter:

The *Kyriale* is now printed. . . . The question of the Preface dragged on with orders and counter-orders right up to the last minute. In the end, the matter was referred to the Holy Father, who clearly ordered it not to be published, since it had not been reviewed by the Commission. Thus the letter that I wrote to the Holy Father on August 28 from Luxembourg did have an effect. Moreover, Dom Pothier was ordered to consult the Commission about the *Liber Gradualis* and, if I have understood correctly, to present the rejected Preface for

the judgment of everyone. If Your Reverence receives this notice, be sure to respond, taking advantage of the opportunity to say what you think. The rest of
us intend to send our responses not to Dom Pothier, but to the Cardinal. Msgr.
Bressan even advised me the other evening to suggest the idea to some of the
most competent Gregorian scholars that they should write to the Cardinal
about recent events, expressing their fears for the success of the edition.

Msgr. Bressan seems preoccupied with the workings of our Commission.
He has assured me that the Holy Father read the letter I sent him from Luxembourg. I conclude from this that the order not to publish the Preface was a consequence of that letter . . .

As soon as the Holy Father learned that I was back, he wished to see me. He
spoke to me of the Catholic Congress, so that I could adroitly move right on to
the Gregorian Congress. But I remained determined not to speak to the Holy
Father any more about chant matters. I clearly told Msgr. Bressan: Since the
Holy Father no longer has the confidence he once had in me, it is not up to me
to broach the subject, except in the event that I should see his honor compromised, as happened regarding the Preface.

The Preface, which was prepared by Wagner,[234] runs three printed
pages in length. Of particular interest is the following remark:

> Now that the previous error has been overcome, because of which, indeed, the
> ancient musical monuments of our fathers were consigned to oblivion or held
> in contempt, we must take care not to err in the opposite extreme, we should
> be more balanced and less meticulous in investigating the more ancient manu-
> scripts.

This was, in fact, a recalling of the painful quarrels of the previous
months, all the more so in that the text dwells, at other places, on subsequent tradition:

> With regard to what is called the Gregorian tradition, it is not right to compress
> it within the limits of some number of years, nor to consider it as the work of
> some individual author, seeing that it embraces all centuries which, indeed, cul-
> tivated the Gregorian art with greater or lesser zeal and success.

Msgr. Respighi, for his part, kept Dom Mocquereau up to date on
everything. He, too, was thoroughly exhausted. He no longer went to
the Vatican, and he did not go to Strasbourg (August 1 to Dom Mocquereau). He approved of Dom Mocquereau's attitude. He said that if,

---

234. "Father de Santi has instructed me to tell you that the author of the famous Preface of
the *Gradual* is the very learned Doctor Wagner." Bas to Dom Mocquereau, October 28, 1905.

after the Letter of June 24, Solesmes was to continue its cooperation, "this fact should be stated publicly; otherwise it is more than just for Solesmes to keep its distance. . . ." He invited Dom Mocquereau to publish whatever Dom Pothier did not accept for the *Kyriale* (August 16).

Msgr. Respighi wrote another letter to Father de Santi on August 25, asking him to pass the letter along to Dom Mocquereau, the same letter to which Father de Santi referred above. In it, Msgr. Respighi said that the Pope and the Cardinal had approved the Preface of the *Kyriale*, but that Msgr. Piacenza and Msgr. Sardi thought it unacceptable. He himself felt that it was unacceptable for the Preface not to include any allusion to the difficulties inherent in the *Kyriale*, and no mention at all of the Editorial Board. Finally, he said that if the Preface were published, he would resign from the Commission.

On September 20, he also told Dom Mocquereau that Msgr. Bressan was preoccupied with the way things were going, and he invited "the various sides to write about the matter to the Cardinal Secretary of State to keep him informed." Finally, he, too, stated that the Preface had been suppressed: "The *Kyriale* will appear without a Preface. The Pope has said that the Commission must review the Preface, because he supposes that nothing has changed with the exception of broader powers given to Dom Pothier." There was, no doubt, another reason why Pius X decided to reject this Preface: was it not too openly referring to the quarrels of recent months?

Msgr. Respighi and Father de Santi were continuing to discuss with Dom Mocquereau various questions relating to the chant. Decrees were in preparation regarding the Vatican Edition, namely the decrees of August 11 and August 14, 1905, imposing a *ne varietur* edition, and making it mandatory for all the Churches of the Roman rite. Although these new provisions were specifically aimed at the editions of Solesmes, they assured Dom Mocquereau that there was no animosity at the Congregation of Sacred Rites against the Abbey. All the Congregation had done was to approve the texts submitted to it. These decrees will be discussed in greater detail below (No. 86).

Articles by Dom Janssens on the Vatican Commission published in *Germania*, the *Kirchenzeitung,* and the *Giornale d'Italia*, were also of concern to Msgr. Respighi and caused him great displeasure. He added that Perosi, Kanzler, and Dom Gaisser shared his discontent (letter to Dom

Mocquereau dated the Feast of St. Andrew, 1905). He also wrote to Dom Amelli about this matter on December 3:

I also would have liked to discuss the *res gregoriana* with you. I don't know how to create mysteries. I will tell you frankly that I find the esthetic theories presented by Father Janssens and Dom Pothier ridiculous and unacceptable, and there will be at least ten other members of the Commission with me . . . I say at least, because I know how those ten think for certain; I have not troubled to find out what the others are thinking. With these new theories, the Gregorian restoration will come to a halt, as it did during the sixteenth century, but under the special conditions of today. Frankly, I bow to the manuscripts, but I have no intention of submitting to the personal taste and esthetics of Dom Janssens. . . Dom Janssens' article is truly an unfortunate and misplaced thing: it has produced a disastrous impression even among his supporters, which, of course, I am not. I don't know if you have read the other article by Dom Gaisser. The eleven of us subscribe to it completely, because it is in keeping with the proper ideas for the Gregorian restoration. Furthermore, it is calm, composed, and may perhaps open the door to a solution . . . (*Musica Sacra*, 1963, 3, p. 82, note 414–416)[235]

Father de Santi, for his part, was harsh in his assessment of Wagner's articles on the same topic:

We must suppose that he does not really know the facts, for they are too different and, at certain points, entirely contrary to what he writes, to the extent that we could prove it with documents and unimpeachable authorities. Wagner's publication is singularly inopportune, and clearly written in a partisan spirit. It neither defends nor favors the truth, but rather discord, which everyone, without exception, wishes to see abated, in truth and justice. (*Rassegna Gregoriana*, 1907, col. 381;—Moneta-Caglio, *Musica Sacra*, 1963, p. 49, note 382)

In this respect, it is also interesting to note what Father Dechevrens wrote to Dom Mocquereau on July 26, 1905: "I have been told that disagreement has already broken out between Dom Pothier and Wagner; Wagner wants, at all costs, to return to his idea of a Gregorian edition based solely on the German manuscripts, St. Gall excluded. . . ."

235. The reference is to an article by Dom Janssens published in the *Giornale d'Italia* (November 25, 1905) and reprinted in the *Giornale di Roma* on November 26, 1905. Dom Gaisser's article was published in the *Katholische Kirchenzeitung* and was reprinted in the *Giornale di Roma* on December 3, 1905 and in the *Rassegna Gregoriana* 1905, col. 543–545.—See also an article by Dom Janssens, which was published in *De Tijd* on March 28, 1908 (excerpt from the *Deutsche Revue*, April 1907), in which the Reverend Father justifies his actions, but which, written long after the events, does not seem to us to correspond to reality (cf. Nos. 45, 66, 70, and 73).

The Vatican *Kyriale* was published in October 1905.[236] Msgr. Respighi liked to comment that the *Kyriale* of the Editorial Board was already prepared in March, and so it had taken more than six months to publish it after it was modified (September 20). It had the decree of August 14, 1905, at the front, but it bore no title. It contained the *Ordinarium Missae* and, in the Appendix, a large selection of pieces prepared at Appuldurcombe. The book was deeply criticized and Msgr. Moneta-Caglio reports a variety of harsh assessments that appeared in numerous places in Germany, Italy, and in England (*Musica Sacra*, 1963, p. 78). The critiques of Father H. Bewerunge, a professor at St. Patrick Seminary in Maynooth (Ireland), were especially effective and unleashed the anger of his opponents. Msgr. Respighi invited his friends to send a letter of protest to the Pope. We have the letter of Mr. H. Worth, who complained that the Solesmes version had been set aside, despite the approval that the majority had given it:

Although certain individuals who are allegedly authorized to speak in the name of the Commission publicly declared that the official *Kyriale* represented the work and science of the entire Commission, it never received the approval of the majority of the members of the Pontifical Commission (letter to the Holy Father).

Worth specifically cited the *Kyrie Fons bonitatis*, studied by Dom Beyssac in the *Rassegna Gregoriana*, and from which the version of the *Kyriale* diverged. On January 11, 1906, he wrote that he "no longer agreed to examine the sheets of any edited text in which Solesmes did not have a role." Father Holly was of the same view, for he sent a very harsh memorandum to Dom Mocquereau in 1906, which we have touched upon several times above. Holly, too, was no longer reviewing the proofs of the *Liber Gradualis* (cf. letter to Dom Mocquereau dated December 21, 1906).

Father Baralli, too, was preparing a memorandum intended for the Pope, but it may never have been sent. This memorandum (seven handwritten pages of 30 lines) was written at Appuldurcombe, during his stay there in summer 1905 (cf. No. 82) to consult the work of the Editorial Board. It is well known that his skills in paleography were such that

---

236. The edition of 1908 (the complete *Liber Gradualis*) made about forty corrections to it. Cf. Dom Jean Claire, *Dom André Mocquereau, Cinquante ans après sa mort*, in *Études Grégoriennes* XIX (Solesmes, 1980), p. 6.

he could judge the work for himself. Dom Mocquereau and Dom Cagin made some small changes to it, perhaps the very few corrections written into the manuscript (in this case, twenty-six words added or crossed out). The memorandum is dated October 5, 1905, but a note from Father Baralli at the top of the documents states that it had not yet been sent to the Pope as of December 10, 1905, and that it might never be sent, "for the hope of success is becoming more and more problematic." However, it is possible that the memorandum was sent, when Msgr. Respighi invited the members of the Commission who were faithful to the Editorial Board to write to the Holy Father in late 1905. Father Baralli did state in the document (and the tone is firm, yet even-handed), that in April 1905, the vast majority of the Commission was supportive of the Editorial Board, and that this was not taken into account at all. He also emphasized that the published *Kyriale* was not the *Kyriale* of the Editorial Board. Finally, he objected consequently that he could no longer cooperate in a work that is no longer in keeping with the thinking of the Pope. Here are the two main passages:

Last April in Rome, I took part in various meetings of the Commission, in which, *by a great majority* [emphasis by Father Baralli], the scientific criteria that served as the rules for editing were accepted; several practical standards were established, and various significant musical teachings (which I could enumerate, if necessary) were admitted in conformity with the most highly respected manuscripts and pure Gregorian esthetics. (P. 2)

Most Holy Father, in publishing an edition created in this way, I feel that Your Holiness has been compromised. This is my heartfelt conviction. And so I could not keep silence, I could not allow others to believe that I was an accomplice in a work that strives toward a goal that is utterly contrary to the ends for which you wanted this work undertaken. (P. 7)

Finally, of the twenty members of the Commission, only six continued to work with Dom Pothier, namely: Dom Janssens, Dom Horn, Father Grospellier, Abbé Perriot, Dr. Wagner, and Professor Amédée Gastoué. Later on, Pothier placed Dom R. Andoyer on the Commission, whom he had known at Solesmes before he went to the Abbey of Ligugé, as well as Dom L. David.

In November 1905, Dom Pothier again asked Dom Mocquereau for his continued cooperation. The request came at the very moment when the quarrel against the rhythmic editions of Solesmes was beginning, a quarrel that was to occupy music journals for several years. So this was not the best time to speak of cooperation, particularly since the situation in the Vatican Commission had not improved at all. Nonetheless, there was a monastic meeting in Rome in December between the Abbeys of the Congregation of France, chaired by the Abbot Primate of the Benedictines, a meeting attended by Dom Delatte and Dom Pothier. One issue that arose was the fact that Solesmes was preparing a critical edition, since Dom Pothier's edition was necessarily temporary:

The monks of Solesmes will continue the work of collating the various manuscripts that they have gathered, in order to establish an absolutely critical edition of the *Gradual* and of the *Antiphonal*. This edition will take at least five full years to complete, without the approval of the Sovereign Pontiff. This edition will not be used in opposition to the Vatican Edition . . . (Minutes)

The Abbot Primate presented the project proposed by the Abbot (of Solesmes): temporary edition by Dom Pothier, definitive edition by Solesmes (Solesmes Notes, December 7 and 13, 1905)

At first, the project pleased Father de Santi, it seems, but he soon expressed strong opposition to it—and the business went nowhere. The *Journal* of Father de Santi is dated December 14:

Dom Delatte came. He told me that it had been agreed among the Abbots that a temporary edition would be prepared, which would be left up to Dom Pothier, while the critical edition would be prepared at Solesmes. . . . The Abbot Primate will propose this plan to give the Holy See a way out of this imbroglio.

But Father Bauducco, who quoted this passage, adds the following note: "There is a typewritten copy of the long note that Father de Santi sent to Cardinal Merry del Val against the plan for a temporary edition."[237]

We have referred to an article by Father H. Bewerunge: *The Vatican Edition of Plain Chant, A critical study*, published in *The Irish Ecclesiastical Record*, January 1906 (French translation: *L'Édition Vaticane du Plain-Chant, Étude Critique*, Brest, Kaigre, 23 pages). The author had worked on the tables at Appuldurcombe, and his critique is certainly a most judicious one, aside from the strong, polemical tone that was in such favor at the time. His critique echoes, to a certain extent, that of the paleography atelier of Solesmes. Here is the conclusion that he came to, despite his criticisms:

---

237. Cf. F. M. Bauducco, *Il. P. Angelo de Santi, s.j., e l'edizione vaticana dei libri gregoriani dal 1904 al 1912*, in *Civiltà Cattolica*, 1963, I, 249 and 250, note 28. The first quote was repeated by Moneta-Caglio, in *Musica Sacra*, 1963, p. 84, note 420.

If we compare it [the Vatican Edition] to the *Kyriale* of the *Liber Gradualis* [Solesmes 1895] or of the *Liber Usualis* [Desclée 1903], we find not only that their melodies have been significantly improved, but also that a considerable number of new melodies has been added, among which some are exceptionally beautiful, especially the most ancient and simplest forms of the *Asperges me* and of the *Kyrie de Beata* and *Kyrie in Dominicis per annum*. The work of the monks of Solesmes has not been in vain. But I still hope that it will not be long before the return to the tradition, without conditions or mixtures, which was so happily begun by the acts of our reigning Pontiff, is completed.

85. Paleographical Wanderings in Spain and Germany

The paleographical research undertaken in Italy by Dom Mocquereau in 1904, for the Vatican Edition, continued into 1905. A trip through Spain began in April 1905. To that end, Dom Mocquereau had obtained a letter of recommendation from the Cardinal Secretary of State, dated February 15, for Dom Maur Sablayrolles and Dom Michel Gabin, monks of En-Calcat. Dom Romain Banquet, who had taken refuge with his community in Parramon (Catalonia) had graciously made them available to the Abbot of Solesmes. Thus the team of the Solesmes scriptorium could continue its task of transcribing the manuscripts. Dom Maur Sablayrolles came to Appuldurcombe from January 9 to 19, to seek Dom Mocquereau's advice. Dom Dominikus Johner, of Beuron, was there at the same time, as was the choirmaster of Maria-Laach (both of them were supposed to be laying the groundwork for a tour in Germany by two monks from Solesmes). Dom Johner had insisted on meeting with Dom Mocquereau before putting the final touches on his work on Gregorian chant.

The trip to Spain was done in two parts. The first trip, which began on April 15 and lasted until July 19, brought the monks in their search for manuscripts to Barcelona, Vic, Gerona, Montserrat, Lerida, Huesca, Zaragoza, Burgos, Las Huelgas, Leon, Oviedo, and Valladolid. The second trip took place from October 12, 1905, to January 20, 1906, with stops at Madrid, Toledo, Cordoba, Seville, Valencia, Tortosa, and Tarragona. This time, to ward off some of the problems encountered during the first trip, Dom Mocquereau had asked for a letter of recommendation from the King of Spain. The King responded through Count de Andino, on November 24, 1905, stating that he was acceding to the request, and that he recommended the travelers to the Archbishop of Toledo.

Dom Maur Sablayrolles wrote two accounts of this paleographical travel, one in Catalan (in the *Revista Catalana* 1906–1907), the other in French: *A la recherche des manuscrits grégoriens espagnols, Iter hispanicum* (in *Sammelbände der Internationalen Musik-Gesellschaft*, April–June 1912, pp. 401–432, and July–September 1912, pp. 509–531). The trips procured for Solesmes 6,000 double photographs. In addition to its primary goal, the trip also made it possible to identify the Catalan notation, which Dom Mocquereau had already glimpsed in 1891 in a manuscript from Tech.

In the meantime, Dom Paul Blanchon, who had already made a tour through England and Italy in 1904, had taken off for Germany, accompanied by Dom Benoît de Malherbe. They remained there from July 21 to December 15, 1905, passing through Antwerp, Cologne, Koblenz, Darmstadt, Wurzburg, Munich, Salzburg, Nonnberg, Mehrerau, Innsbruck, Beuron (where, at Dom Mocquereau's request, Dom Johner had collected manuscripts from Colmar, Karlsruhe, Metz, Trier, Dresden, Zurich, Einsiedeln, Graz, and Vienna, and even from Bamberg and Stuttgart, where the travelers were scheduled to visit), Stuttgart, Bamberg, Frankfurt, Wiesbaden, Maria-Laach (where the choirmaster had gathered manuscripts from Cologne and from Aachen, and from Colmar, Zurich, Bamberg, and Trier), Andenne, and Brussels. The travelers were unable to secure manuscripts—at least this time—from Berlin, Leipzig, and Wolfenbüttel.

Of the long chronicle that the travelers kept, we will cite only this melancholy remark:

At X . . . , the manuscripts were not long in coming, but here, as nearly everywhere else, many of the manuscripts that had been judged unreadable have been sacrificed to be used as bindings or for other more profane uses: of all the ancient riches of X . . . all we have left is a large fourteenth-century *Antiphonal* and a hymnary, several more recent books which we are not going to consider. Finally, there are fragments, protective sheets or book covers, which show that neumed manuscripts of the eleventh to twelfth centuries once existed at X. . . .[238]

Their efforts brought a harvest of 16,360 double photographs.

238. Cf. *Revue du Chant Grégorien*, March–April 1905, p. 137.

VI ■ THE VATICAN COMMISSION

FROM 1905 TO 1913

86. The Quarrel over Rhythm

At the time when the two monks returned from Germany, Solesmes was no longer involved in the task of editing the Vatican Edition, which was being done without its cooperation or that of its friends and defenders. In 1905 and over the following year, several attempts at reconciliation were made between the Commission and the Editors, without result. But before mentioning anything more about this, a word must be said about the relentless wrangling directed against the Solesmes rhythmic editions, for the monks were challenged even with respect to the rights that had been graciously given them by Pius X, as thanks for the publication benefits generously consigned to the Holy See in the matter of establishing the Vatican Edition. As we shall see, the facts that will be presented had some influence on the decision made by Pope Pius X in 1913 to entrust the editing of the Vatican Edition of Gregorian chant to Solesmes. Based on the unimpeachable testimony of Father de Santi and of Msgr. Carlo Respighi, it is clear that the Holy See never allowed itself to be intimidated by the violence of the attacks made against the rhythmic editions.

Decrees of August 1905

In August 1905, two decrees from the Congregation of Sacred Rites appeared back to back. The first, on August 11, demanded specifically that the traditional form of the notes and other signs, their intervals, their grouping, and the correspondence of the notes and syllables, be retained in the Vatican Edition. Furthermore, the decree stated that it

is up to the Ordinary to give the declaration of conformity to the typical edition, on the testimony of authorized examiners. The second decree, on August 14, promulgated the Vatican Edition as the typical edition, and stipulated that nothing should be added to it, deleted, or
changed: *Nihil prorsus addito, dempto vel mutato adamussim sint confor-
mandae etiamsi agatur de excerptis ex libris iisdem*. Further, it declared
that the Pope's wish is that all other editions of Gregorian chant of the
Roman Rite already approved, even for religious, should be removed
from the Churches little by little, gradually, but as soon as possible, in
such a way that "use is made only of the liturgical books of Gregorian
chant composed according to the preceding rules and in complete conformity with this typical edition." (All the documents discussed here
are found in F. Romita, *Jus Musicæ Liturgicæ*, Rome, Desclée, 1947, pp.
189ff.)

This last decree especially, by imposing a *ne varietur* edition, canceled
out one intention of the *motu proprio* of April 25, 1904 (paragraph *d*),
which permitted reproducing the Vatican Edition containing varying
melodies taken legitimately from ancient manuscripts. The Vatican
Commission of Gregorian chant, meeting at Appuldurcombe, had
made a decision (decision no. 6), expressing the hope that the Vatican
Edition would be declared obligatory in all churches of the Roman
Rite, yet at the same time, another decision (no. 5) had upheld the paragraph of the *motu proprio* of April 25, 1904.

Father de Santi had wanted this paragraph *d* of the *motu proprio* especially to be aimed at the Solesmes editions already in use (cf. *Rassegna
Gregoriana*, May–June 1904, col. 260), and which had been declared in
conformity with the *motu proprio* of November 22, 1903 (approbation of
February 24, 1904). At that time, these editions were the only ones to en-
joy this privilege. Frankly, this arrangement could have nullified the unity of Gregorian chant, but it was uppermost in the mind of Pius X, who
valued the idea that each major Church could have its very own chant,
drawn from its own manuscripts (cf. *supra* Nos. 55 and 68).

According to the testimony of Msgr. Carlo Respighi and Father de
Santi, the Congregation of Sacred Rites did not want to target the
Solesmes editions in particular by approving the decrees of August 1905
which were submitted to it, and which practically imposed on all a uni-
form edition of Gregorian chant (Respighi, September 20, and Father de
Santi, September 21, 1905, to Dom Mocquereau; these references apply

to all letters cited here unless otherwise noted).[239] On the other hand, the Vatican Commission, divided as to the criterion for the restoration of the Gregorian melodies, feared that Dom Mocquereau might produce an edition that would be in competition with the typical edition.

Even less did the Congregation of Sacred Rites wish to take aim at the rhythmic indications themselves in the Solesmes editions, because the *nihil prorsus addito, dempto vel mutato (absolutely nothing may be added, removed, or changed)* applied to the very substance of the Gregorian melodies, i.e. to the melodies themselves, to which nothing whatsoever may be added, removed, or changed. Moreover, the Congregation of Sacred Rites quickly issued its *imprimatur* for the *Kyriale* of Solesmes, as soon as the Vatican *Kyriale* was published. In fact, the *Kyriale* of Solesmes came out first with the *imprimatur* of the Bishop of Tournai on October 30, 1905, then with the *imprimatur* of the Congregation of Sacred Rites, on November 16, 1905.[240]

Solesmes had not sought this last approval, and had even strongly suggested to its publishers not to seek it, but to stay with the bishop's approval, as the matter had been settled at the meeting of the Vatican Commission at Appuldurcombe (decision no. 5). It was Desclée's agent in Rome who had gone to great length to obtain the approval of the Congregation of Sacred Rites.

This approval, of course, made the opponents of the rhythmic editions quite unhappy. In particular, the musician Widor wrote to the Cardinal Secretary of State to complain about the Solesmes *Kyriale*. Dom Pothier responded to him in a public letter dated January 16, 1906, in which he stated that, on the one hand, the rhythmic editions altered the typical edition, and on the other hand, the "concordat" of the Congregation of Sacred Rites had been withdrawn. There followed a series of violent polemics in the journals and reviews, some taking sides against

239. De Santi, September 21, 1905: "And even at the Congregation they do not understand this, seeing that they send requests to Msgr. Respighi so that he might recommend answers, and he, of course, knows less than they do, or more, as you will."—Respighi, September 20, 1905: "They sent me a curious question: what is the meaning of the famous decrees! I do not know whether I can answer them, for the very simple reason that there is no one in Rome who could do so conscientiously and with certainty."

240. Note that a "draft agreement was drawn up and suggested to the Benedictines by the Congregation of the Propagation of the Faith. It entrusted to the monks of Solesmes . . . the preparation and correction... of a reproduction of the Vatican edition planned by that Congregation" (Cardinal della Volpe to Dom Delatte, February 4, 1905).

the editions, other favorably interpreting the most recent decision of the Congregation of Sacred Rites. Aside from all commentary, the decision merely stated that in the future, the Congregation would no longer approve such editions, but that the editions had to be approved by the Ordinaries under the usual conditions. This interpretation would be confirmed, in fact, by a decree then in preparation, which came out on February 14, 1906.

Decree of February 14, 1906

This decree governed the conditions for approval by bishops of editions of liturgical books of Gregorian chant. The typical edition had to be reproduced without any alteration or modification. As for rhythmic or other signs, they had to be written in such a way that they were clearly distinct from the typical notes, and that there could be no possible confusion with those notes. Thus, the decree upheld the principle of rhythmic editions, and even alluded to the approval granted in February 1904 for the Solesmes editions *(Whatever other edition may be recognized by the Ordinary or by the Congregation of Sacred Rites itself)*.

Msgr. Respighi and Father de Santi were involved in bringing about this success. Knowing that a decree had been in preparation since January,[241] they had taken on the responsibility of illuminating the authorities on the harmless nature of the rhythmic indications, and on their usefulness. Father de Santi wrote to Msgr. Bressan on February 18, 1906, and Msgr. Respighi wrote to the Cardinal Prefect of Sacred Rites on February 22. Father de Santi said, among other things:

All those who purchase the rhythmic editions are perfectly well aware of what the signs mean, and there is no risk of misunderstanding. Furthermore, they help greatly in the proper performance of Gregorian chant, and in the past, they were an excellent aid in spreading the chant. Here, in the colleges of Rome, Msgr. Rella has introduced them everywhere, as I did in my own day, so great was the benefit that we experienced for an easy and rapid introduction of the chant, and for the uniformity of performance.

Dom Mocquereau himself had thought, at one point, of writing to Msgr. Bressan to remind him of the authority spontaneously granted to Solesmes by the Holy Father with respect to the rhythmic editions, and

---

241. An initial text is said to have been signed on January 13 (Zucconi, Desclée's agent, February 8, 1906).

to protest against the accusation that these editions altered the typical edition. In the end, he decided not to write.

The decree of February 14, 1906, was commented on favorably in the *Giornale d'Italia* and the *Rassegna Gregoriana*.[242] It stirred lively debate, so much so that it is hard to know what to admire more: the obstinacy of the opponents of the rhythmic editions, or the wisdom of the Congregation of Sacred Rites, which did not allow itself to be intimidated. At the Vatican Commission, the friends of Solesmes said that they were prepared to provide any favorable statement legitimately requested by the Ordinary of Tournai, in conformity with the decree.[243]

Later, in May 1906, the Paris publishers obtained a statement from the Congregation of Sacred Rites affirming that the Vatican Edition is perfect in and of itself, but without prejudice to the principle of the rhythmic editions, which were *tolerated* (the word is not used in any pejorative sense, it is simply contrasted to *officially approved*). This document appeared in all the reviews of sacred music (Msgr. D. Panici to Mr. Biais . . . May 2, 1906. Cf. *Romita*, op. cit., p. 193).

What were they going to do in practice at Solesmes, because the Benedictine editions used signs that attached to the notes (and some special neumes, such as the *apostropha* and the *oriscus*)? Despite the advice of his Roman friends, who told him not to change anything, Dom Mocquereau preferred to modify the signs in the Solesmes editions by detaching them entirely from the notation of the typical edition. He explained his viewpoint in a pamphlet published in August 1906: *Le Décret du 14 février 1906 de la S. Congrégation des Rites et les signs rythmiques des Bénédictins de Solesmes* (Desclée 1906, 26 pages). In passing, Dom Mocquereau noted that in March and April 1904, the Holy See granted Solesmes the authority to use its rhythmic indications in reproductions of the typical edition (p. 6). (See Plate 9, the Gradual *Universi*, in the rhythmic editions; the St. Gall neumes have been added by hand above the staves to enable the user to see that the rhythmic indications translate nuances that are actually expressed in the notation of the ancient manuscripts.)

A few months later, in November, Msgr. Dubois, Bishop of Verdun (and future Archbishop of Paris), who had adopted the rhythmic edi-

242. *Rassegna Gregoriana*, February 1906, col. 73 (quoted in the *Giornale d'Italia* of February 23, 1906).

243. The Censor Deputatus said that he was prepared to give his Imprimatur, as he had done previously for the latest Solesmes editions (Bas, March 21, 1906).

tion of the *Kyriale* for use in his diocese, received full assurance on this matter from the Pope, on November 18, and from the Cardinal Secretary of State: "For us, this was the most authentic and surest practical interpretation of the decree of February 14, 1906," he wrote in a letter to the choirmaster of his Cathedral, on March 25, 1907 (this letter was included in the second edition of the pamphlet by Dom Mocquereau, cited above, pp. 25–27).[244]

Congresses of Padua (1907), Sables-d'Olonne, and Pisa (1909)

For several months, Father de Santi had been thinking about having a decree issued that would be more favorable to the rhythmic editions, and that would put an end to all the polemics. One day, he even went to the Pope with a draft in hand, but he kept it to himself (Bas, July 9, 1906). The Congress of Padua (June 10–12, 1907) afforded him the opportunity to do something along these lines.

At the Congress, Father de Santi gave a lecture, after Professor Cheso, on the rhythmic editions, and he proposed the following resolutions: the *ad instar* editions of the typical edition should present the text without additions of any kind, but private editions could add signs for the use of the chant schola. On June 29, he wrote to Dom Mocquereau that upon his return from Padua, on June 19, he had informed the Pope of these resolutions, and that the Pope had seemed quite happy with the solution, hoping that all opposition would end. On June 29, again, Father de Santi explained that he had prepared a summary report on the Congress for *Civiltà Cattolica* (of July 6, 1907, p. 102),[245] the text of which had been presented to the Pope, and approved by him. Nonetheless, Father de Santi noted, the Pope was not inclined to issue an official communiqué on the matter, because he had already had to say and retract so many things on the whole subject.

On July 19, Father de Santi announced that the solution had been greeted with enthusiasm by the Congregation of Sacred Rites:

---

244. It seems that the following note, which the Vatican Press sent to publishers of pontifical documents, was directed particularly at the Benedictine editions, which had the great misfortune of being too successful: "The edition reproduced by a publisher may bear only the name of that publisher, because the authorization was given to it alone: consequently, it is expressly forbidden to add, as front matter to the edition, any other names or titles of companies whose owners have not subscribed to the conditions imposed on each individual publisher" (cited by Bas, August 13, 1906).

245. Cf. *Rassegna Gregoriana*, 1907, col. 353–357.

Msgr. Piacenza was very happy with the resolutions, and will have them includ-ed in the next issue of *Ephemerides Liturgicae*, which is the quasi-official publica-tion of the Congregation of Sacred Rites.

However, there were still some reviews and journals that rejected the distinction drawn by Father de Santi, and once again an all-out battle ensued. After an inaccurate article in the *Osservatore Romano*, Father de Santi wrote to the Pope to remind him that he himself had approved the article that appeared in *Civiltà Cattolica:*

No sooner had I received the article from the *Osservatore Romano* (April 19: *Per le edizioni di canto gregoriano*) than I wrote a Memorandum immediately, which was given to the Holy Father and read by him. . . . In it, I pointed out . . . that before publishing the Padua resolutions, I had submitted them to His Holiness, who approved them in a most explicit fashion, stating that they perfectly ex-pressed his own thinking, and that he had never had any intention of forbid-ding the rhythmic indications and the editions containing them, or of having them forbidden, and finally that His Holiness had even read and approved the article in *Civiltà Cattolica* in the printer's proofs, specifically approving the brief commentary that provides assurance of his august approval. (July 26, 1907)

Finally, Rome demanded silence on the matter. On September 2 the Di-rector of the *Bien Public de Dijon* notified one of his editors:

Dear Father:

Thank you for your letter dated yesterday, regarding the chant. It is quite in-teresting. Unfortunately, as a consequence of a letter from Rome (specifically intended for us), *Bien Public* has promised the pontifical authorities not to print anything, one way or the other, any more (R.M. = *René Moissenet*, included). I hope that you will not hold it against me for speaking frankly to you about this decision. Very truly yours . . . signed: L. Dumarché, Secretary of the Editorial Board.

In August, nonetheless, Dom Mocquereau submitted the changes to Dom Pothier that he had envisaged since the decree of February 14, 1906, and in October, Dom Pothier sent a response stating that he ap-proved of the changes (letter of Dom David, October 6, 1907). Yet in August, Dom David had already taken note of an item published in the *Rassegna Gregoriana* on the rhythmic editions (*Rassegna Gregoriana,* July–August 1907, col. 319). As Dom David pointed out to Desclée: "From an official perspective, the editions made in accordance with this specimen *will not encounter any obstacles"* (Dom David to Desclée, August 8, 1907; the emphasis was added by Dom David himself).

In his study *Il padre de Santi, s.j., e la questione dei "segni ritmici" dal 1904 al 1912*, Father Bauducco includes the following comment on the audience of June 19, 1907, according to the *Journal* of Father de Santi:

Audience with the Holy Father. We spoke at length about Padua, the Congress . . . specifically, I informed him of my resolutions on the rhythmic indications. The Holy Father praised them highly, and approved of them as an expression of common sense, saying that he had always thought along these lines, and that he never dreamed of condemning these signs. (P. 79)

In 1908, the first volume of *Nombre Musical Grégorien* was published. Father de Santi wrote a review in *Civiltà Cattolica*, expressing some reservations, and thus demonstrating that he was capable of maintaining his independent judgment (*Civiltà Cattolica*, 1908, pp. 714–723).[245bis]

Similarly, the *Liber Gradualis* appeared in the early part of the year. The decree of publication is dated August 7, 1907, but the edition did not come out until March 1908 (The tribute sent to Dom Mocquereau is dated March 26, 1908). (See Plate 8, the Gradual *Universi* in the Vatican *Gradual:* it is an exact reproduction of the version in Dom Pothier's *Liber Gradualis*, Solesmes, 1883, Plate 6.)

In 1909, Dom David went even further than in 1907. Following a trip to Quarr Abbey in June—the second place of refuge for Solesmes in England—he spoke with great benevolence of the rhythmic editions in the *Revue du Chant Grégorien* (July–August 1909, p. 191). Immediately, through the offices of Msgr. Bressan, Father de Santi shared the article with Pius X, who was very pleased with it. The response came back that his letter to Msgr. Bressan was "most opportune" (de Santi, September 16). Yet Dom David did not care for the article by Father de Santi in the *Rassegna Gregoriana* (September–October 1909, col. 434: *Ritrattazioni;* cf. col. 350 of November–December 1909), in which Father de Santi noted the new position, the cause of much contentment at the offices of the Secretary of State: "The Cardinal Secretary of State and Msgr. Canali have expressed their satisfaction regarding the article in the *Rassegna* on the *Ritrattazioni*" (de Santi, November 22, 1909).

It was during that same summer of 1909 that the Congress of Sables-d'Olonne was held (July 6–9). Despite the resolutions made there, the

---

245bis. An English translation of this first volume was provided by Mrs. Aileen Tone and Mrs. Justine B. Ward in 1932 (Part I) and 1951 (Part II).—In 1906, the start of a Dutch translation was published in *De Koorbode*, under the title *Theorie en Praktijk van den Rythmus van het Gregoriaansch*. See above, note 127.

Congress was far from peaceful, even though Father de Santi considered it "a sort of withdrawal." Not only was Dom Mocquereau not invited to attend, "neither he nor his signs," but there were various attacks against the rhythmic editions. With respect to the melodies, as well, someone demanded that the (800) Solesmes improvements to the *Paroissien Romain* be banned from the *Roman Antiphonal* then in preparation (Le Roy letter, July 30, and August 19, 1909).[246] In contrast, the following Resolution was passed at the Congress of Pisa in October. Dom Mocquereau had been invited to attend the Congress in person (although he did not go), or at least to send the Congress his thoughts on the questionnaire sent to the bishops of Tuscany (letter of Father Athanasius, C. Sc., promotor of the Congress, September 10, 1909).

5. With respect to anything having to do with the Gregorian melodies at Mass and at Vespers, at Matins, etc., the Vatican Edition shall be imposed absolutely, and the method of performance of the School of Solesmes (*Rassegna Gregoriana*, 1909, col. 550ff.: *Pisa. Il Congresso sinodo toscano di Musica sacra;* cf. *L'Univers*, October 28, 1909, *Le Congrès de Musique Sacrée à Pise*).

Father de Santi was elected acting President of the Italian Cecilia Society at that Congress, as well.

Letter of Cardinal Martinelli (1910)

In 1910, Father de Santi had regained the Pope's trust in matters of Gregorian chant, which had fallen off after the events of June 1905. He had already given Dom Mocquereau several demonstrations of the influence he had regained. The Holy Father now entrusted Father de Santi with the task of drawing up the letter which Cardinal Martinelli, Prefect of the Congregation of Sacred Rites, would send to Msgr. Haberl, President of the St. Cecilia Society of Germany, on February 18, 1910, to condemn mensuralism in the performance of Gregorian chant. In France, there has been a trend to view this letter as a condemnation of the rhythmic editions of Solesmes. Not only is this opinion contrary to the truth, but in the letter, Father de Santi managed to include a discreet word of praise for the work of the Abbey, as he explained to Dom Mocquereau himself,[247] and as is clear from the *confident* commentary that

246. Nonetheless, the *Graduale* retained an imposing number of improvements taken from the *Liber Usualis* (or *Paroissien Romain*). Cf. below, *Conclusion,* and note 253.

247. The letter sent to Dom Mocquereau has been lost, but we have the testimony of Don Julio Franceschini, of the School of Sacred Music in Rome (May 17, 1910). Above all, the letter

he published in the *Rassegna Gregoriana* (March–April 1910, col. 150). He wrote:

We must say, rather, that the letter contains something in favor of rhythmic indications. What are the new and useful studies in which the best Gregorian theoreticians are currently illustrating the free rhythm of the Gregorian melodies? We really do not know which are the new and useful studies produced by the opponents of the monks of Solesmes, whereas the monks have published entire volumes, and continue, in the *Paléographie*, to show the value and correctness of their signs by dint of the romanian "codices" . . . Nevertheless, we affirm, *with full confidence* (emphasis added) that neither through its tone nor through the purpose for which it was written can the pontifical Letter be interpreted or twisted as the opponents of Solesmes, with incredible stubbornness, are intent on doing.

This last sentence was addressing the end of Cardinal Martinelli's letter on the Gregorian restoration,

as the Holy Father understood it, and, as far as rhythm goes, as it has not only been admitted and increasingly well clarified thanks to new and useful works by the most renowned Gregorian theoreticians, but also practiced with full and encouraging success by countless choirs in all parts of the world.

This statement clearly echoes what Father de Santi had written to Msgr. Bressan on February 18, 1906, a sure sign of Father de Santi's authorship of the letter.

Despite everything, the opponents of the rhythmic editions marshaled their forces once again to obtain a condemnation. In June 1910, at the urging of Professor Gastoué, "the Typographers of Paris sent a memorandum to His Eminence the Secretary of State to protest the rhythmic indications, calling for their official condemnation" (de Santi, May 17 and June 2, 1910).[248] But this time, the Cardinal asked that the memorandum go without a response (June 2). To the contrary, on September 7, Father de Santi added:

We can be sure that the Holy Father will not allow such a condemnation, and I have had his express word on this. His Eminence, the Cardinal Secretary of State has already responded to the Typographers of Paris, saying that their de-

---

sent to Msgr. Haberl bears the hallmarks of Father de Santi, who often returned to the fact that the Solesmes editions achieved a *full and encouraging* result. Cf. *infra,* Letters to Msgr. Bressan and *Rassegna Gregoriana,* January–February 1911, col. 59–61.

248. In the letter of June 2, Father de Santi explained to Dom Mocquereau that they had wanted to stop the printing of his popular Manual in modern notation, at the Vatican Press.

mands will not be met. Msgr. Piacenza is on our side, and the new Secretary of the Congregation of Sacred Rites, Msgr. La Fontaine, has also told us that the matter is settled, and that there is no reason to return to it any more.

Father de Santi added:

There is also the attitude adopted regarding this matter by the St. Cecilia Society. I told the Holy Father, and I repeat it to everyone who speaks to me about it: the condemnation of the rhythmic indications would be a disaster for our Gregorian propaganda in Italy, because nearly everything that we have achieved so far, which is quite a lot, has been accomplished thanks to the rhythmic indications, which are an enormous help in teaching and performance.

In the *Bolletino Ceciliano*, Father de Santi explained how Solesmes had been authorized to publish its own editions in March–April 1904 (1910, August, p. 151) (cf. *supra*, No. 65).

The groundwork for founding the *Revue Grégorienne* was done in 1910, as well. The first issue came out in January 1911. Similarly, the College of Sacred Music in Rome, founded by Father de Santi, opened on January 5, 1911.[248bis] On September 7, 1910, he told Dom Mocquereau:

We are working tirelessly to open a school of sacred music. For the moment, the Holy Father is not inclined to provide the necessary funds. We have approached two American millionaires, but we have not had any reply yet. In the meantime, we have been offered a magnificent study organ for the school, if it opens this year. We do not want to lose this gift. So, I have proposed to the Holy Father that we open, for the time being, a course of sacred chant of only four months, from December 1 to April 1, for practical, theoretical, and scientific teaching of Gregorian chant.

This is evidence that the Pope's confidence in Father de Santi was fully restored, and it goes a long way toward explaining the Pope's determined attitude with respect to the opponents of the rhythmic editions.

The book by the Abbé Rousseau, co-founder of the *Revue Grégorienne*, on the *École Grégorienne de Solesmes*, was also published by Desclée in 1910. The book presented the fundamentals and principles of the Solesmes rhythmic approach.

248bis. See Dom P. Combe, *Les origines de la Revue Grégorienne*, in *Études Grégoriennes*, V, 1962, pp. 99–108. That article outlines the impact of the events of January 1911.—*L'Édition Vaticane*, in *Études Grégoriennes*, VIII, 1967, p. 220. One interesting detail regarding the College of Sacred Music: at one point, Father de Santi wanted Solesmes to take charge of the school, or at least of a chair of studies. Two letters from Father de Santi to Dom Delatte bear this out, one dated April 17, 1913, from Padua, the other dated May 15, 1913, from Rome.

Decrees of January 25 and April 11, 1911

Yet the founding of the *Revue Grégorienne* was to arouse a more violent assault than the earlier ones against the rhythmic editions. Even as Msgr. Dubois, who had become Archbishop of Bourges, was seeking the Pope's blessing for the new review—without Solesmes' knowledge—on December 10, 1910 the opponents, including Professor A. Gastoué, deeply alarmed by the announcement of the first issue (which would be dated January 1911),[249] was seeking the condemnation of our edition in Rome. They suggested that the editions already in the marketplace should be left alone, but that the reproduction with rhythmic indications of the Vatican *Antiphonal*, which was in preparation, should be forbidden (Father de Santi, January 14, 1911; and, to Abbé N. Rousseau, January 22, 1911), and finally that all new rhythmic editions should be forbidden. The decree of January 25, 1911, would answer these attacks.

Yet Father de Santi had already informed Dom Mocquereau and Msgr. Dubois that the Pope had assured him that nothing would be done against our editions (cf. *supra*, September 7, 1910). Obviously the life of the *Revue Grégorienne* depended entirely on this issue. Thus Msgr. Dubois, who remained very devoted to Solesmes, wrote to the Cardinal Secretary of State to inform him of the true reasons behind all this opposition (Msgr. Dubois to Dom Mocquereau, January 28, 1911). For his part, Father de Santi alerted the Pope, through Msgr. Bressan, on February 6, reminding him, on his oath (see *supra*, No. 65) of the role that he had played in March 1904 as the intermediary between the Holy See and Solesmes. Moreover, he told the Pope that all these quarrels were not based on any scientific foundation, and that the Benedictine editions were widely distributed throughout Italy, thanks to the St. Cecilia Society:

Nearly all of Italy is using these editions with the rhythmic indications. They have been adopted by the Pontifical Choir, by nearly all the seminaries and colleges in Rome, and by all the seminaries in Italy. All the propaganda now being done in many regions of Italy to get the people to participate in the liturgical chant is being done with the rhythmic editions. Without them, it would be

---

249. "Msgr. Piacenza told me that Professor Gastoué sent a Memorandum to the Cardinal Secretary of State seeking that the signs be abolished in the *Antiphonary*. It seems that they will win this stupid concession, and that we will just have to make do." Msgr. Baudrillart, Rector of the Catholic Institute of Paris, was also approached.

much more difficult to achieve the harmony that is so important between the teachers doing the teaching and the various groups of the faithful who are preparing to sing together in a public church. (Father de Santi to Msgr. Bressan, February 6, 1911)

At the same time, Msgr. Dubois informed Solesmes that "the increasing success of the rhythmic editions was the primary cause of this whole business," because the rhythmic editions were being used in opposition to the typical edition, or at least the two were being confused with each other (Msgr. Dubois, February 10, 1911).

The Desclée company could not remain on the sidelines. Its agent in Rome was extremely zealous under the circumstances, and he, too, received assurances that nothing would be done against the rhythmic editions, but that an effort had to be made not to have them come across as the official editions (Desclée, February 8, 1911).

Baron d'Erp, the Belgian Minister, contacted the Cardinal Secretary of State. On the eve of the publication of the decree of January 25, 1911, he received the reply that nothing had changed with regard to previous dispositions, and that the decree of February 14, 1906, remained in full effect (Desclée, February 16, 1911). A few days later, however, the decree was issued that forbade the rhythmic editions in the future *contrariis non obstantibus quibuscumque* (anything else to the contrary notwithstanding). The reason given was that these editions altered the typical edition, even though Dom Pothier himself had acknowledged that this was utterly untrue (cf. *supra*). Thus Father de Santi wrote, in the *Rassegna Gregoriana* (1911, col. 59–61) that

on this point, the Solesmes editions with the rhythmical indications have nothing to fear, for they do not alter the traditional notation in any way, as it is found in the Vatican Editions, and they contain the strictly Gregorian traditions, taken from the very best manuscripts. On this same point, the publishers have received, in the most explicit and broadest manner, assurances that they are perfectly within the rules. (French text in the *Revue Grégorienne*, 1911, pp. 40–43)[250]

Father Bauducco reports many other steps taken by Father de Santi, of which we were unaware, in approaching the office of the Secretary of State and Dom Pothier. A note sent to Desclée, which Desclée men-

250. Obviously the School of Sacred Music founded by Father de Santi and opened in January 1911 used the rhythmic editions in its instruction (*Revue Grégorienne*, 1911, p. 159).

tions (April 30, 1911), cast doubt on the authorization granted to Solesmes in 1904. It is interesting to discover that this note was written by Dom Janssens, a fact that Msgr. Respighi had already hinted at (Respighi, March 22, 1911) (cf. Bauducco, *op. cit.*, p. 88).

The controversy was in full swing, and it was the solution that Father de Santi proposed at the Congress of Padua that provided a way out. Father de Santi and Msgr. Respighi drew up a text, with the full agreement of Msgr. La Fontaine, Secretary of the Congregation of Sacred Rites, and Father Haegy, consultor of the Liturgical Commission (Abbé Rousseau, May 20, May 1911 Note). The text consisted of two *declarations* that would enable the bishops to approve reproductions of the Vatican Edition with rhythmic indications, and to acknowledge the use of these signs intended to facilitate the performance of Gregorian chant. N. Rousseau, as director of the *Revue Grégorienne*, was invited to ask the questions that were intended to elicit these responses, i.e. the declarations mentioned above (Desclée, April 30; Abbé Rousseau, May 1911 Note). The text of the declarations was finished on April 8, and Abbé Rousseau notified Dom Mocquereau, on April 10, from Rome (Respighi, April 8, to Abbé Delaporte, secretary of the *Revue Grégorienne;* Abbé Rousseau, April 10, to Dom Mocquereau).

But what had happened? We have information from those who were in on the behind-the-scenes maneuvering. Msgr. Respighi wrote:

The decree was truly published in error, without the knowledge of the Congregation of Sacred Rites, which had planned either to suppress it, or to modify it fundamentally. Of course, someone maliciously led those who gave the order to publish it astray. (March 4)

It is true that the text had been submitted to the Belgian Minister. However, it is probable that he did not see its full import. It is also possible that he did not see the definitive version of the text, a view shared by Msgr. Respighi (March 22, 1911).

For his part, Abbé Rousseau learned the details given below from Msgr. La Fontaine in person, when he met him in Rome in April. Rousseau immediately sent word of these details to his brother, a Carthusian monk, in a letter dated April 6. As soon as Desclée's representative received assurances that no action would be taken against the rhythmic editions, he wrote hastily to Dom Pothier to express his satisfaction. Dom Pothier—the author of the decree—played on the ambiguity and brought the letter to the Secretary of State, assuring him that

Desclée and Solesmes were now agreeing with the conclusions of the document, and the order was given to publish it. Yet when the Secretary of the Congregation of Sacred Rites learned of the matter, he was indignant. In concert with several consultors, he prepared the declarations discussed above, to annul the decree.

An inquiry was ordered, and was entrusted to Father Haegy. At the order of the Holy Father, the file on the rhythmic indications was given to him, and his conclusion was as severe as possible: "everything has been dictated by jealousy, contrary to justice and truth," and in the name of science. It was Msgr. La Fontaine who brought Father Haegy's report to the Pope, along with the *declarations* that the Pope approved immediately. This was on April 11 (Father Haegy, July 1, 1911, to Dom Mocquereau).

Here are the key points of the letter that Father Haegy wrote to Dom Mocquereau on July 1, 1911:

I must tell you that, were I not in this position, I might well have been indifferent to this issue. But in performing my duties, I had to examine this issue as thoroughly as possible. I was the judge, and in that role, I had a very large file at my disposal, which the Secretary of State was required to give me. So I read a succession of essays and lengthy letters sent to the Holy Father, to the Congregation of Sacred Rites, and to the office of the Secretary of State. I saw that everything had been dictated by jealousy, contrary to justice and truth. One document, in particular, ill treated the venerable religious of Solesmes, attributing false intentions to them with regard to the rhythmic indications. My indignation reached new heights. Thus my conclusion was as severe as possible, and at my express request, it was included in the large file. My memorandum to the Holy Father clearly set forth the depraved means employed by your opponents. In substance, it said that the motive for their conduct could only be jealousy, which was aimed at men whose sole concern was to work for the glory of God in their contemplation, and whose exceptional competence was widely recognized.

Providence stepped in to help the cause of justice to triumph. I dictated, or rather composed, the two declarations with which you are familiar. In light of the famous decree, on which no one was consulted and that was hatched by a small group, the Liturgical Commission did not want to approve publication of my conclusions. So I strongly urged the Secretary to bring them to the Holy Father's attention, along with my memorandum. That was done, and the Holy Father approved my text, and gave permission to publish it. That is how I came to be involved in this business, which has been so unpleasant for you, from which you have emerged victorious. I am happy to have been the instrument of your success, and you may be assured of my full devotion in the future. Your opponents are moving the heavens and the earth, and would like an official response to the January decree that abolished the previous declarations, but their efforts are in vain.

The official declarations to which Father Haegy refers were sent to Abbé Rousseau on April 29 (the date of the official text: S.R.C., L.C.N. 69/911 *Prot.*). Received at 11:00 AM by Msgr. La Fontaine; he had the declaration by 5:00 PM that same evening (Desclée to Dom Mocquereau, April 30, 1911). However, the second response concerning instruction was in answer both to Abbé Rousseau's request and later to a similar request from the Bishop of Padua dated April 21, 1911 (cf. *Revue Grégorienne*, 1911, pp. 43 and 108). Msgr. La Fontaine went so far as to show Abbé Rousseau "the Pope's handwritten *placet*" given at the audience on April 11 (Desclée, April 30, 1911).

For the moment, Msgr. La Fontaine did not think it possible to publish the Declarations in the *Acta Apostolicae Sedis*, since the text was in such "disharmony" with the decree of January 25, 1911 (Rousseau, Note of May 1911). The Declarations were not published there until 1917, but they were included in the *Decreta authentica S.R.C.* in 1912 (Vol. VI, Appendix, no. 4,263), bearing the date of the Holy Father's April 11 audience. The decree of January 25, 1911 was published in the Acta, but Msgr. Respighi noted that "the commentary in the *Rassegna* concerning the decree is the only one that is correct and authentic," meaning Father de Santi's commentary, discussed above (Respighi, April 8, 1911). Moreover, the text of the decree of April 11, included in the *Decreta authentica*, was issued *ad majorem declarationem Decreti no. 4259, 25 Januarii vertentis anni.*

Thus the plot had failed, a plot summed up by Abbé Rousseau in these terms:

The Gastoué report was an accusation against the rhythmic editions—the decree of January 25 was the crushing blow that was supposed to finish off the accused—and the Congress of Paris [June 12–15, 1911] was to be the solemn burial, to the cries of joy from all the Paris chant scholae. Unfortunately, the corpse had the bad taste to rise up, once again, on the eve of the burial. (June 9, 1911)

Regulation on Sacred Music—Vatican Antiphonal (1912)

In early 1912, a *Regulation on Sacred Music* was issued in Rome, signed by the Cardinal Vicar on February 2. It was clearly inspired by the Pope

("It is His Holiness's express wish . . ." etc.). The Regulation recommended the rhythmic editions:

For greater uniformity in the performance of Gregorian chant in the various churches of Rome, they may be adopted with the addition of the rhythmic indications of Solesmes (no. 19). (*Revue Grégorienne*, 1912, pp. 59ff. and 98ff.)

Of course, Father de Santi was involved. On March 30, he told Dom Mocquereau:

The recommendation to adopt the editions with the rhythmic indications is not at all intended as a polemic; it is merely the result of practical necessities, and of the fact that in Italy, the rhythmic indications pose no problem because absolutely everyone, from the Alps to the Gulf of Sicily to Libya, has adopted the rhythmic editions. Here, singing with other editions could very simply lead to the ruin of our chant.

In April (April 15–18), the Italian St. Cecilia Society held its Tenth Congress of Sacred Music. The chant was sung from the books of Solesmes, and *not otherwise*. The *Revue du Chant Grégorien* published an article stating that the Congress had not used the books of Solesmes, and Father de Santi sent a correction on this point. The *Revue Grégorienne* published it in French translation (*Revue Grégorienne*, 1912, p. 168).

By the end of 1912, Dom Pothier had finished editing the Vatican *Antiphonal*, which he dedicated to the Pope on December 23 (letter from Father Franck, December 22, 1912). The book was published without a preface. The preface that had been prepared for it was rejected at the last minute (Father Franck, December 22; Father Haegy, December 29; cf. de Santi, November 20, 1912).[250bis] It was introduced by a decree that echoed the decree of April 11, 1911 (the declaration concerning authorization of the rhythmic editions, approved by the Pope on April 11). No mention was made of the decree of January 25, 1911. This time, in fact, the Congregation of Sacred Rites was not going to be taken unawares, even though an effort in that direction was made while the Secretary was away (Father Franck, October 9, 1911). Given three wordings for approving this decree for the *Antiphonal*, the Pope rejected one that was unfavorable to the rhythmic editions, and a second one. He chose the third one, which was more favorable than the second:

250bis. "It is certain that D. P. did not manage to have adopted either his preface or the decree that he prepared for the new *Antiphonary*" (de Santi, November 20, 1912).

The Pope placed his *placet* at the bottom of this last page. What more loyal deed could the Congregation of Sacred Rites possibly have done? (Abbé Rousseau, April 2, 1913, from Rome)[250ter]

Yet a *Bulletin pastoral* (cf. *Revue Grégorienne*, 1913, p. 62) discussing this decree of the *Antiphonal*, saw it as "an abrogation of the rhythmic indications." It was quite the contrary, since the decree of January 25, 1911, was not mentioned in it, and the decree of April 11, which was mentioned, had been confirmed in the Decreta authentica, along with the wording quoted above, *ad majorem declarationem Decreti no. 4259, 25 Januarii vertentis anni* (1911).[251]

Thus, on repeated occasions, the opponents sought to have the rhythmic editions of Solesmes condemned. We have seen that, thanks to the critical testimony of Father de Santi and Msgr. Carlo Respighi, the Holy See opposed those efforts consistently. Father Haegy wrote:

Let us allow our opponents to hatch their plots. We are on the alert here, and will keep a watchful eye. Once again, it is true, they have fooled us. But now we see their spirit, and we understand that they are not motivated by feelings of the spirit of faith. (to Abbé Rousseau, June 11, 1911)

87. The Commission's Tribulations

In July 1905—immediately following issuance of the June 24 letter from the Cardinal Secretary of State (cf. No. 82)—Dom Pothier sought the assistance of Solesmes:

250ter. The decree of the Roman *Antiphonal* is dated December 8, 1912.

251. Father Bauducco notes that the Instruction of the Congregation of Sacred Rites dated September 3, 1958, on Sacred Music and the Holy Liturgy in accordance with the spirit of the Encyclicals *Musicae Sacrae disciplina* and *Mediator Dei* of Pope Pius XII, did not mention the decree of January 25, 1911: "Can we rightly conclude that this decree was abrogated? This is not improbable, because in this Instruction, the Congregation seems to be manifesting its intention to gather—into a sort of Code—the legislation in force concerning the chant books" (*Il Padre de Santi, s.j. e la questione dei "segni ritmici" dal 1904 al 1912*, in *Bollettino Ceciliano*, 1964, pp. 74–92, note 46). But that is not all. The text of the Instruction explicitly states that the so-called rhythmic indications introduced under private authority into Gregorian chant are permitted under ordinary conditions: "However the signs, known as *rhythmic* signs, introduced by private authority into the Gregorian chant are permitted provided that the size and shape of the notes found in the Vatican books of liturgical chant are maintained" (*Instructio . . .* , nos. 56–59).

Personally I have always applauded your research, and I have viewed your collations as extremely valuable . . . I also intend to take full account of the comments and information already provided by the members and consultors of the Commission. (To Dom Mocquereau, July 3, 1905)

Therefore, as in the past, I am counting on your devotion to the cause and to the Holy Father, and on the support of the members of the Commission. (To Dom Mocquereau, July 14, 1905)

After the Congress of Strasbourg, Dom Pothier wrote to Dom Mocquereau on behalf of the members and consultors who were present (there were ten of them), saying that they hoped "that you will continue to allow the Vatican Edition to benefit from the valuable fruits of your collations of manuscripts" (August 26, 1905). Dom Pothier repeated his request, on November 23, to Dom Delatte himself. Dom Delatte responded that cooperation was proving to be as difficult as before (which Dom Mocquereau had explained at length to Msgr. Respighi on September 15). Besides, the campaign against the rhythmic editions had just begun, and was not creating the most ideal environment for an understanding. Finally, the monastic meeting at St. Anselm in December 1905 ended in failure particularly because Father de Santi opposed the concept of a temporary edition.

Attempts at rapprochement

In early 1906 (January 2 and February 17), Dom Pothier again sought the cooperation of Solesmes. Dom Mocquereau answered him on January 20, repeating the same message. A long *Note* from Msgr. Respighi, Secretary of the Commission, printed in Italian on seven large-format pages, also was published around the same time (January 28, 1906). In the *Note*, Msgr. Respighi criticized the work of the Commission harshly, and outlined its responsibilities. Dom Pothier responded to the publication in *Quelques Remarques à propos d'une Note* (six printed pages, no date), which was received at Appuldurcombe on February 15. These two documents gave clear proof that tensions remained high within the Commission and that, for lack of a Regulation governing its operation, there was no reason to hope that the situation would improve. The criticism leveled against the *Kyriale* as soon as it was published in October 1905 once again showed that Dom Mocquereau was right to keep his guard up.

On December 19, 1906, Father de Santi was afraid that the *Gradual* would suffer the same fate as the *Kyriale*. He wrote to Dom Delatte and Dom Mocquereau. Father Minetti, S.M., the corrector of the edition, had already written on December 4, and wrote once more on December 29. The pontifical publisher was dragging out the schedule for printing, and said that he was prepared to enter the corrections sought by the Editorial Board himself (which seems to indicate that the initiative for this action came from Scotti, director of the Vatican Press). Finally, on December 20, Dom Gaisser wrote to Solesmes, as well. The word from Solesmes was that they were prepared to cooperate, but under certain essential conditions of impartiality. They proposed that, while awaiting the definitive edition, one of the Solesmes editions should be used (filling in what was missing from the 1903 edition, intended for Sundays and feast days). On January 27, 1907, Father Minetti told Dom Mocquereau that he had spoken about the matter with the Cardinal Secretary of State from the beginning, and that it was the Cardinal who had selected Dom Gaisser as the intermediary. Dom Gaisser went to see the Cardinal three times, who referred him to the Pope. Yet the Pope wanted to keep the *status quo*, since he foresaw that new complications would inevitably arise. Father de Santi had written to the Holy Father, and had received the same response through Msgr. Bressan (de Santi, January 26, 1907, to Dom Delatte).

Father Minetti concluded:

The outcome of these discussions has not been the result we hoped for. Be patient! This business did not depend on us. Besides, they will always be able to say that the monks of Solesmes were prepared, once again, to work together with the Commission and with the assistance of Dom Pothier, on behalf of the Vatican Edition. This attitude is and will always be to the honor of the monks of Solesmes, whom I love with all my heart. I am sure that this position will gain the sympathy of all those who, later on, will understand their generosity. (January 27, 1907)

Father de Santi had suggested a solution to reach an understanding among Gregorianists with respect to the rhythmic editions at the Congress of Padua in 1907. He tried again to achieve a rapprochement within the Commission on January 23, 1908. This time, the initiative certainly came from Scotti at the Vatican Press, who was fearful that the criticism of the *Kyriale* would hurt the edition. So, following Scotti's advice, Father de Santi had agreed to meet with Dom Pothier's secretary, Dom David, who had informed Father de Santi on January 22 of what the Abbot of Saint-Wandrille was looking to achieve. The proposals were as follows:

The Editorial Board must have the right to present the manuscript for the edition; the manuscript must be examined and discussed fairly, and definitively accepted by the Commission. Then, everything depends on an amicable and conciliatory understanding between the office of the President, the Editorial Board, and a small group of arbitrators, as necessary [Dom Pothier suggested three members elected by the President, the Editorial Board, and the Commission]. Only then, after the manuscript has been studied and discussed in this way, is it presented for printing and given to each reviser on the Commission.

Once Dom Pothier had agreed to this plan, Father de Santi asked Dom Mocquereau to say what he thought of it (Father de Santi, January 23, 1908, to Dom Delatte). On February 3, Father de Santi repeated his request. But Dom Mocquereau had already sent his reply on February 1 (February 2, according to the Minutes). His answer reached Rome on February 5, and Father de Santi shared it immediately with Dom David, on February 6. In it, Dom Mocquereau said that the failure of previous discussions, even though the Pope and the Cardinal Secretary of State were aware of them, and the Pope's determination to maintain the provisions created in the Letter of June 24, 1905 (i.e. staying with Dom Pothier's *Liber Gradualis* as the basis for the work), obliged Solesmes to remain very reserved. The project was all the more doomed to failure as the initiative came from the pontifical publisher, who had no official role within the Vatican Commission. On February 15, Dom Delatte made the same comments to Dom David, who had written to him directly. Dom Delatte noted, advisedly (after all, Dom David was reported to be the author of the Letter of June 24), that since Solesmes had been asked to step aside, it would have to remain there. Of course, Father de Santi regretted this refusal on the part of Solesmes (to Dom Cagin, February 18, 1908), but he added that he very well understood the reasons given.

There were no more attempts at cooperation between the Commission and the Editorial Board until 1913. By then however, the involvement was unofficial, and conditions had changed considerably.

It is true that on January 2, 1909, Msgr. Respighi told Dom Mocquereau that Dom Pothier wanted to renew contact with the Commission, and was planning to send a circular letter to the members of the Commission who were scattered all over; but nothing was to happen.

Dom David even went to Quarr Abbey in June. He published an article at the time that would not make matters any easier. Dom David later argued that he did not ask for Dom Mocquereau's assistance at that time (cf. *Revue du Chant Grégorien*, 1911, p. 61). Dom Delatte and Dom Mocquereau, however, are quite clear on this point (the letter from Msgr. Respighi mentioned above is dated January 2, 1909).

Meanwhile the situation was improving gradually for Father de Santi. At the Pope's request, he drafted the letter from Cardinal Martinelli to Msgr. Haberl dated February 18, 1910. The letter condemned mensuralism in the performance of Gregorian chant and, with the Pope's approval, Father de Santi undertook to found the School of Sacred Music in Rome later that year. At the same time, the credibility of Dom Janssens, whom the Pope used to consult readily on the Gregorian question, was on the wane. During the trip of former United States President Theodore Roosevelt to Rome, he lost the Pope's confidence, as he himself admits, in going to visit the President, while the President was not scheduled to visit the Vatican (*Msgr. Janssens, éloge prononcé par Dom H. Quentin, le 7 juin 1926*, direct quote from Dom Janssens himself). As we have seen, Dom Janssens could hardly be counted as one of Dom Mocquereau's supporters.

The Edition in 1913—Research in Germany and Austria

Starting in 1911, following publication of the decree concerning the rhythmic editions, Solesmes (then at Quarr Abbey) began to realize that the situation had changed. The consequences of the decree of January 25, 1911, have been addressed above. It was from that point on that a variety of events showed a renewal of confidence in and good will toward Solesmes.

In June 1911, Dom Mocquereau was consulted on various matters relating to the chant by the Congregation of Sacred Rites itself (for example, on the interrupted mediants, the Martryology, psalmody, etc.). He was asked to prepare the chants for the *Pontificale* (Dom Mocquereau's reply is dated June 29, 1911). In August 1912, it was announced at Solesmes that the Declarations of Padua had been confirmed in the form of a decree *ad meliorem declarationem Decreti no. 4259, 25 Januarii vertentis anni* (1911). This new decree dated April 11, 1911, the date of the audience with the Sovereign Pontiff, allowed the bishops to approve the printing of the Vatican Edition with rhythmic indications (*Decreta au-*

thentica S.R.C., no. 4,263, Appendix I, vol. VI, p. 114). That is what Father de Santi had requested at the Congress of Padua in 1907.

Besides, the Pope's thinking with respect to Solesmes and its abbot were now known:

Msgr. Dubois, Archbishop of Bourges, told me something that was very consoling for me, and certainly for Your Reverence, as well. The Holy Father, in the audience granted to the Archbishop, spoke with high praise, esteem, and affection, of Your Reverence. Thus I hope that the enormous prejudice leveled against your excellent monks through human misfortune will begin to dissipate. We have a saying: lies have short legs. Truth will outpace the lies eventually, and stride to victory. . . . (Father de Santi to Dom Delatte, November 20, 1912)

On February 7, 1911, Father de Santi had written to Dom Mocquereau to say that the Pope had said to him:

Why do the Benedictines of Solesmes not have recourse to the Holy Father? Why do they remain silent? They are wrong to act in this way. I responded: How can they do so, when they feel so humiliated, and even in disgrace with the Holy Father!

On January 5, 1913, Father Haegy had sent a confidential questionnaire to the Abbot of Solesmes, on behalf of Msgr. La Fontaine, Secretary of the Congregation of Rites, with the following remarks:

As the enclosed letter has official status . . . the importance of the invitation that is extended through my good offices does not escape me . . . The strict secrecy that the Secretary is requiring of you does not provide dispensation for informing Dom Mocquereau of this matter [concerning the chant].

Father Haegy visited Quarr Abbey from August 9–13, 1913. (His visit was preceded by one from Father Franck, another consultor of the Congregation of Sacred Rites, on August 20–21, 1912.) Father Haegy said that from then on, he was responsible for chant at the Congregation and that he had been personally delegated by Msgr. La Fontaine to examine all questions relating to the chant. At Quarr Abbey, Father Haegy received a lengthy explanation of how the Gregorian melodies were being restored. When he returned to Rome, he reported on it to Msgr. La Fontaine, and he, in turn, discussed it with the Pope (Father Haegy, November 5, 1913). A few days later, August 25–28, the Very Reverend Dom Maur Serafini, Abbot of Subiaco, came to Quarr Abbey. He spoke at length with Dom Mocquereau, and with Dom Delatte starting in the second session. Minutes of these conversations were prepared, and Dom Serafini asked for a summary of the minutes on September 3.

Dom Serafini immediately declared that he had come at the urging of the Pope and the Congregation of Sacred Rites, and that he was carrying an official letter from Msgr. La Fontaine. Then he stated that the Vatican Commission, which had not existed *de facto* for a long time, now no longer existed *officially*. He said that Solesmes was being asked to continue the work of the Gregorian restoration begun by Pope Pius X (as a formality, he first asked them to work with Dom Pothier, but he did not stress the point). Then the Offices of Christmas and Holy Week were discussed. They had already been prepared by Dom Pothier (cf. Abbé Rousseau, April 5, 1913, from Rome, to Dom Mocquereau). Msgr. La Fontaine had already written to Dom Delatte about the Offices of Christmas and Holy Week, on April 8, 1913, and Father Haegy had written on May 14. A little later, the Abbot-Primate of the Order of St. Benedict also asked Solesmes to prepare a new Monastic *Antiphonal*, with the authorization of the Congregation of Sacred Rites (letter of November 19, 1913).

The Abbot of Solesmes said that he was happy to refer to a message that he had received from the Abbot of Subiaco. He expressed a few wishes: that we would work alone, that we would not receive any financial compensation, and that there would be no question of our being officially involved.

Consequently, on June 5, 1914, the Right Rev. Dom Ferretti, professor at the School of Sacred Music in Rome—Father de Santi was ill—wrote to Dom Delatte to tell him that the Congregation of Sacred Rites had entrusted him with the publication of Holy Week. Therefore, he would have to visit Quarr Abbey because he was seeking our cooperation in his work. On June 15, after receiving the response from Solesmes, Dom Ferretti noted that the Congregation of Sacred Rites was in complete agreement with him, and that he would come to Quarr Abbey during the summer (he visited from July 28 to August 15, 1914). From Quarr Abbey, he sent a Memorandum to the Congregation on August 5.

Dom Ferretti wrote the following to Dom Delatte in a letter dated June 5, 1914, which provide a good summary of the situation:

I would like the Abbey of Solesmes to have a role in this work, a role that, although it does not emanate directly and officially from the Congregation of Sacred Rites for reasons of tact that are readily understood, remains a true, real and *key* role, so that all the merit of the work would reflect on the good and wise Fathers. [The emphasis was added by Dom Ferretti himself.]

It must be made clear that on his return to Quarr Abbey, Dom Serafini had gone to Belgium where Dom Pothier sought refuge with his community (owing to the anti-religious laws in France). Dom Serafini had met with Dom Pothier at Maredsous and had requested a memorandum from him, and from Dom Mocquereau. Dom Pothier declared himself ready to collaborate with Solesmes, and Rev. Haegy had again written to him on June 21, 1914 to ask him to prepare the chants of Holy Week. The result was that the fate of the Vatican Commission was not definitively settled until after Fr. Ferretti's trip to Quarr Abbey in August 1914. However, from the beginning of 1914, Fr. Haegy (January 30), Father de Santi (January 1), and Msgr. Respighi (February 14) had warned Dom Mocquereau that the recent *Motu Proprio Quanta semper* of January 14, 1914, had suppressed all the Commissions and that this suppression had been aimed most especially, "precisamente per excludere," at the Vatican Commission for the chant books (Respighi, January 14, 1914) (Archives of Solesmes and of Saint-Wandrille).[251bis]

The search for manuscripts that ceased in late October 1905 immediately began again. This time, the main objective was the *Antiphonal*. Dom Paul Blanchon-Lasserve and Dom Amand Ménager traveled throughout Germany, Austria, and a part of Italy not visited in 1905, from April 13 to August 17, 1914. Archduchess Zita, future Empress of Austro-Hungary, was so gracious as to recommend the travelers to the librarians of the Empire. The photographs could not be forwarded to Quarr Abbey until after the Great War, around 1920. The main stages of their travels, which encompassed a number of monasteries with rich library collections, were: Cologne, Maria-Laach, Koblenz, Trier, Stuttgart, Karlsbad, Tepl, Prague, Brno, Raigern, Vienna, Zwettl, Göttweig, Klosterneuburg, Melk, Seitenstetten, Wilhering, Linz, St. Florian, Kremsmünster, Admont, Vorau, Graz, St. Paul im Lavanttal, Gorizia, Cividale, Udine, Venice, Vicenza, Verona, Brescia, and Milan.

The Gregorian books of the Vatican

The Commission presided over by Dom Pothier published the *Kyriale* in 1905, the *Liber Gradualis* in 1908, the *Officium pro Defunctis* in 1909,

251bis. Dom Pothier was received one last time by the Pope on December 23, 1912, as discussed above (Jean de Valois, *Le Chant Grégorien*, Paris, 1963, p. 119).

the *Cantorinus seu Toni Communes* in 1911, and the *Liber Antiphonarius* in 1912. Professor Gastoué set forth the principles that guided the editors in *Société Internationale de Musique* (Paris): *L'Édition Vaticane*, 1909, vol. 2, pp. 1025–1035. He lists the instances where they followed the *textus receptus*, and not the oldest variants, and adopted the later tradition of *Do* rather than *Si*.

After 1913, Solesmes published the *Cantus Passionis* in 1916, the *Officium Majoris Hebdomadae et Octavae Paschae* in 1922, the *Officium et Missae in Nativitate Domini* in 1926. It also published the new Offices or Masses that the Holy See requested directly from Solesmes, necessarily following the principles used in the *Gradual* and the *Antiphonal*. These included, for example, the Offices and Masses for the Feasts of the Sacred Heart, Christ the King, the Assumption, etc., as well as the new melodies required under the current liturgical reform. They did not produce Offices or Masses that already existed in the diocesan or religious Propers (such as those of St. Therese of Lisieux, for example). The Commission also published three books for use of the Monastic Order, which were actually new, revised, and corrected editions of the corresponding Vatican books: the *Antiphonale Monasticum* in 1934 (and the *Antiphonale Solesmense* in 1935), *In Nocte Nativitatis Domini juxta ritum monasticum* in 1936, and *In Agendis Mortuorum juxta ritum monasticum* (except for the Mass, which necessarily followed the Vatican Edition) in 1941. These three books included a variety of improvements in terms of the neumes, the melodies (the ancient modal recitations were re-established), and the rhythm (cf. J. Jeanneteau, *L'Antiphonaire Monastique*, in *Revue Grégorienne*, 1952, pp. 209–217; see Plate 11, for an example of a response with a great deal of text in the *Antiphonal* of Solesmes; the St. Gall neumes have been added by hand above the staves). Dom Gajard later explained his point of view on modal recitation in the office in *Les récitations modales des 3ᵉ et 4ᵉ modes et les manuscrits bénéventains et aquitains* in *Études Grégoriennes* I, Solesmes 1954, pp. 9–45 and some 13 tables of 30 manuscripts.

After the Second Vatican Council

Ever since the Second Vatican Council, Solesmes has been officially assigned to oversee the editing and even the printing of Gregorian chant books. Dom Eugène Cardine, professor at the Pontifical Institute of Sacred Music in Rome, was first named President of the Coetus XXV, one of the commissions for the application of the Conciliar Constitution on the Sacred Liturgy. Coetus XXV was concerned with Gregorian Chant and includes a variety of persons, not only Solesmes monks. It is thus that the *Kyriale Simplex* appeared in 1965, and, in 1967 the *Graduale Simplex* for use in small churches, but composed for the most part of short and ancient Antiphons. Several editions of these two books were printed by the Vatican's Polyglot Press. On the other hand, the *Graduale Romanum*, the former Vatican Edition, adapted for the new *Ordo Cantus Missae* of the Congregation of Divine Worship and the *Ordo Missae in cantu* (prefaces and chants for concelebration) were published by Solesmes in 1974 *(Gradual)* and 1975 *(Ordo)*, as well as the second volume *(Tomus Alter)* of the *Antiphonale Romanum*, namely the *Liber Hymnarius cum Invitatoriis et aliquibus Responsoriis* in 1983. The first volume, which will be more extensive—the reason for issuing the publication in two volumes—and contains all the other chants of the *Liturgia Horarum* (Sundays and Feasts for the A, B, C Years and Ferials for the Years 1 and 2), is in preparation. There are also the *Psalterium Monasticum* (Solesmes 1980) and the *Missel Grégorien* (Sundays and Feasts, Solesmes 1985). As in the time of Dom Pothier, but with success this time, there was difficulty in including ancient texts which do not correspond to those of the *Liturgia Horarum*.

All these tasks are carried out in full accord with the Congregation of Divine Worship, which offers suggestions and gives approval. The Coetus XXV has been in session at Solesmes several times. Msgr. Bugnini and Msgr. Noé, successive secretaries of the so-called Consilium, came to the Abbey later. Very soon, a book will appear containing specially the Passions according to the Neo-Vulgate, and with two melodies as options. The work was done at Solesmes, but the publication will be issued by the Vatican Polyglot Press.

Since 1966, Solesmes has also been commissioned officially to oversee the critical editions of the Gregorian chant books requested by the Constitution on the Sacred Liturgy (nos. 116–117). The work is enormous, and the preliminary tasks completed. They comprise hundreds, and doubtless more, of single sheets and tableaux: forming a basic calendar, the disposition of the Masses, critical literary texts and critical music texts (for this last, there are exactly 1,900 tableaux, with 17 musical lines in staffless neumes or on lines, selected from 300 ancient Graduals after their variants and genealogical relationships were established). Three volumes have already been published, but the continuing work requires first, a profound study of the neumes, which was undertaken by Dom Cardine and continued by other musicologists.

Here is the list of books published so far: *Graduel Romain, Edition critique* [Roman Gradual, Critical edition] (Solesmes) Part I. *Les Sources* [The Sources] (1957), Part IV, Vol. I, *Le Groupement des manuscrits* [The Grouping of Manuscripts] (1960), Vol. II. *Les relations généalogiques des manuscrits* [The Genealogical Relationships of the Manuscripts] (1962), all out of print. Then there are the books by René Jean Hesbert: *Antiphonale Missarum Sextuplex*, Vroment 1935, and the six volumes of the *Corpus Antiphonalium Officii*, Herder, after 1963. Also *La Sémiologie Grégorienne* [Gregorian Semiology] (1979) by Dom Eugène Cardine, translated into various languages, the *Graduale Triplex* (1979), and the volumes of the *Études Grégoriennes* (Solesmes), especially Volume XV by Dom Jean Claire: *Les répertoires liturgiques latins avant l'Octoéchos I. L'Office ferial Romano-franc*, [Latin Liturgical Repertoires before the Octoechos I. The Franco-Roman Ferial Office], 1975. It is interesting to recall that Dom Mocquereau had undertaken a (semiological) study of the neumes, the first few pages of Volume III of the *Paléographie Musicale*—not for sale—which was interrupted by pressing demands from choirmasters wishing a deeper study of Gregorian rhythm, since the one published by Dom Pothier in the *Mélodies Grégoriennes* was deemed insufficient for practical application.

Conclusion

In the course of this lengthy discussion, we have set forth the facts as impartially as possible. Now, in retrospect, let us take a quick glance at what transpired.

The reform of the chant and the chant books began at Solesmes in 1833, initiated by Dom Guéranger. Its effects were felt shortly after 1856, or thereabouts, thanks to the work of Dom Jausions and especially of Dom Pothier, with the collaboration of Gontier.

By publishing the *Paléographie Musicale*, Dom Mocquereau hoped to prove the authenticity of Dom Pothier's restorations, whose 1883 *Liber Gradualis* had elicited lively opposition. At the same time, he hoped to destroy the prestige of the Ratisbon "Medicean" edition, which had enjoyed official status since 1871. With the help of Father Angelo de Santi and Monsignor Carlo Respighi, Dom Mocquereau forced the adoption of the reform of liturgical chant undertaken at Solesmes, in Rome itself, and throughout the universal Church.

As soon as he became Pope, Pius X joined the cause by giving his support to the restoration of the sacred chant with the *motu proprio* of November 22, 1903, and that of April 25, 1904, and by creating a Papal Commission to prepare the Vatican Edition of the liturgical books of Gregorian chant.

The work of this Commission was impeded by dissension that divided its members. The first signs of discord surfaced in 1904, as soon as Father de Santi raised the question, in March 1904, of assigning the editorship of the Vatican Edition to the Abbey of Solesmes. The dissension did not center on the rhythmic indications, which Dom Mocquereau had already renounced for the official edition, but on the fundamental principle that would act as a guide in the restitution of the melodies: should this principle (as Dom Mocquereau conceived it) of adopting a scientific methodology focus on the evidence of the most ancient manuscripts? Or, on the other hand, should this criterion be practical (as Dom Pothier wished), one that would take into account the musical preference of modern ears and accept the changes that were made in the melodies over the centuries as improvements arising from a "living tradition"?

Given the emotional tension of the situation, the Commission could not accomplish serious or effective work unless a precise principle could be used to define the melodies, and to indicate a procedure to be followed. Dom Mocquereau and his friends understood this better than the others, but they could not prevail until an accord could be reached on the wording of the Regulation indispensable to the future success of the endeavor. The misunderstanding was irreconcilable: an impasse had been reached.

The only way out of the dilemma, and of saving the Vatican Edition, was to be content with using as a model the second edition of the *Liber Gradualis*, published by Dom Pothier in 1895 (1883?). The decision to do this was promulgated in a letter from the Cardinal Secretary of State, dated June 24, 1905. Father de Santi was not the instigator of the document, but had already thought of this as a solution, and he was right in anticipating this decision as the only possible solution.

In order to exclude Dom Mocquereau, his opponents pretended that his work was not sufficiently advanced, despite the fact that he had already presented the *Kyriale* to the Commission in 1905, that the neumatic tables of the entire *Gradual* were already finished, and that the melodic charts were already underway. So he could easily have completed the work in the time allotted. However, the delays that they reproached him for were merely a pretext for excluding him. In all of this, as often happens, the real cause of the dissension was not a technical matter, and personality conflicts played a dominant role.

After 1905, the Vatican Commission ceased to function in the form in which it had been created in 1904, but its work was not interrupted, and the negotiations that continued until 1913 made it quite clear that it was vain to hope for a collaboration between Solesmes and Dom Pothier. The Commission was formally disbanded toward the end of 1913, actually at the beginning of 1914.

At that time, a new Commission was formed, which reassigned the editing task to Solesmes.

Does this mean that the project of the Vatican Edition failed? Certainly not. In fact, it had some very appreciable positive results. Particularly at Solesmes, it gave rise to labors on a grand scale which will not have been in vain. The crisis which the Commission underwent in 1905 also led to some fortunate consequences: it settled immediately the matter of potential criticism that would not have been wanting had the work been too poorly prepared. Instead, there was rejoicing on all sides when the *Kyriale* appeared. From then on, the new editors became more diligent, especially Dom Andoyer, a former companion of Dom Pothier and Dom Mocquereau at Solesmes, whom the Chairman invited to come to Rome for the preparation of the Vatican *Antiphonal*. As for the *Gradual*, did not Dom Pothier himself write to Dom Mocquereau on January 2, 1906 that "he had taken a careful note of the many variants in the *Liber Usualis* of 1903"? The number of borrowings taken from that book is estimated at more than two thousand.[252]

Better than Dom Pothier's previous editions, the Vatican Edition still had room for improvement, especially in the area of modality. This can be noted by comparing the Vatican *Antiphonal* with the Monastic *An-*

252. T. Laroche, *Le Graduel Romain et le Liber Usualis de 1903. Contribution à l'histoire de l'Édition Vaticane* (Desclée, n. d., 80 p.), taken from the *Rassegna Gregoriana* 1910 and 1913.

tiphonal published by Solesmes in 1934. It was to bring about improvement of the liturgical chant books, need of which is felt so much today, that the Second Vatican Council asked for an *editio magis critica*. The post-conciliar Commission on Liturgy confided this critical edition of the Roman *Gradual* to Solesmes, where use is made for this purpose of the immense collection of manuscripts which Dom Mocquereau had previously photographed for the Vatican Edition. The edition by the Solesmes monks is published by the *Libreria Editrice Vaticana*, which officially assumes the responsibility for a task at first undertaken by private initiative. Thus, Vatican II continues and follows the work of Pius X.

Looking back over the years, and considering Dom Mocquereau's intolerance for half-measures, Msgr. Moneta-Caglio wrote in *Musica Sacra* (1963, p. 50):

If we ask ourselves what Dom Mocquereau would have gained by an attitude of complacent condescension, we would have to recognize that he would have been a thousand times better for it. In those days, when exploration was rife, anyone who wanted to prepare a Gregorian edition had to undertake the project and accept compromises without end. Dom Mocquereau, who refused to play that game, failed in terms of tactics, but conquered as a strategist, because today he appears to us as the very symbol of fidelity to the manuscripts.

APPENDIX I. RESOLUTIONS OF THE

AREZZO CONGRESS

[Conclusions and resolutions adopted by the Arezzo Congress Commission (from the brochure by Dom P. Cagin, *Le chant grégorien au Congrès d'Arezzo*, Poitiers, Oudin, 1883, pp. 39–40), cf. No. 38.]

The European Congress, meeting at Arezzo for the purpose of honoring the memory of Monk Guido, of promoting the improvement of liturgical chant, after having undertaken its tasks in the spirit of the most filial submission to the Holy See and opened its meetings under the auspices of the Apostolic Blessing, is happy to be able to tender its most unreserved respect for the supreme authority and its complete filial surrender to the fatherly kindness of Him whom Jesus Christ has chosen to rule over His Church.

Having concluded undeniably, not without anguish, that for a long time, in the various parts of Europe, with few exceptions, the sacred chant has been neglected and is in a deplorable condition, a condition that is due to:

1. the divergent and incorrect choir books being used in the Churches;

2. the difference in modern theoretical works and the variety and paucity of teaching methods in the seminaries as well as in musical organizations;

3. the neglect with which the music instructors of our times treat plainchant, among whom are numerous members of the clergy too little concerned about this subject;

4. forgetfulness of the true tradition for the good rendition of liturgical chant;

the Congress sets forth the following resolutions:

I. That the choral books in use in the churches should conform as closely as possible to the ancient tradition;

II. That the greatest encouragement be accorded and the widest distribution be given to studies and theoretical works already done and to be done, which bring light to bear on the masterworks of the liturgical tradition;

III. That a suitable place for the study of plainchant be given in the education of the clergy, thus re-establishing and applying with the greatest zeal the canonical instructions on the subject;

IV. That for the performance of plainchant with equal and hammered-out notes should be substituted the rhythmic rendition that conforms to the principles set forth by Guido d'Arezzo in Chapter 15 of his *Micrologus*;

V. That to this end, every method of chant shall include the principles of Latin accentuation.

APPENDIX II. BRIEFS ADDRESSED TO DOM POTHIER

[Here is the text of the two Briefs addressed to Dom Pothier, to which reference was made in No. 39. We provide translations of these two documents because it is not easy to gain access to them now, especially the second one, which is rarely cited in the periodicals of the time. The translation of the second Brief is taken from the *Musica Sacra* of Ghent, May 1884. Finally, remember that the decree *Romanorum Pontificum sollicitudo* mentioned in the Brief of May 3, 1884, is dated April 10, 1883, but that it was not confirmed until April 26, the date usually given. (These documents are found in F. Romita, *Jus Musicae Liturgicae*, Rome, 1947, pp. 273, 280, I and II.)]

Brief "Redditum Fuit Nobis" of March 3, 1884

To our dear son Joseph Pothier, religious of the Order of Saint Benedict, at the monastery of Solesmes, France.

Leo XIII, Pope. Dear son, greeting and Apostolic benediction.

Our venerable brother, Jean-Baptiste Cardinal [Pitra, professed at Solesmes], Bishop of Frascati, has delivered to Us the book of sacred chant which you have published. We have received your homage with pleasure and thanks, and because of the value of the work and also from that which the Very Reverend Cardinal has told us, We know, in fact, dear son, with what intelligence you have applied yourself to interpret and explain the ancient masterpieces of sacred music, and how you have put all your zeal into showing those who cultivate this art the very nature and exact form of these ancient chants, as they were composed in ancient times and which your fathers have preserved with great care. We think, dear son, that in this matter not only are your efforts to be commended in pursuing a work fraught with difficulties and labor, requiring several years of dedicated work, but also your love for the Church of Rome that has inspired you, which has considered it worthy always to hold in high esteem this genre of sacred melodies bearing the name of St. Gregory the Great.

For this reason We keenly desire that Our letters should be a testimony of Our recommendation for the remarkable studies which you have consecrated to the history, the discipline, and the beauty of the sacred chant. We wish to give you this testimonial all the more in that, overcoming the adversities of these evil days, you bravely struggle in the service and for the honor of religion and for the Church (an allusion to the religious persecutions in France). Imploring, then, most clement God to strengthen your courage by the power of His grace, so that His light may shine forth more each day before men, and in the love of the Lord as a pledge of heavenly gifts and in testimony of Our fatherly tender love, we accord you, dear son, and your brothers in the religious life, the Apostolic Benediction.

Given at Rome at St. Peter's on March 3, 1884, in the seventh year of Our Pontificate.

Leo XIII, Pope.

Brief (Counter-Brief) *Quamquam Nos* of May 3, 1884

Leo XIII, Pope. Dear son, greeting and Apostolic Benediction.

Although in the response which we made to your letter of December 24th of last year we praised the competence with which you and your brothers have explained and commented on the ancient masterpieces of sacred music, We were considering the Gradual edited by you solely as a work about the historical science of sacred music and written from the point of view of erudition, and this explains the tone of Our letter; nevertheless, in order to avoid having this letter be the occasion of false interpretation, We have decided, very dear son, to let you know by the Present that in the Letter mentioned above, which We addressed to you, We were not thinking of ignoring what is found in the decree published in virtue of Our authority, April 10th of last year, by our Congregation of Sacred Rites and beginning with the words Romanorum Pontificum sollicitudo, and that Our intention was not to approve for use in the Sacred Liturgy the Gradual which was offered to us, the same would necessarily have to be submitted to a careful examination by the same Congregation according to the custom of the Apostolic See in similar cases.

Now that this explanation has been given, by which We wish to declare that the force of this decree mentioned above should be full and complete, We accord to you with affection in the Lord, dear son, and to your brothers, as a sign of Our paternal love and as an omen of heavenly protection, the Apostolic Benediction.

Given at Rome at St. Peter's on May 3, 1884, in the seventh year of Our Pontificate.

Leo XIII, Pope.

APPENDIX III. THE 1893 *VOTUM* OF

CARDINAL SARTO

We must say a little more about the 1893 *votum* mentioned in sections 30 and 35.

Here is how light gradually came to be shed on this *votum*, and on its relationship to the *motu proprio* that Pius X issued on November 22, 1903.

First, the *Revue Grégorienne* published a letter sent by Father de Santi to Dom Mocquereau on January 4, 1904, in which Father de Santi stated that he himself had used this *votum* of Cardinal Sarto to draw up the *motu proprio* of November 22, 1903, but he failed to mention that he himself was its author (cf. Dom P. Combe, "Aux sources du *Motu Proprio*," *Revue Grégorienne* 1953, pp. 234–235; cf. Part 2, No. 56).

In 1954, Msgr. F. Romita, in an anonymous article published in the *Bollettino Ceciliano* (March–April 1954, pp. 67–71) and in *Azione Ceciliana* (Rome, Desclée 1954, p. 17, note 2) confirmed the identical nature of the *votum* of 1893 and the *motu proprio* of 1903 "in their substantial and dispositive portion". In doing so, in fact, he referred to statements of Father de Santi himself (*Bollettino Ceciliano* 1910, p. 188), and to a comparison of the two manuscripts which he had been able to do in person (but at the time, he said nothing of the role played by Father de Santi in writing that document).

It was Msgr. E. Moneta-Caglio who first proved the influence of the writings of Father de Santi on the thinking of Cardinal Sarto in matters of religious music, by means of detailed comparisons and a philological study of the texts. He proved that Cardinal Sarto's 1895 Venice *Pastoral Letter* is a tributary of the writings of Father de Santi, whose involvement is even more evident in the *motu proprio*: "without wishing to, Father de Santi placed his signature on the wording of the pontifical document" (*Le fonti del motu proprio di S. Pio X*, in *Musica Sacra*, Milan 1961, 1, 2, 3). Msgr. Moneta-Caglio also deduced that the *motu proprio* must be a re-working of the 1893 *votum*.

In 1961, Father F. Bauducco, S.J., of *Civiltà Cattolica*, published two letters of

Cardinal Sarto that furnished proof of what Msgr. Moneta-Caglio had announced. In the first letter, written from Mantua on July 9, 1893, Cardinal Sarto
asked Father de Santi to prepare a memorandum for him that he said he wanted to repeat word for word and submit to the Congregation of Sacred Rites, in
response to a circular letter sent to the bishops of Italy. In the second, also written from Mantua, on July 30, the Cardinal thanked Father de Santi for the work
he accomplished so quickly. Father Bauducco also stated that he knew this *votum* and was convinced of its total conformity with the *motu proprio* (*Il P. Angelo
de Santi e la fondazione della Scuola Superiore di Musica Sacra in Roma, Civiltà Cattolica*, September 16, 1961, pp. 583–594).

Finally, also in 1961, Msgr. F. Romita's book was published: *La preformazione
del motu proprio di S. Pio X sulla Musica sacra* (Desclée, Rome 1961, 107 pp.). This
book published the 1893 *votum* and explained, furnishing the evidence for the
claim, how things had come to pass, using for this purpose, in fact, the three
letters mentioned above (*Revue du Chant Grégorien* and *Civiltà Cattolica*). The
book also provides various information that could not derive solely from a
comparison of the documents (cf. Dom P. Combe, *Le Motu Proprio d S. Pie X du
22 novembre 1903 : Études historiques*, in *Études Grégoriennes* V, 1962, pp. 133–135).
(Cf. Part 2, No. 56.)

APPENDIX IV. TRANSLATION OF THE THE ORIGINAL ITALIAN TEXT OF THE DOCUMENTS* RELATING TO THE ORIGINS OF THE VATICAN COMMISSION

Letter from Father de Santi to Dom Mocquereau, Civiltà Cattolica, *October 22, 1903*

. . . the publication of the *Liber Usualis* has been announced to us, too, as accomplished. Thank God that we shall finally leave behind the difficulties of the books and shall be able to satisfy the many friends who are requesting them. Now let us hope that Desclée will not get them to us until after Christmas. . . .

The state of affairs and hence the look of the future appears to be growing more definite. Since the Pope knows the question and decides by himself, he himself thus continues to make clear his ideas without having others suggest them to him. Both to Msgr. Respighi and to me, in the audience that I had on September 23, the Holy Father has said that he would be displeased if we would simply pass from one monopoly of liturgical books to another. He suggests that the principal dioceses which have good manuscripts should publish them in practical hand editions, thus everywhere resurrecting the ancient melodies. "They will be," he said, "a bit different amongst themselves in some small parts of the melody, but when all is said and done we will have the traditional chant in every diocese."

Last Sunday, the Holy Father received Count Lefebvre and he is pleased with the chant editions which are being prepared by yourself and the Benedictine Fathers. The Pope added that it would be good to publish the choir books also in folio because, he said, in many cathedrals and collegiate churches they

---

* Note: The original Italian texts are presented in the 1969 French edition of this book.

use such books in the large size and the canons would have a rather hard time adapting to smaller hand-held editions.

The same day, the Holy Father also received Mr. Pustet from Ratisbon. His Holiness' statement was as explicit as could be. He declared that he had no preferences for anyone and that every publisher would be equally favored by him, but he added, "As far as Gregorian Chant is concerned, the Holy Father, Pope Leo XIII, has opened a new horizon, has laid down a new path, and this is the road that must be followed. In the Church's chant, we must look for truth and art. These two qualities are possessed only by the ancient traditional chant and it is this chant which must now be restored." Afterwards, he urged Mr. Pustet to join in publishing books of the traditional chant, taking the melodies, if he wished, from manuscripts of the German dioceses.

I learned all this from the lips of Msgr. Bressan that very evening and it tallies with the notes which exist of this audience, also from other sources. If the Holy Father's advice be accepted, the race between publishers will be under way. Blest is he who will know how to get out in front first. . . .

Father de Santi to Dom Delatte, Civiltà Cattolica, *December 20, 1903*

Most Reverend Father! Please accept my wishes for the approaching Christmas feast. I write to bring you some news which doubtless will be most consoling to yourself and all your monks. Truth to tell this news is *not* yet to be made public, but I trust myself to *your* discretion, since public documents will not confirm it.

During the Christmas holidays, the Holy Father will publish a solemn *motu proprio* on the restoration of sacred music. In it is taken, at last, the final step in favor of Gregorian chant according to the manuscripts, which is expressed each time the chant is mentioned. This *motu proprio* is given the force of law *as to a juridical code of sacred music* which is why the affirmations made regarding Gregorian chant take on an extraordinary significance.

The Holy Father communicates the new document with a very beautiful letter to the Cardinal Vicar of Rome in which he enjoins in paternal but yet strong terms the observance of his regulations in all the churches and basilicas of Rome. The conclusion is directed to the colleges and seminaries of Rome, and praises Gregorian chant splendidly, recalling its happy restoration through the labors of illustrious personages who have served the cause of sacred art long and well. At the end, he imposes (*enjoins*) upon all the institutions at Rome the study of traditional Gregorian chant, expressing a desire that just as in the past this chant had been spread from Rome throughout the Church, so too the young students educated in the seminaries and colleges of Rome might in their turn go back from Rome to their dioceses. As you see, Father Abbot, the change is total and profound, the return to tradition solemnly affirmed by the

Supreme Pontiff in a most weighty document. The formal revocation of the decrees of the Congregation of Rites is a self-evident conclusion and we have requested the Holy Father to add such a declaration to the documents; all the more because in order to avoid an avalanche of requests to the Sacred Congregation it seems necessary to state that the Ratisbon editions can be maintained, in those places where they are being used *donec quamprimum fieri poterit*—until the earliest possible moment that the traditional chant replaces them.

However, I cannot deny to you that the question of the books is exceedingly important. If a cathedral or collegiate church wishes to introduce the traditional chant, where does one find the texts? The small books we have at present are completely unsatisfactory for great churches, although most useful for seminaries and colleges. In addition the Holy Father complained to Dr. Haberl that these books are rather poorly printed in type which is too small, and he advised Herr Pustet to print the chant in larger type. We earnestly beg you, Father Abbot, to restrain the efforts of the excellent Dom Mocquereau and to order that work be started at once on larger books with larger type, as the *Liber Gradualis* was originally. The rhythmic signs are certainly excellent for instructional purposes, but since they also present at the very least an *occasion for doubt*, we earnestly entreat you and beg that for now, in the typical edition of the chant books, such signs be omitted. Otherwise you will never obtain ecclesiastical approval and indeed will furnish a reason for taking other measures if the monks of Solesmes do not agree. It is absolutely necessary that we receive this promise from Solesmes in order thus to assure the Holy Father that we shall have as soon as possible the typical edition of the chant books as he desires them, and in order to reply to the requests which the various dioceses might make as to which books they should buy. I entreat you with the greatest insistence that in the decisions which are taken regarding the chant, you hear also the view of Rome and not leave us in the lurch, ignorant of your undertakings. You will pardon the liberty we are taking, but believe that nothing else motivates us except the desire to see the triumph of a cause for which so much has been endured. Kissing your hand and presenting my humble wishes to you, Father Abbot, and all your dear monks, I repeat that I am your most devoted servant in Christ,

A. de Santi S.J.

Note: In the third paragraph of this letter, the word imposes *is written in above the word* enjoins, *which it replaces.*]

Father de Santi to Dom Mocquereau, Civiltà Cattolica, *December 31, 1903*

Very Reverend and dear Father!

At present the pontifical documents will bring some joy to the bitter exile of the good Fathers of Solesmes. Worthily and much sooner than one could have reasonably expected, the Lord has crowned your learned labors. And all of us congratulate you from the very depths of our heart. An explicit mention of Solesmes or at least of the Benedictine order might perhaps have been desirable. We had made that request to the Holy Father, since he had deigned to entrust the revision of the document to a few of us who therefore met together with Father Janssens on the Aventine. But His Holiness replied that it was not needful, that there would be no dearth of opportunity for him to show his pleasure at the work of the Benedictines, but that in documents of this type it was necessary to avoid any personal reference, also in order that there would not be the slightest chance of claiming that the Pope showed any preference for particular publishers. Perhaps it will be good to have Rev. Father Abbot write a letter of thanks to the Holy Father in his name and on behalf of the monks. However, they should see that they send it through Msgr. Respighi, for otherwise it might run the risk of falling into the dead letter box at the Secretariat of State.

(Preparation of the Feast of St. Gregory the Great)

The Holy Father has complained to Father Haberl that the current editions of Solesmes are too small both as regards the musical type and the print of the texts. We adjure the Fathers of Solesmes (and I have already written this to Father Abbot) that they should set to work at once on the Gregorian typical editions such as they have already done with the *Liber Gradualis* without dots and rhythmic signs. If a cathedral church asks to introduce the chant desired by the Pope, there is nothing to give them. The current books are the best for seminaries and for parish choirs, but ill-suited for use in a monastic choir.

Father de Santi to Dom Mocquereau, Roma, Ripetta 246, *January 4, 1904.*

Dear Rev. Father!

. . . I thank Father Abbot for the very beautiful letter he has written me. He says that matters have gone farther than anyone foresaw. That is also true for us. I will say that without forgetting how all this came about. Early in November the Cardinal Vicar wished to publish a circular letter on *musica sacra*, to encourage observance of the well-known prescriptions of the Church. When

Msgr. Respighi showed me the printer's proofs, I thought that one could perhaps do a bit more. I knew very well the memorandum which Cardinal Sarto had sent to the Congregation of Rites in 1893. His pastoral letter based on this memorandum had already been published in 1895. Why would it not be possible to publish also a pontifical *motu proprio* based on the same text? I proposed this at once to the Holy Father, who deigned to approve the idea and commissioned me to draw up such a document. There was no need to go looking for a copy of the memorandum: I had one in my files. The work was done in a trice; it was merely a matter of adding the prescriptions concerning Gregorian chant. The letter of the Cardinal Vicar was then written with ideas suggested by the Pope, and all was ready by early December. In view of the approaching Christmas holidays, publication was postponed, with the thought that the unfortunate choirmasters would really be taken completely unawares, and thus unable to have made corrections in such a short time. I also wrote the draft of the decree of the Congregation of Rites and it is now on the Holy Father's desk and I hope that there will be no obstacle to its publication. The one thing that worried all of us was the matter of the books. It is undeniable that books with dots alone are not enough, and at a time of such radical change it seemed absolutely necessary to avoid any discussion of uncertain or doubtful points. But we trust the monks of Solesmes and we have given assurance of it to the Holy Father as well, and for now we are satisfied with the statements of Father Abbot. And so the twelve monks working on the books should set to work and give us as quickly as possible the books of medium size, without rhythmic signs. For my part, I recommend as strongly as possible the Gregorian edition with dots, because I believe it most useful in seminaries etc. I only have a few reservations about certain subdivisions which in my view could also be indicated in some other fashion, except of course where it is clear that the manuscripts have it that way, or that mutual comparison of the different melodies requires it. What I myself can in no way accept is an edition in modern notation. But the recounting of the weighty reasons for that would take much too long, and on the other hand it is inappropriate to diminish, with thoughts of this kind, the joy which we all feel at this grandiose victory. Many regards to all, and believe me, yours devoted in the Lord,

de Santi.

Father de Santi to Dom Mocquereau, Roma, Ripetta 246, February 28, 1904.

. . . With this information I join some more news, communicated last evening by order of the Holy Father to the representative of the Pustet firm at Rome. It is that no further consideration be given to future editions of the traditional chant, in expectation of the Pope's decision. The same message should have been communicated to the representative of the Desclée company but he was out of town last evening and they are awaiting his return. Pustet had sent to the Holy Father a proof sheet containing the *Asperges* and the *Vidi aquam.* . . .

. . . Several matters of the greatest importance are slowly developing to maturity and as soon as I am able to say something, I shall not neglect to inform you at once. For the moment my lips are sealed. But everything comes down from higher up and all will surely turn out satisfactorily. I ask you to keep this information to yourself, even if it be so sibylline. Come to Rome quickly. Maestro Perosi had even given me the news that you had already arrived; I called San Anselmo at once and was disappointed.

Father de Santi to Dom Mocquereau, Roma, Via di Ripetta 246, November 28, 1908

. . . Regarding the events of 1904 there is not much to say beyond that which I have already indicated. Dom Pothier came to Rome without being invited by anyone, but on his own initiative with the intention of proposing to the Holy See an edition under the auspices of the Pope, to appear, if desired, at the expense of the Poussielgue firm at Rome or at Paris, as desired, with the understanding that Poussielgue would publish the edition first, and later other publishers would be permitted to reproduce it. Therefore he came accompanied by an agent of that company. Basically, they wanted to repeat the proposals already made by Védie in 1901. I laid down the explicit condition that the Benedictines of Solesmes would have to take part in the editorial work, and Dom Pothier agreed. Furthermore, I discouraged presentation of the proposal to the Holy Father before knowing Signor Scotti's opinion on it. It seemed to me that by eliminating the difficulties which could have arisen on the part of subordinates, one might more certainly achieve one's purpose. And so I spoke with Signor Scotti and he excluded most definitely any interference of Poussielgue, saying that he was ready to publish the edition himself and proposing his plan to separate the publishers from the question of expenses as had been done before. (The agent of Poussielgue departed Rome as soon as he learned of Scotti's decision.) However, he did raise two questions: ownership of the notation and copyright of the melodies. Dom Pothier said it was unnecessary to worry about the first point; as to the second he declared his readiness to turn over to the Holy See all the rights which he might have had to his labors, adding that certain difficulties might perhaps arise with the French Government, which at that time had confiscated the Solesmes editions. He also added that in order to move ahead without hindrance it would be good to have a statement of renunciation from Solesmes as well for that which was their contribution. At that time I wrote to Pécoul to ask the terms in which the property matters stood at Paris. I had had no connection with Pécoul at all, but after the publication of the *Motu proprio* on sacred music he had written me a letter of congratulation, and Dom Pothier told me that he was able to do a great deal to prevent govern-

ment interference with an edition which one might wish to publish at Rome. I
pointed out that Dom Pothier, although he had advised also contacting
Solesmes for the transfer of their property rights, he did not however put the
matter as absolutely necessary, at least for the greater part of the work already
done. Matters having been settled thus, on the evening of Monday, February
22, I reported on all of this to the Holy Father, formally proposing the preparation of a Vatican edition with the cooperation of Dom Pothier and the Benedictines of Solesmes. The Holy Father welcomed the proposal with great pleasure and lavishly praised the plan of Scotti regarding expenses. In the meantime
Pécoul began to bombard me with letters, which remained unanswered. Dom
Pothier presented a written declaration transferring to the Holy See all his literary rights, and on the evening of March 9, Scotti came to me to say that the
Holy Father had ordered that a letter be written to the Benedictines of
Solesmes inviting them also to transfer their portion of the copyrights, and to
collaborate in the edition. Dom Pothier came to Rome with another monk of
his abbey whose name I do not recall. I do remember that he and Dom David
spoke to me continually of honoraria which one would have to pay, and of percentages on the edition, be they in compensation for Dom Pothier's work, or to
assist the catastrophic financial state of the abbey. Scotti's proposal to publish
the edition in a way that would not cost the Holy See a penny was not at all to
their liking. I spoke of this with the Holy Father, and the Holy Father told me
that he could not pay anything, but if it were necessary, that he would gladly
meet the expenses which Dom Pothier had to incur because of his stay at
Rome. I think that the original idea of Dom Pothier was to strike a bargain
with Poussielgue, putting the Holy See in the middle in order to avoid upsetting Solesmes. But the scheme failed in part [cf. note 161bis and No. 59]. As far
as the guidelines for producing the edition were concerned, it was originally
proposed to make a good edition based on the earlier one. But when the
monks of Solesmes demonstrated that the copyright was theirs and the Holy
Father recognized the need to give them some compensation of honor in return for the transfer of rights by officially declaring them editors of the Vatican
Edition, we thought in terms of a criterion more strictly scientific, such as had
been proposed in the *Motu proprio*.

*The points made in this letter are very well summarized in a note of Father de San-
ti also published in 1908 in a journal which we have been unable to identify: Gregorian
Chant.*

Dom David knows very well these four things: (1) that the Holy Father did
not think at all of publishing a Vatican Edition and therefore could not even
have thought of entrusting its execution to Dom Pothier or to anyone else, for

that matter; (2) that Dom Pothier, without being invited, came to Rome in February 1904, and offered to the Holy Father to make a Vatican edition at the expense of the Poussielgue firm of Paris; (3) that thanks to an agreement of the director of the Vatican Press, Signor Scotti, there was accepted instead in principle the proposal of a Vatican edition; (4) that the copyright of the Gregorian melodies published up to that time belonged exclusively to the monastery of Solesmes and that consequently it was impossible to begin anything without the cooperation of those monks, who had generously transferred to the Holy See their rights and had received in return the task of furnishing the manuscript of the Vatican edition. Dom David does not say how it later proved possible to exclude the monks of Solesmes and to place everything into the hands of Dom Pothier, but history will tell.

Msgr. Giovanni Bressan to Dom Delatte, Vatican, March 10, 1904

Right Rev. Father!

His Holiness has arrived at the decision to publish at the Vatican Press the edition of liturgical books containing the chant of the Roman Church. This edition, produced under the auspices of the Holy See, will not have restricted copyright but any publisher will be permitted to reprint it as may please him best. The edition will be limited to the typical books alone, such as the *Liber Gradualis*, the *Liber Antiphonarius*, the *Pontificale*, the *Ritual*, etc.

At the same time His Holiness has deigned to entrust to the Rt. Rev. Father Joseph Pothier, O.S.B., of the Solesmes congregation, presently Abbot of Saint-Wandrille, the honorable task of furnishing the text of the Gregorian melodies and of directing the editorial labors which, prior to being approved by His Holiness, will be diligently examined by persons regarded as more competent in this material, with final revision by the Liturgical Commission for the publication of Gregorian chant books recently established by the same Holy Father.

Rev. Father Pothier, grateful for the honor conferred upon him, has renounced in favor of the Holy See, by a formal declaration and for the sole purpose of the aforementioned edition, all rights and every copyright which he might have in the melodies copied by him from the ancient manuscripts, or adapted, or newly composed, such as have already been published in the Solesmes edition.

But the Holy Father in his very special predilection for the illustrious order of St. Benedict, recognizing with deep satisfaction the indefatigable labors performed by Benedictine monks in the restoration of the genuine Gregorian melodies, in particular by the religious of the above-mentioned Abbey of Solesmes, has deigned to order that also in future the editing of the Gregorian liturgical books as well as the composition of any new melodies which may occur in eventual new offices, be always reserved to the Benedictine order and in particular to the monks of Solesmes.

His Holiness does not doubt in the least that you and the monks of your monastery will only receive with gratitude this act of sovereign benevolence, remembering well how Your Reverence, writing in 1901 to his predecessor Pope Leo XIII of holy memory, placed at the disposition of the Holy See all of your efforts so that they might serve in their way for the greater glory of God and for the good of the Church.

In communicating to Your Reverence these sovereign resolutions, I have the high honor by the express wish of His Holiness, to invite Your Reverence and the monks subject to you to collaborate diligently and skillfully in the work desired, under the guidance and direction of the Rt. Rev. Abbot of St. Wandrille and in accord with the norms indicated above, which will in due time be made public by means of a special pontifical act.

I take this occasion to present to you, Father Abbot, my sentiments of most profound esteem and I sign myself as the most humble servant of Your Reverence

Giovanni Bressan
Private Chamberlain to His Holiness

Msgr. G. Bressan to Dom Delatte, Vatican, April 2, 1904

Right Rev. Father!

His Holiness was profoundly moved by the piety and filial devotion, by the spirit of disinterestedness and no small sacrifice, as well as by the marvelous promptness with which Your Reverence accepted the invitation of His Holiness to collaborate in the preparation of a Vatican Edition containing the melodies of the Church and intended for the free use of all the churches throughout the world. The Holy Father has consequently ordered me to manifest his august pleasure to you, with the expression of his gratitude, whilst he wholeheartedly imparts to Your Reverence, to the monks of your monastery, and to their labors, as also to the entire Congregation of France O.S.B. which Your Reverence so excellently governs, the Apostolic blessing. In fulfilling this pleasing and honorable task, kissing your hand I have the honor to repeat that I am

Your Reverence's most humble servant

Giovanni Bressan
Private Chamberlain to His Holiness

[*Extracts from 1904 from the diary of Father de Santi published by Msgr. Ernesto Moneta-Caglio in Musica Sacra (Milan), 1962, nos. 4–5, pp. 108–118* (Dom André Mocquereau e la restaurazione del Canto Gregoriano. X.).]

January 13. Dom Lucien David O.S.B. of Saint-Wandrille came to speak with me about the condition of Dom Pothier and about the desolation in which he had been abandoned by the Benedictines of Solesmes. He asks whether a chant edition might be made at Rome. I said what we think about the current Solesmes books.

January 31. Audience with the Holy Father in the evening from 6 until 7:30. A few musical communications. Letters from Dom Pothier and Dom Delatte.

February 5. Dom Pothier will come to Rome to make a counter-edition to Solesmes. This too!

February 6. Dom Lucien David comes and tells me that Dom Pothier is coming to Rome shortly. He would like to make his own edition.

February 13. Dom Pothier arrives and comes to meet me in the evening. The proposal is to make a Vatican edition under his direction. The agent of the Poussielgue firm also comes and the possible methods are discussed. It is decided to draw up a written proposal in which are maintained all due regards to the Benedictines of Solesmes.

February 14. Dom Pothier returns. He says that the Abbot Primate wishes to take the chant business in hand himself in order to assure it for the Benedictine order in the future too. Dom Pothier remains linked with this and the situation changes. The proposal to the Pope must be made in a different manner.

February 15. Signor Scotti comes from the Vatican Press. He is ready to produce the edition at Rome and declares that it will be possible to provide for the expenses. In the meantime he wishes to know the details regarding copyright for the notation and the melodies.

February 22. Audience with the Holy Father. Explanation of the project to print the books at the Vatican. Received magnificently and with a kind of enthusiasm.

February 25. In the evening Msgr. Bressan tells me of the splendid impression made upon the Holy Father by the proposed edition.

March 2. I received a letter of appointment to the Commission for the Revision of the Gregorian books. From the terminology used and the notice in the *Osservatore Romano* it does not appear that the old Commission has been suppressed.

March 9. Signor Scotti comes. He has spoken with the Holy Father, who told him to commission me with writing the letter to Solesmes and to bring it to him.

March 10. Audience with the Holy Father. I bring him the draft for Solesmes and he is satisfied with it.

March 11. Bressan comes and tells me that the letter to Solesmes was sent yesterday.

March 13. In the afternoon Dom Mocquereau, Dom Cagin, and Dom Noetinger come. They are aware of some things and I have told them the rest. The reasons they advance in support of their edition are very weighty and I am impressed by them.

March 15. Dom Mocquereau comes bringing his comparative charts. In the afternoon Dom Pothier comes and I tell him frankly my views on the changed situation.

March 22. I was received by the Holy Father and I brought him the draft of the Pontifical decree on the Roman edition.

March 23. This morning at 11:00 I accompanied the Benedictines of Solesmes to the audience with the Holy Father.

March 24. Dom Guerrin, secretary of Dom Pothier, came and I explained to him the changed circumstances.

March 31. The Holy Father asked that I come at six in the afternoon. He told me that it had been decided to publish the entire edition at Rome.

April 4. Meeting of the Roman Commission to discuss the page proofs. We agree on the first paragraphs. But when we get to the point of the editing by Solesmes we reach a deadlock for one reason or another. The gist of it is that Dom Pothier and Dom Janssens do not wish to be present because they are against Solesmes.

April 18. In the evening I received a letter from Dom Pothier who complains bitterly about Cagin's article which appeared in the *Rassegna*.

April 18. Signor Scotti comes. He says that there is no choice but to put aside the Benedictines.

April 18. . . . Msgr. Bressan came. He says that the Holy Father will decide. Scotti tells me that the Abbot Primate went to the Cardinal Secretary of State who, however, was not favorably inclined toward him.

April 22. Msgr. Bressan comes. He brings me a nice letter to the Holy Father from the Solesmes monks in which they protest against the intrigues of the Abbot Primate. The letter had not been understood correctly but I explained everything. I promised to betake myself to the Holy Father tomorrow morning.

April 23. I have been to the Holy Father. He asked my advice and declared that he held fast to the first proposal, which contained his definitive wishes. Very little love seemed lost on the Abbot Primate. Dom Pothier came all smiles. Dom Mocquereau also came.

April 25. The Abbot of Silos came, Dom Guépin. Discussion of matters relating to the chant. He says that peace has been made.

April 27. Audience with the Holy Father. He charges me with correcting and arranging the *Motu proprio* on the Vatican edition, and orders me to give to Scotti his instructions to prepare everything necessary for the edition. I went to the Press and then in the afternoon I corrected the proofs. The *Motu proprio* bears the date of April 25. On page III note 293 of *Musica Sacra* there is also the date of April 27. The documents for the edition were explained to the Holy Father on February 22.

May 2. Dom Mocquereau came to thank me for all that had been done in favor of Solesmes, and that also in the name of Msgr. Sambuceti, who knows well the affairs of Solesmes.

May 12. Tomorrow Dom Mocquereau and Dom Cagin leave. I went to greet them this evening with Father Rella. Basically, they are departing well satisfied. The conversation with Dom Mocquereau was good and useful, and one sees how knowledgeable he is about the manuscripts.

APPENDIX V. BIBLIOGRAPHY

The major studies on the restoration of Gregorian chant are the articles by Msgr. Moneta-Caglio and Father Bauducco: Msgr. E. Moneta-Caglio, *Dom André Mocquereau e la restaurazione del Canto gregoriano, Musica Sacra*, Milan, 1961–1963; *L'attività musicale di S. Pio X, Bollettino Ceciliano*, the entire issue of November 1964;—Father F. Bauducco, s.j., *P. Angelo de Santi, s.j., e la fondazione della Scuola Superiore di Musica Sacra in Roma, Civiltà Cattolica*, 1961, 3, 583–594; *Il P. Angelo de Santi, s.j., e l'edizione vaticana dei libri gregoriani dal 1904 al 1912, Civiltà Cattolica*, 1963, I, 240–253; *Il Padre Angelo de Santi s.j., e la questione dei "segni ritmici" dal 1904 al 1912, Bollettino Ceciliano*, 1964, 75–92; *Il P. A. de Santi (da un carteggio col Maestro L. Bottazzo), Civiltà Cattolica*, 1968, 3, 243–252.

Msgr. Moneta-Caglio was the first to approach the subject, publishing a series of articles on Dom Mocquereau and the Gregorian restoration in the *Musica Sacra* of Milan (of course with regard to Dom Mocquereau, he covers the entire history of the restoration). Several chapters are devoted to the Vatican edition. Moneta-Caglio relies on the *Journal* of Father de Santi, and the correspondence between Father Baralli and Dom Mocquereau. (Father de Santi's *Journal* is published in this book as Appendix IV.) There is also a substantial bibliography, in addition to that study's extensive notes. As for the events of 1904, we must point out two omissions. First, the letter from Msgr. Bressan dated March 10, 1904, to Dom Delatte, which asks the Abbot of Solesmes not only for permission to use the Abbey's earlier Gregorian editions, but also to work with Dom Pothier in editing the Vatican edition (cf. Part 2, No. 62). Secondly, Msgr. Moneta-Caglio does not discuss the Brief of May 22, 1904, sent to Dom Delatte. Yet Father de Santi had wanted that Brief in order to consolidate Solesmes' position within the Vatican Commission (Part 2, No. 69).

Msgr. Moneta-Caglio's work goes up to 1906, after the dispersing of the Vatican Commission, but in a later article on *L'attività musicale di S. Pio X*, pp. 261–263, he speaks briefly about the circumstances that led Pius X to entrust the Vatican edition to Solesmes once again, in 1913.

Father Bauducco's account of the Vatican edition goes up to 1913. It is much shorter than Msgr. Moneta-Caglio's work. In addition to de Santi's *Journal*, he draws on a number of other writings by Father de Santi, including some items kept in the private archives of the Vatican. In his article on the rhythmic indications, Father Bauducco outlines the role that Father de Santi played in reaching a peaceful solution to the issue. Father de Santi's role in the negotiations that led to the creation of the Vatican Commission has been presented above. In practical terms, it was also Father de Santi who convinced Pius X to grant Solesmes the authorization to continue publishing its rhythmic editions, in recognition of the sacrifices it had made for the Holy See. This helps explain why Father de Santi viewed the peaceful solution to the issue of rhythm as an equitable one. As Father Bauducco explains, Father de Santi gradually changed his mind about this and defended the rhythmic editions from the scientific perspective as well, whereas initially, he saw them merely as practical aids. Father Bauducco emphasizes the role played by Dom L. David in this unfortunate quarrel, and it is clear from his account that Father de Santi was very harsh toward those who opposed the rhythmic editions and toward the way in which they proceeded.

2   Dominica I. Adventus.

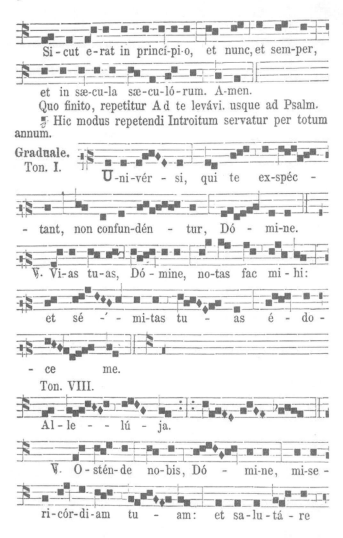

PLATE 4. Graduale Romanum, Pustet edition (Regensburg 1871). The Gradual of the First Sunday in Advent, *Universi:* comparison with Plates 6, 8, and 9 reveals the mutilation of the melody.

Quadragínta annis próximus fu-i genera-ti-óni huic,

et dixi : Semper hi errant corde : ipsi vero non

cognovérunt vias meas, quibus jurávi in ira me-a,

si intro-ibunt in réquiem me- am.

Glóri-a Patri, et Fí-li-o, et Spi-rí-tu-i sancto. Sicut

erat in principi-o, et nunc, et semper : et in

sǽcula sæculórum. A-men.

CANTUS II CUM INVITATORIIS III MODI ASSUMENDUS.

Ve-níte, exsultémus Dómino, jubilémus De-o salutá-

ri nostro : præoccupémus fáciem ejus in confessi-óne ;

et in psalmis jubi- lémus e- i.

PLATE 5. Directorium Chori, Solesmes (Rennes: Vatar, 1864). The first
book of the Gregorian restoration. The traditional neumes are rediscovered.

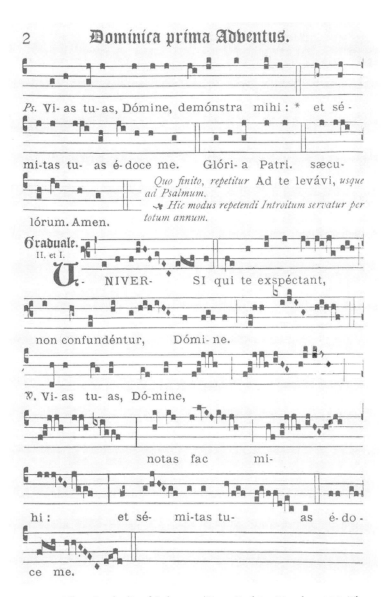

Ps. Vi- as tu- as, Dómine, demónstra mihi : * et sé -

mi-tas tu- as é- doce me.   Glóri- a Patri.   sæcu-

Quo finito, repetitur Ad te levávi, *usque ad Psalmum.*

✳ *Hic modus repetendi Introitum servatur per totum annum.*

lórum. Amen.

Graduale.
II. et I.

U- NIVER- SI qui te exspéctant,

non confundéntur,   Dómi- ne.

℣. Vi- as tu- as, Dó-mine,

notas fac   mi-

hi :   et sé-   mi-tas tu-   as é- do -

ce me.

PLATE 6. Liber Gradualis of Solesmes / Dom Pothier (Desclee 1883). The Advent Gradual *Universi* as restored.

Son but était : (*Paléographie Musicale*)

a) d'étudier le chant grégorien sous toutes ses faces ;

b) de démontrer *par l'exposition des faits paléographiques et histo-riques* que le chant grégorien, chant traditionnel de l'Église Romaine depuis seize siècles, est conservé intact, pur de toute altération, dans les manuscrits de tous les pays et de toutes les époques ;

c) de prouver, par l'étude & le déchiffrement de la notation neumatique, la possibilité de lire les manuscrits, & la solidité des règles d'exécution proposées par les *Mélodies grégoriennes* de Dom J. Pothier ;

d) de mettre à la disposition des savants, afin qu'ils puissent vérifier nos dires, un recueil monumental de paléographie liturgico-musicale, analogue aux grands recueils qui existent pour l'épigraphie, la numismatique, l'archéologie, &c.

Afin de bien montrer que nous étions les fils soumis du Saint-Siège, & que nous n'entreprenions ce grand travail que pour l'honneur & la gloire de la sainte Église, nous avons tourné nos regards vers son Chef auguste, & c'est à ce moment, Très Saint Père, que Vous avez daigné bénir notre œuvre & en accepter l'hommage.

On peut distinguer dans la *Paléographie musicale* :

1° les monuments phototypés.

2° le texte explicatif.

1° LES MONUMENTS PHOTOTYPÉS

Le *Premier volume* publié fut un *Antiphonale Missarum* (142 pages in-4°) de la Bibliothèque de cette abbaye de Saint-Gall qui reçut directement de Rome, vers 790, le chant romain. La comparaison entre ce manuscrit & notre *Liber Gradualis* prouvait que nous avions réimprimé, note par note, groupe par groupe, les vraies mélodies de l'Église Romaine.

Une preuve aussi péremptoire devait convaincre, ce semble, les plus obstinés ; il n'en fut rien. Les adversaires de la Tradition prétendirent qu'un seul manuscrit ne prouvait rien, que d'ailleurs les manuscrits répandus dans le monde entier *ne s'accordaient point entre eux*, & que, vu ces divergences, la restitution du vrai chant grégorien était impossible.

PLATE 7. Memorandum of Dom Delatte to Pope Leo XIII (Solesmes 1901), page 7, dexcribing the purpose of the *Paleographie Musicale*

PLATE 7 – ENGLISH TRANSLATION

Its purpose was: (a) to study Gregorian chant in all its aspects; (b) to demonstrate *by stating the palaeographical and historical facts* that Gregorian chant, for sixteen centuries the traditional song of the Roman Church, is preserved intact and free of any alteration, in the manuscripts of all countries and historical periods; (c) to prove by the study and decipherment of the neumatic notation, that it is possible to read the manuscripts, and to demonstrate the soundness of the rules for performance proposed by the *Mélodies Grégoriennes* of Dom Joseph Pothier; (d) to furnish scholars who wish to verify our claims, a monumental collection of musico-liturgical palaeography analogous to the great collections available for epigraphy, numismatics, archaeology, etc.

In order to make it plain that we were the submissive sons of the Holy See, and that we have undertaken this enormous effort solely for the honor and glory of Holy Church, we have fixed our gaze upon her august Head, and at this moment, Most Holy Father, you have deigned to bless our work and accept it as a gift.

Within the *Paléographie musicale* one can distinguish the documents in phototype, and the accompanying explanatory text.

The Documents in Phototype

The First Volume published was an Antiphonale Missarum of 142 quarto pages from the library of the Abbey of St. Gall, which received the Roman chant directly from Rome around 790 A.D. Comparison of this MS. with our Liber Gradualis proved that we had reprinted, note for note and group for group, the true and genuine melodies of the Roman Church.

It seems that such a completely conclusive proof should have convinced even the most obstinate; but it was in vain! The opponents of Tradition pretended that a single MS. meant nothing, and that in addition, the MSS. scattered throughout the whole world *did not agree with each other.* Hence because of these differences, the restoration of true Gregorian chant was impossible.

¶ *Hic modus repetendi Introitum servatur per totum annum.*

PLATE 8. Liber Gradualis, Editio Vaticana (Rome 1908). The Advent Gradual *Universi:* melody and notation identical with PLATE 6.

PLATE 9. Gradual, Vatican Edition, with rhythmic signs of Dom Mocquereau (Desclée 1908). The neumes of St. Gall have been added by hand
above the staves: the Advent Gradual *Universi* in a notation which more accurately conveys the nuances of the manuscripts.

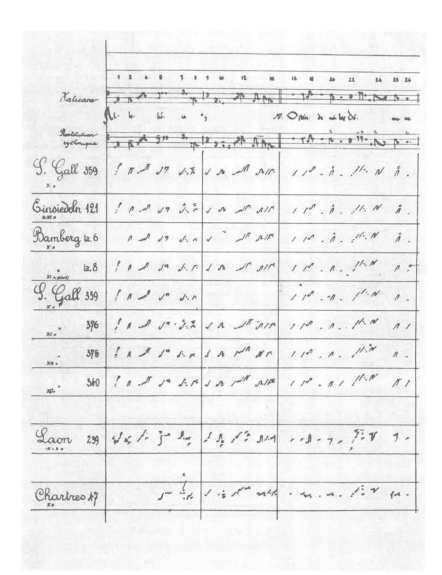

PLATE 10. Alleluja "Ostende nobis" as an example of the *melodic* (and rhythmic) restoration which had been prepared at Solesmes in preparation for the Vatican Edition. – This table gives only the first part of a folding chart published by Dom Mocquereau in "The rhythmic tradition in the manuscripts" = Gregorian Monographs 4 (Desclée 1923). Of course, this chart lists only a small number of the manuscripts transcribed for each piece of the repertory.

PLATE 11. Antiphonale Monasticum of Solesmes/Dom Gajard (Desclée 1934). The responsory *Vidi speciosam*, a "prolix" or longer responsory from First Vespers of the Assumption, with the St. Gall neumes
added by hand above the staves.

INDEX

Since the chief characters in this documentary narrative are named so frequently, and in view of the fact that the detailed descriptive Table of Contents is arranged chronologically, the reader will not be greatly inconvenienced by the omission of personal names such as Guéranger, Pothier, Mocquereau, and de Santi from the Index, which includes many of the important personalities mentioned in the Text, as well as major documents, chant books, and journals frequently cited.

The Restoration of Gregorian Chant: Solesmes and the Vatican Edition was designed and composed in Monotype Dante with Bitstream Engravers Old English display type by Kachergis Book Design, Pittsboro, North Carolina; and printed on 60-pound Glatfelter Natural and bound by Edwards Brothers, Lillington, North Carolina.